Policing the Progressive City

Portland, Oregon, from Settlement to Uprising

Kristian Williams

Policing the Progressive City

ISBN 9781849354288
E-ISBN 9781849354295
Library of Congress Number: 2025935685

AK Press
370 Ryan Avenue #100
Chico, CA 95973
www.akpress.org
akpress@akpress.org
510.208.1700

AK Press
33 Tower St.
Edinburgh EH6 7BN
Scotland
www.akuk.com
akuk@akpress.org

Cover photo by tzen xing
Cover design by John Yates | www.stealworks.com
Printed in the USA on acid-free paper

Contents

Policing the Progressive City

INTRODUCTION
Policing, Portland, Paradox

Portland in the Spotlight

In the summer of 2020, Portland, Oregon, was thrust into a national spotlight when, in the midst of weeks-long racial justice protests, President Donald Trump deployed hundreds of heavily armed federal agents in a theatrical attempt to tame what he would later denounce as an "anarchist jurisdiction."[1]

There were numerous fights playing out simultaneously on Portland's streets that summer. Behind the physical combat between protesters and police, and antifascists and fascists, there was the political conflict of left versus right, liberal versus radical, and reform versus abolition. There was contestation between local, state, and federal governments, and there was division between the cops and the city council. At stake were some issues fundamental to our society: structural racism, the sanctity of private property, the authority of the state, the control of public space, and the political uses of violence. At the center of it all was policing. Each schism and clash vibrated with national significance.

It was in some ways a strange role for an outlying midsize city most famous for a self-parodying sketch comedy and usually overshadowed by its distant neighbors Seattle and San Francisco. But Portland has always had a sort of dual nature. In the early nineties, *Time* magazine described it as a "chamomile and bean-sprout metropolis [with] a Mad Max edge."[2] A century earlier, you could label Portland with equal accuracy as either a sleepy provincial village or as a rough-and-tumble frontier town. In between, it was a center of both the Progressive movement and the Ku Klux Klan, and the site of a continual struggle between moral reformers and political gangsters. In retrospect, it seems almost inevitable that Portland would become and remain both the City of Roses and Little Beirut. What the history makes clear is that for each of these multiple dualities, the two antagonistic halves are intimately connected.

Policing the Progressive City recounts the history of policing in Portland, Oregon, from the period of initial colonization to the aftermath of the 2020 riots. In large part, it is an uninterrupted story of bigotry, corruption, and violence. But there are also features that have won the city and its police their progressive reputation: Portland was among the first cities in the United States to hire a female officer and the first large city with a female police chief; both the Portland Police Bureau and the Multnomah County Sheriff's Office were early and enthusiastic proponents of community policing; and the city has at times adopted policies barring police from participating in immigration raids or enlisting in the FBI's Joint Terrorism Task Force. Rather than view this as a contradiction, I will argue that the progressive veneer is what allows the repressive core to function so effectively, weathering scandals, co-opting critics, and periodically renewing police legitimacy with well-timed and carefully limited reforms.

Since its beginning, the city's animating ideology has been one of progress in several guises: settlement, clean government, rational administration, urban renewal, civic engagement, and livability. In the late-nineteenth and early-twentieth centuries, the Progressive movement was an ecumenical effort to break the dual strangleholds of political machines and corporate monopolies. A century later, "progressive" served as an indistinct moniker signaling a set of vaguely left-liberal inclinations ranging from organic gardening and bicycling to gay rights and labor solidarity. In general, *progress* invokes an idea of continuous improvement and often conflates personal morality and the public good. (Even the language of the Progressives—*vice, corruption, temperance*—implies as much.) And the particular conception of progress has tended to privilege the interests of certain groups of people over others.

Policing as Process

Unlike my first book, *Our Enemies in Blue,* which traced the development of the municipal police as an institution and took as its scope the entire country, *Policing the Progressive City* concentrates on a single city and follows Mark Neocleous's approach of "understand[ing] police as an *activity* rather than an institution, a *function* rather than an entity," namely "the exercise of force for the maintenance of order."[3] What this order consists of is always contested, and the means by which the standards of order are established—always provisionally—together constitute, in the broad sense, *politics*. Policing, then, can be viewed as the application of a particular type of politics, the imposition of a specific social structure.

That process of policing reaches beyond any particular institution, even beyond the full criminal legal system, to include all the means by which surveillance and coercion are used to create a sense of regularity and control. The Portland Police Bureau—having nearly one thousand sworn officers and representing the largest budget item from the city's general fund—features most prominently in my telling, but the police process extends to the Multnomah County Sheriff's Office; the Oregon State Police; the FBI, Homeland Security, and other federal agencies; the district attorney and the courts; jails, prisons, and mental hospitals; and administrative bodies like the Oregon Liquor and Cannabis Commission.[4] Additionally, much of policing is extralegal or informal, conducted by private security companies, independent paramilitaries, freelance detectives, violent mobs, and even organized crime.

Order, importantly, is not law—though the law may be one of the elements that constitute it and one of the tools with which it is fashioned. Policing does not only impose order; it also defines what is tolerated or prohibited, orderly or disorderly.[5] The police do enforce the law, but, when they do, it is always in the service of some other cause. The law is never sacrosanct to those sworn to uphold it. It is a polite fiction, an alibi, a mask for power. An analysis of policing may therefore provide a certain clarifying view of our social structure, highlighting inequality and the role of violence in maintaining it.

Emphasis and Approach

This is not the "secret history" of the Portland Police. My approach has mainly been one of synthesis rather than discovery—distilling a narrative from previously published material rather than excavating archives in search of new facts. The stories I recount ought not to be controversial on epistemic grounds; they just haven't been assembled in a single account, in this manner, or with this emphasis. For the early history, I have relied for the most part on more general studies of the city, county, or state government. For more recent events, I have often turned to the *People's Police Report*, a newsletter published by Portland Copwatch.[6] On the other hand, much of my information has come from the cops themselves—not only official reports but also the memoirs various officers have written over the past hundred years. I have also searched out the impacts of policing and the resistance to it where it appears throughout labor history, Black history, and queer history—anywhere power is challenged or control imposed.

In writing this volume, I have tried, first of all, to convey the history, a sense of *what happened*, addressing theoretical questions only as necessary. I have adhered, as far as possible, to a chronological structure, though inevitably the demands of narrative sometimes complicate this structure. Some chapters therefore overlap in time since several events may have been happening at once, but in the telling it is sometimes necessary to separate them.

Attentive readers may likewise notice an increasingly meticulous attention to detail and a more granular chronology as the narrative approaches the present. To some degree that is a function of the more ready access to sources. But there is also a matter of relevance. The very recent past shades easily into the present, with a greater likelihood that its controversies, practices, and sometimes even individual actors are still with us.

The narrative also periodically expands and contracts—addressing broad-scale institutional and societal changes in one chapter, then focusing on the activities of a handful of people in the next. In a midsize city such as Portland, the actions of relatively few people can set in motion events with an outsized impact. Sometimes these people are police leaders or politicians and sometimes activists or reformers, but often they are ordinary cops whose bad decisions produce a scandal, trigger a crisis, or otherwise draw into question the legitimacy of the agency they represent.

All Policing Is Local

The local focus of this study entails a certain specificity: Portland is not just anywhere. And we cannot pretend that conditions are the same everywhere.

Encompassing 147 square miles at the northern edge of Oregon, Portland straddles one river, the Willamette, and is bordered by another, the Columbia.[7] The area is known for its long, wet, gray winters and generally mild temperatures. The city is home to 652,503 people, as of the 2020 census. Of these, 76 percent are white, 11 percent are Hispanic or Latino, 8 percent are Asian, 6.5 percent are Black, and 1 percent are American Indian or Alaskan Native. About one in six speak a language other than English in their home, the most common being Spanish. And 12.2 percent of the city's residents are foreign-born, most of whom (55 percent) are nationalized citizens. More than 52 percent of adults have a bachelor's degree, and the median household income is $81,119 per year, while 12.7 percent of the city's residents live in poverty.[8] About six thousand people are homeless.[9]

In addition to being the largest city in the state, Portland is also the seat of Multnomah County, though the city limits extend slightly into Washington and Clackamas Counties. (It is generally understood that when one refers to "the county," one means Multnomah.) Since 1983, the city has been responsible for policing, firefighting, transportation (except for bridges), parks, and water and sewer service, leaving the county to handle social services, corrections, taxation, elections, and libraries.[10]

Residents are rightly proud of the city's independent bookstores, movie theaters, and breweries, and they largely take for granted its equally impressive public parks and tap water. Portland is a city of hobbyists and eccentrics, though its "Keep Portland Weird" reputation is increasingly a leftover from an earlier era of temp jobs and cheap rent. Portland is also cloyingly self-conscious of its own publicity, exhibiting an adolescent preoccupation with appearing on annual "most" and "best" lists.

There are undoubtedly some aspects of the city that are unique, but in many more respects Portland is simply typical. While most police histories focus on metropolises such as New York, cities with smaller populations and more modest budgets are more representative of most American's experience with policing. Legal, organizational, and tactical innovations often first appear in these minor urban laboratories, sometimes shaping and sometimes corresponding to broader trends. Local conditions are likewise influenced by—and influence in turn—regional, national, and even international events. So the story I tell in *Policing the Progressive City* will sometimes take us far outside the city limits, often as far as the nation's capital. And several national figures—including Margaret Sanger, Harry Bridges, Robert Kennedy, George H. W. Bush, and Donald J. Trump—will play a role in local events as well.

Being thus obsessed with its own sense of exceptionalism, Portland has a special vulnerability for self-mythology. I have tried as far as possible to adhere to documented historical fact and to leave aside legends, mysteries, and colorful elaborations. So some of Portland's favorite stories about itself will not show up here or appear only in greatly diminished form: I will discuss shanghaiing but not the Shanghai tunnels; the sex trade but not Nancy Boggs's riverboat brothel. Our most famous folk hero, D. B. Cooper, will not be making an appearance (or disappearance) after this point.[11]

Autobiographical Note

Though I have done my best to be fair, telling the truth as I understand it, sticking to the facts and taking as many into account as I can manage, I am not what might be called a dispassionate observer.

I moved to Portland in 1994 and have lived here for nearly my entire adult life. For most of that time I have been involved, to a greater or lesser extent, in organizing against the police. Many of the events discussed in the later chapters of this book I saw unfold at close proximity, and some of the participants I have been proud to know personally. I've been a member of several groups mentioned in these pages, most importantly Portland Copwatch and Rose City Copwatch.

Quite apart from my activism, just in the course of daily life, I have had plenty of opportunity to see the cops at work and have formed some definite opinions about what they do and how. Let me begin by saying that on several occasions I have seen the police respond to potentially suicidal or otherwise "distressed" individuals with remarkable patience, sometimes even bordering on compassion. Once, on a very cold night, I watched as an officer used the phone in a church to call one shelter after another, looking for a bed for a young woman sleeping in the park. I've seen the police respond with calm professionalism in the aftermath of a hate crime. I have seen a sergeant refuse to move a group of striking workers out of a hotel lobby. And I once saw a sheriff's deputy intervene to stop the Portland Police Bureau's mounted patrol harassing a group of homeless teenagers sitting by the entrance to the downtown library. Firmly but politely, the diminutive, rather grandmotherly deputy put herself between the cops and the gutter punks and escorted the cops away. Those moments stand out precisely as exceptions.

More typical are the innumerable times I've seen the police hassle homeless people—on the street, in parks, at bus stops—wherever they happened to be, whatever they happened to be doing. One incident sticks in my mind: Two Portland cops, guns aimed, were shouting at a terrified Black man, who had his hands in the air and what was clearly a fluorescent orange plastic squirt gun in his waistband. Eventually they let him go, but I spent a long time watching helplessly, expecting him to be killed. On another occasion, I watched cops literally drag one of my neighbors to a squad car, leaving his shoes in the street behind him. Late one evening, an elderly Black woman—a total stranger—knocked on my door in a panic and asked to be let inside because the police were following her on her way home from the corner store. These were just events that I happened to witness as I went about my life in this city.

Then, during the 2020 uprising, it became impossible *not* to observe police violence. On most nights my workplace was within earshot, often within sight, and occasionally within tear gas range of hours-long street battles. That is when I decided to write this book.

My hope is that my work here helps the people of Portland to understand their police force, not as benevolent guardians and not as an alien evil but as the clearest manifestation of the inequality that structures our society. It is precisely this inequality that our reputation as "tolerant Oregon" obscures and thus protects.[12]

We are not the city we imagine ourselves to be.

PART I

Pioneers, Progressives, and Professionals

CHAPTER 1

Settlement, Property, and Government

The Clearing and the Enclosure

Before there was a city, there was a meadow in the forest, near the river.

On the west side of the Willamette River, about where Alder and Salmon Streets are today, there came an opening in the wood, about an acre in size. Native peoples referred to it as "the Clearing."[1] Calling this spot a *clearing* should not suggest that it was empty space, however. It was home to numerous plants and animals, of course, but it also likely served an important social use. Such clearings, the product of Native land management practices, were not uncommon throughout the Pacific Northwest. (The later site of Fort Vancouver was another such.) They would be used by various groups as campsites while traveling, during hunts, or seasonally for the harvesting and processing of camas, wapato, and other staple plants, and for fishing during salmon runs as well as for socializing at these times. Some clearings were used as burial grounds.[2]

A few miles north of the Clearing, the Multnomah people lived along the Columbia River, on and near Sauvie Island. About thirty miles to the south, the Clackamas and Tualatin peoples lived along the Willamette River, near the falls, about where Oregon City is today.[3] The groups were culturally and linguistically distinct and organized as autonomous bands. However, trade was common, as was intermarriage, and they shared similar spiritual and ethical beliefs. Communication was facilitated by the Chinook Wawa, a simplified language used throughout much of the Northwest. The Multnomah were exceptional for living year-round in a single location; most other groups traveled along regular routes in warm weather and returned to their villages for winter.[4]

In 1843, two white settlers, William Overton and Asa Lovejoy, claimed sixty-four acres surrounding the Clearing, though Overton soon traded his share to Francis Pettygrove. Pettygrove built a cabin near what is now Southwest Naito Parkway and Washington Street and used it as a store. In 1845, Lovejoy and Pettygrove laid out a grid comprising sixteen blocks, which would come to shape downtown Portland.

Taking this land was not theft in the ordinary sense. It did not violate but rather imposed property relations. The significance of the Clearing was precisely that no one group claimed or controlled it. So when settlers took the area as their own, they did not simply steal the land from any identifiable person or group. What they did was something much worse: seizing this land—their enclosure of these commons—destroyed the possibility for resources to be shared among many, belonging to multiple people or multiple groups, or simply belonging to no one.[5] This may tell us something about the origin of property: rather than theft implying a preexisting property relation, we can see that private property implies a previous theft.

Of course Lovejoy and Overton's claim was only the beginning. The 1850 Oregon Donation Land Act gave 320 acres to every white settler residing in Oregon before December 1851 (later extended to 1855). That was a direct violation of the Organic Act, passed just two years earlier, creating the Oregon Territory. That law had pledged, "Nothing in this act shall be construed to impair the rights of person or property pertaining to the Indian in said territory, so long as such rights shall remain unextinguished by treaty between the United States and such Indians."[6] This provision reaffirmed the earlier promises of the 1787 Northwest Ordinance, which had declared, "The utmost good faith shall always be observed toward the Indians; their lands and property shall never be taken from them without their consent; and in their property, rights, and liberty, they shall never be invaded or disturbed unless in just and lawful war."[7]

Despite these promises, by 1851 half of the Willamette Valley had been claimed by settlers. Across the state approximately sixteen million acres were seized, Native people receiving three cents per acre in compensation. By 1855, 7,437 settlers had claimed land in the Oregon Territory, representing twenty-three million acres, while the majority of the Native population had by then been removed to reservations. The area of those reservations was then systematically reduced over the coming decades. The original inhabitants of the land became almost as prisoners on the reservations, requiring passes to leave. In the course of just a few years, thousands died from the effects of overcrowding and malnutrition.[8]

Government and Pestilence

The first government in the area was a corporation, representing both an economic and a military power. In 1825, the Hudson's Bay Company (HBC) established Fort Vancouver in what is now Washington State, about seven miles from the place where the Willamette flows into the Columbia. The fort itself measured approximately 750 by 450 feet and was surrounded by a tall palisade, with a village of some fifty houses just outside. Altogether about eight hundred people called the settlement home.[9]

Fort Vancouver was governed by Dr. John McLoughlin, the chief factor, whose position, according to an admiring biographer, resembled "that of an old English Baron in feudal times."[10] McLoughlin ruled as an autocrat, though he lacked any formal juridical authority. Appointed largely on the basis of his skill in managing relations with Indigenous tribes, McLoughlin made no attempt to interfere directly with their customs, except insofar as they affected the activities of his corporation.[11] Generally he advocated resolving minor disputes between individual settlers and Natives in accordance to Native custom.[12] But he stood ready to intervene on behalf of all settlers in the region—American, French, and British alike—to help them avoid, or prevail in, conflicts with Indigenous groups. He repeatedly had Indigenous suspects apprehended and hanged for the murder of white settlers.[13] And, under pressure from the Hudson's Bay Company, the Natives themselves punished crimes against white property, usually by flogging.[14] Moreover, McLoughlin employed what one historian characterized as "a policy of . . . 'massive retaliation,' responding severely to any hostile acts by the region's tribes in order to make a highly visible example of them."[15] McLoughlin thus ordered entire villages burned after Hudson's Bay employees were attacked, explaining this policy to his superiors: "To pass over such an outrage would lower us in the opinion of the Indians, . . . & when it is considered the Natives are at least [a] hundred Men to one of us it will be conceived how absolutely necessary it is for our personal security that we should be respected by them." Therefore no offense could be tolerated, and any perceived threat had to be met with overwhelming force: "Everyone acquainted with the character of the Indians of the North West Coast will allow they can only be restrained from Committing acts of atrocity & violence by the dread of retaliation."[16] This approach proved sufficient to generally allow settlers to travel safely, even in remote areas.[17] Its power established, the company would sometimes also intervene in disputes between Natives, either through mediation or by arming select allies.[18]

Apart from outright violence, the settlement at Fort Vancouver also proved to be a public health hazard, with disastrous consequences for the Native population. One fur trader wrote, "Intermittent fever broke out at Fort Vancouver in 1830. All but two of the garrison contracted it. It spread among the Indians. Two villages below Vancouver of at least sixteen families each became afflicted with it. When it had spent itself among them, wolves and vultures fed on the unburied bodies. The whites burned the bodies that were left unburied in these villages."[19] McLoughlin figured that, by 1835, 90 percent of the Indigenous population of the Lower Columbia were dead.[20]

Those farther south, along the Willamette, fared no better. In 1806, the explorers Meriwether Lewis and William Clark estimated that there were eighteen hundred Clackamas people; by 1850 there were fewer than one hundred.[21] Likewise, at the time of the Lewis and Clark expedition, the largest group of Multnomah villages, assembling twenty-four hundred people, was at Sauvie Island.[22] By 1835, that society had been utterly destroyed. One white settler, Nathaniel Wyeth, revisited the island and reported, "A mortality has carried off to a man its inhabitants and there is nothing to attest that they ever existed except their decaying houses, their graves, their unburied bones of which there are heaps." From this no doubt terrifying sight, Wyeth took a strange lesson: "So, you see as the righteous people of New England say, providence has made room for me."[23]

Civil or Military Law

The governments of the United States and the United Kingdom twice agreed (in 1818 and 1827) to occupy the Oregon Country jointly. British subjects were under the authority of the Hudson's Bay Company, while Americans were largely beyond the reach of the law.[24] An 1840 petition to Congress complained that settlers had "no means of protecting their own and the lives of their families, other than self-constituted tribunals, originated and sustained by the power of an ill-constructed public opinion and the resort to force of arms." In this message, historian Charles Carey notes, "The petitioners had put emphasis on their want of protection against crime," though judging from their private correspondence, that was not their main concern. Instead, "there was a growing feeling of apprehension that the natives in eastern and southern Oregon were in an ugly mood toward the settlers, and that a military force might be needed."[25]

The US government's first representative in the territory was Dr. Elijah White. White, a former missionary, was appointed US Indian subagent by the US Secretary of War in 1842. That position gave him generalized legal powers, though its legitimacy was dubious. White's authority derived entirely from that of the US government, but Oregon was not yet officially a US territory; subagents typically served under a governor, but Oregon had no governor. Regardless, White held the position and exercised its powers until 1845.[26]

During that time, his main achievement was the introduction of a "Civil Compact" with Native groups living east of the Cascade Mountains—the Nez Perce, Wallawalla, and Cayuse in particular. The agreement committed Indigenous chiefs to discipline their people, and Dr. White to discipline the whites: "If an Indian breaks these laws, he shall be punished by his chiefs; if a white man break them, he shall be reported to the agent, and be punished at his instance." While in principle mutually constraining, the law clearly favored the interests and values of the settlers, and Natives complained that it was unevenly enforced.[27] Furthermore, the arrangement distorted Native politics by introducing a punitive and authoritarian tendency that had previously been absent. Historians Robert H. Ruby and John A. Brown write, "Chiefs had assumed specialized responsibilities before, for instance, in times of emergency. But now they were being compelled to impose group control, punish nonconformists, and act as official spokesmen for the groups in various matters."[28] Even so, White himself sometimes usurped their authority. In the "Cockstock affair" of 1843, after a dispute about a horse led to a fatal conflict between settlers and some members of the Molalla tribe, White sent armed men to apprehend Cockstock, the man he thought responsible. White's men returned without success, though Cockstock was later killed by Winslow Anderson, a Black settler whose horse had been the cause of the trouble. In another dispute that same year, White himself flogged a Wasco leader named Skiats, allegedly for threatening a missionary. White reported to his superiors, "I believe it morally impossible for us to remain at peace in Oregon, for any considerable amount of time, without the protections of vigorous civil or military law."[29]

Want of Right

The move toward formal government was slow and halting.

On February 7, 1841, a group of settlers met in Champoeg and proposed a new government, consisting of a governor, a probate judge, three justices of the peace, three constables, three roads commissioners, an attorney general, a court clerk, a recorder, and two "overseers of the poor." At the following meeting, on February 18, elections were held, filling every position except that of governor. This election was nullified at the very next meeting, on April 15, though it was also decided to retain the constables, justices of the peace, and probate judge. In practice, they had little power and took little action, though the Reverend Louis H. Judson did deputize John Edmunds as a constable in order to apprehend a fugitive suspect named Joel Turnham. Edmunds's posse killed Turnham in the attempt.[30]

That autumn, the federal government dispatched Lieutenant Charles Wilkes to survey the Oregon Country and issue a report. After conferring with prominent residents, including those calling for a more formal government, Wilkes concluded that only "a small minority of the settlers" were in favor and therefore found a "want of right" concerning its establishment. He also determined that there was no need: "No crime appears yet to have been committed, and the persons and property of settlers are secure." Further, he believed, "any laws they might adopt would be a poor substitute for the moral code they all now followed." Instead, Wilkes surmised, the motivations behind the proposal were more commercial: "[The] principal reasons appear to me to be, that it would give them more importance in the eyes of others at a distance, and induce settlers to flock in, thereby raising the value of their farms and stock." He thus concluded that the "soundest view" was that "there was no necessity for lawyers and magistrates" and advised that the settlers, instead of creating a local government, should "wait until the government of the United States should throw its mantle over them."[31]

From Wolf Meetings to US Territory

A little more than a year later, in February 1843, W. H. Gray, a Methodist missionary and teacher, held an informal meeting in Salem, purportedly in response to predatory animals killing livestock. The only practical outcome was a plan to organize a general meeting bringing together approximately 250 Americans. The second of these "Wolf Meetings," on March 6, 1843, in the view of historian Charles Carey, "constituted the first positive step in the organization of a local government." Those present decided to collect voluntary contributions and pay a reward for killing the predators: fifty cents for a small wolf, a dollar and a half for a lynx, two dollars for a bear, three dollars for a large wolf, and five dollars for a panther. Native Americans could also collect bounties but at half the rate.[32]

The meeting further resolved to appoint a twelve-member legislative committee "to take into consideration the propriety of taking measures for civil and military protection of this colony."[33] On May 2, this committee met at Champoeg, where it was declared a provisional government, "until such time as the United States of America extend their jurisdiction over us."[34] The meeting included both American and British residents, but no Natives, French-Canadians, or representatives of the Hudson's Bay Company were present. The government was established by a vote of 52 to 50, the prevailing faction led by a trapper named Joseph L. Meek.[35] Meek was elected chief law officer, though for a time the position (called alternately *sheriff* or *marshal*) and its duties were rather vague. The prevailing law, it was decided, would be the legal code of the state of Iowa, for the simple reason that a volume happened to be at hand. However, as the provisional government possessed but a single printed copy, it proved necessary to produce abridged manuscript versions to circulate throughout the territory.[36]

The Hudson's Bay Company's chief factor, John McLoughlin, refused to recognize the authority of the new body.[37] As the historian Frederick V. Holman explains, he surely had a point: "The Oregon Provisional Government was not a government in the true meaning of the word, it was a local organization, for the benefit of those consenting. It had no true sovereignty. And yet it punished offenders."[38] It also waged war against the Native peoples. On March 9, 1844, the provisional government created the Oregon Rangers, a military unit consisting of twenty-five mounted riflemen. The Rangers' first mission was to track down Cockstock's accomplices, but they contributed little to this end. A more important, though unstated, purpose was to intimidate the Hudson's Bay Company.[39]

After a Native band murdered a family of missionaries and took fifty captives at Walla Walla in 1847, the provisional government launched an attack against the Cayuse people, doing so entirely on its own authority and raising its own volunteers. (The counterattack was purely retaliatory: the HBC had already arranged for the release of the captives.) Seeking federal assistance, Joseph Meek traveled to Washington DC, presenting himself as "Envoy Extraordinary and Minister Plenipotentiary from the Republic of Oregon to the Court of the United States," and requested that Oregon be granted territorial status. That August, President James Polk signed the Oregon Territorial Act. General

Joseph Lane was appointed territorial governor, and Meek, newly named as US Marshal, oversaw the hanging of five Native men in Oregon City.[40]

The following year federal mail service reached Oregon, and the US Army established bases at Fort Nisqually and Fort Vancouver, two former Hudson's Bay Company sites. (The HBC relocated its headquarters to Fort Victoria on Vancouver Island, in what is now British Columbia).[41] The territorial legislature created Multnomah County in 1854, naming William McMillan as interim sheriff. The legislature designated the sheriff as "conservator of the peace and ministerial officer of the courts" and specifically required him to execute warrants and other court orders, "pursue and apprehend all felons, and persons charged with any crime or misdemeanor," operate the jails, and collect taxes. To achieve these ends, he was empowered to appoint deputies and could compel anyone to assist him in his duties. McMillan enjoyed two terms as sheriff and served simultaneously as the president of the Portland City Council. He would eventually be forced out by an antisemitic campaign led by the *Oregonian*, resulting in the election of the paper's favored candidate, Addison Starr. Starr, a businessman with investments in the local liquor industry, had two months earlier been elected mayor, making him the only person ever to serve in both positions simultaneously.[42]

City and Marshal, County and Sheriff

In 1851, the territorial legislature issued a charter "incorporating 2.1 square miles of fir forest, stumps, and houses as the city of Portland."[43] Section 18 of the charter declared the city marshal the "principal ministerial officer," with instructions to collect taxes, maintain the jail, and enact all orders issued by the mayor in his role as justice of the peace. For this work, he would be paid by a system of fees.[44] That same year, the legislature allocated $85,000 for a new prison, located in Portland, built of brick and measuring 114 x 50 feet, with three tiers of twenty-eight cells each. It replaced the original Oregon Territorial Prison, a simple wooden building in Oregon City, where prisoners were kept in a windowless room only accessible through a trap door. Built in 1845 at the cost of $875, it burned down a year later—reportedly a case of arson, though no arrests were made.[45]

The Portland City Council first met on April 14, 1851. Its very first order of business—Ordinance No. 1—was the appointment of "a competent, and discrete person to act as Marshal." The process did not go smoothly, requiring seven rounds of voting before reaching a majority decision in favor of Hiram Wilber.[46] The difficulty of this first appointment was a taste of what would come, as the staffing and control of police agencies would prove a regular source of controversy and conflict. Throughout the 1850s, the city went through a marshal every eleven months on average.[47]

In July 1867, the council had to vote forty-four times before electing a marshal. Councilman A. Rosenheim eventually won the majority, but sitting Marshal Henry Hoyt contested the legitimacy of the proceedings and refused to vacate the office. For three months, Portland had *two* marshals, each with his own deputies, neither recognizing the authority of the other. The Oregon Supreme Court sided with Hoyt, ruling that one could not both sit on the city council and serve as marshal. The case settled, Rosenheim remained on the council, and both men resigned from the position of marshal. On October 2, the council elected an interim marshal, David Jacobi, who only served for a few weeks, to be replaced by James Lappeus.[48]

Lappeus had served as marshal previously and had dealt before with such twisted lines of authority. An incident from 1859 illustrates the precarious status of the law and the means by which conflicts were sometimes resolved. Amid a controversy as to who would control the levee along the Willamette—the city government or private owners—former mayor George Vaughn, who claimed the land between Alder and Stark Streets, began construction of a wharf. The city government secured a court order demanding he halt the operation, but he ignored it and hired additional men in hopes of completing the project before the case could be heard. Marshal Lappeus and Mayor Stephen McCormick went to confront Vaughn, but they were met at the site by Multnomah County sheriff (and former mayor) Addison Starr, who arrested them both and charged them with "intent to destroy private property." Within hours, they were released from custody and returned with a crowd of sympathizers, who then tore apart the nearly completed dock. A year later, Judge Matthew Deady ruled in Vaughn's favor.[49]

To Protect Persons and Property

As soon as the city government was in place, however tentatively, the *Oregonian*—long the most influential newspaper in the state, and consistently a mouthpiece for the conservative business class—was demanding action to establish a new sense of order. Just days after the council's first meeting, in 1851, the editor wrote, "The city council has been duly organized, but what progress has been made by way of creating ordinances, we are not informed. It is to be hoped, however, that something will be speedily done to protect the persons and property of our citizens from lawless violation, at the hands of desperadoes, which come here to gamble, cheat, rob, and steal and to murder if it suits their fancy or serves their interests."[50] Another editorial a year later called for urgent action against gamblers, demanding "a city marshal who would ferret out those sporting gentleman" and recommending a "few days in the 'block house' on bread and water" as a remedy.[51]

Portland at the time was neither orderly nor especially dangerous. Historian Jewel Lansing observes that in its first five years (1851–56), "The city had no natural disasters, no murders, no big scandals." The major public order problems were "free-flowing alcohol" and "endless mud."[52] Accordingly, the city's earliest laws dealt with public health, street improvement, firearms, gambling, drunken disturbances, riots, and traffic safety; these issues came to define the marshal's work as well. Early on, most of the marshal's activities involved the demolition of disused buildings and the disinterment of graves to clear a path for planned thoroughfares.[53] But being nearly the only municipal employee, his duties were broad and vague and tended to accumulate over time. For instance, on April 29, 1851, at the fifth council meeting, a law was passed requiring the removal of "all animal or vegetable substances, rubbish or filth of any kind whatever in any house, cellar, yard or other place which the city marshal shall deem necessary for the health of the city." On May 6, at the council's ninth meeting, they created an *ad valorem* tax of 1.5 percent of goods for sale; the marshal was then empowered to board ships to determine the value of their cargo.[54] Later assignments concerned the purchase of furniture for the jail, the heating of the council's chambers, lighting streetlamps, and killing stray dogs.[55]

Still, elite opinion was impatient to see the authorities establish new standards. Thomas Dryer, publisher of the *Oregonian* and former member of the territorial legislature, complained, "Our city of late . . . has been the scene of disgraceful midnight rows and bacchanalian revelry, disgusting to every sober mind, by a group of vagabonds hanging around the low groggeries in the day time and destroying property at night."[56] The paper recommended armed vigilante action should the authorities prove unwilling to act.[57]

Not only internal disorder was at issue. On March 27, 1856, the Portland City Council received a petition urging the creation of a night watch "to protect our lives and property from the depredations" of a "common enemy"—namely, the Indigenous population. The discovery of gold in the Rogue River valley had drawn miners into Native territory, leading first to friction and then to fighting.[58] Multnomah County contributed four companies to this war effort, comprising sixty enlisted men and five officers, one of whom, Lieutenant Hiram Wilber, had served as Portland's first city marshal. Operating outside the federal command structure, these Oregon Mounted Volunteers took Native leader Piópio-maksmaks prisoner when he approached them to negotiate a peaceful resolution. When his warriors tried to rescue him, the volunteers killed Piópio-maksmaks and then proceeded to mutilate his corpse: removing his scalp and skinning his back, preserving his ears in alcohol, and breaking his skull into pieces from which they made buttons.[59] US Army general John E. Wool, who was sent in to settle the conflict by means of imposing the reservation system, accused the volunteers of "brigand actions" that risked "uniting all of the tribes of the region" against the white settlers.[60] Anticipating retaliation, the city council directed the marshal and mayor to find "eight reliable, sober and trustworthy men to stand watch within the city limits at such places as they shall deem most proper and necessary." For this service, the watchmen would be paid five dollars a night.[61]

This arrangement was in many respects typical: only in times of emergency did the marshal have any staff to speak of.[62] Indeed, what stands out most starkly from this early period is not only how provisional but also how improvisational the arrangements of government were. Positions of authority were invented without clear limits or duties, and laws adopted solely because a given published volume happened to be available. Local militia engaged in warfare independent of any military authority. The institutions of policing, property, and local government, which would come to seem immutable, were first established *ad hoc,* sometimes by force of arms, sometimes by force of numbers.

CHAPTER 2
Exclusion Acts

Negroes, Slave or Free

Even as they displaced and dispossessed the Indigenous population, the settlers were faced with the task of defining their new society. Among the first but also most enduring questions was that of who would belong. Their eventual answers did much to form the notions of race and citizenship that continue to structure our lives today.

Slavery had been prohibited in Oregon since the Northwest Ordinance of 1787, a fact reaffirmed by the 1843 Organic Code.[1] The following year, 1844, the first exclusion law was passed, requiring all Black people to remove themselves from the territory within three years or "receive upon his or her bare back not less than twenty nor more than thirty-nine stripes, to be inflicted by the constable of the proper county," with such punishment repeated every six months.[2] Later, this penalty was withdrawn. Instead, neatly illustrating the limits of the ban on slavery, Black people failing to depart the Territory would be hired out at public auction, with their new bosses assuming responsibility for removing them when the term of service was at an end.[3]

The preamble to a subsequent 1849 exclusion law set out the legislators' reasoning: "Situated as the people of Oregon are, in the midst of an Indian population, it would be highly dangerous to allow free Negroes and mulattos to reside in the territory, or to intermix with Indians, instilling in their minds feelings of hostility against the white race."[4] Some cited the "scientific" racism of the period, with its attendant theories of white advancement and black stagnation. N. V. Holmes of the territorial legislature argued, "If niggers are allowed to come among us and mingle with the whites, it will cause a perfect state of pollution. Niggers always retrograde, until they get back to that state of barbarity from whence they originated."[5]

Much of the debate over slavery reflected a dispute between rich farmers (who could afford slaves) and small farmers (who could not). Small farmers wanted to avoid competition from plantations with slave labor; rich farmers wanted to buy slaves and save on labor costs. The rights of Black people hardly figured into the matter.[6] Additionally and irrationally, George H. Williams, chief justice of the Oregon Supreme Court, did not merely argue against slavery, but advised the state's residents to "Keep as clear as possible of Negroes." Historians E. Kimbark MacColl and Harry H. Stein sum up the thinking: "Slave labor was both involuntary and lazy, while free black people would degrade the labor market."[7] The fallacy here is obvious. As Noel Ignatiev observed in a somewhat different context, "Blackness was the badge of the slave, and in a perfect inversion of cause and effect, the status of the Afro-American was seen as a function of their color rather than of their servile condition."[8]

Three times in the 1850s, residents of the Oregon Territory voted against convening a constitutional convention, the first step toward statehood. However, after the US Supreme Court ruled in its 1857 *Dred Scott* decision that neither Congress nor territorial legislatures—rather only states—could ban slavery, Oregonians voted to pursue statehood by a margin of seven to one. When they voted for statehood in 1857, the questions of slavery and racial exclusion were posed separately. The state constitution was approved by a vote of 7,195 to 3,195. Slavery was prohibited by a vote of 7,727 to 2,645. But Blacks were excluded from residence by the largest margin of all, 8,640 to 1,081.[9] The settlers, as a body, were more committed to maintaining their near-total white majority than to either free labor or the fundamental system of government.

Emancipation and Expulsion

Neither the bar on slavery nor the exclusion laws were strictly enforced. In 1850, 135 Black people lived in Oregon, fourteen of whom were enslaved.[10] There is only a single recorded case of the courts intervening to grant anyone their freedom, when in 1853's *Holmes v. Ford*, Justice Williams returned the children of a former slave to the custody of their father rather than their purported owner. He reasoned, "In as much as these colored children are in Oregon, where slavery does not legally exist, they are free."[11] Similarly, there was also only a single successful prosecution under the exclusion act.[12] In 1851, Jacob Vanderpool, the owner of a saloon, restaurant, and boardinghouse in Salem was arrested, jailed, and deported for the sole crime of being African American in Oregon Territory.[13] It is likely that the complaint against him was filed by a business competitor.[14]

That same year, in 1851, a Black couple in Portland, Abner Hunt Francis and his wife, Sydna, who likewise ran a boardinghouse, were also ordered out of the territory under the provisions of the exclusion law. But the Francis family was well positioned to resist their expulsion. They had been an important and respected presence in Portland since its founding. Abner, along with his brother, O. B. Francis, had participated in the 1843 meeting that created the local government. (Neither was permitted to vote, but Abner did speak.)[15] Abner had also figured into the deliberations when the exclusion law was debated. Thomas Dryer, editor of the *Oregonian* and himself a member of the legislature, had argued against the law, noting, "There are some free Negroes now in Oregon. Mr. Francis living in the City of Portland, is a black man and a good citizen. A man of property who attends his own business and does as much for the country as any other man in the country."[16]

Furthermore, Abner and Sydna Francis, having both been active in the abolitionist and women's rights movements before settling in Oregon, had the skills of experienced organizers. They canvassed their neighborhood, circulating a petition to overturn the law. More than two hundred people signed, among them Dryer, Robert Newell (a member of the provisional government), and H. W. Corbett (later a US senator). This was one of several similar petitions, circulated on behalf of particular individuals or families but seeking a general repeal of the law. The legislature refused to reconsider the ordinance, but the Francises remained in the city for more than a decade without penalty.[17] In 1863, they moved to Victoria, British Columbia, where Abner Francis became the first Black person elected to the city council.[18]

Even unenforced, the exclusion law had its effect, discouraging Black migration and preserving white dominance.[19] Oregon's broader legal framework was much like that of the segregationist South, with Blacks barred from voting, testifying in court, or marrying whites.[20] In 1862, the state legislature instituted a new tax, charging people of color five dollars per year; if they were unable to pay, they could be impressed into service working on state roads for fifty cents per day.[21] "Taken all together," a later study conducted by the Bosco-Milligan Foundation concluded, these laws and similarly discriminatory measures "were extremely effective": "They kept the African American population small by discouraging immigration. They contained African Americans in the urban areas, removing them from competition for the potential opportunities and wealth of an agrarian society. They placed restrictions on the ability of African Americans to become economically independent and competitive with whites even in the urban areas. Finally, they placed African Americans outside of the normal protections and guarantees of civil and legal institutions of society, making their place in Oregon life tenuous and vulnerable to the dictates of the dominant white culture."[22]

The most effective measure discouraging Black immigration may have been the 1850 Oregon Donation Land Act, which granted 320 acres to any white settler in the Oregon Territory but deliberately excluded Black pioneers.[23] Yet even there, enforcement was spotty: George Bush, a Black man from Missouri, staked a claim near Brush Prairie; after Washington separated from Oregon in 1853, among the provisional government's first acts was to recognize his property rights.[24]

What do we make of this obvious inconsistency? Perhaps, optimistically, it goes to show that the othering logic of exclusion can find purchase with regard to anonymous strangers but is rather harder to apply to one's very neighbors. But more likely, or in any case more importantly, it may instead show that, the exclusion law having had its general effect, there was little point in attending to individual cases, there being so few. When racial minorities were encountered in greater numbers, the attempt to exclude or expel them was more energetically pursued.

Every Principle of American Civilization

While the new state's Black population remained tiny, beginning in the 1860s the Chinese population began growing. In 1861, there were twenty-seven Chinese people living in Portland. By 1865, there were two hundred. By 1872, the number reached one thousand. In the 1880s, Portland had the second-largest Chinese population in the United States after San Francisco, topping five thousand.[25]

In July 1873, several prominent Portland business owners received anonymous notes, passed under their doors in the night, threatening them if they did not cease employing Chinese workers.[26] The *Oregonian* received two letters threatening to burn down Chinatown.[27] Then, on August 2, 1873, the city suffered a catastrophic fire, which burned twenty-two blocks near the waterfront, mostly in Chinatown. As Chinese residents fought the blaze, they were subjected to racial abuse, including some at the hands of the state militia. Ultimately, damages from the fire were estimated at $927,625. Thousands of Chinese immigrants were left homeless. [28] It was never determined how the conflagration started, but Judge Matthew Deady thought it "the work of an incendiary and most likely of some wicked anti-Chinese fanatics."[29]

Chinese immigrants, mostly manual laborers and overwhelmingly male, were viewed by whites as an unassimilable, suspicious, and sometimes menacing presence. At a large public meeting calling for anti-Chinese legislation, presided over by the Multnomah County distinct attorney, the chief justice of the Oregon Supreme Court, and the governor, a resolution was passed: "Chinese are . . . alien to every principle of American civilization, foes to the interest of our industrial population, who have not assimilated and never can assimilate with our people, who bring with them all the debasing vices of their effete social life, who contribute nothing to the wealth of our country, and who serve as a constant drain on our prosperity."[30]

Chinese workers were treated as a cheap and expendable source of labor to be exploited by businesses and thus were seen as a threat to the wages of white workers. Although technically contract workers, they were viewed as "coolies"—practically the equivalent of slaves—and the effort to keep slave labor out of Oregon became conflated with the anti-Chinese cause. Chinese labor thus symbolized a threat not only to white wages but also to the white idea of freedom.[31] (Ironically, much of the anti-Chinese sentiment came not from nativists but rather from another maligned immigrant group: the Irish.)[32] Employers offered discriminatory wages, often paying Chinese men (and women regardless of race) half as much as white men. White workers responded by seeking to exclude the Chinese workers from the labor market altogether, turning to race to resolve what was essentially a class issue. The strategy was foolish as well as unjust, misdirecting anger away from bosses and toward a more vulnerable set of workers, guilty only of being exploited.

Legal Discrimination

Beginning in the 1860s, state and local governments pursued a series of anti-Chinese laws patterned on the South's Black Codes. Local ordinances regulated the cutting of kindling and the hauling of trash and barred anyone from carrying buckets or baskets on a pole across their shoulders or playing bells, drums, or wind instruments. As a result of such laws, and of selective enforcement, in 1873, nine hundred of the approximately one thousand people arrested in Portland were Chinese.[33]

In 1882, responding to widespread agitation, the US Congress passed the Chinese Exclusion Act, denying any Chinese laborer entry to the United States.[34] The law marked an unprecedented extension of federal authority and required new means for enforcement.[35] It thus produced a great deal of confusion, both among the Chinese community and among the government's own agents. In October 1882, two Chinese seamen were arrested by a federal marshal in Portland and accused of violating the exclusion law. But Judge Matthew Deady found that, since "they [were] not brought here to remain and enter into competition with the labor of the inhabitants of the country," they fell outside the law's intended scope.[36]

Exclusion also precipitated new abuses of power. Federal officers with the Bureau of Immigration sometimes conducted strip searches in public view. Inspector in Charge John H. Barbour was sued by the Chinese Consolidated Benevolent Association for illegal searches and arrests and accused by other bureau staff of "incompetence and general unfitness." Fessenden Chase, a customs interrogation stenographer, wrote to their bosses in Washington DC, accusing Barbour of improper procedure, absenteeism, and neglect of duty as well as deporting migrants without any basis in law. (He also noted that Barbour had never passed a civil service test.) Despite the complaint, Barbour remained inspector in charge for another fifteen years.[37]

Some of the Portland officers had been off-loaded from other branches after incidents of incompetence or misconduct. For example, Benjamin F. Jossey had previously been convicted of assaulting a fellow officer in Port Townsend, Washington. After arriving in Portland, he was the subject of complaints from both the Chinese Chamber of Commerce and his fellow immigration officials. Jossey was accused of making arbitrary arrests, including those of legal residents. The Chinese Consolidated Benevolent Association sued him for $10,000 after he trashed a Chinese laundry and lodging house. Jossey said that he was searching for drugs. Under pressure from the Chinese government, the US attorney general and the secretary of the treasury ordered an investigation. But since the officer they appointed, Special Agent Caleb West, had accompanied Jossey on the same raids, exoneration was a foregone conclusion. Jossey was later sued by the On Hing Company after a raid in which their customers and staff were held hostage and much of their merchandise destroyed. The government managed to avoid a trial and simply transferred him again, this time to Tucson.[38]

Whenever possible, the authorities put the responsibility of enforcement onto third parties. For instance, ship captains had to cover the cost of a return trip if their passengers were turned back by immigration authorities. When the steamer companies objected, the Treasury Department issued a pamphlet explaining immigration law and instructing them to enforce it at boarding. It later became a misdemeanor offense to knowingly transport a Chinese laborer to the United States, punishable by a $500 fine and a year in jail.[39]

Populist Pogroms

The exclusion act did little to appease those opposed to the Chinese presence but seemed instead to embolden them to more violent action.[40] In Portland, anti-Chinese militancy was led by Daniel Cronin, an organizer with the Knights of Labor. After orchestrating the expulsion of Chinese residents from Humboldt County, California, and Tacoma, Washington, Cronin arrived in Portland in January 1886 and publicly called on the local government to "rid the country of the heathen Chinese."[41] Together with Burdette G. Haskell, who had helped organize anti-Chinese campaigns in San Francisco, and Sylvester Pennoyer, who later became Oregon's governor and then Portland's mayor, Cronin formed the Merchants' and Laboring Men's Anti-Coolie League, and—on the basis of no authority whatsoever—ordered the Chinese to leave Oregon within forty days.[42]

On February 22, 1886, a thousand men staged a torchlit march through downtown Portland chanting "The Chinese must go!"[43] The leaders of this contingent were arrested, but that night a group of thirty armed men raided a camp of Chinese woodcutters in the nearby town of Albina, forcing them onto a ferry to Portland. A few days later, a few miles to the northwest, a similar attack was matched with looting and gunfire at Guilds Lake. East of the city, a hundred Chinese loggers were driven from Mount Tabor, and farmworker barracks were burned at Mount Scott. Mob violence continued for two weeks, until the arrival of two militia companies.[44]

Mayor John Gates, Judge Matthew Deady, and even some private employers took steps to protect Chinese workers.[45] City leaders, while not exactly favoring the immigrants, were at least committed to minimum standards of civil order.[46] Mayor Gates called a meeting to urge the citizens of the city to unite against this outside agitation: "The city is full of men without any visible means of support . . . attracted here evidently for the purpose of riot when the time comes for the exodus of the Chinese. Our citizens are being assaulted and robbed, and there is general apprehension or outrage. It seems to be high time for all good people to come out and show the disreputable outlaws that the local authorities will be sustained by the people and that law and order must and will be maintained in Portland."[47]

In advance of the Anti-Coolie League's deadline, Gates doubled the size of the police force and swore in three hundred armed volunteers to defend Chinatown. Many companies hired private guards to protect their workers.[48] Still, dynamite attacks against Chinese businesses, as well as more minor vandalism, occurred periodically until the end of the year.[49] Historian Malcolm Cark writes, "Despite the best efforts of the authorities, the armed deputies, the patrolling militia, [and] the arrests and indictments, the violence was never actually brought under control. It simply wore itself out."[50] In the end, the anti-Chinese forces were less defeated than exhausted; the pace and scale of conflict proved unsustainable, and their activities tapered off.

The 1880s anti-Chinese campaign and the official reaction to it operated simultaneously in two dimensions: both as a struggle between economic classes and, as importantly, as a conflict between two versions of white supremacy. While the police seem to have played a laudable and protective role in this episode, fundamentally they were simply following the priorities of the most powerful group in the society. The opposition to the Chinese presence was largely economic, the product of resentment over their use as cheap labor, undermining the position of other workers. At the same time, the business class sought to protect Chinese workers so that they could continue to exploit them. They only extended this protection to the subordinate group on the condition that they remain subordinate. The ruling classes' defense of the Chinese population was therefore itself a defense of the racial hierarchy. Foolishly pitting the workers against each other, the Knights of Labor and their allies helped to maintain the degraded position of the Chinese immigrants and thereby suppressed wages for everyone.[51] The authorities, meanwhile, could present themselves as the benevolent protectors of precisely the people they exploited most ruthlessly.

The Citizenship Crisis

Beyond the economics, there was an underlying question of citizenship and inclusion that had been opened by the abolition movement and only partly resolved by the Civil War. As historian Beth Lew-Williams argues,

> [The] Chinese became aliens at a time when the federal government was dramatically re-making the concept of the citizen. After the Civil War, Congress constructed a new form of national citizenship with the Fourteenth Amendment, explicitly granting citizens certain rights and immunities, and extending formal citizenship to broader numbers of African Americans and Native Americans. At this critical moment, the social and legal meaning of alienage was also transformed. During a period known for the invention of the modern American citizen, the forces of local expulsion, national exclusion, and overseas imperialism produced the modern American alien and an illegal counterpart.[52]

This new understanding of *the citizen* imbued rights quite apart from the traditional privileges accompanying statuses based on race, sex, family, religion, and wealth—threatening to unsettle traditional hierarchies and thus stoking racial fears. It was in amid these anxieties that the anti-Chinese agitation took shape, and laws were passed to bar Chinese immigrants. Lew-Williams concludes: "These histories of rigid exclusion and radical inclusion are two sides of the same coin. The post-bellum period saw both the creation of the modern American citizen and the modern American alien, a synchrony that was not coincidental."[53]

If that is right, then the process of exclusion was essential to the creation of the polity: The concept of the citizen in some respect implied the concept of the alien. Likewise, where *freedom* and *slavery* were both racially construed, *freedom* meant not merely the absence of slavery but also the rejection of those groups that had been enslaved. Settlement too had required dispossession—through force, through pestilence, but perhaps most of all through the imposition of property relations, under which land could be held as an exclusive and legal right. This series of exclusions—and others that followed—continue to shape the demographics of Portland and, even more, the city's racial hierarchy. Indigenous, Black, and Chinese people did not disappear, despite the laws. Society did not exclude them in an absolute sense, but it did marginalize, subjugate, and exploit them. This system of inequality took shape sometimes under the law and sometimes outside of it, but it was always accompanied by violence. Often the practices and rituals of the law, and participation in its violence, became a means of defining and solidifying the political community, strengthening the affective ties between its members and securing their status while simultaneously excluding those defined as outsiders or punishing those who violated important norms.

Hangings

Historian Amy Louise Wood considers the social significance of public executions as way of both legitimating state power and cementing the loyalty of the population—especially as such macabre pageants were racialized: "By allowing white crowds to witness the punishment of a criminal, to grab souvenirs, and, in some cases, to take photographs, public officials created a continuum between the state and the people; the people were not merely onlookers to the imposing power of the state's punishment but [also] participants in the enactment of that punishment. The execution thus established a visceral identification between white spectators and the power of the state. The act of witnessing bestowed a sense of authority in the white spectator, as did his or her identification with the state's authority to judge and condemn wrongdoing."[54]

Multnomah County's first execution was that of Danford Balch, convicted of shooting and killing Mortimer Stump after Stump eloped with Balch's fifteen-year-old daughter, Anna. Balch was hanged on October 18, 1859, near Front and Salmon Streets. Six hundred people attended. Some energetic entrepreneur had built bleachers in front of the gallows, but anonymous citizens deposited them in the river the night before the execution.[55]

There was a kind of social ambivalence or moral ambiguity about such spectacles. "Hangings were meant to be a public display of contrition and consequence, a moral lesson against civil disorder," historian Diane Goeres-Gardner writes. But they sometimes paradoxically created a "festival atmosphere. . . . The executions gradually lost their moral example as crowds became larger and more unruly."[56] "Hangings were high entertainment in the nineteenth century," Dick Pintarich and Ray Stout explain, "like going to a ball game or attending a wedding. Invitations often were sent out by the sheriff to friends, officials and dignitaries. Some of them were stunning: elaborate script done in gold on a thick black card. The confession of the victim might be printed up and sold to the crowd. After the hanging, souvenir hunters would try to get a piece of the rope."[57]

After Balch, the county's next dozen executions were held at the courthouse, which was built in 1864.[58] Some attracted thousands of spectators and required several companies of militia to keep order. Children would climb trees and utility poles to gain a better view. Some of the condemned, like Chee Gong, went to their deaths proclaiming their innocence; others joked and sang for the entertainment of the assembled crowd. Afterward, the corpse was sometimes displayed on the street.[59] Governor George Chamberlain, formerly the Multnomah County district attorney, expressed his disapproval: "Such scenes are demoralizing, and ought not to be tolerated in any civilized community."[60]

The county's last public hanging was that of George Smith on June 5, 1903. Sheriff William Storey sent out invitations, reading in part: "George Smith (colored) murdered his white wife, Annie Smith, by shooting her through the breast on the 22nd of August 1902. He was tried, convicted and sentenced to be hanged on the 19th day of December 1902."[61] While awaiting execution, Smith spent his days knitting shawls and blankets as gifts to the wives of his jailers. He comported himself with dignity as he walked to the gallows and stood at attention as his hands were bound, and the noose placed around his neck. In contrast, one journalist reported, among the spectators, "Curses, coarse jokes and bestial jibes were to be heard. . . . [The] air reeked of tobacco smoke and drink-tainted breath." Afterward, a deputy distributed pieces of the rope, which uncomfortably recalls the grisly southern practice of collecting trophies from the bodies of lynched men.[62]

Beginning in 1903, by law, "all executions [had to] take place within the walls of the penitentiary . . . out of hearing and out of sight of all except officials."[63] It was a more decorous arrangement, certainly, but the rate of executions thereafter more than doubled. For the half-century before the state government took charge of executions, Oregon averaged one a year. In the ten years following the change, twenty-four prisoners were hanged.[64]

Transition

As inequality became entrenched over the turn of the century, violence became increasingly institutionalized.

Government in Oregon had only recently emerged from a contradictory patchwork combining the Hudson's Bay Company's corporate rule, the informal democracy of the Champoeg meetings, and a variety of appointed, self-appointed, or newly elected officials of uncertain jurisdiction and legitimacy. The organizations intended to provide a sense of regularity to social life were themselves highly irregular—provisional, often opportunistic, and sometimes criminal. The process of solidifying and legitimating local governance would be a long and uneven one, suffering numerous reversals in the course of ongoing reform.

CHAPTER 3
Charters and Corruption

The Peace and Quiet of the City

Almost as soon as Portland was founded, it began the process of reform.

The city's original 1851 charter was soon revised, and each subsequent change in the system of government carried with it changes in policing. A new charter was adopted in March 1853, creating a nine-member common council that was authorized to, among other duties, "license, tax, restrain, prohibit, and suppress billiard tables, tippling-houses, gaming and gambling houses, and . . . bawdy houses . . . ; to prevent and restrain any riot, noise, disturbance or disorderly assemblage, in any street, house, or place in the city; to erect a work-house or house of correction . . . ; to establish and regulate a night watch and patrol; [and] to establish and regulate a police."[1] The new charter removed from the mayor his judicial duties, investing them instead in the office of the recorder.[2] Rather inconsistently, an elected marshal was made responsible for "superintendent control over the peace and quiet of the city."[3] Only a year later, a third charter was introduced. It changed the rates of compensation for the marshal, removed the mention of tippling-houses and billiards, and authorized the regulation of indecent and immoral practices.[4]

The means for law enforcement were slow to develop. In the mayor's annual address to city council in 1859, S. J. McCormick announced, "[A] small body of city police . . . shall be paid for their services out of the City Treasury, and shall at all times be under the control of the City Marshal. Heretofore and at present a few locations in our City are guarded at night by private watchmen, but experience has proved that there is neither safety nor economy in this placing of the guardianship of the city in the hands of parties not answerable for their acts to the corporation."[5] However the council seemed reluctant to take up these measures. In the early 1860s, the marshal employed eight occasional deputies, all paid by fee, who supplemented their income by working as private watchmen for businesses. Each had arrest powers and the keys to the jail, but not until 1862 were the deputies issued badges.[6]

In 1864, the state legislature passed a new criminal code that encouraged, but did not require, police to patrol "exposed places" in order to prevent crime. That same year, Portland adopted yet another new charter with the aim of improving policing. The marshal was made responsible for executing all legal processes, attending all meetings of the Recorder's Court, managing the jail, collecting delinquent taxes, maintaining the peace, and enforcing the law.[7] For the first time, the council tried to create a full-time police force with salaried officers ($125 a month for the marshal, and $100 for each of his two deputies).[8] This began a long period, lasting almost to the end of the century, of continual reorganization, policy changes, and political maneuvering, as the city council, the mayor, the state legislature, and the governor—and the various political factions backing them—all competed for influence. Each sought to maximize their control over the new police force, such as it was, while also trying to minimize their responsibility for the concomitant expenses. Through this messy push and pull, a combination of organizational improvisation and political compromise, the Portland Police Bureau began to take its modern shape.

A Thorough Revision

"Our present police force is too small to be thoroughly efficient," Mayor Bernard Goldsmith told a newly elected common council on June 30, 1870. "The Marshal and his assistants do all they are able to do, but a force of three men is not enough for a city of ten thousand inhabitants, and I therefore recommend an increase of two more policemen to be appointed on the recommendation of the Committee on Health and Police; also a thorough revision of our police ordinances."[9] The council took this advice and went further. A new police department would provide twenty-four-hour-a-day service and comprise three bodies: 1) a regular police force, consisting of the marshal and six deputies, paid $100 each month; 2) an auxiliary force to be mobilized during emergencies, earning $3.33 hourly; and 3) private watchmen, funded by voluntary subscription but enjoying the same public authority as the rest of the force. The marshal and his men would be tasked with arresting lawbreakers, keeping prisoners in custody, assisting the city attorney in prosecutions, attending council meetings and executing the mayor's orders, attending the

Recorder's Court and delivering processes issued there, collecting delinquent taxes, and protecting property from looting after a fire. The mayor would have the final authority over all police matters.[10]

This proposal was passed by the council on September 7, 1870, and signed by the mayor on September 12. Two days later, Chief Marshal Phillip Saunders submitted the "General Rules and Regulations for the Government of the Police Force," which were approved by the council. This new structure employed a police chief, a lieutenant, and six officers, dividing the city into three patrol areas (north of Oak Street, between Yamhill and Oak Street, and South of Yamhill). Before the month was out, on September 28, the council further approved construction of a two-story building to serve as police headquarters, city jail, and courthouse.[11]

In its first year, the new department made a record number of arrests—1,838, nearly tripling the number from the previous year (636). The rate of arrests among the Chinese community increased by *five times*.[12]

But the department had barely begun its work when, in October 1870, the governor signed a charter amendment for Portland, giving control of the city's police to a newly formed Board of Police Commissioners appointed by the governor himself. It was a partisan power grab typical of nineteenth-century politics. (The city council was Republican-controlled; the governor was a Democrat.)[13] The same amendment eliminated the positions of marshal and city recorder, replacing them with a chief of police and police judge, respectively. The board was empowered to appoint the chief, establish the department's rules and regulations, set staffing levels, and approve the budget. The city council, however, was responsible for the expenses.[14] In 1874, yet another charter revision gave voters the power to elect the Board of Police Commissioners, though now it put the common council in charge of staffing and pay.[15] Such reversals were common in the early years of the city's police force. Authority shifted back to the mayor in 1880, then again to a new police board in 1885.[16]

The establishment of a police board, while allowing for a great deal of political interference, also provided a measure of accountability. The board instructed the chief to document and report all complaints alleging police misconduct.[17] In 1873, officers were instructed to appear in uniforms consisting of a "dark blue coat, vest, and pantaloons and black hat of uniform style with cord and tassel." The coat was to be single-breasted, with velvet collar, and the vest also single-breasted, and both were to be trimmed with brass buttons."[18] But this greater professionalism may have only raised public expectations, while the board itself, according to historian E. Kimbark MacColl, lay "at the center of much of the local political corruption and bribery."[19]

Gambler, Marshal, Police Chief

There was a lot at stake in the organization of a police force, perhaps the least of which was any concern for the law.

The first set of police commissioners were Absalom Hallock, a former councilman and ardent volunteer firefighter; William Burke, a carpenter who immediately had his son-in-law appointed to the rank of police captain; and John Hayden, who was habitually absent from the board's meetings. All three were committed Democrats—as were all of the officers employed during their tenure.[20]

Though the incumbent Marshal Phillip Saunders had been noted for his honesty, he was immediately replaced by a new marshal who was not. Before serving as town marshal and then police chief, James Lappeus had made a career on the other side of the law, mainly as a gambler.[21] He then opened an upscale parlor, the Oro Fino, which offered food and drink, a stage on which chorus girls danced suggestively, and private rooms, which were convenient for those looking to exchange money for sex. Nor did Lappeus discourage the playing of poker or (more often) faro.[22] He continued to run the Oro Fino during his time as chief, meaning that (as one historian put it), "the man charged with enforcing the Portland city council's prohibition on houses of gambling within the city limits ran a house of gambling very much inside city limits."[23]

In March 1883, the *Portland Weekly News* accused Lappeus of having solicited bribes years earlier, during his time as marshal. The city council investigated and cleared him of wrong-doing, but the mayor fired him just the same. The council then appointed a new chief, William Watkinds.[24] In the background of this relatively minor drama there lurked a whole system of corruption: Mayor James Chapman confessed to the weekly *Mercury* that he had promised top jobs to two men if they could rig the election in his favor. One was Lucerne Besser, former councilman and marshal. In exchange for his services and $1,000, Chapman made him superintendent of streets, with the explicit agreement that Besser had "no obligation to [the] citizens." The other conspirator was Thomas Connell, who paid $1,000 to become police chief. The whole arrangement was spelled out in a written contract, but the deal fell apart when the council named Watkinds chief instead, and Besser endeavored to blackmail the mayor. "You know that such bargains are made before every election," the mayor told the press, quite truthfully, when the affair came to light.[25]

Many of these same individuals would rotate through the same set of positions year after year, election after election, and scandal after scandal. By 1877, Lappeus was again police chief, and his position became the main issue in the election of the new police commissioner. Control of the board moved to Republican hands, and Lappeus was again replaced, this time with Besser. However, in October 1879, the Board of Police Commissioners fired Chief Besser, and the city sued him for $937 in fines that he had collected but never turned in. (The Oregon Supreme Court found in the city's favor, but for a lower sum of $235.) Lappeus then returned as chief, replacing Besser.[26]

Though Lappeus would be removed from his position over allegations of corruption, he faced practically no consequences for his regular use of violence, both in and out of office. In 1872, he had assaulted Eugene Semple, the editor of the *Oregon Herald*. In 1881, Lappeus was sent to quarantine Mary Sullivan, an Irish immigrant who worked in the sex trade. Witnesses reported hearing a struggle, after which Lappeus departed. The next morning Sullivan was found dead, her body naked and bruised. The coroner ruled her a victim of violence, but no further investigation was conducted.[27]

When Lappeus died in 1894, the *Oregonian* eulogized: "His administration was eminently satisfactory, and he enjoyed the confidence of the people, and the respect and obedience of his subordinates."[28]

Machine Politics

Self-interest had been the animating force of Portland's political economy since the city's founding. For some politicians, like John McCracken, it was almost a matter of principle: "I believe the bestowal of public patronage is and ought to be partisan."[29]

Historian Charles Abbott Tracy describes the cumulative effect of this philosophy:

> Portland was . . . a corrupt city—a city largely controlled by the gambling and liquor businesses whose commercial interests would continue to dominate enforcement polices and the use of the police throughout the remainder of the 19th century. . . . The police were frequently involved in

> bribery and illegal voting schemes. Twelve different police chiefs came and went before the end of the century, and the complete replacement of the still small force occurred with regularity after municipal elections. Charges of malfeasance and criminal conspiracy were common, and by the end of the 19th century the Portland police were completely controlled by the prevailing political-economic power.[30]

Portland functioned as a political machine, drawing together politicians, business owners, and organized crime, these categories often overlapping.[31] Bribery, voter fraud, and intimidation were common.[32] This was, in effect, corruption as the very form of government. The machine served well the interests of various "trusts" and monopolies—railroads, timber, private utilities—as well as those of assorted racketeers and purveyors of vice. It was in some respects a coalition between robber barons and neighborhood gangsters. As historian Robert Fogelson described the system common throughout the country at the time:

> A highly decentralized outfit, the machine was an association of loosely affiliated and largely autonomous ward organizations whose power depended on their ability to get out the vote on election day.... [Ward bosses] gave out contracts to local businessmen, found and if need be created jobs for recent immigrants, provided opportunities for aspiring politicians, and otherwise exchanged material inducements for political loyalty. In return for delivering the vote, the ward bosses demanded a good deal to say not only about the policies of the mayor's offices and city councils but also about the operations of the police departments and other municipal agencies.[33]

The police were an excellent source of power for the machines. Politicians promised police jobs to their loyal supporters.[34] Police could exercise significant influence over elections, intimidating voters and stuffing ballot boxes.[35] And the police set the conditions under which illicit businesses operated, providing the machine both with a source of payoffs and the means to shut down any firm aligned with their competitors or whose competition proved inconvenient for their own supporters.[36]

The October 1872 election, for instance, was a festival of fraud, with open bribery, ineligible voters casting ballots, repeat voting, and the like. The *Oregonian* estimated that a quarter of the votes that year were tainted. Two federal grand juries investigated. The first was disbanded when it was revealed that jurors had themselves been bribed; the second proved impotent when, in the midst of the investigation, the US Attorney was dismissed.[37] Two decades later, little had changed. The *Oregonian* said of the election of 1891, "The conduct of the police was positively shameful. Not only did they protect rowdies and encourage rowdyism, but they became rowdies themselves. . . . several fights enlivened the proceedings as the day wore on."[38] Again, in 1896, the paper complained that police "intimidated voters, threatened and even assaulted judges, and abetted and connived in violence, fraud and outrage." It concluded, "The entire police force of the city was devoted to the use of the [mayor's political] ring." That should have come as no surprise, however, since, after he took office in 1894, Mayor George Frank had reorganized the police department to increase his own control and eliminate his opponents from its ranks.[39]

Jonathan Bourne Jr. used his position on the police board to extort payoffs from Chinese gamblers and saloonkeepers, bringing in $10,000 in a single year. He used the money to buy political influence, and that influence was in turn for sale. Bourne accepted $225,000 from Southern Pacific Railroad with which to place their chosen candidates in Congress.[40] He paid Larry Sullivan, the owner of a sailor's boardinghouse, $2.50 for every vote he supplied, and would further provide political and legal cover for Sullivan's various illicit enterprises. As Sullivan virtually controlled the supply of labor to the docks, he was well positioned to recruit sailors and other migrant laborers as repeat voters. Sullivan was put in charge of a polling station at his boardinghouse, which he would guard with a shotgun in hand. One newspaper described the crowd on election day as a "vast mob of heelers, thugs, vagrants . . . with business men sandwiched in between hoboes and morphine addicts."[41]

The *Oregonian* wrote of Larry Sullivan: "He associated with politicians, helped elect mayors, and picked police chiefs who would wink at his practices."[42] He was repeatedly arrested for violent assaults—including an attack against a prosecuting attorney and the harbormaster—and released without charges.[43] Sullivan once bragged, not without cause, "I am the law in Portland!"[44]

Ethnic Politics

Beginning in 1880, and for thirty years following, Joe Simon—simply "The Boss" to his political opponents—served as chair of the Republican Party, a position that gave him de facto control over both the mayor's office and the district attorney's. He also served at various points as a state senator, US senator, mayor, and chair of the Board of Police Commissioners.[45]

Simon vied for the support of both the Black and the Chinese communities and incorporated them into his apparatus.[46] The machine system held a special significance for newly arrived immigrants, racial minorities, and similarly marginalized groups. It could provide them jobs, welfare services, protection from police, and a political outlet for neighborhood pride and ethnic identity. In return, these groups joined the relevant party's constituent base and supplied blocs of votes.[47] Additionally, Chinese gambling and smuggling operations were a good source for bribe money.[48]

While never egalitarian, the system provided a means for inclusion and a kind of representation. The New Port Republican Club, founded in 1892 by the Black employees of the Portland Hotel, supplied the mayor with a list of Black candidates suitable for city jobs. These included Moody E. Scott (for employment in the recorder's office), George Hardin (patrolman), Henry Taylor (detective), and Joe E. Banks (mail carrier). Their efforts met with some success. Scott was hired as a clerk in the auditor's office, becoming the first Black woman to find employment in the city government. Two years later, in 1894, George Hardin and John Harry Hooper were hired by the Portland Police Bureau as "colored patrol drivers." Though Hooper was fired after a few weeks when he lost control of a patrol wagon and caused an accident, Hardin remained with the bureau until 1915, then worked as a Multnomah County sheriff's deputy until 1938.[49] With a single exception—M. M. Stephenson worked as a patrolman for one week in 1896—no other African Americans would be hired by the Portland Police until World War II.[50]

Fix the Policeman

As one feature of the machine system, there was a general leniency about organized crime. Though the city council passed an 1871 ordinance stipulating that sex workers be fined $5 (with instructions that police should give particular attention to Chinese women), arrests were rare, totaling only sixteen in the police department's first six years.[51] That could only be the result of deliberate indifference. Women who sold sex for money were not hard to find: the 1880 census counted fifty-eight.[52] Far from being secretive, their trade was openly advertised. In 1894, several brothels jointly published *The Guide: A Description of Amusement Resorts of Portland, Oregon and Vicinity*, featuring the names, addresses, and descriptions (in verse!) of the city's more prominent courtesans.[53]

Even shanghaiing—the practice of impressing unconscious or inebriated men into service aboard ships—was often accomplished with police connivance.[54] In the 1890s, the chief of police was fired for shanghaiing a jail prisoner to serve aboard the *Sierra Blanca*. Generally, such extreme measures were unnecessary, as sailors were typically trapped in an economy of credit and debt. The practices of "crimping," by which they were advanced the cost of room and board while at port—at extortionate prices—meant that they generally owed more than they earned and had no choice but to sail again. A ship captain would settle the debt with the boardinghouse owner and more or less buy a crew for the next voyage. Once a man signed up, the contract was as binding as enlistment in the armed forces and could be enforced by federal marshals if need be.[55] In principle there were also a number of officials whose duty it was to keep crimps within lawful bounds, ensuring that sailors signed of their own volition and while sober. Among these were the British vice-consul (for British ships), the US shipping commissioner (for American ships), customs officers, harbor police, and US Marshals. But aside from exceptional figures like Vice-Consul James Laidlow, many of these authorities were implicated in the racket themselves. Those scrupulous about the law, like Portland Police Officer John Byrne, often found themselves dismissed, to be replaced by an officer named by well-connected crimps.[56]

The cops' lax attitude was greatly facilitated by a system of regular payoffs. In 1903, the *Morning Oregonian* reported that Deputy Sheriff Tim Hoare collected one dollar a week from every sex worker in the North End (what is now the area spanning Old Town to Slabtown) and similar payoffs from gambling houses. That same year, five Japanese sex workers testified that they paid patrolman Jack Roberts both to avoid arrest and for protection against violent clients.[57] Edward Chambreau, a saloonkeeper, explained that when he opened his business, "Among the first things I did . . . was to fix the policeman on my beat."[58] Bribes could likewise be arranged to encourage the police to overlook illegal gambling, even rigged games.[59] Chambreau explained that when an unhappy mark, suspecting himself cheated, would go to the police, the responding officer would stall the complainant while claiming to investigate, until the victim gave up or left town. "Not one case in a hundred . . . ever comes to trial."[60]

A cartoon from the time showed a period policeman, in frock coat and bobby hat, wearing dark glasses and carrying a cane. Crime occurs all around him as he walks the street unawares, holding a sign reading "Please help the blind."[61]

Wholesome Arrests and Vicious Influences

When the police did enforce the law, it was often in a capricious and discriminatory manner. Periodically the public would demand action, and the cops would make a show of raids in working-class immigrant neighborhoods. An 1851 law against gambling went largely unenforced until 1883, when William Watkinds became chief. Five thousand arrests were made that year. But, in keeping with the rise of anti-Chinese sentiment, the cops ignored whites playing poker and faro and instead raided the fan-tan clubs in Chinatown.[62] Likewise, when police responded to public pressure by arresting scores of sex workers in 1895, the *Oregonian* observed that only "negresses and other low types were convicted"—no madams among them.[63]

The Chinese were particularly useful scapegoats, though the arrests did little to slow the pace of illicit trade. After a series of raids against Chinese lotteries in December 1887, the *Oregonian* reported, "With a contempt of the police force bred by a familiarity with its method, proprietors of Chinese lotteries are running wide open. Drawings are made as usual every night. Policemen, as formerly, are heavy players. The understanding between the breakers of the law and its sworn enforcers appears to be as thorough as ever. . . . In point of fact, the lotteries were never shut down. The wholesome arrests Monday night were made as a bluff."[64]

Chief C. H. Hunt blamed the police board for his agency's poor performance, saying he was "constantly hindered in enforcing the laws by political interference," but he also admitted that he could not count on the discipline of his men.[65] Both would become perennial complaints. In the early-twentieth century, when a subsequent chief, A. M. Cox, was indicted for malfeasance in office, he similarly argued that he was powerless to enforce vice laws because of orders from "higher up."[66] Police chiefs often took advantage of the opportunities presented to them in their position, lawful or not. Yet the chiefs' complaints that they had limited power are not easy to dismiss. Their men *were* undisciplined and corrupt. Political bosses *did* hamper any efforts at impartial enforcement.

No one individual—police chief, mayor, or district attorney, let alone a patrol officer or common citizen—was capable of altering the overall nature of the machine system. That would take a social movement.

CHAPTER 4

Class Interest and the Public Good

Democracy and Policing

By the end of the nineteenth century, a reform movement was taking shape in opposition to the spoils system and political machines. The Progressive movement emphasized honest and efficient administration and promised to put government in the service of the public's interests, rather than those of party bosses.[1] Notably, their model for efficiency was the private corporation.[2] Equally notably, it was native-born members of the professional and business classes who initiated and led the movement.[3]

At issue were two different conceptions of democracy. Under the first, an election was seen as a contest between self-interested factions each trying to assemble majorities to take power; the prevailing party had every right to treat the government as its exclusive property, and the constituency it represented could expect a share of the spoils. Under the second view of democracy, candidates appealed for support based on a combination of values, policy proposals, and personal competence; the winner was obligated to represent not any one group's interests but rather, in a broad sense, the public interest and the common good. The first view produced the political machine, essentially a system of patronage and loyalty. The second view, that of the Progressive movement, would produce the modern bureaucracy—dispassionate, impartial, professional, and highly rationalized. These two views of democracy imply not only different systems of government but also different *publics*. The machine appealed to specific and identifiable groups: political parties most obviously but also particular trades, ethnic neighborhoods, and criminal networks. The Progressives conceived of the public as an abstraction, comprising all the residents of the city without favor or distinction.

For politics to change, policing had to change. Control of the police would play a dual role in Progressive strategy. First, honest policing would deprive the machines of an important source of power and income. And second, once the police were removed from the system of organized corruption, they might begin to enforce laws impartially, especially vice laws.[4] The Progressives wanted to stamp out corruption; they also wanted to eliminate the "vice" that corruption served to protect—drinking, gambling, the sex trade. Viewing social problems as moral problems, questions of public order weighed heavily on their civic consciences. And as their movement gained strength, the campaign against vice intensified, and the demands on the police increased. Expectations rose.

There remained, however, a persistent gulf between the ideal of the orderly city and Portland's reputation as a wide-open town. As the police became increasingly active in the city's anti-vice efforts, complaints against them began to accumulate: brutality, false arrest, drunkenness, sexual impropriety, and racial bias.[5] Whatever attitude they took with regard to vice crime, the cops could not escape criticism, and from the perspective of an individual officer it was easier simply to look away and do nothing, especially if one could earn a little extra on the side. The policy of paying police by fee had been abandoned in favor of a salary system in the later nineteenth century, but the culture it had created persisted.[6] Police expected to be rewarded for specific services, not merely salaried for their general duties. They continued to be more responsive to immediate incentives than to the law as such. This fact was hardly surprising, since in 1903 Portland's fifty patrolmen worked 365 days a year and were paid only $1,020 annually—considerably less than the police of other cities and even less than their counterparts had been paid a decade before.[7] Routine bribery, half-hearted enforcement, and frequent turnover were natural consequences. The cops remained on both sides of the law.

Honesty and Decency

In 1891, a popular vote consolidated the cities of Portland, East Portland, and Albina into a single municipality covering twenty-six square miles and sixty-two thousand residents. The new charter provided for sixteen city council members from eight wards and set limits on their authority to borrow and spend money.[8] The *Oregonian* called the election "a triumph" for "honesty and decency," marking "the end of municipal misrule and the defeat of bossism," along with "insolent policemen and hoodlum firemen."[9] This assessment was, of course, too optimistic.

The new mayor, William S. Mason, the reform candidate, soon grew frustrated at his inability to suppress vice or control the police.[10] On November 11, 1891, he complained to the city council, "We lack the power to enforce the laws. . . . [We have] no control. . . over the police force of our city." He noted that liquor and gambling laws were "a dead letter on [the] statute books" and wondered if the police themselves were "sharers in the spoils." Finding the police board unresponsive, Mason suspected that the corruption started at the top.[11]

In 1898, when Mason, backed by the chamber of commerce, returned for another term as mayor, he replaced the entire police force—all eighty-four officers. He also appointed all-new commissioners and a new police chief. He ordered intensive patrols in the North End, where the vice district was centered, and ordered the police to shut down brothels and gambling houses.[12] These efforts had little lasting effect, however. By 1900 the police were again merely containing vice within specified areas, tolerating gambling and the sex trade in certain "primrose precincts."[13]

Another reform candidate, George H. Williams, was elected mayor in 1902. At the age of seventy-nine, he had already enjoyed an illustrious career: as a judge in the Oregon Territory, a voting member of the Oregon Constitutional Convention (where he had argued against slavery), a US senator, and the US Attorney for Oregon under President Ulysses S. Grant.[14] He ran for mayor on a promise to beautify the city and control vice—"the removal of the vicious class from the prominent streets of the city"—but once in office his strategy scandalized his supporters.[15] Rather than prohibit gambling and the sex trade, Williams regulated the practices, though he would always say otherwise: "No binding contract has been made between the Mayor or the police and the gamblers of Portland, nor are the gamblers licensed," he stated, by way of explanation, "the method adopted, instead of a number of irregular raids and irregular fines, being a regular monthly raid and a regular monthly fine."[16] The practical effect was the transfer of payoff money from the pockets of corrupt officials into the city treasury. Nevertheless, the representatives of public morality were outraged.[17] Protestant clergy attacked Williams in sermons titled "The Mayor of Sodom" and "What Shall It Profit a City to License Crime?"[18]

Tom Word was elected Multnomah County sheriff in 1904, with the support of the progressive organizations and area churches, on a promise that he would crack down on vice. He quickly moved to close all of Portland's gambling houses, Chinese lotteries, fan-tan games, poker tables, and pool halls, often sending his deputies with axes. But Word's raids put seven hundred people out of work and cost the city $5,000 a month in the fines and fees it would have otherwise collected. He soon faced a recall petition featuring almost ten thousand signatures.[19]

The differing approaches—Word's crackdown versus Williams's regulation—caused considerable tension between the two local governments. When Word appealed directly to the chief of police for assistance, the reply was terse: "Go to hell." On January 4, 1905, Mayor Williams was indicted for his refusal "to direct the chief of police or some other officer to arrest the propitiators of a certain club for running a gambling house." District Attorney John Manning declined to prosecute Williams, though he had also authorized Word's raids.[20]

When Word again ran for sheriff in 1912, city police forced store owners to remove his campaign signs from their windows, replacing them with those of his opponent. Word was elected regardless.[21] The *Oregon Journal* said of him in 1914: "He has the reputation of being one of the most aggressive law enforcers that has ever filled the office." Word left the sheriff's office that same year but continued his anti-vice crusade for seven more years as a special agent to the federal government. When he died in 1929, the paper lamented, "There never was a better sheriff in any county, anywhere."[22]

The truth is, there was a limit to what any one official could accomplish. In 1904, reform candidates had filled both the sheriff's office and that of the district attorney, with the intent of prosecuting political corruption. Still, they found their efforts frustrated by county judges, who remained in the service of the reigning machine.[23]

Cleanse and Uplift

Despite these difficulties, under the leadership of attorney William U'Ren and the People's Power League, Progressives saw a remarkable string of victories during the first decade of the twentieth century. In 1901, Oregon adopted the secret ballot. A year later, the initiative and referendum system was introduced, allowing the public to propose and approve legislation.[24] The civil service was created in 1903, leading to the replacement of fourteen of the police department's fifty-one patrolmen after they had failed the test.[25] In 1904, the People's Power League helped institute the direct primary and the popular election of US senators. Then, in 1908, campaign spending limits were imposed, public campaign financing was introduced, and a mechanism was put in place for the recall of elected officials.[26]

In 1905, Dr. Harry Lane, a Democrat and a member of the People's Power League, was elected mayor, pledging "integrity in office" and promising "to go up against moneyed interests."[27] He had a record to stand on. For four years he had served as superintendent for the Oregon state asylum. His opposition to nepotism and refusal to grant contracts as political favors had cost him his job at the asylum but earned him a reputation for honesty.[28]

Lane's attitudes were progressive—with a small p—in the sense that they were in many respects ahead of his time. Working as a physician, he had declined to charge impoverished patients. In 1905, as mayor, he hosted a convention on women's suffrage. He spoke out in support of the 1912 Lawrence textile strike and vocally protested the 1915 execution of radical labor organizer Joe Hill. He appointed a socialist as his assistant and advocated for the nationalization of telephones and mines. An anti-imperialist, he opposed the occupation of the Philippines.[29] Later, as the first US senator from Oregon elected by popular vote, Lane was a reliable advocate for the rights of Indigenous peoples and for their political autonomy, introducing a bill for "the complete emancipation of the American Indian from the control, supervision, and management of the United States Government."[30] He was one of only six senators to vote against the Great War, taking a position that was antimilitarist as well as antiwar: "I am opposed to the creation of a large standing army which . . . I fear will later along be used to override the liberty and rights of the citizens of this country."[31]

Nevertheless, Lane also shared many of the biases and faults more typical of the period. He opposed Chinese immigration and declared himself frankly in favor of white supremacy: "I want to vote for any measure which will keep the Caucasian race in possession of its own country."[32]

As mayor, Lane wanted to "cleanse and uplift the evil city, and make it physically and morally safe for families, single working women, and children."[33] But he would be frustrated in his efforts. He sought to use the city's licensing authority to close businesses that served as fronts for criminal activity, hitting them financially rather than relying on the arrest of low-level operators. The city council refused. He then had the police break up red-light districts, which merely dispersed the sex trade throughout the surrounding neighborhoods. At last his faith in the police grew so dim that in September 1906 he ordered Chief Carl Gritzmacher to replace the entire detective bureau. But without the support of the rest of the council, there was only so much he could do. During his two terms, he issued 169 vetoes and was overruled 90 times.[34]

The Timber Swindle and the Teapot Dome Scandal

In the fight against corruption, Francis H. Heney had more success than most. As a specially appointed federal prosecutor, he secured thirty-three convictions in a case involving the manipulation of federal land claims.[35]

The federal Timber and Stone Act of 1878 provided free land for homesteaders on the condition that they live on the plot themselves. Instead, grants were often claimed by individuals in the pay of timber companies, which enabled the corporations to gain large tracts of profitable land while paying government officials to look the other way. Nearly four million acres of public land, representing almost a third of the state's timber, were transferred to private ownership in this manner.[36]

In 1904, Heney arrived in Portland, accompanied by William J. Burns, a Secret Service agent on loan to the Department of the Interior. Heney made it clear that he was aiming for the big crooks: "One millionaire in the penitentiary is worth a thousand poor devils he has bought as an example to the world."[37] His first step was to arrange for the removal of those authorities who had proved insufficiently aggressive in enforcing the law, specifically US Attorney John H. Hall and US Marshal Jack Matthews. By the time he left town, Heney had won convictions against Hall, Senator John Mitchell, US Representative John Williamson, former judge Albert Tanner, former US Attorney and state senator Franklin P. Mays, and state senator Robert Booth.[38] The press dubbed his investigator, William Burns, the "star of the Secret Service."[39]

Years later it was revealed that Burns and Heney had themselves engaged in a variety of dodgy tactics to win these convictions, including stacking juries and interfering with the assignment of at least one judge. Many of their convictions were vacated on appeal. Such revelations did little to slow the ambitious rise of the prosecutor and his investigator, however. Heney became a superior court judge in Los Angeles County. Burns joined and then led a successful private detective firm with offices in several countries. He later headed the Justice Department's Bureau of Investigation, the forerunner to the FBI.[40]

The Bureau of Investigation was founded in 1908, a direct response to the Oregon timber scandal. President Theodore Roosevelt wanted a federal agency capable of enforcing the laws against government corruption and corporate monopolies, with power to "secure the conviction of the wealthiest and most formidable criminals," especially those with "wide political and social influence." In making his case, he specifically pointed to the conviction of "a Senator and Congressman for land fraud in Oregon."[41]

This anti-corruption origin story would prove ironic when, in 1924, Burns was fired from the Bureau of Investigation because of another scheme involving the fraudulent sale of public resources—this time, of oil reserves in Teapot Dome, Wyoming, and Elk Hills, California. Albert Fall, the US secretary of the interior, had sold the oil in no-bid sweetheart deals and had received generous kickbacks from the purchasing companies. When Senators Burton Wheeler and Thomas Walsh called for hearings to look into the affair, the Bureau of Investigation initiated its own investigation—against the senators. Federal agents opened the senators' mail, tapped their phones, and broke into their homes and offices. They persuaded a grand jury to indict Wheeler for corruption, but the case fell apart when it was shown that the Justice Department had fabricated much of the evidence and that key witnesses admitted to lying under oath. In 1924, Attorney General Harry Daugherty was forced to resign. His successor, Harlan Fiske Stone, fired Burns and replaced him with a young attorney named J. Edgar Hoover.[42]

Disappointments

With time, the reformers grew disappointed. In April 1911, Portland's police chief was indicted for malfeasance, as evidenced by his tolerance for "disorderly houses."[43] A year later, David Pattullo, the president of the local Municipal Association, published a letter in the *Oregon Journal* accusing the district attorney of "negligence and inefficiency" and the police chief of "culpable dereliction."[44] On June 1, 1912, a statement from the grand jury demanded that the police chief take action against vice crime "at once." The grand jury lamented, "[In] all past endeavors it has been the experience in reform movements that the first obstacle encountered is the Police Department. Strange paradox that it may seem, those who are paid to suppress crime are in a sense fostering it."[45]

The following year, a group of civic-minded citizens contracted the New York Bureau of Municipal Research to provide a thorough review of Portland's government. A progressive organization founded in 1907 with funding from

Andrew Carnegie and John Rockefeller, the bureau employed accountants, statisticians, engineers, and business administrators, and it provided consultants to improve the efficiency of local and state governments.[46] After receiving an invitation from the Taxpayer League of Portland, the bureau undertook a review of both the city and county governments, with particular attention to the criminal legal system. It found the police department "vicious for its irresponsibility" and remarked: "There is practically not one single earmark of proper organization or efficient method."[47] The bureau's consultants recommended replacing the coroner with professional medical examiners overseen by the judiciary and transferring the constable's responsibilities to the sheriff. The visiting experts particularly objected to the use of repeat jurors: one man had served on eight juries, another on nine, and yet another on eleven. "The sense of justice is outraged at the idea of having the verdict on murder, personal injury, and other important cases returned by 'professional' jurors [where] conditions of employment naturally makes them subservient to the coroner or deputy coroner," the reviewers reasoned. Half of all coroner juries were in this way compromised.[48]

The report helped to fuel yet another attempt at charter reform.[49]

The Galveston Plan

The Galveston Plan—a progressive scheme for restructuring government, instituted in over two hundred municipalities nationwide—was adopted by the City of Portland in 1913.[50] It replaced all fifteen city councilors with four city commissioners and a mayor. The mayor would be responsible for assigning each commissioner a set of bureaus to manage, and laws would be passed by the full council as a body. All citizen boards were disbanded, excepting the civil service.[51]

Historian E. Kimbark MacColl describes the Progressive ideology behind this change:

> To those who yearned primarily for more government efficiency, or "professionalism," as some call it, the need for functional centralization overrode geographic loyalties and neighborhood ties. Many business and professional reform leaders, supported by the chamber of commerce, tended to identify their concerns with the whole city, or with the public interest, a favorite progressive term. Others, like B.S. Josselyn, the

> president of Portland's giant utility monopoly and largest private property owner, wanted city-wide decision making organized along corporate lines so as to promote a smoother and more efficiently administered urban economy over which they hoped to exercise a greater degree of control than in the past. By centralizing decision-making in fewer hands . . . commission government made it easier for business to influence the council . . . non-partisan commissioners became more accessible than the old councilmen to contributors—and more indebted to them.[52]

The Progressive movement represented the consensus of an emerging professional and commercial class: merchants, lawyers, clergy, business executives, university professors, office workers, and skilled laborers. This was the "middle" class, in the sense that its members were neither proletarians nor millionaires, though they understood themselves as a technical, intellectual, and even moral elite. In favor of the Galveston Plan were middle-class Democrats, liberal Republicans, Roosevelt Progressives, the Portland Municipal Association, the Greater Portland Planning Association, the *Oregon Journal*, and local notables like attorney C. E. S. Wood and the Reverend Thomas Lamb Eliot. Opposed were working-class Democrats, conservative Republicans, the *Labor Press*, and prominent suffragist Abigail Scott Duniway.[53]

The move from ward-based machine politics toward the centralized commission system shifted power out of the neighborhoods and concentrated it, not geographically but institutionally. When the government was divided into wards, the councilors were expected to represent interests that were local and particular.[54] With the wards dissolved, politicians were less dependent on constituencies in specific areas and more dependent on (and indebted to) the major donors capable of funding citywide campaigns. Because immigrants generally lived in distinct neighborhoods, they had been well placed to influence the ward-based machines. New, citywide elections made minority and labor representation in government less likely.[55] The centralized bureaucracies the plan strengthened were likewise generally controlled by native-born professionals of the middle and upper classes.[56] Bureaucracies could provide a stable structure for enacting public policy even as elected officials came and went; but as those bureaucracies solidified, developing their own interests and their own sense of authority, they also blunted the power of the electorate. "Although reformers used the ideology of popular government," historian Samuel Hays explains, "they in no sense meant that all segments of society should be involved equally in municipal decision-making. They meant that their concept of the city's welfare would be best achieved if the business community controlled city government."[57]

Under the new system, the cops were no longer to be the lackeys of the political machine, vulnerable to the vacillations in power from one election to the next. The police now were to be the servants of the law rather than the hired muscle of political entrepreneurs. But this theory obscures as much as it illuminates. It fetishizes the law but leaves aside the question of whom the law serves; it trumpets impartiality but ignores the inequality that drives these ostensibly impartial institutions.

The Progressive Movement and the Professional Class

By its own lights, the Progressive movement was democratic and egalitarian. But its notion of equality was entirely formal, "equality under the law," the equality of impassive bureaucracies and indifferent market forces. Democracy too was a matter of formal procedure rather than popular power, of structure rather than movement, of representation rather than participation.[58] Representation itself was of a special sort. Elected officials were to represent the interests not of distinct neighborhoods or specific constituencies but rather of the city as a whole; this broad "public interest" was naturally taken to coincide with the demands of the business class and inevitably sidelined those of racial and ethnic minorities.

A handbill from the period entitled "The Shame of It" practically seethes with class contempt:

> The disgraceful spectacle of Oregon's Senior Senator frequenting the slums in the North End of the City in search of votes to carry the coming primaries ought to cause every self-respecting citizen to hang his head in shame. . . .
>
> The Simon Machine, under the direction of Joseph Simon, is engaged in rounding up and registering the purchasable element, men who have no property in the city and who pay no taxes. . . .
>
> Why is it that this man ignores the respectable element of the community?[59]

The early history of Portland was animated by an ideology of progress. This trajectory should make it clear exactly what is meant by *progress*, encompassing not merely urbanization and industrialization—or even rational administration and technical efficiency—but also a set of social relations that stands behind these values. Progress, in the relevant sense, did mean—at least in principle—impartial government, social stability, and economic efficiency. But it meant, even more, the ascension of a white, Protestant, native-born, professional class. It is by the values of this class that *progress* was to be defined and through control by this class that it would be achieved.

CHAPTER 5

Vice, Degeneracy, and Inversion

The Women's Police

The dual nature of the Progressive movement is neatly illustrated by the career of Portland's first female police officer.

In 1904, Lola Baldwin moved to Portland from Lincoln, Nebraska, where she had worked as a volunteer social worker and served on the board of the Florence Crittenton Home, a charitable organization that provided assistance to unwed mothers and attempted to rehabilitate sex workers. After arriving in Portland, she again joined the board of the local Crittenton Home, which assigned her to work in the disreputable North End, meeting with madams and convincing them to refer underage girls to the agency.[1]

She was then hired by the Young Women's Christian Association's Travelers Aid Society to lead a group of volunteers, recruited from area colleges, in assisting women and children during the 1905 Lewis and Clark Centennial Exposition. Along with the million and a half tourists, the event also attracted a great many young women, lured with promises of work only to find themselves practically indentured and sometimes pushed into the sex trade. The Traveler's Aid Society offered to help with money, clothing, and lodging, and it provided volunteer chaperones for single women attending the expo.[2]

That same year, the city established its first juvenile court, partly as a result of Baldwin's advocacy. Judge Arthur L. Frazer appointed Millie Reid Trumbull as the head of its probation department and Baldwin as a volunteer probation officer. The police began regularly referring cases involving young women to this tiny department. For the first three years, it received no funding from the city. Finally, in 1908, Baldwin wrote to the mayor, requesting $3,000 from the police budget, noting pointedly that "there was $5,030 used this year for the dog pound." She likewise petitioned to have her work incorporated into the police department. Scoring 95 percent on the civil service exam, she was hired as a "female detective" to head the Women's Auxiliary (later renamed the Women's Protective Division). At first she oversaw a staff of one (Lucy May Sargent, a clerk), and continued to work out of the YWCA offices rather than police headquarters. The Women's Protective Division wore no uniforms. Baldwin kept her badge and gun in her purse.[3]

Women had worked in law enforcement before. Since the 1870s, they had served as matrons in the local jail, guarding female prisoners.[4] In 1905, Mayor Harry Lane appointed Sarah Evans—a journalist, suffragist, and member of several Progressive organizations—as the city's market inspector, responsible for ensuring food safety and sanitation. When she met resistance, Lane made her a special officer with arrest powers.[5] But there had only been one other female police officer in the United States before Baldwin, Detective Sergeant Marie Owens of the Chicago police, who started work in 1891.[6]

Under Baldwin's leadership, the Women's Protective Division (WPD) provided food, lodging, transport, and job placement assistance to young women who found themselves in difficulties.[7] It helped find runaways, and parents would come for guidance on handling difficult children, especially daughters. Young women would sometimes ask for legal advice or help in recovering wages they were owed.[8]

Louise Bryant, writing for the *Oregonian* and not yet a notorious radical, praised the WPD as "a wonderful experiment in the police service" and "builded upon different principles than ordinary policing." She noted especially "the care taken of the girls after the case ha[d] been handled in the courts and when the cause of the trouble ha[d] been removed." After that it was "a matter of mothering, not policing."[9] Baldwin worked hard to cultivate this image. She said, "The effectiveness of the protective work is due to its quietness, lack of show or publicity and its sincerity and sympathetic approach." Her officers, she went on, were "friends in time of trouble."[10]

Baldwin soon became a national figure, consulting with departments around the country. In 1912, together with matron Mary Brown of Seattle, she organized the first national conference of policewomen, which was held in Portland.[11] Baldwin used her position to advocate for better education and job training for women, minimum-wage and maximum-hour laws, workplace safety regulations, and legal reforms such as a public defense system to provide representation for those who could not afford their own lawyers.[12] But beneath this progressive altruism there also lay a conservative moralism.

Baldwin was an advocate for women's rights, though chiefly their right to be protected.[13] In her quest to defend female virtue, she initiated prosecutions for statutory rape and abortion.[14] She scrutinized dancehalls, saloons, restaurants, and boardinghouses for signs of the sex trade.[15] She investigated astrologers, massage parlors, movie arcades, taxi services, motorcyclists, beggars, and swimming pools.[16] In one two-year period (1911–12), the Women's Protective Division took action against 216 establishments and made nineteen hundred arrests.[17] Baldwin called for laws to ban "immoral" dancing and prohibit women from working in bars.[18] She particularly objected to settings in which men and women of different races might intermingle: "Public exhibitions of intimacy between Japanese patrons and these [white] girls . . . were positively disgusting to all persons with a sense of decency."[19] During the First World War, she was appointed supervisor for the Pacific Coast and Arizona divisions of the Commission on Training Camp Activities, which was responsible for maintaining moral standards in the areas surrounding military bases, including enforcement of rules against the sex trade and homosexuality.[20] By the time she retired in 1922, she had served as a special agent under six governors.[21] She lamented the decline in public morals, symbolized especially by flappers and cigarettes, and saw this as "the result of too much freedom."[22]

Whipping Boys

The state's measures for the protection of women took more direct and brutal forms as well. In 1905, the Oregon legislature passed a "whipping post law" prescribing twenty lashes for any man convicted of beating his wife.[23]

Six years later, in 1911, the law was repealed. John Buchanon, a conservative representative from southern Oregon, introduced the bill to remove flogging as a penalty, calling the whip "a relic of slavery days," and quoting the Prison Reform League that such punishment "deprives a man of self respect without reforming him." Buchanon recalled having witnessed a man being flogged. "When the process was over there were a dozen gaping wounds on his bare back. . . . Is that civilization?"[24]

Perhaps owing to its very severity, the penalty had almost never been employed. There are only four documented cases of men in Oregon being flogged after convictions for domestic assault (three in Portland, and one in Baker County). All were manual workers or unemployed, and half were immigrants. "[A] poor man would feel the whip, while a richer man would escape with a fine," State Representative Robert S. Smith had warned.[25]

The flogging cases represented a small portion of already uncommon prosecutions. During the six years that the law was in place, there were 157 arrests in Portland for domestic assault, but only seventeen were taken to court. Less than a quarter of these prosecutions resulted in punishment, as compared to 45 percent of other assault cases—though the penalties were typically harsher when the victim was a spouse. Those at the bottom of the social hierarchy—immigrants, Black people, and workers generally—were arrested at disproportionate rates, but wife-beating remained common across all classes of society. A review of five hundred divorce petitions from Multnomah County reveals that, in almost three-quarters of the cases, wives accused their husbands of violence. Thirty-four percent reported police intervention, and many more relied on help from neighbors, landlords, tenants, and even servants—as well as self-defense.[26]

Rather than respond to the very real problem of domestic violence, the whipping post law had more to do with anxieties over increasing numbers of immigrants and the growing independence of women.[27] The stereotyped narrative featured in the legislative debates and newspaper columns—that of state violence being necessary to protect weak and helpless women from the brutality of foreign-born working-class men—served a number of ideological purposes. It placed the blame for a widespread social problem on an already marginalized population; it legitimized state violence and reinforced the presumptive male role as the protector of women; and it handily discounted any possibility for the agency of the women themselves. "The handful of wifebeaters who suffered a flogging were classic scapegoats," historian David Peterson del Mar concludes, "marginalized men selected by community leaders to bear the larger group's mostly unacknowledged flaws."[28]

An Inquiry into Vice

The anxieties represented and mitigated by the whipping post soon found another outlet.

In August 1911, Mayor Allen Rushlight appointed fifteen well-respected citizens to investigate vice crime in the city. Led by the Reverend Henry R. Talbot of St. David's Episcopal Church, the Vice Commission of the City of Portland included four ministers, four physicians, and the WPD's Lola Baldwin.[29] Two of those appointed requested police badges.[30]

The commission's first report, which appeared the following January, was mainly concerned with the prevalence of venereal disease, counting 1,360 cases in a single month.[31] The second report, on the sex trade, appeared in August 1912; it cited 431 properties "wholly given up to immorality," many of which were owned by government officials, bankers, doctors, lawyers, churches, and even members of the Vice Commission appointed to investigate them. Prominent citizens and city leaders were thus actively profiting from the sex trade.[32]

The Vice Commission's second report revealed a deep ambivalence in Progressive attitudes about sex workers, a combination of pity and disdain. On the one hand, the authors seemed to sympathize with them as "being knocked about with the butt of stupid laws." On the other hand, they described the sex worker as "a nuisance to herself; in all cases a menace to the community, and in no case with any chance of improvement."[33] Official efforts to protect young women likewise typically imposed on them a middle-class morality enforced by law.[34]

Clean the City

The same month that the Vice Commission released its second report, August 1912, a grand jury published a report of its own: "We found the city practically an open town. . . . Gambling and vice flourished under the very eyes of the mayor and chief of police. The north and south ends of the city were infested with dissolute women who plied their trade from open doors, windows and on the streets. . . . The evidence that we have acquired leads this body to believe that graft has permeated nearly all departments involving a great many of our public officials."[35]

Governor Oswald West, confident in having recently led anti-vice crusades in the towns of Redmond and Huntington, announced on August 20, "I am going to clean up Portland next." Two days later, he raised the stakes: "I will clean the city or quit my job." West made it clear he was not interested in ordinary street crime but rather in corruption: "The real prostitutes . . . are the prostitutes in office."[36]

West called a meeting with the Vice Commission, the Municipal Reform Association, Mayor Allen Rushlight, Police Chief Enoch Slover, and District

Attorney George Cameron. (Multnomah County Sheriff Robert Stevens was summoned but declined to attend.) West told the assembled leaders, "I'm prepared to go down the line on the enforcement of the law in Portland and I am here today to ask your cooperation. If I don't get it here, I will go it alone, and from now on I will be on the job every minute as long as I am in office." He announced a plan to appoint "special prosecutors" to handle vice cases and threatened to jail any public official who didn't go along. "I'm to do this work if I have to take charge of the offices of the Sheriff and District Attorney by force with the militia." He appointed Walter H. Evans as a special prosecutor, and he deputized Lola Baldwin, as well as all the 1912 candidates for sheriff, as "special agents" with power "to act in any county in the state."[37]

Chief Slover wryly remarked that he would "welcome the Governor's interference." But George Cameron refused to allow the appointment of special prosecutors to the DA's office. West then tried to remove him, going so far as to appoint a new district attorney, but the courts ruled against him. Defeated, the governor closed his Portland office and abandoned the attempt.[38]

Vice Clique

The Vice Commission, meanwhile, continued its investigations.

In November 1912, one of its volunteer detectives, Benjamin Brick, a woolens merchant and "special police officer," interviewed an elevator operator at the Young Men's Christian Association, who pointed him toward a "suspicious" character named Harry Rowe. Around the same time, a teenager arrested for shoplifting told the police he had been "corrupted" by older men, specifically naming Harry Rowe alongside some of the city's more notable citizens.[39] In the following days, the police arrested fifty men.[40] Fifteen were prosecuted, under indictments presenting variations of the same stereotyped narrative: an exploitative relationship featuring an older perpetrator and a young victim. This framing did not fit the facts: all of those involved were willing participants, and few were minors. But absurdly, Roy Kadel (age thirty) was described as the "boy victim" of Edward McCallister (age forty-five), and John Moffett (age thirty-four) was listed as the "boy victim" of Fred Clark (age thirty-nine). Some men were cast as "victim" in one case and perpetrator in another.[41] The *Oregon Journal* referred to the "organization of degenerates" unearthed by these investigations as the "vice clique."[42]

A number of the accused fled Portland. But news traveled, and police in other cities soon began their own anti-gay witch hunts, as well as finding and arresting those implicated in the Portland affair. Two Portland Police detectives, John Abbott and Carrol Tichenor, spent more than a month traveling from city to city, searching for the fugitives. Men were extradited from as far away as Vancouver, British Columbia, and Los Angeles, California.[43]

The idea that men might have sex with men was nothing new, and the fact of such encounters occurring locally was well enough known among the police if not the broader public. Seven people from Multnomah County had been imprisoned for sodomy before 1913, and many more had spent a few months in the county jail for disorderly conduct, vagrancy, indecent exposure, indecent and immoral acts, or being a lewd and dissolute person.[44] These arrests had disproportionately involved migrant workers or ethnic minorities—people already presumed to be uncouth, immoral, and, in the language of the time, "degenerate."[45] Immigrants represented 44 percent of those arrested for same-sex activities. Approximately three-quarters were manual workers, and less than 10 percent were office workers or professionals.[46] In contrast, of those enmeshed in the YMCA scandal, 80 percent were white-collar professionals, a novel development that lent the affair its tone of scandal and panic.[47]

From Sodomy to Identity

Three of those convicted filed appeals, objecting to District Attorney Frank Collier's tactic of calling numerous witnesses to testify about sexual encounters not alleged in the indictments. Collier responded that such evidence demonstrated a particular disposition and showed that the defendants were the sort of person who would engage in such crimes. He cited Richard von Krafft-Ebing's *Psychopathia Sexualis* to argue that the "sex invert" whose "normal sexual passions and instincts have become inverted" exists as a "male body with a female mind." Inversion, by this theory, was a medical condition and an immutable destiny; the invert was essentially different from other men. The sexologists, Collier explained, "have all agreed . . . that the phenomena which mankind has laid to the door of viciousness alone, are in truth and in fact the result of an abnormal state of mind, in the majority of cases, present from birth." Therefore, "When the state charges a man with the crime against nature, or sodomy . . . it, in effect, charges that he is a sexual invert." There was no suggestion on Collier's part that an inborn trait might qualify as a mitigating factor. And he contrasted the invert with the low-class immigrant degenerate, who simply lacked ordinary moral restraint.[48]

Subtly here, Colliers redefined the crime. The act of sodomy, and any proof thereof, became in a sense secondary to the identity of *the homosexual.* Rather than demonstrate that a specific penetrative encounter had occurred, it was more important to consider the accused person's character—his psychology, desires, and inclinations. In the trial of the physician Harry Start, Judge Calvin Gantenbein ruled: "A normal man could not by any possibility commit a crime of this character. This involves the question of the state of the mind, and it seems to me that evidence of other acts may be admitted, even with other people, for the purpose of showing the state of his mind, as to whether or not it was so perverted that he could be capable of committing this sort of crime."[49]

The Oregon Supreme Court ruled against Colliers's method and overturned three of the convictions.[50] Nevertheless, many of the defendants' lives were ruined. Three had been imprisoned, one died in a mental hospital, at least four lost jobs, one attempted suicide, a few drank themselves to death, one became homeless, and thirty-two left Portland, most changing their names.[51] Though Colliers's arguments did not prevail in court, the conceptual shift he articulated nevertheless took hold. In 1917, the Oregon State Penitentiary ceased the use of the term "degenerate" in its official records and adopted "homo-sexual" instead.[52] Homosexuality crystalized as an identity in the context of, and partly through the process of, its criminalization.

Oregon's sodomy law, passed in 1853, had been broad but uncertain: "Every person who shall commit sodomy, or the crime against nature, either with mankind or any beast, shall, on conviction, be punished." In January 1913, the state legislature, without a dissenting vote, broadened the law to apply to "any act or practice of sexual perversity." The new language applied not only to oral sex, but as the courts ruled in 1928, to mutual masturbation as well. It also increased the maximum penalty from five to fifteen years. Consequently, even as the number of convictions fluctuated, the length of sentences grew progressively longer. Before 1906, fourteen men had been imprisoned in Oregon for the crime of sodomy, serving on average 18.5 months. From 1907 to 1916, twenty-three were sentenced for sodomy, spending 21.5 months in prison. Then, between 1917 and 1926, sixteen men averaged 32.7 months.[53]

Immoral Boys and Vicious Greeks

The outrage caused by the YMCA scandal was quickly directed back against the working class.

In April 1913, the authorities received a tip that the Monte Carlo pool hall was serving as "a clearing house for immoral boys who pander to the passions of vicious Greeks." The police chief dispatched two detectives, R. H. Craddock and John Goltz, who over the course of ten days brought five teenagers in for questioning. On April 18, the detectives followed Andrew Dillige, a thirty-five-year-old transient worker and Greek immigrant, as he left the pool hall in the company of Grover King, a nineteen-year-old native-born laborer. The two men went to the Fairmont Hotel, located between Burnside and Couch on Sixth Street, and a few minutes later the detectives burst into room 29, to witness Dillige's "private parts . . . against [King's] rectum." Dillige was convicted of sodomy and jailed for fifteen months. King was charged with vagrancy but never tried; at nineteen, he was still considered a juvenile.[54]

In enforcing the law, the police engaged in a kind of profiling. As historian Peter Boag explains, they "purposely concentrated their surveillance of male-male sexual activities in transient working-class neighborhoods. In so doing, the local authorities clearly utilized laws against same-sex sexual activities as only one part of a larger middle-class campaign to persecute working-class men of racial and ethnic minority backgrounds, particularly the foreign-born." Suspicion fell principally, and peculiarly, on Greeks. Though they represented only about 1 percent of the city's male population, they accounted for 11 percent of arrests for same-sex vice offenses.[55]

Degeneracy and Eugenics

Lurking in the background of the panic over homosexuality were Social Darwinist ideas about biological hierarchies, middle-class anxieties about labor militancy, and a widespread suspicion of Catholicism. It was common for native-born, Protestant whites to blame working-class immigrants for a general moral decline, the prevalence of the sex trade, and outbreaks of venereal disease.[56] And so one result of the successive queer scandals was an increased support for eugenics.[57]

A eugenics-informed sterilization bill had failed in 1909.[58] But after the scandals of 1912 and 1913, Governor Oswald West voiced his opinion that "moral degenerates should be subjected to . . . emasculation." A proposed law, HB69, introduced in 1913 by Representative L. G. Lewelling, a former prison guard, prescribed sterilization for "habitual criminals, moral degenerates, and sexual perverts . . . [such as] those addicted to the practice of sodomy or the crime against nature, or to other gross, bestial and perverted sexual habits."[59]

Eugenics cut sideways across our usual understandings of left and right. Advocates included white supremacists and Social Darwinists but also Progressives like Theodore Roosevelt, Woodrow Wilson, H. G. Wells, Williams Jennings Bryan, Margaret Sanger, and Victoria Woodhull. Opponents included contrarian writers like G. K. Chesterton and H. L. Mencken, the anarchist Emma Goldman, the Hearst newspapers, and the Catholic Church. There was neither a unified bloc in support nor a cohesive opposition. When Oregon's eugenics bill passed, two prominent attorneys, William U'Ren and C. E. S. Wood, joined anti-vaccine activist Lora Little to form the Anti-Sterilization League and force the measure to the ballot. In November 1913, the eugenics law was repealed by a vote of 56 percent to 44 percent.[60]

Unfortunately, the issue did not die there. A January 1917 report from the Commission to Investigate the Oregon State Penitentiary noted "the existence of vice among inmates" in "alarming proportions," and recommended assertive steps against "congenital homo-sexuality," including "a well guarded law, providing for castration."[61] That same year a new law created the State Board of Eugenics to oversee "the sterilization of all feeble minded residents of state hospitals and prisons." By 1918, sixteen inmates of the State Hospital had been sterilized, twelve men and four women, all described as "flagrant masturbators or sex perverts." Three years later, the number had climbed to 127 (68 men and 59 women). Sixty-six of the men had been castrated. The majority were homosexuals. By the time the law was finally repealed in 1983, at least 2,648 people had been involuntarily sterilized; 65 percent of these were women, and about a third were mentally ill.[62]

Prudish Portland

Alongside its ethnic and class-coded aspects, sexual repression carried implications for freedom of speech.

Writing in the anarchist magazine *Mother Earth*, George Edwards recounted an incident from 1915, when Emma Goldman and Ben Reitman lectured in Portland and were arrested for distributing Margaret Sanger's birth control pamphlet *Family Limitation*.[63] Defending the pair was C. E. S. Wood, who called several doctors to testify that the same information was readily available in medical books. Unmoved, the judge convicted the anarchists and fined them each $100. During the appeal, however, it emerged that the complainant, Josephine De Vore Johnson, had not herself attended the talk in question but had received the pamphlet from the staff at the mayor's office and filed charges at their suggestion.[64] Dismissing the case, Circuit Court Judge William Gatens remarked, "The trouble with our people today is there is too much prudery."[65] The anarchists agreed. "Portland is a prude," Edwards wrote in *Mother Earth*. "A certain prudish woman detective who figured in the case was the very personification of old Madam Portland."[66]

Sanger herself was later arrested for distributing the same pamphlet, as were a local physician, Dr. Marie Equi, and three others. Wood again served as counsel for the defense. The judge ruled the pamphlet obscene, reasoning that material suitable for a doctor's office might not be appropriate for distribution at a public lecture. He issued suspended sentences for Sanger and Equi and fined the others ten dollars apiece.[67]

The Politics of Virtue

While Progressive reformers viewed themselves as modern and rational, architects of a sane and prosperous order—the very word *progressive* implies as much—their preoccupation with vice hints at a set of underlying attitudes that were less visionary than Victorian: a view of foreigners as uncivilized, the lower classes as criminal, women as weak, and sex as sinful and degrading. Conflating corruption and vice, they likewise conflated moral reform and political reform. The Progressive movement—or factions thereof—thus battled against drunkenness, gambling, the sex trade, promiscuity, homosexuality, immigration, and political radicalism, alongside municipal corruption and poor sanitation. They formed alliances not only with social workers and suffragists but also at times with racists and eugenicists. No doubt they considered their own authority as benevolent and enlightened, a civilizing and protective force. Yet in addressing their intertwined anxieties over sex, class, and nationality, their accumulated solutions tended in the direction of intensified control. This tendency became especially pronounced when women, workers, and immigrants dared to take action on their own behalf.

CHAPTER 6
Sex, Wobs, and War

What Makes Prostitutes

Amid the furor over sex, class, and immigration, on June 27, 1913, nearly a hundred workers—all of them women or girls and none of them members of an established union—walked off the job in protest of low wages and unsanitary conditions at the Oregon Packing Company.[1]

Mayor H. Russell Albee blamed the cannery strike on "outsiders" and "hired agitators," especially members of radical labor union the Industrial Workers of the World. The *Oregonian* wrote, salaciously, "IWW agitators, many of them rough men from the North End sections, mingle freely with these girls, talk with them . . . and in general affect some intimacy."[2] Critics accused the Wobblies (as IWW members were called) of corrupting young women and leading them to the sex trade.[3] In response, the strikers carried signs reading "40¢ a day is what makes prostitutes."[4]

Reaction to the strike reflected a range of anxieties relating to ethnicity, class, and the growing independence of women, as well as the Progressives' desire for public order and their preference for bureaucratic and managerial solutions to social conflict. Progressives wanted to see labor issues resolved by the Industrial Welfare Commission, an appointed body consisting of a retired schoolteacher, a factory owner, and a Catholic priest. In the cannery case, the commission urged an end to picketing and attempted to negotiate a settlement without the workers' participation; the strikers entirely rebuffed these efforts.[5]

The reaction to the strike was further sharpened by structural changes to the municipal government, the result of Progressive reforms. For the first few days, police were relatively tolerant of picketing and public speaking. That changed abruptly on July 1, 1913, when Russell Albee became mayor and the commission form of government was instituted.[6] That same day, the chief of police, citing instructions from "those higher up," ordered the striking women: "Quit picketing, quit speaking, quit parading, or else face a jail sentence." The strike immediately became, in addition to a workplace struggle, a free speech fight.[7]

On July 9, with the Employers' Association demanding "definite and decisive action," Mayor Albee ordered police: "Permit no person, striker or other, to use abusive, obscene, vulgar or threatening language. Permit no person to block the street or sidewalk. Permit no rowdyism, threats or violence of any kind. Arrest forthwith all violators of the penal ordinances of the City of Portland or violators of these orders."[8] Arrests began at once, mostly of striking women in their late twenties or early thirties.[9]

The police attacked Tom Burns, an IWW member, on July 16, as he stood atop a soapbox soliciting donations for the strike fund; he was so badly injured that he required surgery. Without a pause, another Wobbly climbed on the soapbox and continued speaking. He too was arrested, and again another took his place—and so on, until having arrested ten speakers, Sheriff Tom Word seized the soapbox, and his men attacked the crowd, clubbing and arresting people indiscriminately, a pregnant woman among them. Dr. Marie Equi, having witnessed this assault, forced her way into the police station—punching two officers to do so—and demanded the release of the pregnant woman. The expecting mother was freed, but Dr. Equi was arrested.[10] She later accused the police of "torture": "I was taken into the county jail, stripped, beaten, and spit upon."[11] Sheriff Word commented: "Certain women . . . cannot expect to be treated as women if they act like hooligans."[12]

Violence continued well into the fall. It was not until November that the mayor lifted his restrictions on public speaking.[13] The strike was ultimately lost, and it set the pattern for how the police would respond to future labor unrest: restrictions on public assembly, mass arrests, and reckless violence.[14]

Immoral Tendencies

While in jail that summer, one young striker, Jean Bennet, met Lillian Larkin, a more typical prisoner. In May 1911, at the age of fifteen, Larkin had gone to the Boys and Girls Aid Society looking for help. Lola Baldwin described her as "bold, with immoral tendencies, . . . [and] an inclination to be dishonest."[15] She was placed with a foster family. At eighteen, Larkin began dating soldiers at the Vancouver Barracks in Washington. As a result, one soldier was charged under the "White Slave Traffic Act" —a 1910 law, commonly known as the Mann Act, which made it a federal crime to transport women across state lines for "prostitution or debauchery, or for any other immoral purpose." Larkin herself was jailed for six months.[16] After her release, she spent the night with another soldier, and her foster mother took her back to Baldwin, who had her examined for venereal disease and charged with vagrancy. When Bennett met her, she was waiting to be transferred to the Industrial School for Girls.[17]

Occupying almost fifty acres a few miles south of Salem, the Industrial School was established by the state legislature in 1913 "to be used as a place of detention for delinquent girls between the ages of twelve and twenty-five years." The inmates there attended school during the weekdays, did Bible study and attended church on the weekends, and were responsible for working in the laundry, garden, and kitchen and doing the cleaning. "Besides being graded on their manual work and studies in school," state superintendent of public instruction Frank Welles reported, "they are also graded on the following: Effort, tidiness, truthfulness, obedience, promptness, honesty, good influence and clean talk." As Welles explained it, "the purpose [was] to protect them, to protect society and if possible to so train and educate them that they [would] become good and useful women." In short, the school aimed to instill in them the values and habits expected of either a productive wageworker or a conscientious housewife. The typical term was three years.[18] The *Daily News* described the institution as "a slave labor camp."[19] In its first three decades of operation, at least one hundred of its prisoner-students were forcibly sterilized.[20]

Lola Baldwin had been instrumental in the founding of the reform school and personally had hundreds of young women confined there.[21] So when Bennett was released, she began circulating a petition to remove Baldwin, calling her "utterly heartless and coldblooded." The IWW undertook a campaign to win Larkin's freedom and sent a delegation to meet with Governor West—all to no avail.[22]

Great War, Mass Hysteria

The repression evident in the cannery strike—of political radicals, striking workers, and female sexuality—would take on more urgency and find a wider application in the context of a world war.

On April 6, 1917—the day the United States declared war on Germany—a Portland police officer was fired, being suspected of disloyalty based on comments he made mocking preparedness efforts.[23] That was just a hint of the paranoia to come: A library assistant was forced to resign after she refused to buy war bonds.[24] A business executive was sentenced to three years in prison for drunkenly ranting "A German can never be beaten by a Yank" and "I could take a gun myself and fight right here."[25] The Secret Service began investigating complaints of hoarding.[26] Oregon's first state police force, the Oregon Military Police, was formed to protect weapons plants.[27]

All non-naturalized Germans were classed as enemy aliens and required to report to the US Attorney's office to be interviewed, photographed, and fingerprinted. Those deemed safe were issued ID cards but were barred from traveling or changing residence without permission. Woodrow Wilson's presidential proclamation 416 forbade them from going within half a mile of an armory or one hundred yards of the waterfront. This proved something of a problem, as hundreds had jobs downtown or in the shipyards. Nationwide, 480,000 were registered and 6,000 interned.[28]

The treatment individual aliens received was determined less by questions of loyalty than by their social standing—by their class position, local ties, family status, political views, and work in war production. Most of those interned were poor, and militant unionists were especially targeted. Labor radicalism was considered even more suspicious than German nationalism. Most of the interned aliens were released soon after the 1918 armistice; a year later, only radicals remained in the camps.[29]

Surprisingly much of the repression was left in the hands of amateurs—especially members of the American Legion.[30] Additionally, a local auxiliary to the National Guard, called the Multnomah Guard, was trained at the Armory by sheriff's deputies and overseen by local police. John Leader, a retired British army colonel and head of the ROTC program at the University of Oregon, lauded the Multnomah Guard: "a magnificent regiment of Portland businessmen, very highly trained and bursting with morale and dash, one of the most 'go get 'em' regiments I have seen."[31] In practice, it was, as historians J. D. Chandler and Theresa Griffin Kennedy describe it, "a six hundred-man paramilitary unit designed to protect the city from radical insurrection."[32] The American Protective League, another group of patriotic businessmen, did their bit as well, conducting surveillance against the IWW.[33]

After George Baker took office as mayor in 1917, he stepped up the effort to move against unionists, socialists, pacifists, and other dissidents, organizing an War Emergency Squad, the city's first red squad. Leon Jenkins headed the unit, overseeing eighty officers, a quarter of the total police force.[34] Jenkins later recalled:

> This work included the policing of all railroad shops, buildings, and tunnels, also all public docks and shipyards and other places where materials were assembled or manufactured for use in the war. My detail had charge of the registering of alien enemies in the city of Portland, and within a radius of four miles outside the city. During this special duty work I uncovered a number of plots against the Government, which resulted in several persons being sent to Federal prisons; [I] also had charge of many raids on radical headquarters during this period. The United States Government appointed several outstanding citizens as secret service agents to assist me. I also worked in conjunction with, and made reports to, the Area Commanders of the United States Army and Navy Intelligence Service regarding alien activities.[35]

One of the secret agents assisting in the anti-subversion campaign was Margaret ("Madge") Lowell Paul, "Informant 53" to the Department of Justice. She befriended Irish nationalist and labor organizer Kathleen O'Brennan, and through O'Brennan she made the acquaintance of Marie Equi. Meanwhile eight agents from Military Intelligence and the Department of Justice kept Equi under surveillance, bugging her rooms, following her visitors, and interviewing acquaintances about her political views. In June 1918, Equi was charged under the Espionage Act after she made an antiwar speech at the IWW hall. That November—after the war had ended—Equi finally went to trial, and O'Brennan was issued a deportation order. As during the cannery strike, sexual morality was used as a weapon against labor radicals. A report from Bureau of Investigation agent William Bryon referred to both Equi and O'Brennan as "perverts and degenerates."[36] In court the prosecutor described Equi, who lived more or less openly as a lesbian, as an "unsexed woman" and railed against "long-haired men and short-haired women."[37] Both Equi and O'Brennan enjoyed the vigorous support of organized labor but with uneven success. O'Brennan's deportation was canceled, but Equi was sent to San Quentin, where she served about ten months of a three-year sentence.[38]

Criminal Syndicalism

That Equi's offense occurred in the IWW hall, before a crowd interspersed with police agents, was not a coincidence. The union was a special target during the war years and after. In September 1917, the US Justice Department launched coordinated raids against IWW halls nationwide and seized five tons of documents, including membership lists. That November, Military Intelligence raided an IWW social in Portland, demanding draft cards from all the men present. Twelve were detained. The following February, Portland police officers under the leadership of a Justice Department special agent raided the IWW hall again. Fifty-one were arrested, six of whom were jailed for vagrancy and released after a few weeks. Frustrated, the judge in the case, George Rossman, began lobbying for stricter laws, especially concerning sabotage: "I believe . . . it would be appropriate to pass an ordinance making it unlawful for any person to advocate the destruction of property and to find in one's possession literature advocating such destruction [should] be made prima facie evidence of the violation of the ordinance."[39]

The Portland City Council had recently passed the Trade Conspiracy Ordinance, criminalizing strike activity. The law defined as a criminal conspiracy any agreement among two or more people to boycott a business, or encourage others to do so, for the purpose of influencing the terms of employment. It specifically banned any effort to "loiter or parade back and forth" in front of a business and any attempt to encourage a boycott by means of "banner, sign, transparency, writing, printing, dodger, card, notice, sticker, button, or sash."[40]

Two years later, on January 30, 1919, the State of Oregon passed a criminal syndicalism law, prohibiting membership in any organization advocating "crime, physical violence, arson, destruction of property, sabotage or any unlawful acts or methods as a means of accomplishing or effecting industrial or political ends, or as a means of effecting industrial or political revolution, or for profit." The Multnomah County district attorney put the matter more simply: "All we demand is proof of membership in the Wobbly organization and we will do our utmost to get a conviction." On February 9, the Portland Police arrested a man carrying a sign to publicize a union meeting. Before the end of the month, they had raided the IWW's hall, smashing the furniture and stealing the union's files. Despite the syndicalism law, however, most of those arrested were charged under simpler and more general statutes such as disorderly conduct or vagrancy.[41]

The following November, the police red squad sent spies to a meeting of the Portland Council of Workers, Soldiers, and Sailors. When the informants reported "sedition," Sergeant Frank Ervin raided the event and arrested fifty-six people, twenty-six of them Wobblies. Two months later, police arrested thirty members of the Communist Labor Party (CLP). All twenty-six Wobblies and six members of the CLP were charged under the Criminal Syndicalism Act; twelve were deported.[42]

Women and War

While the Justice Department and the police were rounding up pacifists, socialists, and assorted immigrants, the military was facing a different internal enemy: 13 percent of new recruits arrived for duty suffering from sexually transmitted diseases. Congress allocated several million dollars to create the Interdepartmental Social Hygiene Board to address the issue. Nationwide thirty thousand women were interned for public health reasons, spending an average of seventy days in detention houses followed by a year in reformatories.[43]

Located next to the Multnomah County Poor Farm, near what is now Sandy Boulevard, the Cedars was the first prison of its kind in the United States.[44] In November 1917, the city council passed an "Ordinance for the Control of Venereal Diseases," including a quarantine mandate. The *Portland Telegram* summarized the law: "Immoral women who are arrested and found afflicted will either be placed in a quarantine station until they are cured or will be required to deposit a bond of $2,000 that they will observe strictly the rules and regulations prescribed by the city health officers. . . . Enforcement of such a measure is considered a war effort."[45] The law required doctors to report all cases to the Board of Health and instructed the city's health officer to conduct "examinations of persons reasonably suspected" of infection. "Owing to the prevalence of such diseases among prostitutes," it said, "all such persons may be considered within the above class."[46] Martha Randall, who had worked previously with the Portland Police morals squad, was hired as a deputy to the state health officer. Beginning in 1918, she interviewed every woman taken into custody and determined which ones required medical exams.[47]

In February 1918, the War Work Council of the Oregon Social Hygiene Society, which controlled the governing board of Cedars, announced a new position, characterized by historian Adam Hodges as a "long-term parole officer." "We feel it is only fair to the girl that someone have her welfare at heart and be ready to assist her in finding an honorable living," the OSHS explained. "This would involve getting the girl's history, learning of the work she is best equipped for, finding employers willing to do their part in this absorbing process, keeping in touch with the girl." Anna Murphy took the job, overseeing more than two hundred former inmates between April 1918 and April 1920. Each young woman had to report in as often and for as long as Murphy judged necessary. She did find them homes and jobs—often in domestic service—but it meant that she took control of these choices. She further intervened in her charges' romantic relationships and social life more generally and enforced nightly curfews with arrests.[48]

Hodges concludes: "The internment program inaugurated during the war era was an escalation of an already institutionalized campaign to contain the sexuality of working class girls and young women in Portland."[49] That the motive behind this program—examination, detention, rehabilitation, probation—was sexual morality rather than public health may be demonstrated by the extent to which it exceeded its nominal justifications. Though initially adopted as a wartime measure to preserve the health of potential conscripts, it continued for years after the end of hostilities. In the early 1920s, there were five such facilities statewide. One of these was the Louise Home in the neighboring city of Gresham. In 1919, that facility received 138 girls, 118 of whom were confined there against their wills. Only half were infected with any sexually transmitted disease. Many of the rest were pregnant or merely "way-ward."[50]

Arresting Bolsheviks

Despite everything, workers kept organizing, and the authorities were right to fear their radicalism. In September 1919, forty thousand workers shut down shipbuilding along the West Coast; seventy-five hundred ship workers struck in Portland. The *Portland News* recorded that on September 26, "nearly 200 police, motorcycle men, deputy sheriffs and special agents" were sent to guard the Willamette Iron and Steel plant. Most of the pickets left when ordered to do so, but twenty-three remained and were arrested. The following day, police, acting on orders from Mayor Baker, broke up a crowd assembled in front of the Boilermakers' union hall. On September 28, the American Federation of Labor organized a public meeting in the city auditorium. The crowd of five thousand—taking inspiration from the Petrograd and Moscow Soviets—passed a resolution calling for the nationalization of shipbuilding industries under worker self-management and on a nonprofit basis. The speakers urged those assembled to continue the fight and were open about the risks: "I believe the only way we men and women are going to win our freedom is to be willing to go on the picket line—and go to jail!" Six hundred signed up for picket duty. Progressive attorney William U'Ren represented thirty-seven pickets arrested in the following days. To exhaust the prosecution, he insisted on separate trials for each. When the first ended in a hung jury, all of the remaining cases were dropped.[51]

The repression had escalated with the war but did not decline after the armistice. At the war's close, Military Intelligence turned its domestic files over to the Justice Department's Bureau of Investigation.[52] These files were surely useful a few months later, when Attorney General A. Mitchell Palmer ordered a series of nationwide raids targeting radical organizations and especially immigrants. Across the county, nearly ten thousand people were arrested and about one thousand summarily deported—including almost one hundred from the Portland area.[53] Radical journalist John Reed's mother wrote to him, urging him to stay away: "They are arresting Bolsheviks out here."[54]

Moralizing Politics

The war effort provided a pretext—and heightened authority—for breaking strikes, persecuting foreigners, and controlling the sexuality of young women. These were in no sense new aims, and many of the repressive measures introduced during the war were retained long after its end.

The Progressives had set out to moralize politics and ended up politicizing morality. This outcome was perhaps inevitable given the uncertainty as to whether they sought to suppress vice in order to eliminate corruption or eliminate corruption in order to best suppress vice. In practice, the efforts stood at cross purposes, the suppression of vice only adding to the opportunities and incentives for corruption. Even after the collapse of the old machine system, bribery and extortion remained endemic to Portland's government. Sometimes corruption was fueled by the very process of reform, especially with regard to the period's most notable instance of idealistic overreach: the prohibition of alcohol.

CHAPTER 7

Prohibition and the Klan

The Politics of Prohibition

In 1914, Oregon voters passed a referendum banning the sale of alcohol, and in 1916 the state prohibited personal consumption as well.[1] After the passage of the Nineteenth Amendment and the 1919 Volstead Act, the Treasury Department was made responsible for federal enforcement; its agents were authorized to close any facility involved in the production or distribution of liquor and to seize any vehicles used in its transport. Bootleggers could be fined up to $1,000 and jailed for six months on the first offense, and as much as $10,000 and five years after further convictions. The Prohibition Bureau's fifteen hundred agents were frequently assisted by the Coast Guard, the Customs Bureau, local police and county sheriffs, and the new Border Patrol.[2] In 1931, Oregon added a state police, combining the agencies responsible for traffic control, arson investigation, prohibition enforcement, and fish and game regulation.[3]

The inscription of prohibition into law was achieved only after many decades of agitation. The temperance movement had brought together suffragists, abolitionists, unionists, and nativists—along with a mass of socially minded Protestants.[4] Their victory owed a great deal to the support of Progressive activists and even more so to the kind of moral and political atmosphere they had created. As historian Richard Hofstadter observed, "It is hardly an accident that the generation that wanted to bring about direct popular rule, break up the political machines, and circumvent representative government was the same generation that imposed Prohibition on the country and proposed to make the world safe for democracy."[5]

The dangers of alcohol—personal addiction, domestic violence, and public disorder—were real enough, but at a deeper level the temperance cause resonated with an array of specific social anxieties, cultural prejudices, and political objectives characteristic of the white Protestant middle class. Drink was disreputable in their eyes, representing the imported customs of recent immigrants, the autonomous culture of industrial workers, and the public face of the illicit economy. Prohibitionists openly appealed to nativist prejudices, noting the cultural associations of Germans with beer, Italians with wine, Poles with vodka, and the Irish with whiskey. They likewise appealed to rural fears about the cities as cesspits of vice, crime, and corruption.[6] As historian Joseph Gusfield explains, the question of drink came to symbolize "a battle in the struggle for status between two distinct styles of life," and prohibition "established the victory of Protestant over Catholic, rural over urban, tradition over modernity, the middle class over both the lower and the upper strata."[7]

In practice, the temperance movement was at war not merely against drunkenness but especially against the institution that was the neighborhood saloon.[8] Historian Lisa McGirr explains: "For a swath of the largely Protestant middle-class in small towns and industrial cities, the workingman's pub was a concrete space that encapsulated a host of threatening developments. Mass poverty, market disorder, crime, and vast inequalities of wealth accompanied the nation's transformation into an industrial powerhouse. The saloon was an appealing foe for self-identified 'respectable' men and women. It provided an easy explanation for these ills without challenging the material underpinnings of these men's and women's lives or requiring more far-reaching change to rebalance social and economic power."[9]

The saloon had a strategic as well as a symbolic value. It was the center of community life for many working-class men. In addition to refreshment, entertainment, and affordable meals, a neighborhood bar provided some essential services for those with few resources: workers could cash their paychecks and could store valuables in the establishment's safe. Migrants, sailors, or others without a stable address could receive mail there. The saloon might have the neighborhood's only available telephone or public restroom. Before anything else, however, it was a place to meet and socialize. Some would host political meetings, and those catering to specific trades served as informal hiring halls.[10] "For politically astute reformers," McGirr observes, "the drive to rein in the saloon was also linked to the saloon's and urban proletarians' role in politics. Ethnic working-class saloons were often informal political institutions, serving as the lowest rung and neighborhood hub of the local urban political party machinery."[11]

Cops and Bootleggers

Temperance crusaders promised a new era of health and prosperity, with a virtual end to crime and corruption. But the main result of prohibition was to deliver the entire liquor industry into the hands of organized crime—which is also to say, the police.

Leon Jenkins began his career walking a beat in the North End. He was soon appointed to the War Emergency Squad, which in addition to its efforts to combat sabotage and subversion also took on vice enforcement. In 1919, he became chief of police. In each new position Jenkins achieved a larger and more active role in the illicit alcohol trade and would strategically use raids and high-profile arrests to advance the department's reputation for strict enforcement while also handily eliminating his competition. By 1925, the police controlled the local liquor trade.[12]

Floyd Marsh joined the Portland Police in 1926. Within six months he was assigned to the "Raiders Squad," and he was eventually placed in command of both vice and the mayor's secret police, a special unit with the stated aim of rooting out corruption—especially in the vice squad. Having one man lead both units was contrary to policy, and rather than provide a layer of accountability it served to do the opposite. Instead of fighting corruption, Marsh was practically in charge of it. "I still have a feeling of guilt for things that I was ordered to do on the Vice Squad," he confessed in his memoir.[13]

Liquor from raids was stored in the basement of the police station at Second and Oak, which served as a wholesale warehouse for the well-connected. "I was in the position to know that the 'so-called higher-ups' got their liquor—and most of the time free—while the ordinary citizen got arrested, tried for a crime, and if convicted paid a fine or got a jail sentence—while someone else was sitting up in his office drinking confiscated whiskey," Marsh wrote. He was particularly troubled by the discriminatory nature of the system: "The poor working class of the Italian people, unable to pay off the authorities, were the ones arrested and prosecuted." In his book, Marsh also admits to participating in a "frame-up," which finally led him to resign in disgust.[14]

The discriminatory enforcement, to which Marsh rightly (if belatedly) objected, was understood and accepted by society as a whole.[15] The police had raided homes in poor and immigrant neighborhoods for years, seeking out the odd stash of homemade wine, and they rarely heard a word of complaint in the local papers; but on the rare occasion that they applied the same standard to middle-class professionals, they found themselves facing a wave of criticism. For instance, in 1924, when the cops arrested a member of the chamber of commerce's board of directors and seized two bottles of whiskey he had provided for a New Year's party, journalists as well as his guests were outraged. He was soon released and the charges dismissed.[16]

Mayor Baker was famous for his own raucous parties, featuring plenty of drinking and gambling and sometimes arranged as semi-official welcomes for visiting dignitaries, political notables, and conventions.[17] Such audacity was typical of Baker's reign, and even legitimate government functions—street repair, garbage collection, and other contracted services—were more or less openly exploited as opportunities for kickbacks and bribery.[18] "No, I am not clean," Mayor Baker once declared, "and I don't pretend to be."[19]

"I had seen the law violated so much around the City Hall and by high-ranking officers at the Police Station that I took it for granted as a way of life," Marsh recalled. He estimated that during his time with the police there were a few dozen stills operating in the Portland area, as well as a hundred speakeasies and another hundred beer and wine bars. Together they were good for about $100,000 in protection money every month, along with cases of whiskey or gallons of moonshine to help maintain good relations with the authorities. Additionally, there were forty or so gambling houses and another fifty Chinese lotteries, together worth $50,000 monthly. The city's thirty-five brothels brought in almost $20,000 more. These bribes would be paid to the local beat cop, who would pass a share on to two plainclothes detectives at the stationhouse, who would deliver the remainder in turn to City Hall.[20]

As part of the overall protection racket, detectives regularly used crooks to spy on crooks, extorting evidence from suspects in exchange for a certain latitude in their own criminal undertakings. The consequences for the informants could vary widely. Johan Fagerlie (aka Handsome Hans), who provided evidence leading to dozens of raids, thousands of dollars in liquor seizures, and long sentences for several bootleggers, was badly injured in a gangland attack. On the other hand, Wee Willie Smith, aka Smitty the Bootlegger, was provided a small police pension when he retired.[21]

Interagency rivalry, jurisdictional disputes, and competing loyalties sometimes led to conflicts, even among law enforcement. In February 1924, Zula Lowe—"maudlin drunk," according to witnesses—crashed her car into another vehicle and injured four people, one of them fatally. She was arrested and charged with manslaughter. That night, her husband, John Lowe—a well-connected gangster—met with two police captains, Harry Circle and Frank Ervin. Circle, who was likely in Lowe's pay, wanted to drop the charges.[22] But Ervin was in the pay of Lowe's competitors and former employers—a bootlegging ring centered on the Pullman porters. He refused to dismiss the case.[23]

The Pullman porters, railway car attendants, held among the best-paying and most-respected jobs available to Black men, and their organization, the Brotherhood of Sleeping Car Porters, was a crucial forebear of the modern civil rights movement.[24] The porters were also very well situated to move alcohol into and around the country. They would bring liquor into town by train, then distribute it from the Golden West Hotel, the largest and most comfortable establishment open to Black guests.[25] When Sheriff Thomas Hurlburt led the War Emergency Squad, he regularly raided Union Depot, making dozens of arrests and seizing hundreds of pints of whiskey.[26] He also sent George Hardin—who in 1915 became the first African American Multnomah County sheriff's deputy, after previously serving as the first Black officer in the Portland Police Bureau—to observe operations at the train station and hotel and identify suspects for arrest.[27] Eventually the porters started paying off the police and sometimes enlisted them in their operations—especially those on the morals squad and the motorcycle patrol. For instance, motorcycle Officer Roy C. Brown was arrested, fired, and later jailed after receiving a shipment of twelve quarts of whiskey from the railway station.[28]

In a series of coordinated raids along the north–south railway line, US Attorney Barnett Goldstein arrested twenty-nine key leaders of the Pullman ring. Filling the vacuum, Tom Johnson took control of local distribution. Johnson was influential both in the underworld and in City Hall. He got his start bootlegging in the 1920s; went on to own nightclubs, speakeasies, and gambling houses; invested in real estate; and in the 1950s, profited greatly by manipulating the process for siting Memorial Coliseum. As historians J. D. Chandler and Theresa Kennedy conclude, Johnson "obviously enjoyed special protection from the Portland Police." Though arrested more than fifty times, he never went to jail. When he died in 1964, the *Oregonian* put a favorable spin on his rather dubious position. While noting that "he was deeply involved in Portland night life," the paper also praised him as "a Negro leader who tried to bridge the gap between members of his race in trouble with the law and the city's White officialdom."[29] That is certainly one way of putting it. Historian Joe Uris was more explicit: in addition to supplying illicit goods and services, Johnson "also served as an agent of social control in the black community.... Through him the police could keep track of activity within the black community. In a relationship (probably unspoken, but certainly understood) of mutual benefit, his operation was generally tolerated in exchange for his cooperation in the policing of black Portland."[30]

Fraternity Party

From beginning to end, the entire project of banning alcohol was beset with difficulties. The Volstead Act's standards were unclear and difficult to enforce. Raids only caught those at the lowest levels of the criminal hierarchy and did little to cut off the supply of booze. Evidence frequently disappeared. Juries proved reluctant to convict.[31] The whole enterprise was an invitation to corruption. Alcohol remained plentiful, and violence proliferated.[32]

In the federal system, prohibition agents were exempt from civil service requirements; appointments devolved to local authorities who gave out jobs as political favors. The agents were paid a maximum of $2,300 annually—less than New York City garbage collectors—but they enjoyed plenty of opportunities for graft: bribery, theft, selling illegal permits, and simple extortion. Between 1921 and 1928, a tenth of prohibition agents were dismissed for cause.[33] Mabel Walker Willebrandt, the assistant attorney general in charge of federal prosecutions, lamented that "hundreds of prohibition agents had been appointed through political pull and were as devoid of honesty and integrity as the bootlegging fraternity."[34]

Some idea of the utter normalcy of lawbreaking may be gleaned from the reminiscence of Len Jorg, who was a child in the Kenton neighborhood during the 1920s. "There were no child labor laws then, so all we kids worked," Jorg recalled. "During the week I racked balls in the pool hall, cleaned the beer parlors and the Chinese restaurant, and ran errands for the madam who managed prostitutes at the Kenton Hotel. I also peddled Chubb Rollie's bathtub gin and whiskey. . . . It was Prohibition, remember. I took the bottles in my wagon, covered them with newspapers, and went to the fire station and the police station, where I got paid fifty cents a bottle."[35]

Hangover

Despite its spectacular failure and seemingly counterproductive results, prohibition nevertheless made a lasting impact on policing, crime, and the broader culture. It opened the private home to unprecedented levels of police scrutiny, especially for the poor. And it increased the scale, power, and role of the federal government in law enforcement, creating new centralized systems of record-keeping, a professional prison bureaucracy, and the Border Patrol. The ranks of the federal agencies swelled: the Bureau of Investigation employed 450 agents; the Border Patrol, 450; and the Prohibition Bureau, 2,278 agents, plus almost 2,000 support staff. Altogether, law enforcement expenditures nationwide grew by five times between 1920 and 1930.[36]

When Volstead and similar laws were finally repealed, the change was largely driven by disappointment and disgust at the waste, corruption, and abuse that the law had engendered. But equally important was a shift in social norms, which Prohibition had ironically accelerated. During the 1920s, the middle class shifted away from Victorian values of faith and self-denial toward a more secular and indulgent consumerism.[37]

Even after alcohol was legalized, some bootlegging continued as a means of avoiding taxes and other regulations.[38] But in general, organized crime adapted to the sudden contraction of a once-profitable market by concentrating on its mainstays, pimping and gambling, and moving into a new field, labor racketeering.[39]

Perhaps most curiously, prohibition had a conservatizing effect on the reformers. Before alcohol was banned by law, Hofstadter reminds us, "leading Prohibitionists had often been leading reformers, and the churches that gave the strongest support to the Social Gospel movement in American Protestantism were all by the same token supporters of the dry cause. The victory of Prohibition, the transformation of the drinker from a victim of evil to a lawbreaker, the necessity of defending a law that was widely violated, drew many one-time reformers toward the camp of the conservatives, while the circumstances of American politics led them into Catholic-baiting and city-baiting."[40] This transmogrification, thereby, also set the stage for the second rise of the Ku Klux Klan.

The Klan Rides In

The atmosphere of repression—political, social, and sexual—that took hold in the teens not only continued but also intensified after (and as a result of) the Great War. Immigrants were treated with suspicion based on nothing other than their origins and were identified, in paranoid fantasy if not in fact, with both Catholics and radicals.[41] By this way of thinking, Catholics, communists, and immigrants were essentially *the same threat* and probably even the same people. As this constellation of prejudices took hold, the Ku Klux Klan enjoyed a renewed relevance.

The 1920s Klan described its ideology as "one hundred per cent Americanism."[42] Its constitution outlined the organization's purposes: "to unite white male persons, native born Gentile citizens of the United States of America, who owe no allegiance of any nature to any foreign government, nation, institution, sect, ruler, person or people . . . to cultivate and promote patriotism toward our Civil Government, . . . to maintain forever white supremacy . . . to conserve, protect, and maintain the distinctions, institutions, rights, privileges, principles, traditions, and ideals of a pure Americanism."[43]

The Klan began organizing in Portland in 1921. By the summer of 1922, the city could claim about ten thousand Klan members, half of the state's total. By the fall of 1923, Portland's Klan No. 1 boasted fifteen thousand members. In those years, there were regular cross burnings on Mount Tabor and Mount Scott. Klansmen in full robes sometimes drove in "kavalcades" through the city, purposefully circling Catholic schools in an intimidating display. Klan lectures regularly overfilled the five-thousand-seat public auditorium and sometimes required dozens of police to manage the crowds spilling into the streets.[44]

When Catholic organizations demanded action from the government, Mayor Baker replied, "Until the Klansmen commit some overt act I must and will not interfere with them."[45]

But overt acts were hardly lacking. The Klan had been responsible for lynchings in Jacksonville and Coos Bay and for attempted or mock executions in Medford and Oregon City. In Portland, their violence was less fatal, but its threat was always present. The Reverend Moses Riley faced harassment and threats after whites began attending his church.[46] An unemployed laborer was threatened with violence if he did not find work, and the editor of the *Labor Press* was threatened with "a Vigilance Committee" because of the paper's scathing coverage of the Klan's activities.[47] A Black woman was beaten and scarred with a K burned into her cheek with acid; a note left at the scene, signed "KKK," warned her family to leave the neighborhood to which they had recently moved.[48] Another woman was branded on her chest so that she wouldn't "wear any more low-neck dresses."[49] The Black Patrol was a secret Klan strong-arm squad consisting of a dozen or so members sworn to "eternal secrecy" and owing absolute obedience to the Imperial Wizard and Grand Dragon. During a 1923 strike they rounded up Wobblies and forced them out of town in boxcars.[50]

Many of the Klan's recruits came from the police.[51] The *Telegram* reported that the Portland Police Bureau was "full to the brink with Klansmen."[52] In 1921, the Klan claimed that 150 Portland cops were active members.[53] A Reed College thesis from 1924 cites an estimate shared by both Klan leaders and journalists that approximately 60 percent of Portland police officers had belonged to the Klan at some point.[54]

On March 3, 1923, newly elected Governor Walter Pierce and Mayor George Baker spoke at a banquet at the Portland Chamber of Commerce, held in honor of Exalted Cyclops Fred Gifford. A famous photograph from the event shows two hooded Klansmen—Gifford himself and King Kleagle Luther Powell—alongside several important law enforcement figures, including Police Chief Leon Jenkins, Sheriff T. M. Hurlburt, District Attorney Walter Evans, Mayor Baker, US Attorney Lester Humphreys, US Department of Justice special agent Russell Bryon, Portland Police captain John Moore, and H. P. Coffin of the National Safety Council. Pierce and Baker later denied knowing that it was a Klan event, and historians are divided as to believing them.[55] Whether Mayor Baker himself ever joined the Klan is also a matter of some dispute. He denied being a member, though he was openly sympathetic with the organization's aims and actively sought their support.[56]

At its peak, the Klan had broad influence in city, county, and state governments. It fully controlled the Multnomah Republican Party and, with it, nominations for school board members, county commissioners, judges, state representatives, the state Speaker of the House, the president of the Oregon senate, the state treasurer, and the governor. In May 1922, twelve (of thirteen) Klan-backed candidates swept the election for the state legislature, two Klansmen were elected to the public service commission, and two (of three) members of the Multnomah County Commission had the Klan's endorsement.[57] That November, with Klan support, Piece was elected governor; the Klan's chosen candidate displaced the sitting US congressman; every circuit court judge with a Klan endorsement kept his position; and a Klan-sponsored public education bill passed, abolishing Catholic schools. The following year, a Klansman was appointed customs inspector at the Port of Portland. The legislature passed two Klan-sponsored bills: one forbade teachers from wearing religious clothing, effectively barring nuns from classrooms; the other prohibited Chinese or Japanese immigrants from owning land.[58] Much of the Klan's legislative success was the work of the improbably named Kaspar K. Kubli, who served in the Oregon legislature from 1919 to 1923 and during that time joined Portland's Klan No. 1. A newspaper campaign ad described Kubli as "a consistent protector of established industry" and the "Father of [the] 'Syndicalism Bill,' which drove the I.W.Ws. out of Oregon."[59]

But the Klan lost power as abruptly as it had won it. In 1924, the Klan-affiliated county commissioners were removed from office after a scandal involving kickbacks for public works projects.[60] That same year, the public school law was declared unconstitutional, and George Baker was defeated in his run for US Senate.[61] By the year's end, membership had fallen to 1,165.[62] Historian Kenneth Jackson attributes this rapid decline to a number of factors, the most import of which was the organization's internal division. Rivalries existed between Baker and Kubli, and between Powell and Gifford. A schism opened between the Klan and its allies in the Federation of Patriotic Societies over the question of corporate control of public utilities. Additionally, the local Klan became known as a haven for grifters and wracked with corruption, including fake charity drives, fraudulent stock sales, and embezzlement.[63] Each of these problems built on the others, and the group's early momentum proved impossible to sustain.

The Making of the White Middle Class

Some Progressives and even left-wing radicals were sympathetic to or collaborated with the Klan—among them, attorney William U'Ren, journalist Eleanor Baldwin, and labor leader Tom Burns.[64] Though the Klan defended the same monopolistic corporations that the Progressives opposed, the two movements had a similar class composition, drawing especially from the upper layers of the working class and the lower layers of the middle.[65] They shared a suspicion of those in the lower strata or on the margins of society. Historian Robert D. Johnston argues that "the Invisible Empire functioned, in complex and complicated ways, to politically mediate—and even help define—the middle of the social order."[66]

Sustained contact between the Progressives and the Klan, in terms of their practical activity, came during the campaign for compulsory public education and the closure of parochial schools—a measure at once anti-elitist and anti-egalitarian.[67] As a result, the Progressives seem to have shifted crucially rightward, adopting what Johnston characterizes as "a liberal, and no longer subversive, populism." He elaborates: "Such liberal populism . . . resonated with the social concerns of the same bloc of low-level white-collar workers, small entrepreneurs and skilled blue-collar workers that had mobilized behind small-propertied radicalism in Portland. Liberal populism spoke to the increasingly tenuous place this set of Americans held in an unequal society. What School Bill defenders ended up demanding, though, was an equal opportunity for all to enter an unequal society through compulsory education—not the transformation of hierarchy itself."[68]

The Progressive movement had always been a kind of cross-class alliance, drawing from the lower and local portions of the capitalist class as well as the more privileged sections of the working class—professionals, office workers, and skilled laborers.[69] Often as not, the thing that allowed for some sense of political coherence was not any common economic interests but rather a shared moral outlook and a racial, ethnic, or national affinity. As much as the Progressive agenda represented an attack on vested interests and gestured occasionally toward a limited anti-capitalism, it often did so by mobilizing in the defense of some other form of dominance: Protestant chauvinism, nativism, or white supremacy.[70] The exchange between the Klan and the Progressives tended to suppress class as a social category and basis for political action.[71] This feat was accomplished, ironically, through the creation and consolidation of a new middle class, which eventually achieved a kind of hegemony. Its concerns came to predominate, its outlook was accepted as common sense, and its values almost defined the public standards of morality.

The triumph of reformers too easily shaded into a reign of reactionaries. Though often in conflict, the two tendencies shared many of the same underlying assumptions. The implicit xenophobia of the reformers was not too distant from the "One Hundred Percent Americanism" of the KKK.[72] The Progressive faith in technical experts and respectable authorities was both rooted in and fed an elitist distrust of the mob, especially groups of a different ethnic or class background than the reformers themselves. The Progressive ideal of the public good generally reflected the perspectives, values, and interests of a middle stratum comprising skilled workers, professionals, and businessmen, which helped also to shape the antiradicalism of the teens and twenties. Their moralistic attitude and paternalistic approach inaugurated a period of sexual repression culminating in prison camps and systematic castration. And the Progressive sense of organizational rationalism, tending always toward an increase in order and stability, discouraged the pursuit of unproductive pleasures and spontaneous joy, as well as any disruptive or conflictual political expression. Viewed from a certain angle, and with particular features highlighted, Progressivism almost seems like a variety of conservatism. The Progressives thus helped to create not only the bureaucratic structures but also the political base, the ideological justification, and even the emotional demands necessary to a policed society.

CHAPTER 8
Depression and Repression

Charities and Vigilantes

Perhaps the strangest and surely the most benign legacy of the Klan's involvement with law enforcement was a charitable operation surviving today as the Sunshine Division.

In 1922, the state tax commission reduced the Portland Police budget by $78,000, reasoning that vehicle patrols could make policing more efficient and require fewer officers. However, they neglected to provide funds for the necessary cars and motorcycles. Forced to lay off forty-one employees and then faced with a staffing shortage, Mayor Baker created "a vigilance committee consisting of one hundred private citizens." He recruited local businessmen to act as an auxiliary, and within a month sixty-three were sworn in and issued badges.[1]

Headed by Inspector C. H. Tichenor, this volunteer force was officially the Portland Police Vigilance Reserve. They were more commonly referred to as "the Vigilantes." All of the original members were Klansmen, personally nominated by Exalted Cyclops Fred Gifford. Though there was little official documentation of the Vigilantes' activities, they seem to have taken a hand in enforcing prohibition and harassing the IWW. In 1926, the name was changed to Portland Police Reserves.[2]

The reserves gradually took over the Police Bureau's charitable functions. In 1920, Captain Harry Circle—who happened to be the highest-ranking police official to join the Klan—had begun an annual tradition of delivering Christmas dinners to poor families, using money his men had deposited in the donation box always on his desk. Chief Jenkins smiled on the project, hoping that it would improve community relations, and after the initial efforts received positive press coverage he instructed his officers to "investigate conditions of poverty... [and] list those families deserving of aid."[3]

The process for determining who was needy and deserving was sometimes intrusive and open to bias. A police officer would interview the family in question about their supplies of food, fuel, and clothing and sometimes search their home. On his second visit, he would ask about employment and use business connections established through the reserves to find jobs for those seeking work. If ongoing help seemed necessary, the police would refer the family to the Public Welfare Bureau. In practice, the police served as a stopgap while poor families waited for more consistent services.[4]

By the end of the decade, the Portland Police Sunshine Division was providing food to more than four thousand people each year, in addition to eight hundred Christmas dinners. Demand only increased during the Depression, as the local unemployment rate neared 30 percent. By 1932, they were feeding more than fifteen thousand people per year and providing hundreds with household goods such as stoves, mattresses, quilts, dishes, and baby carriages.[5]

Both the need and the activity dropped off during the Second World War.[6] But at the end of the forties, the effort was renewed, with Captain Circle resuming control and the new mayor lending support, though the division had long been criticized for duplicating efforts and wasting public resources.[7] As at the start, the aim was only partly altruistic. The minutes from a 1949 meeting of the Sunshine Division board of directors credits "the fine public relations created by the officer on the beat being able to give immediate help to those in distress" as a proven means of increasing "the respect and good will of the people."[8]

Down and Out in the City of Roses

Like everywhere else, Portland was hit hard by the Depression. The Public Welfare Bureau saw its caseload double in 1931 and double again the following year. By 1932 a quarter of Oregonians were unemployed, almost thirty thousand in Portland alone.[9]

The unemployed organized on their own behalf. The Oregon Workers' Alliance monitored the implementation of New Deal programs and advocated for people when their public relief benefits were denied. They called a successful one-day strike for a fifty-cent minimum wage, boycotted businesses that engaged in racial discrimination, and held sit-ins at relief offices when they started recruiting scabs during a timber strike. "We had committees that would first ask the city not to turn off the water for those who couldn't pay the bills," Hamish MacKay recalled, "but if they did we would turn it back on ourselves. Finally, we won when the City stopped turning the water off."[10]

The Portland Police responded by cracking down on vagrancy, breaking up meetings, and sending spies to infiltrate the Communist Party, leading to sixteen indictments.[11] Federal agents also took an interest. On March 3, 1936, Ray Norene, an immigration officer, arrived unannounced at MacKay's home, intimidating his wife and inquiring about ties to the Communist Party.[12] It would be almost twenty-five years before the full effect of that encounter would become clear. On November 18, 1960, MacKay was deported by order of Judge Gus Solomon, citing his membership in a "proscribed organization."[13] A photo from the time shows MacKay's young son carrying a protest sign, "Don't Send Our Daddy Away."[14]

The Battle for the Ports

Those lucky enough to find work faced struggles of their own.

March 9, 1934, marked the first day of a West Coast longshore workers strike, declared by the International Longshoremen's Association (ILA). The workers demanded recognition of their union, control of the hiring hall, a single contract covering the entire coast, an end to blacklisting, and an increase in pay.[15] The strike halted shipping for eighty-two days, paralyzing much of the economy. Fifty thousand Oregon workers were idled, fifteen thousand in Portland.[16] Arthur Farmer, an official with the Portland Chamber of Commerce, described the strike as "a siege on Portland industry."[17] He reported, "It is apparent shipping here will remain at a standstill until and unless protection is given the strikebreakers." Buses used to transport scabs "were rendered useless when fundamental running parts were removed and tires deflated." Scabs' cars were "overturned and damaged" and the scabs themselves "manhandled." All the while, police stood by passively, bringing "no fight to the strikers and no assistance to strike breakers."[18]

Cops sometimes even aided the union. Marvin Ricks, a veteran of the strike, later told an interviewer: "We did have someone in the police department who sent us a list every week of all the special police that were hired, including addresses. So there were specials who happened to run into unfriendly people in the streets." He continued:

> Then we had this detective who used to tell us this and that. Once he says, "They're moving a bunch of scabs this morning. We have been ordered to take them to point X. At point Y, the harbor patrol is to pick them up and guard them the rest of the way. Somebody forgot that there was one block in between those two points. I will see to it that we protect them only to the point that we were told . . . and that none of the harbor patrol go beyond that point." So there was quite a bit of monkey business out in the street that morning in that one block. There were police on both ends, but none made a move because they hadn't any orders. That is what you call having friends.[19]

The ILA cultivated this support and urged the workers not to provoke the cops. The truce lasted about six weeks.[20] Ricks recalled, "When the strike started nearly all the regular police were our friends. They were working men. Then pretty soon, you found all the good guys uptown, directing traffic, and you had every bad one on the waterfront, plus a bunch of special police they stationed at Terminal 4."[21]

The union made it virtually impossible to move strikebreakers to and from the docks, so the employers housed the scabs and the special police who had been hired to protect them either at the worksite or aboard ships anchored nearby. One night, about seventy-five longshoremen raided the *Admiral Evans*, tearing down the fence that had been erected to protect it. The patrolman ostensibly guarding the gate took no action and did not even attempt to discourage them; he merely warned the invading longshoremen to be careful of nails as they walked over the remains of the fence. The two dozen special police aboard the ship were outnumbered and easily routed, as striking workers beat them with broom handles. One of the raiders laughed, remembering, "Some of those specials jumped in the river, got knocked in the river and everything else. That broke up their playhouse." In the end, the *Evans* was cut loose and drifted downstream until it became lodged under the Broadway Bridge.[22]

These "special police" acted almost as a private army. During the strike, the chamber of commerce secretly funded two organizations—the Citizens Emergency Committee and the Citizens Emergency League. These became the principal agencies policing the strike.[23] The Citizens Emergency Committee, a group comprising about a hundred business leaders, collected $300,000 for the hiring of 620 special police officers—many with criminal records—and sponsored a propaganda campaign to build support for the ship owners. The

Citizens Emergency League (CEL), meanwhile, offered its members to be called on "by the constituted authorities in case of emergency." The group's membership application described it as a "voluntary association of able-bodied, patriotic American Citizens, joined together to more effectively discharge our recognized duty as citizens; and to offer our services to a recognized Government authority to be used in cases of extreme emergency to maintain law and order; and for the protection of lives and property." The application asked about pertinent details such as firearms ownership, military training, and "experience with gas bombs." Each of the group's three thousand members was issued a pocket medallion and a red, white, and blue armband.[24] (The official reserves—the Vigilantes—were surprisingly never mobilized during the strike).[25]

On July 11, 1934, Police Chief Burton K. Lawson and three hundred special police accompanied a twenty-five-car train on its approach to Terminal 4, some walking ahead to clear the tracks, others riding in two cabooses and a flat car. When strikers threw rocks at them, the cops—including Lawson—opened fire with pistols and shotguns. Four strikers were hit.[26] But after forcing the strikers back, the cops found it impossible to go on. At an incline along the route, the workers had slicked the tracks with lard, soap, and axle grease. The train had to return to the Albina yards with its cargo.[27]

This skirmish had some far-reaching consequences. When the Communist Party organized a meeting to protest the police violence, Dirk De Jonge and ten others were arrested under the criminal syndicalism law.[28] The prosecutor, Stanley M. ("Larry") Doyle argued at trial that "it was only necessary to show that De Jonge was a communist and had been present at the public meeting to prove his guilt." The judge, Jacob Kanzler, himself a member of the American Legion's Americanization Committee, seemed to agree; all eleven defendants were found guilty. De Jonge appealed, aided by a team of lawyers including future federal judge Gus Solomon, and the US Supreme Court overturned the conviction.[29]

Moreover, the violence led President Franklin Delano Roosevelt to dispatch a US senator from New York, Robert Wagner, to investigate the strike and urge negotiations. On July 18, as Wagner approached Terminal 4 with two union members, a sympathetic attorney, and a journalist, shots were fired at his car. Two company guards were arrested but released that same night. Following the shooting, Governor Julius Meier summoned the National Guard, assembling them at Camp Withycombe in nearby Clackamas County. Emboldened, the shipyard owners tried more aggressively to move their cargo.

The strikers maintained their pickets but carefully avoided violence, and the soldiers remained on base. Perhaps it helped that the Central Labor Council threatened a general strike if they intervened.[30]

On July 20, the owners agreed to arbitration. The workers returned to their jobs at the end of the month.[31] An arbiter raised wages to $1.05 an hour and granted union recognition.[32]

The final battle came after the strike's end. On August 20, 1934, a protest outside the offices of the company-run scab "union" ended in a shootout when Harper Knowles, a man in the employ of the Portland Police, opened fire from inside the hall.[33] One scab was killed and twenty-nine ILA members arrested. Charges were soon dropped. It turned out that another scab, Carl Grammer, had fired the fatal shot.[34]

This strike, which was even more bloody at other West Coast ports, reverberated at the local, state, and national levels. While Chief Lawson resigned in disgrace, Mayor Joseph Carson went on to become the US maritime commissioner.[35] The De Jonge trial led to the repeal of the state's criminal syndicalism law.[36] And, a year after his close call at the Portland docks, Senator Wagner sponsored the National Labor Relations Act, which protected the workers' right to organize, required good faith bargaining, and outlawed a number of specific unfair labor practices.[37] The strike was a defining moment in the history of the longshore union, signaling a new militancy and beginning a transition toward a more democratic organization—the International Longshore and Warehouse Union (ILWU).[38] But, in the view of popular historians J. D. Chandler and J. B. Fisher, "the biggest legacy of the strike" came in the form of "a statewide Red Scare."[39]

Red Squad, Black List, Silver Shirts

The day the strike was settled, the chamber of commerce announced a new Civic Protection Committee "to investigate and study communist activities here in the city and vicinity." Its members included prominent businessmen, attorneys, a sitting judge, a retired general, newspaper editors, and the president of the chamber of commerce.[40] They found a receptive partner in the red squad. According to a report from the Oregon chapter of the National Lawyers Guild (NLG), the red squad was a joint venture of the Portland Police Bureau, the chamber of commerce, and the American Legion. It was originally stationed in a single room in the Railway Exchange Building, its rent covered by private donations.[41]

The unit was led by Walter B. Odale. Though only a patrolman in the Portland Police, he held a "special commission" from the state and was sometimes addressed as "captain," a rank he had earned in the National Guard early in the century. The second-most-prominent member, George Marion Stroup, was not a police officer at all, though he worked out of the red squad's offices and was given access to police files. Also on the detail were a detective, William ("Big Bill") Browne; a patrolman, Merriel R. Bacon; and a clerk, Spencer Raynor. Odale, Stroup, and Browne were all members of the American Legion's Subversive Activities Committee.[42]

Using funds from the Legion, the red squad investigated radicals far outside of Portland—in Marion, Yamhill, Coos, and Columbia counties—and issued reports naming potential subversives, usually union members. A report on Klamath Falls included 135 names and was delivered to local business owners for use as a blacklist—though, ironically, some *employers* publicly protested its inaccuracies.[43] Another report, on Oregon State College in Corvallis and the University of Oregon in Eugene, warned that "many small groups of progressives, liberals, radicals, pacifists, internationalists and others"—the Baptist Youth Council and committees of both the YMCA and YWCA, among them—were being manipulated and used "to build communism with non-communist hands."[44]

This sort of libel was typical of the red squad's work, especially its "Weekly Report of Communist Activities." A bulletin from January 1937 listed several people as "active communist sympathizers and supporters" based entirely on their membership in the ACLU. ("Everyone knows the American Civil Liberties Union is merely another front for the communist party," Odale explained.)[45] Mimeographed copies of the newsletter were sent to the governor, the mayor, other officers in the Portland Police, various other law enforcement agencies, the American Legion, and select business owners.[46] Governor Charles Martin reciprocated by having the state police send their intelligence reports to Odale as well.[47] Martin, a former US Army general nicknamed Old Iron Pants, sympathized with the Klan, had a tendency to rant about "Jew Communists," and opposed public utilities and labor unions.[48] Having once himself overseen the suppression of a peasant revolt in Panama, he wrote an open letter to the state's sheriffs advising them on the handling of strikes: "Beat the hell out of them.... Crack their damned heads. These fellows are there for nothing but trouble ... give it to them!"[49]

Odale insisted that he was not anti-union. But the red squad's major function was the maintenance of blacklists. These were made available to employers but were also compiled with the assistance of conservative union officials eager to rid their organizations of radicals. Stroup's wages were sometimes paid by unions as well—mainly the Teamsters. Private detective firms also enjoyed access to the red squad's files for use in their union-busting efforts. In fact, the red squad office served as a kind of employment referral service for labor spies. Odale told the National Lawyers Guild that "the red squad itself did not employ spies for this purpose, but when asked to do so would send suitable investigators directly to the employer needing the investigation; thus the spy was supplied by the red squad but hired by the industrial employer."[50]

Odale claimed that his unit had files on ten thousand people who had been "active in some phase of communist activity" during the previous six years." His notion of "communist activity" was elastic, however. He estimated that there were 1,000 official members of the Communist Party (CP) in Oregon and another 2,000 supporters, though the CP itself only claimed 260 members in the entire region.[51] The National Lawyers Guild assessed, "[Odale] sees communist efforts as the explanation of almost every social ill, from the loosening of family ties to labor abuses and the current national crime waves."[52]

Even more worrying were Odale's ideas for fighting communism. In one newsletter he offered what sounded very much like a defense of fascism: "When communism has so undermined a government that that government can no longer combat communism, then 'Fascism' is the last resort of an aroused citizenry to overthrow communism."[53] In fact, Odale later joined a fascist organization—the American Defenders, an offshoot of the Silver Shirts, a group modeled on the Nazi Brownshirts.[54]

In 1937, the American Legion's Subversive Activities Committee was disbanded for reaching beyond its remit. That same year, after an *Oregonian* series on the unit, the Portland Police likewise took steps to reign in the red squad. Its office was relocated to police headquarters, it would henceforth be supervised by a captain, circulation of its newsletter would be limited to law enforcement agencies, and Odale was barred from speaking publicly about their work. "Except in these respects, however," the National Lawyers Guild noted, "the activities of the red squad do not appear to have changed materially."[55]

Many of the unit's proscribed activities and even its files were taken over by a new organization called Americans, Incorporated.[56] "Although it is probably not to be identified with the police red squad," the NLG wrote judiciously, "its activities . . . resemble the red squad's closely. . . . [Its] principal known activity

. . . has been the publication of a mimeographed bulletin similar in all respects to the bulletin formerly distributed by the red squad." The new publication was titled *Radical Activities Bulletin* and often cited "information given Americans, Incorporated, by local law enforcement officers."[57]

The Bridges Conspiracy

The Portland Police red squad came to play an outsized role in the attempt to deport Harry Bridges, an Australian-born leader in the longshore union.

On March 5, 1938, Bridges was summoned to a hearing on Angel Island, an immigration facility in the San Francisco Bay, to determine whether he was subject to deportation as a member of the Communist Party. Roy Norene, the head of the immigration office in Portland, and Raphael Bonham, his counterpart in Seattle, had written to Secretary of Labor Frances Perkins to demand the labor leader's arrest and expulsion, attaching four affidavits connecting him to the Communist Party.[58] Bridges consistently denied being a Communist.[59]

The hearing began on July 10, 1938, overseen by James M. Landis, the dean of Harvard Law School.[60] Bridges's attorney Carol King, in her opening remarks, asserted, "The witnesses against Bridges are felons or labor spies, or both, and their evidence is not credible." As part of a scheme "carried out with the active assistance of high public officials," they had been either bribed or blackmailed, she said. "The most prominent participants of this type are Captain [John] Keegan, of the Portland police, Lieutenant 'Red' Hynes, of the Los Angeles police, Clarence Morrill, director of the California State Bureau of Criminal Investigation, and Captain Odale, of the Portland police force."[61] Through tenacious cross-examination, Bridges's lawyers demonstrated that rather than uncover a Communist conspiracy with Bridges at the center, the government had engaged in an anticommunist conspiracy centered on Bridges. In making this case, they also provided a rare window into the operations of the red squad and its affiliates.

The government's first witness was Major Laurence Milner, who as a special agent for the Military Intelligence Battalion of the Oregon National Guard had infiltrated the Communist Party from 1933 to 1937. In that role he wrote daily reports that totaled fourteen hundred pages. Milner had, by his own admission, sometimes acted as an agent provocateur and had served as a defense witness for Dirk De Jonge when he was on trial for violating the state's criminal syndicalism law. Here he admitted to lying in the earlier trial, when he had testified that De Jonge was not a communist. "I considered it my duty as a military intelligence officer," he explained, "to do anything to gain my purpose without being disclosed." Landis was not impressed, dismissing the witness as "a self-confessed liar" and referring the matter for prosecution as perjury.[62]

This was a bad start for the government's case, and it hardly got better. Two of those who had signed the original affidavits either failed to appear or refused to testify. The Portland red squad's Merriel Bacon merely repeated a secondhand account he had heard from an informant only identified as "Mickey." Civilian witnesses admitted to being bribed or threatened.[63] The picture that emerged over the next nine and a half weeks of testimony was that of an inquisition obsessed with its quarry but indifferent to facts.

Harper Knowles, by his own introduction "one of the foremost people on the Pacific Coast who have been demanding a hearing against Bridges," was the executive secretary of the Associated Farmers of California, an anti-union industry group. During the 1934 strike he had been commander of the American Legion branch in San Francisco and organized the Legion's committee to track subversives. He had developed a network of hundreds of informants all over the state and shared intelligence with employers, the military, the State Bureau of Criminal Investigation, and the Los Angeles Police Department. He had repeatedly written to Perkins nominating Bridges for deportation as a communist; when she asked for evidence, he joined with Larry Doyle and the Portland Police to find former party members who might swear out affidavits.[64]

Captain Keegan testified that Doyle—the prosecutor in the De Jonge case, a special agent to the State of Oregon, an employee of the Waterfront Employers Association, and yet another member of the American Legion—had contacted him during a convention of the Maritime Federation of the Pacific, held in Portland in 1937. Keegan assigned Big Bill Browne to help Doyle bug Bridges's hotel room, while Keegan himself took a team of detectives to infiltrate the convention. Since that time, using funds from the Teamsters union, he had sent his officers up and down the coast to interview witnesses and collect information on Bridges.[65]

Though Milner had submitted seventy-seven reports about Bridges over the course of four years, his investigation never amounted to more than reheated gossip. "The evidence," Landis determined, "establishes neither that Harry R. Bridges is a member of nor affiliated with the Communist Party of the United States of America."[66] Folksinger Woody Guthrie offered his own verdict in

"The Ballad of Harry Bridges," vindicating the labor leader and condemning his accusers: "Old Harper Knowles and Captain Keegan / Will someday sleep in a restless grave."[67]

But the federal authorities were not done with Bridges. In 1940, Congress passed the Smith Act, making it a criminal offense to advocate the overthrow of the United States government.[68] Sam Hobbs, a congressman from Alabama, could hardly contain his vindictive glee: "It is my joy to announce that this bill . . . changes the law so that the Department of Justice should now have little trouble in deporting Harry Bridges and all others of similar ilk."[69] The FBI opened an investigation, headed by J. Edgar Hoover personally. The outcome was a foregone conclusion. "Bridges is a Red," Hoover declared, and Francis Biddle—the new attorney general and longtime member of the American Civil Liberties Union—ordered him deported.[70] The US Supreme Court disagreed, however, and in 1945 Harry Bridges became an US citizen.[71]

Class, Conflict

The Great Depression signaled a crisis in the capitalist system at every level—locally, nationally, and even globally—and engendered a multiplicity of responses, including increased support for communism on the left, fascism on the right, and a new type of liberalism centered on the welfare state. Police attitudes were likewise varied, and police behavior when facing rebellious workers was not always what one might have expected. The cops were, however, consistently anticommunist and over time displayed a rightward bias. Whatever the reservations of individual officers, as conflicts escalated, means were found to mobilize the institution for purposes of repression. At times this involved recruiting new officers with fewer scruples and creating and mobilizing auxiliary forces. The role of the chamber of commerce in funding and directing the police and their ad hoc deputies is of singular import. It both illustrates the use of the police as a tool for the capitalist class and points to the limits of their utility in that role. For the police have their own interests, attitudes, and loyalties, which fully align neither with those of the employers nor those of the working class. This ambivalence was apparent in some of the struggles of the thirties, and the resulting tensions would later be contained, if not quite resolved, in that most contradictory of political creatures—the police union.

CHAPTER 9
Professionalism and Unionization

Career Goals

While the Portland police were alternately aiding and repressing the labor movement, they were also engaged in a struggle to establish—and improve—their own class position. First, there was a movement for professionalization, a police-led reform effort to convert their organizations into modern bureaucracies and to reimagine themselves as skilled and respected specialists with a defined field of expertise, akin to teachers or engineers. Beginning somewhat later than professionalization, but continuing concurrently, the cops formed a union of their own.

The Great Depression had changed the composition of the police force, drawing in middle-class recruits, while also suppressing wages and exposing the cops to the illustrative example of militant labor action. The lasting effects of the Prohibition, meanwhile, meant that the cops neither deserved nor received the trust and respect of the broader public. In 1934, an independent committee—the Portland Police Survey Commission—was contracted to study the Police Bureau and make recommendations for improvement. The authors concluded:

> The entire Portland police force has been subjected to severe public criticism and there has for some time been a marked loss of confidence in it in all sections of the community. In spite of the fact that some divisions of the Bureau operate with really remarkable efficiency and that at least 70% of Portland's policemen are the sort of policemen the city should have, there remains much justification for this loss of public confidence in the force. Hampered by ineffective leadership of some officers, defective organization, inadequate training, lax discipline and poor equipment, it is truly surprising that the force performs as well as it does. The pension fund is bankrupt, or nearly so, and the old and physically unfit do not

> retire and cannot be compelled to do so. The disciplinary machinery is and has for years been chaotic, and the inefficient and incompetent have been continued in service. Merit has not been rewarded and sloth has not been punished. Standards of admission have been low, training meager, and standards of promotion conveniently flexible.[1]

The report deliberately said nothing about strikebreaking or internal politics—which was rather a lot to leave out.[2] The longshore strike, with its divergent police responses—inaction, collusion, and brutality—was still fresh in the public's mind. And internally the department was factionalizing. Mayor Joseph Carson had appointed his former commanding officer, Burton Lawson, as chief of police, demoting Leon Jenkins to chief inspector. Jenkins, however, remained popular with the men, while Lawson, as an outsider lacking in police experience, had been greeted with suspicion and disdain. He was known to complain that his own officers deliberately withheld information from him. At the same time, the morals squad was floundering, partly owing to the end of Prohibition and partly as a result of its own corruption and the ensuing scandals. The red squad, on the other hand, was ascendant.[3]

But rather than address the internal squabbles continually undercutting the official leadership, the report focused instead on the changing character of policing and the demands those changes placed on the institution: "Our investigations indicate clearly that police work is now as much a matter of brain as of brawn. Police work has attained the status of a profession."[4] Such declarations were common among the advocates of professionalization; they somewhat inconsistently treated the matter both as an accomplished fact and as an ambitious goal. That is, they would assert that policing was a profession and then detail the changes necessary for it to become a profession. The Survey Commission offered more than a dozen recommendations, centered mainly on improved recruitment, training, and discipline. It also proposed an amendment to the city charter: "The chief of police shall be an experienced police officer and shall have tenure of office. This will insure not only trained leadership, but freedom from political and other outside influences."[5] Such proposals were exactly typical of the movement toward professionalization, and the Survey Commission discovered a ready ally when Harry Niles was appointed police chief in December 1934.[6]

Niles, who was almost seventy when he became chief, had already earned a widespread reputation for his attempts to modernize and professionalize policing. In 1922, he established the first records division in the Portland Police Bureau; in 1927, he led Portland's first police training school. The next year, he took a leave of absence to reorganize the police department in Santa Barbara, California. (He declined an offer to become police chief there.) Also in 1928, he traveled to Washington, DC, to help organize the records system for the Prohibition Enforcement Division of the Treasury Department. In 1931, he helped set up the Oregon State Police, again taking responsibility for the records division, and was appointed assistant superintendent. In December 1934, he became chief of police in Portland, in the aftermath of the bloody and contentious longshore strike. As chief, he formed a disciplinary board with a right to appeal and took other steps to improve the caliber of the officers working in the department. He also attended to public relations, making a weekly radio broadcast on KGW.[7]

A School for Cops

Education was central to the ideology of professionalism, and the Portland Police Bureau had a severe deficit that it would need to overcome. When Niles took charge, the only educational requirement for employment in the police was the completion of grammar school, though as a consequence of the Depression and the reduced prospects of the middle class, during the thirties most new recruits had at least some college education.[8] However, most had no police experience, and the training of new hires had been informal—if it occurred at all.[9] Captain W. C. Epps recalled, "[When I began as a patrolman in 1908,] my training consisted of being assigned with different officers four successive nights, and then turned loose with all the authority of the city, state, and federal government and told to enforce the law." One of his trainers "stopped at every saloon on the way" and then spent the night sleeping in a brewery. (He was later fired for drunkenness.)[10] Sergeant Dana Jewell likewise reported, "When I joined the Portland department, the only education and training I received before I was sent out on a beat by myself was one day's work with a sergeant. He told me to keep my eyes open and, if I saw anything happen, avoid it."[11]

A training school had been established in March 1927 under Niles's guidance. Its course ran for twelve weeks, with classes two hours a day, three days a week. Lectures covered topics in criminology, law, police administration, and first aid. Attendance was optional. The project was abandoned in 1931, having graduated

474 officers (54 failed).[12] A proper academy would not be in place until 1940.[13] However, in March 1937, a statewide police training program was implemented, a joint project of the Portland Police Bureau, the Oregon State Police, and the Federal Bureau of Investigation.[14] Seven officers from these agencies, along with a number of local district attorneys and city attorneys and a dean from the University of Oregon School of Journalism, offered a series of lectures to departments around the state.[15] (Strangely, the training was not offered in Portland, and, aside from the instructors, no officers from the Portland Police attended.)[16] Lectures covered recent developments in police organization, enforcement strategies, legal and procedural matters, and detection techniques, as well as topics such as "What the Public Expects of the Police Officer and His Duties."[17]

In addition to providing local cops up-to-date information and an opportunity to improve their technical skills, the program also sought to instill in its students the ethos of professionalism. The aim of the classes, as an instructor patronizingly put it, was "to pass on . . . some of the more progressive ideas in police work today."[18] One lecture after another insisted: "Law enforcement is no longer just a job; it is rapidly becoming a profession," and "With the coming of civil service in the larger towns of the state, and the removal of politicians from the appointment of public employees, police work will become more and more of a profession,—one for which the young man will begin to fit himself in school and college with the same degree of thoroughness and foresight as if he were entering the practice of law or medicine."[19]

The instructors spelled out not only the means of professionalization but also the advantages for the institution. Sergeant Dana Jewell's lecture emphasized ethics as means for protecting the department's reputation and thus winning improved conditions.[20] Detective Orville Williams predicted, hopefully, that achieving a professional status would also lead to increased police power: "With the development of a higher class of officers and careful obedience of these laws by all officers, we may be able in the future to persuade our lawmakers to entrust us with less limited authority."[21] In short, professionalization was seen as a means of securing more respect and greater discretion. While publicly presented in terms of civic responsibility and public service, it also conveyed a barely concealed sense of grievance over the job's low status and a feeling of resentment against the public at large. "The public," Captain W. C. Epps declaimed, "expects of a police officer certain protection of lives and possessions, and feels that it is entitled to a great deal more, in fact, than it seems to be willing to pay for."[22]

Different Priorities

While police commanders and consulting experts were contemplating the nature of the police institution and the social standing of those within it, the line officers had their own somewhat more earthy concerns. Pay had been frozen throughout the Depression.[23] In 1941, the maximum salary for a patrolman was $186 a month, from which he needed to pay for his own uniform and firearm. He worked six days a week, eight hours each day, and was expected to be always on call. There was no overtime pay for additional hours and no pay for court appearances. The officer could annually expect ten days of vacation and ten holidays but only three sick days.[24]

One patrolman, John D. Hayes, had previously worked as a pinball machine repairman and had organized his coworkers into a union.[25] He decided to do it again in the police department. This would be the first real attempt to unionize police since the Boston cops had gone on strike in 1919, precipitating widespread rioting.[26] (The Portland Police Association thus considers itself "America's oldest continuous police union.")[27] The American Federation of State, County, and Municipal Employees (AFSCME) accepted the new police affiliate on the condition that they never go on strike.[28] The Local 456 constitution of 1942 declared, "Members of the local union will not participate in any strike, and though our full sympathies may lie with the lawful doings of other unions, our first duty shall remain, nevertheless, with the public."[29] This was, in effect, not only a no-strike pledge but also a strikebreaking pledge.

The mayor and the chief refused to recognize the union, and Niles announced that any officer joining it would be fired. He never followed through on that threat, and more than two-thirds of the officers signed up (286 of 427). Their initial demands were recognition of their union, collective bargaining, a forty-hour work week, time-and-a-half for overtime, and equal pay for women. Niles would refuse to even consider any demands put forward by the union, but he would sometimes agree to suggestions—for instance, a uniform allowance—if they were first passed through a third party. Still, by 1945, the union had won a base wage of $205 monthly, afternoon court appearances for night-duty officers, and an additional switchboard operator for the night shift.[30]

Patrolman Hayes, who had initiated the organizing campaign, served as interim president, but once the local charter was approved and elections held, the police chose as their new president an actual Nazi. Otto Meiners, a former member of the German American Bund, was elected by his coworkers to be their representative on April 28, 1942.[31] The Bund, which received funding from Germany's Nazi Party, pledged itself "to honor and defend the Constitution, the flag and the institutions of the United States" but also "to cherish German language and German customs" and "to oppose all racial intermixture."[32] Bund members carried US and Nazi flags together at their rallies. They certainly were not shy about introducing the trappings of fascism to an American context—the swastika, the goose step, the stiff-arm salute, shouting "Sieg Heil."[33] Their paramilitary, the Ordnungsdienst, was modeled on the Sturmabteilung, the infamous Brownshirts, with the stated aim "to exterminate with all their power the stinking poison of red Jewish infection in America."[34]

In 1946, Meiners retired, and Hayes was elected president. That same year, the police and firefighter unions joined forces to win a better pension. As Susan Hauser explains, writing in the Portland Police Association's in-house history, "The thinking was that the fire-fighters had a better chance of winning the voters' favor. They were, after all, the 'good guys' in the public's view, the ones who saved people instead of bossing them around." Together the two unions sponsored a ballot measure and sent two-man teams—one police officer and one firefighter, both in uniform—canvassing for support. The measure passed, and the police and fire pension system went into effect on July 1, 1949. A few months later, the Central Labor Council raised the issue of a forty-hour week, demanding that the city council hold hearings on the matter. Police packed the chambers, and the council voted unanimously in favor.[35]

With Portland's police union as a successful example, AFSCME started organizing cops in cities across the country. They sent Otto Meiners to advise on union drives in Salem, Oregon; Vancouver and Spokane, in Washington; and San Francisco and Los Angeles, in California. By 1952, AFSCME had chartered thirty-six police locals.[36]

Another Report

In 1947, another commission filed yet another report on the police bureau, this time with August Vollmer listed as the principal author.

Vollmer, who had consulted on the 1934 survey, was famous as a forward-thinking reformer. As town marshal and then police chief in Berkeley, California, he instituted numerous changes—such as the first formal police training program in the United States, and the first use of radio cars, forensic investigations, and bicycle patrols—and then worked to spread those innovations throughout the country. In addition to Portland, Vollmer consulted with police in Los Angeles, Chicago, Kansas City (Missouri), Dallas, and Detroit. He taught criminal justice and police science at UC Berkeley and the University of Chicago, received a Public Welfare Medal from the National Academy of Sciences, and served as the president of the International Association of Chiefs of Police. He is often referred to as "the father of modern policing."[37] Historians Gene Carte and Elaine Carte describe him as "the principal author of the professional model of policing," promoting a "model centered upon the concept of an idealized policeman who was a skilled and dedicated crime fighter, rigorously trained to perform a difficult job; who was aggressive in using science and technology in all phases of policing; and who was deeply involved in the community he served."[38]

Some of the reforms Vollmer advocated were those common to the movement toward professionalization: replacement of police boards with tenured chiefs, increased training and formal police academies, higher pay, more stringent hiring standards, improved discipline, and the use of standardized testing for promotions. He also went further, with specific prohibitions against dishonesty and excessive force, with particular attention to the rights of prisoners. The Berkeley Police Department recruited college graduates, and Vollmer hired Elizabeth Lossing, a social worker, to head the Crime Prevention Division. Other innovations were adapted from military practices, including the use of specialized squads and intelligence units. Vollmer established new systems of recordkeeping, assigned analysts to create criminal profiles and identify high-crime areas, and used statistics and mapping to direct patrols.[39]

The military influence was born of Vollmer's direct experience. Prior to his work in Berkeley, he had served in the army, policing Manila during the US occupation of the Philippines. The colonial mind-set carried over to his approach domestically. The police academy he founded included coursework on "racial types," "race degeneration," and hereditary criminality. None of this was coincidental; it was precisely the reason he was hired. Vollmer was appointed chief in Berkeley during an influx of Chinese immigrants and was recruited for the position specifically because of his experience in the Philippines. He was similarly asked to consult with the Los Angeles Police Department during an increase in the number of Italian immigrants, which resulted in a similar racial panic.[40] And his second visit to Portland came after an abrupt rise in the African American population as Black people moved to the city for work in war industries.

The 1947 report noted little improvement in police performance, as evidenced by an increase in crime over the previous ten years, despite a substantial investment in policing.[41] "Police personnel has increased 63.3% during the past twenty years and 40.6% in the past seven years. During the same periods per capita police expenditures have risen 57.3% and 24.7% respectively."[42] Yet, even with more officers and more money (and after a dozen years of professionalization), the force had proved inadequate. During the Second World War, especially, the crime rate soared, including a 50 percent increase in assaults between 1940 and 1945, a 400 percent increase in homicides, and a 700 percent increase in reported rapes.[43]

The Vollmer report pointed to "many factors" contributing to inefficiency, "the more important being: (1) poor organization, (2) inadequate supervision, (3) extremes in specialization, (4) failure to utilize patrolmen to the fullest extent of their ability, (5) inadequate records plus a failure to utilize available records for scientific distribution and assignment of personnel, (6) absence of an adequate training program, (7) totally inadequate pension system with resultant high percentage of personnel who are over age or physically unsuited for active police service, and (8) salary scales which are too low to attract and hold desirable personnel."[44] Additionally, the authors found the command structure to be unclear and inefficient, and discipline "too laxly enforced."[45] Most of these criticisms had been voiced in the report issued thirteen years before, yet the problems remained.

The solutions were equally familiar. The report proposed—yet again—the professional model, with an encouraging tone and the acknowledgement of progress in the attitudes of the officers themselves:

> Policemen are becoming increasingly aware that they are members of a business organization, comparable in size and complexity to large commercial enterprises. . . . There is an increasing appreciation of the public's right to an efficient and economical stewardship of the funds, personnel and equipment entrusted to their use. In the process of attaining business and professional status, progressive police administrators have borrowed extensively from proven methods of commercial organization. In addition, because police units are semi-military in character, it has been found that certain well established policies and procedures used by the armed services are, with suitable variations, equally adaptable to the police service.[46]

The centrality of the business model favored by Progressives is evident here, but so too is the influence of Vollmer's military background. The report identifies a number of principles to guide police administration, including having a "well-established plan," "coordination at the top," "definite and direct . . . lines of authority," "authority . . . commensurate with responsibility," "unity of command," and having a realistic "span of control." Nearly all of these, the researchers found, were lacking in the Portland Police.[47] The report also recommended eliminating residency requirements, recruiting college graduates, using psychological evaluations, "greater emphasis . . . on character investigations," more training, yearly physicals, higher pay, and an improved pension.[48] The ultimate goal, evidently, was a military organization staffed by middle-class professionals.

Reform Paradigms

Professionalization had promised a more efficient and effective police administration but failed to raise the social status or standard of living for the cops themselves. It improved the institution, with little benefit to the officers. Unionization, in contrast, did improve the working conditions for cops and thus also improved their lives.

Professionalization was very much in line with the middle-class ethos of the Progressives, whereas the police union obviously drew inspiration from the decidedly working-class labor movement. This ambivalence speaks to the peculiar class position of the police: their jobs are low-status, often physical, and sometimes dirty, yet much of their work is precisely the disciplining of workers, the repression of the workers' movement, and the defense of the class system. Superficially, they may resemble other workers, but functionally they are more like management.[49] Complicating matters, police departments have their own internal hierarchies, with competing agendas and inevitable conflict. The demands of professionalization, while popular among command staff, may be resented by the lower ranks. Chief Niles's efforts to modernize the Portland Police, for instance, were often frustrated by the recalcitrance of his subordinates. He was a skilled administrator but a poor leader, a bureaucrat incapable of winning the esteem of those who served beneath him and therefore powerless to change the culture of the institution.[50]

As much as professionalization and unionization may compete and conflict, it is notable how much they have in common. Both professionalization and unionization work by analogy, drawing comparisons between the police and doctors and lawyers (on the one hand) or bricklayers and truck drivers (on the other), yet both models insist that policing is a distinctive activity deserving special consideration. Professionals and unionists alike sought increased resources and respect, though the first group was more concerned with social status and the second with economic gains. Perhaps most fundamentally, the thing they had in common was a desire for increased authority and autonomy for the institution as a whole; they diverged on the question of how much that power should be concentrated at the top or invested in the individual officers of the rank and file.

Though each movement liked to emphasize the abstract concept of justice and the social importance of crime-fighting, they were fundamentally, and sometimes even openly, self-interested. Unlike the Progressives, who sought police reform as a means of improving society, both the professionalists and the unionists made demands of society for the benefit of the police. Importantly, though, while the status of the police was in question, the function of policing was not. Neither movement was especially concerned to reduce police violence or to end their role in the maintenance of white supremacy. Those aspects of the work were largely taken for granted.

CHAPTER 10
The Color Line on the Home Front

Enemy Aliens

On December 7, 1941, the military of imperial Japan bombed the US naval base at Pearl Harbor, Hawaii, drawing the United States fully into the Second World War.

The attack produced panic and paranoia throughout the United States, especially on the West Coast. In Portland, the military and police posted guards on bridges, docks, and other critical infrastructure. In an effort to make up for an anticipated staffing shortage, 103 volunteers—all veterans of the Great War, many of them members of the American Legion—were sworn in as a Veterans Guard and Patrol. Within a year, there were thirty-five hundred men serving in this capacity.[1] A similar body, the Multnomah Guard, was formed to aid the sheriff's office in civil defense; after the war, it would be continued as the Multnomah County Sheriff's Reserve.[2]

The FBI wasted no time before going on the offensive. Within hours of the attack, it had initiated a series of warrantless raids and arrested Japanese, German, and Italian nationals, mostly community leaders. FBI agents seized binoculars, radios, guns, and anything featuring Japanese writing. Typically, these suspects—if that is what they were—were arrested in the middle of the night, taken to federal prisons, and held incommunicado. Usually their families did not know where they were.[3] Special agent Alan F. Davis of the FBI's Portland Field Office resigned rather than participate in the roundup.[4]

The feds did not need to improvise these raids. Since September 1939, the Army's G-2 Division and the Office of Naval Intelligence had worked together with the FBI to monitor Japanese Americans. The military took the broad view, tracking activities at the community level, while the FBI focused on the surveillance of individuals.[5] Even before the attack on Pearl Harbor, 770 Japanese had been identified for internment in the event of war; two months after the attack, 2,192 had been arrested throughout the country.[6]

Once war was declared, the *issei* (those born in Japan) became enemy aliens, but official suspicion also extended to the *nisei* (US-born citizens). All "enemy aliens and persons of Japanese ancestry" were subject to an 8:00 p.m. curfew, forbidden to travel, and ordered to turn in radios, cameras, and similar equipment.[7] Their fishing boats were grounded, and Japanese produce markets were closed. Bank accounts were initially frozen; later, withdrawals were permitted within strict limits.[8]

Minoru Yasui, an attorney living in Portland, notified both the FBI and the US Attorney's office that he considered the curfew to be unconstitutional and intended to break the law in order to test it in court. On March 28, 1942, he went for a nighttime walk and presented a patrolman with his birth certificate and a copy of the curfew order. The policeman sensibly declined to arrest him and advised him to go home. Yasui instead entered the Central Precinct station at 11:20 p.m. and demanded to be arrested. He was charged with a federal misdemeanor. Yasui argued in court that the law could not be applied to US citizens, and Judge Alder Fee agreed, though he also determined that by working as a lawyer for the Japanese consulate Yasui had effectively renounced his US citizenship. He was sentenced to a year in prison and a $5,000 fine. The Supreme Court upheld the conviction but restored his citizenship—contradicting the trial court on both points. After nine months in solitary confinement, occupying a six-by-eight-foot windowless cell, Yasui was released from Portland's Rocky Butte Jail—only to be transported directly to a prison camp at Minidoka, Idaho.[9] There he served as an informant for the FBI, reporting on other prisoners suspected of disloyalty.[10]

Concentration Camps

Such camps are usually referred to as *internment camps*. But that is not even a euphemism; it is a misnomer. Presidents Roosevelt and Truman both described them as "concentration camps."[11]

The difference is not merely semantic. Internment is a legal process, with an established procedure. It is recognized by both US and international law and governed under the Geneva Conventions. Legally, internment requires a hearing for each detainee to determine whether their individual behavior might pose a potential threat. These findings could be appealed to the US attorney general. "While the decision to intern an individual may not have been just, internment in the United States generally followed the rules set down in American and international law," according to historian Roger Daniels; the concentration camp program, in contrast, "was simply lawless."[12]

It is estimated that about 11,000 people were interned during the war, including 8,000 Japanese, 2,300 Germans, and a few hundred Italians. Enemy Alien Hearings Boards reviewed the evidence in each case and frequently did recommend release.[13] On the other hand, approximately 112,000 Japanese—two thirds of them American citizens—were imprisoned in concentration camps without any equivalent review and no right to appeal.[14]

There was no military justification for mass confinement, and this fact was understood even at the time. Multiple intelligence reports concluded that there was no evidence of widespread disloyalty, espionage, or sabotage. One report, provided directly to the president, estimated that 90–98 percent of Japanese Americans were fully loyal to the United States.[15] In March 1941, a Naval Intelligence officer, Kenneth Ringle, broke into the Japanese consulate in Los Angeles and stole documents concerning their espionage efforts; they indicated that the overall Japanese community was pro-American.[16] Secret communications intercepted by the US military likewise detailed the Japanese government's failure to recruit agents in the United States.[17]

The most vocal advocate for wholesale detention was General John L. DeWitt, the head of the Western Defense Command, who proposed mass confinement less than seventy-two hours after the Pearl Harbor attack.[18] He explained his thinking in a February 14, 1942, memo: "In the war in which we are now engaged, racial affinities are not severed by migration. The Japanese race is an enemy race and while many second- and third-generation Japanese born on United States soil, possessed of American citizenship, have become 'Americanized,' the racial strains are undiluted." Elsewhere DeWitt employed the logic of a witch hunt: "The very fact that no sabotage has taken place to date is a disturbing and confirming indication that such action will be taken."[19] FBI director J. Edgar Hoover—nobody's idea of a liberal—considered the argument for mass detention "damned nonsense" and privately accused General DeWitt of "hysteria and lack of judgment."[20]

Nevertheless, on February 19, 1942, President Franklin Delano Roosevelt signed Executive Order 9066, authorizing the military to designate areas "from which any or all persons may be excluded." On March 2, DeWitt announced the creation of two such exclusion zones. Military Area 1 covered the western halves of Washington, Oregon, and California, and the southern half of Arizona. Military Area 2 took in the remainder of those same states. German and Italian aliens, and all ethnic Japanese—regardless of citizenship—were to be excluded from Zone 1. (The War Department later abandoned plans to remove the Germans and Italians.) Congress gave this scheme its blessing by making it a federal offense to disobey a military exclusion order. Those who would not comply could be arrested, and the Census Bureau provided an advisor and raw data to help locate Japanese families, street by street.[21]

On May 7, 1942, the Western Defense Command posted notices in Multnomah County ordering "all persons of Japanese ancestry, both alien and non-alien" to report to an assembly center.[22] The new prisoners could only bring what they could carry, leaving them five days to sell their homes, businesses, livestock, automobiles, and other property, often at a fraction of its real value.[23] Richard Neustadt, an official with the Farm Security Administration, denounced this process as a land grab "to give to greedy others the fine gardens and farms that have been developed by these people on land that originally the white men did not care to improve."[24] Estimates of property losses range from $67 to $116 million. About 75 percent of those imprisoned lost everything.[25]

From May to September 1942, more than four thousand Japanese Americans from Multnomah, Hood River, and Washington counties were held at the Evacuee Assembly Center at the Pacific International Livestock and Exposition Grounds. Conditions were intolerable. The inmates were housed in a large cattle barn, hastily whitewashed and divided into living quarters. Each family was assigned a cubicle with plywood walls and a canvas door, furnished only with army cots and straw mattresses. The rooms were eight by twenty or twenty by twenty, depending on the size of the family. Residents complained of the smell, fleas, and flies. "It was filthy, smelly, and dirty," one former inmate recalled. "There was roughly two thousand people packed in one large building." Another added: "It stank. We were there for the summer months. Barns were converted to create these makeshift holdings. It made me sick to think that animals lived there only a few weeks before . . . their smell still was [there]. It was hot, and humid, and sticky. Flies were all over."[26]

Sanitation was inadequate and illness common. Rations were spare and poor in quality. Mail was censored, and the use of the Japanese language was extremely restricted. Inmates did most of the work to maintain the camp. They had their own fire department and an eight-man police force. The installation was surrounded by eight-foot barbed-wire fences and watchtowers mounted with search lights and 30-caliber machine guns. Military police guarded the exterior. The entire facility was subject to search without notice.[27]

In September 1942, the assembly center closed, and the last inmates were sent to more permanent camps further inland. Most Portland-area prisoners were moved to the Minidoka Relocation Center, near Twin Falls, Idaho. The center featured residential barracks surrounding a central mess hall, with communal latrines, showers, and laundry. Prisoners were housed in tar-paper buildings that offered little protection against extreme temperatures, which sometimes reached –20F in the winter and 115F in the summer. Each family was assigned a single sixteen-by-twenty-foot room. Unmarried adults shared rooms with strangers. The camp was surrounded by watchtowers and barbed wire. The interior was patrolled by War Relocation Authority guards and inmate police. Outside the wire, soldiers kept watch. Minidoka held 9,397 prisoners.[28]

The Jim Crow North

While the Japanese were being forcibly expelled from the West Coast, a new workforce was being brought in to support wartime production—including, for the first time in Portland, a substantial number of African Americans. Shipbuilders ran employment ads in eleven states, increasing the city's population by a third in just two years.[29] By the end of the war, the city's Black population had grown from approximately two thousand to more than twenty-one thousand.[30] The arrival of the new workers and the changing demographics of the area produced consternation and anxiety. Mayor Earl Riley openly worried, "Portland can absorb only a minimum of Negroes without upsetting the city's regular life."[31]

Official attitudes toward racial integration in the Northwest had always been somewhat uncertain. The various exclusion acts of the nineteenth century had kept the number of Black people in Oregon so low that, on the one hand, it was impractical to maintain separate facilities for their use, while, on the other hand, it was entirely possible to maintain all-white institutions and neighborhoods. In 1867, after the Portland public schools had refused to admit four Black children, the local government created a separate school, which, over the next five years taught twenty-five Black students. In 1873, however, in the midst of an economic downturn, it proved impossible to sustain the necessary $800 in funding, and the city's schools were quietly integrated.[32]

Social mixing was perhaps even more fraught. Patrolmen passing by a Black-owned restaurant in 1914 spotted a white woman inside and ordered her to leave.[33] In 1922, police raided a cabaret after observing white women dancing with Black men. The city council revoked the establishment's license, though no law had been broken. The National Association for the Advancement of Colored People lodged a formal complaint with the council, and Mayor George Baker urged a new law, arguing, "When you take our white girls and allow them to get drunk in your establishment, and allow then to consort with negro men, I want to say that it is humiliating to the white race and an insult to the decent negro people as well." Ultimately the council simply left the matter for the police to decide, determining "that no additional legislation [was] necessary" and that it was better to "handle the situation through police vigilance."[34]

The police record on segregation was rather ambivalent. In 1909, the cops had ordered a restaurant to remove a sign reading "No Colored Patrons Wanted." In 1933, Beatrice Cannady, a leader in the local branch of the NAACP, convinced Chief Burt Lawson to remove a sign (again at a restaurant) reading, "We cater only to white trade."[35] But during the Second World War, as the Black population increased dramatically, "White Trade Only" signs, like those in the deep South, became more and more common throughout the city.[36]

Vanport

"We must be tolerant and considerate," Mayor Riley advised, "but we must as well be firm. Undesirables—white or colored—are not wanted and if they fail to obey our laws will be unceremoniously dealt with."[37] The Central East Portland Community Club recommended: "If it is necessary to bring large numbers of Negro workers, locate them on the edge of the city. . . . If they are allowed to fan out through the city, it soon will be necessary to station a policeman on every corner."[38]

Anticipating an influx of workers, the city council, as an emergency wartime measure, created the Housing Authority of Portland, which assumed a separate-but-equal stance: "We don't discriminate, but we do segregate."[39]

One solution to the wartime housing crisis was the construction of Vanport—part housing project, part company town, located to the north, just past the city limits. To accommodate the new workforce, industrialist Henry Kaiser and the US Maritime Commission agreed to build six thousand new homes (later increased to ten thousand) and planned for construction without consulting the City of Portland. Kaiser purchased 650 acres of land, and construction started three days later. According to the City of Portland's Bureau of Planning, it was to become "the largest wartime housing project in the United States and the second largest city in Oregon."[40]

At its peak, Vanport was home to forty-two thousand people, almost 15 percent of whom were Black. Housing was segregated building by building, but the schools were integrated. (The first black teachers in Oregon taught there.) The entire development was considered temporary, so construction consisted of cheap prefabricated buildings lacking a concrete foundation. Still, the city included a hospital, library, shopping center, bus station, five elementary schools, and a junior high. Vanport remained unincorporated for the entirety of its existence, neither a part of Portland nor a self-governing municipality. It had no elected officials and was managed instead by the Housing Authority of Portland. At Kaiser's insistence, it had its own fire department, but policing was done by the Multnomah County sheriffs, working out of a broad, one-story building resembling a school. It included a jail, which mostly served as a drunk tank; serious offenders were taken elsewhere. Thirty-four deputies and forty auxiliaries worked from there, with access to two squad cars and five motorcycles.[41]

Four of the deputies were Black, though that did nothing to ensure fair treatment for Black residents. On April 3, 1946, Earl Salls, a Black veteran and Kaiser shipyard worker, reported two Black deputies for being rude to him. In retaliation, they arrested him and beat him so badly he had to be hospitalized for four days. He lost vision in one eye.[42]

When the war was over, much of the workforce was laid off. As workers left, their houses were disassembled. Vanport became proportionally more Black, and, as it did, it gained a reputation for being dangerous, though the crime rate was the same as that of Portland proper.[43] Then, on May 30, 1948, Vanport was destroyed by flood. Much of the city washed away within a few minutes. Seeing the river rise over the course of a week, Sheriff Martin Pratt had already put his officers on twelve-hour shifts. When the levee broke, he immediately issued an emergency call for all available boats. (The Coast Guard refused to assist.)[44] Though Vanport was outside their jurisdiction, the Portland police sent officers to aid the evacuation, and the city council agreed to pay an unprecedented twenty-six cents per hour in overtime.[45] President Truman declared a disaster, and the National Guard patrolled to deter the looting of evacuated homes. At least fifteen people died. Ten others went missing. The sheriff and his deputies were generally praised for their quick response, but some survivors believe that the evacuation had been delayed because it would have meant resettling the Black residents in Portland.[46]

A Potentiality of Unrest

African Americans had been viewed askance throughout Oregon's history, and as their numbers increased so did the suspicion. Even as their labor was desperately needed for the war effort, they were viewed as a potential fifth column.

In June 1942, the FBI began an investigation into "Foreign-Inspired Agitation Among the American Negroes," a program code-named RACON (for "racial conditions"). All fifty-six field offices contributed, and the project resulted in a report titled *Survey of Racial Conditions in the United States.*[47] In its section, the Portland Field Division found that "no inroads were made among the Negro population by the Japanese" and separately that "the Negroes exhibit[ed] a disapproval of the Communist Party." The report generally concluded, "Negroes in this area feel some discrimination but as a whole are loyal to the United States." However, it also conveyed a warning from "a Negro attorney and president of an active Negro organization in Portland, Oregon," who suggested such discrimination gave rise to "a potentiality of unrest and trouble among the Negroes."[48]

Three years later, a City Club of Portland report reiterated: "Many of the causes of social unrest which lead to interracial strife and violence exist in Portland today. We believe that acute social disturbances and outbreaks are likely in this community unless positive and immediate action is taken to avert such calamity."[49] The group's researchers documented discrimination in almost every aspect of life: housing, employment, labor unions, restaurants and hotels, medical care, and law enforcement.[50]

Police Chief Harry Niles denied it: "No racial discrimination is practiced by members of the force."[51] Instead, he suggested (as the report paraphrased) "that Negroes were responsible for more crimes and misdemeanors of all types than white residents of Portland. This impression was shared by other members of the police force who were questioned." Likewise, when the City Club urged that "an effort be made to place qualified Negroes on the Portland police force,"

Niles explained their absence by saying that none could meet the minimum requirements. The City Club further advocated a "course of police training ... to inculcate in the city's police force tolerance and understanding of problems involving racial tensions," a suggestion met with a "lack of enthusiasm" from the chief.[52] Naturally, as Niles saw it, if there was no problem, then there was no need for change.

Making an Example

That same year, two incidents involving the police galvanized the local civil rights movement.

At 2:00 a.m. on August 21, 1945, police broke into the home of Ervin Jones while searching for another man. The cops simultaneously kicked in his front door and broke through a window at the back of his house. Jones, believing he was being robbed, confronted them with a gun, though accounts differ as to whether he fired it. The police shot him in the back, killing him. The Portland Council of Churches and the NAACP demanded an investigation. They got not one but three; however, the cops' internal review, the coroner's inquest, and a grand jury all exonerated the officers.[53]

Then, on Christmas Eve, US Army Sergeant Wardell Henderson was pulled over in a stolen vehicle. The owner of the car, Walter Poole, had been murdered and Henderson soon confessed. He was convicted and sentenced to death. But his guilt was widely doubted within the Black community, and the NAACP believed that his confession was forced. Even jurors expressed doubts about the verdict. The foreman urged clemency, and two others later swore affidavits attesting to the racism of their peers. (One juror had argued: "An example must be made of a Negro ... or they will overrun us.") But Governor John Hall refused to take any action, and on January 1, 1948, Henderson was executed by lethal injection, an outcome the Urban League compared to a lynching.[54]

Continuities

The war years saw numerous changes in Portland, with concomitant implications for policing. Most notable among these was the rapid process of industrialization and with it the increase in population and its diversity. Equally, though, the war crystalized tendencies long present in the life of the city and the institution and conduct of the police.

It is easy enough to draw a line connecting the prejudices underlying the Black exclusion acts to those that compelled Henry Kaiser to build an entirely new city to house his workers. Similarly, the dispossession of the Japanese had been on the Klan's agenda since the 1920s, and the assumption that Asian immigrants were unassimilable can be traced back to the anti-Chinese panic of the nineteenth century. The process of removing the entire Japanese population and holding them in distant prison camps recalled the earlier displacement and consignment of Native Americans to reservations. The federal government's engagement in local policing had been a factor since Indian subagent Elijah White first arrived in 1842, then escalated in stages throughout the periods of Chinese exclusion, World War I, and Prohibition. Police Chief Niles, whose tenure spanned the war years, seemed to discover both the practical and ideological limits of professionalization, an effort that could be thought of as bringing Progressive reforms in-house. Around the same time, class conflict—in which the police often played a contradictory role—was likewise internalized with the creation of the Portland Police Association. Throughout it all, pervasive corruption and the purity campaigns opposing it continued apace.

PART II

The Long Road to Community Policing

CHAPTER 11

The No-Sin Mayor and the Vice Czar

Openly and Notoriously

Early Progressive victories soon proved incomplete if not illusory. Despite decades of reform, mayors Joseph Carson (1933–41) and R. Earl Riley (1941–48) continued to distribute jobs as patronage, award city contracts to their political supporters, and tolerate vice crime.[1] A 1948 City Club report stated that commercial sex and gambling had been conducted "openly and notoriously throughout the city for a number of years."[2] It counted 248 vice spots then in operation, with "protection . . . provided in consideration of a substantial 'pay off' to some police officers and public officials."[3] Monthly rates for the protection of gambling houses were set at $50 per slot machine, $500 for dice tables, and $1,000 for poker.[4] An individual officer could earn between $200 and $500 a week in bribes.[5] The report called Portland an "open town" and stated that "no police officer or public official competent enough to do his job could be unaware of the situation."[6]

The City Club report made crime an issue in the mayoral election and paved the way for the victory of Dorothy McCullough Lee, a former chair of the Oregon Crime Commission.[7] Her slogan was simply, "I will enforce the law." She said, "I am not a reformer, but I believe strongly in the integrity of government."[8] The *Oregon Voter* described her as "decent in private and public life, tenacious, firm" and added: "She is not a crusader, but she will not quail before those who sneer at the law."[9] Though law enforcement and clean government were her main issues, Lee also favored increased school funding, free kindergarten, old age pensions, and legislation prohibiting racial discrimination.[10] "Despite Dorothy Lee's claims that she was not a reformer," historian Paul Pitzer concluded, "she was, in fact, an old-school progressive who vowed to make Portland city government more efficient."[11] Her supporters included a cross section of progressives, churches, and local newspapers, as well as the

Urban League, the Women's Christian Temperance Union, and the Portland Retail Trade Bureau. She won 70 percent of the vote in May 1948.[12]

Lee quickly demoted James Flemming from police chief to night shift supervisor and replaced him with Charles Pray, the retired head of the Oregon State Police who had coordinated strikebreaking under Governor Martin and once deployed a National Guard machine gun unit to a picket line.[13] Pray was generally regarded as honest and competent, and he arrived without political entanglements.[14] However, he never won the trust of the line officers, who cut him off from the information he needed to effectively manage the bureau. He had no control at all over the vice squad.[15] Frequently complaining that he knew less about the department than the average patrolman, Pray resigned in May 1951.[16]

As a candidate, Lee had promised to break the cycle of scandal and complacency "through constant and unremitting efforts of a police department with high standards of efficiency and effectiveness."[17] In practice that meant a constant push against low-level operators. The cops began by raiding Chinese clubs and breaking through their doors with axes.[18] Lee then announced: "Slot machines and other highly lucrative and corrupting devices will be repressed. The law will be enforced against them and it will be enforced impartially, without discrimination and regardless of where the slot machines are located."[19] Mainstream establishments like the American Legion, the Eagles, and other lodges, and even elite institutions like the Arlington Club, were targeted for their slot machines and poker games.[20] The mayor supplied the district attorney with a list of brothels and pressed him to file injunctions to shutter cheap hotels that knowingly accommodated the sex trade.[21] By 1951, the Social Hygiene Association found commercial sex to be an at all-time low.[22]

Moral Crusade

The moral crusade extended to other aspects of sexuality as well. A *Police Journal* article from 1948, covering the "sex deviate problem," mentions a "squad of officers" sent to parks and "other public meeting places, where perverts have been known to congregate." There they took descriptions of suspects and their cars and added them to files to be referenced in investigations of other sex crimes, such as assaults against children.[23]

In February 1949, two Portland police officers, Edna Trout and Sybil Plumtree, went undercover at the Music Hall and waited to be picked up by other women. No one approached them during their three visits to the club, but they did file a report about the entertainment: dirty jokes, a drag queen impersonating Mae West, and a large man named Tiny who performed in the persona of a six-year-old girl. Lee threatened to shut down the Music Hall if they continued to book "men who act like unladylike ladies." She declared, "They have got to get out of Portland, along with the undesirable persons they attract." She eventually persuaded the Oregon Liquor Control Commission to lean on the venue, and, with their liquor license imperiled, the owners canceled the drag shows and excluded gay and lesbian patrons.[24]

At least one cop expressed doubts about this moral mission. Earl Biggs was a Portland police sergeant, an investigator for the sex crime unit, and author of *How to Protect Your Child from the Sex Criminal*. Based on his experiences arresting gay men, he became skeptical of the law he was enforcing. In 1950, he wrote *Sex, Science, and Sin: A Study of Normal and Abnormal Sex Activity of Our Time in Relation to Science, the Law, and Religion*, part of which argued for the decriminalization of homosexual activity. (In conducting his research, he began a correspondence with Alfred Kinsey, who then edited the book.) Biggs noted that same-sex attraction has existed "at all times" and is "neither abnormal nor unnatural." He urged the law to "make allowance for man's sexual nature" and only preclude "those sex acts that are detrimental to the general welfare."[25]

But the moral dragnet only grew broader. On July 6, 1951, thirty-one police officers—accompanied by reporters—launched the largest raid of abortionists in city history, making twelve arrests. (Three more occurred in the following days.)[26] Much of the evidence justifying the arrests had been collected by the *Oregon Journal*'s Rolla Crick, working alongside a Women's Protective Division officer posing as his girlfriend. Under a special arrangement with the district attorney, Crick conducted the investigation in exchange for access to government files and the privilege of accompanying police when they moved in.[27]

The raids came as a total surprise. Abortion had been illegal in Oregon since 1854, punishable by fifteen years in prison and a $5,000 fine. However, there was, as one abortionist termed it, an "unwritten agreement" that so long as there were no fatalities, there would be no prosecutions. The cops preferred that the clinics be located a respectful distance from any police station or church, and some clinics paid them off, which may have provided another layer of security. Throughout the thirties and forties, abortion clinics were treated like any other "vice" operation.[28]

That started to change after the war, for reasons both national and local, both abstract and tactical. On one level, both Mayor Lee and District Attorney John McCourt needed a boost in publicity as they planned for the next election. On another level, an outcry against abortion was one part of a broad campaign to reimpose gender norms that the war effort had disrupted.[29] "Moving against abortion and abortionists in 1951 shored up a lot of traditional notions about women and family," historian Rickie Solinger explains.[30]

Over the next two decades, abortionists faced more frequent arrest and longer sentences.[31] Many moved their practices more or less underground or far outside the city limits.[32] Ruth Barnett, a naturopath who claimed forty thousand abortions over her fifty-year career (and said she had never lost a patient), later reflected: "My practice, once a well-organized clinical affair, had been reduced by my arrests to a 'backstairs' sort of clientele. Ironically, I was forced to adopt tactics of which I would have once been ashamed."[33] The main effect of enforcement was to make abortion not less common but instead more dangerous—for practitioners and patients alike.[34]

Sheriffs, Prosecutors, Racketeers

Facing similar pressures, brothels and gambling houses simply moved their operations out of town. Some moved *far* out of town: Al Winter headed to Las Vegas and opened the Sahara Hotel and Casino, the largest establishment on the Strip at that time. But most set up shop just outside the Portland city limits.[35] There they found an ally in Multnomah County sheriff Mike Elliott.

Marion Leroy (Mike) Elliott was elected soon after Mayor Lee, in November 1948. As a candidate, he promised to bring the sheriff's office up to FBI standards and to reform the juvenile justice system.[36] He tried to visibly align himself with the mayor, announcing a "Dual Drive on Vice" and making a show of tavern raids. Elliott liked to have himself photographed smashing pinball machines with a sledgehammer.[37]

Ironically, Elliott's campaign had been funded by gambling interests. Once elected, he replaced key figures in the sheriff's office, presumably with those more to the liking of his backers. Most significantly—given later events—an organized crime boss named James Elkins had contributed to Elliott's campaign and provided the information for many of the sheriff's raids, usually targeting his racketeering competitor, Stan Terry. Elkins eventually turned on Elliott and gave

Wally Turner, an *Oregonian* reporter, information about the sheriff consorting with sex workers. Elliott had already weathered revelations that he had lied about his education and his military service, but the sex scandal was too much. He was recalled in October 1949, just ten months after taking office.[38] To fill the vacancy, the county commissioners appointed a Portland Fire Department captain named Terry Schrunk.[39] He would become, historians Jewel Lansing and Fred Leeson note, "one of Multnomah County's most popular sheriffs ever." They explain: "He was praised for his efficient running of the county tax collection department, for making Rocky Butte Jail the best in the nation, for his smoothly operating uniform division, for his civil defense work, for his introduction of incentive pay and annual police training schools, for his youth and safety programs, and for establishing a volunteer deputy sheriff's reserve."[40]

A self-described "moderate progressive," Schrunk also earned praise from the Urban League "for his alertness, courage and integrity." After a Black family moved into a previously all-white neighborhood, Schrunk sent plainclothes detectives to monitor racist meetings and posted uniformed deputies by the family's home. The Urban League's Edwin C. Berry declared, "This is the type of enlightened law enforcement required in a progressive community. We need enforcement agents who are 'color blind,' know the law, and who will make no compromise with bigotry. Terry Schrunk fills the bill."[41]

Just months into his term, the *Oregonian* was similarly impressed: "When Sheriff Terry Schrunk was appointed . . . the sheriff's office was a 'shambles' created by the cops-and-robbers antics of his recalled predecessor. . . . [Schrunk] has reestablished the self-respect of his 221 employees, some of whom, a year ago, hesitated to admit that they worked for the sheriff's office. . . . [He] doesn't claim to have eliminated all the gambling and prostitution in Multnomah County, but he is making progress."[42]

But Schrunk's "progress," like Elliot's, proved rather selective, and for much the same reason. It was again criminal interests—specifically, the Teamsters union—that were responsible for putting Schrunk in office, having paid $10,000 to the county commissioners to ensure his appointment.[43]

The Teamsters had been an aggressive force in Portland for quite some time. They started by using their control of trucking to take over liquor distribution—sometimes employing violence even against other unions—then opened brothels and gambling houses and eventually took direct control of bars and clubs. Bribes to local and state officials ensured that they could operate with virtual impunity.[44]

In 1950, both the Teamsters and Jim Elkins supported the candidacy of William Langley for district attorney. Langley, the son of former Multnomah County DA Lotus Langley, was the previous owner of the China Lantern nightclub in Beaverton, which fronted an Elkins-controlled gambling operation. Elkins and the union made an explicit agreement with the future prosecutor that, in exchange for campaign funding, he would offer his protection for their gambling interests, brothels, and strikes.[45]

Then, in 1952, Elkins and the Teamsters funded Fred Peterson's bid to oust Dorothy McCollough Lee.[46]

The Businessman

Mayor Lee's zeal for law enforcement earned her several nicknames, including "Dauntless Dottie," "Dottie Do-Good," "Mrs. Airwick," and "No Sin Lee."[47] These were not always warmly meant. The mayor was subjected to hate mail, harassing phone calls, public booing, and threats, including threats against her children. At one point she received in the mail an alarm clock wired to a dead fish. She began carrying a gun and sent her children abroad.[48]

Her approach proved less and less popular with time. In the view of the *Oregonian*, "Her steely determination is her greatest political asset and her greatest political liability." Lee's 1952 reelection slogan was the same as her first: "I will enforce the law." Her opponent, Fred Peterson, ran with the equally uninspired "Portland needs a businessman." Peterson won: 105,767 votes to 93,230. Lee went on to work for the US Board of Parole, overseeing the Youth Division.[49] Then, in 1957, President Dwight Eisenhower appointed her to the Subversive Activities Control Board, which managed the registration of Communist-affiliated organizations as required by the Internal Security Act of 1950.[50] Lee was later promoted to SACB chair under President Kennedy, and served for five years. In that role, she pledged to drive the Communists out of the labor movement.[51]

On the strength of Elkins's recommendation—and $100,000—Mayor Peterson appointed Jim Purcell chief of police. "Diamond Jim" had already enjoyed a colorful career. As a patrolman, he earned a reputation for recovering stolen cars, a feat he accomplished by coordinating with the car thieves. In the late forties he oversaw the Portland Police "shotgun squads," which along with checkpoints on major roads and bridges were part of the initial response to the postwar crime wave. Later he was appointed chief detective, an ideal position from which to slant investigations and cover up murders. From there he rose to captain and then to acting chief in just six years. Even as chief, Purcell remained part owner, along with a pimp named George Bernard, of a gambling house off Sandy Boulevard, the Penguin Club. He named Carl Crisp the head of the vice squad—which was convenient, since Crisp had both a drug habit and a bribe habit and managed the payoffs for Jim Elkins.[52]

Elkins's Empire

Jim Elkins had a piece of every pie: liquor, gambling, the sex trade, drugs, and jukeboxes and pinball, which were prohibited under the same law that forbade slots. His negotiating style relied heavily on blackmail and violence. The FBI called him Portland's "vice czar." In 1957, nightclub owner Nate Zusman told Senate investigators, "Mr. Elkins ran the town."[53] According to Harry King (aka Harry Huerth), a safecracker and Elkins's one-time business partner, "he had full control of the [police] department," and "nobody got a promotion around there without Jim's OK first."[54] His influence even reached as far as the governor's office. In 1955, when the Oregon Liquor Control Commission's Thomas Sheridan was fired for "accepting gratuities" from the Teamsters, Elkins called the governor and had him reinstated.[55]

Elkins had a symbiotic relationship with law enforcement. He provided information to the Portland Police, the sheriffs of Multnomah and Clackamas Counties, the FBI, the Federal Bureau of Narcotics, and, during the war, the Coast Guard and Navy Intelligence. In exchange, they protected his illicit businesses.[56] Elkins would use the police to shut down his competitors and even have his subordinates arrested if they got out of line, an arrangement that, as one historian has noted, "essentially made Portland's finest Elkins's hit squad."[57]

Elkins and the Teamsters would become closer after the union used its control over deliveries to help him corner the pinball market.[58] In 1954, they together sponsored an $8 million bond measure to build Memorial Coliseum, manipulating the siting process to benefit their business associates, including Tom Johnson.[59] But a partnership between such ambitious and powerful actors could not last long or end well. By August 1955, Elkins had come to suspect that the union was preparing to cut him out or even to kill him. Knowing that he couldn't outmatch them in violence, and lacking any legal recourse, he turned to his familiar tactics of blackmail. He hired Raymond Clark, a former vice cop and one-time police chief in the town of St. Helens, to bug the Portland apartment and tap the telephone of Thomas Maloney, a Seattle-based racketeer on the Teamsters' payroll as an organizer. The resulting tapes recorded District Attorney William Langley counting his bribe money, complaining about his share of the payoffs, and plotting to frame Elkins.[60]

Public Shame

Elkins retaliated by going to the press.[61] He provided the crucial information leading to a 1956 *Oregonian* exposé of the Teamsters' involvement in organized crime.[62] The ensuing scandal garnered national attention, and a Senate committee sent Robert Kennedy to Portland to investigate.

The Select Committee on Improper Activities in the Labor and Management Field consisted of John McClellan (chair), Joseph McCarthy (later replaced by Carl Curtis), Barry Goldwater, Karl Mundt (formerly of the House Un-American Activities Committee), Irving Ives, Sam Ervin, Patrick McNamara, and John F. Kennedy. Robert Kennedy served as chief counsel.[63] The committee had a staff of one hundred and, over almost three years of hearings, called 1,525 witnesses, including Langley, Schrunk, Purcell, and Elkins.[64]

Elkins testified about his own illegal activities and about his arrangements with the Teamsters, the district attorney, and the Portland Police. He claimed that Sheriff Schrunk had pressed him to provide money and liquor for a law enforcement convention in 1955, a story verified by Oregon State Police investigators and by the deputy who handled the finances. It further emerged that three city policemen had witnessed Schrunk accepting a payoff from the manager of one of Elkins's clubs. The committee hearings, and later grand jury investigations, demonstrated pretty clearly that Schrunk had been in league with Elkins, Stan Terry, the Teamsters, and other racketeers and used his position to protect certain favored gambling houses.[65]

"Were it not that the conspirators in this particular case had a falling out," the McClellan Committee intoned in one of its reports, "gambling and law enforcement in Portland would now be completely under the domination of a Teamsters-backed underworld."[66] Indeed, it seems that after the elections of 1952, the mayor, sheriff, district attorney, police chief, and vice squad commander had all been in the pay of organized crime. Senator Karl Mundt suggested Portland "pull the flags down at half-mast in public shame."[67]

Whatever the consequences for Portland's reputation, the McClellan hearings did even worse to that of the Teamsters and the labor movement more generally. In 1959, Congress passed the Landrum-Griffin Act. The law tightened restrictions against secondary boycotts, introduced regulations concerning union finances, prohibited bribery, banned ex-cons from holding union office, guaranteed certain rights for union members, increased penalties for using violence in labor disputes, and made embezzlement a federal crime. Though the reforms encouraged union democracy and limited the opportunities for corruption, they were primarily motivated by a desire to undermine the power of the labor movement. It was the first major change to labor law since Taft-Hartley, the 1947 law that limited a union's right to strike, boycott, picket, or donate to political campaigns and barred Communists from positions of leadership.[68] Landrum-Griffin seems, in many ways, to constitute its sequel.

From McCarthy to Kennedy

The McClellan hearings made Robert Kennedy a national figure.[69] He later took credit for 124 indictments of Teamster officials, members, and associates, leading to sixty-five convictions.[70] But not everyone was pleased by his performance. Muckraking journalist I. F. Stone commented: "Though Bobby helped clean a lot of hoodlums and corrupt dictators out of the labor movement, he acted much as had McCarthy, equating invocation of the Fifth Amendment with confession of guilt and treating a Congressional investigation as a pillory in which people he disliked could be held up to public scorn."[71] Stone's comparison was well-grounded, and not merely because of McCarthy's presence on the McClellan Committee. McClellan himself went on to lead a three-year investigation, beginning in 1967, on "riots [and] civil and criminal disorders," which he blamed on "militant agitators" and "Communists . . . sow[ing] the seeds of discord."[72]

Robert Kennedy had previously worked for the Justice Department's Internal Security Division, which prosecuted espionage and subversion. In 1953, he was hired by the Senate Government Operations Committee's Investigations Subcommittee, just as his family friend, the arch red-baiter Joseph McCarthy, was appointed chairman. Biographers are divided as to how much Kennedy's resignation a month later was a matter of political principle, how much it was an expression of careerist frustration after being passed over for chief counsel, and how much it was prompted by personal distaste for the man who got the job, Roy Cohn. In any case, a year later he returned to the subcommittee when the Democrats took control, and he was appointed chief counsel in 1955. He would remain friends with McCarthy until the senator's death in 1957.[73]

This pattern held as Kennedy climbed to higher office. In 1961—his first year as attorney general, serving in his brother's cabinet—he established an intelligence unit in the Justice Department to coordinate investigations into organized crime, asked Congress to strengthen racketeering laws, and began a series of prosecutions against Teamsters president James Hoffa. That same year, he had the Communist Party indicted for failing to register as the agent of a foreign power.[74]

Indictments

Back in Portland, by September 1957, forty-one people had been indicted by three grand juries, totaling 115 separate charges. Among them were Jim Elkins, the Teamsters' Tom Maloney, Multnomah County District Attorney William Langley, Police Chief James Purcell, and the newly elected mayor, Terry Schrunk.[75] Ironically, Schrunk—in his last weeks as sheriff—had made the initial arrests. He then trumpeted the case in his (Elkins-funded) mayoral campaign, promising a "good, clean, decent police department."[76] Then, on November 1, 1956, just before the election, Chief Purcell held a press conference and read aloud an indictment of Sheriff Schrunk, accusing him of lax enforcement, staging "token and phony" raids for political purposes, and accepting bribes.[77] One way or another, though, Schrunk came out ahead, besting Fred Peterson by 38,000 votes.[78]

Alongside the cynical political maneuvering, some of the indictments were brought about through the efforts of—at last!—an honest policeman. Jack Olsen, an idealistic rookie, was shocked and unnerved when he was first offered a bribe. He suggested reporting the incident to the chief of police, but his partner quickly put him right: "Who do you think's running this thing?" Olsen began accepting the payoffs and documenting every dollar he received; he then took his records to *Oregonian* reporter James Miller. The paper at first refused to run Miller's stories, and the vice squad put a tail on him in an attempt to learn his source. Elkins personally tried to bribe Miller, then quickly resorted to threatening his family. Miller then took his story to the state police.

Olsen's evidence contributed to the indictments of Purcell and Langley, along with those of eight patrol officers. He then found himself ostracized by the other cops and assigned to the graveyard shift in the records division. He left the bureau, attended law school, worked as a prosecutor in nearby Clackamas County, and later became a judge.[79]

Despite years of investigation and national headlines, few convictions resulted: Langley was fined $428 and removed from office, though his conviction was later overturned. Elkins was sentenced to twelve months and fined $2,000 but also won on appeal. (Curiously, the *Oregonian* paid for Elkins's legal expenses until his conviction; the costs of his appeal were paid for personally by the Kennedy brothers.) Clark, the private detective, received six months and a $500 fine. A brothel owner was incidentally fined $250. Purcell resigned as chief and was reassigned to the St. Johns neighborhood, where corruption continued to thrive. Schrunk was acquitted, despite Robert Kennedy's testimony at his trial. He served as Portland's mayor from 1957 to 1972.[80]

The paucity of convictions was itself rather suspicious, even apart from the district attorney's involvement. A grand jury accused state attorney general Robert Thornton of undercutting the criminal investigation through his failure to provide adequate staff and resources.[81] Arthur Kaplan, an assistant to Thornton who would later work as an investigator for the McClellan Committee, published an open letter accusing Thornton of "attempting to whitewash the prosecution for political or personal motives." Howard Lonergan, another of the attorney general's assistants, accused him directly of taking money from Jim Elkins.[82] Later, when the US Department of Justice moved to file federal charges against Elkins, Robert Kennedy ordered that the prosecutor be fired. US Attorney for Oregon Sidney Lezak refused.[83] The case came to set an important precedent: Much of the evidence against Elkins had been seized illegally by local police; but under the "Silver Platter" doctrine, it was admissible in federal court so long as the *federal* authorities had not been party to the illegal search. Elkins's appeal went as far as the US Supreme Court, which overturned his conviction and discarded the Silver Platter rule.[84]

Case Study

Portland, as historian Robert C. Donnelly writes, provides "an exceptional case study of repeated and failed efforts by progressive reformers to clean up municipal government and police morality."[85] This failure says something, surely, about how entrenched the criminal interests were, how strong the temptations to put personal gain over public duty, and how *near* the practices of government always are to those of organized crime. The parallel experiences of Jack Olsen, at the bottom of the hierarchy, and Charles Pray, at the top—both isolated and then exiled—shows the limits of any individual's effect and therefore also of any plan for change that depends on getting the right people into office or into uniform. Similar lessons may be taken from Dorothy Lee's purity campaign and Robert Kennedy's efforts. Lee's tenure demonstrates too the repeated tendency of moral crusades to shade over into simple prejudice and for the dictates of one's conscience to begin, in turn, to dictate to others. Indeed, it is precisely the attempt to legislate morality that creates the market for vice, which is really less about the provision of illicit goods and services, and more about the profitable opportunity for extortion. Corruption is the twin of prohibition, and it makes little difference what it is that is being prohibited: alcohol, sex, gambling, or pinball.

The demand for civic virtue also, it seems, fits nicely alongside a program of political repression. That was true of the Red Scare of the teens, and it was true of the Red Scare of the fifties. And here we find one thing on which the reformers, the racketeers, and the red squad all agreed: they were each in their own ways committed to the capitalist system and opposed to any efforts to overturn it. It was the antiradicalism of the authorities that allowed organized crime to infiltrate the labor movement in the first place. During the turbulent years of the Depression, "labor racketeering was consciously permitted, even chosen," historian James Jacobs argues in *Mobsters, Unions, and Feds*. Employers found self-interested gangsters easier to deal with than ideologically driven militants, and "governments at all levels" were ready to "ally . . . with organized crime figures" in their efforts to de-radicalize the labor movement.[86] The reformers' later efforts to rid the unions of mobsters both resembled and facilitated their ongoing efforts to rid them of reds. But of the two, the reds were always the priority.

CHAPTER 12

Unamerican, Antiwar, Counterculture

Naming Names

During the period of transition following the Second World War, as geopolitics sorted nations into competing blocs, the fear of communism—acute among establishment figures since the Russian Revolution—took on a renewed urgency and an additional weight. While the local red squad continued to play its traditional role blacklisting union organizers, federal authorities were bringing unprecedented scrutiny to elite institutions, determined to drive out any potentially subversive influence. The House Un-American Activities Committee (HUAC) visited Portland in 1954, mostly to investigate Reed College. Homer Owen and Robert Canon, formerly a student and a dean, respectively, testified before the committee and named fifty-three alleged Communists.[1]

In response, on June 1, 1954, the Reed faculty adopted a statement on academic freedom: "The Faculty of Reed College opposes as contrary to democratic liberties any ban or regulation which would prohibit the employment as a teacher of any person solely because of his views or associations." The following day, Stanley Moore, a tenured professor of philosophy, appeared before HUAC. Moore, a Marxist scholar and former member of the Communist Party, had never hidden his views, but in this instance he refused to testify.[2]

The Reed Faculty Council and the college's board of trustees then initiated their own investigations into on-campus communism. Moore objected in an open letter: "I believe that academic officials have no more authority to ask these questions than do Congressmen," he wrote. "It is an abuse of power for an employer to question an employee about his politics." He did agree to meet with the college president, faculty council, and board of trustees but only to discuss his teaching, not his political views. Concerning professional matters, he was on solid ground. The faculty council found Moore "outstanding . . . in terms of scholarly preparation, objectivity in the presentation of material and general effectiveness in the classroom." They recommended "no charges of misconduct" and "no disciplinary action of any kind." The trustees, however, considered communism "beyond the scope of political beliefs and associations and also beyond the scope of academic freedom." They therefore concluded that Moore's refusal to discuss his time in the Communist Party constituted "misconduct." He was fired that August.[3]

"Moore's case was unusual," historian Ellen Schrecker writes, "because he had been so straightforward about refusing to answer political questions . . . [and because] the trustees made that the only grounds for his dismissal. . . . In fact, if we view academic freedom in its functional sense, as the faculty's control over its own hiring and promotion, then Reed may well have had the only real academic freedom case of the McCarthy period."[4]

Two other Reed College professors—Lloyd Reynolds, a tenured professor of fine arts, and Leonard Marsak, a visiting professor of history—were similarly subpoenaed by HUAC and likewise refused to participate. However, they each cooperated with the college's internal investigations. College president Duncan Ballantine relieved Reynolds of his teaching assignments for the summer session, but he returned in the fall. Marsak's contract was not renewed for the following year, and he found himself blacklisted.[5] Those outside a prestigious liberal arts college faced worse. Four Portlanders called before HUAC faced prison time for contempt of Congress, but their convictions were overturned by the US Supreme Court.[6] Nevertheless, they were persecuted for years afterward. The wife of one wrote, "The FBI appeared not only at places we lived but at his jobs . . . as if they were there to get him fired."[7]

HUAC's less-famous cousin, the federal Subversive Activities Control Board, visited Portland a decade later, in 1964 and 1965, focusing again on area colleges and relying on evidence provided by two FBI informers who had infiltrated the Communist Party. Public reaction this time was far less muted. Students from Portland State College and Reed College packed the courtroom, while hundreds more picketed outside—an act itself prohibited under the 1950 McCarran Act. Signs read "End Thought Control Now" and "Defend the Right to Dissent."[8]

Public hearings were just the most visible edge of a much more expansive blacklisting system. Rather than rely on government bodies with subpoena powers, the FBI (and similar agencies) would supply employers with lists of suspected radicals, fully expecting that the institutions would handle the matter internally. Usually they did—abruptly, arbitrarily, without explanation and without controversy. It is estimated that, across the country, between ten and twelve thousand people lost jobs because of their alleged ties to Communism.[9]

Fighting the War

In a 1966 survey, Portland cops ranked "keeping track of subversives" as their eighth-highest priority, above "traffic duties" and "control of vice."[10]

Mason Drukman, a professor at Reed, recalled Charles Trimble, an officer in the Portland Police Bureau's Intelligence Division, approaching him: "He tried to find out what Reedies were up to and what the antiwar students were planning. . . . I wouldn't tell him, but we had interesting conversations."[11] Activists organizing against the war in Vietnam remember surveillance being pervasive.[12] Looking back, one activist, Hugo du Courdray, says, "We were sure there was at least one government informant at every meeting. . . . It was a given for the times."[13] The cops cast a wide net: by 1970, the red squad had 175 informants in area high schools.[14] Police used the information they collected on activists to spread discrediting rumors, damage their personal reputations, and create strife within their organizations.[15]

It is perhaps surprising, then, that authorities were initially reserved in their response to antiwar demonstrations, sometimes comically so. A July 1966 antiwar march featured three hundred protesters under a banner reading "We Mourn the Dead of World War III." One of the organizers, Lynn Meyer, later recalled, "This march was illegal because the city would not grant a parade permit. Our motorcycle escort was arrested. That prompted all of us to march to the police station to turn ourselves in for staging an illegal parade. The police refused to arrest us, so we bailed out those few they had arrested."[16]

"I remember occupying a downtown post office," Professor Drukman said of another demonstration. "We were arrested, and U.S. Attorney Sid Lezak marched us out and released us immediately."[17] Lezak was known for his reluctance to prosecute conscientious objectors. One such refusenik, Jamie Partridge, later thanked him for his measured approach. Lezak replied, "There were some of you on the outside fighting the war and some of us on the inside fighting it."[18] Still, in 1967, the US Attorney's office in Oregon indicted seventy people for refusing the draft; the following year that number was 118.[19]

The cops would reach the end of their patience before 1966 was through. That September 27, two hundred demonstrators filled the sidewalk in front of the Sheraton Hotel, where Vice President Hubert Humphrey was speaking at a fundraiser.[20] The *Oregonian* reported, "What otherwise appeared to be a peaceful demonstration exploded into a club-swinging mêlée by policemen when a cordon of blue-uniformed officers moved out of formation at the entrance to the Sheraton parking lot and began to haul away the demonstrators who had sat down on the pavement."[21] Thirty-one people were arrested. This episode, historians Matt Nelson and Bill Nygren comment, "marked a turning point in police-protestor relations."[22] From here, violence would escalate.

Encountering the Counterculture

The hardening of attitudes against protesters was matched by an official disdain for the emerging counterculture. Indeed, they were often conflated. Many of the draft resisters appeared before Judge Gus Solomon, who described them in a newspaper interview as "bearded, longhaired, drug using hippies" and called the men "dropouts living with women and taking no responsibility for children they had fathered."[23] This slander simultaneously cast antiwar activists as irresponsible losers, and hippies as dangerous subversives.

It followed that hippies didn't even need to be activists to become targets for repression. In January 1967 the Portland Police vice squad, accompanied by federal agents, raided eleven residences in Lair Hill, a low-rent area popular with students and artists—"Portland's answer to Haight Ashbury," as at least one observer described it. Fifty-two people were arrested and an estimated $20,000 worth of marijuana was seized.[24] A year later, prompted by a media panic over a coming flower-child invasion, Parks Commissioner Frank Ivancie declared a "war on hippies" and imposed a curfew for Lair Hill Park, where a committee called the Provos had organized free concerts without engaging the permit process. Numerous arrests followed, though the curfew was twice deemed unconstitutional.[25] On a single night, police raided both the park and The Charix, one of several church-run coffee shops ministering to counterculture youth. Fifty people were arrested.[26]

Throughout his long political career—nine years as Mayor Schrunk's executive assistant, fourteen years on city council, and four as mayor—Frank Ivancie was always a law-and-order figure and relied on his reputation as a tough guy.[27]

As journalist Floyd McKay described, "He could be a bully and was known to intimidate; in political contests he had a nasty edge. . . . He lacked empathy with neighborhood organizers and other activists. . . . He opposed community policing, mass transit, downtown housing, professional planning, and gay rights."[28] Ivancie's hostility extended to those he saw as enabling the dropout culture. He spoke against the creation of Outside-In, a social service agency offering aid to homeless teenagers, telling the city council: "I'm not interested in helping create any hippie heaven here in Portland, and I'm sure the people of Portland are not interested in having that kind of reputation."[29] According to Dr. Charles Spray, who founded Outside-In's medical clinic, the controversy actually "brought us a flood of volunteers and gave us caché."[30] However, the police pressured Outside-In, Youth Ministries, and similar agencies to turn runaways over to the Women's Protective Division (WPD).[31] In effect, that would mean sending them back home and in the process undercutting any basis for trust in the social service agencies. "We . . . built a network of informants among the kids," one WPD officer later wrote. "As a result we were very successful in tracking down some of the runaways and getting them back to their families."[32]

Shut Up Those Kids

The repression of the antiwar movement reached its iconic climax in the spring of 1970, when National Guard troops opened fire on a crowd at Kent State University in Ohio, killing four. The massacre prompted student strikes at four hundred colleges across the country, Portland State University (PSU) among them.[33] Streets were blocked and campus buildings occupied.[34] Frank Ivancie showed his usual compassion and charm: "It's time someone shut up those kids."[35]

The Police Bureau's Captain Norman Reiter took a more judicious view, negotiating with the students to remove barricades from the streets surrounding the campus. Assistant Park Superintendent Robert Gustafson agreed to allow a first aid tent to remain in the South Park Blocks adjacent to the college until after the barricades were cleared away. Everything seemed headed for a peaceful resolution until Ivancie, as parks commissioner, overruled Gustafson's decision. Without notice, the police Tac ("Tactical") Squad arrived on campus, ready to confront two thousand striking students. PSU president Greg Wolfe called Mayor Schrunk, urging him to have the cops stand down. Captain Reiter, too, appealed to his superiors to leave the tent in place. He was relieved of command and escorted from the area.[36] Others likewise tried to reason with the cops. "After the police were in formation in front of the students," professor Steve Kosokoff recalls, "several faculty members, a minister, and I, approached the police officer in charge and pleaded with him to call off the police. . . . He ordered the tactical squad to advance."[37]

One of the students, Lester Lamm, described what happened next:

> Then everything went into slow motion as the TAC squad stiffened, grunted, growled and pointed their clubs forward, stomped their left foot and jabbed straight ahead in this wedge formation. It didn't take twenty seconds before the point of that wedge came into contact with the protestors. That's when the clubs came up, and they started beating people. I saw Jeff go down. Roger was standing adjacent to me, and I heard his head split like a pumpkin. . . . You couldn't run because you were against this mass of people behind the tent. People who were getting pummeled couldn't run anywhere.
>
> I'm telling you the TAC Squad were salivating. You could see it. They were smiling.[38]

Police didn't make arrests but just clubbed wildly into the crowd.[39] Kosokoff found himself in the scrum:

> Next, I was hit myself and turned to get away. I was hit several times on the back by several policemen as I made my way into the street. I was hit on the curb, well away from the tent. I then watched the clubbing continue and ran to the assistance of a former student, who was unconscious. On my way to her aid, I was hit three more times. . . . Four of us picked her up to carry her out of the way of the police. Several times, in carrying her through the ranks, we were threatened by them. We carried her a block away and set her down to await an ambulance.[40]

Photographs and televised footage show the Tac Squad advancing, in formation, with helmets and long batons, clubbing protesters already on the ground. Thirty-one demonstrators were hospitalized. Four cops were injured as well.[41]

A public meeting that evening drew up a list of five demands: 1) a thorough investigation; 2) elimination of the Tac Squad; 3) resignations of the officials responsible for sending in the police; 4) prosecution of police guilty of abuse; and 5) a meeting with Mayor Schrunk.[42] The next day almost five thousand people marched to City Hall to protest the violence. Still, as historian Polina Olsen notes, "the hospital tent's removal signaled the strike's end."[43]

A grand jury was convened to investigate the strike. Though the students refused to testify, the jury ultimately blamed the police for the violence. Establishing a pattern that would continue even until the present, the city council gestured toward a technical fix while refusing to hold anyone to account. The council passed an ordinance instructing the Police Bureau to revise its operations manual on crowd control, but no officers were disciplined.[44]

Into the Vortex

After the PSU strike—to say nothing of the Kent State massacre that precipitated it—tensions remained high. They would only increase when it was announced that President Richard Nixon would visit Portland that summer to address the national convention of the American Legion.[45] Almost at once, an antiwar demonstration was also announced—first called the Revolutionary Festival of Life but later renamed the People's Army Jamboree.[46] The FBI was alarmed: "All current information indicates that thousands of dissidents, hippies, anti-Vietnam [*sic*] and anti-military protestors, and other individuals generally bent on bringing down society, the government, and all its representatives will be gathering in Portland."[47] The feds requested reports from around the country naming activists who might make the trip, infiltrated local meetings, and recorded the license numbers of automobiles parked outside the homes of organizers. They sent regular updates to the Bureau of Alcohol, Tobacco, and Firearms, the US Marshals, and other law enforcement agencies.[48] A few weeks later, the FBI warned Oregon Governor Tom McCall to prepare for fifty thousand protesters and stated that Portland faced the "highest risk of violence in the nation" that summer.[49] Representatives from the governor's office met with antiwar activists, urging them to cancel the protests. The activists refused.[50]

A small counterculture collective called The Family approached Governor McCall with a proposal: Vortex One: A Biodegradable Festival of Life, a weeklong government-funded rock festival.[51] As activist Lee Meier saw it, "We thought, you know, we ought to come up with something else, something not antiwar so much as pro-peace."[52] An August 13, 1970, FBI memo offered a different rationale:

"This festival is to be held during the same dates as the legion convention and is sanctioned as an effort to drain young people from the downtown area in the hope of lessening chances of a violent confrontation."[53] Governor McCall, the Portland City Council, and local business owners all approved. Restaurants donated kitchen equipment, and private businesses paid for the sound stage and sanitation. The governor's Chief of Staff Ed Westerdahl later explained, "The Portland business community financially supported Vortex because they knew it was in their interests to not have downtown trashed."[54]

The location for the event was selected as McIver State Park, twenty-five miles southeast of the city—near enough to attract a crowd, but far enough to avoid any interaction with the Legionnaires. Westerdahl, who had previously served as an officer in military intelligence, has characterized the strategy as containment. "That's why we picked McIver Park. Our intention was to draw people out of the city, put them in a location where they could be contained." The park was surrounded by forest, with only one road in or out. The National Guard was positioned out of sight, on higher ground. The State Police SWAT team was stationed in a Parks Department maintenance building. Undercover cops kept an eye on things within the festival but were instructed to ignore nonviolent offenses. Ivancie was incensed: "You're telling these people, 'You can get stoned at this state park. . . . We will exempt you from our laws and rules.' "[55]

Estimates range from thirty to one hundred thousand people in attendance at Vortex I, while the People's Army Jamboree mobilized between two hundred and seventeen hundred for its demonstrations downtown. Video from McIver Park shows groups of people in the nude—in a steam tent, swimming, sunbathing, and just walking around—as well as clowns, drum circles, and festivalgoers sitting in a field smoking marijuana.[56] "There was a lot of pot smoking and skinny dipping," McCall conceded, "but nobody got killed."[57]

In the end, both sides declared victory. The American Legion held its convention, and an internal FBI memo expressed satisfaction at the "complete lack of violence or any major disruptive incident."[58] The People's Army Jamboree (PAJ), meanwhile, took credit for Nixon's last-minute cancellation. (He was replaced by Vice President Spiro Agnew—nobody's first choice.)[59] "The PAJ was the best thing I ever did," activist Cathy Wood Wyrick would later say. "Nixon canceled his speech because of us. We won."[60]

Attitudes about Vortex, however, remain divided. "Was there a statement being made by walking around naked and smoking dope in McIver Park when young men and Vietnamese [were] dying by the thousands?" historian Matt

Love asks. "And there are people today that still see Vortex as a sell-out, because you could have been protesting the war."[61] Others, however, insist that they *were* protesting the war, but in a more constructive, meaningful, and fun manner than the standard march—and with infinitely less chance of suffering a police-inflicted concussion. Hugo du Courdray takes this view: "Many of my comrades were angry about Vortex, and some still feel that way, but I was delighted. It was far more than one antiwar parade through town, and a lot less dangerous. . . . Of course, the sentiment of the crowd was antiwar, and they expressed that with garb, buttons and slogans. It was a peace convention to contrast with the convocation of rabid warmongers in the legion."[62]

McCall's biographer, Brent Walth, is skeptical that the event had any political impact: "The Vortex crowds were not bought-off protestors. They were local kids who had no interest in political marches, but were interested in a party."[63] Indeed, FBI director J. Edgar Hoover was never convinced of the danger.[64] And People's Army Jamboree organizers have since admitted that the threat of a big demonstration was always a bluff.[65]

On the other hand, the divergent responses from within the peace movement, the differing assessments, the recrimination and divisiveness—those were certainly real enough. At first glance, the controversy would seem to track a political fault line within the antiwar movement: a liberal, discursive politics versus a radical, confrontational politics; or else a prefigurative pacifism versus a revolutionary militancy. But either interpretation leaves out the role of the state in constructing the very dilemma. Viewed one way, Vortex I constituted a "bread and circuses" strategy, a manipulative distraction to ensure that the peace movement would have no practical effect.[66] Viewed another way, it represented a "carrot and stick" strategy: the metaphorical carrot of an utopian holiday versus the literal stick of the riot police. "The problem," as historian Maurice Isserman saw it, "was that in the back of everybody's minds was the violence that had taken place during the strike. . . . no wonder so many young people in Portland decided to head for a rock festival in the countryside rather than march down city streets and potentially get their heads cracked open."[67]

The threat of violence, largely unspoken yet ever present, effectively channeled the protest into actions that were purely expressive, nondisruptive, and "contained," while separating the diehard radicals from their larger base of support. This strategy would be employed repeatedly over the coming decades—programmatically and sometimes with greater sophistication, though rarely with the same degree of unalloyed success.

CHAPTER 13
An Occupying Army and Self-Defense

Sunday in the Park

On July 30, 1967, a Black cultural event billed as "Sunday in the Park" promised a theater performance, a photo exhibit on the work of the Student Nonviolent Coordinating Committee, and a speech by Black Panther Party minister of information Eldridge Cleaver. Anticipating trouble, National Guard troops in jeeps and trucks patrolled the largely Black neighborhood of Albina, police cars endlessly circled Irving Park, and the FBI sent plainclothes agents into the crowd. Cleaver failed to show, and as the sun set, youths at the rally became restless. They chased an FBI agent out of the park, attacked a park supervisor, and then began throwing rocks and bottles at passing cars.[1]

For two nights, angry crowds vandalized nearby businesses, started fires, and attacked whites, sometimes shouting, "Whitey, go home!" Arsonists concentrated on the infrastructure of urban development, setting fire to construction equipment and fuel trucks. The mayor declared a curfew, and four hundred police and sheriff's deputies were deployed, four or five to a car; hundreds more, along with five hundred National Guardsmen, waited in reserve. Each unit was issued a shotgun loaded with buckshot, and the officers were ordered to wear helmets. They sealed off a thirty-block area and arrested nineteen people the first night. On the second night, Mayor Terry Schrunk ordered police to clear Irving Park, where the crowds were gathering: "Start making plenty of arrests." The cops shot one person and arrested ninety-eight, the majority Black and a quarter of them juveniles.[2]

A young patrolman at the time, Tom Potter—later to become Portland's police chief, then mayor—recalls a moment of clarity amid the chaos: "During the night I can remember standing on what was then Union Avenue and

Fremont and every building I could see was on fire. And I could hear the pop-pop of guns. And pretty soon I saw this group of young Black men. And they looked at me and . . . [said] 'We're gone kill you, pig.' . . . And I'm thinking, 'What did I do to these people?' Well, it's not what *I* did, it's what that uniform did at other times and places."

Potter said, "[I saw] how African Americans were treated. I saw people beat up that I did not think should have been beat up. I heard in the locker rooms and out on the street the N-word, repeatedly." Confronted with the anger that such contempt provoked, he realized, "Our job was not to . . . solve problems. It was to suppress things." Simply put, "We were an occupation army."[3]

The Colonial Model

Since the end of the Second World War, discriminatory housing policies had increasingly concentrated the city's African-American population in Albina, which correspondingly became both more crowded and also more predominantly Black.[4] By 1960, there were 15,637 African Americans in Portland, representing 4 percent of the city's population. Almost three quarters (73 percent) lived in Albina—which historian Kenneth R. Coleman characterized as "a two-and-a-half square mile area with substandard housing, resource-starved schools, poor environmental protections, and discriminatory policing."[5]

Policing, as much as poverty, is what makes a neighborhood a ghetto. In Albina, unlike any other part of the city, the cops patrolled in pairs.[6] A City Club report from the late sixties found: "[Police] feel they have the right to stop and frisk someone because his skin is black and he is in the black part of town."[7] "Where else but in Albina do cops hang around the streets and parks all day like plantation overseers?," one young man asked. "Just their presence antagonizes us. We feel like we are being watched all of the time."[8] In fact the Intelligence Division did keep a close eye on Albina, including surveillance of civil rights organizations and a standing policy of breaking up any unauthorized gathering.[9] After the riot, police surveillance intensified; henceforth even routine encounters in Albina would be reported to the Intelligence Division.[10]

At the same time, according to an official history published by the City's Bureau of Planning, "the riot . . . opened dialogue between City officials and residents of Albina." Parks Commissioner Frank Ivancie visited the neighborhood to promote new recreation programs. Mayor Terry Schrunk met with a group of young people who demanded jobs, better schools, better housing, more public services, and fewer police.[11]

But many young activists felt that such negotiations missed the point. Frank Fair described the Albina neighborhood as "a colony, something separate and foreign from the city" yet under the control of a largely indifferent white society. He concluded that the residents would "have to deal with their problems on those terms."[12] Kenneth Coleman elaborates: "The colonial model led black activists in Portland and elsewhere to reject liberal assimilation and integration in favor of advocacy of the redistribution of economic and political power, self-sufficiency, and self-determination."[13]

Community Relations

Hoping to head off future unrest, in 1968, Chief Donald McNamara created the Police Community Relations Division (PCR). Funded through the federal Model Cities program, it consisted of ten sworn officers overseen by a lieutenant, fifteen community service officers overseen by a community service supervisor, and a secretary.[14]

The bureau's annual report from 1971 records, "The Police Community Relations Division was formed in May 1968, when it became apparent that there was a vital need for this type of service. They have been very active in many community programs and have established rapport with minority groups in the Portland area. . . . The project operates a number of programs which are intended to make the uniform officers [*sic*] task an easier one by improving mutual understanding between the citizen and the police. We are attempting to facilitate improved police service by developing a closer working relationship between citizens and the Police Bureau."[15] The 1972 report largely repeated the language of the previous year's, with this addition: "As part of their regular duties, personnel cover situations which have a potential for violence or friction, with the object of lessoning tension."[16] The purpose of the program was clear, and so were its limitations. The PCR was geared around the *cops'* needs: making the job easier, improving their performance, avoiding unrest. In any case, there is no indication that the new unit did much to change the conduct of the police.[17] And so it struggled to win the public's trust. On March 12, 1970, the Police Community Relations office in Northeast Portland was bombed.[18]

Ironically, when the PCR did succeed in building trust with activists, the resulting relationships tended to provoke *distrust* within the bureau. For instance, in 1971, Black Berets founder Roscoe La Verne Anderson was elected to the Model Cities Law and Justice Committee. In that position he worked closely with the Police Community Relations Division and formed a good working relationship with Sergeant John Roe. Superior officers disapproved, and the Intelligence Division opened files on both Anderson and Roe. In short order, and over the objections of the Law and Justice Committee, Roe was transferred, and Anderson resigned. The committee essentially ceased to function.[19]

A review of the Police Community Relations unit conducted by PSU's Lee Brown concluded that the program had achieved nothing beyond "its survival" and suggested that the main source for conflict between the police and the public was the fact that the "police come from a totally different environment" and bring with them a "stereotyped view of . . . residents."[20] The PCR was soon dissolved.[21]

Defend Ourselves

For three nights, beginning Friday, June 13, 1969, police swept through the Albina neighborhood, dispersing groups of young people out enjoying the summer evening. The cops said that they were responding to complaints about rowdy teenagers outside of Lidio's Drive-In, on the corner of Northeast Union and Shaver. A crowd attacked the police, slashing their tires, throwing rocks, breaking windows, and setting fires. However, numerous witnesses—including a member of Governor Tom McCall's staff, speaking on condition of anonymity—blamed the cops for provoking the kids. "The police got rougher than they should have," journalist Jimmy "Bang-Bang" Walker said, "and this is when everything got out of hand." George Davis, the manager at Lidio's, told the *Oregonian* that the cops showed up in leather jackets, without badges or name plates, and the trouble started when one "put his club around a girl's neck and forced her into the squad car" and two others clubbed young men in the head and stomach. "After that the kids broke loose on them and started throwing rocks and smashing windows."[22]

On Tuesday, the North Precinct commander, Captain William Taylor, met with a group of Black leaders and agreed to withdraw the police for forty-eight hours if they would use their influence to urge calm. That night saw twelve arsons, but the police kept their word and only entered the area to escort firefighters. By the following afternoon things had returned to normal.[23]

When he was released from jail, Kent Ford—a young Black man who had been arrested on the first night of rioting—stood on the steps of the downtown police headquarters and announced the formation of a Portland chapter of the National Committee to Combat Fascism, a front group for the Black Panther Party (BPP).[24] "If they keep coming in with these fascist tactics," he declared, "we're going to defend ourselves."[25] However, Percy Hampton, another of the chapter's cofounders, later remarked that the Portland Panthers had deliberately downplayed the armed aspect of their program: "We never did openly display our weapons. . . . We kind of kept that out of the limelight 'cause that could frighten our own folks. . . . We didn't want anyone to perceive us as being out-of-control, gun-toting radicals." Local efforts concentrated instead on the party's survival programs. For five years, beginning in 1969, the Portland chapter provided free breakfasts for schoolchildren, and from 1970 to 1980 managed a free medical and dental clinic.[26]

Still, the Panthers took their self-defense function seriously. When Black students reported harassment at Roosevelt High, Panthers started escorting them to and from school. David Morris, a freshman at the time, describes the impact: "Once the Panthers got involved my fear went away. . . . Kent sent in soldiers to protect us. . . . The first day they arrived, they were wearing army fatigues and marching on each side of us. . . . They had us shouting slogans and everything. . . . I'll never forget that experience."[27]

The Panthers also sought to help people—especially poor and Black people—to navigate the criminal legal system. They distributed a "Pocket Lawyer," a pamphlet explaining one's rights when dealing with the police, and circulated a list of "judges that we and others considered white supremacists."[28] They made a practice of observing arrests and bailing people out of jail.[29] In 1970, in an attempt to increase community control, the BPP circulated a petition to divide the Police Bureau into two divisions—one for Albina and one for the rest of the city.[30]

In all their activities the Panthers sought to build power in the Black community and better meet the needs of that community. As their reward, they endured constant surveillance and harassment, from both the local cops and the FBI.[31] Federal agents watched their homes and harassed their friends, families, and employers. Sometimes cops would contact the parents of young members, saying, "Do you know that your children are involved in the Black Panther

Party? You need to protect them from this, because they're headed the wrong direction."[32] Percy Hampton recalls, "FBI agents would go door to door and ask my neighbors about me and my activities.... Then there were times when I'd look in my rearview mirror and see them following me around town."[33] Kent Ford was repeatedly arrested for jaywalking and minor traffic violations—he was once issued four tickets in a single day, all of which were eventually dismissed.[34] Former Panther Oscar Johnson remembers feeling more bemused than intimidated: "You just wanted to say to them, 'Hey guys, don't you have something better to do?'"[35]

Intelligence Files

By the early seventies, the surveillance extended further than even the Panthers suspected, permeating the community as a whole. A young PSU student named Avel Gordly—who would later serve in the state legislature from 1991 to 2008—took an internship at the Portland Police Bureau, studying the bureau's overtime practices. (She would quickly learn that the cops were averse to even that level of scrutiny.) Looking back on her research, she recalled "some unexpected discoveries in the police files. I came across a series of photographs ... of Black people taken in different circumstances in the community." Those pictured were not necessarily activists, and the pictures were not from demonstrations. Instead, they showed the inside of "clubs or parties in peoples' homes," suggesting a sense of trust or intimacy: "The photographer had to be very close." Gordly found them unnerving. "It made me think: 'informant.'"[36]

The police file on Ron Herndon, chair of the Black United Front, featured no allegations of criminal misconduct but did include family photos. Herndon concludes that the cops weren't just monitoring Black revolutionaries but also "anybody who knew or was friends with them. Before long, they were just keeping watch over black people, period."[37]

In 1975, the ACLU sued the Portland Police for illegal spying. Resolving the case years later, the bureau agreed to destroy the red squad's dossiers. Instead, Officer Winfield Falk took home thirty-six boxes of files, totaling 851 manila folders, and continued to add to them for years. Concentrated mainly on the period 1965 to 1985, the files contained information on 576 groups and more than 3,000 individuals. Many documents had no relationship to any criminal matter at all. Some listed the names of people who had signed human rights petitions; others described community projects like soup kitchens, day care centers, and food co-ops. Some files included financial records and job applications. One named an auxiliary police captain "known to associate and play with the gay crowd."[38]

These reports, often replete with inaccurate, biased, and even libelous information, were sometimes used to get tenants evicted and public employees fired.[39] They were commonly shared between departments, errors and all. For example, a summary report from the Seattle Police, forwarded to the Portland Police Intelligence Division, identified a "Chicano activist" who "advocate[d] terrorist acts," though nothing in the original file would support such a claim.[40] Portland's records were in turn passed on to the Chicago police, who had reciprocal intelligence-sharing arrangements with 159 agencies nationwide.[41] Some of those departments then distributed the information even further. The Los Angeles Police Department shared its files with Research West, a private firm, founded by former FBI agents, which sold intelligence reports to corporate clients.[42]

Winfeld Falk's influence extended beyond the red squad: he also served in the Oregon National Guard, taught seminars on terrorism at the police academy, and was a member of the fanatically anticommunist and intemperately conspiracy-minded John Birch Society.[43] He shared some of his files with the Western Goals Foundation, a far-right operation run by Birch leader (and sitting US congressman) Larry McDonald.[44]

Though the red squad did keep files on reactionary groups like the National Socialist White People's Party and Posse Comitatus (an important forerunner of the militia movement), most of its intelligence concerned left-wing organizations and activists—often described in absurdly paranoid terms.[45] Women's shelters, for example, were described as "safe houses . . . [that] will probably be used for the movement of noted fugitives in the case of further terrorist acts."[46] A clerk with the Police Bureau's Intelligence Division later recalled, "By the time I left, I thought everyone in Portland was a subversive."[47]

Counterintelligence, Anti-Breakfast

Portland's Panthers faced less repression than other chapters. Under the FBI's secret and largely illegal Counterintelligence Program (COINTELPRO), Panther branches around the country were subjected to surveillance, infiltration, police raids and arrests, campaigns of sabotage and disinformation, and even assassination. Events in Portland never reached that same pitch. "The Panthers here were low key," former Chief Richard Walker later explained. "They were busy feeding kids and stuff like that. . . . so there was no need to raid their offices."[48]

Still, the Panthers' survival programs were specifically targeted by both the Portland Police and the FBI. On one occasion, in the spring of 1973, police and sheriff's deputies broke into the Panther's clinic and removed medical supplies, destroying $1,000 worth of refrigerated medicines.[49] The FBI repeatedly sent the programs' volunteers and donors anonymous letters to discourage their participation, essentially harassing doctors for treating poor children and restaurant owners for feeding them. Local police did much the same, pressuring businesses to withdraw support and sometimes raiding those that donated to the Panthers' efforts.[50] When the BPP received funds for food baskets through the Model Cities program, Mayor Schrunk fired the director.[51]

Kent Ford remembers applying for a permit to solicit donations. The required hearing "probably lasted ninety minutes," and the Panthers brought in "a number of well-respected doctors, professionals, and other people, both black and white" to speak in support. But then, "After everyone finished testifying, a city council person asked if there was anyone who opposed granting the Panthers a permit. . . . Right then a white detective from the Portland Police Bureau stood up and introduced himself and then sat down. No questions were asked of him, still we were denied."[52] Later, the group twice faced investigations regarding the clinic's use of federal grant money, but each time the case was quietly dropped. "I guess it was just their way of messing with us," Ford sighs, "interrupting our daily routine so that we wouldn't be able to get our work done."[53]

FBI director J. Edgar Hoover explained the strategy in a memo: "One of our primary aims in counterintelligence . . . is to keep this group isolated from the moderate black and white community which may support it. This is most emphatically pointed out in their Breakfast for Children Program, where they are actively soliciting and receiving support from uninformed whites and moderate blacks." Hoover castigated one agent who expressed reservations: "You state that the Bureau under COINTELPRO should not attack programs of community interest such as the [Panthers'] 'Breakfast for Children' . . . because many prominent 'humanitarians,' both white and black, are interested in the program as well as churches, which are actively supporting it. You have obviously missed the point."[54]

What Hoover understood was that the survival programs were not mere charity; they were a way of building the party and winning the support of the community. By highlighting needs that the government and the market failed to meet, they offered a clear if implicit critique of the existing political and economic system, and by meeting those needs directly they also presented an alternative. The attacks against them were therefore fundamentally political in nature; they had no law enforcement justification. That was true in cities around the country, but it was especially clear in Portland, where the Panthers deliberately de-emphasized the military aspects of their struggle.

Class Action and Internal Investigations

Alongside the riots and the breakfast programs, activists also tried using the courts to force the police to change. In the fall of 1968, Robert Probasco, Kent Ford, and a dozen others filed a class-action lawsuit on behalf of twenty thousand Black residents. It named as defendants Mayor Schrunk, Police Chief McNamara, the members of the city council, and thirty-eight police officers. The suit asked the court to end the systematic harassment of African Americans, saying that police practices created "an atmosphere of fear and persecution" and a "chilling effect upon the exercise of federally protected rights."[55]

The case was settled by consent decree (the "*Probasco* decree") in 1971. The city admitted no wrongdoing but entered into a binding agreement that instructed the cops to cease using "insulting, degrading or ethnically denigrating terms," prohibited the use of lead-knuckled "sap gloves" and weighted batons, and clarified that the police needed warrants before searching people's homes. The Portland Police Bureau additionally agreed to require patrolmen to wear badges and provide their names when asked, to train officers for racial sensitivity, to create an affirmative action plan and increase minority hiring, and to create a body to investigate complaints of police misconduct.[56]

Out of this agreement came the Internal Investigations Division.[57] Though it was designed specifically to avoid civilian oversight, police still opposed it. Some officers, recalling a similar unit in place during Prohibition, referred to it as a "secret police." Others predicted, "Those we arrest will come in here and tell lies." The cops needn't have worried: in the division's first year only 10 percent of complaints were sustained.[58]

Accidents and Justifiable Homicides

Despite the years of struggle and the occasional reforms, police violence and police racism seemed to continue unabated. In August 1974, a woman named Rachel James wrote to Mayor Neil Goldschmidt:

> A week ago a young black man by the name of Cedric Johnson took a brutal beating at gun point by four Portland Police Officers. His head is badly bruised, there are signs of a concussion and even possible brain damage, this type of thing can't go on any longer. . . . For years black people in the Albina area, have been bullied and victimized by our so called law-men, but what it all really boils down to is that [we are] living in a day and age when we ourselves as blacks must protect our own from the very law who vows its protections. . . . Either you in authority get up off your back sides or this too may become a battle ground, as Watts, Detroit, and Jersey City did. . . . As things are today any black man without a gun is a dammed fool. [We are] tired of being accidents and justifiable homicides.[59]

Ms. James's worries were well grounded. Between October 1974 and March 1975, four Black men were killed by the Portland Police. The first of these was Joe Hopkins, a former boxer suffering a psychological crisis and armed with a revolver. Two cops grabbed him and pulled him to the ground, but he wouldn't let go of the gun. A third officer, Gary Harrington, fired twice, hitting Hopkins in the back, killing him. That was October 8, 1974.[60]

Three weeks later, on October 26, the police killed Kenny Allen. The cops, Ed May and John Hren, said that they had been circling a Northeast Portland neighborhood, out of uniform and in an unmarked car, looking to arrest sex workers. Allen approached and offered to take them to a brothel. He then tried to rob them and was shot in the ensuing struggle. The problem with this story is that, according to both his family and the investigating detective, Allen knew the officers and was working as an informant. It can't be proven, former Internal Affairs Division Sergeant Mike Cullivan was careful to say, but based on his interview with the two cops, he concluded that Allen "was a snitch of theirs." Allen's family had additional questions, chief among them: Why was his face bruised as though he had been beaten? In the nights following, Allen's widow started receiving anonymous phone calls, full of racist abuse and threats that if she "talked to anyone" she and her children would be killed. She took her family and moved to California. Mayor Neil Goldschmidt was pleased with the cops' performance: "Maybe it'll get the word to some of these crazies who are carrying handguns around and robbing people," he mused.[61]

On November 20, Charles Menfree, a young man with a history of mental illness, was driving through the nearby town of Woodburn when someone contacted the police to say that he seemed "suspicious" and that the car he was driving might be stolen. Woodburn police tried to pull him over, but Menfree sped up and continued north. At least half a dozen squad cars joined the chase until, in North Portland, one managed to ram Menfree's Buick, causing him to lose control and skid to a stop. Police then swarmed the vehicle and tried to pull him out by his hair. He grabbed a rifle from the floor and shot Officer Kent Perry in the arm. Police then fired from every angle. He was the third young Black man the police had killed in forty-four days.[62]

A few months later, on March 12, 1975, Rickie Johnson was killed in a robbery sting operation, shot by an undercover officer posing as a delivery driver. According to the cop, Kenneth Sanford, Johnson had pointed a gun at him, and refused to drop it when ordered. Sanford then fired twice; Johnson took a few steps and fell. But when the smoke cleared, the scene that remained did not look good: Johnson's body was found pointed away from Sanford's position and toward the building's rear exit. The fatal shot had entered through the back of his head. Johnson's gun, lying about ten feet away, was not loaded.[63]

Questionable

It was probably not Johnson's death alone, but rather the whole series of similar incidents, that spurred the community to action. As the *Oregonian* reflected decades later, "Portland's Black community had faced heavy-handed policing for decades, but never before had so many Black people been killed by police in such rapid succession." The cops had killed just two African Americans in the previous twenty years—then, suddenly, four dead in just a few months.[64] Though only 7 percent of the local population was Black, they comprised 60 percent of those killed by the Portland Police over the course of the 1970s.[65]

An editorial in the *Portland Observer* asserted, "The community must demand an investigation of its police force—not just of this shooting or this officer, but of the attitudes prevailing in the force that make this type of action possible."[66] The NAACP asked for a public inquest—the first in decades. (The DA agreed, but the jury voted five to one that Johnson's shooting was justified. The dissenting vote was that of the sole Black juror.) Members of PSU's Black Student Union met with Chief Bruce Baker to demand that Officer Sanford be fired and the previous three shootings be reinvestigated. Outside the meeting, protesters chanted "Fire Bruce Baker!"[67] A new group emerged, the Black Justice Committee, to focus specifically on the issue of police violence. It joined more than a dozen other organizations to form the Albina Coalition. That April, they met with US Attorney Sidney Lezak, who opened an investigation to see if these deaths pointed to a broader pattern. He did not find one, though he did acknowledge the use of "questionable tactics."[68]

Justice for the victims of police violence remained as elusive as ever. But in the course of its pursuit, the civil rights movement had marked an important development. "It was the first time really there was a coalition of groups to come together to protest a police shooting, at least in my memory," Cullivan, the IAD sergeant, later recalled. "It was a rude awakening."[69]

CHAPTER 14

Full-Service Problem-Solvers

Tiny Fiefdoms and Civil Service

In a career that would come to span decades, taking him from prison guard to patrolman to sheriff to county chair to director of the Housing Authority, Don Clark undertook a prolonged experiment to reinvent policing, beginning with the Multnomah County Sheriff's Office.

It is hard to know, looking back, whether the process of reform began by blind luck or through cunning maneuvering. Francis Lambert had been appointed sheriff in 1956 when the previous sheriff, Terry Schrunk, was elected mayor.[1] Lambert, being part-owner of a brothel in Dallesport, was not an obvious reformer, but he set out to improve the department's efficiency, often skirting civil service rules to do so. Many of his employees never even sat for the required exam, and some worked for years under "temporary" assignments.[2] Eventually, facing consistent pressure from both the Civil Service Board and the police union, Lambert tasked Clark with redesigning the personnel system, formalizing the organization's procedures, creating a training program, and bringing the department into line with civil service rules. At first, Clark saw, "there was almost no training, there weren't any manuals, there was very little written down." He was relieved of all other duties in order to give this project his full attention.[3]

Clark was a surprising and even brave choice. For one thing, he was a mere patrolman—the lowest rank in the sheriff's office—and he was no ordinary cop.[4] College-educated and politically liberal, he was critical of many aspects of the criminal legal system. His prior experience as a guard at San Quentin led him to conclude that "prisons brutalize people and . . . most people come out far worse than when they went in."[5] Soon after joining the sheriff's office, he had taken a job as a counselor at Rocky Butte Jail. Inspired by the work of the reformers in the Oregon Prison Association, the counseling program represented an attempt to move the jails in a more rehabilitative direction. Clark's attention, ironically, soon turned toward reforming the guards. "It became very obvious to me right away," he later recalled, "that probably the most productive thing I could do was change the attitudes of the jailors." This approach did not sit well with his superiors. "Jack Matthews was the chief jailor," Clark explained, "[and] Jack Matthews didn't believe in any of that, thought the whole thing was nonsense, didn't like me there, didn't like me." The jail counselor program survived less than six months and accomplished nothing. Clark resigned and became an elementary school teacher.[6] But then, returning to the sheriff's office a couple years later, he somehow found himself responsible for reorganizing the entire institution.

Under the system Clark designed, the Multnomah County Sheriff's Office started conducting background checks on new recruits and introduced an "ad hoc-ish" training program. But the main problems, Clark saw, were structural: there were "a whole lot of little, tiny fiefdoms in the sheriff's office, each of which had its own manager and they operated almost independently."[7] It would take strong leadership and persistent attention to break these up. When Lambert retired in 1962, Clark decided that he would run for sheriff himself. He won the election, beating Portland Police captain Gene Ferguson by 1,001 votes out of 189,901 ballots cast—less than 1 percent.[8]

A Bomb-Throwing Aspect

If Clark had been an unusual deputy, he was an even more exceptional sheriff.

An active member of the City Club, he gave frequent speeches about beautification, conservation, and other things that, he later admitted, "didn't really have a whole lot to do with being sheriff."[9] He admired John F. Kennedy for his vision and idealism and later worked for Robert Kennedy's presidential campaign, recruiting other law enforcement officers to the cause.[10] He liked to take visiting officials on unannounced tours of the Multnomah County Correctional Institute and Rocky Butte Jail, stopping for lunch in the cafeteria, standing in line with the inmates. (The food was better at MCCI, he thought.)[11] Conversely, when traveling the country, he would ask to stay overnight in local jails to get a sense of the conditions in different jurisdictions.[12]

When Selma, Alabama, Sheriff Jim Clark (no relation) was elected president of the National Sheriffs' Association—just months after his deputies had brutalized civil rights demonstrators—Don Clark put forward a resolution at the Oregon State Sheriffs' Association threatening to withdraw from the national body. The measure passed unanimously, and other state associations seemed poised to follow. Rather than face a humiliating series of defections, Selma's Clark gave up his newly won position.[13]

It wasn't enough for Don Clark to clean up his own agency; he wanted to change the nature of policing writ large. "There's a radicalism involved in this," he said, much later. "It stirred the status quo, the bureaucracies and the 'business as usual' kind of attitude. There's a bomb-throwing aspect to it."[14]

Systematizing Operations

From the beginning, Clark's term was distinguished by his efforts at modernizing the sheriff's office. He centralized recordkeeping and computerized the tax system. He formed a "Scientific Investigation Unit" to process crime scenes, and an "Emergency Squad" whose fifty officers handled both crowd control and search-and-rescue operations. He assigned a specialist to investigate traffic fatalities. He increased the number of jail staff and brought back the counseling program. Jack Matthews, the obstructionist jail commander, resigned.[15]

Seeking to eliminate the "little kingdoms" and "petty jealousies" that had held sway previously, Clark reorganized the command structure and streamlined the hierarchy.[16] At his urging, and with the blessing of the police union, the state legislature passed the 1963 Multnomah County Sheriff's Office Reorganization Bill, which allowed him to bypass civil service and directly appoint an undersheriff, four deputy undersheriffs, and an administrative aide.[17] Clark also took steps to reduce discrimination in the ranks, eliminating the separate track for female deputies and opening all assignments to women.[18] He hired the first women and people of color in the Civil Division and proposed paying jail matrons as much as the male guards, though the Civil Service Board refused to allow it.[19]

The sheriff's office developed a directory of social service agencies and encouraged deputies to form liaisons with other departments as part of a strategy to prevent crime by addressing its underlying causes.[20] "I thought we ran a full-service police agency," Clark later told an interviewer. He wanted the deputies to view themselves "as problem-solvers" with an expansive notion of the police role: "We expected them to act as not only an agent of the sheriff but an agent of the county. . . . [If] welfare needed to know something, then they should figure out how to get welfare involved. . . . You worked with partners in the social service system to get people the help they needed."[21] This broader conception and the collaboration with outside agencies not only expanded the police mission and added to the deputies' duties but also made additional resources available to the sheriff's office. The network effects might increase the power of the police agency while reducing the state's reliance on overt coercion, allowing the sheriff's office to avail itself of the influence and resources of other government offices, or even community groups, and widening its range of intervention beyond citations, arrests, and violence.

Liberal Arts, Liberal Cops

One obstacle Clark faced in pursuing his agenda was the culture of his organization and, he thought, the caliber of its officers. Speaking decades later, he was frank about the problems he saw: "There were lots of folks in the Sheriff's office who probably should not have ever been entrusted with a firearm and a badge. . . . I think a number of them caused far more harm than they did good. You would have been far better off to not have anybody out there than have some of these folks out there doing what they did." To some degree, it was a question of motivation: "You tended to get people who wanted to push people around."[22]

Clark thought that cops would better understand the people they encountered and the problems they faced, make better decisions, and use their discretion more responsibly, if they had more formal education. So, in 1964 the Multnomah County Sheriff's Office (MCSO) started requiring a bachelor's degree for new deputies.[23] "What we wanted," Clark later explained, "were the liberal arts educated people who had been exposed to the history of Western Civilization, who had been exposed to understanding their own institutions, the Constitution of the United States of America, who understood our 20th-century America in context of the flow of western civilization, and who had a tolerance for people who weren't exactly like them, who had an ability to communicate, both written and orally. . . . What we were looking for was the educated person, and so we wanted a liberal arts degree."[24]

There were unintended consequences: The new requirements made it harder to recruit people of color, so the sheriff's office compensated with targeted efforts to attract Black and Native American applicants. In addition to the traditional sources—the military and other police departments—recruiters began looking to local colleges and the Peace Corps. The budding partnerships with social service and mental health agencies presented opportunities for recruitment as well.

Clark believed that one way to make the sheriff's office more service-oriented would be to recruit social workers to serve as deputies.[25]

The composition of the department did change with time, but that presented its own difficulties: the new recruits and the old-timers didn't really get along. "There was a chasm between the two groups," Clark admits, "and a tension that never quite went away."[26]

The Politics of It All

If Sheriff Clark proved to be an effective reformer, it was in large measure because he was a canny politician. He was adept at turning adversaries into allies.

"Was I going to be able to deal with the union?" he wondered. "It was a real concern, because I was going in there, again, with a big broom and I was going to sweep things out and I was going to change things. I was going to do things like raise standards. I was going to do things like fire people who were incompetent, people who were dishonest, people who were corrupt, people who violated their oath. The union was going to have to defend some of those employees, so there was going to be some real tension." He managed that tension by emphasizing the interests they had in common and stressing the benefits of these reforms for the deputies themselves: "Their job could be better if the agency was better and was broadly respected in the community, and got more resources." Or, more plainly: "I was very often the strongest advocate for raising the salary of deputies."[27] By 1966, Multnomah County's deputies were the best-paid in Oregon.[28] This advocacy on behalf of his employees bought the sheriff some loyalty. "The union had not been a very progressive force," he conceded, "but they ended up supporting me as I moved to raise the standards in the Sheriff's Office."[29]

Reform sometimes required some delicate diplomacy. Clark's attempts to crack down on gambling—that traditional Progressive preoccupation—inevitably posed, as he put it, "a question about the politics of it all." Given the overlapping jurisdictions, there were numerous opportunities for conflict. "If you were to aggressively enforce the gambling statutes countywide, then you were going to step on toes and you were going to potentially embarrass people. You were going to embarrass local politicians. You were going to embarrass local police agencies." To mitigate that embarrassment, the sheriff's office made a point of involving other departments when conducting raids, serving warrants, or making arrests, thus giving "an appearance that we were working together," even when both the initiative and the main investigatory work may have come from the MCSO.[30]

The police required special consideration. "I was always concerned that I didn't offend the Portland Police Bureau," Clark said later. The "old-timers" in leadership "didn't really want to change"—the chief, in particular. "Don McNamara was chief of police, nice guy in his own way, but he was from a different era and he was part of the problem. He did not want to be a part of the community. He saw that as meddling, he saw that as threatening, he saw that as a problem." But for the sheriff, that reticence only made the relationship with the police bureau more important: "In many, many ways they were the target of what we were trying to reform, and we were trying to engage them in the process of change."[31]

Ordinary Corruption

It is not hard to see why the police bureau would attract Clark's notice. While he was pushing reform at the county level, ordinary policing in the city of Portland—which is also to say, ordinary corruption—continued much as it always had. In the early sixties, a patrolman's salary was a modest $420 a month, so nearly everyone found a way to supplement it, legally, semi-legally, or otherwise. Some officers simply relied on overtime pay and manipulated their schedules accordingly.[32] Most of the cops assigned to the graveyard shift worked other jobs during the day and slept when they were supposed to be on patrol.[33] Auto theft detectives doubled as repo men. Parking wardens stole thousands of dollars from the meters.[34] Lieutenant Carl Crisp, the head of the vice squad, "moonlighted" (according to retired Detective Don DuPay) "as the operator of several brothels in the north end."[35] (He schooled his officers in "an old rule" for dealing with sex workers, tantamount to sexual extortion: "If you're gonna arrest 'em, don't fuck 'em! And if you're gonna fuck 'em, don't arrest 'em!")[36] Meanwhile Jim Purcell, the disgraced former police chief who had been demoted as a result of Jim Elkins's bribery revelations, made the most of his new position as the captain in charge of North Precinct, collecting protection money from brothels in St. Johns. Those officers who proved overly scrupulous he would put on desk duty or send to direct traffic in the rain.[37] DuPay considered Purcell "a pimp with a badge."[38]

CHAPTER 15

New Leadership, Civic Engagement

The Evangelist

In 1968, former sheriff Don Clark was elected to the Multnomah County Commission. He was at the same time teaching at Portland State University, where he started the criminal justice program and recruited Lee Brown to head the new department. Clark described Brown as "almost a kind of travelling evangelist, selling the concept of police-community relations and community-based policing."[1] Others have since called him the "Father of Community Policing."[2]

Brown began his career in 1960 as a patrol officer in San Jose, California. There he organized a police community relations unit in 1967. The unit conducted a survey of minority communities and held meetings with social service agencies. It started a Community Watch program and a Police Athletic League, recruited young volunteers to the Police Community Relations Aide Program, gave presentations in schools, and published a newsletter. The explicit purpose of the unit was to prevent rioting, and Brown took personal credit for calming tempers twice in 1968, after the assassinations of Martin Luther King Jr. and Robert Kennedy.[3] The chief of police was vocal in his praise: "Sergeant Brown's work was instrumental in preventing riots in San Jose while other cities went up in flames."[4]

Brown earned a bachelor's in criminology from Fresno State, a master's in sociology from San Jose State, and a PhD in criminology from UC Berkeley. From 1968 to 1972 he chaired the Department of Administration of Justice at PSU, where he also volunteered as faculty advisor to the Black Student Union. He lectured on race relations at the Oregon State Police Academy and the Portland Police Bureau's training school. He sometimes consulted with the Justice Department's Community Relations Service, a division largely devoted to avoiding racial unrest. Brown later served as an instructor for Justice Department trainings on the prevention of riots.[5]

When Don Clark was elected county chair in 1974, he asked Brown to serve as sheriff, making him the first African American to lead a large law enforcement agency anywhere in the country.[6] "The first major change I made," Brown later wrote, "was to the department's firearms policy." The law allowed police to shoot any "fleeing felon" (meaning in practice any fleeing *suspect*), but Brown decided that his deputies would only use guns in the defense of life.[7] In short order, Multnomah County's firearms policy became a model for other agencies around the country, including the Portland Police Bureau.[8] Then, in 1985's *Tennessee v. Garner* decision, the US Supreme Court established a nationwide standard that police only use deadly force when they "have probable cause . . . to believe that the suspect . . . poses a threat to the safety of the officers or a danger to the community if left at large."[9]

Team Policing

Lee Brown's signature contribution during his time at Multnomah County was the implementation of the concept of "team policing," beginning in August 1975. Applying a model adapted from military practice, teams of twenty to thirty officers, headed by a lieutenant, would be assigned to specific geographic areas. These neighborhood teams would handle routine investigations, preventive patrols, and community outreach, while a support team consisting of detectives and other specialists could be brought in for investigations requiring scientific methods. Several of the neighborhood teams opened storefront offices staffed by civilian community service officers. These officers performed clerical work, helped crime victims access social services, and met with community groups; some units used them to conduct surveys, track crime statistics, map reported crimes, register bicycles, and engrave property to discourage theft.[10]

Team policing did not merely change how officers were deployed and the duties they were assigned, it also shifted "more responsibility, autonomy and decision-making authority to the lower level (team and unit) of the Department's organized structure." Brown described this as "decentralization as a means of encouraging flexibility." He reasoned that "people, conditions and problems differ from one part of the county to another"; in order to find solutions suitable to the local conditions, decisions should be made "at the level of execution."[11] Therefore, each team would be given "as much autonomy as possible."[12]

"A primary advantage of Team Policing," Brown contended, "is the opportunity it affords both citizens and deputies to work together to identify local problems and find their solutions." This sense of collaboration would both encourage and rely on "positive police–community interaction," which therefore had to be "actively programmed" into the strategy.[13]

Neighborhood Involvement

The restructuring in the sheriff's office—with decentralization and neighborhood focus—was one element of a broader set of changes in local government. In 1967, a new county charter had rebranded the sheriff as the director of public safety, making it an appointed rather than elected position, removing all duties relating to tax collection and process-serving, and leaving three main responsibilities: law enforcement, the custody of suspects and convicts, and disaster preparedness.[14] Over the next few years, the county would further consolidate the bureaucracies in its various departments, reorganize local government services by neighborhood, and grant citizen advisory groups a larger role in setting policy.[15]

The Portland city government was likewise seeking ways to encourage citizen participation, the most notable measure being the establishment of the Office of Neighborhood Associations in February 1974 (now the Office of Community and Civic Life). After repeated amendments at the urging of civic activists eager to ensure neighborhood autonomy, the law creating the agency read: "Any neighborhood association shall be eligible to recommend an action, a policy, or a comprehensive plan to the city or to any city agency on any matter affecting livability to the neighborhood, including but not limited to, land-use, zoning, housing, community facilities, human resources, social and recreational programs, traffic and transportation, environmental quality, open space and parks." The office would therefore provide technical assistance, expert advice, training, and funding.[16] Through this avenue, the historian Carl Abbott explains, the city could "legitimize and partially co-opt neighborhood activists by incorporating independent neighborhood associations as secondary participants in public decisions."[17] By the end of the decade there were ninety neighborhood associations, each representing between four thousand and five thousand residents.[18]

The consequences of this development would be far-reaching, shaping the culture of the city for decades. When the new structure was first adopted, sociologist Robert Putnam points out, Portland's civic engagement was comparable to that in other cities. Over the next twenty years, citizen involvement in Portland would rise impressively even as it declined sharply everywhere else:

> In 1974, 21 percent of Portlanders attended at least one public meeting on town or school affairs, compared to 22 percent for residents of comparably sized American cities. By the early 1990s, the figure for the rest of the country had been cut in half (11 percent), whereas the figure for Portland had risen steadily to 30–35 percent. In 1974, 4 percent of Portlanders reported that they were members of "some group interested in better government," slightly below the national figure of 5 percent. By 1994, the Portland rate had nearly tripled, while the national rate had halved.[19]

Out with the Old

Behind the changes was a new generation of leaders. Between 1969 and 1973, the average age of the Portland City Council dropped by fifteen years. Neil Goldschmidt was thirty when he was elected to city council in 1970; two years later, he became the youngest mayor of any major city.[20] And he had an activist background, having registered voters in Mississippi during 1964's Freedom Summer.[21] In Portland, he worked as a legal aid attorney and then organized against freeway construction.[22]

The generational shift at City Hall, from Schrunk to Goldschmidt, which can seem in retrospect like the changing of the seasons, was in fact precipitated by an earlier change of leadership in the district attorney's office. In 1970, Desmond ("Des") Connall was appointed district attorney for Multnomah County. He had risen to prominence a few years before as the prosecutor in an infamous "lovers' lane" murder case: two college students, Larry Peyton and Beverly Allan, had been found dead, and two young men with a history of legal trouble were convicted of killing them. However, "with the benefit of hindsight," journalist Phil Stanford would write decades later, it is clear that "these boys didn't have anything to do with the savage murders that rattled the city."[23] Their convictions relied on the testimony of a teenage runaway who had initially denied having ever been at the crime scene. To refresh her memory, Connall had her repeatedly interrogated while drugged and hypnotized.[24]

Connall fought dirty, but he couldn't be bought.[25] By the standards of local law enforcement, he wasn't exactly honest, but he wasn't exactly corrupt either.

As DA, he recruited eight officers from various jurisdictions, mostly outside the city limits, and formed a special task force reporting directly to himself. This group met on the sixth floor of the courthouse, in a locked room with butcher paper taped over the interior windows. In this room, they created wall charts tracking the connections that made up the region's criminal underworld—the bosses and henchmen, the financing and logistics, the payoffs.[26] Connall's plan was to aim at those directing illegal enterprises, rather than just the street-level operatives.[27] A few months into the investigation, he took aside a young prosecutor named Michael Schrunk and told him that the evidence was pointing toward the mayor, his father, Terry Schrunk. Michael, of course, passed word along to Terry, who soon announced that he would not be running for reelection.[28]

When it came to prosecutions, however, Connall's campaign was a flop. A raid on a commercial sex ring centered on the Gold Coin nightclub led to only four convictions and sentences of probation. A perjury charge against Lieutenant Jack Strudgeon, the head of the vice squad, resulted in acquittal. Public opinion quickly turned against the crusading DA.[29]

Times had changed, and Connall had not kept up. A decade before, in the early sixties, moral offense laws had been blissfully indifferent to questions of personal liberty. "Lewd cohabitation"—an unmarried couple living together—was a violation of city statues. Adultery was a felony punishable by three years in prison. Plainclothes detectives would pick up men in public restrooms and arrest them for "disorderly conduct"; patrol officers would park outside gay bars and write tickets for jaywalking.[30] Similarly, retired Detective Don DuPay recalls, "We would harass [brothels]; we'd break out the parking ticket book and write tickets for being parked over a foot from the curb, whether they were or not. We'd stop and talk to everybody going in or coming out, writing parking tickets and towing cars and generally disrupting business. Harassing people was one of the ways we did our job."[31]

But by 1972 sexual mores had loosened and Portland was experiencing a "virtual explosion" of dirty bookstores, porn theaters, and massage parlors, leading the Center for Sociological Research at PSU to declare the city "the pornography capital of the West Coast." Fully 85 percent of Portland residents opposed any move to ban sexually explicit material, and a strong majority (60 percent) thought sex work should be legal. The city soon moved to regulate its numerous massage parlors, creating a license for "Relaxation Treatment Therapists" and requiring criminal background checks.[32]

Connall's brand of moralism felt old-fashioned and faintly ridiculous. Newspaper cartoonists depicted him as Mighty Mouse, and he was roundly defeated by Harl Haas in the 1972 election.[33]

Renewal

The new mayor, Neil Goldschmidt, had a different notion of cleaning up the city, focusing on issues of livability: participatory planning, public transportation, neighborhood life, and the redevelopment of downtown.[34]

The mayor's "Downtown Plan"—created in collaboration with the Portland Improvement Corporation (later renamed the Association for Portland Progress, then the Portland Business Alliance, and now the Portland Metro Chamber)—changed the face of the city center. A central transit mall, surrounded by a Fareless Square where the buses were free, encouraged the use of public transportation and eased congestion. A multilane downtown thoroughfare, Harbor Drive, was demolished and replaced with Tom McCall Waterfront Park.[35] Trees were planted along streets, sidewalks widened, and public art—funded by a tax on commercial buildings—was installed.[36] The results were remarkable. "Portland was a near-terminal city in the late 1960s," one study recalls: "a gray, dirty, even boring town."[37] By 1975 all that had changed: the Environmental Protection Agency named it the country's "most livable" city.[38]

Old Town, Old Habits

Despite downtown's facelift, the Old Town area north of Burnside persevered in its traditional role as the city's skid row, a few square blocks of concentrated poverty and despair, blended with alcohol and habitual petty crime.

The relationship of the cops to Old Town's residents was complicated. "Some cops love the people there," police bureau Detective Loren Christensen wrote in *Skid Row Beat,* but "others see them as less than human. Some feel these conflicting emotions in the same shift."[39] Christensen's reflections on his time as a patrolman in the mid-seventies make for strange reading. He expends no effort to hide his contempt for the people living on the streets he patrolled, but he does sometimes imagine his job from their point of view. A homeless person might "scrounge all day for enough coins to buy a cheap bottle of wine, then as he settled into his favorite doorway, all cozy and warm under a Salvation Army blanket, a cop would come along and pull the blanket off his head, pry the coveted bottle out of his hand, and pour its contents into the gutter."[40]

Those arrested for minor drunk-and-disorderly offenses would be tried in a city court, a process that, in former sheriff Don Clark's blunt assessment, "made a mockery out of justice." Judges tried people en masse, a roomful at once. They were asked how they pled, "and they in unison pled guilty to being publicly drunk. Then they were sentenced to the city jail . . . [where] they were not treated very well."[41] People died there regularly; others got lost in the system for months at a time.[42] "The jail was run pretty badly," Clark explained, because the police bureau treated it as "a punishment post for people who didn't serve as good policemen." Newspapers regularly decried the conditions there, and grand juries had repeatedly called for its closure. Shutting it down had been "a major goal" when Clark was sheriff, but he hadn't found a way to do it.[43]

This time things were different. The city and the county—or at least, the mayor and the county chair—were aligned in their priorities. Clark and Goldschmidt worked together to merge the municipal court into the district court and close the city jail.[44] In place of the latter, they opened the David Hooper Sobriety Station and Detoxification Center, named for the last man to die of alcohol poisoning at the old jail.[45] Beginning in 1972, Hooper Detox offered assistance in three stages: a sobering station, medical detoxification, and a recovery program.[46] Thousands of people received services there every year, often brought in by the police.[47]

A patrolman assigned to Old Town later recalled the frequent trips to Hooper, as part of his daily routine: "The first thing we did every morning was to make a sweep of the usual crash sites. . . . We would cruise the doorways, warehouse loading docks, freeway underpasses, and alleys. . . . The detoxification center was a half mile away from the heart of skid row, so we would load one or two drunks into the backseat of our car and make a quick trip to dump them off. Some days we would make half a dozen trips or more before noon."[48] On the other hand, "If no one complained, we would sometimes let drunks sleep it off wherever they happened to fall."[49]

Integrity and Discretion

Goldschmidt had run for mayor on the promise of cleaning up corruption and, once in office, encouraged senior police commanders to retire and tried to recruit more leaders from outside the police bureau. In 1974, he removed Donald McNamara from the chief's office and appointed Bruce Baker, formerly police chief in Berkeley. Tracking similar reforms then unfolding in the sheriff's office, Goldschmidt and Baker together reorganized the bureau to decentralize it and make it more responsive to community concerns. Baker introduced computerized records, implemented in-service training, and brought a new emphasis on crime prevention and long-term planning. He thoroughly revised the bureau's manual of rules and procedures and treated dishonesty as grounds for termination. When a police reservist was caught selling stolen merchandise to other officers, all those involved were disciplined—and those who lied about it were fired outright.[50]

But the new commitment to integrity had its limits.

District Attorney Harl Haas—another of the new crop of leaders entering office in the early seventies—cultivated a tough image by refusing to offer plea deals to repeat offenders.[51] However, when the enterprising Captain Norm Reiter took control of the vice squad in 1975, the deeper loyalties of both the DA's office and the top police commanders soon became apparent, and each did their best to protect prominent citizens from public embarrassment. Reiter was an oddity. An intellectual with two master's degrees, he received top scores in every promotional exam. But while he moved through the ranks, he was never part of the bureau's leadership clique, and his approach was often at odds with that of the district attorney. While Captain Reiter sought to strictly enforce obscenity laws, Haas insisted that they didn't have the resources to prosecute such cases. Vice raids at the Old Chelsea theater led to the arrests of three dancers and eight patrons, but Haas dropped the charges. The vice squad then broke up an all-male commercial sex ring managed by Sandy Director—a well-known drag queen ("Sandra Dee") and gay activist who came to be called "Portland's gay mayor." Haas handled the matter quietly, arranging for a closed hearing, a small fine, and immediate expungement of Director's record.[52]

When the cops recruited Christine Barkdoll, a twenty-year-old licensed "relaxation therapist," to go undercover in the unregulated segment of the sex industry, they unearthed a network involving nightclub manager Billy Moe and city auditor George Yerkovitch. A former bar owner, Yerkovitch made himself especially useful to the city government by setting up visiting dignitaries with female company. Police Officer Daryl Dick filed a report titled "Subject: Prostitution Activity by an Elected Official," which surfaced in the discovery documents when Moe was arrested a few months later. Prosecutors tried hard to keep Yerkovitch's name out of the court proceedings, effectively crippling their own case. Billy Moe was convicted regardless but suffered a relatively lenient $2,500 fine and five years' probation. Captain Reiter, meanwhile, was transferred to East Precinct, a more remote post where he could cause less trouble.[53]

Later, when two vice cops—Daryl Dick and Irv McGeachy—spotted Mayor Neil Goldschmidt outside the home of a former madam, they drew two understandable but erroneous conclusions: that this madam had come out of retirement and that the mayor had gotten involved in her business. (Goldschmidt was actually having an affair with her neighbor, one of numerous illicit liaisons.) The vice squad then put the mayor under surveillance and, seeing how frequently his path crossed with that of Commissioner Charles Jordan—the first African American on city council—they put Jordan under surveillance as well. When his bosses learned about this, McGeachy was transferred out of vice.[54]

Mayor Humbert Humbert

Given the extent of the vice squad's surveillance, they must have known—or at least, strongly suspected—that Goldschmidt was engaged in an exploitative sexual relationship with his babysitter, the daughter of two campaign volunteers. The Intelligence Division, in any case, had definite knowledge: the division supplied the mayor with his drivers, who dutifully taxied him to and from the girl's home.[55]

Mayor Goldschmidt and the girl—identified years later as Elizabeth Dunham—communicated by a series of signals: A light over a basement door indicated that her parents were away. If the mayor's driver flashed his headlights, it meant that she should unlock the door for him. As explained by the journalist Margie Boulé, who interviewed Dunham repeatedly: "She believed for a long time that it was an affair," and she acted accordingly. But her collusion does nothing to alter the fact that when this "affair" began in January 1975, she was only thirteen years old.[56]

Goldschmidt went on to be elected governor in 1987. Dunham dropped out of high school, attempted suicide, and suffered a life of mental illness and addiction. Goldschmidt eventually paid her $250,000, "contingent on confidentiality." But she was not very good at keeping this secret: her mother knew, as did her grandmother. In the 1980s, she had directly told the District Attorney, Dave Peters. She later told police in Seattle. In the early nineties, Dunham was arrested repeatedly and eventually sent to federal prison. There she told her story to a counselor, who sent a report to Multnomah County District Attorney Michael Schrunk. In keeping with the strategy that characterized his career, Schrunk quietly took no action.[57]

Even after he left office in 1991, Goldschmidt remained, in the words of journalist Nigel Jacquiss, "the kingmaker... the most influential private citizen in the state. Many elected officials and corporate officials in the state owed their position either directly to him or indirectly to him." He enjoyed an "unparalleled ... network of influence."[58]

Dunham died from the complications of alcoholism.[59]

CHAPTER 16

Collective Bargaining and Affirmative Action

Labor Relations

Though the Portland Police had been unionized since the 1940s, more than twenty years later they still didn't have a contract. The Portland Police Association (PPA) was, as former Chief Penny Harrington would later say, "a very weak organization" that "did nothing but collect dues."[1]

That began to change at the end of the 1960s. Shifts in both state law and city policy made it more possible for public employees to bargain collectively—including sworn officers. Negotiations began between the City of Portland and the Portland Police Association on April 1, 1969.[2]

Penny Orazetti (as Harrington was known at the time) was a tireless volunteer with the union during those first contract talks and would later serve as the assistant editor of the PPA's newsletter, the *Rap Sheet*.[3] In her memoirs, she reminisced about this early period of unity within the ranks: "Even the command staff was behind our effort. . . . They brought donuts and coffee to the picket lines, and at night they would sneak into the union office to help us out." After almost a year of fruitless bargaining, on January 1, 1970, the police began to picket City Hall. They carried signs reading "Crime Pays, Police Work Doesn't" and "No Pay, No Pigs." In the days following, they expanded their picket to include Memorial Coliseum and the docks. Harrington recalled, "[There were] secret meetings with the longshoremen as we plotted and planned behind the backs of the mayor and everybody else. . . . We convinced the longshoremen to honor our informational picket on the city docks and completely shut down the ports."[4]

For three days, longshore workers refused to cross the picket line, and Teamsters refused to make deliveries. In Susan Hauser's estimation, in the PPA's in-house history, *Pickets, Pistols and Politics*, "The longshoremen's contribution to the police cause was invaluable. As it turned out, their refusal to cross the police informational picket line was what finally brought the City to the table."[5] It broke the impasse and won the PPA its first contract.[6] Signed on December 18, 1970, the agreement included pay raises of $150 a month, a family medical plan, increased vacation time, overtime pay, a grievance procedure, and a no-strike clause.[7]

Despite the "invaluable" support of organized labor, the cops immediately broke ranks. The police local stopped paying dues to its parent organization, the American Federation of State, County, and Municipal Employees, who then responded by revoking the PPA charter. The organization then affiliated with the International Brotherhood of Police Officers (IBPO), as Local 117.[8] The IBPO had been founded a year earlier by John Cassese, the tough and ambitious head of the New York Patrolmen's Benevolent Association, who had recently defeated a proposed civilian review board. A year later, the IBPO rebranded itself as the National Union of Police Officers.[9] In 1972, the Portland local disaffiliated from the NUPO as well, though it also refused an invitation to return to the AFL-CIO.[10] From then on, the PPA would operate as an independent organization.

A Belligerent Turn

Despite the union's growing strength, many cops were unhappy with the contract. It brought them higher wages but traded away the right to work second jobs. A group of a hundred officers sued, and the case went as far as the US Supreme Court. (They lost.) PPA president David Callison had a guard assigned to his home because his union brothers threatened to burn it down.[11]

In the union's 1974 election, Callison lost to a motorcycle cop named Stan Peters, who would go on to serve as PPA president until 1991.[12] Peters, Susan Hauser writes, came to serve as "a symbol for a new kind of police officer who just was not going to take it anymore."[13] Penny Harrington, on the other hand, saw in Peters not a new symbol but rather "the old stereotype." Six foot four, with "short cropped hair, and ramrod straight," he was "an imposing figure," Harrington wrote. "Peters had the 'cop image' I hoped would one day disappear from policing: ultraconservative, a proponent of force, a distrust of the public."[14] Harrington wasn't alone. In the union, other cops complained of his "imperial" style of leadership.[15]

Under Peters, the PPA was fierce in its defense of the police. In a program called "Blue Liberation," the union brought legal action against people accused of assaulting officers, prevailing in twelve civil suits between 1978 and 1982.[16] It likewise attacked the Police Bureau's critics head-on, suing the *Oregonian* in 1981 after the paper published an exposé citing attorneys, civil rights activists, former cops, and Police Commissioner Charles Jordan, all confirming that Sergeant John McNabb, one of the officers named in the *Probasco* suit, had a reputation as a racist.[17] At the same time, the union was becoming more politically involved, donating thousands of dollars to electoral campaigns and forming a separate political action committee. Surveys showed that the PPA's was the endorsement most sought by local candidates.[18]

Peters was also a tough negotiator. He once slammed his gun down on the table during contract talks, declaring: "These are my ground rules."[19] More often, the union relied on that other standard law enforcement tool—blackmail—bringing police files to bargaining sessions in order to intimidate city negotiators.[20] The elected officials were certainly vulnerable. One former city councilor has said (anonymously, of course) that, during the later seventies, three of the five members of the council, including himself, had notable cocaine habits—and the cops knew it. "Look," PPA president Stan Peters once told this particular politician, "we know what you're doing, but we don't really care. What we care about is the police pension vote coming up this week. Can we count on your support?" Yes, they certainly could.[21]

Half the city council was high on cocaine, and at least two members—Mayor Goldschmidt and Police Commissioner Jordan—were regularly under surveillance. Additionally, Goldschmidt was pursuing a years-long sexually exploitative relationship with a teenage girl, which the intelligence unit definitely knew about, which the vice squad likely suspected, and which would become a regular topic of station house gossip.[22] We have to assume that the Police Association would be all too happy to use this sort of information to its advantage.

This period would mark a turning point. Corruption still ran all the way to the top, but the police would no longer be pawns for the power brokers in City Hall. Now the cops themselves were the power brokers, blackmail being just another tool available to their suddenly powerful union.

Ball Busters

Penny Orazetti, the union stalwart, was at the same time engaged in her own struggle in the Police Bureau, which would eventually bring her into conflict with the PPA.

When she had joined the force in 1964, female officers were sequestered in the Women's Protective Division (WPD). Though Title VII of the 1964 Civil Rights Act prohibited gender-based employment discrimination, the women of the WPD were paid less than male officers and were required to have a college degree while men only needed a high school equivalent.[23] The women were instructed to always wear hats and white gloves, and they did not drive patrol cars or carry guns. "Neither the male officers nor the public saw us as real cops," Orazetti recalled.[24] One street cop gave voice to the concerns of his colleagues: "If I've got a dangerous problem on the street and I ask for a cover car and they send a woman, then I've got the *same* problem I had in the first place, plus a female to protect."[25]

In 1971, the civil service adopted the classification of "police officer," making obsolete the previously separate classifications of "policeman" and "policewoman" and opening opportunities for women in the bureau.[26] Then the 1973 Crime Control Act made sex discrimination illegal for any agency receiving funds from the Law Enforcement Assistance Administration.[27] In practice, though, women in the police bureau often had to sue even for the right to *apply* for jobs, and the bureau sometimes left positions vacant rather than promote women to fill them.[28] Annette Jolin, one of the three female officers at the time, sums up the situation: "The men refused to work with us, and the department refused to make them."[29] When Orazetti and her sister, Roberta Ledyard, sued for their right to be hired as regular uniformed officers, other cops started referring to the pair as the "ball busters."[30] When Orazetti made detective, she received a slew of lewd phone calls and hate mail. One letter referred to her as "a female bull" who "carrie[d] her 38 in a hand bag."[31] There were worse affronts. She once interrupted a precinct captain who had pinned a secretary against a filing cabinet, groping her. After Orazetti filed a complaint, the captain called her into his office and pressed her hand against his crotch.[32]

One mechanism for excluding women (as well as most Latino and Asian candidates) was the bureau's height requirement: five foot nine at minimum. When women in the department pushed to change this rule, they met almost universal opposition. A burglary detective, Mike O'Leary, complained of this and other attempts to bring diversity to the police force: "All they'll be hiring is cunts, runts, and niggers!"[33] Even cops' wives protested, with picket signs reading "We want real cops, not midgets" and "If the height requirement goes, our children will die." They handed out leaflets making the gender politics explicit: "We support the concept that men are . . . the protectors of women and children."[34] So far as Orazetti was concerned, these fears represented a fundamental misunderstanding in the nature of police work. As she saw it, the fact that women relied less on violence was an advantage: "We don't go in fighting," she would explain. "We talk, we use reason, and we use our femininity. It defuses situations and brings a softening to police work."[35] The height requirement was eliminated; neither children nor cops died as a result.[36]

Over time, Orazetti started discouraging women from engaging with the union, finding the leadership unresponsive to complaints of discrimination. One issue of the *Rap Sheet* ran a poem mocking the women cops. It closed with the lines, "I like my girls (put it mild) barefoot and with child / and chained to a bed in the kitchen." (The newsletter did at least find space for a poetic rebuttal by Orazetti and Ledyard.) Increasingly, women came to rely on lawsuits rather than the grievance process.[37] In the years 1973–76, the bureau faced forty-two complaints about discrimination in pay and promotions.[38]

Affirmative Action Report

Racial diversity was not faring much better.

In 1974, Charles Jordan, the former director of Portland's Model Cities program, became the first Black person to serve on the city council, and in 1977 he became the first Black police commissioner.[39] Under his leadership, the bureau began a targeted recruitment of minorities, sending officers to recruit at Black churches and featuring people of color in their promotional materials. They moved the location of the civil service exam to the Urban League's offices and offered classes to help people prepare for the test.[40] To encourage diversity among the command staff, Jordan proposed a two-track process for advancement. The PPA sued, saying it would "result in a decline in the quality of the police bureau." A judge ruled against the City on procedural grounds.[41]

White officers were suspicious of any effort to encourage minority representation in the bureau, arguing that the very idea "smacks of racism." One cop said the message seemed to be, "If you are not black or female there is no use . . . coming down to take the test."[42] The PPA too remained opposed to affirmative action. There was a running joke at union meetings: "Affirmative action report: There is none."[43] This attitude was essentially institutionalized in the department, despite changes in policy. Robert Davis Jr., an affirmative action specialist, resigned from the police bureau, complaining of the "racist environment" and reporting that he had been excluded from meetings related to recruitment, hiring, and training.[44]

Marilyn Snowden, a police bureau recruiter, found herself at a loss to explain the lack of diversity: "for some reason minorities are not attracted to police work in their own communities." Dwight Ford, another bureau recruiter, blamed "holdover attitudes from the turbulent 1960s."[45] It was true, as retired Portland Police lieutenant Harry Jackson complained, that Black officers faced criticism from their community: "People say that we need more Blacks on the department. But when you get on the department, you're Uncle Tom."[46] Still, rather than blame the community for the bureau's lack of diversity, recruiters might have done better to consider the "holdover attitudes" of the incumbent officers. One recruit, Tony Newman, later reported: "Every black officer has heard the word 'nigger.' Every black officer has to listen to 'nigger' jokes and doesn't feel he can object."[47] Another recruit kept finding lost property in his squad car at shift change. It turned out his supervisors had taken to leaving things in his vehicle to test his integrity. He turned all the items in as he was supposed to, but the exercise had the effect of undermining his reputation nonetheless. He didn't stay with the bureau for long.[48]

Culture Clash and Power Struggle

Over the course of about a dozen years spanning the 1970s, the Portland Police Association transformed from "a very weak organization" that "did not nothing but collect dues" into a political powerhouse. It won real gains for its members, in terms of wage increases and retirement benefits, but its protections were not uniformly applied. According to the PPA's own (surely understated) account, "The few minorities who were actually hired found very little encouragement or support from the union."[49] And the union seemed actively hostile to the handful of women on the force. Undoubtedly these attitudes reflected the culture of policing in general.

One way to understand the police union, especially as it has developed over time, is to notice where it has served to defend not just officers as individuals or as a group but also the institution of which they are part, insulating it from the pressures of a changing society. The PPA has, as we have seen, opposed affirmative action and diversity initiatives and tried to silence the bureau's critics in the press. They would also, in the decades following, become the single most stubborn obstacle facing any efforts for police accountability.

By the middle 1970s, it was clear that society's expectations of the police were changing. At the start of the decade, the *Probasco* decree mandated specific changes in the cops' treatment of African Americans and led to the creation of the Internal Affairs Division (IAD). In 1975, for the first time, a coalition of Black organizations had joined together and organized demonstrations against police violence. A new generation of leaders had taken seats in City Hall, promising the community a greater role in deciding the practices of government. One of these, Charles Jordan, became the city's first Black police commissioner. At the county level, Lee Brown was serving as the first Black sheriff and experimenting with "team policing" to build closer relationships between his deputies and local residents. Brown hoped the new model might raise standards for police across the country.

The cops themselves, however, were on the whole resistant to change. While social norms were moving, however slowly and unevenly, in the direction of greater equality, police continued to view Black people as suspects and women as weak. As the community demanded greater accountability, the police guarded their autonomy. They resisted any outside constraints and many internal controls as well. This contradiction, between police authority and democratic norms, has surfaced repeatedly since the Progressives first turned their eye to the issue of corruption. As the seventies became the eighties, it would produce a series of scandals, demands for reforms, and subsequent power struggles.

CHAPTER 17

Drugs and Motorcycles

A Drug Problem

A week after taking charge of the Special Investigations Division (SID), covering both drugs and vice, Captain Norm Reiter made a worried report to his superior, Deputy Chief Phil Smith, laying out his reasons for suspecting corruption in the unit. Some narcotics officers were buying expensive new sports cars, motorcycles, and otherwise living above their evident means. The deputy chief ignored him, and Reiter concluded that the corruption had infected command staff as well.[1]

He was smart to worry. Soon after Reiter's departure from SID, a drug dealer accused the police of planting evidence—and doing so ineptly. He was arrested in possession of heroin, but what he sold was cocaine. "We had crooked cops," former SID Detective (and later police chief) Charles Moose would write in his memoirs. "They were . . . making arrests stick by planting drugs, and stealing money—or drugs, and selling the drugs for money—and getting rich on the side." One officer partnered with an informant to sell the painkiller Dilaudid. Another, a woman sent undercover, began a romantic relationship with a suspect; she was later caught trying to smuggle drugs into prison.[2]

Neil Gearheart (aka "Gearshift") and Scott Deppe ("Big Red") were perhaps the most ambitious of the late-seventies drug cops. They would steal drugs from suspects and pocket the "buy money."[3] Some of what they stole they sold to a biker gang, the Free Souls.[4] Sometimes they would arrest people for a small amount of marijuana, then force them to sell pills or heroin. Together the two officers were suspected in five murders.[5]

Moral Peril

Gearheart and Deppe had not set out to be crooks. Both came from devout religious upbringings (Catholic and Mormon, respectively), and both had been attracted to law enforcement as a kind of moral crusade. They started as serious drug warriors and ended as serious drug dealers.[6]

How does this happen? Everybody seems to have a theory.

Retried Detective Don DuPay saw it simply as an occupational hazard: "Vice cops are expected to use cocaine to create an illusion of legitimacy among the criminal drug dealing elite. What happens, obviously, is these police officers become tragically addicted."[7]

Charles Moose thought it had more to do with training, supervision, and support. He described "a flaw in the process," beginning with recruitment: "Most police officer candidates by definition have to come from pretty sheltered, stable, middle-class homes. You wind up recruiting very straight and often very inexperienced young people." Working drugs, especially if they go undercover, they are confronted with temptations that nothing in their lives would have prepared them for. "By putting young, inexperienced police officers in this kind of environment, you run the risk that they'll start acting more like these people [they encounter in the drug trade] and less like the officers you hired them to be."[8]

Somewhat more reflective, Penny Harrington blamed the culture of impunity prevalent in the Special Investigations Division and was not shy about pointing fingers: "Deputy Chief [Jim] Brouillette had been giving the drug unit pep talks. Brouillette wanted drugs out of Portland, and he told the officers to do whatever it took to make it happen—the department would stand behind them. The more the unit pushed the envelope without negative consequences, the braver they got." Given such encouragement, "the officers began to feel the end justified the means—they could do anything to get the bad guys—even break the law."[9]

Journalist Phil Stanford, however, thinks the problem is inherent to drug enforcement: "Since both parties to an illegal drug deal have every interest in keeping it secret," he argues, "the only way to catch anyone is to team up with half the crooks against the other half." One group gets "a virtually free ride" so long as they "turn in their competition." But if the cops start protecting select criminals, "before long, it seems you might as well be in business with them. And before you know it, you are."[10]

Gang Fight

Some things are hard to cover up, even for the police. A shootout with a biker gang leaving a cop dead and his pockets full of drugs is one of those things.

On December 12, 1979, about twenty cops raided the St. Johns clubhouse of the Outsiders Motorcycle Club. As the Special Investigations Division's David Crowther broke down the door, a biker named Robert Jack Christopher ("Pigpen") opened fire with a shotgun. Crowther collapsed outside the door, felled by a fatal head wound. He was found to have been carrying drugs, with the obvious intention of planting evidence inside.[11]

"We had been working them, using informants, trying to make a drug arrest," Charles Moose later recalled. But part of the strategy was pure harassment: "We'd follow them when they went on rides, trying to bust them on whatever we could." As a result, "They had a long-running feud with the Portland police."[12]

This "feud" was not limited to the Outsiders and did not end with the raid in St. Johns. Writing in his memoirs, retired Officer Leonard Collins describes group fights, ambushes, and a giant bar brawl, in addition to routine harassment like towing away whole lines of motorcycles. "As I remember," Collins explains, "there were several altercations where members of local motorcycle gangs would catch a lone police officer and beat him up a little, followed by the police beating up a motorcycle gang member . . . or two. . . . Most of us thought it was great fun. Part of being a police officer is beating up bikers—or at least we thought so, then. Part of being a biker is beating up cops. It all evened out."[13]

Where the Outsiders were concerned, this conflict was not just a matter of "great fun," getting even, or club-spirited rivalry. It was business. Throughout the late seventies, the Outsiders Motorcycle Club provided for the transportation and security of the main methamphetamine distribution network in the Portland area. Their wholesale connection was Harold Penland ("Slick Willie"), a boxer, burglar, drug dealer, and serial rapist convicted of numerous other violent crimes. He had worked at the Gold Coin in its sex-trade days, ostensibly as a parking attendant and informally as security, then went on to manage massage parlors. He was also a police informant, working with Gearhart and Deppe to set up the Outsiders and take over their distribution network.[14]

At trial, the bikers said they thought they were being raided by another gang—which, to be fair, was not exactly wrong. Regardless, Pigpen was convicted of manslaughter and sentenced to twenty years.[15]

Crowther died a villain's death, but he got a hero's funeral. Nine hundred attended. Flags were put to half-staff.[16] His name still appears on memorials to officers killed in the line of duty.[17]

Unraveling

A year and a half later, the Outsiders would be vindicated.

Larry Mastne, who worked as a snitch for Deppe, got himself arrested for selling amphetamines in Boise. He told the cops there about Deppe's dealing, which led Deppe to rat out Gearheart. Gearheart then came clean about the Outsiders' raid. The ensuing investigation uncovered a pattern of perjury, corruption, and evidence-planting going back years. Five members of the Special Investigations Division resigned. Deppe was convicted of writing phony prescriptions and sentenced to thirty days. Gearheart retired with a $37,466 disability payout, compensation for the trauma of seeing his fellow officer killed in the Outsiders' raid.[18]

In the aftermath of the SID scandal, the district attorney's office identified fifty-nine wrongful convictions and thirty-five pending cases that were similarly compromised by police misconduct—including theft (in twenty-eight cases), planting evidence (sixteen), perjury (fifteen), and misappropriation of City funds (eight). All the affected cases had to be dismissed, including that of Robert Jack Christopher ("Pigpen"), the biker who killed Crowther.[19]

District Attorney Michael Schrunk, under pressure from the police, promised to retry Pigpen.[20] Earl Son, a private investigator working for prosecutor-turned-defense-lawyer Des Connall, met with Pigpen and the club president Robert Pagan ("T-Bob") on Christmas Eve, 1981. Son was a former Multnomah County homicide detective who had spent the first part of his career seizing slot machines and burglarizing bars when their owners failed to pay protection money. He then (with Connall) achieved a kind of fame in the Peyton-Allan murder investigation.[21] Son told the bikers not to worry about the trial: "I've got these cops on two murders." A week later, he was found dead in his home, seemingly by suicide. There was no further investigation of his death.[22]

Connall negotiated a short stint for Pigpen, avoiding a second trial, and the file on the SID case was sealed.[23]

Unscathed

Two drug cops would come out unscathed. One was Roberta Webber (née Ledyard), who had only transferred into the drug squad on the day of the Outsiders raid and was, as it happens, the sister of future Police Chief Penny Harrington.[24] The other was Charles Moose, who would himself later advance through the ranks to chief. Coincidentally or not, Moose was the only officer to bring a lawyer to his Internal Affairs interview. He said later that, as the only Black man on the narcotics team, he feared being scapegoated by his colleagues: "I was a natural profile for a drug cop gone wrong."[25]

Profiles aside, there are legitimate reasons that Moose might have warranted some scrutiny. He had been the second person into the breach, after Crowther. Furthermore, he and Crowther were not just coworkers; they were friends, and Moose had recruited Crowther into the SID. "We lifted weights together. . . , and then I had encouraged him to consider working for the police department," Moose later recalled. "In fact, I encouraged him to get into narcotics."[26] The place they lifted weights, Loprinzi's Gym on Southeast Forty-First, served as a hub for the area drug trade. Narcs worked out there and maintained a complicated relationship with another regular, David Owens, a body builder and cocaine dealer. The cops alternately shook Owens down for payoffs and sold him drugs they had stolen from other dealers.[27] How much Moose knew of the goings-on at the gym, whether he knew the extent of the corruption in SID, or whether he knew of the plan to plant drugs in the Outsiders' clubhouse, we cannot say. He admitted only to knowing that "there were guys at Loprinzi's doing steroids," and "some of the guys on the narcotics team were starting to behave strangely."[28]

In his memoirs, Moose did confess to a certain lapse of judgment early in his career. His very first police bureau assignment sent him undercover, buying stolen property, illegal guns, and drugs. At one point he learned of a planned robbery. Seeking protection, he hired a bunch of "street guys"—"people I knew from my undercover work, criminals"—and armed them with illegal guns. When the moment came, Moose's hired muscle confronted the would-be robbers, and the robbers backed down. "Later," Moose writes, "I realized that was the stupidest possible thing I could have done. If someone had started shooting, and a bunch of guys had gotten killed, I would have had some serious explaining to do."[29] Yes, illegally arming known criminals to protect a stash of stolen goods might produce quite a scandal. It almost sounds like something the drug squad might do.

CHAPTER 18

Internal Conflict and External Review

The Possum Posse

In the spring of 1981, as the drug squad was rapidly disintegrating, its credibility and its cases ruined by a seemingly endless series of revelations concerning corruption, perjury, and straightforward gangsterism, the police bureau found itself embroiled in a separate scandal, less baroque but in its own way equally grotesque. At about 10:15 p.m. on March 12, Police Officers Craig Ward and Jim Gallaway put out a radio call for all available cars to meet them at the Burger Barn, a Black-owned restaurant in the Albina neighborhood. Four squad cars and several officers responded. Ward and Gallaway then went on, before their laughing colleagues and numerous other witnesses, to dump four dead possums in the doorway of the restaurant.[1]

Not quite two weeks later, on March 25, almost two hundred people gathered outside of City Hall demanding that Ward and Gallaway be fired. They were. The PPA's Stan Peters called it "the most unjustified termination in the history of the city." The union filed a grievance, started circulating a petition to remove Charles Jordan from his position as police commissioner, and organized a no-confidence vote against both Commissioner Jordan and Police Chief Bruce Baker.[2] On April 3, almost one thousand people, mostly off-duty cops, marched to City Hall. They carried signs like "Reinstate the Blue Two," "Justice Not Politics," and "Cops Have Rights, Too."[3] Counterprotesters carried pigs' heads on sticks and signs reading "No Possum Posse."[4]

The police voted no confidence in Baker (326 to 94) and no confidence in Jordan (411 to 10). Nearly 10,000 people signed the petition to bring back the discharged officers. Ultimately, an arbiter would side with the PPA, reinstating the cops and setting a precedent that would haunt not only the city but also the entire country for decades. According to PPA attorney Will Aitchison (paraphrased by Susan Hauser), for years after the ruling, it remained "the leading police disciplinary case in the United States, and in labor law circles [was] the arbitration decision referenced most often."[5]

On June 1, Mayor Frank Ivancie took over as police commissioner. Jordan always suspected that the move was intended to appease the union and complained that it amounted to "admitting that Stan Peters is running the city."[6] Ivancie also replaced Chief Baker with a union favorite, Lieutenant Ron Still, a vocal opponent of affirmative action and civilian review. Still was, in Penny Harrington's assessment, "an 'old-fashioned, law-and-order police officer,' a 'policeman's policeman.'"[7] He had led the scandal-plagued Special Investigations Division in the late 1970s and before that had headed the bureau's campaign against the Black Panthers breakfast program.[8] As chief, Still announced a "War on Crime" and presented for the council's consideration a slate of new ordinances concerning drunkenness, loitering, and sex work. His proposal overlooked—or blatantly ignored—the fact that its measures were all based on similar measures that had previously been ruled unconstitutional. Furthermore, the jails were at capacity, so more arrests would not represent a net gain. No matter. Still wanted sex workers arrested, and if there wasn't room to hold them in the cells, he suggested keeping them overnight in the paddy wagons. Even his top commanders considered this plan unworkable. The paddy wagons weren't heated and had no plumbing. Some precinct commanders simply refused to make the arrests.[9]

A Review Board, Kind Of

In his last weeks as police commissioner, Jordan, responding to the possum incident, appointed a Police Citizens Task Force on Internal Affairs to evaluate the existing system of accountability. Its report, released July 16, 1981, concluded: "Many citizens have no confidence in the IAD and its procedures and are therefore reluctant to file complaints with the police." The committee offered a series of recommendations, most prominently a proposal for a citizens' panel to hear appeals.[10]

Chief Still, Mayor Ivancie, and the Portland Police Association were all opposed. In this case, they did not prevail. By a 3–2 vote, on April 8, 1982, the city council established the Police Internal Investigations Auditing Committee (PIIAC; pronounced "pie-ack"). The new body consisted of three city councilors and eight volunteers. Its mandate was "to monitor the internal investigations process and to hear appeals of police investigations." It could not investigate complaints or impose discipline but merely offer recommendations.[11] According to Samuel Walker, a scholar studying police oversight, this was the first body of its type and "an important innovation in the field."[12]

The day after the council vote, Citizens for a Safe Portland (a PPA front group) began circulating a petition to force the issue to the ballot. According to Susan Hauser, writing in the Police Association's in-house history, "The union had opposed PIIAC for a number of reasons. Some of the arguments were: it would undermine police morale; police would become less assertive because of a threat of civilian review of their professional judgment; public hearings might subject officers to embarrassment; having City Council members on the committee made auditing a purely political process."[13] The police union outspent accountability advocates $70,000 to $12,000. But that November, a bare majority of voters approved the review board.[14]

The following month, PIIAC began its work. It monitored Internal Affairs and served as an appeals board, but its only real power was to send cases back to the IAD for further investigation.[15] In a Reed College thesis, Colette Gordon offers what may well be the simplest explanation of the review process:

> Under PIIAC, the complainant first complained to IAD and if they were unsatisfied with the ruling they were allowed to file a complaint with PIIAC. The PIIAC staff person and one PIIAC citizen volunteer reviewed each complaint and reported back to the citizen group which would vote on whether to accept or deny the appeal. If they accepted it, the full committee, including City Council, would provide a hearing. The hearing was an audit and not an investigation and as such the complainants could not give new information but rather just answer questions and comment on the committee's description of the case. City Council members asked questions, commented, and voted whether to affirm IADs finding, refer [the case] back to IAD for further investigation, or rule that IAD's finding should be changed at which point it was the chief's decision as to how to respond.[16]

Complainants were often understandably confused by this procedure and frustrated that PIIAC did not conduct independent investigations. Moreover, PIIAC put greater emphasis on organizational problems than on individual officers, which had the potential to change the practices and conditions leading to abuse but offered no real remedy to specific injustices. Worse still, of twenty-eight recommendations offered over the course of eight years, the IAD accepted just two of them.[17] The Police Association discouraged cops from cooperating with the review process. Some refused to testify, even defying subpoenas.[18] "Despite its innovative role," professor Walker concludes, sadly, "PIIAC was widely regarded as ineffectual."[19] Some members resigned from the board in frustration after being denied the right to conduct independent investigations, despite having subpoena power. One complained, "it's a failure because it's not meant to do anything. . . . It's totally ineffective. It's absolutely ignored."[20]

Despite PIIAC's obvious shortcomings, other jurisdictions—including San Jose and Los Angeles County—soon adopted Portland's auditing model.[21]

Woman of the Year

With back-to-back scandals fresh in the public's mind, tavern owner Bud Clark ran for mayor in 1984 with a promise to make the police more responsive to community concerns.[22] ("I wanted to fire the whole department and start over again," he later said, "because how do you change the culture?")[23] Clark beat Frank Ivancie in 235 out of 291 precincts and took office in January 1985.[24] He soon appointed Penny Harrington chief of police. She was the first woman to hold the position in any major US city, and it made national news. *USA Today, Good Morning America, The MacNeil/Lehrer News Hour, NBC Nightly News, Ladies' Home Journal, People,* and the *New York Times* all ran stories. Harrington was named one of Harvard Law School's "Most Influential Women in Law" and *Ms.* magazine's "Woman of the Year." The *Downtowner*, a local weekly, produced a Penny Harrington paper doll.[25]

In her prior role as East Precinct commander, Harrington had built a reputation as both community-focused and proactive. She would later write, "[I had] decided to work with the neighborhood associations and get them involved in police work. The first thing I did was set up a 'citizen advisory council' that included a representative from each of the twenty neighborhood associations in my precinct. I also included representatives from the various populations: senior citizens, teenagers, African American[s], and business owners. About forty to fifty people attended our monthly meetings." As much as these advisory council members represented the community to the police bureau, they also represented the police bureau to the community. "I wanted each council member to go back to his or her respective neighborhood association and explain how the department worked and what resources were available to the communities—to establish a real rapport between the precinct and the citizens."[26]

Based on what they heard from the advisory board, the police had undertaken a series of programs focused on crime prevention and public order. Cops installed locks for poor and elderly people. They added traffic dividers on Eighty-Second Avenue and enforced a late-night curfew to discourage drag racing. They organized residents and business owners to photograph cars that picked up sex workers. A new unit enforced truancy laws in an effort to reduce daytime burglaries.[27]

"We went out into the community and worked with the businesses and the homeowners," Harrington recalled. "Citizens became our eyes and ears and then reported back to us. . . . Our arrest rate increased. Crime rates dropped by about fifty percent, and citizen complaints dropped significantly."[28] The approach also brought distinct political advantages: "The program worked well, and the communities became strong supporters of the police bureau—and of me. . . . They were our advocates, which made a real difference when certain items came up for a budgetary vote."[29] In essence, the police created a neighborhood-level law-and-order lobby, and Harrington developed a personal constituency. Success was measured by public support, which in turn offered compounding benefits. Increased support increased power. Politics showed up in another way as well: the police, by selecting their partners in this endeavor, also worked to *define* the community, deciding who would and would not belong and hardening class-coded distinctions between community members and outsiders (e.g., "the businesses and the homeowners" versus sex workers and their clients).[30]

Unlucky, Unpopular

Despite or because of her community-based approach, Harrington was never popular with the line officers, and the union had opposed her promotion to chief. Sexism was surely one factor, and her several lawsuits against the bureau only fostered additional suspicion and resentment. She also cut an unlucky break. In her first month, just as a new agreement between the City of Portland and Multnomah County added thirty square miles and sixty thousand residents to the Portland Police jurisdiction, an arbiter settled a union dispute by increasing officer salaries by 10 percent. To balance the books, Harrington eliminated sixteen positions and left sixty others vacant. Then, when she discovered that the Police Association was only reimbursing the City for half of the union president's salary, she ordered Stan Peters to report for duty twenty hours a week. He accused her of union-busting, and the PPA voted to pay his full salary instead.[31] Other points of friction were more avoidable: Harrington required that all officers attend a diversity training ("Cross Cultural Communications") and banned smoking—even off-duty.[32] At times, it must have seemed like she was *trying* to make herself unpopular.

Most importantly, Harrington reorganized the drug and vice squads, incorporating them into the detective division and placing them under closer supervision. The PPA opposed the restructuring.[33] As Harrington saw it, "There were people in the police bureau that didn't want things to change—officers who didn't want to be looked at closely."[34] Surely so—but Harrington's reorganization put drug and vice enforcement into entirely new hands, disrupting investigations for more than a year.[35] Stan Peters accused her of making Portland "the drug capital of the Pacific Northwest."[36]

Harrington certainly knew how the cops felt about her agenda. "I was getting death threats all the time," she later wrote. "Most of them were anonymous threats from inside the department."[37]

Choke Point

The conflict between the union and the chief reached the crisis stage when an officer employing a carotid artery "sleeper hold" killed a Black man named Lloyd Stevenson. "Tony" (as he was known) was a Marine Corps veteran, a department store security guard, and the father of five. Details of the confrontation remain murky even now, but at a public inquest an all-white jury ruled the death a homicide. The grand jury, on the other hand, failed to indict Gary Barbour, the officer responsible.[38]

"I feared the community would explode into riots," Harrington recalled. Stevenson was killed on a Saturday night, and the chief stayed up calling all the church leaders she knew, some as late as 4:00 and 5:00 a.m. In the weeks that followed, she "went to every possible meeting, spoke to every group," Harrington wrote. "I took officers with me to demonstrate the carotid hold. I told them exactly what occurred on that night [of his death]." The US Justice Department dispatched agents of the Community Relations Service to help assess and calm the situation. They provided the Portland Police with information on other carotid hold fatalities, and Harrington appointed a committee to study the technique, suspending its use in the meantime. The PPA opposed the ban.[39]

Two officers—Richard Montee and Paul Wickersham—then had T-shirts printed with the slogan "Don't Choke 'Em, Smoke 'Em," appearing above the image of a revolver with smoke drifting from the barrel.[40] They sold the shirts in the precinct break room, beginning April 26—the day of Stevenson's funeral.[41] Some cops then wore them under their uniforms.[42]

When news of the T-shirts appeared in the media, there was a general sense of outrage. Signs went up on telephone poles all over the city, showing a police car with a circle and a slash through it and the words "Smoke them before they smoke you."[43]

On May 7, Mayor Bud Clark fired Montee and Wickersham. That August, the case went to arbitration. Will Aitchison, the PPA's attorney, argued that the cops didn't know that the funeral was that day, that the phrase was common among police throughout the country, and that the possum case had set a precedent. The arbiter agreed, and the officers returned to work after a six-month suspension. Commissioner Mike Lindberg called the arbiter's decision "a devastating blow to the police chief and city council and our ability to manage the police department. . . . It's almost an unsupervisable (police) force at this point in time."[44]

Town Hall

Crisis followed crisis, one after another. Almost as soon as the T-shirt controversy passed, an armed standoff devolved into a shootout, and the cops mistakenly killed an eighty-five-year-old woman as she tried to flee the gunfire. Unrest seemed imminent, and, for the second time in Harrington's brief tenure, the federal Community Relations Service was dispatched to Portland. The Black United Front (BUF) responded with a public meeting at a local school and invited the mayor and chief to attend. The city officials offered a twenty-minute presentation, distributed copies of their preliminary report on the incident, and then took questions. Finally, they asked for suggestions as to how the police could handle things differently, and patiently wrote down what people told them. At the end, the police chief and the mayor received a standing ovation. "I had been worried that [BUF cochair Ron] Herndon arranged the meeting to foment more problems," Harrington later admitted, "but he actually brought us to the school to clear the air and buy me time—and it worked. . . . we avoided a potential racial explosion."[45]

A subsequent investigation found that the captain in charge on the night of the shooting had left in the midst of the crisis; he was fired. The lieutenant who authorized lethal force was also disciplined. No other officers were punished. There were no riots.[46]

Tarnished Penny

While the police bureau was mired in front-page controversy, a federal drug task force began quietly investigating cocaine trafficking in the Portland area. One target of the investigation was Bobby Lee, the owner of Rickshaw Charlie's. As it happens, Chief Harrington knew Lee. She and her husband Gary were regulars at his restaurant; they had even gone there to celebrate her promotion.[47]

When she learned of the federal probe, Penny told her husband, Gary, who was himself a police officer, and months later he warned Bobby Lee against allowing drug dealers to hang out in his dining room. When the drug task force finally questioned Lee, he was very cooperative and mentioned in passing this piece of advice. The investigation then took a turn. That very night District Attorney Michael Schrunk met with Chief Harrington to inform her that her husband was being considered a suspect, and detectives interviewed them both.[48]

Schrunk eventually determined that there wasn't enough evidence to indict Gary Harrington, but he did also find a number of violations of department policies. The mayor appointed an independent committee to look into the matter, and this body was headed by former US Attorney Sidney Lezak. Lezak immediately expanded the scope of the inquiry to include Chief Harrington's reorganization of the drug squad, and the PPA lined up a series of witnesses to testify against the chief, mostly in secret. In the committee's final report, Gary Harrington was found to have violated rules against associating with and providing information to criminal suspects. He would be suspended for twenty-five days and placed on probation for a year. Penny Harrington was exonerated of any wrongdoing, but Lezak recommended replacing her anyway, arguing that "she lost the confidence of her command" and was "unlikely to ever regain the confidence of a working majority of the bureau."[49]

Mayor Clark had every reason to distance himself from the drug allegations. One of his top aides was already under investigation for cocaine trafficking and embezzlement.[50] And rumors swirled around the mayor himself, some suggesting that he had ignored drug use at his bar, the Goose Hollow Inn.[51] So, following the committee's recommendations, on June 2, 1986, Clark announced Harrington's resignation.[52] *Time* magazine called her "Portland's Tarnished Penny."[53] She went on to become assistant director of the Office of Investigations for the California State Bar and later worked as the first director of the National Center for Women and Policing.[54]

"[As] I think about how my story unfolds," Harrington wrote in her memoirs, "I think the key to my being removed as chief was some sort of link between the district attorney's office, the union, and some of the members of the bureau with ties to the original narcotics unit I dismantled." More basically: "I got fired because the union hated me."[55] *Oregonian* columnist David Sarsohn thought that real reason was rank-and-file disaffection after the Stevenson T-shirt controversy.[56] Or, as an anonymous cop told the *Observer*, "Peters and his cronies couldn't handle a strong woman police chief, especially one who was pushing through reforms that threatened the 'old boys network' in the bureau."[57]

CHAPTER 19

Community Policing and Public Housing

The Most Dangerous Place

Portland's first fatal drive-by shooting occurred at the Columbia Villa housing project on August 17, 1988. The victim was Joseph "Ray-Ray" Winston, a promising young student, athlete, and leader in the Columbia Villa Crips. He was seventeen years old. Almost overnight, Don Clark recalls, "Columbia Villa became, in the public mind, the most dangerous place in the State of Oregon."[1]

Clark, the former Multnomah County sheriff, had been hired as the executive director of the Housing Authority of Portland (HAP) that February, and was almost immediately confronted with the numerous ways that crack cocaine was altering the culture of public housing, producing a more prominent gang presence and increased reports of violence.[2]

Columbia Villa was the city's largest public housing project, with sixteen hundred low-income residents almost evenly divided by race: 48 percent white and 42 percent Black. More than 80 percent of households there were headed by a single woman under the age of thirty. Easily half the residents were under eighteen, and a quarter were younger than eight. The complex comprised 598 units, mainly arranged in duplexes and fourplexes. In 1988, nearly a quarter of the apartments (141 units) were vacant, and many of the remaining residents requested transfers to other housing projects.[3]

The police were, if anything, part of the problem. The cops were aggressive when they weren't negligent. They represented both an overbearing presence and indifferent absence. Clark remembers them "assembling outside of Columbia Villa, sending in an army of police cars, . . . and then leaving. . . . And when they left, there'd be retaliation to anybody who cooperated with the Portland Police." The answer, Clark believed, was greater consistency—"a continuing presence." But this the cops absolutely did not want to provide. Housing Authority staff had repeatedly requested more regular patrols, but

Police Chief Richard Walker had always declined. Clark described the cops as unsympathetic and "unresponsive," putting the blame first of all at the chief: "Dick Walker didn't want to have anything to do with Columbia Villa."[4]

When the police did engage, their approach was generally counterproductive. John Angell, Multnomah County's justice services director, moved his family into the Villa in December 1988, partly to counter the perception that the neighborhood was being abandoned. Living there, he witnessed numerous confrontations between residents and cops and was even involved in one himself. He became increasingly critical of the Portland Police Bureau—the hostile attitude of the officers, the practice of sending battalions of police for routine calls, and the tendency to search or arrest whole groups of people, treating all residents as presumptive suspects. He once heard an officer threaten a teenage neighbor, "This bullet has your name on it."[5]

Clark could certainly believe it: "[The] Portland police, historically, they had a hard-nosed attitude toward the kids at Columbia Villa," he said. "They'd throw kids down on the ground, and put a gun up to their head. . . . That stuff actually went on."[6]

Root Problems

Feeling that the situation was deteriorating, and recognizing that he couldn't count on the police, Clark appointed a team, including several members with criminal justice backgrounds, and they took charge of managing the housing project.[7] Clark identified three goals: "The first one was, we wanted to reduce the fear of crime, because the fear of crime changed everybody's behavior, made people stay in, and it built on itself. . . . [Second,] reduce the actual amount of crime. . . . And [third] we wanted to give people hope for the future. We wanted people to feel they had a potential for upward mobility, and a better life."[8]

The Columbia Villa Community Services Project was a collaboration between the city, the county, the Housing Authority, and several private agencies. Norm Monroe was appointed service coordinator.[9] Among the existing programs the committee sought to expand were counseling and addiction treatment; visits from Health Department nurses; nutrition classes; and the Black United Front's Saturday School, which covered basic math, literacy, and Black history. New initiatives included reduced fees for Parks Bureau programs, movie nights, dances, day camps, and job training. Juvenile Justice set up an office in the Villa, as did the the county parole and probation office, the Youth Gang Task Force, and the Oregon Employment Department.[10] "But I still wasn't getting anything out of the Portland Police Bureau," Clark complained.[11]

In February 1989, Clark—the former sheriff—approached Sheriff Robert Skipper for help. Skipper assigned Lieutenant Rod Englert, a former homicide detective with twenty-seven years in law enforcement, to conduct a security review of the housing complex. Englert's report described a pervasive sense of fear—fear of crime and gangs, yes, but also fear of the Housing Authority and the police. He argued for a community policing approach ("individual contact must be made with citizens," he said), and he recommended bringing in an agency apart from the police bureau.[12]

Safety Action Team

In April 1989, the Housing Authority of Portland contracted with the Multnomah County Sheriff's Office, which then—drawing from its experience with team policing—assigned a lieutenant, three deputies, and two unsworn community safety officers to Columbia Villa, full-time. Englert was made head of this new Safety Action Team (SAT).[13]

The Housing Authority later summarized "SAT's three-step approach: 1) make contact, 2) establish communication, and 3) build up trust."[14] Each SAT member had a quota of ten resident contacts per day. On a typical shift, the officers would ride bicycles through the neighborhood, stopping to chat and emphasizing casual, friendly interactions with people in the community. In the evening, they would close the playground and other public areas, sending away groups of young people hanging out there. The next morning, any incidents from the previous day would be reported to the community safety officers, who could follow up with those affected, victims and suspects alike, and offer referrals to social service agencies.[15]

"If you don't have anything else going on," Englert would tell his officers, "reach out and hug a kid." SAT officers sometimes took neighborhood kids fishing or arranged outings to the zoo, and deputies attended Villa social events on their off hours, bringing their families with them.[16]

The program also brought residents more tangible benefits. Working with the federal Job Corps and the state employment department, the Columbia Villa Community Service Project found jobs for 106 residents in the first year.[17] One tenant, Sheila Daniels, credited the deputies with helping her get out of an abusive relationship. "Even now when I have problems I can go over and talk to them and they give me advice," she said. "They're kind of like counselors."[18]

In principle, the Portland Police Bureau was still responsible for 911 calls from the Villa, but as a practical matter the Safety Action Team often arrived at the scene first. Englert described the relationship between the two agencies as "very strained." City cops openly mocked his officers and offered no assistance. "They wouldn't back us, they didn't want us to back them." True to form, Englert organized interagency potlucks to help ease tensions. Relations slowly improved, and after a time regular cops began volunteering with Columbia Villa programs.[19]

Evictions, Arrests, and Other Interventions

But even while they were hugging kids and organizing potlucks, the Housing Authority and the sheriff's office were also planning evictions.

Following Englert's recommendations, the Housing Authority instituted stricter lease requirements, mandating evictions for drug or gun offenses and setting paternalistic limits to the number of nights a guest could stay (a maximum of seventy-two hours per visit, and no more than fourteen overnight stays in the course of a year). Deputies were authorized to issue trespass orders for rule violations.[20] In effect, the landlord's authority and the policing authority were merged.

Despite these extraordinary new powers, though, enforcement seems to have been de-emphasized in practice. In 1989, there were four drug-related evictions; in 1990, there were zero; and in 1991 there was only one.[21] Of the first five hundred contacts between residents and deputies, only fourteen resulted in arrest.[22]

More remarkably, members of the Safety Action Team sometimes advocated on behalf of Columbia Villa residents in their difficulties with other parts of the criminal legal system, urging leniency and winning second (or third) chances. Englert personally intervened twice to keep one resident out of jail, promising to monitor her behavior and help find her a job.[23] Sergeant Mel Hedgpeth helped another regain custody of her son following a drug relapse. Afterward, SAT members visited her almost daily to support her in her recovery and check on the child. "My parole officer was ready to throw me back to jail," she said, "but the Safety Action Team keep trying to help me."[24]

The service-oriented approach seemed to have the desired effect. Reports of gang-related crimes dropped from 153 for the period of May 1988–March 1989, to fifty-six for April 1989–March 1990, and then to thirty-eight for April 1990–March 1991. Assaults declined from 252 to 204 and then 193 over the same periods.[25] The *feeling* of safety also made a difference. Truck drivers began making deliveries again, and the fire department would respond without a police escort.[26] In a September 1989 survey, with 211 residents responding, about half (49.3 percent) said that things were improving.[27] Almost three years later, in January 1992, 73 percent of residents indicated that the Villa was safer. Perhaps most tellingly, people moved in. The occupancy rate increased to 98 percent.[28]

Transition

The police bureau's Captain Tom Potter took note. "This has really demonstrated to me the effectiveness of community policing," he said. "If it could work here, it could work in other areas of the city."[29] Potter had recently been assigned responsibility for drafting a community policing plan, and in November 1990 he was appointed chief of police.[30] By that point, community policing had been adopted as the official doctrine of the bureau:

> Community policing is based on a philosophy which recognizes the interdependence and shared responsibility of the police and community in making Portland a safer, more livable city. It is a method of policing which encourages a partnership that identifies community safety issues, determines resources, and applies innovative strategies designed to create and sustain healthy, vital neighborhoods. Community policing will coordinate with efforts being made by private, non-profit, and public agencies to bring a comprehensive approach to Portland's problem of crime and disorder. Community policing reflects the values of: community participation; problem solving; officer involvement in decision making; police accountability; and deployment of police personnel at a level closer to the neighborhood.[31]

Potter's transition plan called for three demonstration projects to test the theory before its citywide implementation. Jodi Pitre, the director of housing management at the Housing Authority, helped select Iris Court as one of the demonstration sites, based on the prevalence of drug sales and gang violence at the complex. The housing project was already known to police as a trouble spot. A year before, two cops had been surrounded by a crowd and pelted with rocks and bottles as they tried to make an arrest.[32]

Lieutenant Charles Moose, the project facilitator, described the neighborhood: "[It] was a place filled with crime and violence. . . . There was a lot of drug activity. . . . There were constantly rapes and assaults. There were always people standing around drinking and fighting. It was rough and unsafe, and the violence and criminality of it was starting to bleed over into the surrounding neighborhoods. It was the worst kind of urban blight."[33]

Three goals were identified for the Iris Court campaign, echoing those from Columbia Villa: a) improve the quality of life of the residents; b) reduce the fear of crime; and c) reduce the level of actual crime.[34] To pursue these aims, the police created a coalition called the Metro-Life Enhancement Team (MET). Member organizations included a wide array of government agencies—both law enforcement and social services—as well as the Iris Court Residential Committee, the Humboldt Neighborhood Association, the Urban League, and the Albina Ministerial Alliance. A steering committee set the overall direction, and Moose drew up an action plan.[35]

The twenty-one elements of Moose's plan could roughly be sorted into four categories: enforcement, prevention, organizing, and services. *Enforcement* included "assertive . . . prosecution" and "immediate action against tenants found in violation of tenant agreements." *Preventive* measures covered "information sharing, neighborhood watch, court watch, and workshops on drug and gang enforcement"; "environmental design" efforts to slow traffic, increase outdoor lighting, and improve home security; an "on-site Neighborhood Police Office"; "one-to-one outreach to gang impacted youth"; "training in conflict management"; and "law-related education" to "assist young people with [their] decisions." *Organizing* involved "a survey of all tenants," a "residential committee," and "regular meeting[s] with residents [and police]." *Services* would include "structured recreation"; "employment counseling"; GED classes; youth programs; an "on-site Health Fair"; "support groups . . . [and] counseling" for the victims of domestic violence; "on-site drug and alcohol treatment"; and child care.[36]

In practice, enforcement received top priority.

Tactics, Services, and Results

Moose started by having the streets converted into cul-de-sacs, "so people would be less likely to try and drive through . . . to buy their drugs." He took control of a pair of apartments, turning one into a police substation, "so it would look like police were around all the time." (Getting the cops to use the substation was another matter. Eventually he installed cable television, assuming, if nothing else, "the officers would stop by to watch football games.") The second apartment was converted to a new laundry room, and the MET hired women from the neighborhood to "supervise" the facility and "do little clerical jobs for the police substation."[37] The MET also sponsored barbecues, holiday parties, and outings for neighborhood children. They resurfaced the basketball court. They opened a day care center and arranged for visits from a community health nurse. When no one would come to see her, the nurse turned her hand to bicycle repair. The MET hosted a job fair and brought in an employment specialist for twenty hours a week. Oregon State University started offering nutrition classes. The police began teaching women self-defense.[38]

At the same time, the cops stepped up enforcement. Following the Columbia Villa model, Moose sought enhanced police powers, persuading "various local agencies to give us the right to evict anyone who was not technically on the lease for an apartment," as well as "the power to arrest people for trespassing."[39] Right away the police served ten drug warrants, followed by evictions. There were thirteen evictions in 1989, and ten in 1990, but none the year following.[40] "[The] remaining tenants had started to be aware of the relationship between their behavior and their housing," Moose explained in his 1993 doctoral dissertation. He recounted an episode when "there were three individuals visiting and living in and about the complex although they were not on a lease agreement and were generally seen as troublemakers. At the request of police officers, HAP sent letters to all of the Iris Court tenants informing them that continued association with these individuals could lead to eviction."[41] In short: if the cops didn't like your friends, they could take away your housing.

Between August 15, 1989, and March 31, 1990, the police wrote ninety-four exclusion orders, barring people from the complex for rule violations. These exclusions did not require convictions or even arrests; the standard of proof was very low. If an excluded person returned to the property, he could be arrested for trespassing. Ninety-eight percent of those excluded were Black. More than half (58 percent) were excluded for drug violations and another 10 percent for drinking in public. Only four individuals were barred because of violence. Between April 1990 and August 1991, there were only three exclusions, all Black men and all for fighting.[42] This was just one fewer than the previous year, suggesting that while there may have been less out-in-the-open drinking and drug use, there was no significant reduction in violence.

Regardless, during the period of the pilot project, the percentage of residents who said they were "very afraid" fell from 40 percent to a still unacceptable 33 percent. Reported offenses declined by an impressive 55 percent, though the concentrated enforcement "potentially displaced a problem to another location."[43] By Moose's reckoning, the campaign was a success. "The Iris Court project became a nationally observed experiment in community policing," he boasted. "And a lot of citizens in Iris Court—and a thousand places like it, all over the country—[wound] up having better lives because of it."[44]

Charles Moose wrote his doctoral dissertation about community policing at Iris Court and received his degree in 1993.[45] That same year, he was appointed chief of police. Iris Court's community center would later bear his name.[46]

Slippery Slopes

The Portland Police Bureau's much-lauded embrace of community policing came only after decades of experimentation carried out by the Multnomah County Sheriff's Office. There was a clear progression from Clark's version of professionalism—wedding, as it did, rational administration with humane and democratic values—to Brown's more programmatic application of team policing, to the bold experiment at Columbia Villa and its more heavy-handed sequel at Iris Court.[47]

Columbia Villa was the test case. It showed that community policing could work, that liberal social services and judicious law enforcement could bring down crime and improve people's lives. It then became a model—replicated elsewhere in Portland and referenced by police agencies around the country as they designed their own programs.[48] But where the Columbia Villa Project was service-oriented, later iterations tended to be not only police-driven but also police-centered.[49] One need only compare the Safety Action Team's restrained use of exclusion, eviction, and arrest powers at Columbia Villa with the Metro-Life Enhancement Team's more aggressive enforcement at Iris Court to recognize the slippery slope and predict where it might lead.

That difference—pronounced even between agencies that shared the same tactics, strategy, and stated goals—points to the fundamental importance of organizational culture in shaping the behavior of the police.[50] The sheriff's office had already undergone three decades of reform before it undertook the audacious experiment at Columbia Villa. The Portland Police never had any equivalent experience. They took the Villa model as a template, but they were left trying to adopt a new approach without really changing the organization. They tended to retain the priorities of law enforcement, with social services added as a kind of sweetener. The Columbia Villa Community Services Project was an exemplar and therefore also an outlier. It is probably the best we could hope for from liberal policing, which illustrates the limits of even the most thoughtful and heroic efforts and underscores how little we expect of ordinary policing.

The contrast between the implementation at Columbia Villa and Iris Court likewise points to the responsibility of those in leadership for setting the tone for the organization as a whole—though it equally shows the limits to any top-down approach to change. Progress imposed by fiat can just as easily be reversed by fiat. One lesson, then, is that we would be wise to forestall any attempt to widen the scope of police attention, to broaden their sphere of authority, or to increase their resources or influence.

Charles Moose, writing in his dissertation, inadvertently revealed how sweeping and even totalitarian the implications of community policing can be:

> Addressing the problem [of crime] requires a lot more than just cops. It requires the participation of every agency available. . . .
>
> You have to get the Department of Sanitation to get all the garbage off the streets. You have to make sure the Bureau of Street Maintenance fills the potholes and keeps lines painted on the streets and replaces all the burned-out street lights. . . .
>
> You have to create after-school programs so that bored teenagers have somewhere to go and something to do.
>
> You have to send DARE teams into the schools so that at-risk kids learn what drugs and alcohol will really do to them.
>
> You may need housing revitalization, to create more affordable housing for poor people in the community. You may need the cooperation of local judges, to get them to understand that they have to start sentencing people to maximum terms if they're going to keep them from creating more crime in the community.

> You have to get the authorities to move in on the public housing areas, to make sure no one is living there that shouldn't be living there. You have to get the probation department to move in on the area, too, to make sure there are no parole violators on the street.[51]

Even as he foregrounded the social service aspects, Moose took it for granted that the full resources of the government should be available to the police to deploy as they see fit. He assumed that law enforcement could and should set the agenda for transportation, housing, education, and even the judiciary. The picture that emerges is one of the welfare state in the service of the police state.

CHAPTER 20

Enforcing Quality of Life

Flashpoint

On a hot August night in 1992, Arleen Curths called 911 to report a "bloodcurdling scream" coming from Laurelhurst Park, followed by the sounds of "body blows," someone being "pounded and pounded," and desperate cries of "Help me, help me." "I believed somebody was getting killed," she later recalled. It turned out to be the sound of police work.[1]

Curths was just one of several witnesses to complain of the violence accompanying a crackdown against men having sex in the park. T. J. Browning, a longtime neighborhood activist, thought the busts counterproductive. She told the *Oregonian* that the presence of gay men had always made her feel safer walking alone in the park, since she trusted that they would help if there was ever trouble. "Now the gay men don't come here anymore," she said. "[And] we no longer trust our police department."[2]

Though Emily Simon—a defense attorney and member of the Police Internal Investigations Auditing Committee—described the park raid as "the flashpoint," it was merely one of a series of incidents undermining public confidence in the police. A year before, when a mentally ill man took twelve-year-old Nathan Thomas hostage in his own home, the police opened fire and killed them both.[3] Then, in 1993, Officer Doug Erickson fired twenty-two rounds at a fleeing suspect—he emptied his clip, reloaded, and kept shooting. The suspect, Gerald Gratton, was struck by three of Erickson's bullets but survived. Erickson was initially fired, but the Police Association spent $100,000 to take the case to arbitration and he was ultimately reinstated.[4] The *Oregonian* asked, "If you can't dismiss a police officer for firing 22 times at a fleeing man who isn't shooting back, what can you fire him for?"[5]

Internal Investigations wrote a report on the Laurelhurst roundup, which PIIAC sent back for further review after members of the board complained about what they saw as deliberate obfuscation. Meanwhile, Lieutenant John McNabb, who oversaw the operation, was transferred to North Precinct—historically the dumping ground for problem officers—and retired soon after.[6]

Mayor Bud Clark then asked the city auditor to examine the whole accountability system, both Internal Investigations and PIIAC. The review concluded that PIIAC had "not accomplished its objectives" and had "failed to adequately monitor, review and report on the police internal investigations system as required by City Code." The mayor recommended some changes, including an increase in the number of citizen advisors, the hiring of part-time staff, and the creation of an outreach program. City Council finally approved the proposal in January 1994, a year after Clark had left office.[7]

Chief's Forums

The move to strengthen the review board fit well with Tom Potter's management style as chief. Potter scaled Penny Harrington's advisory board strategy up to the city level. He began the practice—which would continue under subsequent police chiefs into the next decade—of establishing committees to represent the interests of specific identity groups with the aim of improving police relations: Asian Law Enforcement Advisory Council (1991), Hispanic Advisory Council (1992), Sexual Minorities Roundtable (1992), Developmental Disabilities Advisory Council (1993), African American Advisory Council (1996), and the Arab and Muslim Police Advisory Council (2001).[8]

In 1990, Mayor Clark invited Richard Brown, co-chair of the Black United Front, to join the Chief's Forum. Brown later recalled:

> Potter's idea with the Forum was to give civilians a real say in policing. It was a biweekly meeting, with two dozen participants. There were heads of neighborhood associations, high-level officers, beat cops, the head of the PPA (Stan Peters, still), and several Black and Brown folks, including Avel Gordly and me. Basically, we'd all sit at a giant table, and we'd go around bringing up concerns. Potter, too, would ask questions—how to deal with dope houses, what constitutes use of force,

> what cars cops should drive—and we'd talk until we'd found a solution we all could stomach.[9]

Though it was in some respects a deliberative body, the Chief's Forum had no real decision-making authority. It provided the cops' critics an opportunity to voice their complaints and argue for improvements in policy, but—though reforms might occasionally result—the main function of this process was to legitimate the chief's decisions. The Chief's Forum represented, as cynical observers described it, a "rubber stamp [for] Bureau initiatives."[10]

Front Group

The gesture toward inclusion—a literal seat at the table—might make advisory boards seem like an inviting prospect and a real exercise in democratic engagement. But participation in the Chief's Forum also inevitably pulled the leadership of the Black United Front—which had previously organized civil disobedience actions against apartheid and boycotts of the public schools—more and more into the orbit of the police, which had a rather distorting effect on the civil rights agenda.[11] In his autobiography *This Is Not for You,* Richard Brown described himself: "[I'm] a civilian who's spent years working with cops. . . . I've ridden along in squad cars hundreds of times. . . . I've been on more search warrants than most active officers." And, beginning in the summer of 1994, Brown wrote, he "led a citizen foot patrol every night for a year-plus in a gang-addled area."[12] Nightly from six to eleven, a highly visible group of volunteers would walk along Beech Street between Williams and Mississippi. They received training from police, lawyers, and EMTs. Once a night, the beat cops would stop by and check in. But to the disappointment of the organizers, local residents did not want to participate.[13]

These relationships undoubtedly shaped Brown's perceptions of the police and shifted his approach: "In those days, I was getting all sorts of calls, many of them from folks who'd had a bad run-in with cops and wanted me to raise a stink on their behalf. Sometimes I would. But more often I'd try to explain why the cops did what they did."[14] Brown would later help develop the curriculum and teach classes at the police academy and then at the FBI Academy at Quantico, Virginia.[15] In 2007, he suggested that the police should enforce the long-dormant youth curfew. The cops conducted a sweep in Northeast Portland over spring break, rounding up teenagers and ticketing their parents. Seven were cited and fined $750. All were Black. When the effort was denounced as implicitly racist, Deputy District Attorney Jim Hayden pointed out that it had been Brown's idea.[16]

Richard Brown undoubtedly felt that by partnering with the police he was gaining influence. And establishment groups fed that impression. He was awarded the Spirit of Portland Award and the Citizens Crime Commission's Distinguished Service Medal. But his increasingly police-adjacent role also affected his reputation in the community. He complained of being called an Uncle Tom and was sometimes accused of being a snitch.[17]

An Example Not to Follow

The reform of the review board represented a kind of extension of Chief Potter's strategy of using advisory councils to both encourage citizen participation and contain dissent. In the ideal case, these boards could tame the cops' critics and, by virtue of the inclusive process, bring a sense of legitimacy to policing. But the most important fact about any advisory board is precisely that it is advisory. Policy makers are free to ignore them and often do.

PIIAC did have some minor successes, leading the bureau to print complaint forms in multiple languages and limiting the use of leading questions in Internal Affairs interviews.[18] But the review board rarely challenged the police. In 1990, PIIAC sided with Internal Affairs in seventy-eight out of seventy-eight cases; the following year, they upheld the police findings in seventy-four cases out of seventy-six. Even in the rare event that a complaint was forwarded to the city council, the process had to no real impact. The council voted three times between 1997 and 2001 to sustain allegations against an officer, and each time the police chief disregarded the finding.[19] As the PIIAC process relied entirely on police investigators, the bias was built-in. By 1998, IAD had four investigators, one for every 225 officers; one of these four was Jeff Barker, the police union president.[20]

The inherent weaknesses of the PIIAC model, its reliance on and deference to the police, the biases of IAD investigations, the resistance of the police union, and the ultimately advisory role of even the city council all added up to a review system that failed to provide even the appearance of accountability. According to Human Rights Watch, PIIAC "was singled out by national police abuse experts as an example not to follow in creating a review board."[21]

Too Much Fun

Toward the end of the twentieth century, the discourse about policing began to change, though enforcement activity continued to follow some established patterns. The Laurelhurst Park raid, which once would have been justified in terms of morals or vice, could now be absorbed into the community policing model as a means of improving the quality of life.[22]

As a noun, *quality of life* would seem virtually synonymous with Portland's highest civic ideal—livability. But like *community, quality of life* also appears as an adjective attached to *policing*. Where *community* poses questions of inclusion and exclusion, the concept of the *quality of life* seems already to assume the answers. We are expected to know immediately and without any need for argument which features of a city will enhance the quality of life and which ones will diminish it. *Whose quality of life?* and *Quality by whose standards?* are not questions that are meant to arise. The idea is bound up with a very specific conception of public order: business-friendly and family-oriented; rationalized, regulated, and predicable. Anything unexpected or unusual is a potential threat; simple spontaneity is treated with suspicion. When combined with coercive force, the overall effect can sometimes feel less like an exercise of law and more like a war against fun.

In his memoir *Portland Police Stories,* Leonard Collins recalls one of the city's seasonal crackdowns on cruising, that adolescent practice of driving repeatedly along the same length of street for the sake of showing off, laughing with friends, and trying to find dates. "I have always suspected," Collins wrote, "that the department didn't like the kids occupying downtown because they were having too much fun." Regardless, he admits, "I gave out a myriad of uniform traffic citations to kids doing nothing wrong, really, but there was always the broken taillight, failure to use a turn signal to change lanes[,] . . . illegal use of a motor vehicle horn. . . . Harassment was the name of the game, and the kids knew it."[23] The display of police power sent a clear signal about who was welcome downtown and for what purposes, about who the city belonged to and what it was for. Still, it sometimes left the public to wonder about the cops' priorities. In 1988, as the police bureau was enduring one of its periodic staffing shortages, crime victims complained that the bureau wouldn't dispatch officers to investigate burglaries or car theft, but it did deploy forty cops every weekend to stop kids from driving along Broadway.[24]

Likewise, during the first decade of the twenty-first century, the bureau carried on a years-long contest of wills against the so-called Zoobombers, a group of daredevils who took to racing children's bicycles downhill on Highway 26, from the zoo to downtown, at speeds approaching forty miles per hour. The cops wrote tickets, seized bikes, detained "bombers," and even asked the transit authority to interrupt light rail service to impede travel to the race's starting point.[25]

In the spring of 2001, Mayor Vera Katz announced a new project to rid the city of posters on telephone poles. Police would step up enforcement against this long-tolerated but technically illegal practice, and inmate work crews would strip utility poles throughout the city, tearing off all the concert notices, political agitprop, lost cat posters, and yard sale signs. It wasn't long before the cops confronted a musician, DJ Seiss, as he was putting up posters for a show. When he refused to let them search his bag, they jumped him and slammed his head against the ground. He was charged with interfering with an officer and resisting arrest, but the charges were later dropped.[26]

Broken Windows

From one perspective, the opportunity for unauthorized, self-organized, spontaneous, and noncommercial activity—skateboarding, zoobombing, cruising (of both sorts), and raves—is exactly what makes a city vibrant, attractive, interesting, and fun. From another point of view, it is a challenge to public order, a half-step from chaos, and a precursor to crime.

This second attitude received its most decisive articulation in a 1982 *Atlantic Monthly* article by James Q. Wilson and George L. Kelling titled "Broken Windows." The idea, as they explained it, is that small signs of disorder create an environment that seems "untended," uncared for, and ultimately ungoverned, leading to serious crime. The job of the police, then, is to enforce community norms as well as (or even instead of) the law, to act quickly and with as much force as needed to counteract any sign of disorder before the weeds of chaos can take root and spread.[27]

"There is no good evidence to support the broken windows theory," the criminologist Bernard Harcourt argues at length in his book *Illusion of Order*. "The existing social-scientific data [suggest] that neighborhood disorder is not significantly related to homicide, burglary, physical assault, rape, or purse-snatching/pocket-picking victimization when the antecedent neighborhood characteristics (such as poverty, stability, race, and collective efficacy) are held constant."[28] Yet the broken windows idea has been incredibly influential in police circles, probably because it corresponds to the way the cops *already* understood social order and their role in preserving it. What Wilson and Kelling offered was not really a theory, which would be judged against evidence and revised accordingly, but a Hobbesian just-so story. It proved particularly popular among the very administrators who did the most to bring community policing to Portland. Charles Moose explicitly credits the "broken windows" concept as guiding his approach.[29] Don Clark too invoked the idea in its most literal form, making a point of "eradicating both broken glass and graffiti" at Columbia Villa, seeing these as signs of gang activity.[30]

"Broken windows" thinking informs much of what the police do, and, often as not, the practices of order-maintenance are less about prohibiting particular types of behavior than about distinguishing between orderly and disorderly *people*. Enforcement practices then come to define the categories (orderly and disorderly) and the perceptions of the individuals and groups so classified. Police do not only punish certain types (or groups) of people; in the process they also stigmatize them, mark them in the public mind as disorderly, as dangerous, as suspects, as offenders, as criminals, as people deserving punishment.[31]

Sit/Lie, Appeal, Repeat

Predictably, the most frequent object of enforcement in quality-of-life campaigns has always been the city's large and growing homeless population.[32]

For decades, the City of Portland has sought after some acceptable (and constitutional) means of making it illegal for homeless people to appear in public—despite the fact that, more or less by definition, they have no other place to be. Camping bans, "sidewalk use ordinances," "street access" codes, crackdowns on panhandling, and mandatory "services" backed with the threat of incarceration have each been instituted one after another, enforced for a while, then rejected by the courts, only to be revised and reintroduced.[33]

It can be hard to know which rules are in effect at any given time, but there is no question whom the laws are meant to control. Speaking in 2009, Central Precinct Commander Mike Reese (who would later become police chief and then sheriff) was open about targeting homeless teenagers: "The folks we're really having a problem with are these *Road Warrior* youth." In fact, Mike

Kuykendall—then vice president of the Portland Business Alliance and cochair of the mayor's Street Access for Everyone (SAFE) committee; later director of services in the police bureau—told the *Portland Mercury* that the "Street Access" law was designed with these kids in mind: "The behavior of many of the teenagers and young adults who spend their days on Portland streets was the impetus behind the SAFE ordinance, as many businesses were impacted by the negative impression they were giving downtown. . . . So it makes sense this group is receiving a majority of the warnings and citations."[34]

Portland Copwatch argued that the "sit-lie" ordinance, which made it illegal to take up space on the sidewalk, invited selective enforcement by its very nature: "Many people obstruct pedestrian traffic . . . people waiting for buses, people stopping to talk or windowshop, people who camp out for a cherished spot on parade routes, people who stop to listen to or watch street performers, people who wait in line to buy food at the food stands, etc."[35] In 2008, 133 of the 170 sit-lie citations went to homeless people; no citations were issued in connection to signboards or sidewalk cafes, which equally obstruct the pedestrian right-of-way.[36]

Sometimes the police undertook a more concerted effort. In the spring of 1998, police instituted a "Street Youth Mission" to enforce truancy laws in the downtown area. Fifty-two kids were apprehended in a single day. Six were arrested for drugs or on outstanding warrants, and the rest were returned to their parents' homes.[37] In the winter of 2005–06, about thirty reserve officers were dispatched to the downtown area and to the retail strip along Northwest Twenty-Third Avenue; citing the sit-lie ordinance, they issued warnings to move people away from commercial areas. A police bureau memo outlined a "holiday plan" consisting of "selective enforcement and aggressive hospitality."[38]

The use of warnings rather than tickets is typical and telling. The real purpose was not to win convictions but to push poor people out: to force them out of commercial areas, then out of neighborhoods, out of parks, out of whatever remote nook they might find, and so on, endlessly. The ordinance cited—in whichever form, with whatever parameters and exemptions and constitutional niceties—was mainly a signal about who was welcome and who was undesirable.

Who Is My Neighbor?

The one-sided class war often targeted those who helped poor people meet their basic needs.

Beginning in the late nineties, St. Francis of Assisi Parish, which treated its property as a park and allowed homeless people to spend time there, came under increasing pressure from neighborhood businesses and police. Anne Hughes, owner of a nearby coffee shop, kept records of drug dealing, fights, and other illegal activity she observed in the area of the church.[39] Police persistently harassed staff and clients at the St. Francis Dining Hall, especially asking Latino people for immigration papers. One officer, Mary Wheat, frankly stated to an observer from Portland Copwatch that the police were "after the Hispanics."[40] In September 2003, police declared the facility a "chronic nuisance" and forced the church to close the park and suspend some of its services.[41]

During the same period, a similar campaign led by the Sunnyside Neighborhood Association focused on Sunnyside Centenary United Methodist Church. The church had served meals to the hungry for almost two decades, but the Sunnyside neighborhood had lately been, as the *Oregonian* put it, "rediscovered."[42] Later the paper was more forthright: "In fact, tensions between the church and neighborhood have grown more pronounced in recent years as Sunnyside experiences a renaissance. That renewal is fueling gentrification, a process in which downtrodden neighborhoods with low property values gradually transform into upscale enclaves with rising values—and taxes—as homeowners with greater disposable incomes move in."[43] As the neighborhood changed, so did the character of the neighborhood association. Citywide, participation in these organizations had peaked in the 1980s, but as popular enthusiasm waned, control over them was increasingly captured by business owners and others pushing a "not-in-my-backyard" agenda.[44] David Leslie, head of the Ecumenical Ministries of Oregon, said that such attitudes raised a biblical question: "Who is my neighbor?"[45]

Sunnyside Methodist tried to compromise, holding meetings with concerned homeowners and suspending services for three months in 1999. When they began serving the meals again, they hired a security guard and organized a volunteer foot patrol. It was not enough. A few months later, the city revoked the church's permit for the meals. Elizabeth Normand, the land-use hearings officer responsible for the decision, pointed to "police call-data" showing fewer reported crimes during the three-month hiatus and concluded that the "program . . . seriously reduce[d] the safety and livability of that neighborhood."[46] She suggested without any sense of irony: "Those who have been getting meals at Sunnyside can go to St. Francis."[47]

Special Treatment

For some cops the harassment of the destitute was practically a specialty. Officer Richard Olson, for example, was awarded a "Commendation Medal" in 1998 for breaking up over 350 homeless encampments.[48] When the head of the Mounted Patrol, Sergeant David Pool, retired in 2002, Portland Copwatch reflected on his nineteen years in the saddle: "His approach to homeless people involved verbal abuse, habitual harassment, and selective enforcement of loitering, littering, and trespassing laws, among others. Copwatch members have documented dozens of incidents between Pool and street youth. In each, he belittled them and their problems, calling them 'worthless,' 'low-lifes,' and 'whores.' Pool also routinely confiscated property without cause and threatened to beat suspects."[49]

Probably no Portland police officer has been so innovative and systematic about his harassment, however, as Jeffrey Myers, who came to Portland in 2000 specifically because he was "interested in community policing." But he did not like what he found when he arrived. "I thought the whole system . . . was broken. It was very dysfunctional . . . and I sought a holistic approach." As Senior Neighborhood Officer, he decided to focus on "livability issues" on the west side. Over the course of a few months in late 2003, Myers initiated several efforts to secure his own view of public order. He had the Oregon Department of Transportation dig up a community garden maintained by the First Presbyterian Church, and he began a program to track trespass warnings for people found camping in the landscaped strip alongside the freeway. But Myers's singular contribution was the creation of a secret list of downtown's most-arrested people—"the dirty thirty"—which he then distributed among officers patrolling the area.[50]

The program was biased in at least two respects. Of the thirty-five people on Myers's initial list, at least twelve were homeless and twenty-four were Black.[51] Regardless, under the Neighborhood Livability Crime Enforcement Program, this "Chronic Arrestee List" was soon expanded to include four hundred persistent low-level offenders, 52 percent of whom were Black. Those on the list would be singled out for special attention—surveillance, enforcement, and prosecution. Even minor offenses would automatically be charged as felonies, and they would face a choice between a trial and mandatory drug treatment.[52]

The *Oregonian* was enthusiastic about the idea: "This list epitomizes community policing."[53] But public defender Chris O'Connor saw the obvious problems: "It's a sad state of affairs when you force someone to commit a felony in order to get mental health or drug treatment. . . . Not to mention that the fundamental lesson of the 20th century seems to me to be that we shouldn't put people's names on lists, and then target them for special treatment."[54] In 2010, it was revealed that, after almost a decade in action and at a cost of nearly $2.5 million each year, the program had managed to place only seventy-seven people in recovery programs.[55]

Defining Disorder

Who defines order? Who decides what behavior is acceptable? It is clear after just a moment of thought that no neutral definition of *order* is possible. As Harcourt asks, "Why is it that eccentric clothes, youthful exuberance, or loitering is disorderly? . . . And why should we distinguish so sharply between street disorder and other forms of disorder? Everyday forms of tax evasion—paying cash to avoid sales tax, paying workers or household help under the table, using an out-of-state address—are also disorderly. Insider trading, insurance misrepresentation, police corruption, and police brutality: these are all disorderly. Yet they fit nowhere in the theory of order-maintenance policing. How come?"[56]

The answer is very simple: police tend to follow the visible lines of power. The standards they enforce will, in general, be those of the business class rather than the working class, of homeowners rather than the homeless, of adults rather than adolescents, of established and assimilated whites rather than immigrants and people of color.

Neighborly Prosecutions

Building on the idea of community policing and responding to demands from business owners to more aggressively prosecute minor "quality-of-life" offenses, in 1990 District Attorney Michael Schrunk launched the first-of-its-kind community prosecutor program in the Lloyd District. "Portland was going through a redevelopment phase on the east side of the river," Schrunk later explained. "It was an under-utilized area, but it was also a high crime area for street robbery, prostitution, dumping, and car thefts. A group of people got together and formed a safety action committee and . . . asked if they could have a lawyer who would be there all the time."[57]

Wayne Pearson, the first neighborhood DA, held public meetings to win the trust of residents and to identify their problems. He convinced the Lloyd District Community Association to write to judges, urging stricter penalties for minor offenses. And he trained private security companies and volunteer "citizen-informers" to collect evidence and build prosecutable cases. Local businesses paid his salary.[58]

Crime fell in the Lloyd District, and the program was soon replicated around the city. By the time it was discontinued in 2016, the Multnomah County DA's Neighborhood Unit was prosecuting about five thousand misdemeanor cases per year. Nearly a quarter of those charged with quality-of-life offenses (24 percent) were Black.[59]

The Ruling Class

In the downtown area, the standards the police enforce, the priorities they follow, and the interests they defend, have for years been to a startling degree those identified by the Portland Business Alliance (PBA).

Created during Mayor Neil Goldschmidt's efforts to revitalize the city center in the 1970s, the PBA (renamed the Portland Metro Chamber in 2023) serves as the chamber of commerce for downtown Portland and enjoys a quasi-governmental right to tax area businesses. In terms of either dollars spent or visits to public officials, it has long been the city's most active lobby group—and its most powerful. By the PBA's own account, it is "the primary advocate for the business community and active in all aspects of public policy which could adversely effect [*sic*] that community." In this role it has drafted legislation criminalizing homelessness, argued against bike lanes, fought tax increases, and opposed a city council resolution against the US invasion of Iraq.[60]

The PBA has long taken a role in enforcement as well. Since 1988 it has operated the "Clean and Safe" program in a designated 212-block area of downtown. Funded by their business tax, the program arranges for sidewalk cleaning, graffiti removal, and a group of "Portland Guides" or "Downtown Ambassadors" who offer directions to tourists while alerting police to panhandlers and other signs of disorder.[61] Derisively nicknamed "Pickleheads" in the 1990s for the bright green hats they wore, the guides are essentially low-wage hall monitors for the urban core.

The PBA has sometimes leased sworn officers from the city—including direct access to the Mounted Patrol—to focus on "order maintenance problems" and has contracted with Portland Patrol, Inc. (PPI), a private company whose agents carry guns and wear uniforms almost indistinguishable from those of the PPB.[62] In addition to writing exclusions for suspected drug dealers, sex workers, or others violating city ordinances, the private guards (as specified in their contract) endeavored to "wake up all individuals who use the sidewalk, and business doorways, as sleeping locations."[63] In 1997, Sheriff Dan Noelle deputized PPI guards, granting them the power to make arrests.[64]

The transfer of the state's authority to a private entity worried, among others, the city auditor: "The problem arises when security, enforcement, and management of public spaces are decided by one paying sector of the community without the city's oversight and public input." Sociologist Johanna Brenner put it more starkly, describing Clean and Safe and similar "Enhanced Service Districts" as "part of a larger decades-long process of the privatization of the commons [in which] underfunded city governments have allowed commercial property owners to take control over city space."[65]

Livability and Exclusion

The emphasis on livability has led the police to focus not so much on crime as on disorder, bringing coercive attention to minor offenses and even violations of social norms that may not themselves be illegal. Fables about "broken windows" have simply offered an intellectual pretext for the cops' traditional preoccupations—drugs, sex work, homelessness, noisy teenagers, and graffiti. The standards police enforce tend to be those congruent with business interests and middle-class propriety, such that the activities—or even the *presence*—of the young, the poor, and people of color may be regarded presumptively as disorder. In fact, this process has often been surprisingly literal and linear, with business groups setting and even enforcing the rules.

All of this, over time, has had the effect of increasing inequality, a fact that worried Chief Moose, not only for its implications in terms of justice but also for its consequences for the stability of society. Delivering his farewell address to the City Club, Moose took the opportunity to castigate Portland's liberal elite, urging them to find more funding for social services, especially in housing, education, and drug treatment. The alternative, he warned, was more and more spending on police and prisons, with more arrests, more inmates, and "more violent confrontations when the police come up against the people that you have decided to make have-nots."[66]

CHAPTER 21

Militarizing Prohibition, Sexual Misconduct, and Exclusion Zones

Charles Moose became chief of police in 1993, making him the first Black person to hold the job.

Before Mayor Vera Katz made her selection, she went to several community groups—including the PTA, business groups, and fraternal organizations—and asked them what they wanted from the police bureau's leadership. Moose later wrote that what tipped the scales in his favor, he thought, even more than his experience with community policing, was his support for gay rights. He had been one of a very few officers willing to join Chief Potter in marching in the annual gay pride parade. "I thought it was important for the police to show they supported civil rights," Moose explained, "everyone's civil rights." It was a courageous gesture and a good career move; it won the mayor's favor. But it did not win him any points with the line officers. Many took the image of their commanders marching in uniform amid throngs of joyous and flamboyant queers as (in Moose's words) "a real affront."[1]

Inevitably too, much of the distrust of Moose's leadership was overtly racist. When he and his wife moved to 422 Northeast Going Street—in the neighborhood that then had the highest homicide rate in the city—graffiti appeared inside one police stationhouse: "The chief's moving in his ho' and turning her out." One night when Chief Moose was away, his wife, Sandy, a white woman, received a menacing early-morning phone call: "Nobody fucks niggers." She called the police, and the officer who took the report commented, "What did you expect, moving into that neighborhood like you did?"[2]

Moose's term as chief in many respects resembled an extension of his efforts at Iris Court. The Gang Resistance Education and Training (GREAT) program sent officers to give presentations in elementary and middle schools and sponsored a basketball team coached by Gang Enforcement officers.[3] A day care opened in the Justice Center. Moose created a Crisis Intervention Team to respond to people suffering from mental illness. He required new recruits to have a four-year degree and reduced the number of supervisory ranks in order to flatten the hierarchy.[4] He also made an effort to improve relations with the union. The PPA was provided drafts of new policies to review before they went into effect, and the union's suggestions were usually incorporated.[5] At the same time, Moose took steps toward the militarization of the police force, making ballistic vests mandatory and purchasing 225 AR-15 assault rifles.[6]

It was notably at the height of "community policing" that Portland saw an abrupt and seemingly permanent increase in deadly force. Police killed twenty-four people during the nineties—more than twice the number of any previous decade.[7]

Community Policing and Mass Incarceration

Moose was not the only police leader to militarize community policing. After leaving Oregon in 1978, former Multnomah County Sheriff Lee Brown—"the father of community policing"—went on to become the public safety commissioner in Atlanta, then police chief in Houston, police commissioner in New York, and director of the Office of National Drug Control Policy ("Drug Czar") under President Bill Clinton. He would later be elected the first Black mayor of Houston, where he sought to apply the principles of community policing to other public services under the moniker "Neighborhood Oriented Government." He was a founding member of the Police Executive Research Forum and the first African American president of the International Association of Chiefs of Police. In every position he held, Brown promoted and refined his model for law enforcement. But in addition to community policing staples like storefront offices, victim assistance programs, and neighborhood watch patrols, in Houston he established special squads for drug and prostitution enforcement, a Zero Tolerance Unit, and a Mounted Patrol. In New York he introduced the federal "Weed and Seed" program, which paired strict enforcement with development aid. And he implemented a mapping system that supplied the foundation for CompStat, the technology that later facilitated Mayor Rudolph Giuliani's zero-tolerance crackdown.[8]

As the federal "Drug Czar," Brown continued seeking to "expand community policing, putting more police on the streets and taking guns out of the hands of criminals," while increasing the penalties for first-time offenders ("particularly young offenders").[9] He is proud to claim responsibility for the inclusion of the Community Oriented Policing Services (COPS) in the 1994 Violent Crime Control and Law Enforcement Act. But that law also eliminated prison education programs, introduced sixteen new capital crimes, established mandatory sentences, and increased prison time for offenses in specially designated "drug free zones."[10] The law represented, in the view of historian Elizabeth Hinton, "the largest and most draconian crime bill in American history."[11] It was also a massive spending bill, allocating $8.8 billion for local police departments to hire one hundred thousand additional officers, purchase new equipment, and implement community policing; $3 billion for the Border Patrol to hire more agents, buy surveillance equipment and weaponry, and build new immigrant detention facilities; and another $7.9 billion for the construction of new state prisons.[12] By the estimate of the Government Accountability Office, the multibillion dollar investment reduced reported crimes by about 1 percent.[13]

That is not to say that the crime bill had no effect. Clinton's policies amplified trends that were already well established, including especially the criminalization of drugs and the concomitant expansion of the prison population. In 1970, there had been fewer than 200,000 prisoners nationwide. By 1990, there were 1.1 million, and by 2000 there were 2.3 million.[14] The Justice Policy Institute later concluded, "The Clinton Administration's 'tough on crime' policies resulted in the largest increase in federal and state prison inmates of any president in American history."[15]

Mandatory Minimums

Also in 1994, Oregon voters passed Measure 11, establishing minimum sentences for sixteen violent offenses and requiring that juveniles aged fifteen and older be charged as adults for those crimes. The introduction of mandatory sentencing shifted power from the judge—who could assign a term of incarceration based on a view of the total circumstances—to the prosecutor, who could select charges to fit the penalty he wanted to exact. This arrangement allowed prosecutors to practically extort guilty pleas by systematically overcharging and then offering defendants the opportunity to plead to a lesser offense. More than 70 percent of Measure 11 cases were resolved with guilty pleas to reduced charges; in Multnomah County it was 74.6 percent.[16] The net result was more people in prison for longer terms. "In 1996 an offender indicted for a M11 offense was 36 percent more likely to go to prison than an offender indicted in 1994," the Oregon Criminal Justice Commission found. "The differences are even larger for the median length of stay, with an 81 percent increase from 1994 to 1996."[17] After Measure 11, Oregon's sentencing practices ranked among the most severe in the country, reversing a three-year decline in incarceration.[18] By the end of the 1990s, the state's prison population had surpassed ten thousand inmates, up from six thousand at the beginning of the decade. Approximately twenty-nine hundred of those were in prison as a result of Measure 11.[19]

Though the "typical M11 offender [was] white (74 percent)," the Criminal Justice Commission found "important racial disparities" in the law's application. Latino and Native men were each 1.6 times as likely to be indicted on Measure 11 offenses as white men, and Black men were an astonishing 4.4 times as likely. For women, Latinas were 1.1 times as likely to be indicted as white women; Native women were 2.3 times as likely; and Black women, 3.5 times as likely. In Multnomah County, from 2013 to 2018, 2.5 percent of those indicted under Measure 11 were Native Americans, 13.4 percent were Latino, and 33.4 percent were Black.[20] For comparison, 1.5 percent of the county's population was American Indian or Alaska Native in 2020, 12.9 percent Hispanic or Latino, and only 6.2 percent Black.[21]

Mass incarceration carried several opportunity costs, the price we paid in services not funded so that prisons could be built, maintained, and staffed. "While school districts cut hundreds of teachers," Governor John Kitzhaber lamented in a 1996 speech, "we will be hiring almost 1,000 new prison guards—many at youth correctional facilities. So, we won't be teaching your kids—but we'll be able to guard them well."[22] On balance, and looking back, it is hard to feel that the trade-off was worth it. According to a 2021 review by the Criminal Justice Commission, the effect of Measure 11 on crime was "relatively small, diminishing close to zero" over time.[23]

War Footing

Another device for sweeping millions of people into prison cells was the prohibition of drugs—an effort generally referred to as a war. This framing did a lot of work, carrying with it the suggestion of an existential conflict, promoting a military model for addressing it, and offering an a priori justification for violence.[24] No surprise, then, that the campaign involved the Portland Police in any number of constitutionally questionable practices.

For instance, the police set a "trap and trace" on the phone of a gardening supply company, collecting the numbers of all incoming calls without either party's knowledge or permission. They then monitored electricity usage at the homes of the garden center's customers, identified some they suspected of growing marijuana, and then conducted "knock and talk" searches, showing up unannounced and bullying their way into people's homes. Over the course of four years in the 1990s, the Portland police identified and interviewed almost five hundred suspects by these means.[25] In another case, police targeted a medical marijuana dispensary with a sting operation, followed by a raid.[26]

The obsession with drugs sometimes had deadly consequences. On the morning of January 27, 1998, members of the Marijuana Task Force approached a Southeast Portland home, hoping to talk their way inside and search it. When no one answered the door, Sergeant Jim Hudson picked up a paving stone and used it to smash the lock. Gunfire erupted from inside the house, injuring Hudson and Officer Kim Keist and killing Officer Colleen Waibel. The cops returned fire, hitting the occupant, Steven Dons, once in the chest. Hours later, the paramilitary Special Emergency Reaction Team (SERT) fired tear gas into the house and moved in. They found Dons shirtless and bloody on his kitchen floor. They hit him repeatedly with less-lethal shotgun blasts and removed his pants, then dragged him to their armored vehicle. A photograph from the scene shows police with automatic rifles standing over his naked body.[27]

A month later, on February 25, Dons was found dead in the Justice Center's medical unit. Guards say they discovered him at 4:45 a.m. with one end of a sheet wrapped around his neck and the other end tied around the frame of his adjustable hospital bed. Investigators concluded that, though he was paralyzed from the waist down and heavily medicated, he had rigged the sheet so as to strangle himself and then used a wad of paper and strip of tape to hold down the button and raise the bed. No explanation was offered as to how the surveillance camera in his room came to have toothpaste smeared over the lens. Within twelve hours, the medical examiner ruled the death a suicide; a grand jury agreed. Others remained skeptical, but Deputy DA Jim McIntyre candidly admitted that he just didn't care what had happened to Dons: "It is ridiculous in this day and age that we can only judge guilt in a courtroom trial."[28]

Hostile Work

The photograph of Dons—naked and prone on the bumper of a truck, displayed almost like a slain deer—is disturbing in several respects, but it fits with what we know about the culture of the elite Special Emergency Reaction Team.

In his memoir *Hunting Men*, Mike Davis of the Oregon State Police (OSP) reminisces about multi-agency paramilitary training at Camp Rilea, near Seaside. SEAL Team 2 trained local police on shooting under stress. The Sixth Army Group offered instruction on tactical entries. The OSP and FBI ran "scenarios . . . to practice hostage rescue." Davis clearly enjoyed playing soldier, but he does admit that summer camp antics sometimes got out of hand. "When you get that many guys working and playing together the pranks start to escalate. On one occasion Portland [cops] found an unlocked door to the barracks and then an unlocked room. They attacked one of our SWAT members[,] biting him all over and growling like a pack of dogs."[29]

Predictably, this sort of frat-house mischief sometimes took an unseemly and specifically gendered form. In May 2001, Officer Liani Reyna, the first woman to join the Special Emergency Reaction Team, filed an official complaint alleging a hostile work environment and discrimination based on her gender and sexual orientation. The *Oregonian* described a pattern of hazing that included "strip club outings, masturbating, [pretending to be a] supervisor having a bowel movement, [and] a form of discipline in which SERT members would force an officer to the ground while another officer would sit naked on the officer's face." New recruits would get themselves tattooed with the team symbol (a bat), were responsible for washing the dishes and cleaning the weapons of senior officers, had to haul the gear, and were made to sing for the squad's entertainment. They were also on occasion forced to wear dresses, carry purses, and perform strip teases. Commanding officers had known about the hazing for years. But despite the misogyny ingrained in many of these practices, a jury of five women and three men somehow concluded that such actions did not constitute a "hostile work environment" for the sole female officer.[30]

Exclusions

In its combination of legally dubious drug war tactics and rank misogyny, SERT merely concentrated features common throughout the police bureau.

Perhaps the most persistently unconstitutional weapon in the drug war arsenal was the designation of so-called drug free zones. The City of Portland established these zones in 1993, authorizing police to exclude a person from all such areas for ninety days after a drug arrest and a year after a conviction. If found in an exclusion zone during that period, one could be charged with criminal trespassing.[31]

Equally questionable "prostitution free zones" (PFZs) were created around the same time, with the aim of excluding sex workers and their clients. Brian Duddy, the "prostitution coordinator" in Southeast Precinct—nicknamed "the Ho King" by other cops—explained the focus on workers and customers rather than bosses: "Pimps are just real hard to work."[32]

Advocacy groups—*Danzine*, Scarlet Letter, and the Portland Women's Crisis Line among them—generally opposed the PFZ approach. Explaining her opposition, Teresa Dulce, creator of *Danzine* (both a nonprofit and a magazine by and for sex workers) noted that trespassing carries a stiffer penalty than prostitution and is no doubt easier to prove.[33] Indeed, one officer said the exclusions were a "great tool" because no real evidence was required to move someone along: "Even if they didn't do anything, I just get them off *my* street."[34]

The criminalization of the sex trade left workers more vulnerable to abuse—from pimps, clients, and cops. Women in the industry took steps to protect themselves. *Danzine*, founded in 1995 as a forum for sex workers to tell their stories, also operated a "Bad Date Hotline."[35] And in 1998, Invisible Fringe circulated a flier with a photo of Sergeant David Howe, warning, "WATCH OUT! This cop has been harassing dancers and other women in the biz." They cited a pattern of intimidation, unlawful searches, and name-calling (specifically, "fucking bitches").[36] A few months later, Howe arrested a woman for trespassing in a PFZ; once he had her in the car, she says he forced her to masturbate while he watched. Commander Rosie Sizer (later police chief) recommended a ten-day suspension, but Chief Moose only reprimanded him for failing to radio his location. Less than two weeks later, Howe received the National Association of Police Organizations "Top Cop" award.[37] In 2007, he would resign after being arrested in a prostitution sting.[38]

Sexual Offenses

Howe was just one of a series of officers to be fired, indicted, or forced to resign for sexual offenses. In late 2003, Officer William Moffenbeier was arrested for criminal trespass, official misconduct, and third-degree sex abuse after uninvited contact with a woman he'd met on patrol. Rodney Murdock resigned amid accusations that he had inappropriate contact with sex workers while on duty. Jason Wood pled guilty to official misconduct related to his practice of asking women at traffic stops to show him their tattoos and underwear. He was placed on probation and lost his law enforcement certification. Matthew Kohnke was convicted of official misconduct after sexually assaulting a homeless woman while searching for drugs. She sued and received $25,000 from the city and $5,000 from Kohnke personally. Jason Faulk was convicted of official misconduct after taking advantage of a woman experiencing an emotional crisis, an abuse of power Portland Copwatch characterized as "an on-duty rape." Joseph Wild pled guilty to twenty counts of telephonic harassment and forty-one counts of official misconduct after making sexually explicit phone calls—sometimes threatening rape—to teenage girls he met in the course of his duties, female recruits at the police academy, and a domestic violence victim. In January 2012, former School Resource Officer Ryan Graichen was sentenced to ten years in prison for trading money, drugs, and alcohol to underage girls in exchange for sex. He had resigned in 2003 after he was caught videotaping female students, zooming in on their breasts, and making the tapes available for others. Also in 2012, Police Bureau Officer Scott Elliott was arrested for "luring a minor and online sexual corruption of a child." He was one member of a task force monitoring registered sex offenders.[39]

This is not a problem unique to the Portland Police Bureau. Multnomah County Sheriff's Deputy James Miller was arrested in 2012 after sexual contract with a prisoner.[40] And Deputy Christopher Green pulled over several women and ordered them to remove their clothing, saying that he was searching for a suspect with a flower tattoo. (That was a lie.) Nationwide, sexual offenses are the second-most-reported category of police misconduct, after excessive force.[41] Between 2009 and 2014, one thousand officers across the US lost their law enforcement certification because of sexual violence.[42] These sorts of abuses do not emerge from a vacuum. They speak, first of all, to the sense of impunity the police enjoy, as well as to the sexist, macho attitudes characteristic of cop culture. But more disturbingly the pattern would seem to point to an organization in which abuse, exploitation, and misogyny are institutionalized. To some degree this is probably inherent in the criminalization of sex work and other forms of policing sexuality. In the spring of 2010, it was revealed that cops were providing funds for informants to hire sex workers, whom they then arrested. District Attorney Michael Schrunk defended the practice: "Prostitution as you know exploits women, degrades neighborhoods, degrades people."[43] It is strange, then, to essentially subsidize a crime, only then to prosecute the purported victim.

Zone Out

Since their inception, the exclusion zones (like the sit-lie laws) were continuously subjected to legal challenges, ruled unconstitutional, reworked, and then reintroduced. The City's single-minded commitment to the strategy seems peculiar, since it is not clear that the program reduced crime in any way. *Danzine*'s Teresa Dulce noted that the prostitution free zones were exactly where one would be *most* likely to find sex workers.[44] And, according to Deputy District Attorney Jim Hayden, the Beech Drug Free Zone showed a 30 percent decrease in drugs arrests—but so did neighboring areas. The Alberta Drug Free Zone, in contrast, showed a 50 percent decrease, while nearby neighborhoods experienced a 15% *increase*, suggesting that concentrated enforcement simply dispersed drug sales to a larger area.[45]

But while the exclusion zones may not have had any effect on crime, they had a measurable impact on the lives of Black people. In 2007, after a consultant's report found enforcement in the drug free zones and prostitution free zones to be racially biased, Mayor Tom Potter allowed the ordinances creating them to expire without pursuing renewal. The mayor's office explained: "In all zones, African Americans are excluded 68 percent of the time, compared to 54 percent for Whites."[46]

Some neighborhood groups, in Montavilla in particular, demanded that the PFZs be reinstated and conspicuously photographed people they suspected of involvement in the sex trade. Mayor Potter and Police Chief Rosie Sizer settled on a plan to keep pressure on sex workers and their clients, stepping up patrols and asking for exclusions from particular neighborhoods as a condition of probation. Police also began a series of undercover stings along Southeast Eighty-Second Avenue, with male officers posing as customers and female officers as sex workers.[47] The city then created the 82nd Avenue Prostitution Advisory Council, which made recommendations to shape city policy. Based on the committee's guidance, instead of sex workers being tried in community court and sentenced to community service or a short stay in jail, they would henceforth be given a choice between mandatory counseling or a criminal trial. Public defenders and representatives of the Portland Women's Crisis Line objected to the coercive help model. On the one hand, they asked, couldn't counseling just be made available to those who felt like they needed it, without having to be arrested first? On the other hand, the critics pointed out, the proposed counseling "solution" did not actually address the root problem, which was poverty. The cops' own data supported this point. According to a survey conducted by the police bureau, most people who engage in sex work do so because they lack money. Crystal Tenty, the Crisis Line's sex industry outreach coordinator, went further and asked sex workers what they needed. Most of the answers came down to one thing: living-wage jobs. At a community forum, she pointed out that the discussions about sex work were being framed by cops, politicians, and the neighborhood associations but were leaving out the people most directly affected. No sex workers served on the advisory council.[48]

The drug free zones were eventually brought back at the urging of downtown business owners. In 2011, Mayor Sam Adams met with business leaders and then announced new "Illegal Drug Impact Areas," from which those convicted of a drug offense could be excluded by a judge's order. Those excluded would also be eligible for assistance from the Service Coordination Team, the group of police, corrections officers, and social workers who had previously managed the Chronic Arrestee List.[49] At the same time, the city council also created new "gun free zones." By August of that year, thirteen people had been excluded: one Latino, one Asian, three white, and eight Black—in a city that was 75 percent white.[50]

The Dangers of Community Policing

The drug free zones and prostitution free zones derived, in a sad fashion, from Don Clark's strategy at Columbia Villa, which emphasized social services but fused landlord and police authority and allowed the cops to formally exclude people they saw as undesirables. Equally so, the shift in Portland government toward democratic participation at the neighborhood level paved the way for NIMBY campaigns against sex workers and churches that fed the homeless. Lee Brown started by urging sheriff's deputies to solve neighborhood problems at the neighborhood level; scaling up to federal policy, he became convinced that the drug war could be won with one hundred thousand new cops and a million more people in prison.

The pattern shows something of the radioactive nature of policing, its tendency to poison everything with which it has contact. Things that, in another context, might be harmless or even beneficial—youth sports or neighborhood meetings—take on a different hue as the police convert them to means for their own ends. This speaks too to the problems with police reform—not only the futility but also the real danger. Measures taken to make the police more responsive to community needs inevitably become new sources of intelligence, legitimacy, and thus power. As police networks become increasingly embedded in the life of the community, the community, sometimes without realizing it, surrenders some of its power to the police and makes its resources available for the cops' purposes. However benevolent the intent, and however narrow the initial objective, each new power the police acquire will contain the temptation to expand, find new outlets and novel applications, feel its own strength, and extend its reach ever further.

In practice, community policing tends to emphasize not the ways the police might help the community but the ways the community can help the police. In his 1994 book *Skinhead Street Gangs*, Portland Police gang Detective Loren Christensen devoted a chapter to "Working with the Community," offering advice on public presentations, partnerships with neighborhood organizations, and use of the media. "As a result of Portland officers giving hundreds of presentations to myriad audiences in the community," he wrote, "citizens are now much more informed about gangs and thus better able to give the police good information."[51] From the detective's perspective, this was the purpose of community engagement: more cooperation, better intelligence.

In 1994, the police bureau obtained its first search warrant "based solely on observations and statements from trained neighbor observers."[52] A few years later, a front-page photo in the *Portland Tribune* showed ten cops in helmets, bulletproof vests, combat boots, and blue fatigues aiming pistols and assault rifles at a suspect's house. These cops—members of the Northeast Precinct senior neighborhood officer unit, a team focused on quality-of-life enforcement—had received a warrant based on six months of intensive surveillance conducted by neighbors. The police admitted that the raid would probably not produce criminal convictions but would more likely lead to the tenants' eviction and homelessness. Regardless, Police Chief Mark Kroeker pointed to this exercise as an example of the promise of community policing: "We have a police bureau that is understaffed, underfunded and overwhelmed. But we have a community that is willing to work, willing to help."[53]

PART III

Public Order and Popular Resistance

CHAPTER 22

Skin City and Little Beirut

Klan Mentality

In 1981, after a labor arbiter reinstated the two cops fired for leaving dead possums in the doorway of a Black-owned business, the Reverend C. T. Vivian, director of the National Anti-Klan Network, traveled to Portland to help local organizers prepare for what would come next. Accusing the police of having a "Klan mentality," he warned that the arbiter's decision would surely embolden white supremacists and lead to violence. The police bureau's Intelligence Division responded by opening a file on Vivian.[1]

It would not be long before his fears would be realized. In 1988, a racist skinhead gang murdered an Ethiopian immigrant named Mulugeta Seraw, beating him to death on a Southeast Portland street.[2]

Portland for years had been a center for skinhead activity, much of it racist and much of it *anti*racist, and conflict between the two was frequent and bloody. The subculture grew so prominent that Portland was sometimes called "Skin City."[3] But whenever possible, the police bureau's Gang Enforcement Team—and especially its resident skinhead specialist, Loren Christensen—downplayed the political dimension and framed the conflict as a gang rivalry, insisting on a kind of equivalency between racists and antiracists. In his 1994 book *Skinhead Street Gangs*, Christensen asserted unambiguously, "The antiracist skinheads are just as violent as the racist—at times, even more so."[4] The cops' investigative priorities reflected this attitude. Though the police would conspicuously surveil the homes of antiracist skinheads and take pictures of anyone visiting, on at least two occasions they failed to investigate shots fired into these same houses.[5]

For Jon Bair—who, as a young man, went to prison for killing a racist skinhead—the cops' biases made perfect sense. "I believe the police exist to protect the powerful," he told an interviewer decades later, "and our groups existed to protect those who don't have power. So the motivations are really different right from the beginning, which puts us at odds with the police. White supremacy is not a threat to the police. People who hold racist views, they're not a threat to law enforcement. So it makes sense that they'd be treated as less of a threat."[6]

Mulugeta Seraw's murder shocked the conscience of the liberal city, and the police were suddenly—if briefly—moved to act. Extra staff were assigned to answer phones, conduct interviews, and perform surveillance. The FBI joined the effort, and the district attorney empaneled a grand jury. Three members of East Side White Pride went to prison, and White Aryan Resistance (WAR) founder Tom Metzger was held liable in a civil trial. Even as WAR was bankrupted, Metzger remained defiant. "The movement will not be stopped in the puny town of Portland," he boasted. "Don't you understand? We're in your colleges. We're in your armies. We're in your police forces. . . . Where do you think a lot of the skinheads disappeared to?"[7]

In her book *A Hundred Little Hitlers*, Elinor Langer compares this sequence of events to a morality play. By focusing on Nazis—in particular, a despised youth subculture and an outside agitator—liberal Portland was able to avoid facing the racism of its own history, culture, and institutions.[8]

Antiwar, Anti-Bush

During the same period, at the end of the eighties and the start of the nineties, unruly demonstrations would occur any time President George Herbert Walker Bush or Vice President Dan Quayle came to town. Police regularly responded with arrests and violence.[9]

That most prolific of Portland Police memoirists, Loren Christensen, recalls: "On every [presidential] visit, the protestors came out in force, and every time they ripped up the streets. . . . [They would] vandalize property and fight the police. They carried out their resistance with lots of laughter, cheering, dancing. . . . It was party time for all of them." As Christensen tells it, it was less of a party for the cops, who worked "for 12 to 14 hours without a break, without water, and without using the restroom. During a couple of the big anti-Bush riots downtown, we worked from 6AM to 2AM." The fatigue was corrosive to discipline. "After 14 hours of intensity, squad leaders, sergeants, and lieutenants can have trouble controlling troops pushed to their physical and emotional limits. In fact, supervisors can have trouble controlling themselves."

The resulting violence was sometimes counterproductive. "There were times when an overly aggressive police officer or sergeant in charge of 10 officers would ignite a peaceful protest into a riot."[10]

Compared to the protests against the 1991 Gulf War—which reached upward of 15,000 people—demonstrations against presidential (or vice-presidential) visits were relatively small, though they generated a lot of arrests. When 150 people blocked the path of Dan Quayle's limousine in September 1989, twenty were arrested. The following May, 300 protesters threw eggs, fruit, and small explosives at President Bush, who was in town for a fundraiser. Seventy-five cops attacked the crowd, producing a prolonged brawl and twenty-five arrests. In September 1990, Quayle returned and was greeted by about 300 protesters. Fifty-one were arrested, one of whom successfully sued for $25,000. When Bush returned a year later, about 400 protesters were met with almost two hundred cops. The *Oregonian* reported, "Flags were burned, rocks and eggs were thrown at police, Republicans were spat upon and jeered at, 30 protestors were arrested and two policeman were slightly hurt."[11]

It was during this period that a White House staffer gave Portland the nickname "Little Beirut."[12]

The Hokey-Pokey at the X-Ray Cafe

A small collective that helped with logistics for the protests took *Beirut* as their name—"Boisterous Extremists for Insurrection against Republicans and other Unprincipled Thugs."[13] One member of this group, Douglas Squirrel, was identified in police files as the "leader of the anarchists," which then led to his arrest when the cops attacked a punk show in the summer of 1993.[14]

Based on an informant's tip that a disturbance was imminent, police amassed all available officers and lined up in helmets outside the X-Ray Cafe, an all-ages club located just past the west end of the Burnside Bridge. A standoff ensued, which was later mischaracterized as "the Anarchist Riot." Mostly kids from the club just taunted the police. The X-Ray's DJ played "The Hokey Pokey" over the club's outside speakers, and video from the incident shows a few people doing the dance. (The cops did not dance.) When some of the kids tried to leave through the police lines, a ruckus ensued; then the crowd reversed course, taking a side street, marching through downtown and leaving a total of two broken windows in its wake.[15] Some riot.

Thirty-one people were arrested, but only Squirrel was held for as long as five days. Files released as part of the resultant lawsuit revealed an extensive pattern of political surveillance, with informers infiltrating meetings and collecting intelligence unrelated to any criminal investigation, in violation of Oregon law. One file included notes from a 1992 meeting of the People Overseeing Police Study Group (POPSG), discussing possible reforms to the civilian review board.[16] Resolving the lawsuit, a judge's order further restricted police intelligence activity, but the surveillance continued—often against the same targets.

POPSG founder Dan Handelman was named in a 1998 "Criminal Intelligence Report" that surfaced after police arrested twenty-five people protesting the bombing of Iraq and then questioned them about their political activities and about the leadership of the demonstration.[17] The document identified Handelman as the "Leader" of the Peace and Justice Works Iraq Affinity Group and expressly classified him as a "non-criminal," while noting that he had been "very active in calling for, arranging, and sponsoring these demonstrations concerning U.S. involvement with Iraq."[18] The continuity here was pretty tight: POPSG—which would later become Portland Copwatch—was itself an outgrowth of the antiwar movement, founded soon after the Gulf War as a committee of Portland Peaceworks (later Peace and Justice Works) representing a domestic expression of the organization's antimilitarist ideals.[19]

Collecting political intelligence without any justifying law enforcement pretext clearly violated both state law and the judge's prior order, but remedies remained elusive.

Anarchist Bicyclists

A few weeks after the X-Ray Cafe episode, the cops started targeting what their files called "Anarchist bike rallies."[20]

Beginning in October 1993, dozens of cyclists gathered together once a month for a Critical Mass group ride. "Come ride your bike or board," one flier suggested, "for a sustainable, environmental future and against the death culture of cars." For more than a decade, these rides would be subject to continual police harassment. Mostly, cops would arrive in numbers and write tickets—*lots* of tickets. The January 1994 ride featured eight cyclists, eight cops, and eight citations. A memo from Sergeant B. L. Mulvihill to Central Precinct Commander

Mike Garvey explained, "Because this group continues to demonstrate or rally each month, and because no approach we have made alleviates the problems associated with each demonstration, it is time to pick up our pressure and issue citations for every violation that occurs."[21]

Police would often aggressively flank or follow the Critical Mass ride, trying to control its direction or break it up into smaller groups. These tactics could be extremely dangerous. In January 1999, a cyclist was struck by a squad car. But one police sergeant explained the bureau's priorities: "Safety is not the issue. Following the law is more important."[22]

There was a moment of hope in January 2005, when the new mayor (and former police chief) Tom Potter joined the Critical Mass ride himself. A spokesman for the mayor explained that Potter wanted to show his support for bicycling and "see for himself the dynamics of the evening's ride, and witness the interaction between bicyclists and police officers." As Potter saw it, these events called for "some problem-solving, not for some enforcement." The attempt to point the cops in a new direction worked—for exactly as long as the mayor was present. No citations were issued the night that Potter joined the ride. The next month, however, the cops arrived in larger numbers, mostly on bikes, and escalated enforcement. The mayor had clearly overestimated his influence, and his efforts at amelioration largely backfired. The cops saw his overture to Critical Mass as a sign of disrespect. "They were a little upset with me for being there," Potter admitted. The policing of the event thus took on a renewed significance and became part of a power struggle over the control of policing. "There is *intense* hatred between the mayor's office and the police bureau," Mary Volm, a former spokesperson for the Portland Bureau of Transportation, explained. "And so Potter goes out and makes an effort, and then all of a sudden the Traffic Division is out cracking down. So who runs the city?"[23]

By 2007, the overbearing police presence, innumerable citations, and frequent arrests came to be too much, and the rides finally ceased.[24] Ironically, though, bicycling had by that point become much more mainstream, and, as Critical Mass faded out, other large group rides were gaining acceptance. "These group rides are becoming more common," a 2009 police bureau training video, *Bicycle Traffic Enforcement*, explains. "At first glance, the groups may resemble Critical Mass, but they are often nothing like it. These aren't protests aimed at traffic disruption, but are semi-organized processions of good-humored fun-seekers who don't want confrontation with law enforcement."[25]

Think Global

In the latter half of the nineties, the left enjoyed a growing upsurge of activity on several fronts—the labor and environmental movements especially, and the two together in the antiglobalization movement.[26] Demonstrations became more frequent, larger, and more lively, featuring drum corps, giant puppets, and Radical Cheerleaders. They also sometimes included a civil disobedience or direct action component, aimed not just at making a statement but also at interfering with the operations of some business or government agency—or disrupting the smooth functioning of the city more generally. Anti-sweatshop activists swarmed into Niketown so often that the store would sometimes preemptively close when a demonstration just happened to occur nearby.[27]

Police violence was common, usually at the level of pushing and shoving. Looking back on this period, Portland Copwatch recalled the special role of the Mounted Patrol, which was "routinely called in to break up protests" and responded in ways that were "aggressive, dangerous, and often out of control." Between 1997 and 2002, Copwatch documented "scores of indiscriminate horse charges, pepper sprayings, illegal orders to disperse, and a few tramplings that . . . endangered bystanders almost as often as protestors."[28] Sometimes token arrests occurred, usually at the very end of a march, triggering a long and stressful standoff, often prolonging the event for hours.[29]

Two things happened right at the end of the century that moved the police to take a more aggressive approach to public assembly of all kinds. One was the November 1999 World Trade Organization protests in Seattle, where tens of thousands of demonstrators outmaneuvered and overwhelmed the police, blockading the streets and effectively delaying the ministerial meeting. Police in Portland, as much as anywhere, were determined not to let their city become the next Seattle. The other precipitous event was Mayor Vera Katz's selection of Mark Kroeker to be the chief of police.

Kroeker was hired in December 1999, having spent most of his career in the Los Angeles Police Department—where he had been second in command during the 1992 riots—then moving on to advise policing missions in Bosnia, Haiti, Rwanda, and Burundi, and working with the Palestinian-Israeli Anti-Incitement Committee. In other words, after decades in leadership at the famously militaristic LAPD, he spent several years as a police strategist in conflict zones, or in post-conflict societies, and then brought his skills to Little Beirut.[30]

Church, State, and Family

Throughout his time in Portland, Chief Kroeker would be continuously ensnared in controversies of his own making. Early on, he managed to alienate both his officers and the public by imposing a new dress code that prohibited long hair, beards, and earrings, while at almost the same time reducing the bureau's education standards.[31] Portland Police Association vice president Kurt Nelson worried that the haircuts marked a step toward militarization and might create an "us-vs.-them" mentality. PPA secretary-treasurer Tom Mack similarly worried about the police becoming "an occupying army" and thought that he detected something more sinister underlying the increased regimentation. "Will I be able to keep my own hair and eye color," Mack asked, "or has Chief Kroeker decided that blonde and blue will present the best uniform appearance?"[32]

The most pronounced of Kroeker's scandals came at the end of his first year, in November 2000, when the *Portland Alliance* ran a front-page story about comments he had made to a conference of Christian cops a decade before, denigrating queer people and urging patriarchal discipline in the family. "We are increasingly becoming a valueless, a lawless society," he told the assembly of pious lawmen, "and we become so more as we move to that day [when] 'alternative lifestyle' is being used for certain forms of perversion." He went on, solemnly and apocalyptically: "On this terrible issue of homosexuality, the other clear evidence in our society shows that, as we have moved away from control of certain criminal activities, the result has become a disaster."[33]

This was not mere prejudice; it was a *philosophy* of prejudice, a social theory, and a political program. In his speech, Kroeker articulated a coherent and deeply conservative worldview, in which the stability of the broader society depends on the authority that the father exercises over the family. He urged that each woman learn "how to be a submissive wife" and advocated corporal punishment, reminiscing about striking children with a three-foot paddle at a Christian summer camp.[34]

Springtime for Kroeker

Nowhere was Kroeker's authoritarian and militarist program more in evidence than when his troops confronted crowds.

On May 1, 2000, a parade advertised as a family-friendly celebration of worker power and the coming of spring only made it a few blocks before it was attacked by the Mounted Patrol. Some in the crowd responded by throwing things at the cops, and the police declared a "street-level emergency." Riot cops then pushed the group to Waterfront Park and ordered it to disperse. But as the marchers left the park, police attacked again and again, dividing the crowd into smaller and smaller groups. Dozens were injured—clubbed, pepper-sprayed, hit with less-lethal munitions, or trampled by horses.[35]

The police and their media apologists immediately began making excuses, focusing especially on the absence of a parade permit, the presence of "people dressed as anarchists," and reports of vandalism and violence. But *Willamette Week* conducted a careful analysis of the cops' video evidence and found that they were lying on almost every point: no broken windows, no barricaded streets, no terrified schoolchildren. Even the *Oregonian* came to decry the use of "riot control where a riot didn't exist." Complaints poured into the mayor's office.[36]

A week later, the mayor and police chief held a public forum at the Maranatha Church of God. Nearly five hundred people attended, and dozens demanded answers that the officials on stage were unwilling or unable to provide. Kroeker's only response to the controversy was to promise better "command and control."[37] His feeling, apparently, was that the problems on May Day derived not from too much militarization but rather from too little. His solution was to create the Rapid Response Team (RRT), which drilled in "Mobile Field Force Tactics."[38] The RRT comprised between sixty and seventy officers, organized into squads made up of one leader, twelve officers, a videographer, and a medic from the fire bureau. Over time, Portland's riot squad would be looked to internationally for its expertise, advising and training similar units around the world.[39]

Reclaim the Streets, Protect Our City

May Day 2000 was an early example of an emerging police strategy that scholars would later describe as "strategic incapacitation." Under this theory, Patrick Gillham writes, "police distinguish between two categories of protesters—contained and transgressive—in order to target those perceived most likely to engage in disruptive activities. Contained protesters, often referred to by police as 'good protesters' are generally known by police, use conventional and legal tactics, negotiate with police, make self-interested demands, and are generally older. By contrast, protesters considered 'bad' or transgressive articulate more abstract demands, use unpredictable and often illegal tactics, do not negotiate with police, and are generally younger."[40] The "contained" protesters would be allowed to proceed with their demonstrations, albeit within strict boundaries. The "transgressive" protesters would be met with coercive force. The process of classification would depend, in the ideal case, on extensive intelligence into all the protesting groups.[41] At the start of the new century, however, the Portland Police often relied on the permitting system as a blunt instrument dividing the "good protesters" from the "bad."

In the year following May Day 2000, the riot cops got plenty of practice with their new approach.

A September 26, 2000, Reclaim the Streets (RTS) event in downtown Portland was scheduled to coincide with similar events worldwide, including demonstrations outside the joint meetings of the International Monetary Fund and the World Bank in Prague. The RTS organizers, mostly young people who lived on the streets, closed off a city block for an unlicensed dance party. As Copwatch observers described it, police aggression then "turn[ed] what had been a pleasant, mildly disruptive gathering into a tense stand-off that degenerated into indiscriminate police violence.... Police attacked RTS participants and bystanders alike with horses, pepper spray and clubs." Regardless, the protesters held the street, and the size of the crowd grew to over three hundred as hours wore on. The police action itself seemed to draw people to the demonstration. By 7:30 p.m., the cops were standing impotently in back-to-back skirmish lines. The crowd then started to march, weaving its way through downtown as the cops struggled to keep up. At least thirty people were arrested over the course of the day, and dozens were injured, two with concussions.[42] Commissioner Jim Francesconi praised the police for their "amazing restraint."[43]

A few weeks later, the October 22 March Against Police Brutality proceeded without incident, a rare success that the police would cite again and again to show the ease and utility of the suddenly crucial permitting system. What they neglected to mention was that the permit cost the organizers hundreds of dollars, granted police control over the timing and route of the march, and required one marshal for every ten protesters. Police used the application process to collect intelligence on the participating organizations, and the demonstration itself was subjected to conspicuous surveillance and a heavy police presence.[44]

Less cooperative were the two thousand or so champagne-happy revelers filling Pioneer Square on New Year's Eve, as 2000 turned to 2001. Police claimed that members of the crowd, disappointed to hear that there would be no fireworks, started spontaneously breaking windows and attacking cops. Nine were arrested and an unknown number injured as police tried to break up the crowd. Witnesses told the *Portland Alliance* a different story, saying that the disturbance began when the police suddenly attacked a pair of drunk but harmless teenagers, leaving a pool of blood and several teeth on the sidewalk as they dragged them away—*then* people started throwing bottles.[45]

Despite or because of his officers' uneven record, when Kroeker appeared before the city council a few weeks later to explain the bureau's crowd control strategy, the downtown business class showed up in support, packing council chambers and wearing stickers reading "Protect Our City."[46]

Counterculture Crackdown

As winter turned to spring and everyone started to think again about May Day, the police brought new pressure to bear against the anarchist counterculture. Early 2001 saw an increase in police harassment of the local anarchist punk scene, with cops regularly stopping, questioning, and photographing young people in black clothing, paying particular attention to patches and tattoos. That March, forty cops raided a party at a punk house in the Alberta neighborhood, charging in with guns drawn and beating numerous people with their fists, flashlights, and nightsticks. Police took Polaroids of everyone present and asked what they knew about two underground direct-action groups, the Earth Liberation Front and Animal Liberation Front. Nine people were taken to detox, though most were sober. Three were arrested, and two—Chad Hapshe and Bjorn Einertsen—were charged with assault and, amazingly, kidnapping. (The police alleged the two young men jumped Sergeant Michael Fort and dragged him into the house, locking a door behind him.) When the suspects were arraigned on April 2, two plainclothes police officers—later identified by Portland Copwatch as Officer James Stradley and Detective Sergeant Neil Crannell, both of the Gang Enforcement Team—videotaped everyone entering the courtroom.[47]

Just before trial, Hapshe and Einertsen were offered a plea deal. To avoid risking a nine-year mandatory minimum sentence, they pled guilty to Assault

III and were sentenced to ninety days, divided between jail and a forest camp, followed by three years of probation.[48] The prosecuting attorney admitted that the evidence for the original charge was lacking: "As the case progressed, it became more problematic whether the kidnapping could be sustained at trial." "Why," then, the *Portland Mercury* asked, "did the DA take a routine assault charge and for six months aggressively prosecute it as a trumped-up kidnapping?" The paper supplied its own answer: for the sake of "putting a scare on the punks and activists."[49]

May First, Again

May Day threatened a repeat of the previous year's police riot. Chief Kroeker stated flatly that, unless a permit was in place, everyone on the street would be subject to arrest. The May Day Coalition resolved to call his bluff, refusing on principle to apply for the permit. The demonstration organizers cannily tied their free speech rights to the much broader issue of police violence, and they had spent the entire year expressing solidarity with other victims of police brutality, seeking to discredit the police bureau not merely as the regulators of public speech but also as a racist institution. Police violence took a place alongside workers' rights as the theme of the demonstration—an historically appropriate addition, given the holiday's origins commemorating police attacks against the movement for an eight-hour day.[50]

Kroeker's ultimatum and the coalition's recalcitrance left the city council in a bind, which they resolved through a brilliant if absurd bit of lateral thinking: they simply took out the permit themselves. "Could we have kept 1,000 people on the sidewalk, and do we arrest 1,000 people if we can't?," Mayor Vera Katz asked. "There was going to be a march whether we took out a permit or not." Katz's Chief of Staff (and later mayor) Sam Adams detailed a plan to minimize confrontation: horses and ATVs would be kept out of view, police would only enter the crowd to make arrests, and they would not videotape the demonstration. He refused to say whether they would send undercover officers. (Portland Police Association president Robert King was spotted in the crowd early on and quickly ejected from the march.) The police mostly kept their word, though two separate riot squads—the police bureau's Rapid Response Team and the Oregon State Police Mobile Response Team, together comprising more than one hundred officers—were each staged a few blocks away. Approximately fifteen hundred people marched from the North Park Blocks to Portland State University, flanked by a relatively spare contingent of thirty-six bike cops. No one was arrested, and no one was hurt.[51]

New Bush, New War

That fall produced a seismic shift in politics at every level. After Islamist terrorists flew hijacked planes into the World Trade Center and the Pentagon on September 11, 2001, and as the United States raced to war—first against Afghanistan and two years later against Iraq—antiwar protests again became a regular feature in the life of the city. In the winter of 2001, the police mainly responded by using the riot squad to keep protesters far from their targets, rather than trying to forcefully disperse crowds, resulting in relatively few arrests and injuries. However, when President George W. Bush visited a youth employment center in Northeast Portland, the police essentially locked down the entire neighborhood. Residents received automated phone calls warning them to remain indoors. At least two people were arrested when they tried to leave their homes.[52]

The following summer, the cops grew more aggressive. On August 12, a bike contingent was on its way to Waterfront Park to join a rally in support of locked-out longshore workers. Motorcycle cops hemmed then in, tackled a journalist who was taking photos, and issued numerous citations. On August 22, police used force to clear the entrance to a fundraiser featuring President Bush. After making a virtually inaudible announcement ordering the thousand people collected there to disperse, they pushed the crowd with batons, and then fired a variety of less-lethal munitions and used pepper spray, sometimes against unresisting protesters and even mere bystanders. Among the injured were journalists, observers representing the civilian review board, and an infant.[53] Graffiti started appearing around the city: "They pepper-sprayed babies."[54]

By the time the United States invaded Iraq, the antiwar movement had grown to historic proportions, and police were regularly responding to demonstrations with arrests and violence. Cops were given photos of activists to watch out for at protests, and the sheriff started reserving jail beds for demonstrators.[55]

The police attacked a February 15, 2003, antiwar protest that was blocking traffic in front of the Portland Center for the Performing Arts, using pepper spray to force people out of the street. A month later, when a smaller march broke away from a rally of thirty thousand people at Waterfront Park and approached the Morrison Bridge, the cops raced to head it off, striking one man with a vehicle and pepper-spraying several others. On March 20, after the US invasion of Iraq, the streets downtown were full of angry, militant crowds. A few protesters threw rocks at the police or damaged property, but the cops were relatively restrained, arresting individual people but using little force and no pepper spray. On the second day of demonstrations, however, riot cops formed lines in front of numerous buildings downtown and took a firm hand from the start. An attempted march was immediately halted with pepper spray and arrests. That set the tone for the week following, as the cops forcefully arrested anyone stepping off the sidewalk, often throwing them to the ground. A widely circulated photo showed two cops cornering a young woman, smiling as they pepper sprayed her face from inches away.[56]

Dave Schlegel was one of the officers who went undercover in the crowds, where he kept an eye out for weapons, bulging bags, gas masks, and people in hooded sweatshirts. He also took photos and tried to "identify leaders." On at least a couple of occasions, Schlegel experienced firsthand the violence of fellow officers who presumably did not recognize him. One cop tripped him during an antiwar march, and others laughed when he fell. Later, a group of cops drove by the crowd, pepper-spraying out the windows. From the perspective of the crowd, Schlegel later recalled, the Rapid Response Team "all looked alike.... they began to beat their nightsticks against their shin guards.... it was scary." Schlegel later infiltrated a follow-up meeting where activists discussed suing the City.[57]

Somehow It Comes Back to Nazis

As lawyers prepared a suit, they uncovered a number of unsavory facts about one of the officers named as a defendant. Captain Mark Kruger, who had been photographed blasting a young woman in the face with pepper spray, had also been photographed (off-duty) dressed in an historical Nazi uniform, complete with swastika. Two of Kruger's high school friends came forward to confess that as teenagers the three of them liked to drive around town listening to recordings of Hitler's speeches, tagging buildings with Nazi graffiti, and harassing people of color. After joining the police, Kruger had built a shrine at Rocky Butte honoring five Nazi soldiers, including a Waffen SS Obersturmfuhrer and the commander of a regiment that massacred thousands of POWs.[58]

Kruger would eventually be disciplined for the Nazi memorial and for retaliating against one of the investigators in the case—only to have the discipline reversed and his record expunged, while receiving a $5,000 settlement. Lieutenant Kristy Galvan, the victim of the retaliation, also sued, and received $50,000. The cops' violence against demonstrators resulted in $300,000 in settlement payments for twenty-four people. None of the officers responsible were disciplined.[59]

CHAPTER 23

The Local War on Terror

Prime Suspect

Portland got a head start in the War on Terror. On February 2, 2000, the Federal Bureau of Investigation; the Bureau of Alcohol, Tobacco, and Firearms (ATF); and the US Forest Service launched simultaneous raids against the downtown office of the Liberation Collective—an activist group with broad interests but best known for organizing anti-fur protests—and the home of one of its founding members, Craig Rosebraugh. Federal agents seized computers, photographs, audio and video tapes, books, cameras, and a mailing list of almost five thousand people. The agents also destroyed much of Rosebraugh's personal property, including his girlfriend's artwork and the announcement of his grandfather's funeral.[1]

The feds had had their eye on both Rosebraugh and the Liberation Collective for several years. In 1997, FBI and ATF agents went to Rosebraugh's house repeatedly, first inquiring about the Animal Liberation Front, an underground group famous for freeing captive animals, and then "asking . . . about the Liberation Collective organization, [its] ideology, and [its] organizational structure." Months of conspicuous surveillance followed, as well as surreptitious searches of Rosebraugh's residence. (Address books went missing, and Rosebraugh would sometimes come home to find the door unlocked—or standing open.) Over the next couple of years, the FBI and ATF regularly visited the Liberation Collective offices, harassing volunteers and pestering them with questions. The IRS also opened an investigation and revoked the organization's nonprofit status.[2]

Local police had their own role. Cops intercepted Rosebraugh on his way to a 1997 demonstration marking Buy Nothing Day—an anti-consumerist holiday created by the magazine *Adbusters*, which would later issue the original call for Occupy Wall Street—apparently because they believed him to be the event's organizer. (He was not.) Riot police then formed a line in front of the Justice Center, where he was being held, in case the protesters decided to assemble there and demand his release. (They didn't.)[3] Two years later, Rosebraugh was arrested, along with five others, and his arm was broken when police attacked an October 1999 demonstration demanding freedom for Mumia Abu-Jamal, a former Black Panther convicted of killing a Philadelphia police officer in a trial widely regarded as farcical.[4]

For several years, this is what Rosebraugh's life was like. He was regularly visited by various law enforcement agencies, including the FBI, the ATF, the Oregon State Police, and the Eugene Police Department. His home and place of business were repeatedly raided. In search after search, computers, fax machines, and address books were seized.[5] A poster from the time showed a photo of Rosebraugh holding a sign reading, "U.S. Out of My Living Room."[6]

Forest Crimes

The main source for this intense interest was Rosebraugh's work as a spokesperson for the Earth Liberation Front (ELF), an underground group devoted to destroying property to slow environmental destruction. Though ELF-style sabotage never killed anyone *and was designed not to*, in 2005 John Lewis, the FBI deputy assistant director in charge of counterterrorism, declared, "The number one domestic terrorism threat . . . is the eco-terrorism, animal rights movement. . . . There is nothing else going on in this country, over the last several years, that is racking up the high number of violent crimes and terrorist actions, arsons, etc., that this particular area of domestic terrorism has caused."[7] That was a stunning assertion when, that same year, the FBI counted 7,163 hate crime incidents, involving 8,380 criminal offenses, 5,190 of which were crimes against persons—including six murders and three forcible rapes.[8] But for the FBI "hate crimes" are not considered "terrorism," and they receive a lower priority.[9]

One might likewise contrast the government's concern over property destroyed in defense of the forest, versus the illegal destruction of the forest itself. According to the FBI's estimate, the ELF and similar groups caused $110 million in damage over the course of fifteen years, which, as journalist Jeffrey St. Clair points out, is "about the same amount that timber companies steal from national forests each year."[10] Timber companies working on public land regularly reach outside the boundaries established by the terms of sale and cut healthy trees under the auspices of "salvage" logging. US Forest Service documents estimate that 10 percent of the trees harvested from federal land are cut illegally. Though this industrial-scale fraud destroys hundreds of thousands of trees, worth approximately $100 million, every year, it rarely receives any law enforcement attention. When it has, the results have been less than inspiring. In 1995, the US Forest Service's Timber Theft Task Force discovered the Weyerhaeuser corporation engaging in such practices and Forest Service officials working to cover it up, but the task force was abruptly dissolved and its investigators reassigned. No charges were ever filed.[11]

One might conclude that the ELF was a problem less because it committed crimes and destroyed property than because it *impeded* corporate crime and the destruction of public property.

Inquisitions

And so Craig Rosebraugh, a vegan baker who distributed the ELF's communiqués, became, in the words of the *New York Times*, "The Face of Ecoterrorism."[12] He repeatedly found himself subpoenaed to testify before grand juries—and once summoned to appear before Congress.[13]

Special grand juries are secret investigative bodies entirely controlled by prosecutors. Their hearings are closed, and witnesses cannot even have an attorney present. The usual rules of evidence, like those barring hearsay, do not apply, and a judge can jail witnesses without trial if they refuse to cooperate.[14]

Rosebraugh reluctantly complied with the subpoenas and appeared before multiple grand juries. Most of the prosecutor's questions seemed directly related to arsons claimed by the ELF or to the group's methods of delivering communiqués. But some were more ideological. ("What is your philosophy on arson?" "You once supported nonviolence, have you had a change in philosophy?") Others concerned Rosebraugh's political associations. ("Were you still with Liberation Collective in December of 1999?") The congressional questions were predictably more McCarthyist: "Are you currently affiliated with the ELF?" "What are the sources of money?" "Has the North American ELF Press Office ever received financial support from animal rights groups?" "Would you take this opportunity to ask these groups to stop what they are doing?"[15] Rosebraugh carefully walked a line between collaboration and contempt, agreeing to answer questions that "asked specifically for my opinion or were theoretical in nature" while refusing to answer questions that might aid a criminal investigation.[16] He barely managed to avoid prison, and he lived with the threat of it for years.

Others fared worse. During the winter of 2005–06, nineteen people were charged in connection with twenty ELF actions. Most were arrested, tried, and sent to prison for as long as thirteen years. One killed himself after being taken into custody. Other saboteurs, knowing they had been identified, fled the country. Only one remains at large.[17]

Joint Terrorism

Less than a year after the raid on Liberation Collective, the Portland City Council voted in November 2000 to renew the police bureau's participation in the FBI's Joint Terrorism Task Force (JTTF), at the same time expanding the Criminal Intelligence Unit (the "red squad") from two officers to eight. The police bureau had joined the FBI task force three years earlier, but the public hadn't been made aware of that fact until Portland Copwatch's Dan Handelman spotted the renewal hidden among a number of no-debate formalities on the council's "consent" agenda. Once the matter came to light, a broadly felt outrage forced a full hearing on the issue, with almost five hours of public testimony. Activists spoke of police surveillance and harassment. Japanese Americans told about being sent to concentration camps as children. The only people to speak up for the secret police were the representatives of downtown business interests. Regardless, the motion passed unanimously. Eight police officers would be deputized as federal agents and work out of the Federal Building, with little local oversight.[18]

Right away, the federalized red squad zeroed in on a traditional enemy: organized labor. In 2001, the Carpenters Union received a call from a JTTF investigator, asking about an organizing drive at a construction site and warning about the possible participation of the Cross-Border Labor Organizing Committee, a labor solidarity group. When union organizers showed up to hand out flyers to the workers, they found that everyone had been sent home for the day, leading them to believe that the management had also been warned by the police. Twenty-one union locals passed resolutions demanding that the city withdraw from the Joint Terrorism Task Force. And when the agreement was again due for renewal, hundreds of people packed the council chambers, rising together and turning their backs on their representatives as they voted to approve it.[19]

It would be years before such pressure would have an effect. By 2002, the JTTF employed forty full-time investigators, including agents from the IRS, INS, Postal Service, Secret Service, and the US Department of Agriculture, as well as the FBI and local police agencies.[20]

Security Theater and the PATRIOT Act

Of course, the repression faced by labor organizers or even radical environmentalists paled in comparison to that directed against the Muslim community.

It is hard to overstate the consequences of the attacks of September 11, 2001, when hijacked airliners collided with buildings in New York City and Washington, DC. They led directly to a twenty-year war with Afghanistan, the invasion of Iraq, the creation of an extralegal torture base at Guantánamo Bay, and the US military's renewed interest in counterinsurgency. They also inspired the most monumental bureaucratic realignment since the creation of the Defense Department, as the new Department of Homeland Security absorbed 170,000 federal employees and combined the functions of twenty-two agencies, including the Immigration and Naturalization Service (INS), Customs, the Coast Guard, the Federal Emergency Management Agency, the Secret Service, and the Border Patrol.[21] Congress was quick to pass the Uniting and Strengthening America by Providing Appropriate Tools Required to Intercept and Obstruct Terrorism Act (the "USA PATRIOT Act"), expanding the definition of "terrorism," formalizing guilt by association, restricting the rights of immigrants, and authorizing secret searches and electronic surveillance while limiting judicial oversight.[22] The National Security Agency expanded its already massive electronic surveillance program, intercepting the communications of Americans at the rate of 1.7 billion *per day,* and forwarding what it found to other intelligence and law enforcement agencies.[23] Attorney General John Ashcroft ordered the FBI to "shift its primary focus from investigating and prosecuting past crimes to identifying threats of future terrorist attacks."[24]

Locally, the government's immediate response to the September 11 attacks took the form of highly visible but arbitrary actions. Reciting a litany of security measures—some sensible, most pointless—an *Oregonian* article captured something of the feeling from that first day:

> Local officials fell back on training and worst-case scenarios. No one sensed immediate danger to Portland or the state of Oregon. But they sought to reassure local residents.
>
> The FBI mobilized an emergency command post in Portland with direct contact to the governor's office. . . .
>
> Federal buildings throughout Oregon were closed. . . .
>
> The FBI recommended that the managers of Portland's tallest building, the Wells Fargo Center at 1300 S.W. Fifth Ave., evacuate. Several thousand employees from more than 30 companies filed out of the skyscraper. . .
>
> Police and fire bureaus restricted access to public buildings and ratcheted up security along Tri-Met bus and MAX light-rail lines.
>
> County workers were ordered to inspect and search all of the bridges under county jurisdiction. . . . The Multnomah County sheriff's river patrol kept guard from the waters.
>
> Uniformed Portland police officers stood stone-faced outside police precincts and public buildings.[25]

A few weeks later, however, when the FBI asked local police to assist with the interviews of young men from the Middle East, the Portland Police Bureau declined to do so. In November 2001, the city attorney issued an opinion that some of the FBI's questions would violate state law, specifically ORS 181.575, which barred the police from collecting intelligence on people who were not suspected of criminal wrongdoing.[26] This was the right call: those questioned by the FBI reported that they were mainly asked about their political beliefs and details about their mosques. FBI training materials suggested that these sorts of meetings were useful not only for identifying suspects but also for recruiting informers. Nationwide, the FBI conducted five thousand such interviews.[27]

Threat Assessment

Unfortunately, this moment of restraint was not typical of the Portland Police and even less so of the JTTF. Perhaps because of its controversial start, the unit was always eager to prove its worth and announce its accomplishments. And the task force did have several successes, though in each case the terrorist threat turned out to be less impressive than initially advertised. A local cleric was arrested at the airport, to the joy of headline writers, when his luggage tested positive for explosives. Subsequent tests were negative, however, and after a long investigation he was only convicted of using a fake Social Security number on his application for the Oregon Health Plan. Another man was convicted on weapons and immigration charges—but no connection to terrorism was ever discovered. Police Chief Kroeker, however, pointed to the arrest as showing the value of local police in fighting terrorism, leading the suspect's family to receive anonymous threats and be evicted from their home.[28]

Even the greatest victory in the local front of the Global War on Terror—the case of the "Portland Seven"—turned out to be more smoke than fire. Six of the seven were arrested in October 2002 and accused of conspiring to travel to Afghanistan and wage war against the United States; the seventh was arrested the following March. Only one ever made it to Afghanistan, where he was killed in a battle against Pakistani soldiers. One other—the sole woman—was only accused of sending the group money while they were abroad. The remaining defendants insisted that they were delivering humanitarian aid, but they accepted plea deals and received sentences ranging from three to eighteen years.[29]

Without rival the JTTF's greatest blunder was the arrest of attorney Brandon Mayfield, who came under suspicion because he attended the same mosque as the Portland Seven and had represented one of them in a child custody case. On May 7, 2004, the JTTF arrested Mayfield, claiming that his fingerprints had been found in a van parked outside a Madrid train station on the day of a terrorist attack that killed 191 people. On May 20, they released him with an apology. The *Portland Tribune* described the incident as a "headline-grabbing arrest . . . in which an explosive piece of supposedly objective evidence turned out to be embarrassingly wrong."[30]

The FBI had mistaken a partial print found at the bombsite for Mayfield's and pushed ahead despite cautions from Spanish investigators. An article in the *Journal of Forensic Identification* blamed human error for the mismatch and more disturbingly found that once an FBI supervisor had settled on Mayfield as a suspect, his subordinates were unwilling to point out the mistake. In the weeks before the arrest, federal agents had broken into Mayfield's home, office, and car, monitored his mail, and tapped his phone. Mayfield eventually settled for $2 million, and the Patriot Act's authorization of secret searches was ruled unconstitutional.[31]

Withdrawal Pains

Mayfield's arrest led City Commissioners Randy Leonard and Erik Sten to openly discuss withdrawing from the Joint Terrorism Task Force.[32] They were soon joined by incoming mayor Tom Potter. "In this country, there's an old-fashioned principle, that the police or the military have to be answerable to civilian oversight," Potter said. "The president has to have that control over the United States military. The police commissioner has to have that oversight over the Police Bureau."[33]

In April 2005 Potter (the former police chief) and Leonard (a former firefighter) put forward a motion to withdraw the police bureau from the JTTF. (Exceptions remained for investigations approved on a case-by-case basis and in the event of an emergency.) On April 28, 2005, the city council voted 4–1 to withdraw.[34] The move soured relations between the local authorities and federal law enforcement. "Only in Portland has there been such an uproar," an FBI spokesperson complained.[35] A few months later, Mayor Potter revealed that the FBI had tried to recruit an informer inside City Hall, asking a City employee if they would pass along information about their coworkers. Potter had his own office swept for bugs, with inconclusive results. "I believe the FBI's recent actions smack of Big Brother," he said.[36]

The removal of local cops from the federal partnership provoked hysterical and apocalyptic predictions from both the Justice Department and the conservative press. "We have people here in Oregon," special agent Robert Jordan warned, "that have trained in jihadist camps . . . [and] taken oaths to kill Americans and engage in jihad."[37] But a year later, US Attorney Karen Immergut admitted that she couldn't cite "a bad incident or concrete example of where the system failed as a consequence" of the City's withdrawal.[38]

That simply would not do. If jihadists weren't going to keep the people of Portland scared and thus accepting of new and intrusive government powers, the government would just have to do it for them.

Imperfect Entrapment

In November 2010, the FBI arrested a Somali-American teenager for trying to bomb a Christmas-tree lighting ceremony in Pioneer Square.

A year before, Mohamed Osman Mohamud, a student at Oregon State University, had emailed a man in Pakistan, asking for information about a religious school in Yemen. Monitoring their communication, the NSA tagged Mohamud's correspondent as a terrorist recruiter. Mohamud was then placed on a no-fly list and interviewed by the FBI. Soon after, an FBI informant sent him an email, pretending to be a representative of al-Qaeda. Mohamud agreed to meet and (according to the informant) said he "wanted to wage war in the U.S." The recruiter/informer offered him a range of options: he could live a pious life and spread the message of Islam; become a doctor and provide medical aid; raise funds for overseas terror operations; or become a martyr. According to the FBI, Mohamud chose martyrdom and selected Pioneer Square as a target. Over the course of several months, two agents helped him plan his mission, taught him how to detonate a bomb, recorded a martyrdom video, gave him $2,700 to cover his rent, and supplied both the van and a phony car bomb. The agents then drove him from Corvallis to Portland, parked the vehicle near the Christmas celebration, and gave Mohamud a cell phone which they said would serve as a trigger. Then, on November 26, 2010, as Pioneer Square filled with people eager to watch the lighting of the city's Christmas tree, Mohamud twice dialed the phone to detonate the bomb. The FBI then surrounded his vehicle and took him into custody.[39]

Mohamud's attorney argued that he had been set up, but a jury convicted him, and the judge—who agreed that the FBI's actions amounted to "imperfect entrapment"—sentenced him to thirty years.[40]

"At first glance, the plot appeared to be dangerous and deadly," journalist Trevor Aaronson later observed. But in reality, "Mohamud was an underachieving, penniless young man whose alleged act of terrorism was only made possible by the FBI."[41] "This is a kid," retired FBI agent James Wedick said of Mohamud, "who . . . barely had the capacity to put his shoes on in the morning."[42]

Another former FBI agent, Mike German, who spent years undercover in white supremacist organizations, faults the bureau for taking things too far and needlessly frightening people. He believes that the investigators had enough evidence for a conviction weeks before the attempted attack. Staging a bombing "did nothing but increase public fear and tension between Christians and Muslims." (Two days after Mohamud's arrest, a self-described "Christian warrior" firebombed a mosque in retaliation.) Looking at the full arc of events, German concludes that the government's "theatrics" served a purpose that was more political than legal, that the whole episode was meant "to aggrandize the accomplishments of the FBI and scare Portland citizens and officials into having the PPB rejoin the JTTF."[43]

That was the effect: the incident became a major talking point for the Department of Justice, a propaganda story in the War on Terror. A few months later, the Portland City Council voted to allow the police to work with the Terrorism Task Force on a limited basis. The exact nature of that relationship remained uncertain, even to the councilors who approved it: Randy Leonard voted in favor specifically because it did not represent a new JTTF partnership, while Dan Saltzman voted in favor precisely because it *did*. Predictably, the council's decision did nothing to resolve the controversy. Soon after the measure was adopted, the Arab and Muslim Police Advisory Council disbanded. In the years following, the Portland police would repeatedly join the task force and then leave again, and that pattern may continue indefinitely.[44]

This debate has run parallel to a similar one, also concerning local-federal law enforcement partnerships—specifically, about the use of police to enforce immigration law.

CHAPTER 24

North Star, Whistle-Blowers, and Cover-Ups

Job Corners

The nineties saw an abrupt and dramatic escalation in immigration enforcement, especially following the passage of the Illegal Immigration Reform and Immigrant Responsibility Act, which was signed by President Clinton in 1996. According to immigration scholar Roxanne Lynn Doty, the new law "departed from previous legislation in its overwhelmingly exclusionary nature, its diminution of the rights of immigrants, and the hardening of lines between citizens and noncitizens." The law expanded the range of deportable offenses and expedited the deportation process. It banned anyone with prior criminal convictions from entering the country, no matter how minor the offense or how long ago it occurred, and closed many routes toward legal status for people already living in the United States. Anthropologist Ruth Gomberg-Muñoz reports that the law is "widely considered to be the most punitive U.S. immigration bill to date."[1]

Nationally, the number of INS enforcement officers doubled over the course of the decade, and the budget for the Portland office swelled to $6 million per year. Arrests and deportations increased accordingly. Between October 1995 and September 1996 (the agency's fiscal year), the INS's Portland District arrested 2,045 people. Between October 1996 and September 1997, the same office arrested 3,100 people, a record high and a 50 percent increase. Likewise, the annual number of deportations doubled from an average of two hundred early in the decade, to 414 in 1996. The very next year, it doubled again, to 841.[2]

This crackdown came just as day laborers were organizing to improve their wages and conditions, and the workers were subjected to regular harassment and occasional large-scale sweeps. Much of the enforcement activity was concentrated at "job corners," where day laborers waited for work, especially the one at East Burnside and Grand. INS agents would descend on corners where the workers gathered and arrest them *en masse*, often with unnecessary violence. Sometimes as many as fifty people would be arrested in a single operation. Most were deported, but many others were released because they were in the country legally. Ramon Ramirez, an immigrant rights advocate and union organizer, described the overall effect: "These raids have created a reign of terror in our community."[3]

A broad coalition supported the workers and opposed government harassment, including the Workers Organizing Committee, Causa of Oregon, the Oregon Council for Hispanic Advancement, the American Friends Service Committee, Jobs With Justice, the Hispanic Metropolitan Chamber of Commerce, and the Catholic Church. The Workers Organizing Committee initiated a Copwatch-style MigraWatch program to document INS activity. Observers reported seeing agents brandish firearms, apply choke holds, and use pain holds against suspects already in restraints. INS agents responded by threatening to arrest or sue MigraWatch volunteers. In May 1997, one hundred people picketed the INS district office in Portland, and Causa released a statement detailing a series of abuses. INS district director David Beebe was unperturbed: "What I see here is a two-page statement that we are doing our job."[4]

The framing of immigrant rights as a labor issue, indicated by the involvement of groups like the Workers Organizing Committee and Jobs With Justice, is remarkable precisely because immigrants are so often blamed for undercutting wages, an allegation presented as justifying and even necessitating strict border control. But this argument confuses causes and effects. "[It] isn't migration, but border policing and enforcement, that weakens workers and drives wages down," political theorist Geo Maher explains. "By casting many migrants into a gray area—no labor protections, no minimum wage, no right to unionize—criminalization creates an ideal situation for capitalists. . . . A defenseless and deportable class is in no position to demand higher wages, and the bosses know it." The bad consequences are not only felt by those who are themselves criminalized. "By holding down the wages of undocumented workers, immigration enforcement suppresses wages across entire branches of industry, impacting both documented and undocumented workers." Therefore, Maher concludes, "Criminalization is the *cause* of low wages, not the solution."[5]

North Star

Oregon law had long prohibited the use of local "agency money, equipment or personnel for the purpose of detecting or apprehending" people who might be in the country illegally but who were not suspected of any criminal offense.[6] However, while state law prohibited local cops from joining INS operations, nothing prevented INS agents from joining Portland Police operations. There were fifty-eight joint operations in Portland in 1997, a 25 percent increase from the year before. The most dramatic of these was a raid that year at the Tiffany Court apartments in the suburb of Tigard. Sixty cops, including officers from nearby Tualatin and Canby, searched the apartment building and seized six pounds of cocaine and heroin, a handgun, and $7,000 cash; 130 people were arrested, a few for drugs charges, the rest for immigration violations.[7]

The Tiffany raid came as the result of a Portland police investigation concerning drug sales in the downtown area, part of a multiyear series of stings called Operation North Star.[8] Running from September 1996 to March 1999, North Star was a collaborative campaign involving the FBI, the INS, and local cops.[9] On the street level, it targeted ordinary users. Cops would go undercover and offer to sell drugs to passersby, arresting them if they said yes. "If there are no buyers there will be no dealers," Central Precinct Commander Ed May reasoned.[10] Thousands were arrested in the program's first year.[11] Observing one day's activity, which resulted in thirty-five criminal arrests and a much greater number of deportations, MigraWatch reported that "the sting targeted all brown-skinned, Spanish-speaking people who were in downtown Portland at the time."[12]

The federal government provided $457,000 in funding for North Star. But it was later discovered that, by the police bureau's own estimate, thirty cops assigned to the program had falsified time sheets, claiming $165,000 of unearned wages. The cops employed a variety of tricks: Supervisors told officers to leave early without clocking out. Cops frequently went out drinking while still on the clock. Some just didn't show up to work and were paid anyway. It was not just a matter of workers fudging their hours or goofing off on city time. An internal investigation affirmed that these practices "involved management decision-making and direction."[13]

A few officers reported the fraudulent practices to the chief's office.[14] Both the district attorney and the US Department of Justice opened investigations, which Interim Chief Lynnae Berg described as "a crucible for our organization."[15] Ultimately, no criminal charges were filed, for the damning-in-itself reason that the police bureau's record-keeping was so poor that there was no way to definitely prove how much had been stolen or by whom. Prosecutors said that bad accounting and the established practices in the bureau presented "insurmountable legal and factual obstacles."[16]

Two cops were suspended in connection to the overtime scandal, one for claiming wages for hours he did not work, one for misleading investigators. Central Precinct Commander Robert Kauffman was demoted and transferred to the training division. Lieutenant James McDaniel voluntarily took a demotion and was reassigned to investigate fraud, putting his skill set to good use. One sergeant, Richard Barton—who had previously been transferred out of another unit for similar behavior—was fired. Another sergeant, Rocky Balada, was demoted. Fourteen officers were issued written reprimands.[17]

Sergeant Balada later sued, arguing that nothing about North Star was unusual, that sending cops home early was a common practice, widely known, generally accepted, and of long standing: "Successive chiefs of police who have risen through the ranks, virtually every commanding officer who has risen through the ranks, and virtually every supervisor for the past 40 years have participated in the utilization of 'cuff time' and 'short nights' and have approved it, acquiesced in it, used it as a reward, and have been the recipients and beneficiaries of the practice."[18] (The lawsuit did not prevail.)[19]

If nothing else, it was clear that the bureau had budgeting and accounting problems. An audit found that police overtime costs had ballooned from $5.4 million in 1992 to $9.4 million in 2000 and that the cops had exceeded their budget every year during that time, usually by a million dollars or more. Seventeen officers had each been paid $30,000 in overtime in a single year. Many engaged in some questionable accounting to inflate their wages, such as billing as overtime the period between the end of the night shift and a court appearance the following day. The *Oregonian* decried the state of police accountancy as "abysmal," and attorney Spencer Neal wrote a letter urging criminal prosecution. The city auditor recommended a variety of changes, including better timekeeping practices, reevaluating assignments based on total costs, assigning desk jobs to lower-paid civilian staff, limiting the use of comp time, and requiring ethics training.[20]

Fucking Rat Snitches

Another pervasive problem that North Star brought to light was the culture of impunity within the police bureau and the preservation of that culture through intimidation. One cop who reported the payroll irregularities was given a month's leave for his own protection. Another was ostracized by fellow officers.[21]

A third, Damon Woodcock, reported the timesheet fraud in February 1999. He was interviewed by Internal Affairs on May 19. Three days later, Officer Kelvin Knudson vocally complained, in Woodcock's presence, about the "fucking rat snitches" in the precinct and stated that he had enough bullets to take care of them all. Woodcock reported the comment to the IAD. A month later, Chief Charles Moose ordered him to switch locker rooms, which he did on June 26. (Woodcock had begun a gender transition two years earlier, changing names, pronouns, and undergoing surgery.) Almost immediately, his locker was vandalized, with a circle and a slash through the "cock" in his name. Another officer reported the vandalism to Internal Affairs, but they never investigated it. Instead, as one cop later put it, Woodcock was made "the target [of the investigation] instead of the victim." He was disciplined for violating the bureau's dress code by wearing a tongue stud, and reprimanded for switching locker rooms. (Moose denied ordering him to do so, but Officer Katie Potter, daughter of former Chief Tom Potter, testified in support of Woodcock's account.) In this atmosphere, Woodcock began to worry that he would receive "no cover" or "slow cover" if dispatched to a dangerous call. He requested desk duty, but the request was refused. In July, he applied for stress-related disability. Several officers testified at the eligibility hearing, detailing the hostility sexual minorities faced at Central Precinct.[22]

Not everyone on the pension board was sympathetic; the vote ended in a tie, with all police representatives voting against Woodcock's claim. His benefits were denied. City Auditor Gary Blackmer—who, it should be stressed, was responsible for overseeing the civilian review process—explained his position: "You have to expect that you're going to run into difficulties and that things are going to happen, some of it in the workplace." Others, especially women officers, seemed to take the situation more seriously. Lori Smith, an African American cop, characterized the vandalism of Woodcock's locker as "a hate crime," similar to leaving a noose at someone's desk. Detective Amber Lewis agreed, stating that she read the graffiti as a "death threat."[23]

Woodcock's disability claim was approved on appeal. He received a $205,000 payout from the city and spent the rest of his life working as a private investigator, usually with defense and civil rights attorneys.[24]

A Culture of Cover-Ups

The intimidation of whistle-blowers was an established practice in the bureau. Loren Christensen recalls that when he joined the Portland Police in the early seventies, "rookies didn't say anything if they wanted to keep their jobs."[25] Two decades later, in 1993, Officer Dawn Urban settled a $25,000 claim after receiving death threats; she had reported a sergeant who instructed her to write a false report, and another officer who kept the drugs he seized from a suspect.[26]

Often, as in Woodcock's case, retaliation overlapped with other types of discrimination. After Officer Gina Hoesly filed a lawsuit over sexual harassment suffered at the hands of her coworkers, she started receiving death threats, and other cops stopped providing backup. (She was eventually awarded $20,000.) Two years later, while she was on medical leave and preparing to retire, she filed assault charges against an ex-boyfriend, Joshua David Rodriguez. When the cops arrested him, they found methamphetamine in his possession. Her former colleagues (and, in the case of Assistant Chief Andrew Kirkland, a former boyfriend) then promptly opened an investigation on Hoesly, targeting her with the use of informants and searching her trash. There they found drug paraphernalia and a bloody tampon, which they had tested for DNA, drugs, and (inexplicably) semen. In June 2002, she was arrested on felony drug charges, but the case fell apart when the courts ruled the trash search illegal.[27]

In 2011, a police bureau trainee, Lindsay Hunt, reported a slew of violations committed by her field training officer, Quency Ho—among them, conducting warrantless searches, doctoring police reports, and destroying evidence. Ho admitted to driving without a seat belt and accepting free sodas from 7-Eleven, but nothing more. Hunt was then questioned by the chief of police, and the training division opened an investigation *against her*. She resigned a few days later, fearing that she would not receive backup if she needed it. She sued, unsuccessfully, but at trial another recruit, Erin Lewis, testified to witnessing numerous uses of excessive force, both by her own field training officer and by other cops at Central Precinct. In one instance, she reported seeing Officers Matthew Delenikos and Matthew Manus leave with a handcuffed teenager who had been swearing at them and then returning "with this kid, blood all over his face, crying."[28] Hunt's lawyers described "the environment in the training division" as "toxic with regard to complaining about officers."[29] The free sodas, it turned out, were part of an arrangement originally negotiated by Charles

Moose in an effort to draw cops to the neighborhood and discourage low-level crimes. Hunt's complaint forced a change of policy.[30]

Gross Negligence

The feeling of impunity was common to both the line officers and command staff. It was enforced both from the bottom up and from the top down.

Perhaps the most illustrative example was the attempted cover-up of an off-duty beating in January 2002. Two cops, Grant Bailey and Craig Hampton, were out drinking when one of them made some remark about another man's suspenders, and that man, James Ladd, took offense and pushed one of the loud-mouthed drunks. The bar's bouncers threw Ladd out, but the two off-duty cops followed him and then beat him in front of a dozen witnesses while identifying themselves as police to keep others from interfering.[31] So far, so dumb.

The first officer to respond to calls about the fight, Ryan Lee, was a rookie who clearly didn't know how these things were handled. He proceeded to take photos, interview witnesses, call his supervisor, and write up the incident. When Lieutenant Gabe Kalmanek arrived, he ordered the officers present *not* to file reports. One officer—Matt Stimmell—disposed of Ladd's bloody shirt rather than keeping it as evidence. Three days later, Lieutenant Kalmanek wrote his own report, claiming that the victim had only suffered a bloody nose. (It was in fact broken, and his eye was swollen shut.) Kalmanek didn't refer the case for a criminal investigation and assumed the matter finished. Three weeks later, the Independent Police Review (IPR) Division—the civilian review board—received an anonymous complaint describing the fight.[32]

Sergeant Dirk Anderson, who filed the complaint, did everything he could to hide his identity and to conceal the fact that the report came from within the bureau. He deliberately misspelled words, called the cops names, and made sure that he didn't touch the paper so as to avoid leaving fingerprints. The ensuing investigation involved a Multi-Disciplinary Team, including IPR director Richard Rosenthal and representatives of the city attorney's office, the Oregon State Police, the Oregon Department of Justice, and the police bureau's personnel and detective divisions, as well as Internal Affairs. A grand jury heard testimony from thirty witnesses, and expressed as much concern about the cover-up as the initial crime. In a letter to the district attorney, jurors accused police commanders of "gross negligence" and concluded that they were not "interested in or capable of ascertaining the facts."[33]

Craig Hampton pled guilty to third-degree assault and was sentenced to twenty-one months in prison. Grant Bailey pled guilty to second-degree assault and was sentenced to eighteen months. Matt Stimmell received a written reprimand for destroying evidence. Sergeant Lawrence Baid was suspended for ten days, and Sergeant Ken Whattam was suspended for thirty. Lieutenant Steve Hollingsworth and Lieutenant Gabe Kalmanek were each demoted to sergeant. Captain Rosie Sizer was issued a written reprimand. (She would later become police chief.) Ladd sued and received $75,000. Both Anderson and Lee were transferred to other precincts for their own protection. Even at his new post, the other cops shunned Anderson, and he was suspended for five days because he had failed to challenge Lieutenant Kalmanek's order not to file an official report.[34]

The bureau's treatment of whistle-blowers—formally and informally—shows us something of the culture of impunity that exists in policing and the ways it sustains itself. It also points to an insular, paranoid, us-versus-them mindset such that, whatever the official rhetoric might imply, the cops view themselves as apart from the community at large. And thereby it also points to the fundamentally lawless nature of policing, the tendency to apply the law selectively and rarely to themselves or their colleagues, as well as hinting at the ruthless lengths to which they will go to punish anyone they see as threatening their power.

"If the police will do this to a police officer," Stephen Houze, Gina Hoesly's attorney asked, "who won't they do it to?"[35]

Feudal Lords

While the police bureau was enmeshed in the North Star scandal, the INS was facing problems of its own.

"Step into the detention and deportation section of Portland's U.S. immigration office," an *Oregonian* exposé began, "and enter a world of racism, sexism and questionable conduct." "[The] Portland unit seethes with hatred," the paper continued. This was built on a "decades-old culture of abuse and ineptitude" preserved by a "feudal" organizational structure.[36]

Charity Reeves, a former INS detention enforcement officer, told reporters that the Portland Division was rife with racism and a culture that encouraged abuse. She accused Roger Pelletier, a detention officer who had recently been promoted to supervisor, of sexual harassment and recalled that he liked to say there were "two things that he could not stand, and that was niggers and white trash." (Another officer confirmed the quote.) Other agents regularly referred to immigrants as "wets" (for "wetbacks") and "tonks" (reportedly the sound made when a person is hit on the head with a metal flashlight).[37]

This culture produced a series of scandals, large and small, stretching back at least a decade. The internal auditor opened an investigation on an inappropriate weapons discharge that occurred in 1995 but wasn't reported for nearly five years. Oscar Villa, a deportation officer, was arrested on July 29, 2000, for driving an INS vehicle while drunk. Most shocking, Olen Ray Jones, the former district head, was convicted in 1992 of sexually abusing an eleven-year-old girl whose parents had applied for work permits. By the year 2000, the office was facing simultaneous investigations by the INS internal auditor, the Equal Employment Opportunity Commission, the Federal Labor Relations Authority, and the Justice Department's inspector general.[38]

A few months after the exposé, INS Portland District director David Beebe resigned amid controversy over the strip-search of a Chinese woman. Guo Liming was searched at the airport, then jailed for two nights because INS agents believed (wrongly) that her passport was a forgery. An internal investigation determined that the search was appropriate. But, around the same time, another internal report found the Portland office to be mismanaged in several respects, citing a lack of supervision, an absence of written policies, a shortage of interpreters, poor recordkeeping, low morale, and an overreliance on local police.[39]

After September 11, 2001, Beebe's resignation would be followed by much broader changes, as the Immigration and Naturalization Service was converted into Immigration and Customs Enforcement (ICE) and moved from the Justice Department to the brand-new Department of Homeland Security.

Much more remained the same, however. In the summer of 2007, almost one hundred ICE agents raided the Fresh Del Monte Produce plant in North Portland, detaining 165 workers and arresting three managers.[40] The raid came after the resolution of a class-action lawsuit filed on behalf of eighteen hundred workers, relating to a range of company practices including the failure to pay overtime, denying workers legally required breaks, and firing anyone who raised safety concerns. Del Monte settled for $400,000.[41] "The most publicized case of low-wage immigrant workers complaining became the site of the largest immigration raid in the state," former attorney and Willamette University professor Keith Cunningham-Parmeter noted. "The message from all of this: Immigrant workers who complain get deported."[42] Tom Leedham, the secretary-treasurer of Teamsters Local 206 explained the cumulative effect of immigration enforcement: "As a practical matter, it's impossible to organize large groups of undocumented workers . . . because the companies use fear tactics, like the fear of a raid."[43]

Two years later, in 2009, Del Monte was subjected to another class-action lawsuit, and a Multnomah County jury ordered the company to pay $800,000 to 330 workers, along with $1.4 million in attorney's fees. But some parts of the law move more swiftly than others. By the time the case made it to court, several of the plaintiffs had already been deported.[44]

CHAPTER 25

Accountability and Reform

Hospital Shooting

On March 30, 2001, José Santos Victor Mejía Poot, a Mexican national, suffered an epileptic seizure while boarding a TriMet bus and didn't respond when the driver asked him to deposit his fare. The driver contacted police who, not recognizing a medical emergency when they saw one, proceeded to drag Mejía off the bus and beat him in front of numerous witnesses. He was then taken to the Justice Center, charged with harassment and resisting arrest, and beaten again. When he was released, he simply sat outside the jail crying. Police eventually drove him to Providence Crisis Triage Center for a mental health evaluation. Though he had been to Providence just a few days earlier regarding a prior epileptic episode, the staff there transferred him to a private psychiatric facility, Pacific Gateway Hospital. On April 1, a nurse called police because Mejía had escaped from his room and, she said, was "attacking staff, grabbing patients, and writing on walls." When the cops arrived, Mejía confronted them with an aluminum rod he had stripped from a door. They shot and killed him.[1]

Members of the Latino community picketed the courthouse while a grand jury investigated Mejía's death. When the jury failed to issue any indictments, members of the clergy and representatives of the American Friends Service Committee, the Hispanic Chamber of Commerce, the student groups MEChA and Gennacción, the Coalition of Black Men, and the Mexican consulate held a press conference at City Hall and called for a federal civil rights investigation. A "Justice for José Mejía Poot" march followed on Cinco de Mayo, with nearly one thousand people taking part. Featured speakers included members of Mejía's family and leaders from the African American and Asian American communities, marking the emergence of a cross-racial coalition. Portland Copwatch called the event "the largest march for police accountability in recent Portland history."[2]

A few changes were immediate: Pacific Gateway Hospital was closed. Multnomah County ended its contract with Providence Triage, which then also closed. TriMet introduced a new policy, archiving all video of arrests or other confrontations. The police, however, went a different direction. In November 2002, Portland Police Chief Mark Kroeker awarded medals to the two officers who had killed Mejía. Representatives of the Latino Network, the Hispanic Police Advisory Council, the Hispanic Chamber of Commerce, and County Commissioner Serena Cruz spoke at a rally in response, demanding that Kroeker resign. Other demonstrations followed at the mayor's office and the chief's home.[3]

Weapons as Reforms

The Portland Police did adopt one reform after Mejía's death. In June 2002, Kroeker told the Chief's Forum that he would be arming a dozen Portland cops with tasers, weapons that deliver a 50,000-volt electric shock to overwhelm the nervous system, causing considerable pain and temporary paralysis. Ostensibly the new weapons would give the police an alternative to firearms—though, notably, the taser's manufacturer recommends *against* using the device on a subject with epilepsy.[4] Most likely, Kroeker was simply using Mejía's death as a pretext to introduce new weaponry—a good reminder to be suspicious of any reforms proposed by the police themselves.

In their first eighteen months with tasers, the Portland police used them 447 times, including twenty-five times when the suspect was already in handcuffs. Eight were shocked in the groin area.[5] In 2004, *Willamette Week* published a report showing that the police were specifically trained to use the taser to shock nonviolent and handcuffed suspects so as to hurry them into police cars.[6] Four years later, the *Mercury* found that the weapons were still "being used more often by officers to gain compliance from uncooperative subjects, and less often as a 'less-lethal' alternative to deadly force."[7] During the same four-year period, the police used tasers about five hundred times annually. In roughly a fifth of those cases, the weapon was used to shock people suffering from mental illness. The police bureau's own reporting verified that, contrary to official policy, tasers were regularly used as "compliance tools": one report showed that in sixty-one cases police tasered people who were simply not following instructions and that in another sixteen the victims were offering *no resistance at all*.[8] In March

2006, the city had its first fatality related to the use of the electroshock weapon after Officer Paul Park tasered Tim Grant, a disoriented man who had been walking in traffic.[9]

By 2012, the City had paid out over $1.3 million in taser-related lawsuits, including one case that involved police tasering a woman in her own bed.[10] In a single month (February 2011), the city paid more than $180,000 to settle three taser claims involving unresisting victims, two of whom were on their knees when the police shocked them.[11] In another case, three cops tasered and beat a man whom they suspected of spraying graffiti. (In truth, he was just walking by a wall that already had graffiti on it.)[12] A seventy-one year old woman was awarded $145,000 after police pushed her down, tasered her repeatedly, and then struck her in the head so hard that her glass eye popped out. Soon after, the police bureau released a new directive urging "consideration" when using tasers against "children, women who are known to be or obviously [are] pregnant and the elderly." Contradicting all previous propaganda, the 2012 police bureau directive explicitly stated, "The Taser is not meant to take the place of deadly force options."[13]

Review Board Review

The controversy surrounding Mejía's death occurred amid a larger debate about immigration and border enforcement, and the organizing in response to his killing built on the momentum of the immigrants' rights movement. It also coincided with a transition, already underway, in the structure and direction of the police oversight system.

City Auditor Gary Blackmer had taken control of the Police Internal Investigations Auditing Committee in 1999. From his perspective, PIIAC's greatest shortcoming was not its lack of public confidence or ultimate impotence but its failure to achieve creditability *with the police*, which he attributed to the biases of the committee members. The following year, the mayor appointed a group to "review the [oversight] process and propose recommendations" for reform. Its eighteen volunteers included current and former members of PIIAC, and representatives from Portland Copwatch, the NAACP, the National Lawyers Guild, the League of Women Voters, and the Portland Police Association. The group met for five months and issued two conflicting reports. The "Majority Report" commended PIIAC's mediation program, community outreach, and monitoring reports but criticized its process for handling complaints—the board's main purpose. The report found that the problems were structural and called for "major reforms." Among its twenty-seven recommendations were suggestions that PIIAC conduct its own investigations, that its findings should be binding, that it recommend discipline, and that it propose changes in police policy. In contrast, a dissenting "Minority Report" found that PIIAC followed "the best form of civilian oversight available" and offered only minor technical adjustments.[14]

In January 2001, the city council asked Blackmer to conduct an audit of the program he had overseen. He praised PIIAC's "relatively less adversarial and legalistic" approach and said again that its greatest weakness was its lack of credibility in the eyes of the police. He suggested creating a new body, the Division of Independent Police Review (IPR), which would accept civilian complaints, and then pass them to IAD for an investigation. Appeals would go before a nine-member Citizen Review Committee, with the final decision to be reached at a city council hearing. The new body would have no authority over shootings or fatalities and no role in deciding discipline. The proposal passed unanimously on June 6, 2001.[15] The city council was under some external pressure to show results, not only because of outrage over Mejía's murder but also because activists were preparing a ballot measure to create a completely new review system.[16]

But from the beginning, the freshly minted IPR was beset with problems. Volunteer committee members and even the Portland city council seemed reluctant to use their new powers. (It wasn't until 2019 that the city council found an officer to have violated bureau policy.) The IPR accepted fewer complaints than the old board, and its annual reports focused on quantitative measures, like the number of investigations and the amount of time before an investigation was closed.[17] When committee members took a more expansive view of their mandate, they were often thwarted by IPR staff. At one point Director Richard Rosenthal, himself a former prosecutor, joined in the cover-up of an earlier cover-up, concealing the fact that the police had for years been violating state law by destroying the original investigatory records in lethal force cases, including interview tapes and officers' notes.[18]

The events leading up to Mejía's death would later produce a crisis in this new oversight system. In 2003, over the objections of Director Rosenthal, seven of the nine members of the IPR's Citizen Review Committee (CRC) voted to look into the violence accompanying Mejía's arrest, though they were barred from examining the later shooting. Rosenthal then refused to work on the case or to allow the IPR staff to assist, essentially killing the review effort.[19] A majority of CRC members resigned, describing the accountability process as a "mockery" and a "sham."[20] In January 2004, six former members held an independent hearing on the Mejía case and found that Officer James Ferner had used excessive force while removing Mejía from the bus. It was an inspired piece of political theater but, as Director Rosenthal was quick to point out, legally "irrelevant."[21]

The Labyrinth

The IPR was the main, but by no means the only, body responsible for monitoring and advising the Portland Police Bureau, and over time the oversight system became more labyrinthine, disorienting all who entered. An imperfect list of those agencies, committees, subcommittees, work groups, and officials appointed by the police chief, city council, state government, or federal judiciary to examine, oversee, or revise some aspect of policing during the first two decades of the twenty-first century would include the Office of Equity, the Use of Force Review Board, the Racial Profiling Committee, the Bias Based Policing Work Group, the Office of Accountability and Professional Standards, the Community Oversight Advisory Board, the Community Police Organizational Review Team, a compliance officer/community liaison, a force inspector, a Mental Health Work Group, the Portland Committee on Community Engaged Policing, the Community/Police Relations Committee, the Police Review Board, the Human Rights Committee, the Department of Public Safety Standards and Training, the Police Equity Advisory Committee, the Behavior Health Unit Advisory Committee, and the Training Advisory Council, as well as the IPR, the CRC, the bureau's own Internal Affairs Division, and a coalition of advisory groups representing distinct populations.[22] A later study by the US Department of Justice concluded, "[The Portland Police Bureau] has a number of fragmented processes for review of uses of force, none of which result in timely individual or systemic corrective action."[23]

In a typical year, the IPR declined two-thirds of the complaints it received prior to any investigation. The remaining third were passed on to Internal Affairs, which then declined about a fifth of the complaints reaching its desk—still without investigation. Of the remaining cases, Internal Affairs treated the majority (51–60 percent) as "service improvement opportunities," generally resulting in "non-disciplinary" advice or coaching—meaning again "not subject to a full investigation." Less commonly, if both parties agreed, "the complaint [could] be resolved through mediation"—yet another way to avoid a full review, an official finding, and possible discipline. "[But] for those complaints that result in full IA investigations," the Justice Department wrote, reassuringly, "we found the investigations to be thorough."[24]

Once the IAD did its work, or failed to, either the citizen-complainant or the officer could appeal its findings to the Citizen Review Committee made up of nine volunteers. Importantly, the CRC would only consider the *finding*, not the actual discipline, and even then they had limited authority to compel any change. More often, if the CRC disagreed with the IAD's conclusions, it would send the case back for more work. Absurdly, though the CRC held its own hearings, it was "prohibited from using this new evidence" and was expected to "opine on the propriety of a prior finding without consideration of all the evidence before them."[25]

If the CRC found itself ultimately disagreeing with the IAD's assessment, it could forward the case to the city council, which, after further hearings, would issue a final finding. The chief of police would then make a recommendation concerning discipline, with the authority to order disciplinary action resting with the police commissioner (usually the mayor). The chastised officer could subsequently appeal any discipline through the union's grievance procedure, with the final decision coming from an arbiter. "This process is so lengthy and attenuated," the Justice Department noted, "that the efficacy of corrective action is invariably undermined."[26]

Describing this process as "cumbersome" and "grueling," the DOJ argued, "The established systems have become so complex and so time consuming that the objectives—officer accountability and public confidence—have been lost." Thus it was a "Self Defeating Accountability System."[27]

Eternal Recurrence

The Justice Department's assessment is devastating but also, in a funny way, naïve.

These review systems, with their constituent parts and numerous repetitive processes, do not exist because of any real or intended effect that they might have on policing, which is always minimal. They are created instead to exercise a pacifying influence over activists. As Colette Gordon argues in

Mobilizing Beyond Crisis, it is very difficult to continually build pressure through a grassroots campaign. And so, with scarce resources and facing an often hostile political climate, when organizations are unable to "sustain mass-based tactics," they tend to pursue their "grievances through responsive institutional channels" afforded by a "pluralistic power structure."[28] At its best, this approach allows for modest gains without the challenges and risks of disruptive action; at its worst, committed activists and other concerned citizens lose time and momentum in a seemingly endless series of exhausting and ultimately pointless committee meetings.

As the police endure periodic crises in public confidence, the demand for improved oversight predictably resurfaces. Sometimes, as we have seen, the authorities respond to this demand by creating a new committee to monitor some specific aspect of policing. Sometimes they propose adjustments to an existing oversight body—new processes, new powers, always falling far short of anything that accountability advocates might recommend. Regardless, the changes may come to inspire a brief moment of cautious optimism, only to be followed by a long and confusing transition period, leading eventually to frustration and disappointment, typically marked by the resignations of those who were once the project's most enthusiastic participants. At the beginning, such reforms might be enough to create the appearance of progress, of movement, of a system willing to examine itself and engage in necessary correction. In fact, the process represents just the opposite, a kind of stasis, a predictable cycle, a continual return to the prior condition, albeit with a new constitutional, democratic, or social-science gloss.

What seems at first like forward motion is instead a slow turning back, drawing us ever further into the labyrinth.

CHAPTER 26

Deadly Profiles

Punctuated Escalation

Looking back, it seems the death of José Mejía represented a turning point.

Local organizing against police brutality had ebbed and flowed throughout the nineties but remained a kind of niche concern, never achieving any sort of mass character. There were an increasing number of demonstrations about the issue as the decade went on, but these were mostly organized by ad hoc groups or coalitions that did not survive past the end of the protest. Policing was a primary concern for a relative handful of dedicated activists, grieving families, crusading lawyers, and tiny organizations. Chief among these was Portland Copwatch, which during this period helped the victims of misconduct navigate the complaint system, educated members of the public about their rights when dealing with police, pushed for an independent review board, and occasionally went on patrol to observe the cops and document their activities.[1]

Beginning in 2001, the "Justice for Mejia" movement helped unify ongoing efforts against police violence, while building on the immigrants' rights movement and the attempts to organize day laborers. Both the pace and the magnitude of activity began to change, with large demonstrations and multiracial coalitions expanding the sense of what was possible. It marked the starting point for an emerging pattern of periodic crisis and punctuated escalation that would continue through 2020. Over the course of two decades, each subsequent upheaval seemed to draw its energy from the scale, intensity, and disruptive force of the one before, despite intervening periods of apparent calm.

Mourn, Organize

A pair of police shootings in 2003 and 2004—both of unarmed African Americans—further galvanized the movement.

Kendra James was shot and killed in the course of a May 2003 traffic stop. Police pulled over the car in which she was riding, and arrested the driver. They then ordered James out of the car, but she climbed into the driver's seat and started to pull away. Officer Scott McCollister claimed that he was leaning into the vehicle as it began to move. "I made the decision to pull the trigger . . . 'cause I knew I was gonna get run over . . . or dragged down the street." Other evidence, however—eyewitness accounts, including the initial statements of other officers; forensic analysis showing that James was shot from a distance of two feet; and McCollister's own assertion that he "started to fall . . . and [then] fired"—would all seem to contradict this version of events.[2]

James's death inspired the largest demonstration against police brutality that the city had seen in almost two decades, mobilizing about two thousand people—though Pastor Robin Wright later admitted that its purpose was mainly cathartic, supplying an outlet for community anger while waiting for the official investigation to conclude.[3] Adding to the tension, that August the Police Assessment Resource Center (PARC) released a 222-page report, commissioned by the city government, examining thirty-two shootings and two deaths in custody from the period January 1997–June 2000. PARC found that there was *no* command-level review in 31 percent of the cases it examined and that an additional 13 percent failed to adhere to the standards of review established by policy. Among the problems the report identified were neglect in securing the scene and preserving physical evidence, failures to conduct forensic analyses, a standard three-day delay before interviewing police, and off-the-record "pre-interviews" conducted before taking official statements from the cops involved.[4] "There's no administrative review in this organization," a senior officer told PARC. "People are afraid to ask hard questions." As a result, the report concluded, command staff "did not seek to draw lessons from the shooting incidents. . . . Many did not comment on tactics, even when they were questionable," and it "was not unusual" for a review to produce "no recommendations concerning policy, procedure or training."[5]

It was in this context that, a few days later, Police Chief Mark Kroeker announced that he would be suspending Officer Scott McCollister for nine hundred hours (a little less than six months)—not for the use of lethal force but for exercising poor tactical judgment and placing himself in danger. This outcome naturally satisfied no one, as the cops thought that *any* discipline was too severe, and in effect an attack on their entire profession, whereas a good portion of the public felt that McCollister should have been dismissed and possibly prosecuted.[6]

Mayor Vera Katz immediately issued a quit-or-be-fired ultimatum to Chief Kroeker, and he resigned. Neither the chief nor the mayor cited specific reasons for his departure, but there were plenty to choose from, his handling of the James shooting being only the most obvious. The list of complaints about Kroeker, from all sides, stretched back years: the manhandling of protesters, his patriarchal and homophobic sermons, the awarding of medals to the cops who killed José Mejía, and his imperious and authoritarian management style.[7] By the time he left, it was doubtful that his popularity could possibly sink any lower among the public or the police.

Kroeker went on to lead an international police force in Liberia, speaking in his sanctimonious way about his "deep desire to serve the cause of peace."[8] Scott McCollister continued his career in the Portland Police Bureau and in 2008 was involved in another fatal shooting.[9]

New Chief, New Crisis

Kroeker was replaced by Derrick Foxworth, a Black officer who had risen through the ranks of the police bureau, working in drugs and vice as well as on the Gang Enforcement Team, then being appointed public information officer, Northeast Precinct commander, and assistant chief. His record on the use of force was mixed. In 1998, he had ordered police to fire less-lethal shotguns at a mostly Black crowd protesting in front of the home of Chief Charles Moose—the bureau's first use of the new weapon.[10] On the other hand, he had specifically ordered officers *not* to use deadly force when Tyrone Waters confronted them with what turned out to be a pellet gun. In Portland Copwatch's estimation, "it's likely that Foxworth's involvement saved the young man's life." (Waters was the son of State Senator Avel Gordly, which may have been a consideration.)[11] Foxworth's reputation was equally mixed. While some activists said that he was held in reasonably high esteem, Foxworth himself admitted to being called "Uncle Tom" and "a sellout." Police largely viewed him as a firm-but-fair disciplinarian, an image shared by those who knew him personally. His ex-wife called him "a by-the-book person." He once ticketed his own mother for speeding.[12] However, he also had a history of impropriety that would later prove portentous. In 1997, he had been placed on administrative leave during an investigation into his on-duty cell phone use. He had called the same number 370 times in four months, claiming that it belonged to an informant. He was still married at the time, but the "informant" would later become his second wife. He eventually reimbursed the city for the cost of the calls.[13]

As chief, Foxworth reintroduced some of the old community policing staples: a "Citizens Police Academy," where volunteers could receive police training so as to better understand the decisions officers make; bike patrols to get the cops out of their cars and encourage friendly in-person contact; and recruitment focused on communities of color. He lifted Kroeker's ban on long hair, earrings, and beards. And he introduced a reform of his own, requiring police to file a report any time they pointed a gun at someone.[14]

But Foxworth had barely settled into his new role when the bureau was again thrust into controversy. On March 28, 2004, Officer Jason Sery shot and killed an unarmed Black man, James Jahar Perez.[15] As usual, a grand jury failed to indict. In this case, however, District Attorney Michael Schrunk ordered a public inquest. Three days of televised hearings allowed an unprecedented look into the decisions leading to the shooting. Sery's partner, Sean Macomber, explained that Perez's car had drawn his attention because it looked out of place in the St. Johns neighborhood. Sery ran the plates, and Macomber deduced that the driver was too young to be the registered owner. The cops then doubled back to follow the car. The police claimed that when Perez pulled off Fessenden Avenue into the parking lot of the Lucky Day laundromat, he signaled with fewer than the one hundred prescribed feet. The officers approached, and Macomber opened the driver-side door. When Perez reached into his pocket, presumably to show his license, Macomber grabbed his arm and forced his head against the steering wheel. Both cops ordered him to show his hands, and, as Perez removed his hand from his pocket, Sery fired three times. Macomber then fired his taser, which continued to cycle until it overheated three minutes later.[16]

Statistics and Denials

Since the criminal case had already been dismissed, the inquest was largely a matter of public relations—as Sery's lawyer described it, "a three-day press conference." But the jury, on its own initiative, wrote a letter to the City of Portland, questioning police tactics and directly asking whether Perez had been the victim of racial profiling.[17]

Study after study had demonstrated that the Portland police were stopping, searching, arresting, and taking other coercive action against Black and Latino people at rates far exceeding their portion of the population. According to a 2006 report, Black people were stopped at 2.4 times the rate of whites, and Latinos at 1.7 times the white rate. African Americans, making up 6 percent of the local population, accounted for 13 percent of police stops; Latinos, also 6 percent of the population, accounted for 9 percent of stops; and whites, at 79 percent of the population, represented 69.5 percent of stops. In the same period, police searched 27 percent of the Black people they stopped, compared to 26 percent of Latinos and 12.5 percent of whites.[18]

In the previous ten years, 19 percent of the people shot by the Portland Police had been Black and 15 percent Latino.[19] In the years immediately following, from 2004 to 2008, police statistics showed that almost a third of use-of-force reports (29 percent) identified the subject as African American.[20] A 2006 survey showed that more than half of all Portlanders—53 percent of all those interviewed and 71 percent of African Americans—believed that the police regularly stopped people without justification.[21] That same year, for the first time, the Police Bureau acknowledged the existence of racial profiling.[22]

One group that actively disbelieved the evidence of statistics was the Portland Police Association, which responded to accusations of bias by denying the existence of racial profiling and/or by justifying it as an investigative technique. The PPA's newsletter, the *Rap Sheet*, regularly ran letters defending the practice.[23] Retired Captain Jim Harvey, for example, asserted that "there's no such thing as racial profiling," while admitting that "race may be an element of a profile" and expressly defending its use against "gangs of young Hispanic or black men" and against people with "Arabian or Muslim names" in the "war on terrorism."[24]

Since the cops represent the first point of contact between the public and the penal system, disproportionate police scrutiny can have far-reaching consequences, which are then compounded by (as one study put it) "disparities . . . at each stage of the criminal justice system: arrest, prosecution, verdicts, and sentencing."[25] By the middle of the decade, African Americans made up 27.6 percent of felony bookings in Multnomah County and 25.3 percent of misdemeanor bookings.[26] Statewide, in 2005, the incarceration rate for Black Oregonians was 2,930 per 100,000 (nearly 3 percent of the Black population); for Hispanics, it was 573; and for whites, 502. That meant that Black people were 5.8 times as likely to be incarcerated than white people.[27]

Marching and Copwatching

Three demonstrations occurred in the month following Perez's death. The first, on April 4, 2004, was organized by the Albina Ministerial Alliance, the Coalition of Black Men, and the Urban League. The same groups organized another march on April 23, following the grand jury's announcement that it would not indict. The next day, the avowed revolutionaries of the Arissa organization (founded by former Earth Liberation Front spokesman Craig Rosebraugh) led a march to the mayor's house, though both the Perez and James families distanced themselves from the action. Arissa's posters carried the provocative slogan: "The only thing the police understand is an eye for an eye."[28]

That summer a Black-led group called the Portland Community Liberation Front (PCLF) began frequent patrols in North and Northeast Portland, observing the police and documenting abuses. "We decided that we were going to start an organization where we held the police accountable," Caine Lowery later explained. "Every time we saw the police stop somebody we would get out and observe what was happening."[29] About once a week, the PCLF was joined by Rose City Copwatch—an organization founded in 2002 by former members of Portland Copwatch looking to move the work in a more community-focused and less institutional direction, while developing a radical abolitionist politics.[30]

The patrol tactic—"copwatching," using direct observation to deter police misconduct—was not new to Portland, but it occurred with greater frequency in this period. Portland Copwatch had conducted sporadic patrols in the late nineties, largely focused on the cops' treatment of the homeless population. A joint effort between Portland Copwatch and Sisters of the Road led the City to cancel a scheduled sweep of a homeless camp in 1998. Portland Copwatch similarly assisted the Workers Organizing Committee with their MigraWatch project, documenting INS treatment of day laborers. The tactic was sometimes deployed in a support role in other sorts of actions: Rose City Copwatch first mobilized its observers to accompany a picket line blocking access to a job site during a strike.[31]

When Scott McCollister returned to work after his six-month suspension, Rose City Copwatch (RCCW) covered the neighborhood surrounding his precinct with posters warning the community—"Armed and Dangerous Killer Released to North Portland"—and offering a free bag of groceries to anyone who could provide a picture of him.[32] Police, politicians, and the press all generally responded to the posters as though they constituted a threat of violence, when in fact they only suggested that the community should be able to identify killer cops.[33] A few weeks later, RCCW blanketed the city with new posters, this time featuring photos of both McCollister and Sery, renewing the controversy.[34]

The Fire Some Time?

Throughout the summer of 2004, the city was tense, charged with anger and grief—a physical sensation, like electricity in the air. There was an ominous sense of impending cataclysm that some people longed for and some people feared, and nobody could predict when it might begin.[35]

Polite society—press, politicians, the clergy—carefully avoided the word *riot,* as though the mere mention might summon it into being. Detective Peter Simpson came close to breaking the taboo when he worried about the investigation into the Perez shooting: "What will people do if we go all the way through this and the officers are exonerated? How will they react?"[36] Others were thinking the same thing. A group of teenagers—all boys, all Black; truants, smoking cigarettes in the park—debated the possibilities:

> "There about to be a riot, bro. There about to be a riot."
>
> "I don't think it'd be as big as a riot. . . . Yesterday I seen the little rally on the news [and it] seemed pretty peaceful. But I think, you know, probably, man, it could get out of hand, though. But they don't want that, they really don't."
>
> "I hear people talking that if they kill one of us, then we gonna kill two of them."
>
> "People in the hood is pissed, man."
>
> "If nothing happens . . . to this policeman, if nothing happen, bro, then everybody gonna get even madder, bro, cause this has happened [and] that's twice in a row they didn't do nothin', bro. . . . So of course everybody gonna start gettin' mad, and everybody going to start throwing a riot. . . . I swear to God, there gonna be a riot, bro. Watch."[37]

A former city official, speaking on condition of anonymity, thought it a realistic possibility. The first thing that came to his mind after the Perez shooting, he said, was rioting: "Man, many more of these, you know, there are going to be riots. You can only take so much as a people, as a community. . . . I give us two or three more and people are gonna get tired."[38]

The recognized Black leadership, especially the clergy, warned against "hate" and "retaliation." At the April 4 Coalition of Black Men rally, one speaker after another talked about the need for change while also urging a commitment to nonviolence. State Senator Avel Gordly both called for reform and pledged her "full support" to Police Chief Foxworth. But the tone set from the speaker's platform did not match the mood of the crowd. Caine Lowery, who would soon found the Portland Community Liberation Front, said at the time, "I don't think it's necessary to chill people out. I think there needs to be a fiery response from the community to the police department, because every single day people are being harassed . . . And when they get a strong response from the community, that's going to stop everything that goes on, I believe—hopefully."[39]

The riots did not materialize—not that summer. But in August 2004, Jason Sery resigned. He was later hired by the police department in the neighboring suburb of Beaverton.[40]

Two years later, Foxworth was removed from his position as chief, after a civilian clerk filed a complaint accusing him of sexual harassment. They had engaged in what Foxworth called a "brief, but intense" affair, and after it ended she objected to his repeated phone calls and "sexually disgusting email." Mayor Tom Potter called this a "serious lapse of judgment" and demoted Foxworth to captain.[41]

Foxworth was replaced by Rosie Sizer, the commander implicated a few years before in the cover-up of an off-duty beating that landed two cops in jail.[42] As Black United Front co-chair Richard Brown tells it, as soon as Sizer took over, "she set about snuffing out any trace of community policing," even disbanding the Chief's Forum.[43]

Near Chaos

Meanwhile, the Multnomah County Sheriff's Office seemed to be in permanent freefall.

In a single year, 1999, the sheriff's office received 189 complaints of excessive force in the booking area of the Justice Center. But the facility did not come under meaningful scrutiny until July 2000, following two deaths and a brutal beating. John Beckel, owner of the Montage restaurant, died after being forcibly restrained by a deputy. The medical examiner determined that he had hit his head when he fell down in the street prior to his arrest, but accountability advocates pointed to the lack of medical attention in the jail. James Ludto, who had been arrested for drunk driving after crashing his car into a concrete barrier, died in jail from a ruptured spleen. Doctors reported that his body had been covered with bruises inconsistent with the low-speed collision, and the medical examiner determined that he died as a result of the "use of force." Soon after, Dennis Poe was beaten, while in handcuffs, by several deputies: Rodger Cross, James Borja, John Montoya, and Sergeant Jeremy Risvet. He was then strapped to a restraint board and beaten again. One of those implicated, Cross, was responsible for training new hires in the use of force.[44]

It later emerged that, earlier on the day that Poe was beaten, Deputy Michael Foster had taken Borja and Montoya to get matching tattoos, an emblem reading "Brotherhood of the Strong." Foster apparently arrived in Oregon with a similar tattoo, having been part of a deputy gang in Hawaii. He was fired, ostensibly for lying about his employment history, and the FBI opened a civil rights investigation. The four deputies who beat Poe were eventually fired, and Risvet was convicted of harassment and official misconduct. He was sentenced to fifteen days in jail and two years of probation. Sheriff Dan Noelle offered a public apology, added video cameras to intake areas, increased training for deputies, and began teaching civilian employees to recognize and report excessive force.[45]

Almost ten years later, the sheriff's office, and the jails specifically, were again facing scrutiny. Over the course of 2007, Deputy Alexander Weise pled no contest to a charge of official misconduct related to a romantic (though nonsexual) relationship with an inmate. Another deputy, Erich Watson, was sentenced to eighteen months of probation after he was caught smuggling cocaine into the jail. A pair of lawsuits focused on beatings deputies delivered in the jail's intake area. Corrections Deputy David B. Thompson was transferred away from inmates after bragging online: "I crushed a dude's eye socket from repeatedly punching him.... He took a plea to get away from me." The increase in violence coincided with a decline in oversight. Since the election of Sheriff Bernie Giusto in 2002, the sheriff's office had averaged just nineteen disciplinary investigations each year, down from fifty under his predecessor.[46]

The agency's finances were similarly mismanaged. When former Sheriff Dan Noelle conducted an evaluation of Giusto's administration, he found $5.5 million in waste.[47] The county auditor and a grand jury similarly criticized the spiraling overtime costs—up from $3.6 million in 2003 to $6.15 million in 2005.[48]

Giusto additionally allowed deputies to use their uniforms and patrol cars while moonlighting as security guards, in violation of policy.[49]

In 2006, District Attorney Michael Schrunk released an extremely critical report on the state of the jails, describing facilities in a state of "violent and costly near-chaos because the elected officials responsible for overseeing them refused to do their jobs." The report faulted jail staff for admitting injured prisoners without adequate medical care, accused guards of obscuring security cameras while taking unauthorized breaks, and concluded that Giusto was reluctant to enact discipline even when it was recommended by commanders. Giusto responded the next day with a press conference, where he defended his management style: "This is a jailin' system, j-a-i-l-i-n, no 'g'—we're all about being the Arkansas of the West Coast." Apparently the Multnomah County Commission disagreed. Chair Ted Wheeler took control of jail spending and discipline for the next six months.[50]

At the same time, Giusto was facing charges that he had misused his office by intervening in a marital dispute between Jim Jeddeloh, the former head of the Citizens Crime Commission, and his wife, Lee Doss, with whom Giusto was having an affair. Jeddeloh's family confronted him about his drinking while Giusto's deputies waited outside. When the family was finished, the deputies entered and presented Jeddeloh with a choice: go to rehab or be served with divorce papers and a restraining order. In January 2007, Giusto was exonerated, and the *Oregonian* dubbed him "The Teflon Sheriff." Deputies called him "Porno Pants."[51]

Inappropriate

Giusto's legal troubles weren't over, however. Just a few weeks later, a citizen complaint filed with the state's Department of Public Safety Standards and Training (DPSST) listed numerous allegations from throughout the sheriff's decades-long career. It made the case that Giusto was not morally fit to hold office, since state law prohibited "acts and conduct which would cause a reasonable person to have substantial doubts about the individual's honesty, fairness, respect for the rights of others or the laws of the state." When Giusto learned of the complaint, he ordered Detective Todd Shanks to run a background check on the person who filed it, in itself an illegitimate and illegal use of government databases. At the same time, suspecting a leak from within his own agency, Giusto ordered an internal investigation to find the source. Adding heft to the allegations, Fred Leonhardt, a former speechwriter for Governor Neil Goldschmidt, submitted a statement asserting that, as the governor's bodyguard and driver in the late eighties, Giusto had learned about Goldschmidt's sexually exploitative relationship with a minor a decade before. Giusto claimed that he did not report the abuse because the statute of limitations had expired, but Leonhardt believed that he blackmailed Goldschmidt in order to keep his job while carrying on an affair with the governor's wife. In the end, the DPSST concluded that Giusto had lied to investigators about that relationship, and in June 2008 he resigned, forfeiting his law enforcement certification.[52]

Bob Skipper was appointed sheriff in July 2008 and elected that fall. The *Oregonian* was hopeful: "Skipper's humble, old-fashioned style is in marked contrast to [Giusto's] swagger and tangled personal life. . . . Skipper earned praise for bringing stability, integrity, and credibility to an agency currently much in need of all those things."[53] Yet a year later, Skipper was gone, having twice failed certification tests, even after being exempted from the physical fitness requirements.[54]

In November 2009, Dan Staton replaced Skipper.[55] In many ways, Staton's term was a repeat of Giusto's: Staton used Multnomah County funds to purchase a $33,623 Dodge Charger with leather seats, a sunroof, and polished aluminum wheels; Chief Deputy Linda Yankee accused him of sexual harassment, resulting in a $300,000 settlement; and there were accusations of bribery.[56] He fired an analyst after she released a report showing that African Americans made up only 5 percent of county residents but 27 percent of inmates in the county's jails and 40 percent of those against whom force was used. Continuing the long-established pattern of investigating and harassing the MCSO's critics, Staton ordered background checks on the advocates of an appointed-sheriff system and intimidated members of the charter committee. The Oregon attorney general opened a criminal investigation, looking at his "violent threats" against political opponents.[57] Even the Oregon State Fraternal Order of Police published a letter expressing concern about Staton's "alleged inappropriate behavior" and the "hostile work environment" that might result, then pointedly asking, "Should the sheriff continue to be sheriff or should he step down?"[58]

CHAPTER 27

Public Order and Mental Disorder

A Terrible Fear

On September 17, 2006, two transit cops—Portland Police Officer Christopher Humphreys and Multnomah County Deputy Brett Burton—spotted James Chasse Jr. on the street in the upscale Pearl District. "He caught my attention initially because he [was] disheveled," Humphreys told investigators. "I just assumed he was probably transient."[1]

Chasse was not homeless, but he lived with poverty and suffered from schizophrenia. A recognizable figure in the counterculture and alternative music scene since the 1970s, "Jim Jim" was known to sometimes behave strangely but was widely regarded as harmless.[2] Two of the city's most notable seventies punk bands, the Wipers and the Neo Boys, had written songs for or about him—"Alien Boy" and "Nothing to Fear," respectively. Chasse had been beaten by the cops as a teenager, and, according to his mother, "from about that time on, he had a terrible fear of the police."[3]

And so, in 2006, when Humphreys and Burton approached him, Chasse ran. They chased him and, joined by Portland Police Sergeant Kyle Nice, caught up with him up at the intersection of Northwest Thirteenth and Everett, where they tackled him, then punched and kicked him, tasered him, and hogtied him.[4] A bartender at the Blue Hour later told an interviewer: "I saw knees to the chest, punches to the face. . . . the officer behind him was striking downward at him . . . a haymaker, . . . when you're just bringing your arm all the way back and bringing it down full force." Another witness recalled, "He's clearly not a dangerous person, he is a frightened person. . . . the hit on the pavement, the twisting and turning, the kicks, the hit, the taser. . . . After a few minutes I wondered if he was dead."[5]

The medical examiner, Karen Gunson, found: "Chasse suffered 46 separate abrasions or contusions on his body, including six of the head and 19 strikes to the torso. . . . Fractures to Chasse's rear ribs . . . likely resulted from a kick or a knee-drop."[6] Sixteen ribs were broken in twenty-six places; some had punctured his lungs. His collarbone was also broken and his spleen ruptured.[7] Gunson compared his injuries to those caused by "a high-speed car crash." Still, she thought, "If he had been transported to the hospital at this point he would have had a long recovery but he probably would have survived."[8]

The police failed to tell paramedics about the level of force they had used or that Chasse had lost consciousness, and misled them by suggesting that he had been taking drugs. Once medics determined that his vital signs were normal, the cops dismissed them and took Chasse to jail, where they again failed to disclose the prior use of force. But on examining him, a nurse at the jail ordered transport to a hospital. Rather than call an ambulance, the cops loaded him into a squad car and drove unhurriedly toward the most distant hospital in the city, using neither lights nor sirens. He died on the way.[9]

Gresham Police Sergeant Terry O'Keefe, who was supervising the transit officers, sent them a text: "Nice work boys. Glad U R OK N HE ISN'T."[10]

The Boundary

There is no evidence that James Chasse committed any crime. The police initially claimed they suspected him of urinating in public, but Transit Police Commander Donna Henderson later admitted that that was just a "pretext." She pointed more generally to the Transit Division's quality-of-life mission, with its emphasis on small nuisances and signs of disorder—things like panhandling, sleeping on the sidewalk, and peeing in public.[11] By and large these are class-coded offenses, and thus the real targets of enforcement tend to be poor people as such. Jason Renaud of the Mental Health Association of Portland later explained the political geography: "Portland spent over a hundred and twenty years ghettoizing people who were poor and in trouble into the inner part of the downtown area, what we call Old Town. Well, recently, the City has allowed the urbanization [gentrification] of a large industrial area adjacent to Old Town. Now it's called the Pearl District. . . . The police patrol the boundary between the Pearl District and Old Town very rigorously."[12]

The Pearl District, exemplified "a successful urban renewal project," in the words of one developer. "Working together, both the private and public sector transformed an old manufacturing-industrial area into a lively urban community with a strong arts cultural overlay . . . a destination playground for those seeking a unique urban getaway experience." That transformation had begun in the late seventies, as artists converted industrial space into studios and lofts. They were priced out over time, to be replaced by yuppies in condos, along with restaurants, bars, boutiques, and storefront galleries. The epicenter of this change, and the "heart and soul" of the development project, was Northwest Thirteenth Avenue—where the cops beat Chasse.[13] The creation of a "Pearl District" out of a swatch of warehouses and breweries was largely a matter of economics, but reserving it as a "playground" for the rich, alongside an area of concentrated poverty, required a certain amount of violence.

All Cops Are Humphreys

The Portland Police Bureau took three years to complete its investigation into Chasse's death. In the end, the Use of Force Review Board determined that the cops did not use excessive force when they tackled, kicked, beat, and tasered him but that they should have immediately taken him to the hospital. Chief Rosie Sizer proposed a one-week suspension for Sergeant Kyle Nice; Police Commissioner Dan Saltzman increased it to two weeks for Nice and Humphreys both. Their discipline was eventually reversed in arbitration. In the meantime, Deputy Burton was hired by the Portland Police.[14]

Portland Police Association president Scott Westerman explained the case against discipline: "If they're going to pull those three officers from patrol, the city may as well pull all police officers from the street, because any officer on the Portland Police Bureau that was present in that situation would have likely had the same outcome."[15]

Chris Humphreys made headlines again on November 14, 2009, when he was caught on video firing a less-lethal shotgun at a twelve-year-old Black girl who had boarded the light rail train in violation of a previous exclusion order. Commissioner Saltzman immediately placed him on paid administrative leave while the incident was being investigated.[16]

The police union cried foul. The *Rap Sheet* ran at least nine articles defending Humphreys's tactics. Echoing their earlier response to the possum scandal, the PPA called for a no-confidence vote against Saltzman and Sizer and organized a large public demonstration. On November 24, 2009, about seven hundred cops marched to City Hall wearing T-shirts and carrying signs reading "Safety! Not

Politics," "I Support the Police!," and, most tellingly, "I Am Chris Humphreys"—putting to rest the argument that we cannot judge all officers by the violent actions of a few. In the end, a compromise was reached: Humphreys would be assigned desk duty, and the union would not release the results of its vote.[17]

Humphreys was later exonerated by the chief of police, and the Training Division started showing the video to demonstrate the correct use of the less-lethal shotgun. Regardless, he soon left the Portland Police Bureau. In 2012, he was elected sheriff in Wheeler County, Oregon.[18]

Terribly Wrong

Following the Police Association's show of strength, the difficulty of disciplining killer cops would be proven repeatedly.

On the evening of January 29, 2010, Aaron Campbell's family called 911 asking that someone check on him. His brother had died earlier in the day, and they feared Campbell might be considering suicide. Soon after the police arrived at the Sandy Terrace Apartments, they contacted the despondent man by phone and two hours later persuaded him to come outside. Campbell walked out to the parking lot with his hands on his head. Officer Ryan Lewton ordered him to put his hands in the air but then fired less-lethal rounds, hitting him half a dozen times. Reacting to the pain, Campbell's hands went to the area where he had been hit, and he started to run. Officer Ron Frashour then fired his AR-15, killing him. PPA president Scott Westerman was uncharacteristically frank about the shooting: "Basically, we shot an unarmed black guy running away from us."[19]

A grand jury determined that there was no basis for criminal charges against the officers but, in an unusual move, published a letter to the district attorney to clarify their feelings: "What we found was that Officer Frashour's actions were consistent with the relevant laws and statutes regarding the use of deadly force by a police officer. . . . This was very difficult for us. . . . Our sympathies lie with the Campbell family and the mood of the community. As a group, we are outraged. . . . We know something went terribly, terribly wrong at Sandy Terrace and that Aaron Campbell should not have died that day."[20]

In addition to the decisions of individual officers, the grand jury pointed to systemic problems with police tactics, training, communication, and command and control. For instance, Captain Bob Day had arrived on the scene without his ballistic vest, necessitating that the incident commander leave the scene to brief him. When she did, Sergeant Liani Reyna failed to appoint a proxy, and during this moment without leadership everything had gone awry.[21]

Cops, Pigs, Murderers

Campbell was killed amid a regional upsurge in resistance to police violence, beginning with the death of Oscar Grant, in Oakland. Grant—another unarmed Black man—was killed by transit police in front of numerous witnesses on New Year's Day 2009, shot in the back while on the ground. Riotous demonstrations followed, and Officer Johannes Mehserle was convicted of manslaughter and sent to prison.[22] For most of the next two years, West Coast cities regularly responded to police violence with militant protests and riots—as well as occasional arson, sabotage, and ambush attacks.[23]

A series of rallies and marches followed the Campbell shooting, including one with about twelve hundred people, led by the Reverend Jesse Jackson. Jackson first met with Mayor Sam Adams and Police Commissioner Dan Saltzman, telling them that it was "insulting" that Frashour remained on the force. That night, he urged an audience at Maranatha Church: "Make this a matter of conscience, a matter of right and wrong and not just a matter of black and white." The next day hundreds of people marched into City Hall and confronted the mayor.[24]

Two months after Campbell's death, Officer Jason Walters shot and killed Jack Dale Collins, a homeless man, as he exited a public restroom holding an Exacto knife and covered in his own blood.[25] Boisterous demonstrations began that same night, with overturned dumpsters, a few broken windows, and graffiti. Crowds chanted, "Cops! Pigs! Murderers!" April 8 and 9 were declared "West Coast Solidarity Days of Action," with protest marches and civil disobedience events in Olympia, Seattle, Oakland, and Portland. In Portland, anarchists blockaded the intersection at Thirteenth and Everett, where James Chasse had been beaten three years before; the next day they arranged a public discussion "about the role of police in their communities, alternatives to the police, and the viability of different tactics of resistance."[26] Increasingly the question of policing was framed not in terms of how to control them, but how to get rid of them altogether—not police accountability but police abolition.

As the weeks went on, a range of tactics were employed: community forums, leafleting, street-corner demonstrations, and—with surprising regularity—black bloc actions in which windows were broken, numerous people were arrested, and, reportedly, several cops were injured. Nighttime sabotage also occurred: police substations, a community corrections office, and the headquarters of the Portland Police Association all had their windows broken.[27] Brian Michael Bendis, a Portland resident and, at the time, one of the most popular comics creators in the world, started publishing *Scarlet*, a series set in Portland, featuring a young woman who gets fed up with police corruption and just starts killing cops.[28]

Bernie Foster, the publisher of African American newspaper the *Skanner*, wrote a sober editorial titled "Having an Emergency? Don't Call the Police." "The fact is, we at *The Skanner News* simply have to warn our readers away from calling the police when they are in a crisis situation. We cannot have faith that innocents won't get caught in the firing line." He called on the Black community to develop better skills and resources to "solve problems and de-escalate potential violence" rather than relying on "some force outside ourselves to fix our situation."[29]

Feminists, especially those near anarchist subcultures, were thinking along the same lines, and began experimenting with "restorative" or "transformative" forms of justice, particularly to address sexual assault and intimate partner violence. Praxiss, the Pink Tape Collective, and other small volunteer organizations—along with several unnamed ad hoc interventions—sought to work with both survivors and perpetrators to repair harm and build the skills for healthier, more respectful and egalitarian relationships.[30]

In the first months of 2010, the resistance to policing began to take the form of a genuine popular movement—a fact evinced by the variety of approaches animated by a common underlying sentiment. The mounting anger, frustration, and sense of crisis both echoed and built on earlier cycles of protest, especially those following the shootings of José Mejía, Kendra James, and James Jahar Perez. And in several respects—the pervasive distrust of police, the disruptive and confrontational demonstrations, the embrace of illegal tactics, the rhetorical shift toward abolition, and the tendency for unrest to spread from city to city—the struggle of 2010 foreshadowed the climactic events to come in 2020.

Another Fatality

Facing increasing scrutiny, widespread calls for accountability, and escalating unrest, the government was eager to seem responsive. In March 2010, the city council passed a proposal to increase the authority of the civilian review board, adding subpoena powers, expanding the scope of investigations, and granting it jurisdiction over any interaction between civilians and police.[31] Two months later, on May 10, the City of Portland settled with James Chasse's family for $1.6 million. It was the last of a series of settlements, after Multnomah County paid $925,000 and American Medical Response paid $600,000.[32] Also on May 10, with spectacularly poor timing, Police Chief Sizer held a press conference in which she, flanked by her top commanders, complained about constraints to the police bureau's budget.[33] Two days later, Mayor Adams announced that he was taking over as police commissioner, promising to steer the bureau in "a different direction." He fired Sizer and appointed Mike Reese as chief.[34] Adams explained, "Too many Portlanders express concern about their own safety—not because of crime, but rather fear of their own police force."[35]

By cruel coincidence, another young Black man was killed by police that same day. Keaton Otis was driving his mother's car in the area of the Lloyd Center mall on May 12, 2010, when the police pulled him over. According to a witness, this encounter at first seemed like "a fairly calm situation," but it went wrong quite suddenly. "They were just talking to the guy and wanted him to get out of the car and when he wouldn't they reached in and they grabbed him . . . and then it just escalated very, very, quickly, this all occurred in a matter of I would say a minute[,] two minutes at the most." At that point, one officer "fired the Taser," and Otis "slumped over or leaned over . . . and very quickly after that, there were shots fired." Another witness was more specific: "Then a shot rang out, heard one shot, officer [Chris Burley] went down. And then all the officers on scene . . . opened fire on the vehicle." The police fired more than thirty times, shooting recklessly in a densely populated neighborhood. Officer Pat Murphy, on the opposite side of the car, had to dive for cover. The wall behind him was left pockmarked by bullets. One round landed inside a store two blocks away. Keaton Otis died at the scene.[36]

In January 2012, the Police Review Board ruled, almost unanimously, that all officers involved in Keaton Otis's death were acting within policy. No one was disciplined.[37]

In a different year, in another context, Otis's death would hardly have been controversial. A cop had been shot and, though he survived, for most people, including journalists and even many activists, that would settle the matter. But coming so soon after Campbell's death and in the midst of what was already a crisis of legitimacy, another fatality could only deepen the sense of public mistrust. Fred Bryant, Otis's father, never accepted the cops' version of the story and insisted that his son did not own a gun.[38] His doubts were often echoed in the Black community, drawing from long historical experience, though witness statements overwhelmingly corroborate the police narrative. More surprisingly, some people accepted the facts as presented and still believed that the cops were in the wrong. Given "the overwhelming number of officers," their readiness to resort to violence, their misuse of the taser in this very case, and a recent court ruling (*State v. Oliphant*) establishing the right to defend oneself against excessive force, even the avowedly pacifist Portland Copwatch had to ask, "Isn't it possible that . . . [Keaton Otis] had a right to self-defense?"[39]

Reasonable Suspicion

Underlying the community's suspicion was a sense that the traffic stop itself was illegitimate. "Keaton Otis did not have to die and Officer Christopher Burley did not have to be shot," Reverend LeRoy Haynes said at an Albina Ministerial Alliance press conference. "Keaton Otis, a citizen of this community, was pursued on an erroneous assumption that he was a gang member on the basis of his racial identity and attire."[40]

Haynes was not guessing as to the cops' motives. He was simply repeating the story as the police themselves told it: spotting Otis, a young Black man in a hooded sweatshirt driving his mother's Toyota Corolla, Officer Ryan Foote had decided to run his plates, thinking that he looked "like he could be a gangster." Even Foote's partner, James DeFrain, was skeptical: "Are you serious?," he asked. "You're going to run that Corolla?" Though the car had not been reported stolen, they decided to pull it over anyway.[41]

Foote and DeFrain were members of the Hotspot Enforcement Action Team (HEAT), "a citywide street crimes unit," which DeFrain described in classic community-policing style: "A big part of our job is to refer kids . . . to counselors who then, through the Office of Youth Violence Prevention go out and see the kids and try to help 'em. We do a lot of that. . . . [We] gather a lot of intelligence and information for GET [the Gang Enforcement Team]. . . . [We] also do enforcement . . . to get guns off the street."[42] HEAT was aggressive in the pursuit of its mission, logging an impressive twenty-five thousand contacts and thirty-five hundred arrests in the previous two years—averaging thirty-four stops and five arrests daily.[43]

Later, police bureau spokesperson Detective Mary Wheat assured the public that the cops "were not racial profiling"—which the bureau defined as "the inappropriate reliance on race as a factor in deciding to stop and/or search an individual."[44] Naturally, that formulation left plenty of room for the cops to decide which racial considerations *were* appropriate. For instance, more than a year before Otis was shot, James Pitkin, a reporter for *Willamette Week*, tagged along during "Operation Cool Down" as the police increased their presence in gang-affected neighborhoods. He reported that the cops passed by groups of white people without notice but stopped, searched, and questioned Black and Latino men when they saw them. "Profiling—I'm not scared of that word," Gang Enforcement Officer Russ Corno commented. "If you're profiling people based just on their race, that is an issue. We're profiling people based on crime." Yet Pitkin wrote: "Corno is frank about who they're targeting: young black men." Corno explained, "Statistics don't lie. You gotta go where the numbers go."[45]

By the police bureau's own reporting, African Americans made up only 6 percent of the city's population in 2010 but 12 percent of motor vehicle stops. Of the drivers they stopped, police searched 14 percent of African Americans and 11.4 percent of Latinos but only 6.5 percent of whites. Moreover, 20 percent of pedestrian and bicycle stops were of African Americans. Again, people of color were searched at twice the rate of whites: 9 percent of Black pedestrians and 6 percent of Latinos, compared to 3.5 percent of whites.[46]

Such numbers indicate more than just the personal biases of individual officers. They demonstrate an institutional orientation that treated Black people as suspects, as hazards, and as targets for violence. Between 2000 and 2010, twenty-six people were killed by the Portland Police, eight of them (30 percent) people of color. A further result was the overrepresentation of people of color in all parts of the criminal legal system. Only 5.2 percent of Multnomah County's population was Black, but they composed 24.1 percent of those under the supervision of the corrections system and were more than six times as likely to be in prison as whites (3 percent of the Black population; 0.4 percent of the white).[47] By a kind of circular logic, that overrepresentation was then cited to justify the heightened scrutiny that had originally produced it.[48] ("You gotta go where the numbers go.") Perhaps not surprisingly, in 2007, two-thirds of Oregon's Black population said they believed the police often or always engaged in racial profiling.[49]

Music and Dress

This discriminatory suspicion extended also to Black cultural events and even commercial enterprises. "The Portland Police have continuously shut down hip-hop clubs," the musician G_Force told *Vice*.[50] Mac Smiff agrees: "They really just used the city's resources—the police, the fire marshals, the OLCC [the Oregon Liquor Control Commission, since renamed the Oregon Liquor and Cannabis Commission]—to really, like, shut down hip hop, and really any black-led event."[51] The organizers for PDX Pop Now! told investigators with the Independent Police Review that, during their multi-day music festivals, hip-hop acts received greater scrutiny and attracted a larger police presence than other artists.[52] Luck-One made the point more forcefully: "The police are sent out to every rap show to terrorize concert-goers."[53]

In March 2014, the Gang Enforcement Team, concerned about a scheduled performance by rapper Mikey Vegaz, asked the police bureau's entertainment detail to do a walk-through at the venue, the Blue Monk. Noticing an overcrowding issue, the police contacted the fire inspector, who conducted a formal count. Finding the basement concert space full beyond capacity, he ordered a portion of the audience to leave. While no doubt frustrated and disappointed, the audience was cooperative, and a large group exited the building. But seeing a crowd spill out onto the street, the cops called for backup. Within minutes, fourteen officers were on the scene, their cars blocking the streets surrounding the club and their overhead lights flashing. The police presence became so intimidating that the musicians refused to perform. A month later, the Blue Monk closed for good, pointing to the canceled show as the coup de grace.[54]

Throughout the 2010s, the Gang Enforcement Team (and its successor, the Gun Violence Reduction Team) trained bar owners, managers, and bouncers to profile and exclude gang members, often by imposing strict and ostensibly race-neutral dress codes. The rules generally banned red and blue clothing, sports jerseys, ball caps, and baggy pants—all items the police associated with Black gangs like the Bloods and the Crips. (The training was silent concerning the Gypsy Jokers, European Kindred, and other white gangs.) The strict standards were selectively enforced, serving, as one security guard put it, "as an excuse to not let people in they don't want in there anyway."[55]

When bar owners eschewed such racist practices, the pressure they faced could be intense. Soon after Samuel Thompson opened his bar, Seeznin's, in 2011, he noticed that the place was receiving an unusual amount of police attention. “The police used to come . . . and sit in front of the damn bar with their lights on for hours,” he recalled. When cops explained that they were suspicious because of the building’s blue decor—the color being associated with the Crips—Thompson repainted. Still, when a shooting occurred across the street, the OLCC imposed new restrictions on Seeznin’s: four security guards on busy nights, searches at the door, a strict dress code, and no alcohol sales after 11:00 p.m. “It seems like they want me to be the police and do their job,” Thompson said. Unable to meet the new requirements and turn a profit, Seeznin’s soon went out of business.[56]

This pattern spans decades. In 1997, after an unrelated shooting outside the concert venue La Luna, Detective Bill Calder advised its owner that the solution to violence was “not having hip-hop shows.” For months afterward, it was virtually impossible to book such shows anywhere in the city.[57] More than twenty years later, in 2019, the *Mercury* reported on another club driven out of business after police started posting themselves by the door, passively discouraging entry.[58]

Pattern or Practice

In November 2010, Officer Ron Frashour was fired for the shooting of Aaron Campbell. Three other officers were suspended for two weeks: Officer Ryan Lewton, who had inexplicably hit Campbell with the less-lethal rounds as he tried to surrender; Sergeant John Birkbine, who had failed to communicate with fellow officers when he ordered Campbell out of the house; and Sergeant Liani Reyna, who had been in charge at the scene and neglected to delegate authority when she went to brief senior officers. The PPA preferred to blame Captain Day for arriving without protective gear, thus requiring Reyna to step away—but he was not disciplined. He would later become the head of the Training Division and then chief of police.[59]

In March 2012, two years after Campbell’s death, his family received a settlement of $1.2 million. That same month an arbiter ordered that Frashour be reinstated with back pay.[60] This outcome was as predictable as it was frustrating. “It broke my heart and burst a blood vessel in my head,” Mayor Adams later recalled. “The whole thing was sad and infuriating and proof positive that the civilians who run the city of Portland do not have control over their police bureau.”[61]

Having encountered one dead end after another in the local system, a truly impressive assortment of individuals and organizations—including the Urban League, the Albina Ministerial Alliance, Police Commissioner Dan Saltzman, US Representative Earl Blumenauer, and US Senator Ron Wyden—wrote to the Department of Justice to request a civil rights investigation.[62] And on June 7, 2011, Assistant Attorney General Thomas Perez announced that the Civil Rights Division would embark on a "pattern and practice" investigation to determine whether the cops' treatment of people with mental illness violated their constitutional rights. Many critics, including Portland Copwatch and Jo Ann Bowman (a former state senator who would later be elected to the city council as Jo Ann Hardesty) objected to the exclusive "mental illness" focus and urged that race should also be included in the scope of the inquiry.[63]

Concluding its investigation in September 2012, the Department of Justice sent Mayor Adams a forty-two-page letter outlining its findings, including:

> (1) Encounters between PPB officers and persons with mental illness too frequently result in a use of force when force is unnecessary or in the use of a higher level of force than necessary or appropriate, up to and including deadly force. We found instances that support a pattern of dangerous uses of force against persons who posed little or no threat and who could not, as a result of their mental illness, comply with officers' commands. We also found that PPB employs practices that escalate the use of force where there were clear earlier junctures when the force could have been avoided or minimized. . . .
>
> (2) In particular, we found that PPB officers use electronic control weapons ('ECWs' (commonly referred to as 'Tasers')) in circumstances when ECW use is not justified. . . .
>
> (3) . . . [We] found that PPB officers use more force than necessary in effectuating arrests for low level offenses involving people who are or appear to be in mental health crisis.

Crucially, this violence was not simply the product of individual biases but resulted "from deficiencies in policy, training, and supervision," including "(1) deficiencies in responding to persons with mental illness or in mental health crisis; (2) inadequate reviews of officers' use of force; and (3) inadequate investigations of officer misconduct." Specifically, the Justice Department found inadequate supervisory review of use-of-force cases and a reluctance to fault officers for using violence. "Our analysis and review of hundreds of police reports revealed that rarely was the use of force found to be out of policy, even when the force used was clearly excessive."[64]

To remedy this state of affairs, the Justice Department negotiated a binding agreement with the City of Portland stipulating new "guidance [for officers] when encountering someone with mental illness," stricter timelines for misconduct investigations, and the creation of a new "body to ensure increased community oversight of reforms."[65]

Police Chief Mike Reese, however, was stubborn in his refusal to accept responsibility or hold his officers to account. Speaking at the press conference announcing the agreement, his main aim was to excuse the behavior of his troops. "What we're talking about today are processes and systems, not about our police officers," he said. "They're not the folks to blame. They are out in the community doing their very best and in the majority of cases are highly successful, saving lives and making a positive difference. I support them and what they do."[66]

Reese would go on to be elected Multnomah County sheriff in 2016. During his time there, jail guards colluded with criminal gangs, including the Hoovers and the Gypsy Jokers, offering them special privileges and in return relying on gang members to discipline other prisoners. It was "the culture in these units at that time," one guard explained, "where if you let them handle their own business, then the units would run smoothly." Or, as one gang member put it, speaking on a recorded phone line, "We take care of shit for them, they gonna take care of shit for us in here."[67]

Reese is now head of the Oregon Department of Corrections.[68]

CHAPTER 28

Redevelopment, Homelessness, and the Occupy Movement

Re-Commoning

On October 6, 2011, several thousand people marched through downtown Portland, and a couple hundred set up camp in two adjacent parks at the Chapman and Lownsdale Squares—the Plaza Blocks—between the Justice Center and the federal courthouse on one side and the county courthouse and the Portland Building on the other. (City Hall is only one block south and well within sight.) Though organizers had refused to apply for a permit, the police took a nonconfrontational approach, and Mayor Sam Adams granted the group permission to stay the night, provided they leave by 9:00 a.m. the next day. Protesters ignored the deadline and maintained the camp for more than a month.[1]

This was Occupy Portland, one of hundreds of similar encampments worldwide. The first, New York City's Occupy Wall Street (OWS), began with a civil disobedience action near the Stock Exchange on September 1, 2011, and was quickly ended with a few arrests. A couple weeks later, however, on September 17, OWS set up camp in Zuccotti Park and used it as a base from which to launch daily protests.[2] "[The] tactics of Occupy Wall Street," radical geographer David Harvey explained, "are to take a central public space, a park or a square, close to where many of the levers of power are centered, and, by putting human bodies in that place, to convert public space into a political commons—a place for open discussion and debate over what power is doing and how best to oppose its reach."[3] Occupy was many things: a belated response to the 2007 to 2008 financial crash; a protest against economic inequality; a re-commoning of public space; an experiment in direct democracy; and a prefigurative model for a new society.[4]

In Portland, Occupy held two parks for about five weeks. Some people lived there full-time for as long as it lasted. Others stopped by, regularly or sporadically, just to hang out or to help with specific tasks like cooking or facilitating seemingly interminable meetings. But by mid-November the City of Portland had had enough. On November 10, Mayor Adams issued an ultimatum giving the protesters two days to clear out. This time, they did not simply ignore the mayor's demand, they defied it. As the deadline approached, nearly five thousand people filled the parks to defend the camp. The police withdrew. When the appointed hour arrived and nothing happened, the crowd started to thin. By morning, there were far fewer people, and the police returned. Cops with loudspeakers warned of arrests, as well as "chemical agents and impact weapons." Demonstrators chanted in reply: "We are a peaceful protest!" and "The whole world is watching!" Most of those remaining left when ordered, though a few stayed to be arrested. When the cops moved in, they beat those still in the park. City workers then cleared away the remaining tents and erected fences around the suddenly vacant space.[5]

Many within the movement experienced the eviction as a kind of betrayal. Occupy's police and City Hall liaisons resigned, having worked for weeks to establish direct lines of communication with the mayor and the police chief. Some individual campers had likewise tried to maintain friendly relations with the cops, offering regular expressions of gratitude or collaborating on security measures. For their part, the cops had done their best to maintain the appearance of nonviolence and restraint, and Portland Copwatch reported that "Occupy Portland had a mostly good relationship with the police until about two days before the eviction."[6]

Still, there had been plenty of signs of what was coming. The police had maintained an almost continuous street presence near the Occupy site, and they released daily reports detailing such trivial incidents as drug use, fights, and overflowing toilets—establishing any number of pretexts for intervention. The *Oregonian* and the Portland Business Alliance publicly urged that the parks be cleared.[7]

Very likely, the decisive factor inclining the government to act rather than simply wait the protesters out, was the worry that the "Occupy" tactic would spread further, to other parks or to vacant buildings, or escalate to more disruptive actions (as Occupy Oakland already had, closing down the port).[8] Mayor Adams had agreed to tolerate the existing tent city, but he specifically warned against establishing new encampments elsewhere. Heedless of his threats, one group tried exactly that on October 29, striking camp at Jamison Square in the recently gentrified Pearl District. After about twelve hours, police in riot gear pushed the protesters out and arrested twenty-seven people.[9] Exactly two weeks later, the city's law enforcement agencies swept through the encampment at Chapman and Lownsdale Squares.

Coordinated Assault

This final eviction at the main camp, in the early hours of November 13, was just one operation in a nationwide campaign. Fifteen raids—including those in Portland, Oakland, Seattle, and New York—occurred in just the five days of November 11 to November 15. Across the country, municipal and federal authorities coordinated timetables and agreed on common messaging to try to minimize the public outcry. The Department of Homeland Security and the FBI, in discussions facilitated by the US Conference of Mayors, offered advice to the elected leaders of eighteen cities. "There had been two calls hosted by the organization," Mayor Adams told the *New York Times*, "to share information about the occupying encampments around the country" and to discuss tactics. The Police Executive Research Forum (PERF) likewise organized conference calls involving representatives from forty law enforcement agencies. Chuck Wexler, PERF's executive director, said the idea "originated from Boston and Portland. The police chiefs in those cities asked to just compare notes."[10]

Perhaps more than anything else, these calls helped to develop a common narrative, seizing on the longstanding association of order with sanitation and hygiene, and disorder with filth and disease. The equation works in both directions: dirt as disorder, disorder as dirt. "The trope was useful," sociologist Mike King explains, in depicting the "encampments as untenable and dangerous" and the activists as "dirty and irresponsible." This rhetoric depoliticized the police action. "There [was] a deliberate avoidance of frames of repression," suggesting instead that "the cities had no choice and were forced to raid the camps due to their obligation to maintain public health and safety." The same story was told by mayors in city after city—New York, Los Angeles, Oakland, Denver, and Philadelphia as well as Portland—generally accompanied by liberal platitudes about free speech and even expressions of sympathy for the movement they were preparing to repress. And so officials in Portland expressed concern over the state of the camp's kitchen, and the mayor worried that "crime, especially reported assaults, ha[d] increased in an area around the camps."[11] (This was likely true but also misleading: a park with people in it is bound to have more crime than a park with no people in it.)

Still, there were evident limits to the legitimating narrative. A few days after the eviction, Police Chief Mike Reese announced the end of his campaign to become the next mayor.[12]

Those Other Tent Cities

Occupy had embodied a collective claim to public space—both as a tactic and as a kind of prefigurative gesture, symbolically instantiating a different kind of society. For increasing numbers of people, however, occupying public space is not a tactical choice but a material inevitability: there simply is no other place for them to go. They are not *claiming* public space so much as they are thrust into it.

In the late 1990s, Portland had been famously inexpensive, especially compared to other West Coast cities.[13] That would change, gradually but dramatically, over the course of the following decade, and by 2012 a majority of the city's residents (59 percent) felt that housing was unaffordable. The average cost of a single-family home was $400,000. Rents increased an average of 50 percent in *a single year* (2014–15), and by 2015 there were about three thousand homeless people living in the city.[14]

This situation, even apart from social or moral concerns, was economically irrational. Homelessness is expensive, as R. Bruce Stephenson explains: "The price of keeping a homeless person in the streets ranges up to $40,000 a year when factoring in the various levels of city assistance, crisis intervention, emergency medical support, and the demand on correctional facilities." The solutions are obvious but politically unacceptable: "improved access to mental health care, additional low-skill jobs and higher wages, more options for fighting addiction and, most of all, more permanent affordable housing." As usual, the City of Portland was making inconsistent, tentative, and incremental moves toward the provision of services, alongside immediate, sustained, and decisive leaps toward criminalization.[15]

In May 2010, the city council had adopted yet another version of the sit-lie law prohibiting stationary use of the sidewalk, arguing this time that it was required by the Americans with Disabilities Act (ADA). Disabled people did not necessarily agree: several testified at the council's hearing on the matter, objecting to this framing and saying that they did not want to be used as props to justify the abuse of the homeless. The eventual "Sidewalk Use" ordinance required six feet of navigable space surrounding any building, pushing to the curb anyone who needed to sit down and rest. However, the rules only applied in select commercial districts—downtown, in the Lloyd District, and in the Rose Quarter—which would seem to undercut the ADA rationale since federal law necessarily applies throughout the entire city, and people with disabilities also live in other neighborhoods. Likewise, the law was not applied to non-homeless obstructions, such as sidewalk cafes, signboards, or newspaper boxes.[16]

The Portland Business Alliance was more forthright about the aims of the renewed restrictions. In the April–May 2010 issue of its downtown "Business Improvement District" newsletter, *BID News*, Michelle Martin explained the problem from the PBA's perspective: "We have seen a group of individuals, who some refer to as 'Road Warriors' or 'Summer Travelers,' begin to return to downtown Portland. They are approximately 18–30 years old, can be very unkempt, often have unlicensed or un-leashed dogs, and regularly engage in illegal or aggressive behavior." She then identified the steps the PBA was taking as part of its "Clean and Safe" program, beginning with the new law: "First, we have been working with Mayor Adams the past few months on a new Sidewalk Use Ordinance, which was passed by the Portland City Council on May 6.... Second, Central Precinct Commander Dave Famous has instituted a 'zero tolerance' program to deal with individuals committing livability offenses downtown."[17] Much of the subsequent enforcement was enacted by private police, including those employed by the PBA, making public accountability near to impossible.[18]

Most sit-lie citations issued by the police bureau were written by the Mounted Patrol and received by people without addresses. Many of these pretextual encounters led to arrests when the cops took the opportunity to run warrant checks, conduct searches, and otherwise work up criminal charges out of thin air. In keeping with another discriminatory pattern, 14 percent of those subjected to sit-lie enforcement were Black, more than twice their percentage of the local population.[19]

Crisis or Panic? Panic or Plan?

Housing and homelessness demanded increasing attention from the mayor's office as the decade wore on. In October 2015, Mayor Charlie Hales declared an emergency, based on the increase in homelessness. It was still in place when he left office more than a year later.[20]

Driving the new sense of urgency was a controversy over the use of the North Park Blocks, a series of three consecutive parks just north of Burnside, serving as a kind of buffer between the gentrified Pearl District and the Old Town area closer to the river. That summer, by one count, an average of 36.1 homeless people used some part of the park over the course of a day. Though there was no data to indicate that the figure had recently increased or that it exceeded that of other comparable downtown spaces, it was used to create something of a civic panic. KATU News ran a story on August 25 warning of "the breakdown of the North Park Blocks: drugs, public sex, and off-leash dog attacks." The next week, the *Northwest Examiner* managed to sound even more hysterical: "Civility Collapses in North Park Blocks." A website-cum-lobby group called Northparkblocks.org (later incorporated as the nonprofit North Park Blocks Conservancy) started running sensationalistic photographs of incidents in the park and petitioning the City of Portland for increased policing. Predictably, business owners were the loudest voices.[21]

"It was not a park problem, but a societal failure," R. Bruce Stephenson later wrote. "In the midst of an unprecedented real estate boom, the city faced a situation not seen since the Great Depression. The issues of housing affordability and homelessness are intertwined."[22] Indeed, Portland's real estate boom—the increased profitability of speculation in land and housing—was practically coextensive with the homelessness crisis. It is not even enough to say that one caused the other; in a real sense they were *the same phenomenon*. Housing costs more; fewer people can afford it. That is two ways of saying the same thing.

Though the budding housing crisis was fundamentally an economic issue, the political and business classes invariably framed it as a crisis in public order and thus a police matter. The problem, as they saw it, was not homelessness but rather the homeless, not poverty but instead the poor. To conclude otherwise would require fundamental changes in the way essential goods—necessities for survival—are distributed in our society. Doing so would at least threaten to diminish the wealth and power of those same political and business classes. A punitive response, on the other hand, had none of these disadvantages and, if anything, would amplify that inequality. The poor, under this approach, not only suffer from material deprivation, they also are stigmatized, discriminated against, and targeted for coercive enforcement and violence, while the wealthy are secure, not only in terms of personal safety and private property but also in their comfortable distance from the lives of the dispossessed and from the consequences of their own policies.

As one developer recalls, beginning in the 1990s,

> [Portland Development Commission chair] Don [Magnuson], other downtown business people, and property owners used to meet informally to discuss what to do about the presence of homeless individuals and this growing street drug problem. One member of this group came up with the phrase "the solution is dilution." The idea was to add new activities that would result in more people visiting local shops and businesses. The objective was to reduce the visual concentration of street people and, hopefully, influence them to leave the area as more and more newcomers took over the environment. If Old Town were full of more shopkeepers, shoppers, and, perhaps, tourists; then people who were homeless would go somewhere else because they wouldn't feel comfortable.[23]

The ultimate aim was the transformation of Old Town from a skid row to a second Pearl District. Old Town had been a problem for the proper and propertied classes since the nineteenth century, when it had been called the North End. Historically, police had mainly pursued a strategy of containment, keeping the crime, vice, filth, noise, and disorder within some tolerable limits, and most importantly keeping it within some well-delineated geographic borders. Since the 1980s, an informal agreement had limited development in the area so long as local charities put on cap on the available shelter space. (When nonprofits pushed those limits, they faced attacks in the media and found their donations dwindling.)[24] More recently, however, developers and business owners had started eyeing the area with greedy frustration. Here were several blocks of prime real estate in the very center of the city, with historic buildings and a view of the river. The problem, of course, was the people.

This may tell us something about the housing market, that it is a political as well as an economic project, that it does not merely produce and distribute material goods but also aims at creating specific social relations. It is notable that real estate developers, people in the business of building housing, would look at an unhoused population and see not an opportunity but rather a problem and then think that the solution was not to provide affordable housing but instead to simply make the unhoused people go away—though the means for doing so remained purposefully vague: What would "influence them to leave"? Why "wouldn't [they] feel comfortable"? The answer, or a large part of it, was policing.

All of which brings us back to the North Park Blocks. This strip of public land had served as an intuitive border between the Pearl District and Old Town. By the mid-aughts, however, developers hoping to extend their reach from the Pearl to the river proposed a "creative corridor" along Couch Street, intersecting with the Park Blocks. The city council approved the idea in 2015. And, thanks to a real estate deal brokered by the Portland Development Commission, the Pacific Northwest College of Art opened new facilities that same year, occupying the area between Union Station (to the north of Old Town) and the Park Blocks (to the west).[25] The dispute over the North Park Blocks occurred in this context, one part of a concerted effort to claim the surrounding area for the respectable classes.

Safe Sleep, Cesspool

You can't make people less homeless by punishing them. But you can make them leave—provided there is somewhere else for them to go.

A new city policy, "Safe Sleep," was announced by Mayor Hales in February 2016.[26] It allowed camps of up to six people to occupy public spaces in designated areas between the hours of 9:00 p.m. and 7:00 a.m. The aim was to regulate homeless people so as to minimize the inconvenience to property owners and businesses, but the rules were poorly understood and rarely enforced. The Portland Business Alliance sued the City of Portland, and Hales's popularity sank. By August, public pressure forced him to abandon the idea. The PBA gloated: "Mayor Hales' policy failed, in part because he ignored the voices of the affected Portland residents, neighborhood communities and businesses."[27] It was not a mistake that the next mayor was inclined to repeat. In 2017, Mayor Ted Wheeler held a closed-door meeting with seventy-five members of the Portland Business Alliance, representatives of the Multnomah County government, the district attorney's office, and the police. Afterward, the city added eight blocks to a "pedestrian only" zone, in which camping was prohibited.[28]

Homeless people represented 52 percent of arrests that year and 44 percent of police use-of-force reports, though they were less than 3 percent of Portland's population. Confronted with these numbers, Mayor Wheeler expressed his concern and—whether disingenuous or plain oblivious—failed altogether to connect this outcome with his administration's policies. "The police should be focused on policing criminal activity, and that's sort of the beginning, the middle and the end of it for me," he said. "The criminal justice system is not the right place ... to provide addiction or mental health services.... The police should be addressing car break-ins and burglaries and things like that."[29] The Police Association's president Daryl Turner disagreed, speaking forcefully about the bureau's quality-of-life mission: "Our City has become a cesspool. Livability that once made Portland a unique and vibrant city is now replaced with human feces in businesses [*sic*] doorways, in our parks, and on our streets. Aggressive panhandlers block the sidewalks, storefronts, and landmarks like Pioneer Square, discouraging people from enjoying our City. Garbage-filled RVs and vehicles are strewn throughout our neighborhoods. Used needles, drug paraphernalia, and trash are common sights lining the streets and sidewalks of the downtown core area, under our bridges, and freeway overpasses."[30] This description of generalized urban decay, in Turner's view, more than amply justified the punitive targeting of the homeless. It is as though the poor not only cause the city's problems but also *personify* them.

A Livable Place

This sense of dehumanization predictably led to harassment and violence.

Both city cops and private cops—the Portland Police; Portland Patrol, Inc.; and Pacific Patrol Services—would often seize the meager belongings of people who were already desperately poor, including essentials such as tents, clothing, sleeping bags, identification, and medicines. Retrieving these items was in principle possible but in practice rarely achieved. Police often failed to catalog the seized property, which they then stored in an unmarked building far from the center of town.[31]

Homeless residents in Southeast Portland told Portland Copwatch that homeowners were often worse than the cops: the police mainly left them alone, but entitled strangers would wake them up and tell them to move. Throughout the later teens, NIMBY groups organized call-ins to City Hall to complain about their homeless neighbors, videotaped clients visiting a needle exchange or receiving other services, and organized to prevent the City of Portland from opening sanctioned camping areas.[32]

The Oregon Department of Transportation started placing huge boulders under overpasses to prevent camping.[33] Then, between January and October 2017, the police coordinated with the Portland Bureau of Transportation to tow approximately three hundred recreational vehicles that had been parked on city streets, a third of which had been serving as residences.[34] Unlike camp sweeps, the seizure of these vehicles required no notice and could be accomplished with remarkably little legal process. "We didn't have any clear-cut rules," East Precinct Neighborhood Response Team Sergeant Randy Tieg admitted. Criminal charges or public complaints were unnecessary so long as the police were acting in a "caretaking" role in the interest of "health and safety." Anyone who had been living in one of these impounded RVs would be left without shelter until they could find the money to cover the costs of towing, cleaning, and storing the vehicle, in addition to registration fees and the fines for the original parking violation. In the program's first three months, *no vehicles* were successfully reclaimed by their owners.[35] Transportation Commissioner Dan Saltzman justified the practice of extorting money from extremely impoverished people and robbing them of their only shelter: "One of our jobs is to make sure our city is a livable place," he said.[36]

Enforcing Homelessness

Policing does not deter homelessness, because, in the overwhelming number of cases, homelessness is not a choice. But the point is not to solve homelessness through policing. It is instead, in part, to force the homeless into invisibility in order to remove apparent and uncomfortable reminders of public disorder, social inequality, or both. Basically what the police do is force homeless people to move—a lot. "They would wake you up in the dead of sleep," one man reported, "and you have to walk around in the cold and rain trying to find a new place. When you finally get settled, an hour later, they move you again."[37]

That is inhumane, but it is also emblematic of the contradictory nature of policing. Police create order, stability, security, and safety for some by imposing disorder, instability, insecurity, and harm on others. On another level, these practices illustrate the intimate connection of police with the concept of private property. By periodically forcing the destitute to relocate, the police disrupt their capacity to build routines or form relationships centered on a specific place, to act and be seen as neighbors, to integrate with their surroundings, to find belonging—both in the interpersonal sense and in the sense that they are understood to belong in some particular place. That is a short step from feeling that that place belongs to them, if not exactly as property than at least in so far as they have the right to use it and feel a special responsibility for it. This feeling, that a person might have a right to a place they do not own, threatens the very basis of the property relation, though usually in a nascent, unstated fashion. The police, by continuously moving the poor along, preserve the exclusive concept of private property precisely by enforcing the exclusion. And by denying the very poor any place that they might rightly claim, anywhere that they have a presumptive right to be, policing renders them not merely unhoused but actually homeless.

CHAPTER 29

Between Occupy and Uprising

After Occupy

Occupy-themed demonstrations continued for some months after police broke up Portland's encampment, but these did not have the same vitality. The movement had lost not its sense of purpose but rather its center of gravity. It became diffuse, indistinct. Its force dissipated. It came to resemble any other protest movement, with predictable marches and little leverage. The police watched the demonstrations closely and acted quickly to preclude any attempt to create a new tent city—for example, pepper-spraying and beating people when marches approached the Plaza Blocks, where the first camp had been established.[1]

The cops' response to other public protests became increasingly unpredictable—sometimes passive or even accommodating, sometimes aggressive and forbidding, not adhering to any evident pattern. The full range was on display on May Day 2012. Police took a hands-off approach at a demonstration of students protesting funding cuts to public education and even kept their distance at a reverse-eviction when demonstrators illegally moved a woman back into her home. But they used horses, bikes, and old-fashioned pushing and shoving to break up a crowd gathered under the Burnside Bridge calling for a general strike. A march later in the day proceeded without incident, only for police to attack a dance party afterward. Altogether thirty-six people were arrested that day, and many others were injured.[2]

Targeting Anarchists (Again)

Political repression was not limited to crowd control. On the morning of July 25, 2012, FBI teams outfitted with assault rifles, helmets, and olive drab uniforms broke down the doors of three Portland homes, searching for paint, sticks, road flares, cell phones, "diary and journal entries," address books, black clothing, and "anti-government or anarchist literature." Similar raids occurred simultaneously in Seattle and Olympia, and four people were subpoenaed to testify before a federal grand jury. Those appearing before the tribunal reported a McCarthyite proceeding in which, without the rights to remain silent or to have an attorney present, they were asked about their political views, the beliefs of their friends, and which of their acquaintances knew one another. Those refusing to answer such questions were cited for contempt of court and jailed for as long as five months. Eventually Judge Richard Jones ordered them released, observing, "Their physical health has deteriorated sharply and their mental health has also suffered from the effects of solitary confinement."[3]

Ostensibly the grand jury was investigating damage done to a federal courthouse during May Day demonstrations in Seattle that year. But those imprisoned as part of the inquiry were not in any meaningful sense criminal suspects; most were not even in Seattle on the day in question. And, in the end, the grand jury produced no indictments. In fact, the entire ordeal hinged on a pretext. Even before the subpoenas were delivered, a young man new to the anarchist movement had already admitted to breaking the windows at the courthouse. He pled guilty to a misdemeanor charge, paid $500 in restitution, and was released with "time served."[4]

FBI documents show that a group of Portland anarchists was under surveillance well before the May Day demonstration and was followed by federal agents as its members traveled north toward Seattle. It is hard to know precisely when they had come under scrutiny, but a month before the raids Portland police had broken up squats where some of these people had been living. One was arrested for thirty-six acts of vandalism, mostly targeting banks and dating back as far as 2010. Though vandalism is typically a misdemeanor offense, these were charged as thirty-six counts of felony criminal mischief and thirty-six counts of felony conspiracy; they were reduced to five counts as part of a plea agreement, leading to twenty days in jail.[5] Though we can't be certain, it seems most probable that the local police, and even the FBI, had been monitoring this group of friends for two years—since the policing crisis of 2010, with its numerous militant demonstrations—all the while letting charges accumulate and only moving in when they thought they could make a federal case.

Ending Protests

Despite the state's efforts, radical organizing continued, and disruptive protests recurred—often in response to police violence.

In late 2014, the deaths of two unarmed Black men—Michael Brown in Ferguson, Missouri, and Eric Garner in Staten Island, New York—ignited anti-police demonstrations in more than 170 cities across the country, including Portland.[6] These demonstrations, which helped to popularize the slogan "Black Lives Matter," fundamentally changed the debate about policing and the resistance to it. *Time* magazine ran a piece titled "In Defense of Rioting."[7] *Rolling Stone* offered suggestions for building a "Cop-Free World."[8] Radical politics suddenly had a mainstream audience.

In Portland, protests—mostly peaceful—occurred on and off for months, and the cops responded in a variety of ways, seemingly without a consistent strategy. Some demonstrations did not attract a police presence even as they blocked traffic, while others were met with pepper spray, clubs, horses, and newly acquired flashbang grenades. The cops kept a respectful distance on November 25 as the Albina Ministerial Alliance led nearly three thousand people on a march, but they attacked several small groups that tried to break away for independent actions. Four days later, on November 29, police surrounded the entire crowd and arrested ten people at a demonstration organized by Don't Shoot Portland. Police Chief Mike Marshman defended the tactic, called "kettling," as a "successful way to end a protest peacefully"—as though ending protests represented a legitimate aim for law enforcement in a functioning democracy. The district attorney declined to press charges.[9]

Trumped

Both Occupy and Black Lives Matter were triggered by events elsewhere in the United States, then grew into international movements while taking on distinctive local features. The 2016 election of Donald Trump—a "reality television" star and real estate heir who gained a political following by peddling conspiracy theories and racist invective—served to further escalate, accelerate, and polarize local as well as national politics.[10]

Immediately after the election, about four thousand people took the streets of Portland, chanting "We reject the president-elect." Demonstrations continued nightly for more than a week, producing numerous broken windows and ninety-seven arrests. Throughout the winter, police would regularly counter small-scale property destruction with the indiscriminate use of tear gas, pepper spray, and less-lethal munitions, pushing the city into headlines internationally.[11] The Associated Press declared Portland the "epicenter" for anti-Trump protests, and the ACLU observed that "no other police force in America use[d] crowd control weapons with the regularity of the Portland Police Bureau." As arrests accumulated, the district attorney announced that most defendants would be released without charges—which, Portland Copwatch noted, would seem to support "the theory that officers arrest protestors to end demonstrations, but not to prosecute people engaged in criminal activity."[12]

An unpermitted march on Inauguration Day drew nearly ten thousand people. Once the crowd had dwindled to a few hundred, cops attacked with flashbang grenades and pepper spray, arresting six.[13] In contrast, the police were broadly cooperative with the Women's March, a permitted event that attracted nearly one hundred thousand people to downtown Portland the following day. Police activity there mainly consisted of directing traffic, posing for photos with demonstrators, and wearing the march's trademark "pussy" hats. These divergent police postures would seem to fit with the "strategic incapacitation" model of crowd control—accommodating (and regulating) cooperative groups but preemptively attacking those viewed as disruptive.[14] Margaret Jacobson, one of the local Women's March organizers, more or less accused the police of extortion, comparing the permit system to a protection racket: "It was odd to basically *buy* safety for our marchers," she said. "[The] night before the policemen who were 'keeping us safe' attacked protestors because they were protesting without a permit."[15]

Main Stage

It was not only the left that mobilized. Trump's victory emboldened the far right, who undertook a campaign of organized violence both locally and nationally. In Portland, the local and national levels more and more became one, as right-wingers from around the country repeatedly traveled to the city intending, as one researcher explained, "to incite violent confrontations with counter-protesters, blame any resulting violence on the left, and press for further repression and retaliation against those they consider[ed] their political adversaries."[16]

The first notable instance of what would become a dismal pattern came on June 4, 2017, at a rally organized by Joey Gibson and his group, Patriot Prayer. The group's name, as scholar David Neiwert notes, "reflect[ed] both its militia movement and Christian nationalist orientations," combining constitutional originalism and conspiracy thinking with specifically pro-gun and anti-abortion positions. Tactically, with its emphasis on provoking the left and engaging in brawls, Patriot Prayer most closely resembled the Proud Boys, the self-described "Western chauvinist street gang." And Proud Boys nearly always attended Patriot Prayer events, sometimes serving as security.[17]

Tensions were high ahead of the June 4 rally. An earlier "March for Free Speech," organized by Patriot Prayer on April 20, had been largely uneventful, producing only three arrests and a level of conflict that the *Mercury* characterized as "pushing and a lot of yelling." However, police management of the event left many observers with a sense that the cops were granting the far right special privileges by, for example, providing buses to transport them to and from the rally.[18] Antagonism between police and protesters only deepened on May 1, when the cops revoked the permit for a May Day rally after members of the crowd started pelting cops with cans of Pepsi—a clever detournement of a recent ad featuring a young protester sharing a soda with a police officer. What began as a rally of about a thousand people, listening to speeches in English and Spanish, ended as a running battle, with twenty-five arrests, damage to numerous businesses, and fires in the streets.[19] Then, over Memorial Day weekend, a Patriot Prayer hanger-on named Jeremy Christian confronted a Black woman aboard the Max light rail, striking her in the head with a bottle. She pepper-sprayed him, and, when the police arrived twenty minutes later, witnesses identified him as the assailant. The cops let him go with a warning. The next day, again on the light rail, Christian launched into an anti-Muslim tirade against two teenaged girls. When three men—Ricky Best, Micah Fletcher, and Taliesin Myrddin Namkai-Meche—stepped forward to defend them, Christian attacked with a knife, stabbing all three men. Only Fletcher survived.[20]

Fearing that a double murder portended worse violence to come, Mayor Ted Wheeler urged the federal government, which controls Terry Schrunk Plaza, to rescind its permission for Gibson to use the park. The federal authorities refused. Wheeler then met with Gibson personally and tried to persuade him to cancel the event himself. He also refused. The controversy drove attention toward the "Trump Free Speech Rally," helping to make it the first Patriot Prayer event to draw significant numbers—bringing together Trump Republicans, assorted militiamen, and alt-right internet celebrities, all opposed by a broad left/liberal coalition organized in counterprotest. The Federal Protective Service (FPS) took responsibility for containing the primary demonstration while the Portland Police Bureau attended to the more numerous counterprotesters in the adjacent city parks.[21]

The ACLU's Mat dos Santos described the day's events: "For the first four hours of the demonstrations, law enforcement successfully kept groups separated in an effort to avoid conflict. . . . Things took a dangerous turn as police deployed flashbang grenades, chemical irritants, and less-lethal bullets at the antifascist gathering—to the cheers of the alt-right group." When the left retreated, the cops gave chase, eventually surrounding the counterprotesters. The police detained 389 demonstrators, journalists, and bystanders and held them long enough to identify and photograph each one.[22]

The next day, the Portland Police Rapid Response Team's Lieutenant Jeff Niiya received two messages. One was from a progressive activist, Nora Colie, requesting a meeting and an explanation: "I know there are some bad seeds with protest gatherings who can ruin it for the rest of us by throwing stuff, but still the harsh return from the police makes it pretty terrible for those of us not there to battle you, which is always the majority of the crowd. It was weird yesterday to get attacked by the police suddenly and see standing behind them white supremacists cheering the police on." The other message was from Lawrence Cavallero, who worked security for Patriot Prayer: "It goes without saying, but a huge 'thank you' from my group. Your officers did an outstanding job and we are extremely grateful."[23]

Proxy War

The June 4 rally set a pattern that would continue for years, well into 2020. Right-wing toughs would come to the city looking to instigate violence. Organized antifascists—some affiliated with Rose City Antifa, some with other organizations—and a much larger number of everyday people would show up to oppose them. The police would try to keep the two groups apart, typically standing with their backs to the fascists and their weapons pointed at the antifascists. Then, and usually without warning, the cops would indiscriminately attack the left while leaving the violence of the right practically unchecked.[24] "Gibson's rally was a proving ground of sorts for what was to come," journalist Andy Campbell wrote. "After that, he and the Proud Boys knew they could host violent rallies in the city limits . . . and even expect support from responding law enforcement."[25]

This support would take multiple forms in the coming years and over the course of numerous encounters. The police were repeatedly accused of standing aside during right-wing attacks: "Ignoring racist and right wing thugs," as City Commissioner Chloe Eudaly described it, "and arresting left wing activists for no reason."[26] On at least one occasion, Portland Police even made an arrest at Gibson's direct request.[27] At another event in June 2018, police disarmed antifascist protesters as they arrived but allowed Patriot Prayer and the Proud Boys to keep wooden dowels and metal pipes. When they used these as clubs to attack the counterprotesters, the Portland Police revoked their permit and ordered them to disperse while Homeland Security officers fired less-lethal rounds at the antifascists.[28] When cops found armed militiamen on a rooftop overlooking a later demonstration, they confiscated their rifles but made no arrests.[29] At times, the police bureau provided personal security for Proud Boys leaders.[30]

At a 2019 "End Domestic Terrorism" rally, police escorted hundreds of Proud Boys across the otherwise-closed Hawthorne Bridge but declared a civil disturbance when left-wing counterprotesters later blocked a street.[31] Police Chief Danielle Outlaw defended the approach: "We determined it would be in the interest of everyone's safety to allow [the Proud Boys] to remove themselves from the area. We did not show preferential treatment but rather facilitated a de-escalation of potential conflict."[32] "But," the *Mercury*'s Alex Zielinski countered, "for anyone watching the swarm of men—wearing 'Make America Great Again' hats and shirts advocating for violence against LGBTQ+ people and Muslims—cheering as they took the Hawthorne Bridge completely unopposed, PPB's decision felt more like an endorsement."[33]

From the White House, via Twitter, President Trump made it clear which side he was on: "Major consideration is being given to naming ANTIFA an 'ORGANIZATION OF TERROR.' Portland is being watched very closely." Legally, this was gibberish: under federal law, only foreign groups could be officially designated as terrorist organizations.[34] But the real purpose of this and Trump's numerous similar pronouncements was to identify antifascists as official enemies, signal to far-right activists that they had his ear, and legitimize reactionary violence.

The Portland Police likewise used social media in their attempts to discredit the left. At a June 29, 2019, antifascist demonstration that observers described as "carnival-like," police attacked crowds with pepper spray and pepper balls. The police then posted a tweet warning that the vegan milkshakes being served by PopMob's antifascist party planners "contained quick-drying cement." Though hundreds of people were merrily drinking the shakes without ill effect, the lie was immediately circulated by the major news networks, as well as Fox News and US senator Ted Cruz.[35]

At times the cops were willing to act as proxies for the right; other times they saw the right-wing paramilitaries as an extension of law enforcement. Video from one protest showed militia members assisting Homeland Security officers with an arrest.[36] Before another far-right action, Lieutenant Niiya wrote to Brian Krogmann, a former cop who had since joined the Oathkeepers: "I would like pictures of those who will be armed. I don't want a blue on blue issue."[37] Krogmann was just one of dozens of Oregon cops who had joined the far-right militia—a current Portland Police officer, an instructor at the Corrections Academy, and six current or former corrections officers among them.[38]

The Left Problem

It was clear that the police saw the left as the problem. When Chief Outlaw appeared on local radio host Lars Larson's show a few days after a 2018 skirmish, she accused the antifascist counterprotesters of coming with "the intent . . . to cause physical harm and confrontation." She added, "They got confrontation, but it's not who they wanted confrontation with" (meaning that the police had attacked in lieu of the Proud Boys). Outlaw smugly compared antiracist activists to kids who lost a schoolyard fight and then "wail off and whine and complain."[39]

The Independent Police Review Division later found that police planning documents described antifascist groups as "more confrontational" and "volatile" than the far-right brawlers. One lieutenant described Patriot Prayer and its menagerie of nationalists as "much more mainstream" than those opposing them. "Law enforcement's tacit sanctioning of far-right violence during these protests encouraged an escalation," former FBI agent Mike German concluded. "It appeared that years of demonizing anarchists and other left-wing protestors in law enforcement intelligence reports had led the police to believe black-clad anti-fascist fighters were somehow as bad or worse than the far-right extremists who were organizing these disruptive events."[40]

It was later revealed that police training materials on "Protests & Riots" prominently featured a Proud Boys meme titled "Prayer of the Alt Knight."

(The Alt-Knights were the gang's "tactical defense" unit.) The image features an armored cop striking a protester, paired with quasi-biblical language:

> Woe be unto you, dirty hippy. . . .
> I shall send among you,
> My humble servants with hat, and with bat
> That they may christen your heads with hickory
> And anoint your faces with pepper spray.[41]

Sergeant Jeffrey McDaniel—who had previously been named in four lawsuits for protest-related violence—was suspended for ten days for inserting the meme into the presentation.[42]

Collusion

For some—including city council member Jo Ann Hardesty—the symbiotic relationship between the Portland Police and the far right looked an awful lot like "collusion."[43] Such accusations would only gain force when *Willamette Week* revealed text exchanges between Patriot Prayer's Joey Gibson and the Rapid Response Team's Lieutenant Jeff Niiya. The messages show Niiya providing Gibson with real-time intelligence on the locations of left-wing protests, the movement of antifascist fighters, and details of police deployment.[44] Niiya further offered advice to help notorious Patriot Prayer brawler Tusitala ("Tiny") Toese avoid arrest despite having an active warrant: "Just make sure he doesn't do anything that may draw our attention. . . . I don't see a need to arrest on the warrant unless there is a reason."[45]

Assistance with avoiding arrests seems to have been a defining feature of Niiya's relationship with Patriot Prayer. Video from a June 3, 2018, demonstration shows a conversation between Sergeant Kevin Allen and Joey Gibson. Allen says, "I just talked to Jeff Niiya, and he asked me to tell you that he has probable cause to arrest a couple of the guys here. . . . They've arrested the other side, so it's not singling you guys out. . . . But it's time to go. If you guys can go home, there won't be any arrests."[46]

On the face of it, this sort of friendly warning would seem to violate Police Bureau policy, specifically the directive that "members should not provide information directly or indirectly that may enable any person to avoid arrest."

But a subsequent investigation by the Independent Police Review confirmed that incident commanders, assistant chiefs, two consecutive police chiefs, and the mayor were all aware of Niiya's contacts with Patriot Prayer. The IPR exonerated him.[47]

Soft Power

The IPR report provides a fascinating look at the cops' use of soft tactics to try to manage protests. "I understand how this looks," Niiya conceded, "but you don't get cooperation by, bluntly, being an asshole to people, right[?]" As he saw it, the goal was to persuade demonstration organizers to discipline the crowd: "If you want to assign peacekeepers, liaisons, or some type of security detail, we encourage that. That way we, the police, don't have to get involved."[48]

"We're always . . . looking for alternatives to being in a control setting," Assistant Chief Ryan Lee explained. "So, to delineate between crowd management and crowd control, *crowd management* is fundamentally the concept that you are going to manage, negotiate, facilitate activity and . . . help people identify and carry out lawful expressions of their rights that they are exercising." That stands in contrast to the older "philosophy" of *crowd control,* which "was about reasserting authority."[49] Lee expressly compared Niiya's approach to the Swedish model of "dialogue policing"—under which, as one study explains, police seek "to avoid confrontation through genuine dialogue, communication, identifying potential risks to public order, the facilitation of protestors' legitimate interests, and creating self-policing among the crowd." Specially designated officers "act as a communication link between demonstrators and police commanders."[50] They typically go unarmed and appear in civilian clothes (though wearing high-visibility vests). They do not participate in any enforcement activity, do not collect evidence for prosecution, and do not share what they learn with the intelligence unit.[51] Niiya's work diverged from this model in several respects. He appeared at demonstrations armed and in uniform, had a role in directing enforcement activity, and passed information on to police bureau commanders, the mayor's office, the Washington State Patrol, the FBI, and other agencies.[52] The only real similarity with dialogue policing is with the aim of using protest leaders to advance the cops' agenda.

Between Patriot Prayer and the police, however, there is a real question as to who was co-opting whom. Niiya's stated intention was to establish rapport to moderate the group's behavior. "I've always kind of pushed [Joey Gibson] that you are a leader in that group. You need to set the tone and expectations and that has I think at times reduced some of the violence."[53] But did it? Given the group's history of public brawling, the evidence that Niiya helped nudge them toward lawful action is exceedingly thin. In fact, one could make a stronger case that the police tempered *their own* activities—repeatedly foregoing arrests, for example—in order to maintain good relations and keep open the lines of communication. Or—what seems to me most likely—it may be that the cops were just never inclined to forcefully act against the far right. Gibson certainly understood Niiya's attempts at "dialogue" as conveying legitimacy and offering encouragement. He told his minions at one Patriot Prayer rally: "[The cops] have our back."[54]

Courting the Left

The police did try to establish similar contacts on the left, using well-known activists to marginalize the militants. For instance, Niiya met with Nora Colie ahead of 2017's May Day demonstrations to express his concern that anarchists might take over the protest. During the demonstration itself, he contacted her again to get the march's peacekeepers to stop people from throwing things at the police. During another event the following month, Niiya texted Jamie Partridge, a well-known labor activist: "being told black Bloch [*sic*] made their way into your group FYI. Can the peacekeepers get them out?" Partridge replied: "We're doing our best. . . . we're asking them to unmask & give up weapons." Niiya: "Great thanks."[55]

In fairness, it seems the police did occasionally reciprocate. Niiya told investigators of an exchange with one progressive activist:

> I still remember a time, a rally at Terry Schrunk Plaza. The left and the right were both there. The police bureau has RRT in full PPE which is, you know, full protective gear and there was pushing and shoving going on and I can tell you that June [Davies] was messaging me directly and saying, hey don't bring in the hard squads. It's going to set the tone off and we're going to lose control. . . . I trusted her . . . and we didn't. We did not bring in police in that situation and it ultimately resolved itself.[56]

When these messages were made public, Davies was shunned by other activists and even threatened. Niiya expressed his frustration: "I lost a lot due to one of my sources getting outed on FB [Facebook]. Calling her a snitch and saying I used her. Doubt most are going to want to talk to me now." He later concluded, "I believe my effectiveness for getting any human intel from anyone on the left will now be compromised." That was correct. Exposure essentially ended friendly contact. Sergeant Kevin Allen recalled one demonstration where he was supposed to serve as a liaison to the protesters, but no one would take his business card.[57]

Zero Tolerance in the Sanctuary City

President Trump, all this while, was pursuing his own agenda, declaring a new "zero tolerance" approach to immigration. On January 25, 2017, only a few days after his inauguration, he issued an order withholding federal funds from so-called sanctuary cities, where local officials do not participate in immigration enforcement. Two days later, he barred travel from several majority-Muslim nations. Immigration and Customs Enforcement officers began detaining visitors at airports, prompting disruptive demonstrations at airports across the country. More than one hundred people gathered at PDX on the first day of protests, and more than six hundred on the second.[58]

That spring, the city council passed a resolution affirming Portland's status as a sanctuary city—an entirely symbolic gesture that simply restated the requirements of the Oregon Revised Statutes. Police Chief Mike Marshman reminded his officers that they could not enforce immigration law, and Sheriff Mike Reese pledged not to hold prisoners for ICE. Reese explained: "I believe we have a responsibly to nurture a relationship of trust with everyone in our community. ... When our community trusts us, they share information about crime ... and that makes us all safer." An ICE official later complained, "Cooperation from Multnomah County Sheriff's Office and probation has recently been reduced from limited to nonexistent."[59] But other agencies—including the Portland Police Bureau, the district attorney's office, the Oregon State Police, and the Department of Corrections—were later found to be sharing information with ICE, likely in violation of Oregon law.[60]

American Values

In response to Trump's policies, blockades started appearing at ICE offices, first in Portland, then across the country. On June 17, 2018, a large group of activists established an encampment outside of the Immigration and Customs Enforcement building on Southwest Macadam Avenue.[61] At its peak, the Occupy ICE camp comprised ninety tents and about two hundred people, with a kitchen, a first aid station, and child care.[62]

Surprising the left and outraging the right, Mayor Ted Wheeler initially expressed support for the protest and said that the Portland Police would not interfere. "The policy being enacted by the federal government around the separation of very small children from their parents is an abomination," Wheeler wrote. "I do not want the [Portland Police] to be engaged or sucked into a conflict, particularly from a federal agency that I believe is on the wrong track[,] that has not fully lived American values of inclusion."[63]

Two days into the action, protesters barricaded the entrance to the building, and ICE employees called 911. The Portland Police did not respond, referring the matter instead to the Federal Protective Service. The next day the ICE office was closed. Protesters removed the US flag from the building and hoisted one of their own, reading "Refugees Welcome."[64]

The National ICE Council, the union for immigration officers, sent Mayor Wheeler a letter accusing him of violating the Fourteenth Amendment's "equal protection" clause by holding back the police. "Your policy has created a zone of terror and lawlessness," the letter said, directly foreshadowing the president's rhetoric two years later. Wheeler clarified that the police would respond if there was a "life safety concern" but reiterated that he "did not want the Portland Police Bureau to be engaged or sucked into a conflict for the purpose of securing federal property that houses a federal agency with their own federal police force."[65]

At a dawn raid on June 28, Federal Protective Service officers tore down the barricade at the ICE building's entrance and made several arrests. Robert Sperling, the spokesperson for the FPS, told the media that most of the protesters were cooperative, and the camp would be allowed to remain so long as it did not impede access to the facility. "It's been very, very peaceful," he said. "No one has thrown anything or hit anybody. There's been no violence." Numerous arrests occurred over the next few weeks, for trespassing on federal property or blocking vehicles as they tried to enter the site.[66]

Mayor Wheeler revised his laissez-faire approach when Patriot Prayer leader Joey Gibson announced that he would be visiting the Occupy ICE site on July 20. "Given recent past incidents of violence between groups of demonstrators," Wheeler explained, "I asked Portland Police to maintain a presence near the facility to ensure those present can safely express their First Amendment rights." Not even a week later, on July 23, the mayor further announced that Portland Police would in fact be sweeping the Occupy ICE camp and arresting any protesters. They removed those remaining two days later. Wheeler said he made the decision because of the Patriot Prayer visit, seeming not to recognize that that would effectively allow the far right to set the limits for official tolerance.[67]

Police Chief Outlaw, however, pointed to sanitation and safety concerns at the Occupy camp and further contradicted Wheeler's account by insisting that the decision to sweep the camp had been hers and not the mayor's. She told conservative radio host Lars Larson that she had informed Wheeler of the impending raid but "wasn't asking for permission."[68]

Superficially, it might almost seem like a repeat of the original Occupy script: a liberal mayor expressed sympathy with the protest only for the police to intervene under the auspices of preserving public health and safety. But a novel element here was the open conflict between the local and federal governments, and specifically between Mayor Wheeler and President Trump. In broad strokes, that tracked an ideological conflict between left and right, but it also revealed a deeper dispute over the control of policing—which ended with the local police not only aligning with the far right but openly declaring their independence from the mayor.

CHAPTER 30
Can't Breathe

Pandemic

It was during 2020 that the words *apocalyptic* and *dystopian* lost their literary chime and became ordinary adjectives.

On February 28 that year, Oregon registered its first confirmed case of the severe acute respiratory syndrome coronavirus 2 (SARS-CoV-2, or Covid-19).[1] Almost a month later, on March 23, Governor Kate Brown issued a statewide stay-at-home order, closing businesses and schools. Conservatives voiced fears about "violations of civil rights," but in reality there was almost no enforcement of the rules. A month into lockdown, Portland police had written zero tickets, though they had received reports of 469 violations of the stay-home order.[2] Police and Multnomah County sheriff's deputies were themselves so resistant to public health measures that they would later be exempted from the local governments' vaccine requirements.[3] And Governor Brown had to meet personally with state troopers to try to persuade them to comply with her indoor mask mandate.[4]

Law enforcement's response to the pandemic was wildly inconsistent, between or even within agencies. As a precaution to slow the spread of the virus in jails, the sheriff's office released low-level offenders, reducing the inmate population by 32 percent.[5] Police switched to writing citations for misdemeanor offenses rather than taking people into custody, and the bureau ceased dispatching officers to most calls, excepting violent crimes, car crashes, and burglaries. Cops stopped sweeping homeless camps nearly altogether.[6] Governor Brown, however, resisted calls to release aged or infirm prisoners, commuting the sentences of only 187 state inmates over the course of the year. (In contrast, Washington State, just to the north, released 1,100.)[7] President Trump, meanwhile, simultaneously downplayed the dangers of the disease and opportunistically used the pandemic as an excuse to close the borders.[8]

Covid-19 brought into stark relief, and drew into question, some fundamental features of our society that are ordinarily taken for granted—about work, wealth, housing, and medical care. Inequality proved fatal, and the profit motive appeared to be unerringly at odds with public health.[9]

Mutual Aid, Collective Grief

Confronted with a growing sense that both the state and the market economy were failing to meet our needs, people increasingly turned to each other for help. Neighbors looked in on the elderly and ran errands for those in fragile health. A gift-economy cottage industry arose practically overnight, as individuals with sewing machines made masks for their friends, family, neighbors, and strangers. Numerous groups started delivering free meals. Rosehip Medics ("a group of volunteer Street Medics and health care activists") partnered with other organizations to produce seventeen thousand bottles of hand sanitizer. *Mutual aid,* previously anarchist jargon, was suddenly a term in vogue.[10] One thing we learned, in the midst of disaster, was that we could count on each other. We had to.

By May, Covid-19 had killed 137 people in Oregon, 103,700 in the United States, and 362,705 globally.[11] Psychologically too the pandemic had its victims: depression, heavy drinking, and domestic violence all increased.[12] Everyone was in grief. People were confused, fearful, frustrated, angry. After two months in lockdown, many felt helpless. They longed for connection, a sense of community. Many were also idle—without work, stuck at home.[13] Their days felt empty, lacked structure, seemed pointless. There was an unnerving combination of stress and stasis. As the cultural critic Jesse Kavadlo observed, "Everything changed, and nothing happened."[14]

And then something happened.

In this period of painful reflection and deep uncertainty, just as spring was turning to summer, Minneapolis police killed a forty-six-year-old African American man named George Floyd.

Gonna Kill Me

George Floyd—Perry to his family—was arrested on May 25, 2020, after using a counterfeit bill in a neighborhood store, probably unwittingly. Floyd, who suffered from claustrophobia, was handcuffed and left sitting in the back of a squad car; he began to panic. Deciding to apply further restraints, the cops pulled him from the car, pushed him facedown onto the street, and piled on top. For nine minutes and twenty-nine seconds, Officer Derek Chauvin kneeled on Floyd's neck, while other cops pressed down on his back and legs. Video from a witness's smartphone shows Floyd pleading for his life and saying repeatedly, "I can't breathe" and "They're gonna kill me."[15]

He lost consciousness after four minutes, but the cops held him down for five minutes longer until an ambulance arrived and medics drove him away. He was dead before he reached the hospital; probably he was dead before they loaded him onto the gurney.[16]

In the weeks following, there were demonstrations in more than twenty-four hundred cities and towns in all fifty US states and at least sixty other countries. Between May 25 and July 1, the Major Cities Chiefs Association recorded eighty-seven hundred mass protests—more than two hundred each day, on average. Approximately twenty million people took part. Most demonstrations (51 percent) were "peaceful and lawful," and just 7 percent of the events were violent. However episodic, illegal action was also widespread: 62 percent of jurisdictions reported looting, and 72 percent reported injuries to police officers. Perhaps surprisingly, some of the largest protests occurred in mid-size, majority-white cities: Minneapolis (63.8 percent white), Seattle (65.7 percent), and Portland (72.2 percent).[17]

The Crisis Before the Crisis

Police in Portland were already "operating from a trust deficit." A year earlier, the police bureau had released a report showing that 71 percent of the city's residents felt some level of distrust toward the police. More than two-thirds (69 percent) thought that accountability was lacking, and almost three-quarters (73 percent) believed that officers considered race and ethnicity when enforcing the law.[18] Suspicion was particularly intense in the African American community, among whom 85 percent doubted the bureau's fairness and only 25 percent said they felt "comfortable and safe" engaging with the cops.[19] Small wonder: in 2019, Portland police used force against Black people almost twice as frequently as they used it against whites—that is, in 2.7 percent of arrests when the suspect was white and 3.9 percent when the suspect was Black. Compounding matters,

African Americans were already overrepresented in total stops and arrests, making up 18 percent of drivers and pedestrians stopped by police and 22 percent of those taken into custody, though only 6 percent of the city's population.[20] A review of fifty police shootings and in-custody deaths over an eight-year period found that 26 percent of those shot or killed were Black.[21]

Moreover, deadly force was on the rise. Portland Copwatch noted with alarm that the Portland Police had "shot, shot at or caused the death" of seven people in just under one hundred days. Three more lethal-force incidents followed in the next three months, making 2019 the most deadly year, in terms of police violence, since 2001.[22]

Riot Nights

As soon as the video of George Floyd's death began to circulate online, a small group gathered on the steps of the Multnomah County Justice Center. A handful of people maintained a vigil overnight on May 28, and about fifty others joined the next day. On the evening of Friday, May 29, a crowd of about one thousand marched the five miles from Peninsula Park to the Justice Center, chanting "No good cops in a racist system." Police flanked the march on parallel streets while remaining out of view. They continued to keep their distance even as protesters spray-painted the Justice Center's walls and smashed its windows. Before long, though, a group had broken into the building and began ransacking offices and setting small fires. The police eventually pushed them back with tear gas, but dispersing the rioters only spread the riot. Angry crowds rushed through the streets breaking windows and looting stores. May 29 was dubbed "Riot Night," but it was just the first of many.[23]

The next day, police responded to demonstrations in riot gear, firing tear gas, swinging clubs, and throwing flashbang grenades. But when ten thousand people marched across the Burnside Bridge, the cops had no option but to retreat.[24]

By June 2, fencing appeared around the Justice Center and the neighboring Mark O. Hatfield United States Courthouse. Police would attack anyone who approached the barriers. They repeatedly fired tear gas, not only into the crowd of protesters but also into surrounding streets, disrupting traffic and causing numerous collisions. Gas drifted into the Justice Center, leading inmates to file a lawsuit. An analysis by Forensic Architecture found that on June 2—nicknamed

"Teargas Tuesday" by activists—"the city's downtown was blanketed with gas at more than 50 times the level federal regulators consider 'immediately dangerous to life or health.'"[25]

The Diversity of Tactics

Relatively quickly, an organic division began to develop between daytime and nighttime protests. During the day, marches led by a new group, Rose City Justice, would leave from a concert venue called Revolution Hall and wind through neighborhoods, mostly on the east side of the river. Some of these marches were estimated to involve eighteen thousand people and generally managed to avoid directly engaging with the police. But by night, mass gatherings downtown took a more confrontational tone, often attacking the Justice Center and the federal courthouse. Apart from the first "Riot Night," there was relatively little damage to area businesses. Even in riotous demonstrations, most participants engaged in neither violence nor property destruction, and the largest share of the violence was always committed by the police—who do, after all, claim a legal monopoly on it.[26]

The police response often appeared entirely arbitrary, having no real relationship to the behavior of the crowds. On one occasion, police fired less-lethal munitions at a group tossing around a beach ball. Officer Brett Taylor testified that he fired fifteen less-lethal rounds at protesters holding a banner, because he believed that it could be used as a weapon. Cops regularly conducted "bull rushes," in which a line of officers would suddenly charge a crowd, knocking down anyone in their way. There were 236 protest-related arrests in June, and the police bureau recorded using force 2,378 times that month. By the end of the summer, the total would reach 6,249 documented uses of force—an admitted undercount, given that not every instance would have been reported. These included 438 uses of riot-control agents like tear gas and 1,380 uses of "direct impact" munitions (e.g., rubber bullets).[27]

It is impossible to know how many people were injured, but a representative of Legacy Health Systems estimated that one or two protesters sought hospital care each night, and by 2024, the City of Portland had paid $2,702,745 in lawsuits and settlements.[28] The liability included $300,000 to a man who suffered a broken arm; $250,000 for the illegal use of tear gas; $100,000 to a man who was pepper-sprayed and arrested while trying to register voters; $95,000 to a man who required surgery after being pushed down while walking away; $75,000 to a man hit fourteen times with less-lethal munitions, nine times after he was on the ground; $55,000 for two reporters who were arrested while covering the protests; $47,500 to a medic who required surgery after being pushed down by police; $40,272 to another medic who suffered a broken arm; $30,000 to a woman who was shot, repeatedly and at close range, with plastic buckshot; and $5,000 to a man arrested for violating curfew when there was no curfew in effect.[29]

More Confrontational

An independent review commissioned by the City of Portland found numerous problems related to police planning, training, organization, communication, and supervision during the demonstrations. Rules of engagement were not clearly communicated to line officers and generally went unenforced.[30] Investigators found an overreliance on "unlawful assembly" declarations and "overuse of riot control agents." Aside from any humanitarian or civil liberties concerns, the violence was ultimately self-defeating. "When the community comes to believe that police are responding to protest in ways that are unfair or heavy-handed, it is radicalizing and draws more people into the crowds, which only makes them exponentially harder to police. It also cements a sense of collective identity among crowd members as *adversaries* of the police, rather than partners, making them more oppositional. . . . crowds grow and become more confrontational with each passing night."[31]

Faced with repeated violence, protesters were quickly schooled in the art of street fighting and learned to regroup as the tear gas cleared. They adopted tactics from the pro-democracy movement in Hong Kong: using umbrellas to deflect police projectiles and pepper spray; trapping tear gas canisters under traffic cones and dousing them with water; using laser pointers to blind video cameras and harry officers. As the summer went on, protesters started arriving increasingly armored and armed. Some carried hockey and lacrosse sticks with which to send tear gas canisters sailing back toward police lines. Others used slingshots to fire missiles, either at the cops or at the windows of government buildings.[32]

Mutual aid groups redirected their efforts to support the protests. The Rosehip Medics converted their hand sanitizer production line to make chemical wipes for the removal of pepper spray. Symbiosis Hub and Resource Exchange (SHARE) distributed personal protective equipment, likewise expanding from Covid masks to protest gear. Snack Mamas and Riot Ribs provided food and water.[33]

The police saw what was happening—the tactical innovation, the development of infrastructure—and they didn't like it. "Each evening," Officer Tommy Clark wrote, "they become more organized, more prepared, and more hostile." The police adapted as well. They increasingly targeted smaller groups on the periphery of demonstrations. Every day, a patrol combed the park to collect rocks, bottles, and other potential projectiles, and they eventually started confiscating traffic cones. Police also took to targeting cars that they thought might be supplying the protests, sometimes writing citations but more usually stabbing their tires and even smashing their windows. They singled out medics for arrest and for violence, and they seized or destroyed first aid supplies.[34]

Both protesters and police took steps to assure their anonymity. For the protesters, that meant wearing a mask and dressing entirely in black, blending together to avoid arrest. The cops received special permission to cover their name tags.[35]

Battle Fatigue

It was clear that the cops were feeling embattled—or, as one report later put it, "betrayed."[36] Officer Tommy Clark claimed that he could "sense the hostility" while driving through East Portland: "The typical 'Fuck you!'s and 'Pigs!' had turned into silent stares and a finger gun to the head." He also sensed that his colleagues were starting to tire, feeling "the effects of prolonged duty hours, physical exertion, lack of sleep, and adrenaline fatigue from going call to call defending the city against the violent extremist groups known as Antifa and Black Lives Matter."[37]

"It's been especially hard for our frontline folks," Police Chief Chuck Lovell told the Police Executive Research Forum. "They get pelted with rocks, commercial-grade fireworks, and very harmful green lasers shined in their eyes. . . . Some officers are off for a protracted period of time due to their injuries." There was also a problem with morale: "You come to work and your buildings are all boarded up and there's horrible graffiti spray painted all around your work area. It really takes a toll . . . personally and emotionally."[38]

The protesters too were nearing exhaustion. Demonstrations continued nightly, but by late June they rarely attracted more than two or three hundred people. Most nights there were only a few dozen. The police bureau demobilized its incident management team on June 23. Rose City Justice disbanded a week later.[39] It seemed that the protests had just about run their course.

But then the president of the United States decided to get involved.

The Fed War

On June 18, a group of teenagers with the Pacific Northwest Youth Liberation Front had gathered outside of the Portland German American Society to burn flags and pull down a statue of George Washington. President Donald Trump was outraged: "Two days ago leftist radicals in Portland, Oregon ripped down a statue of George Washington and wrapped it in an American flag and set the American flag on fire. . . . We ought to come up with legislation that if you burn the American flag you go to jail for one year."[40] A flag-burning ban would of course be unconstitutional, so the president did the next best thing, signing Executive Order 13933, "Protecting American Monuments, Memorials, and Statues, and Federal Property" and dispatching 755 Homeland Security officers to Portland.[41] "Almost overnight," a report commissioned by the city government later recounted, "the protests and riots, which had largely self-extinguished, reignited, and their focus shifted to federal buildings, including Portland's Mark O. Hatfield United States Courthouse."[42]

For the next few weeks, the federal government became the protesters' main adversary. On July 7, a squad of federal officers dressed like soldiers launched flashbangs and impact rounds against a candlelight vigil. Three days later, a US Marshal fired an impact round directly into the face of Donavan LaBella, a young man armed only with a boom box, nearly killing him and causing permanent cognitive damage. On July 18, when Christopher David, a fifty-three-year-old US Navy vet, approached the riot line and calmly asked the assembled federal officers, "Why are you violating your oath to the Constitution?," one responded by pushing him; another drew his gun; a third doused him with pepper spray; and one repeatedly swung his baton—two-handed, like a baseball bat—striking him five times. Video shows David standing motionless until the beating ends, then walking away with his middle fingers raised. He later required surgery.[43]

Federal agents would sometimes blanket an area with tear gas, then charge into the cloud and beat people while they were incapacitated.[44] Medics saw increasing numbers of injuries from less-lethal rounds and described federal agents "shooting [tear gas] canisters directly at people . . . at head-level in a straight line." "We are now seeing more head wounds," acknowledged Michelle Ozaki, the coordinator for OHSU4BLM (Oregon Health Sciences University for Black Lives Matter). "The federal officials and local police do not seem to be wanting to disperse protestors anymore, they seem to be wanting to hurt protestors."[45]

By mid-July men in military fatigues were pulling demonstrators into unmarked vans. Those they detained report being searched, photographed, and released without paperwork after about ninety minutes. Generally they had little idea who had taken them prisoner. It turned out to be the Border Patrol Tactical Unit (BORTAC)—a group whose training is modeled on that of the Army Rangers and the Navy SEALs.[46]

The more outrageous the police violence, the more people turned out to oppose it. Protesters pelted the cops with pink squeaky-toy pigs. They tore down the courthouse fence, or portions of it, repeatedly. When the feds emerged from the courthouse, activists would form a shield wall. Those in the back would throw bottles and tear gas canisters while the front line advanced. Repeatedly, police were forced to fall back. Later, a "Wall of Moms" created a human barrier between the riot squad and the protesters. Police responded by pepper spraying them and firing less-lethal rounds at close range. "When you tear gas moms, what happens?" the City Council's Jo Ann Hardesty asked, rhetorically. "Twice as many people show up the next night." Soon suburban dads arrived with leaf blowers, which they used to push the poisonous clouds back toward the cops.[47]

By July 20, Homeland Security officers had reported 689 injuries. The US Marshals Service said that nineteen deputies had sustained "multiple traumatic injuries," resulting from hammers, lasers, or other weapons. The police bureau estimated that 450 of its officers had suffered injuries, including cuts, bruises, concussions, and broken bones.[48]

Lacking Intelligence

All the while, the intelligence services watched from the courthouse, monitored livestreams of the protests, and deployed undercover agents in the crowds. An FBI counterterrorism "Fly Team" interviewed those arrested and handled the "initial exploitation of [suspects'] phones, or other communication devices." The Department of Homeland Security's Office of Intelligence and Analysis Operations (I&A) sent sixteen intelligence collectors and two analysts to Portland (with additional support from six contractors working remotely). This unit produced operational background reports (OBRs), brief profiles commonly known as "baseball cards." Distributed to "federal, state, and local law enforcement," OBRs sum up an individual's "past criminal history, travel history, derogatory information from DHS or Intelligence Community holdings as well as any relevant publicly available social media potentially relevant to identity indicators of domestic violent extremism or coordination among violent actors."[49]

Such reports are not usually produced for US citizens unless there is a "demonstrated terrorism nexus." But top officials, including acting DHS secretary Chad Wolf, "wanted I&A to create OBRs against everyone participating in the Portland protests." When it was explained that this would be both impractical and illegal, Wolf asked for reports on everyone who was arrested. A great many of the resulting documents listed only nonviolent offenses such as trespassing or failure to comply with a lawful order. Some included information on constitutionally protected activities: three "reported on the activities of U.S. journalists engaged in ordinary journalism" and, by the government's admission, "should not have been published."[50]

The I&A staff repeatedly raised concerns about their assignments, and some refused to take part. Acting undersecretary Brian Murphy, however, would not be deterred. "Convinced that there was a coordinated effort to commit violence," he hoped to "identify a single individual or group that was 'masterminding' the attacks." When multiple analyses failed to uncover any such coordination, what developed was a fight over constitutional rights filtered through the medium of office politics, with the leaders' political objectives pitted against the staff's professional standards:

> In many conversations, Mr. Murphy stated that violent protesters in Portland were connected to or motivated by ANTIFA . . . but I&A did not have collection (evidence) to show it. . . . For weeks, the analysts had been telling Mr. Murphy that because ANTIFA was not in the collection, it could not be put into the analysis. Notwithstanding this feedback from the I&A analysts, on July 25, 2020, Mr. Murphy sent an email to his senior leadership instructing them that henceforth, the

> violent opportunists in Portland were to be reported as VAAI [Violent Antifa Anarchists Inspired extremists], unless the intel "show[ed] something different."[51]

Homeland Security's internal review of the I&A operation provides, in the words of Senator Ron Wyden, "a stunning analysis of the incompetence and mismanagement and abuse of power during the summer of 2020."[52] The internal review cites numerous problems with the operation's planning, priorities, training, supervision, "tradecraft," and administrative procedures, along with a "toxic atmosphere" characterized by "demeaning, dismissive, and degrading treatment of I&A employees."[53]

A separate audit of the Portland Police Bureau's intelligence efforts likewise found that they frequently ignored policies intended to protect individual privacy and prevent political spying. Assembling photographs, video, license plate numbers, and social media screen captures, "Portland officers collected personally identifiable information about protestors in police records without documenting suspected criminal activity." Much of the behavior they reported was constitutionally protected, and some of it was hilariously trivial. The intelligence unit filed reports about a planned demonstration against the state attorney general, "a vehicle playing anti-law enforcement music," internet posts critical of the prosecutor's office, and complaints about police antisemitism. One report described a man simply looking at a police building. Without undergoing the legally required review, most reports were consequently filed in a statewide database and will be available to other law enforcement agencies for twenty years.[54]

Tear Gas Bans

The federal presence stoked the protests, but it also provided some relief for Mayor Ted Wheeler, who would try to present himself as a brave liberal standing up to President Trump—a pose met with almost universal scorn. When he showed up at the protests, the feds teargassed him and the demonstrators heckled him, chanting "Ted shot us, too," and dumping a bag of Portland Police riot munitions at his feet.[55]

To be fair, though, it is not clear that Wheeler—or anyone—could control the Portland Police. On June 6, the mayor had restricted the use of tear gas to circumstances in which there was a "serious and immediate threat to life safety, and there is no other viable alternative for dispersal." Three days later, a federal judge issued a restraining order, prohibiting the use of gas unless "the lives or safety of the public or the police are at risk." And on June 30, Governor Kate Brown signed a law reserving it for officially declared riots. The total result of these three orders was that the police did not reduce their use of tear gas but *did* declare riots more frequently. The bureau would later be found in contempt for ignoring the court order.[56]

Home Rule

On July 29, Governor Kate Brown announced that, under a deal negotiated with Vice President Mike Pence, Homeland Security would be reducing its presence in the city and the Oregon State Police (OSP) would take their place. "[It] is obvious the current strategy is not sustainable and has the high probability of serious injury or death, as officers and community members clash," the State Police said in a statement. "OSP hopes to de-escalate the tensions around the Mark O. Hatfield Courthouse, facilitating peaceful free speech and proportionate response if criminal activity is observed." July 30, the first night under the new arrangement was relatively calm, and the state cops did not even show themselves.[57]

Protests started to shrink again. Where there had been thousands in July, a couple weeks later there were only hundreds. Police took advantage of the smaller numbers, rushing into crowds and beating people without making arrests, or else kettling whole groups and arresting everyone.[58] They settled on a single approach after August 11, when District Attorney Mike Schmidt announced that his office would "presumptively decline to charge cases . . . that do not involve deliberate property damage, theft, or the use or threat of force against another person." The cops responded by escalating direct violence while making fewer arrests.[59]

Protesters adjusted to the new circumstances, moving away from mass actions and adopting more hit-and-run tactics. They diversified their targets, attacking smaller precinct buildings, ICE offices, and the Portland Police Association's union hall, then fleeing before the cops could respond. Police took to filling entire neighborhoods with tear gas and beating residents when they came out of their homes.[60]

Back the Blue

August also saw the arrival of daytime "Back the Blue" rallies, often featuring Proud Boys and other far-right militants. Fairly quickly, these demonstrations supporting the police started to collide with those *against* the police, and the police bureau announced that it would not intervene in violence "between willing participants." As a policy, that had every appearance of inviting the far right to attack the left-wing protests with impunity, almost as though they were acting on the cops' behalf. True to their word, the police stood aside when, on August 22, about two hundred Proud Boys and other assorted rowdies gathered at the Justice Center and a huge, hours-long brawl ensued. Eventually, left and right sorted into two groups, each behind their own shield wall. For a while, they exchanged barrages of eggs, bottles, fireworks, and paintballs. Some Proud Boys tried attacking with pepper spray, but the wind was against them, and they only blinded their own team. Someone from the left took the opportunity to throw a large firework into the opposing crowd, which caused immediate panic. The right-wing shield wall broke formation, and the crowd fled in an undisciplined retreat, with some members running to the nearby federal building and begging for help. The Federal Protective Service declared an unlawful assembly and moved in against the remaining demonstrators, those of the left.[61]

A week later, as part of a "Trump Cruise," almost a thousand trucks wound through the city, flying US and Thin Blue Line flags and firing paintballs and mace from their moving vehicles. Afterward, two men affiliated with Patriot Prayer, Jay Danielson and Chandler Pappas, were walking through downtown, armed with guns, bats, and pepper spray, when they encountered Michael Reinoehl, a self-described antifascist. Though the confrontation was captured on video, it is not entirely clear what happened next, except that Reinoehl shot and killed Danielson.[62]

Reinoehl was himself killed the following week. The US Marshals Service Pacific Northwest Violent Offender Task Force tracked him north to Lacey, Washington, boxed in his car with two SUVs, and fired between thirty and fifty shots without warning.[63] In numerous statements over the following days, Trump gloated over the killing. "We sent in the US Marshals," he bragged. "Took 15 minutes, it was over. Fifteen minutes, it was over. We got him. They knew who he was, didn't want to arrest him, and fifteen minutes that ended." He later told Fox News: "This guy was a violent criminal, and the US Marshals killed him. And I'll tell you something—that's the way it has to be. There has to be retribution."[64]

Fire Exit

What finally ended the summer's unrest was not tear gas but smoke. Beginning September 7, forest fires raged within a few miles of the city. More than a million acres burned, and entire towns were completely destroyed. More than forty thousand people had to be evacuated. Seventeen died.[65]

Conspiracy-fantasists spread unfounded rumors that the fires were being set by Antifa—to what end, they never said. Officially, law enforcement agencies, from the Douglas County Sheriff's Office to the Federal Bureau of Investigation, did their best to squelch these rumors; unofficially, some of their own officers helped to spread them. Small groups of armed men set up roadblocks in rural areas throughout the Northwest, sometimes with police support. Ostensibly aiming to stop arsonists and prevent looting, they mostly harassed people of color and impeded the evacuation.[66]

The fires never reached Portland, but the air in the city became unbreathable. The atmosphere was an unyielding bank of smoke, blotting out the sun and giving everything a sickly, sepia-toned look. It was dangerous just to be outside, and the demonstrations abruptly ceased.[67]

When racial justice protests resumed a couple of weeks later, the momentum had clearly been lost.[68] A report commissioned by the city government described the demonstrations occurring in the last part of the year as "more sporadic, less sustained, and more likely to be resolved peacefully."[69]

Hindsight

Three things set 2020 apart. First, it was an election year, in which the incumbent candidate was Donald Trump, a man who thrives on conflict, whose politics both fuel and are fueled by polarizing division, and who has no scruples about using government authority and coercive force to gain some momentary advantage in pursuing his personal ambitions. Second, there was the Covid-19 pandemic and, with it, widespread economic insecurity, social anxiety, and existential dread, a simultaneous feeling of solidarity and isolation, pervasive uncertainty and active distrust, and a desperate need for control alongside a certain sense of fatalism. Finally, there was the very scale of the moral outrage gripping international society in the face of yet another police murder.

Even so, Portland was an outlier. "What we have in Portland," Homeland Security Secretary Chad Wolf intoned, "is very different than what we have in any other city."[70]

Why Portland? All of the elements fueling the revolt had in fact been building for years. Since the beginning of this century, the city had seen successive waves of organizing and unrest, specifically against the police, with increasing frequency, escalating militancy, and ever more radical agendas. The pattern really took hold after the death of José Mejía in 2001 and built until after James Jahar Perez was killed three years later, then picked up again after the murder of Aaron Campbell in 2010. Alongside this movement, almost as its shadow, there was also a series of halfhearted, disingenuous, or sincerely failing reforms—review boards, diversity training, less-lethal weaponry. And, as a reaction (and often overreaction) the police union stood stubbornly opposed to any outside controls, any limits to police authority and officer discretion.

Surely these factors could be found in similar proportion in other cities with liberal leaders and brutal police. What made Portland unique, I think, was the very recent and prolonged experience with street fighting, created by the persistent and aggressive incursions of fascistic groups like Patriot Prayer and the Proud Boys. The resulting confrontations, often including police attacks against left-wing counterprotesters, discredited the Portland Police and normalized political violence. Over time, the almost routine nature of this conflict created the conditions such that, under the right circumstances and given the right provocation, fighting the cops would appear not only as an obvious response but as a necessity.

CHAPTER 31
Aftermath

Reforms and Resignations

Rioting brought immediate results.

Even as the protests were ongoing, and for a couple of years after they ended, change seemed inevitable. Demands that would have been inconceivable a short while before—defunding the police, cops out of schools—appeared now as reasonable, even mild. Facing such broad and fierce public outcry, agencies at every level of government enacted a flurry of reforms, long overdue, suddenly urgent.

On June 17, 2020, the Portland City Council redirected $15 million from the police bureau to other programs, eliminating eight positions from the Special Emergency Reaction Team and disbanding the gang/gun squad.[1] The Oregon state legislature passed laws requiring cops to report misconduct, mandating new bias crime training, banning choke holds, restricting the publication of mug shots, restricting the cops' ability to lie when questioning juveniles, limiting the offenses for which police can stop a vehicle, and requiring cops to inform people of their right to refuse a search, alongside reforms of prisons and the courts.[2] Both Portland Public Schools and the TriMet transit agency announced that they would be reducing their reliance on police and shifting toward unarmed guards, outreach workers, and counselors instead.[3]

There were also sudden changes in leadership. On June 8, barely a week into the demonstrations, Police Chief Jami Resch abruptly resigned, nominating Chuck Lovell, a Black police captain, to take her place.[4] Resch was openly acquiescing to demands from civil rights groups, resigning one day after she received a letter jointly signed by the Coalition of Black Men, the Black Male Alliance, and Word Is Bond criticizing her "all-white leadership team."[5] Once he took over, Lovell immediately set up meetings with community leaders.[6]

District Attorney Rod Underhill likewise resigned, leaving office a few months early in favor of the newly elected Mike Schmidt, who had campaigned on a reform platform and received 76 percent of the vote.[7] Underhill presented his departure as a principled move to ensure continuity during what he expected to be a period of long, high-profile prosecutions related to the protests. But it is equally plausible that he hoped to hand Schmidt a poisoned chalice, forcing him to choose between displeasing his reform-minded supporters by aggressively prosecuting demonstrators or spoiling his relationship with police by adopting a more lenient approach. Schmidt took the latter option, dismissing 520 of 682 protest cases, or 85 percent.[8]

Attempted Accountability

Schmidt would spend his entire term under fire from conservative lobby groups, police unions, and his own staff.[9] Cops publicly labeled him as "Antifa" and claimed that his campaign was funded by billionaire philanthropist (and conspiracy-theory bugaboo) George Soros. East Precinct Commander Erica Hurley, in uniform and on duty, urged a neighborhood meeting to vote Schmidt out of office—a violation of the law, the secretary of state determined. Someone even leaked Schmidt's home address on a pro-police website, leading to death threats and forcing him to temporarily relocate his family.[10]

His relationship with the police was further strained when he turned his attention to their own lawbreaking. The district attorney's office reviewed twenty-one protest-related cases against police officers, but more than a third were dismissed because individual cops could not be identified. Furthermore, Schmidt explained, "The law is on a police officer's side in doing their job, they can use force." In the end, only two were charged. The first, Scott Groshong, had been working in an unmarked van when he saw people breaking into a skate shop. He drove after them, hit one with the vehicle, and failed to report it. He retired while the investigation was ongoing and later pled guilty to felony assault and official misconduct, receiving three years of probation and eighty hours of community service.[11]

The second officer, the Rapid Response Team's Corey Budworth, had been caught on video pushing photojournalist Teri Jacobs to the ground and clubbing her in the face as she tried to get up. When Budworth was indicted for misdemeanor assault, the entire Rapid Response Team resigned in protest—a "particularly disquieting" development, an independent review later noted, "as a seemingly wholesale and organized repudiation of formal accountability measures." Instead of going to trial, Budworth's case was diverted into a restorative justice program, leading him to record a public apology with the flat delivery typical of a hostage video. Jacobs sued and received $50,000.[12]

While the DA met with only minor success, the review system remained an abject failure. Though the Independent Police Review received more than one hundred complaints related to the demonstrations, the agency ultimately found no police misconduct. The "vast majority" of complaints were dismissed because the cops couldn't be identified—a predictable result of management allowing officers to cover their nametags. But even when the officers were known, IPR director Ross Caldwell explained, police bureau rules made it impossible to hold individual officers accountable in crowd control situations.[13] The US Department of Justice suggested another strategy: holding supervisors responsible for the behavior of their troops, specifically citing North Precinct Commander Brian Ossenkop for authorizing force that violated policy. Chief Lovell promoted him instead, naming him assistant chief.[14]

Before the 2020 protests, the Department of Justice (DOJ) had been poised to release the Portland Police Bureau from federal oversight, resolving the 2012 consent decree. But based on the bureau's performance at the demonstrations, the DOJ instead imposed new requirements related to training and command responsibility, a review of crowd control operations, and the adoption of body cameras.[15]

The public also took action. The November 2020 elections saw the passage of a citywide ballot measure, 26-217, which scrapped the existing and ineffectual Independent Police Review system and created a new review board that could investigate the use of force (including deadly force), discrimination, and violations of constitutional rights. It would be given subpoena power and the authority to fire officers. The measure passed with 82 percent approval.[16]

Half Measures Availed Us Nothing

In that same election, Oregon voters approved the decriminalization of all drugs. On the theory that "people suffering from addiction are more effectively treated with health care services than with criminal punishments," Ballot Measure 110 eliminated criminal penalties for simple possession—though it stopped short of full legalization. Possession of small quantities of any drug would constitute a Class E violation punishable by a $100 fine; however, the ticket could be dismissed with a phone call to a drug counseling hotline. The law simultaneously increased funding for addiction services by 500 percent.[17]

Unfortunately, the government did not even *try* to get decriminalization right. When Measure 110 first passed, advocates with the Oregon Health Justice Recovery Alliance sent the governor a set of recommendations for the law's implementation, calling for new police training, a citation form prominently featuring the drug counseling number, and coordination between treatment providers and the courts. This document was utterly ignored. The cops were not retrained, the ticket was not redesigned, and there was no effort to coordinate operations. Mike Marshall, the director of Oregon Recovers and an opponent of decriminalization, was dismayed by the bureaucratic indifference: "They simply tried to do the least amount of work to administer it to the letter of the law."[18] Worse still, though the money was there in the budget, funding for treatment lagged disastrously. The legislation dedicated $300 million in marijuana taxes to be put toward addiction treatment and recovery every three years. But after eighteen months, only $2.8 million had been spent—less than 1 percent of the budgeted funds. Six months later, the figure had risen to $31 million, still leaving $270 million moldering in state coffers.[19]

The police hated decriminalization. A study published in the *International Journal of Drug Policy* found complete unanimity on this point: "All law enforcement interviewees were frustrated that Class E violations appeared to have little to no impact on the person receiving the citation."[20] (The interviews have been anonymized, so it is impossible to know which officers, if any, worked in Portland.) The cops also insisted that Measure 110 triggered a crime wave, though data did not support that claim.[21]

It seems that the thing the cops hated most about decriminalization was its interruption of their usual methods. Researchers found that the police saw Measure 110 as "resulting in an erosion of their authority. . . . They expressed frustration that they could not use drug possession as a 'tool' for investigations to pursue and build cases, establish probable cause, and impose what they believed necessary for social order." Moreover, "interviewees noted that B[allot] M[easure] 110 ha[d] virtually eliminated the informant networks that they once cultivated and relied on to build larger cases." "Drug users hate jail," one officer explained. "If they're there and can't use, they'll get dope sick. . . . [But] I won't lodge you at the jail today if you can help me find somebody that's dealing. . . . we kind of use that as leverage." Another officer said, "It's not so easy anymore as to go out and get the dope, put the person in jail, and then they'll get 27 warrants after the fact for failing to appear on that one dope charge. That's how we used to keep that population in check. . . . So now we need to hang them up on real crimes."[22] Notice that by this way of thinking, solving "real crimes" is a needless hassle and secondary to "keep[ing] that population in check."

One police chief, expressing frustration, argued that it was a mistake for Measure 110 to involve the police at all. "[Just when] we're trying to back out of these [drug enforcement] situations . . . now we're asking our law enforcement professionals to reinsert themselves." That approach, as he politely put it, "seems counterintuitive." It probably was confusing to the police that the law decriminalized drugs but did not legalize them, proscribing but not penalizing their use. Drugs were prohibited, and the police were expected to intervene—but without arrests or incarceration. As they saw it, they were given a job to do but no tools with which to do it. One officer complained, "We lost our ability to hold people accountable in a jail cell. . . . How else am I going to get through to somebody that would rather get high over and over and over again?"[23]

In 2024, after an alarming rise in overdose deaths, the Democrat-controlled state legislature reintroduced criminal penalties, making personal possession punishable by 180 days in jail.[24] There was no good factual basis for doing so. Studies found "no evidence of an association between drug policy changes that remove or reduce criminal penalties for drug possession . . . and fatal overdoses."[25] In fact, the rise in overdoses began before decriminalization. (The state medical examiner recorded 298 deaths from methamphetamine use in 2019, 391 in 2020, and 291 in 2021; for fentanyl the figures were 75 in 2019, 230 in 2020, and 237 in 2021.)[26] The promised benefits of recriminalization were purely a matter of conjecture, shading easily into delusional moralism and wishful thinking. As there were already more people seeking drug treatment than the existing system could accommodate, recriminalization would only lead to more people going to jail. The state's Criminal Justice Commission estimated that recriminalization would add 1,333 convictions and send 533 more people to jail every year statewide, with a disproportionate impact on people of color.[27]

The "defunding" of the Portland Police—which had merely returned the budget to 2016 levels—proved similarly short-lived. In 2021, the City added $5.2 million to the police budget, and Mayor Ted Wheeler promised to hire two hundred more cops over the following three years. By 2022, the bureau was receiving $12 million above its (already inflated) 2019 level, reaching a record $249 million annually.[28]

In September 2023, the city council likewise took steps to roll back the changes to the police review board, reducing the number of members, limiting the scope of complaints the board could consider, involving the police in the appointment of board members, putting investigatory hearings behind closed doors, and eliminating appeals. The Albina Ministerial Alliance's LeRoy Haynes accused the council of trying to "dilute the police oversight charter." "The public sent a clear message when it approved Measure 26-217," Carolyn Buppert, president of the League of Women Voters, reminds us. "Portlanders want a community-centered oversight system with the independence to do its job, free from political or police bureau interference. . . . the city's proposed code undermines that goal."[29]

Street Roots and Cahoots

The most ambitious reform of the period, the creation of a nonpolice first-responder unit, was already in the works before the uprising.

In 2019, the homeless advocacy organization and newspaper *Street Roots* published "Portland Street Response: A Plan for the Future of Crisis and Disorder Intervention in Public Spaces."[30] It proposed a new organization modeled on a long-standing program in Eugene, Oregon, CAHOOTS: Crisis Assistance Helping Out on the Streets.[31] The CAHOOTS web page explains: "CAHOOTS workers are not trained in law enforcement and do not have the same authority as police. We are a mobile crisis intervention team, designed as an alternative to police response for non-violent crises."[32] The group would send a nurse or EMT and a mental health professional to emergency calls involving intoxication, psychological distress, self-harm, and the like. Their mission was to de-escalate crisis situations and connect people to needed services. The response team administered first aid, provided food and water, and transported clients to detox, a medical clinic, or a psych ward as needed. Unlike police, CAHOOTS workers did not use restraints and went unarmed; they didn't even carry pepper spray. Operating with only 2 percent of the Eugene Police Department budget, CAHOOTS handled 20 percent of the city's emergency calls (approximately twenty-four thousand a year).[33]

The idea got the attention of Portland City Commissioner Jo Ann Hardesty, and the city council approved a pilot project to operate out of the fire bureau.[34] The city auditor describes it: "Portland Street Response's mobile crisis response teams are made up of mental health crisis responders, community health medical responders, community health workers, and peer support specialists. The teams are unarmed and respond in a van to nonemergency 911 calls with mental health, behavioral health, substance use, and/or general welfare components. Community Health Workers and Peer Support Specialists offer continued support to help connect clients to needed services. . . . Portland Street Response is largely focused on reducing police contact with people who are experiencing mental health crises and have not committed a crime."[35]

In its first year of operations, Portland Street Response (PSR) handled 1,219 separate incidents; by its second year that number had grown to 7,418. Nearly all of these (97.6 percent) would have previously been handled by the police. Only one incident in its first two years led to an arrest, and none resulted in injuries. More than two-thirds of the people PSR assisted (68.4 percent) were homeless, and nearly as many (60.2 percent) showed signs of mental illness.[36]

The program was immediately popular with the public. After its first year, a survey of area voters found that 87 percent thought that a "non-police first responder" would be better trained to address a crisis involving mental illness, drugs, or a homeless person; 86 percent thought that they would be better prepared to conduct welfare checks. A petition urging the expansion of the Street Response program later received ten thousand signatures.[37]

Somewhat surprisingly, researchers also found police to be supportive and even enthusiastic about the new system. "The majority of PPB staff we spoke with acknowledged the clear value of having PSR respond to issues involving people experiencing mental health crises or homelessness." One officer stated, "I think it's a better, more humane solution to the problem [of homelessness] than us giving them a resource card and telling them to leave." Another expressed his hope that the program could expand: "We would love it if they take all the mental health calls. . . . we're not psychologists, we're not therapists, that's not our wheelhouse, so to speak." In fact, the cops' main complaint is that the program is not doing *more*. "The primary areas for improvement discussed by PPB staff pertained to PSR staffing capacity and availability, the need to expand call types and criteria, and working on communication and collaboration between PSR and PPB."[38]

Perhaps the greatest obstacle facing Portland Street Response was the opposition of Commissioner Rene Gonzalez, who took control of the fire bureau in January 2023. Almost immediately, Gonzalez imposed a hiring freeze, preventing a planned expansion to twenty-four-hour service. A month later he ordered PSR staff to cease their distribution of tents, taking away what researchers described as "one of their most important tools." (The following week, Portland was hit with the worst snowstorm in eighty years, and at least one person died from hypothermia.) Gonzalez later announced budget cuts limiting the unit's ability to distribute food and clothing.[39]

Gonzalez's concerns about Portland Street Response were mainly ideological. He considered it "problematic" that "a police abolitionist as a city employee [would be] involved in first responding." As abolitionist scholar Alex Vitale argues, "[Politicians] can't really allow these alternatives to flourish because they come into conflict with their governing logic."[40] It is an open question, though, whether Portland Street Response advances the cause of abolition by demonstrating the real possibility for functioning alternatives or whether it supplements policing by freeing up officers to respond to other calls, proactively patrol, or conduct investigations. Does the existence of a working alternative erode our society's dependence on the cops, or by relieving the police of some of their more challenging and controversial assignments, does it help to maintain their legitimacy? *Street Roots* certainly promised that the program could be good for the police: "A better response to people on Portland's streets might be the linchpin to creating the space for more effective policing . . . freeing up critical time for officers to meet community expectations."[41] Though the cops seemed to feel that PSR helped rather than hurt them, Gonzalez worried about a drift toward police abolition and was committed to halting it.

Betrayed

Ultimately the most durable effect of the 2020 uprising may be the widespread demoralization of police personnel. "The Bureau's morale is low in ways that arise from and perpetuate antagonism with part of the Portland community—including local elected leaders," one assessment found. "Portland officers report feeling less respect and compliance from their community. With the loss of legitimacy (or, even, power), comes a loss of morale; their desire to engage with the community is lost, too." One cop commented anonymously: "City leaders, elected officials, and [the] community need to know officers feel betrayed."[42]

According to a 2021 poll, nearly all Portland police (97 percent) felt that the "city government has made the work of the Bureau more difficult over the last year or two." A very large majority (80 percent) agreed with the statement

"Community members are less likely to treat Bureau officers with respect than they were a year or two ago." And 83 percent agreed that "community members are less likely to comply with [police] instructions."[43]

If nothing else, Portlanders did an excellent job making the cops feel unwelcome. The Police Association's offices were set on fire so often over the course of 2020 that the union relocated to an anonymous building in the suburbs.[44] Even years after the demonstrations ended, officers complain of being ostracized, shunned in their neighborhoods, churches, and children's schools.[45]

These hard feelings have had real impacts on recruitment, retention, and the willingness of the cops to get out of their cars. "We had more officers resign than in any time in recent history," Chief Lovell lamented—160 in 2020 alone. Another 115 left the following year.[46] In exit interviews, most officers blamed elected officials, police bureau leaders, the Department of Justice, and public disrespect. "The community shows zero support," one officer complained. "I felt worthless and not appreciated," another confessed. "For the first time in my life," wrote a third, "[I] hated the job that I worked so hard to get."[47] Replacing these officers has been difficult and slow. Four years later, the Portland Police Bureau was operating with 75 vacancies out of 881 budgeted positions.[48] Those still on the job have cultivated a reputation for avoiding the work. "When Portlanders call 911," *Willamette Week* reported in the summer of 2022, "they can't rely on police to show up." Residents and politicians alike often remark that the police are essentially on strike.[49] But a more hopeful interpretation is also available. Rather than view police disengagement in terms of the officers withholding their labor to protest social conditions, we could instead view it as an example of the public, by refusing to grant the institution legitimacy and withholding cooperation, successfully (if temporarily) suppressing police activity.

Threshold

As I write this, Portland is at the threshold of a new period in its history. In 2025 the commissioner system that had structured city government for more than a century was replaced by a larger city council, districted elections, and ranked-choice voting. The reconstituted council is expected to be more responsive to neighborhood concerns, and thus to the city's working classes and racial minorities, and less dependent on campaign funding from major business interests.[50] At the same time, a new system of police oversight—with both investigatory and disciplinary power—began its work. It is too early to know how these changes will affect the city, whether or how soon they will be either captured or undermined by the Portland Business Alliance, the Portland Police Association, and other entrenched interests, or whether they might have a real effect on the way policing is done. Likewise, we do not yet know whether Portland Street Response will survive and, if it does, whether it will become simply an appendage to normal policing or grow into a new paradigm for public safety.

What we do know is that the work of justice is far from complete, that even the most ambitious reforms fall short of what is necessary to achieve a minimally decent society, to say nothing of the ideals of freedom and equality.

The problem is not that reforms are impossible. They are only too possible and all too tempting. The problem is that reforms so rarely touch the deeper relations of power. Instead, they refine the expression of authority, direct it, make it more effective, more lawful, more acceptable. The very limit to police power, imposed over the objections of the officers themselves, can be the thing that supplies its legitimacy. Yet that limit can always be transgressed if the need arises. To the extent that reforms cover policing with a veil of legality, they may help to excuse violence even as they seek to control it. Attempts to limit the excesses of an unjust system tend by implication to justify the remainder. Unless the fundamental injustices of our society are addressed—especially race, class, and gender inequality—all efforts to ameliorate the suffering they cause, however well-meaning and even necessary, will only alleviate some of the symptoms while prolonging the underling condition.

CONSPECTUS

Policing and Progress

A Paradox Revisited

Let us return at the end to the paradox with which we began: the progressive city with the repressive police force. The key to resolving the apparent contradiction lies, I think, in the particular ethos of progress that has guided Portland's development. *Progress* has been treated as nearly synonymous with prosperity in its narrowly economic sense, though it has also been associated with democratic governance and a host of related social norms, cultural practices, and moral assumptions. Progress implies change, but it also implies order. Inevitably, then, the notion of progress has itself changed over time, and at every stage its particular conception of order has shaped the practices of policing. Progress has at times meant colonization, urbanization, gentrification, economic profit, technical and technological advances, moral uplift, good government, rational administration, public utilities, public education, public parks, social hygiene, and Social Darwinism. Connecting all of these was an enthusiasm for order and a faith in government intervention as the means to achieve it. The results often appear, especially in hindsight, as puritanical. The Progressive spirit is the Protestant ethic, animated by a missionary zeal and a civic-minded *noblesse oblige*.[1]

Put simply, progress, in Portland's special sense of the term, is identified with capitalism, democracy, and white supremacy. Together, these three supports have structured the city's public life. There is nothing necessary or inevitable about the combination of these three factors; no one of them requires the other two. Yet they work together more or less well, reinforcing one another and providing a minimum of stability to the overall system. Of course they do not do so perfectly. The demands of each may sometimes conflict with those of the others, and each one has its own way of raising expectations that the whole set cannot meet and of stoking resentments it cannot always contain.

Of the three, democracy is by far the weakest element; it has been, throughout the city's history, more form than substance, more promise than fact. While in theory, or at least in fantasy, democracy should imply popular power and public participation, in practice the very structures of representation serve to limit engagement and to concentrate power, and elections have been determined as much by the writing of checks as by the casting of ballots. Liberal democracy, it turns out, is neither particularly liberal nor especially democratic.

New Crises

The paradox of abolition is this: The police exist to preserve the inequalities of our society. To abolish the police, we must also eliminate those inequalities. And to eliminate those inequalities, we must overcome the police.

For the past quarter century, Portland's resistance to policing has arrived in waves, each one more forceful than the last. Each new effort builds on what has come before and sometimes draws new energy from events at the national level. The response to the death of José Mejía drew from ongoing immigrants' rights organizing. It helped to form a coalition that would return in larger numbers after the police killed Kendra James and James Jahar Perez a few years later. When the cops killed Aaron Campbell in 2010, local unrest helped feed a regional policing crisis that began with the Oscar Grant rebellion in Oakland a year before. Occupy ICE drew inspiration from both Occupy Wall Street and Black Lives Matter, while channeling the anger over Trump's immigration policies into a direct-action campaign that in many ways prefigured Portland's later clash with the Department of Homeland Security. The unrest of 2020 drew from all of these sources and others. Most recently in the background was the regular street fighting that had periodically gripped the city over the previous several years, which can itself find origins in the skinhead wars of the eighties and nineties. The city's history may not have made the events of 2020 inevitable, but it did make them possible and certainly helped to determine the shape of that conflict.

There was also a measure of happenstance. Without the Covid-19 pandemic, it is doubtful that the unrest would have reached the same scale, embraced the same militancy, or endured for quite so long. It may be tempting, then, to think of this as a once-in-a-lifetime occurrence, a generation's opportunity for revolution—which we bungled. That, however, assumes that with the Covid crisis behind us, the future will return to a kind of predictable stability. It will not.

If nothing else, climate change is enough to guarantee that there will be future crises, which will strain our existing systems, overburden our physical and social infrastructure, and interrupt the routines of daily life.[2] Pairing that with continued inequality, it seems likely that 2020 will not be remembered as an anomalous year in history, like 1968, but as a prologue to the city's future—and the country's.

Acknowledgments

Several people offered advice and comments on earlier drafts of this book, for which I am very grateful. Among them: Effie Baum, Emily-Jane Dawson, Colette Gordon, Peter Little, Tabatha Millican, Will Munger, Gabriel Ryder, Josef Schneider, Kevin Van Meter, Geoff Wichert, Alex Vitale, and Dolores Williams.

Notes

Introduction: Policing, Portland, Paradox

1 The Trump administration named Portland, Seattle, and New York as cities "that have permitted violence and the destruction of property to persist and have refused to undertake reasonable measures to counteract these criminal activities (anarchist jurisdictions)." Quoted in Eric Laursen, *The Operating System: An Anarchist Theory of the Modern State* (Chico, CA: AK Press, 2021), 12.

2. David S. Jackson, "Skinhead Against Skinhead," time.com, August 9, 1993.

3. Mark Neocleous, *A Critical Theory of Police Power: The Fabrication of Social Order* (London: Verso, 2021) 59, 212. Emphasis in original.

4. Nigel Jaquiss and Tess Riski, "For Nearly 80 Years, the Portland Police Association Has Wielded Power in a Town That Doesn't Like Cops. That Power Is Now Under Siege," *Willamette Week*, June 24, 2020.

   In *Our Enemies in Blue*, I posited the defining characteristics of police as "(1) the authority to use force, (2) a public character and accountability (at least in principle) to some central governmental authority, and (3) general law enforcement duties (as opposed to limited, specified duties such as parking enforcement or animal control)." Here I am taking a broader approach. Kristian Williams, *Our Enemies in Blue: Police and Power in America*, 3rd ed. (Oakland: AK Press, 2015), 53.

5. Bernard E. Harcourt, *Illusion of Order: The False Promise of Broken Windows Policing* (Cambridge, MA: Harvard University Press, 2001), 18.

6. Though the organization is open about its agenda, Portland Copwatch is generally reliable as to the facts and, if anything, painfully fair-minded (sometimes, for instance, offering cops a "Spike Lee Do-The-Right-Thing Award"). They have provided detailed summaries and analyses of virtually every report, study, and policy document relating to the Portland Police Bureau for nearly three decades. For more information, visit portlandcopwatch.org.

7. Jewel Lansing, *Portland: People, Politics, and Power, 1851–2001* (Corvallis: Oregon State University Press, 2003), 461.

8. "Portland City, Oregon [2020]," data.census.gov, accessed March 28, 2024.

9. Countywide, the point-in-time measure for January 2023 registered 6,297 homeless individuals. Multnomah County, "News Release: Chronic Homelessness Number Falls Across Tri-County Region in 2023 Point in Time Count," multco.us, May 10, 2023.

10. Jewel Lansing and Fred Leeson, *Multnomah: The Tumultuous Story of Oregon's Most Populous County* (Corvallis: Oregon State University Press, 2012), 178.

11. For a debunking of tall tales about Nancy Boggs's floating bordello, see Joe Streckert, *Storied and Scandalous Portland, Oregon: A History of Gambling, Vice, Wits, and Wagers* (Guilford, CT: Globe Pequot, 2020), 29–30. Concerning the misattribution of downtown's tunnels to shanghaiers, see Barney Blalock, *The Oregon Shanghaiers: Columbia River Crimping from Astoria to Portland* (Charleston, SC: The History Press, 2014), 143–45.
12. Dead Kennedys, "Night of the Living Rednecks," in *Give Me Convenience or Give Me Death* (Alternative Tentacles, 1987).

Chapter 1: Settlement, Property, and Government

1. Jewel Lansing, *Portland: People, Politics, and Power* (Corvallis: Oregon State University Press, 2003), 6; Gordon DeMarco, *A Short History of Portland* (San Francisco: Lexikos, 1990), 31–32; J. D. Chandler, *Hidden History of Portland Oregon* (Charleston, SC: The History Press, 2013), 13; Percy Maddux, *City on the Willamette: The Story of Portland, Oregon* (Portland: Binford & Mort, 1952), 11.
2. Douglas Deur, *An Ethnohistorical Overview of Groups with Ties to Fort Vancouver National Historical Site* (Seattle: National Cultural Resources Report, 2012), 9–12.
3. Erin Goodling, "Our River, Our Future: More-than-Local Grassroots Activism in the Portland Harbor," in *Urban Cascadia and the Pursuit of Environmental Justice*, edited by Nik Janos and Corina McKendry (Seattle: University of Washington Press, 2021), 147; and DeMarco, *A Short History of Portland*, 5. See also the map in Jeff Zucker, et al., *Oregon Indians: Culture, History and Current Affairs: An Atlas and Introduction* ([Portland]: Press of the Oregon Historical Society, 1983), 9.
4. Chandler, *Hidden History*, 14–15, 17; and Dell Hymes, "Languages and Their Uses," in *The First Oregonians*, edited by Laura Berg (Portland: Oregon Council for the Humanities, 2007), 252.
5. "Village, hunting and berry picking sites were usually 'owned' in common by the tribe. Fishing spots were owned sometimes by families and sometimes by the whole tribe. But this 'ownership' was very different from the concept of property and ownership in current American society. In traditional Indian thought, land was sacred and was never actually owned, although rights for the use of a particular piece of land could reside in certain people." Zucker, *Oregon Indians*, 14.

   For more on the imposition of private property, including a comparison to the period of "enclosures" in England, see Roxanne Dunbar-Ortiz, *An Indigenous People's History of the United States* (Boston: Beacon Press, 2014), 34–36.
6. Quoted in Stephen Dow Beckham, "Federal-Indian Relations," in *The First Oregonians*, edited by Laura Berg (Portland: Oregon Council for the Humanities, 2007), 211.
7. Quoted in Beckham, "Federal-Indian Relations," 209.
8. DeMarco, *A Short History of Portland*, 41; Beckham, "Federal-Indian Relations," 212–33, 223; and Samuel R. Thurston, "Oregon," in *Becoming Oregon: From Expedition to Exposition*, edited by Robert Lewisohn Hamm (Lake Oswego, OR: Mossy Brae Press, 2015), 216–17.

   The Grande Ronde Reservation, to which the Willamette Valley peoples were confined, was established in 1856, covering 59,759 acres. In 1901, that was reduced to 33,648 acres. By 1954, only 597 acres remained, with an additional 800 acres of individual allotments still held in trust. Zucker, *Oregon Indians*, 112.
9. DeMarco, *A Short History of Portland*, 19; Lansing, *Portland*, 2; Frederick V. Holman, *Dr. John McLoughlin, the Father of Oregon* (Cleveland: Arthur H. Clark, 1907), 28–30; Charles

H. Carey, *General History of Oregon Through Early Statehood* (Portland: Binford & Mort, 1971), 245; and Stewart H. Holbrook, *The Columbia* (New York: Holt, Rinehart and Winston, 1956), 67–68.

10. Holman, *Dr. John McLoughlin*, 31. Charles Carey likewise described Fort Vancouver as "an American feudal state." Carey, *General History of Oregon*, 243.
11. Kenneth R. Coleman, *Dangerous Subjects: James D. Saules and the Rise of Black Exclusion in Oregon* (Corvallis: Oregon State University Press, 2017), 81; and Holbrook, *The Columbia*, 66.
12. Coleman, *Dangerous Subjects*, 100.
13. Holman, *Dr. John McLoughlin*, 35–39; and, Carey, *General History of Oregon*, 317.
14. Deur, *An Ethnohistorical Overview*, 54.
15. Deur, *An Ethnohistorical Overview*, 52.
16. Quoted in Deur, *An Ethnohistorical Overview*, 52. For details of McLoughlin's retaliatory practices, see Deur, *An Ethnohistorical Overview*, 52–54.
17. Holbrook, *The Columbia*, 70–71.
18. Deur, *An Ethnohistorical Overview*, 54.
19. Quoted in Melvin Clay Jacobs, *Winning Oregon: A Study of an Expansionist Movement* (Caldwell, ID: Caxton Printers, 1938), 29.
20. Lansing, *Portland*, 2. McLoughlin's estimate is in keeping with evidence from elsewhere. For instance: "The best scholarly estimates are that, in any given area, the initial epidemics typically reduced native numbers by half or more and that populations did not stabilize until successive waves of disease had reduced them by a factor of 90–95 percent." Daniel K. Richter, *The Ordeal of the Longhouse: The Peoples of the Iroquois League in the Era of European Colonization* (Chapel Hill: University of North Carolina Press, 1992), 58.

    Even the effects of disease, as Roxanne Dunbar-Ortiz reminds us, cannot be viewed in isolation from the other aspects of colonization, including the loss of territory and the disruption of traditional hunting, fishing, and trade practices leading to shortages of food and other essentials. Dunbar-Ortiz, *An Indigenous People's History of the United States*, 40–41.
21. Robert H. Ruby and John A. Brown, *Indians in the Pacific Northwest: A History* (Norman: University of Oklahoma Press, 1988), 98.
22. DeMarco, *A Short History of Portland*, 15.
23. Quoted in DeMarco, *A Short History of Portland*, 25–26.
24. Carlos Arnaldo Schwantes, *The Pacific Northwest: An Interpretive History*, rev. ed. (Lincoln: University of Nebraska Press, 1996), 113.
25. Carey, *General History of Oregon*, 318.
26. Coleman, *Dangerous Subjects*, 81–82.
27. Coleman, *Dangerous Subjects*, 83–86; Carey, *General History of Oregon*, 524–25; and Ruby and Brown, *Indians of the Pacific Northwest*, 96. Quote from Coleman, *Dangerous Subjects*, 85.
28. Ruby and Brown, *Indians in the Pacific Northwest*, 97. See also Carey, *General History of Oregon*, 525–26.
29. Coleman, *Dangerous Subjects*, 90–93, 100; Carey, *General History of Oregon*, 522–23; Franz M. Schneider, "The 'Black Laws' of Oregon" (master's thesis, University of Santa Clara, 1970), 6–8; and Kenneth R. Coleman, "Cockstock Incident," *Oregon Encyclopedia*, oregon encyclopedia.org, accessed January 5, 2025. Quote from Coleman, *Dangerous Subjects*, 100.
30. Carey, *General History of Oregon*, 319–22.
31. Quoted in Carey, *General History of Oregon*, 322–23.
32. Carey, *General History of Oregon*, 326–28.
33. Quoted in Carey, *General History of Oregon*, 328.

34. Quoted in Carey, *General History of Oregon*, 336.
35. Carey, *General History of Oregon*, 329–30.
36. Ken Bilderback and Kris Bilderback, *Law and Order at the End of the Oregon Trail* (kenbilderback.com, 2015) 8–10; and Carey, *General History of Oregon*, 335.
37. Schwantes, *The Pacific Northwest*, 114.
38. Holman, *Dr. John McLoughlin*, 40.
39. Coleman, *Dangerous Subjects*, 100; Ruby and Brown, *Indians of the Pacific Northwest*, 99; and Carey, *General History of Oregon*, 523.
40. Holbrook, *The Columbia*, 85–91. Quoted in Schwantes, *The Pacific Northwest*, 119.
41. Schwantes, *The Pacific Northwest*, 120; Coleman, *Dangerous Subjects*, 139; and Holbrook, *The Columbia*, 91.
42. John Gordon King, "The History of the Office of Multnomah County Sheriff, Multnomah County, Oregon" (undergraduate thesis, Lewis and Clark College, 1965), 5–9, 53; and Jewel Lansing and Fred Leeson, *Multnomah: The Tumultuous Story of Oregon's Most Populous County* (Corvallis: Oregon State University Press, 2012), 19–20. Quotes from King, "The History of the Office of Multnomah County Sheriff," 5, 7.
43. Quoted in DeMarco, *A Short History of Portland*, 39.
44. Charles Abbot Tracy III, "Police Function in Portland, 1851–1874: Part I," *Oregon Historical Quarterly*, Spring 1979, 9.
45. Diane L. Goeres-Gardner and John Ritter, *Oregon State Penitentiary* (Charleston, SC: Arcadia, 2014) 7; and King, *The History of the Office of Multnomah County Sheriff*, 38.
46. Lansing, *Portland*, 42; Tracy, "Police Function in Portland, 1851–1874: Part I," 10. Quote from Tracy, "Police Function in Portland, 1851–1874: Part I," 10.
47. Finn J. D. John, *Wicked Portland: The Wild and Lusty Underworld of a Frontier Seaport Town* (Charleston, SC: The History Press, 2012), 92.
48. Lansing, *Portland*, 123–24; and Charles Abbot Tracy III, "Police Function in Portland, 1851–1874: Part II," *Oregon Historical Quarterly*, Summer 1979, 15–19.
49. John, *Wicked Portland*, 99–100; and Lansing and Leeson, *Multnomah*, 27.
50. Quoted in Lansing, *Portland*, 43.
51. Quoted in Tracy, "Police Function in Portland, 1851–1874: Part I," 15.
52. Lansing, *Portland*, 80.
53. Tracy, "Police Function in Portland, 1851–1874: Part I," 10, 26; and E. Kimbark MacColl and Harry H. Stein, *Merchants, Money, and Power: The Portland Establishment, 1843–1913* (n.p.: Georgian Press, 1988), 68.
54. Lansing, *Portland*, 44.
55. Tracy, "Police Function in Portland, 1851–1874: Part II," 145, 151; and Lansing, *Portland*, 43, 44, 47, 88.
56. Quoted in MacColl and Stein, *Merchants, Money, and Power*, 69.
57. Tracy, "Police Function in Portland, 1851–1874: Part I," 19.
58. MacColl and Stein, *Merchants, Money, and Power*, 70–71. Quote from Lansing, *Portland*, 78.
59. Ruby and Brown, *Indians of the Pacific Northwest*, 149–50; and Carey, *General History of Oregon*, 582–85.
60. Quoted in Chandler, *Hidden History*, 28–30.
61. Quoted in Lansing, *Portland*, 78. Such vigilance proved unnecessary: the fighting never came within forty miles of the city. MacColl and Stein, *Merchants, Money, and Power*, 70–71; and Lansing, *Portland*, 78.
62. J. D. Chandler, *Portland Rogue's Gallery: A Baker's Dozen Arresting Criminals from Portland's History* (n.p. America Through Time, 2021), 13.

Chapter 2: Exclusion Acts

1. Elizabeth McLagan, *A Peculiar Paradise: A History of Blacks in Oregon, 1788–1940* (Portland: Georgian Press, 1980), 25; and Quintard Taylor, *In Search of the Racial Frontier: African Americans in the American West, 1528–1990* (New York: W. W. Norton, 1998), 75.
2. Gordon DeMarco, *A Short History of Portland* (San Francisco: Lexikos, 1990), 48; Elinor Langer, *A Hundred Little Hitlers: The Death of a Black Man, the Trial of a White Racist, and the Rise of the Neo-Nazi Movement in America* (New York: Picador, 2003), 209; and McLagan, *A Peculiar Paradise*, 24–28. Quote from City of Portland Bureau of Planning, *History of Portland's African American Community* (Portland: Portland Bureau of Planning, 1993), 5.
3. Portland Bureau of Planning, *History of Portland's African American Community*, 5.
4. Quoted in McLagan, *A Peculiar Paradise*, 26.
5. Quoted in Langer, *A Hundred Little Hitlers*, 208.
6. Portland Bureau of Planning, *History of Portland's African American Community*, 6; DeMarco, *A Short History of Portland*, 48; and Langer, *A Hundred Little Hitlers*, 209.
7. Quoted in E. Kimbark MacColl and Harry H. Stein, *Merchants, Money, and Power: The Portland Establishment, 1843–1913* (n.p.: Georgian Press, 1988), 91. In 1871, Williams was appointed US attorney general. Two years later he was nominated to the Supreme Court but withdrew from consideration under southern pressure. He would later become president of the Direct Legislation League, an important Progressive organization. Roy E. Roos, *History of Albina, Including Eliot, Boise, King, Humboldt, and Piedmont Neighborhoods* (n.p., 2008), 6; and Paula Abrams, *Cross Purposes:* Pierce v. Society of Sisters *and the Struggle over Compulsory Public Education* (Ann Arbor: University of Michigan Press, 2009), 19.
8. Noel Ignatiev, *How the Irish Became White* (London: Routledge, 1995), 111–12.
9. Dick Pintarich and J. Kingston Pierce, "The Achievement of Oregon Statehood," in *Great and Minor Moments in Oregon History: An Illustrated Anthology of Illuminating Glimpses into Oregon's Past from Prehistory to the Present*, edited by Dick Pintarich (Portland: New Oregon Publishers, 2003), 79–80; and Charles H. Carey, *General History of Oregon through Early Statehood* (Portland: Binford & Mort, 1971), 511. For the text of the exclusion laws and excerpts from the state constitution, see McLagan, *A Peculiar Paradise*, 185–87. For a timeline of laws and policies affecting the rights of Black people in the early period, see Ralph Hayes and Joe Franklin, *Northwest Black Pioneers: A Centennial Tribute* (n.p., 1994), 9–12.
10. Portland Bureau of Planning, *History of Portland's African American Community*, 4.
11. Fred Leeson, *Rose City Justice: A Legal History of Portland, Oregon* (Portland: Oregon Historical Society Press and the Oregon State Bar, 1998), 20; and McLagan, *A Peculiar Paradise*, 36. Quote from Taylor, *In Search of the Racial Frontier*, 77. Concerning other court cases involving slavery after its legal prohibition, see McLagan, *A Peculiar Paradise*, 57.
12. Portland Bureau of Planning, *History of Portland's African American Community*, 8; McLagan, *A Peculiar Paradise*, 24; and Franz M. Schneider, "The 'Black Laws' of Oregon" (master's thesis, University of Santa Clara, 1970), 16–17.
13. DeMarco, *A Short History of Portland*, 48; McLagan, *A Peculiar Paradise*, 23; Portland Bureau of Planning, *History of Portland's African American Community*, 8.
14. Kenneth R. Coleman, *Dangerous Subjects: James D. Saules and the Rise of Black Exclusion in Oregon* (Corvallis: Oregon State University Press, 2017), 154.
15. J. D. Chandler, *Hidden History of Portland Oregon* (Charleston, SC: The History Press, 2013), 81–82.

16. Quoted in Portland Bureau of Planning, *History of Portland's African American Community*, 7.
17. DeMarco, *A Short History of Portland*, 50; McLagan, *A Peculiar Paradise*, 27, 88; Portland Bureau of Planning, *History of Portland's African American Community*, 8; Tracy J. Prince and Zadie Schaffer, *Notable Women of Portland* (Charleston, SC: Arcadia, 2017), 18; and Schneider, "The 'Black Laws' of Oregon," 17–18. Concerning other petitions, see Schneider, "The 'Black Laws' of Oregon," 18–20.
18. Chandler, *Hidden History of Portland*, 82.
19. Portland Bureau of Planning, *History of Portland's African American Community*, 8; and Darrell Millner, "Blacks in Oregon 1888–1940," in *Blacks in Oregon: A Statistical and Historical Report*, edited by William A. Little and James E. Weiss (Portland: Black Studies Center and the Center for Population Research and Census, Portland State University, 1978), 26.
20. Portland Bureau of Planning, *History of Portland's African American Community*, 7; Schneider, "The 'Black Laws' of Oregon," 46; and Millner, "Blacks in Oregon," 26.
21. Portland Bureau of Planning, *History of Portland's African American Community*, 7; Charles Abbot Tracy III, "Police Function in Portland, 1851–1874: Part II," *Oregon Historical Quarterly*, Summer 1979, 140; and Schneider, "The 'Black Laws' of Oregon," 41–42.
22. Darrell Millner et al., *Cornerstones of Community: Buildings of Portland's African American History* (Portland: Bosco-Milligan Foundation, 1995), 8.
23. McLagan, *A Peculiar Paradise*, 18; and Coleman, *Dangerous Subjects*, 144.
24. Hayes and Franklin, *Northwest Black Pioneers*, 3–5.
25. Jewel Lansing, *Portland: People, Politics, and Power* (Corvallis: Oregon State University Press, 2003), 146; DeMarco, *A Short History of Portland*, 53; MacColl and Stein, *Merchants, Money, and Power*, 238; McLagan, *A Peculiar Paradise*, 89; and Chandler, *Hidden History*, 119.
26. Chandler, *Hidden History*, 111–12.
27. Joe Streckert, *Storied and Scandalous Portland, Oregon: A History of Gambling, Vice, Wits, and Wagers* (Guilford, CT: Globe Pequot, 2020), 45.
28. MacColl and Stein, *Merchants, Money, and Power*, 174–75; and Chandler, *Hidden History*, 112–13.
29. Quoted in Marie Rose Wong, *Sweet Cakes, Long Journey: The Chinatowns of Portland, Oregon* (Seattle: University of Washington Press, 2004), 243. Three Chinese volunteers had disappeared while fighting an earlier fire, on December 23, 1872. It was rumored that they had been thrown into the river and drowned. Chandler, *Hidden History*, 108–9.
30. Quoted in Lansing, *Portland*, 170–71.
31. Beth Lew-Williams, *The Chinese Must Go: Violence, Exclusion, and the Making of the Alien in America* (Cambridge: Harvard University Press, 2018), 31–32; Carlos A. Schwantes, "From Anti-Chinese Agitation to Reform Politics: The Legacy of the Knights of Labor in Washington and the Pacific Northwest," *Pacific Northwest Quarterly* 88, no. 4 (Fall 1997): 181; and *The Chinese Exclusion Act*, directed by Ric Burns and Li-Shin Yu (PBS Distribution, 2019).
32. MacColl and Stein, *Merchants, Money, and Power*, 238–40; and Kristofer Allerfeldt, *Race, Radicalism, Religion, and Restriction: Immigration in the Pacific Northwest, 1890–1924* (Westport, CT: Praeger, 2003), 77.
33. *The Chinese Exclusion Act*; and MacColl and Stein, *Merchants, Money, and Power*, 167.
34. Lansing, *Portland*, 170–71.
35. Wong, *Sweet Cakes, Long Journey*, 84.
36. Quoted in Lew-Williams, *The Chinese Must Go*, 61.
37. Wong, *Sweet Cakes, Long Journey*, 94–97.

38. Wong, *Sweet Cakes, Long Journey*, 82–3, 86–93.
39. Wong, *Sweet Cakes, Long Journey*, 80–81.
40. Wong, *Sweet Cakes, Long Journey*, 43–44; and Schwantes, "From Anti-Chinese Agitation to Reform Politics," 177–78.
41. Quoted in MacColl and Stein, *Merchants, Money, and Power*, 238–39. On Cronin's earlier campaigns, see Chandler, *Hidden History*, 118; and Wong, *Sweet Cakes, Long Journey*, 44.
42. Robert D. Johnston, *The Radical Middle Class: Populist Democracy and the Question of Capitalism in Progressive Era Portland, Oregon* (Princeton: Princeton University Press, 2003), 95; Wong, *Sweet Cakes, Long Journey*, 45; Lansing, *Portland*, 186–87; DeMarco, *A Short History of Portland*, 52; and Malcolm Clark Jr., "The Bigot Disclosed: 90 Years of Nativism," *Oregon Historical Quarterly* 75, no. 2 (June 1974): 130.

    Pennoyer was a Populist, elected on the "People's Party" ticket after a campaign centered on Chinese immigration. He defended slavery and supported the Confederacy during the war. Perhaps the most one can say for him is that he did try to rid the government of corruption and that his support for (white) labor was not merely rhetorical. When railway workers marched on Albany, Oregon, in 1888 to demand wages they were owed, Pennoyer announced that he would not send the militia—even in the event of rioting—until the men had been paid. For a profile, see Dick Pintarich, "His Eccentricity," in *Great and Minor Moments in Oregon History: An Illustrated Anthology of Illuminating Glimpses into Oregon's Past from Prehistory to Present* (Portland: New Oregon Publishers, 2008).
43. Quoted in Percy Maddux, *City on the Willamette: The Story of Portland, Oregon* (Portland: Binford & Mort, 1952), 81.
44. Lansing, *Portland*, 186–88; MacColl and Stein, *Merchants, Money, and Power*, 239–40; Maddux, *City on the Willamette*, 81–83; Wong, *Sweet Cakes, Long Journey*, 45; Chandler, *Hidden History*, 118; and Clark, "The Bigot Disclosed," 129. A third militia company, the Emmett Guards, made up entirely of Irish Americans, proved unreliable and was disbanded. Only twenty-five of its members reported for the muster, and fifteen of those refused the oath. Clark, "The Bigot Disclosed," 128.
45. Lew-Williams, *The Chinese Must Go*, 126; and Wong, *Sweet Cakes, Long Journey*, 42, 45, 47.
46. "[The] merchant class . . . saw their defense of the Chinese as an assertion of their right to uphold civic order rather than as an expression of any special regard for an ethnic minority." William Toll, *The Making of An Ethnic Middle Class: Portland Jewry Over Four Generations* (Albany: State University of New York Press, 1982), 83.
47. Quoted in Wong, *Sweet Cakes, Long Journey*, 47.
48. Wong, *Sweet Cakes, Long Journey*, 42–43, 49; and Clark, "The Bigot Disclosed," 128.
49. Lansing, *Portland*, 186–88; MacColl and Stein, *Merchants, Money, and Power*, 239–40; Maddux, *City on the Willamette*, 81–83; Wong, *Sweet Cakes, Long Journey*, 45; Chandler, *Hidden History*, 118; and Clark, "The Bigot Disclosed," 129.
50. Clark, "The Bigot Disclosed," 130.
51. Moreover, a recent study from the National Bureau of Economic Research found that by slowing growth the expulsion of Chinese workers generally *reduced* opportunities for white workers—an effect that continued until the Second World War. Joe Long et al., "The Impact of the Chinese Exclusion Act on the Economic Development of the Western U.S.," NBER Working Paper Series (Cambridge, MA: National Bureau of Economic Research, 2024).
52. Lew-Williams, *The Chinese Must Go*, 9–10.
53. Lew-Williams, *The Chinese Must Go*, 236–38.
54. Amy Louise Wood, *Lynching and Spectacle: Witnessing Racial Violence in America, 1890–1940* (Chapel Hill: University of North Carolina Press, 2009), 38–39.

55. Jewel Lansing and Fred Leeson, *Multnomah: The Tumultuous Story of Oregon's Most Populous County* (Corvallis: Oregon State University Press, 2012), 20–21; Eugene E. Snyder, *We Claimed This Land: Portland's Pioneer Settlers* (Portland: Binford and Mort, 1989), 13; Dick Pintarich and Ray Stout, "Execution Oregon Style," in *Great and Minor Moments in Oregon History: An Illustrated Anthology of Illuminating Glimpses into Oregon's Past from Prehistory to the Present*, edited by Dick Pintarich (Portland: New Oregon Publishers, 2003), 263; and Diane L. Goeres-Gardner, *Necktie Parties: A History of Legal Executions in Oregon, 1951–1905* (Caldwell, ID: Caxton Press, 2005), 32–33. For a short biography of Balch, including an account of the murder and execution, see Snyder, *We Claimed This Land*, 9–15.
56. Goeres-Gardner, *Necktie Parties*, xx.
57. Pintarich and Stout, "Execution Oregon Style," 263.
58. Lansing and Leeson, *Multnomah*, 22.
59. For accounts of specific executions, see Goeres-Gardner, *Necktie Parties*, 84–89, 107, 113, 245–49; and Pintarich and Stout, "Execution Oregon Style," 264. On Chee Gong and his likely innocence, see Paul Susi, "Here Lies: Honoring Chee Gong in a City That Would Forget Him," *Oregon Humanities* (Summer 2022): 22–25; and Goeres-Gardner, *Necktie Parties*, 152–53.
60. Quoted in Pintarich and Stout, "Execution Oregon Style," 264.
61. Quoted in Lansing and Leeson, *Multnomah*, 40–41.
62. Goeres-Gardner, *Necktie Parties*, 271–72; and Lansing and Leeson, *Multnomah*, 41. On the taking of souvenirs from lynchings, see Philip Dray, *At the Hands of Persons Unknown: The Lynching of Black America* (New York: Random House, 2002), 14, 78, 79, 82, 168, 174, 181, 218. Between 1882 and 1903, nineteen people were lynched in Oregon: fifteen white, one Black, and three from other racial groups. James Elbert Cutler, *Lynch-Law: An Investigation into the History of Lynching in the United States* (Montclair, NJ: Patterson Smith, 1969), 180.
63. Quoted in Lansing and Leeson, *Multnomah*, 37.
64. Lansing and Leeson, *Multnomah*, 41.

Chapter 3: Charters and Corruption

1. Quoted in Charles Abbot Tracy III, "Police Function in Portland, 1851–1874: Part I," *Oregon Historical Quarterly* (Spring 1979): 17.
2. The charter instructed him "to recommend to the common council the adoption of all such measures connected with the police. . . ; to be vigilant and active in causing the laws and ordinances of the city government to be . . . enforced; [and] to exercise a constant supervision and control over the conduct and acts of all subordinate officers." Quoted in Tracy, "Police Function in Portland, 1851–1874: Part I," 17.
3. Quoted in Tracy, "Police Function in Portland, 1851–1874: Part I," 18.
4. Tracy, "Police Function in Portland, 1851–1874: Part I," 20–21.
5. Quoted in Charles Abbot Tracy III, "Police Function in Portland, 1851–1874: Part II," *Oregon Historical Quarterly* (Summer 1979): 134–35.
6. Tracy, "Police Function in Portland, 1851–1874: Part II," 139, 145.
7. Jewel Lansing, *Portland: People, Politics, and Power* (Corvallis: Oregon State University Press, 2003), 116; and Tracy, "Police Function in Portland, 1851–1874: Part II," 146–47.
8. Lansing, *Portland*, 116; E. Kimbark MacColl and Harry H. Stein, *Merchants, Money, and Power: The Portland Establishment, 1843–1913* (n.p.: Georgian Press, 1988), 167; Tracy, "Police Function in Portland, 1851–1874: Part II," 154–55.

9. Quoted in Tracy, "Police Function in Portland, 1851–1874: Part II," 164.
10. Tracy, "Police Function in Portland, 1851–1874: Part II," 165.
11. Tracy, "Police Function in Portland, 1851–1874: Part II," 164–67. A map appears in Tracy, "Police Function in Portland, 1851–1874: Part II," 168.
12. Charles Abbot Tracy III, "Police Function in Portland, 1851–1874: Part III," *Oregon Historical Quarterly* (Fall 1979): 296, 309. This pattern is typical of newly policed cities. The number of arrests rise, though usually for less-serious offenses. See Kristian Williams, *Our Enemies in Blue: Police and Power in America* (Oakland: AK Press, 2015), 109–10.
13. MacColl and Stein, *Merchants, Money, and Power*, 168.
14. Lansing, *Portland*, 137–38.
15. Tracy, "Police Function in Portland, 1851–1874: Part III," 320.
16. Lansing, *Portland*, 166, 175; and MacColl and Stein, *Merchants, Money, and Power*, 245.
17. Tracy, "Police Function in Portland, 1851–1874: Part III," 293.
18. Quoted in Tracy, "Police Function in Portland, 1851–1874: Part III," 297.
19. E. Kimbark MacColl, *The Shaping of a City: Business and Politics in Portland, Oregon, 1855–1915* (Portland: Georgian Press, 1976), 192.
20. Lansing, *Portland*, 138; and Tracy, "Police Function in Portland, 1851–1874: Part II," 292. These subordinates included a former deputy sheriff (Captain Joseph R. Wiley), a former marshal (David Jacobi), a former deputy marshal (A. B. Brannon), a former jail guard (W. M. Ward), and Daniel Norton, who had previously been convicted of assault. Tracy, "Police Function in Portland, 1851–1874: Part II," 290–91.
21. J. D. Chandler, *Murder and Mayhem in Portland Oregon* (Charleston, SC: The History Press, 2013), 33.
22. Tracy, "Police Function in Portland, 1851–1874: Part II," 135; and Joe Streckert, *Storied and Scandalous Portland, Oregon: A History of Gambling, Vice, Wits, and Wagers* (Guilford, CT: Globe Pequot, 2020), 11, 15.
23. Streckert, *Storied and Scandalous Portland, Oregon*, 13.
24. Lansing, *Portland*, 175–76; Streckert, *Storied and Scandalous Portland, Oregon*, 13. Watkinds is notable as the only delegate to the state constitutional convention to speak out against the Black exclusion law. Kenneth R. Coleman, *Dangerous Subjects: James D. Saules and the Rise of Black Exclusion in Oregon* (Corvallis: Oregon State University Press, 2017), 155; and Elizabeth McLagan, *A Peculiar Paradise: A History of Blacks in Oregon, 1788–1940* (Portland: Georgian Press, 1980), 53.
25. Streckert, *Storied and Scandalous Portland, Oregon*, 17–18. Both quotes from Lansing, *Portland*, 178.
26. Lansing, *Portland*, 158, 162. In 1900, Besser was implicated in a $200,000 scam involving a forged deed. J. D. Chandler, *Hidden History of Portland Oregon* (Charleston, SC: The History Press, 2013), 138–39.
27. J. D. Chandler, *Portland Rogues Gallery: A Baker's Dozen Arresting Criminals from Portland History* ([Charleston, SC]: America Through Time, 2021), 13–17.
28. Quoted in Chandler, *Portland Rogues Gallery*, 17.
29. Quoted in MacColl and Stein, *Merchants, Money, and Power*, 87.
30. Tracy, "Police Function in Portland, 1851–1874: Part III," 321–22.
31. Tracy, "Police Function in Portland, 1851–1874: Part II," 160.
32. MacColl and Stein, *Merchants, Money, and Power*, 322–25.
33. Robert M. Fogelson, *Big-City Police* (Cambridge, MA: Harvard University Press, 1977), 17.
34. Lansing, *Portland*, 162; and Robert C. Donnelly, *Dark Rose: Organized Crime and Corruption in Portland* (Seattle: University of Washington Press, 2011), 32.

35. Chandler, *Hidden History*, 138; and Chandler, *Portland Rogues Gallery*, 13.
36. Fogelson, *Big-City Police*, 18–21.
37. Lansing, *Portland*, 144–45.
38. Quoted in Lansing, *Portland*, 200.
39. Chandler, *Portland Rogues Gallery*, 47–48.
40. Lansing, *Portland*, 185–86; and Donnelly, *Dark Rose*, 30. Bourne later became a reformer, instrumental in securing such directly democratic devices as the ballot initiative and the referendum. As a US senator during Teddy Roosevelt's administration, he advocated for campaign finance regulations, women's suffrage, oversight of public-service corporations, direct primaries, and the direct election of US senators, along with a host of other Progressive reforms. It is not clear what motivated this rehabilitation, and his politics swung toward the right after he left office, attacking (among other enemies) labor unions and the League of Nations. Leonard Schlup, "Jonathan Bourne and the Politics of Progressivism, 1908–1912," *Oregon Historical Quarterly* 87, no. 3 (Fall 1986): 229, 238–40.
41. Barney Blalock, *The Oregon Shanghaiers: Columbia River Crimping from Astoria to Portland* (Charleston, SC: The History Press, 2014), 116–17; Finn J. D. John, *Wicked Portland: The Wild and Lusty Underworld of a Frontier Seaport Town* (Charleston, SC: The History Press, 2012), 84–85, 119; Chandler, *Portland Rogues Gallery*, 48–49; and Barney Blalock, *Portland's Lost Waterfront: Tall Ships, Steam Mills and Sailors' Boardinghouses* (Charleston, SC: The History Press, 2012), 78–79. Quote from Blalock, *Portland's Lost Waterfront*, 79.
42. Quoted in Dick Pintarich, "Shanghai City," in *Great and Minor Moments in Oregon History: An Illustrated Anthology of Illuminating Glimpses into Oregon's Past from Prehistory to the Present* (Portland: New Oregon Publishers, 2003), 116.
43. Blalock, *Portland's Lost Waterfront*, 78–79. Sullivan later worked in Los Angeles as a detective for attorney Clarence Darrow and was accused of trying to bribe jurors. When he returned to Portland in 1916, he entered the growth market of illegal alcohol sales. He was arrested, convicted, and ultimately pardoned. Afterward he worked as a guard in the shipyards. Blalock, *The Oregon Shanghaiers*, 135–37.
44. Quoted in John, *Wicked Portland*, 85.
45. Gordon DeMarco, *A Short History of Portland* (San Francisco: Lexikos, 1990), 70; Lansing, *Portland*, 203–6; and MacColl, *The Shaping of a City*, 62–63.
46. Historian Elizabeth McLagan writes, "One of the most lucrative opportunities for blacks as well as whites was in the underworld that flourished in Portland in the late nineteenth century, tolerated by a corrupt city government. Gambling and prostitution were practiced openly; the police force took bribes and ignored illegal activities. . . . Black men owned saloons and gambling houses . . . and were able to wield political influence. Bribery was an accepted practice, and black businessmen were often paid to deliver the black vote." McLagan, *A Peculiar Paradise*, 91.
47. Richard Hofstadter, *The Age of Reform: From Bryan to F.D.R.* (New York: Alfred A. Knopf, 1961), 176.
48. Chandler, *Hidden History*, 88.
49. Chandler, *Hidden History*, 89–90; Chandler, *Murder and Mayhem in Portland Oregon*, 109–10; Martha Anderson, *Black Pioneers of the Northwest* (n.p., 1980), 96; and City of Portland Bureau of Planning, *History of Portland's African American Community* (Portland: Portland Bureau of Planning, 1993), 21–22. These were the first Black members of the Portland Police Bureau, but not the first to work in law enforcement. As early as 1862, Adam Augustus Waterford—already the city's first Black firefighter—was made a deputy US Marshal under Penumbra Kelly. He later twice served as an elections judge. Anderson,

Black Pioneers of the Northwest, 96; and Ralph Hayes and Joe Franklin, *Northwest Black Pioneers: A Centennial Tribute* (n.p., 1994), 16.

50. Chandler, *Hidden History*, 90.
51. Tracy, "Police Function in Portland, 1851–1874: Part III," 294; and Lansing, *Portland*, 141.
52. Chandler, *Murder and Mayhem in Portland Oregon*, 27; and Diane L. Goeres-Gardner, *Murder, Morality, and Madness: Women Criminals in Early Oregon* (Caldwell, ID: Caxton Press, 2009), 115.
53. Jan MacKell Collins, *Good Time Girls of the Pacific Northwest: A Red-Light History of Washington, Oregon, and Alaska* (Guilford, CT: Twodot, 2020), 123.
54. John discusses the practices of shanghaiing in some detail. John, *Wicked Portland*, 71–90. The police role is addressed on pages 83–86.
55. The US Supreme Court recognized the essentially involuntary nature of this arrangement when it ruled in *Robertson v. Baldwin* that sailors did not enjoy the full protections of the Thirteenth Amendment, which outlawed slavery. Blalock, *The Oregon Shanghaiers*; Streckert, *Storied and Scandalous Portland, Oregon*, 24–28; Blalock, *Portland's Lost Waterfront*, 48; Pintarich, "Shanghai City," 116; and Chandler, *Portland Rogues Gallery*, 44.
56. Blalock, *The Oregon Shanghaiers*, 8, 23, 34, 48, 106, 110–11. Crimping was eventually eliminated through a combination of reforms to maritime law, unionization, and technological changes (specifically the introduction of steam power). Richard H. Engerman, *The Oregon Companion: An Historical Gazetteer of the Useful, the Curious, and the Arcane* (Portland: Timber Press, 2009), 107.
57. Collins, *Good Time Girls*, 133–34.
58. Quoted in John, *Wicked Portland*, 43.
59. Lansing, *Portland*, 132.
60. Quoted in John, *Wicked Portland*, 49–51.
61. Reproduced in MacColl, *The Shaping of a City*, 193.
62. Carl Abbott, *Portland in Three Centuries: The Place and the People* (Corvallis: Oregon State University Press, 2011), 60.
63. Quoted in MacColl, *The Shaping of a City*, 199.
64. Quoted in Streckert, *Storied and Scandalous Portland, Oregon*, 42.
65. Quoted in MacColl and Stein, *Merchants, Money, and Power*, 290.
66. Quoted in MacColl and Stein, *Merchants, Money, and Power*, 433.

Chapter 4: Class Interest and the Public Good

1. "Historians of the United States have labeled the late nineteenth and early twentieth century the 'Progressive Era,' after the energetic group of Protestant and largely elite men and women, self-identified as Progressives, and to the reform wave they launched. . . . They worked to improve health, hygiene, and urban sanitation, to beautify their cities, and to provide social centers for immigrants. One central concern of these reformers was ending the municipal power of urban political machines. Meshed in networks of graft, kickbacks, and patronage, and providing routes for upward mobility for ethnic political brokers, this form of politics offended reformers' sense of the civic public good." Lisa McGirr, *The War on Alcohol: Prohibition and the Rise of the American State* (New York: W. W. Norton), 16–17.
2. James F. Richardson, *Urban Police in the United States* (Port Washington, NY: National University Press and Kennikat Press, 1974), 62. B. S. Josselyn explained the rationale: "Safe, economic and businesslike government of municipal affairs should follow the lines of what

has been considered best in large business affairs, which, if good for the investor, should also be good for the taxpayer." Quoted in E. Kimbark MacColl, *The Growth of a City: Power and Politics in Portland, Oregon, 1915 to 1950* (Portland: Georgian Press, 1979), 32.

3. Robert M. Fogelson, *Big-City Police* (Cambridge, MA: Harvard University Press, 1977), 40. "Their ideal leader was a well-to-do, well-educated, high-minded citizen, rich enough to be free from motives of what they often called 'crass materialism,' whose family roots were deep not only in American history but [also] in his local community. Such a person, they thought, would be just the sort to put the national interest, as well as the interests of civic improvement, above personal motives or political opportunism." Richard Hofstadter, *The Age of Reform: From Bryan to F.D.R.* (New York: Alfred A. Knopf, 1961), 140.
4. Fogelson, *Big-City Police*, 41–42.
5. George Painter, *The Vice Clique: Portland's Great Sex Scandal* (Portland: Espresso Book Machine, 2013), 16.
6. J. D. Chandler and Theresa Griffin Kennedy, *Murder and Scandal in Prohibition Portland: Sex, Vice and Misdeeds in Mayor Baker's Reign* (Charleston, SC: The History Press, 2016), 35.
7. MacColl, *The Growth of a City*, 11; E. Kimbark MacColl, *The Shaping of a City: Business and Politics in Portland,. Oregon, 1855–1915* (Portland: The Georgian Press Company, 1976), 257; and Painter, *Vice Clique*, 12.
8. E. Kimbark MacColl and Harry H. Stein, *Merchants, Money, and Power: The Portland Establishment, 1843–1913* (n.p., Georgian Press, 1988), 288; and Roy E. Roos, *The History of Albina, Including Eliot, Boise, King, Humboldt, and Piedmont Neighborhoods* (n.p., 2008), 24.
9. Quoted in Jewel Lansing, *Portland: People, Politics, and Power* (Corvallis: Oregon State University Press, 2003), 200.
10. Lansing, *Portland*, 203.
11. Quoted in MacColl and Stein, *Merchants, Money, and Power*, 288–99.
12. Lansing, *Portland*, 227; and MacColl and Stein, *Merchants, Money, and Power*, 328.
13. Quoted in MacColl and Stein, *Merchants, Money, and Power*, 342.
14. Jewel Lansing and Fred Leeson, *Multnomah: The Tumultuous Story of Oregon's Most Populous County* (Corvallis: Oregon State University Press, 2012), 42; and "A Bad Apple in a Rotten Barrel," in *Great and Minor Moments in Oregon History: An Illustrated Anthology of Illuminating Glimpses into Oregon's Past from Prehistory to Present*, edited by Dick Pintarich (Portland: New Oregon Publishers, 2008), 139.
15. Lansing and Leeson, *Multnomah*, 42. Quote from MacColl and Stein, *Merchants, Money, and Power*, 348.
16. Quoted in Barney Blalock, *The Oregon Shanghaiers: Columbia River Crimping from Astoria to Portland* (Charleston, SC: The History Press, 2014), 118.
17. Lansing and Leeson, *Multnomah*, 43.
18. Quoted in Lansing, *Portland*, 256.
19. Lansing and Leeson, *Multnomah*, 43–44; and John Gordon King, "The History of the Office of Multnomah County Sheriff, Multnomah County, Oregon" (undergraduate thesis, Lewis and Clark College, 1965), 66–68.
20. Lansing and Leeson, *Multnomah*, 44 (both quotes); and Lansing, *Portland*, 257.
21. Lansing and Leeson, *Multnomah*, 50.
22. Quoted in Lansing and Leeson, *Multnomah*, 51, 66.
23. MacColl and Stein, *Merchants, Money, and Power*, 366.
24. Stewart Holbrook, "Oregon," in *The Pacific Northwest*, edited by Anthony Netboy (Garden City, NY: Doubleday, 1963), 24; and J. D. Chandler, *Hidden History of Portland Oregon* (Charleston, SC: The History Press, 2013), 148.

25. Ruby Fay Purdy, *The Rose City of the World: Portland, Oregon* (Portland: Binford & Mort, 1947), 51.
26. Robert D. Johnston, *The Radical Middle Class: Populist Democracy and the Question of Capitalism in Progressive Era Portland, Oregon* (Princeton: Princeton University Press, 2003), 123–24.
27. Quoted in MacColl and Stein, *Merchants, Money, and Power*, 372 ("integrity"); and Johnston, *Radical Middle Class*, 32 ("moneyed interests").
28. MacColl and Stein, *Merchants, Money, and Power*, 381; and Diane L. Goeres-Gardner, *Inside Oregon State Hospital: A History of Tragedy and Triumph* (Charleston, SC: The History Press, 2013), 55.
29. Johnston, *Radical Middle Class*, 32–37. On Joe Hill and his execution by the state of Utah, see Lisa DiPetto, "In Search of Joe Hill," in *Wobblies! A Graphic History of the Industrial Workers of the World*, edited by Paul Buhle and Nicole Schulman (London: Verso, 2005), unpaged; and Howard Zinn, *A People's History of the United States, 1492–Present*, rev. ed. (New York: HarperCollins, 1995), 326–27. On the Lawrence textile strike, see Zinn, *A People's History of the United States*, 327–30.
30. Quoted in Johnston, *Radical Middle Class*, 38.
31. Quoted in Johnston, *Radical Middle Class*, 42.
32. Quoted in Johnston, *Radical Middle Class*, 35.
33. Quoted in Robert C. Donnelly, *Dark Rose: Organized Crime and Corruption in Portland* (Seattle: University of Washington Press, 2011), 38.
34. MacColl, *The Shaping of a City*, 328; MacColl and Stein, *Merchants, Money, and Power*, 391–92; and Chandler, *Hidden History*, 149.
35. Fred Leeson, *Rose City Justice: A Legal History of Portland, Oregon* (Portland: Oregon Historical Society Press and the Oregon State Bar, 1998), 67–72; MacColl and Stein, *Merchants, Money, and Power*, 369–71; and MacColl, *The Shaping of a City*, 288–97.
36. Leeson, *Rose City Justice*, 67–72; MacColl and Stein, *Merchants, Money, and Power*, 369–71; MacColl, *The Shaping of a City*, 288–97; and Williams Boly, "How They Stole the Oregon Land," in *Great and Minor Moments in Oregon History: An Illustrated Anthology of Illuminating Glimpses into Oregon's Past from Prehistory to the Present*, edited by Dick Pintarich (Portland: New Oregon Publishers, 2003), 159.
37. Quoted in Boly, "How they Stole the Oregon Land," 161.
38. Leeson, *Rose City Justice*, 67–72; MacColl and Stein, *Merchants, Money, and Power*, 369–71; MacColl, *The Shaping of a City*, 288–97.
39. Quoted in Frank Morn, *"The Eye that Never Sleeps": A History of the Pinkerton National Detective Agency* (Bloomington: Indiana University Press, 1982), 173. Heney and Burns went on to lead an anti-corruption investigation in San Francisco, winning convictions against Mayor Eugene Schmitz and political boss Abe Ruef and bringing about the resignations of eighteen other city officials. Morn, *The Eye that Never Sleeps*, 173.
40. Leeson, *Rose City Justice*, 67–72; MacColl and Stein, *Merchants, Money, and Power*, 369–71; MacColl, *The Shaping of a City*, 288–97. One of those pardoned was John Hall, who continued to practice law and later refashioned himself as an anti-radical crusader. MacColl, *The Growth of a City*, 157.
41. Quoted in Mike German, *Disrupt, Discredit, and Divide: How the New FBI Damages Democracy* (New York: New Press, 2019), 4, 113. See also Tim Weiner, *Enemies: A History of the FBI* (New York: Random House, 2012), 10–11; and Morn, *The Eye that Never Sleeps*, 180.
42. Athan G. Theoharis, *The FBI and American Democracy: A Brief Critical History* (Lawrence, University of Kansas Press, 2004), 31–32; Weiner, *Enemies*, 57–58; and Morn, *The Eye that Never Sleeps*, 181–82. Aside from the Justice Department's role in this affair, the

Burns Detective Agency began investigating the jurors in Fall's conspiracy trial, leading to a mistrial. Fall was later convicted and sentenced to a year in prison. He served not quite ten months, most of that time in the infirmary where he was treated for tuberculosis. Burl Noggle, *Teapot Dome: Oil and Politics in the 1920's* ([Baton Rouge]: Louisiana State University Press, 1962), 185, 210, 213.

43. Painter, *Vice Clique*, 12.
44. Quoted in Painter, *Vice Clique*, 29.
45. Quoted in Painter, *Vice Clique*, 30.
46. Lansing and Leeson, *Multnomah*, 54.
47. Quoted in Lansing, *Portland*, 290–91.
48. Lansing and Leeson, *Multnomah*, 56–59. Quote on p. 57.
49. Lansing and Leeson, *Multnomah*, 54, 59.
50. Joseph S. Uris, "Trouble in River City: An Analysis of an Urban Vice Probe" (PhD diss., Portland State University, 1981), 52.
51. MacColl and Stein, *Merchants, Money, and Power*, 446.
52. MacColl and Stein, *Merchants, Money, and Power*, 446–47, 449.
53. MacColl, *The Shaping of a City*, 443.
54. Samuel P. Hays, "The Politics of Reform in Municipal Government in the Progressive Era," *Pacific Northwest Quarterly* (July 1964): 161–62.
55. James Weinstein, *The Corporate Ideal in the Liberal State: 1900–1918* (Boston: Beacon Press, 1968), 109.
56. Fogelson, *Big-City Police*, 37.
57. Hays, "The Politics of Reform in Municipal Government," 160.
58. "According to the liberal view of the Progressive Era, the major political innovations of reform involved the equalization of political power through the primary, the direct election of public officials, and the initiative, referendum, and recall. . . . But they provided at best only an occasional and often incidental process of decision-making. Far more important in continuous, sustained, day-to-day processes of government were those innovations which centralized decision-making in the hands of fewer and fewer people." Hays, "The Politics of Reform in Municipal Government," 163.
59. Quoted in MacColl, *The Shaping of a City*, 249.

Chapter 5: Vice, Degeneracy, and Inversion

1. Robert N. Ullman, *The Gift of Policewomen* (Redmond, OR: Nutcracker Publishing, 2018), 11–12, 17.
2. Ullman, *The Gift of Policewomen*, 13–16; Tracy J. Prince and Zadie Schaffer, *Notable Women of Portland* (Charleston, SC: Arcadia, 2017), 33; Cara Rabe-Hemp, *Thriving in an All-Boys Club: Female Police and Their Fight for Equality* (Lanham, MD: Rowman & Littlefield, 2018), 7; Michael Helquist, *Marie Equi: Radical Politics and Outlaw Passions* (Corvallis: Oregon State University Press, 2015), 60; Joe Streckert, *Storied and Scandalous Portland, Oregon: A History of Gambling, Vice, Wits, and Wagers* (Guilford, CT: Globe Pequot, 2020), 69; J. D. Chandler and Theresa Griffin Kennedy, *Murder and Scandal in Prohibition Portland: Sex, Vice and Misdeeds in Mayor Baker's Reign* (Charleston, SC: The History Press, 2016), 34; and Jan MacKell Collins, *Good Time Girls of the Pacific Northwest: A Red-Light History of Washington, Oregon, and Alaska* (Guilford, CT: Twodot, 2020), 134.
3. Lawrence M. Lipin, *Eleanor Baldwin and the Woman's Point of View: New Thought Radicalism*

in *Portland's Progressive Era* (Corvallis: Oregon State University Press, 2017), 73–74; Ullman, *The Gift of Policewomen*, 18, 23–25; Allan T. Duffin, *History in Blue: 160 Years of Women Police, Sheriffs, Detectives, and State Troopers* (New York: Kaplan, 2010), 29; Streckert, *Storied and Scandalous Portland, Oregon*, 69–70; and J. D. Chandler, *Hidden History of Portland, Oregon* (Charleston, SC: The History Press, 2013), 155. Quote from Ullman, *The Gift of Policewomen*, 24.

4. Chandler, *Hidden History*, 155; and Rabe-Hemp, *Thriving in an All-Boys Club*, 1.
5. Chandler and Kennedy, *Murder and Scandal in Prohibition Portland*, 38–40.
6. Owens was hired by the Chicago Department of Health in 1889 to inspect the city's factories and tenements, enforcing child labor and safety laws. In 1891, she was promoted to police detective, a position she often used to locate men who had abandoned their families. Ullman, *The Gift of Policewomen*, 6–7.
7. Chandler, *Hidden History*, 156.
8. Louise Bryant, "Portland's Pioneer in Municipal Protective Work for Women," *Oregonian*, January 14, 1912; and Ullman, *The Gift of Policewomen*, xiii.
9. Quoted in Bryant, "Portland's Pioneer in Municipal Protective Work." On Bryant's eventful life, see Mary V. Dearborn, *Queen of Bohemia: The Life of Louise Bryant* (Boston: Houghton Mifflin, 1996).
10. Quoted in Duffin, *History in Blue*, 29.
11. Chandler, *Hidden History*, 161.
12. Bryant, "Portland's Pioneer in Municipal Protective Work."
13. Chandler and Kennedy, *Murder and Scandal in Prohibition Portland*, 36.
14. Baldwin began collecting evidence against abortionists before joining the police, and such prosecutions were already increasing due to the Progressive movement's almost missionary zeal and the medical establishment's efforts at professionalization. Before 1903, Portland saw only three prosecutions for abortion. From 1905 to 1908, there were nine. Altogether, by 1920, there had been twenty-seven trials, with 30 percent ending in conviction. During the same period, there were approximately six thousand abortions performed in the city. Helquist, *Marie Equi*, 88–89, 92.
15. Chandler, *Hidden History*, 156; and Rabe-Hemp, *Thriving in an All-Boys Club*, 8.
16. George Painter, *The Vice Clique: Portland's Great Sex Scandal* (Portland: Espresso Book Machine, 2013), 10. One establishment that Baldwin shut down—under the pretext of a fire code violation—was Cotillion Hall, operated by Montrose Ringler at Twelfth and Burnside. It would later become the Crystal Ballroom, first owned by Portland Police Officer Chester Rinehart. It is now owned by McMenamins and includes a restaurant named Ringler's and a bar called Lola's Room. Streckert, *Storied and Scandalous Portland, Oregon*, 75, 78, 163.
17. Streckert, *Storied and Scandalous Portland, Oregon*, 72.
18. Chandler, *Hidden History*, 156; and Rabe-Hemp, *Thriving in an All-Boys Club*, 9.
19. Quoted in Streckert, *Storied and Scandalous Portland, Oregon*, 73.
20. Peter Boag, *Same-Sex Affairs: Constructing and Controlling Homosexuality in the Pacific Northwest* (Berkeley: University of California Press, 2003), 80–81; and Chandler, *Hidden History*, 161.
21. Ullman, *The Gift of Policewomen*, 62.
22. Quoted in Streckert, *Storied and Scandalous Portland, Oregon*, 76. See also Chandler and Kennedy, *Murder and Scandal in Prohibition Portland*, 36.
23. David Peterson del Mar, "'His Face Is Weak and Sensual': Portland and the Whipping Post Law," in *Women in Pacific Northwest History*, 2nd ed., edited by Karen J. Blair (Seattle: University of Washington Press, 2001), 62–63.
24. Quoted in Peterson del Mar, "'His Face Is Weak and Sensual'," 64.

25. Peterson del Mar, "His Face Is Weak and Sensual," 63, 66–67.
26. Peterson del Mar, "His Face Is Weak and Sensual," 71–76, 79–80.
27. Peterson del Mar, "His Face Is Weak and Sensual," 59.
28. Peterson del Mar, "His Face Is Weak and Sensual," 66–73.
29. E. Kimbark MacColl, *The Shaping of a City: Business and Politics in Portland, Oregon, 1855–1915* (Portland: Georgian Press, 1976), 402.
30. Painter, *Vice Clique*, 17.
31. MacColl, *The Shaping of a City*, 402.
32. E. Kimbark MacColl and Harry H. Stein, *Merchants, Money, and Power: The Portland Establishment, 1843–1913* ([Portland]: Georgian Press, 1988), 435–36; Jewel Lansing, *Portland: People, Politics, and Power, 1851–2001* (Corvallis: Oregon State University Press, 2003), 282–84; Collins, *Good Time Girls*, 136–37; and Jewel Lansing and Fred Leeson, *Multnomah: The Tumultuous Story of Oregon's Most Populous County* (Corvallis: Oregon State University Press, 2012), 50. Quote from Lansing, *Portland*, 283.
33. Quoted in MacColl, *The Shaping of a City*, 409.
34. Heather Mayer, *Beyond the Rebel Girl: Women and the Industrial Workers of the World in the Pacific Northwest* (Corvallis: Oregon State University Press, 2018), 68.
35. Quoted in Lansing, *Portland*, 285–86.
36. Quoted in MacColl, *The Shaping of a City*, 403, 404, 408.
37. Quoted in Painter, *Vice Clique*, 39–40. See also MacColl, *The Shaping of a City*, 404. West did not follow through on his threat to use the militia in Portland, but he did declare martial law in Copperfield and had the National Guard arrest the elected council. The town was held under military occupation for two years. Richard H. Engerman, *The Oregon Companion: An Historical Gazetteer of the Useful, the Curious, and the Arcane* (Portland: Timber Press, 2009), 98–99.
38. Painter, *Vice Clique*, 31, 39–41.
39. Quoted in Painter, *Vice Clique*, 50. See also Boag, *Same-Sex Affairs*, 89, 267n12. The young shoplifter has been variously identified as Hazen Wright (age fourteen) and Benjamin Trout (age nineteen). See Painter and Boag, respectively.
40. Helquist, *Marie Equi*, 110.
41. Painter, *Vice Clique*, 63; and Boag, *Same-Sex Affairs*, 108. Three of those indicted were nineteen years old and thus legally minors. Painter, *Vice Clique*, 63.
42. Quoted in Painter, *Vice Clique*, 51.
43. Painter, *Vice Clique*, 63; and Boag, *Same-Sex Affairs*, 157–58.
44. Painter, *Vice Clique*, 6; and Boag, *Same-Sex Affairs*, 48.
45. Boag, *Same-Sex Affairs*, 137–38.
46. Boag, *Same-Sex Affairs*, 48–50.
47. Boag, *Same-Sex Affairs*, 3, 91.
48. Boag, *Same-Sex Affairs*, 139–43. Quotes on 142–43.
49. Quoted in Boag, *Same-Sex Affairs*, 141.
50. Boag, *Same-Sex Affairs*, 143–44. In 1944, the court would reverse itself and allow extraneous testimony in sodomy cases. Painter, *Vice Clique*, 192.
51. Painter, *Vice Clique*, 102, 133.
52. Quoted in Boag, *Same-Sex Affairs*, 149.
53. Boag, *Same-Sex Affairs*, 203–5.
54. Boag, *Same-Sex Affairs*, 45, 49.
55. Boag, *Same-Sex Affairs*, 46–47, 52.
56. Boag, *Same-Sex Affairs*, 59.

57. Boag, *Same-Sex Affairs*, 208.
58. Mark A. Largent, "'The Greatest Curse of the Race': Eugenic Sterilization in Oregon, 1909–1983," *Oregon Historical Quarterly* 1, no. 2 (Summer 2002): 195.
59. Quoted in Boag, *Same-Sex Affairs*, 210.
60. Boag, *Same-Sex Affairs*, 208–10; Painter, *Vice Clique*, 171, 177; Robert D. Johnston, *The Radical Middle Class: Populist Democracy and the Question of Capitalism in Progressive Era Portland, Oregon* (Princeton: Princeton University Press, 2003), 202; and Largent, "The Greatest Curse of the Race," 197–98.
61. Quoted in Boag, *Same-Sex Affairs*, 212.
62. Painter, *Vice Clique*, 181–84; Adam J. Hodges, *World War I and Urban Order: The Local Class Politics of National Mobilization* (Houndmills, UK: Palgrave Macmillan, 2016), 116; and Diane L. Goeres-Gardner, *Inside Oregon State Hospital: A History of Tragedy and Triumph* (Charleston, SC: The History Press, 2013), 149. Quotes from Hodges, *World War I and Urban Order*, 116 ("sterilization") and Painter, *Vice Clique*, 181 ("flagrant").
63. George Edwards, "A Portrait of Portland," *Mother Earth*, November 1915, 312, 314. See also Boag, *Same-Sex Affairs*, 199–200.
64. Robert Hamburger, *Two Rooms: The Life of Charles Erskine Scott Wood* (Lincoln: University of Nebraska Press, 1998), 222–32.
65. Quoted in Helquist, *Marie Equi*, 135.
66. Edwards, "A Portrait of Portland," 312, 314.
67. Hamburger, *Two Rooms*, 236–37; and Sherry L. Smith, *Bohemians West: Free Love, Family, and Radicals in Twentieth-Century America* (Berkeley: Heyday, 2020), 210.

Chapter 6: Sex, Wobs, and War

1. Dennis E. Hoffman and Vincent J. Webb, "Police Response to Labor Radicalism in Portland and Seattle, 1913–19," *Oregon Historical Quarterly* 87, no. 4 (Winter 1986): 342; Heather Mayer, *Beyond the Rebel Girl: Women and the Industrial Workers of the World in the Pacific Northwest, 1905–1924* (Corvallis: Oregon State University Press, 2018), 70–71; and Michael Helquist, *Marie Equi: Radical Politics and Outlaw Passions* (Corvallis: Oregon State University Press, 2015), 116.
2. Quoted in Mayer, *Beyond the Rebel Girl*, 82, 83.
3. Mayer, *Beyond the Rebel Girl*, 70.
4. Quoted in Mayer, *Beyond the Rebel Girl*, 63. The strike followed soon after two homosexual scandals and coincided with a nationwide panic over "white slavery." The exaggerated claims about sexual slavery, as historian Heather Mayer put it, "combined the moralistic attitudes of Progressive reformers with the Victorian fear of sexual impropriety." They also incorporated a fair measure of antisemitic and anti-Chinese racism: "White slave" rings were alleged to be run by Jews in the East and the Chinese in the West. Mayer, *Beyond the Rebel Girl*, 66–67.
5. Mayer, *Beyond the Rebel Girl*, 63–66, 73–74; and Helquist, *Marie Equi*, 118.
6. Hoffman and Webb, "Police Response to Labor Radicalism," 354.
7. Quoted in Hoffman and Webb, "Police Response to Labor Radicalism," 343.
8. Employers' Association quoted in Hoffman and Webb, "Police Response to Labor Radicalism," 356; Albee quoted in Mayer, *Beyond the Rebel Girl*, 74.
9. Hoffman and Webb, "Police Response to Labor Radicalism," 344; and Mayer, *Beyond the Rebel Girl*, 74–75.

10. Mayer, *Beyond the Rebel Girl*, 76; Helquist, *Marie Equi*, 118–19; and J. D. Chandler, *Hidden History of Portland Oregon* (Charleston, SC: The History Press, 2013), 178–80.
11. Quoted in Helquist, *Marie Equi*, 120 ("torture"), 177 ("I was taken").
12. Quoted in Mayer, *Beyond the Rebel Girl*, 76. More than anything else, it was the experience of the cannery strike that converted Marie Equi from a progressive reformer to a radical. Helquist, *Marie Equi*, 121; and Mayer, *Beyond the Rebel Girl*, 142.
13. Jewel Lansing, *Portland: People, Politics, and Power, 1851–2001* (Corvallis: Oregon State University Press, 2003), 296; and Hoffman and Webb, "Police Response to Labor Radicalism," 344–45.
14. For details, see Hoffman and Webb, "Police Response to Labor Radicalism."
15. Quoted in Mayer, *Beyond the Rebel Girl*, 84.
16. Quoted in Beverly Gage, *G-Man: J. Edgar Hoover and the Making of the American Century* (New York: Viking, 2022), 95. Though intended to impede sex trafficking, the law was soon applied to *any* irregular sexual activity: commercial, adulterous, under-age, or interracial. Gage, *G-Man*, 95. See also Mayer, *Beyond the Rebel Girl*, 67.
17. Mayer, *Beyond the Rebel Girl*, 84–85.
18. Frank K. Welles, "Our Oregon State Institutions: Oregon State Industrial School for Girls," *Oregon Teachers Monthly* (January 1916): 270–71.
19. Quoted in Chandler, *Hidden History*, 160.
20. Diane L. Goeres-Gardner, *Inside Oregon State Hospital: A History of Tragedy and Triumph* (Charleston, SC: The History Press, 2013), 167.
21. Chandler, *Hidden History*, 156.
22. Mayer, *Beyond the Rebel Girl*, 85–86; Chandler, *Hidden History*, 160.
23. Lansing, *Portland*, 301.
24. Lansing, *Portland*, 307; E. Kimbark MacColl, *The Growth of a City: Power and Politics in Portland, Oregon, 1915 to 1950* (Portland: Georgian Press, 1979), 149–52; and Adam J. Hodges, *World War I and Urban Order: The Local Class Politics of National Mobilization* (Houndmills, UK: Palgrave Macmillan, 2016), 53.
25. Quoted in Fred Leeson, *Rose City Justice: A Legal History of Portland, Oregon* (Portland: Oregon Historical Society Press and the Oregon State Bar, 1998), 100–101.
26. Hodges, *World War I and Urban Order*, 54.
27. *The History of the Oregon State Police, 50th Anniversary—1981*, edited by William H. Freele and Edna R. Killmeyer (Dallas: Department of State Police, State of Oregon, 1981), 20.
28. Hodges, *World War I and Urban Order*, 106; and MacColl, *The Growth of a City*, 143.
29. Hodges, *World War I and Urban Order*, 106, 110–15, 123; and Paula Abrams, *Cross Purposes: Pierce v. Society of Sisters and the Struggle over Compulsory Public Education* (Ann Arbor: University of Michigan Press, 2009), 63.
30. J. D. Chandler and Theresa Griffin Kennedy, *Murder and Scandal in Prohibition Portland: Sex, Vice and Misdeeds in Mayor Baker's Reign* (Charleston, SC: The History Press, 2016), 112.
31. John Leader, *Oregon Through Alien Eyes* (Portland: JK Gill, 1922), 76.
32. Chandler and Kennedy, *Murder and Scandal in Prohibition Portland*, 64. See also Hodges, *World War I and Urban Order*, 136–37.
33. Kristofer Allerfeldt, *Race, Radicalism, Religion, and Restriction: Immigration in the Pacific Northwest, 1890–1924* (Westport, CT: Praeger, 2003), 127. The American Protective League was authorized by Attorney General Thomas Gregory to assist the Bureau of Investigation. It became "the nation's most prominent right-wing vigilante organization," in Mike German's assessment. "Boasting more than two hundred fifty thousand members nationwide,

the APL functioned as a private army of informers and thugs for hire." Mike German, *Disrupt, Discredit, and Divide: How the New FBI Damages Democracy* (New York: New Press, 2019), 117.

34. Hodges, *World War I and Urban Order*, 108; and Gordon DeMarco, *A Short History of Portland* (San Francisco: Lexikos, 1990), 113.
35. Quoted in MacColl, *The Growth of a City*, 143.
36. Helquist, *Marie Equi*, 164–67 (quote on 167). The Espionage Act forbade anyone to "willfully utter, print, write, or publish any disloyal, profane, scurrilous, or abusive language" or to "cause or attempt to cause, or incite or attempt to incite, insubordination, disloyalty, mutiny, or refusal of duty, in the military or naval forces of the United States." Quoted in Jules Boykoff, *Beyond Bullets: The Suppression of Dissent in the United States* (Oakland: AK Press, 2007), 158–59.
37. Quoted in Helquist, *Marie Equi*, 176–77.
38. Hodges, *World War I and Urban Order*, 98–102.
39. Hodges, *World War I and Urban Order*, 90–92; and Eric Thomas Chester, *The Wobblies in Their Heyday: The Rise and Destruction of the Industrial Workers of the World During the World War I Era* (Santa Barbara: Praeger, 2014), 163. Quote from Hodges, *World War I and Urban Order*, 92.
40. Hodges, *World War I and Urban Order*, 60–61, 65 (quote).
41. DeMarco, *A Short History of Portland*, 113–14; Lansing, *Portland*, 309; and Robert L. Tyler, *Rebels of the Woods: The IWW in the Pacific Northwest* (Eugene: University of Oregon Books, 1967), 150–52. Quotes from Tyler, *Rebels of the Woods*, 150 (text of law), 151 (district attorney's statement).
42. Michael Munk, *The Portland Red Guide: Sites and Stories of Our Radical Past* (Portland: Ooligan Press, 2007), 56–57; and Chandler and Kennedy, *Murder and Scandal in Prohibition Portland*, 80.
43. Hodges, *World War I and Urban Order*, 107–8.
44. Hodges, *World War I and Urban Order*, 116; and Sharon Nesbit and Tim Hills, *Vintage Edgefield: A History of the Multnomah County Poor Farm and McMenamins Edgefield* ([Portland]: McMenamins, 2002), 10.
45. Quoted in Jewel Lansing and Fred Leeson, *Multnomah: The Tumultuous Story of Oregon's Most Populous County* (Corvallis: Oregon State University Press, 2012), 72.
46. Quoted in Hodges, *World War I and Urban Order*, 117.
47. Hodges, *World War I and Urban Order*, 123.
48. Quoted in Hodges, *World War I and Urban Order*, 119–21. Founded in 1908 by Mayor Harry Lane, Governor George Chamberlain, the Police Department's Lola Baldwin, and a group of physicians, the OSHS sponsored sex education lectures around the state and published information about sexual health, with particular attention to stopping the spread of disease. Its approach had always been somewhat moralizing, seeking to instill a sense of sexual restraint in men and advocating laws to regulate the public morals. It became more assertive after the YMCA scandal, receiving $20,000 from the state government to fund programs educating boys about heterosexuality, deliberately ignoring homosexuality in an attempt to steer their orientation. Peter Boag, *Same-Sex Affairs: Constructing and Controlling Homosexuality in the Pacific Northwest* (Berkeley: University of California Press, 2003), 189–91, 197; Hodges, *World War I and Urban Order*, 119; and Tracy J. Prince and Zadie Schaffer, *Notable Women of Portland* (Charleston, SC: Arcadia, 2017), 32.
49. Hodges, *World War I and Urban Order*, 118.

50. Hodges, *World War I and Urban Order*, 122. Distressingly, this pattern of non-specific criminalization was typical for young offenders. Of the 4,331 boys confined in the Oregon State Reformatory between 1891 and 1942, 1,110 were not held for specific crimes but rather for being "incorrigible." This was in fact the most common offense. Hannah Hoffmann, "The Lost Boys of MacLaren: 124 Years of Records," statesmanjournal.com, April 18, 2015; and, J. D. Chandler, *Portland Rogues Gallery: A Baker's Dozen Arresting Criminals from Portland's History* (n.p.: America Through Time, 2021) 113.
51. Hodges, *World War I and Urban Order*, 57, 65–67. Quotes from 66 ("nearly 200") and 67 ("the only way").
52. Hodges, *World War I and Urban Order*, 137–38.
53. Boykoff, *Beyond Bullets*, 162–65.
54. Quoted in Mary V. Dearborn, *Queen of Bohemia: The Life of Louise Bryant* (Boston: Houghton Mifflin, 1996), 127.

Chapter 7: Prohibition and the Klan

1. Fred Leeson, *Rose City Justice: A Legal History of Portland, Oregon* (Portland: Oregon Historical Society Press and the Oregon State Bar, 1998), 76.
2. Thomas R. Pegram, *Battling Demon Rum: The Struggle for a Dry America, 1800–1933* (Chicago: Ivan R. Dee, 1998), 151, 158; Lisa McGirr, *The War on Alcohol: Prohibition and the Rise of the American State* (New York: W. W. Norton), 123; and Herbert Asbury, *The Great Illusion: An Informal History of Prohibition* (Mineola, NY: Dover Publications, 2018), 141.
3. *The History of the Oregon State Police, 50th Anniversary—1981*, edited by William H. Freele and Edna R. Killmeyer (Dallas: Department of State Police, State of Oregon, 1981), 24. The Oregon State Police got out of the booze business with the creation of the Oregon Liquor Control Commission in 1933. Freel and Killmeyer, *The History of the Oregon State Police*, 28.
4. Organized opposition to the temperance movement included brewers, distillers, bar owners, and machine bosses but also principled conservatives suspicious of state intervention. Edward Behr, *Prohibition: Thirteen Years that Changed America* (New York: Arcade Publishing, 2011), 25, 29, 48; and J. D. Chandler and Theresa Griffin Kennedy, *Murder and Scandal in Prohibition Portland: Sex, Vice and Misdeeds in Mayor Baker's Reign* (Charleston, SC: The History Press, 2016), 24.
5. Richard Hofstadter, *The Age of Reform: From Bryan to F.D.R.* (New York: Alfred A. Knopf, 1961), 17.
6. Adam Woog, *Prohibition: Banning Alcohol* (San Diego: Lucent Books, 2003), 13; and Pegram, *Battling Demon Rum*, 90. "Beyond the debate on the rights of reformers to regulate social behavior by force, restricting individual freedom in the name of better health, morality, and godliness, Prohibition was the rearguard action of a still dominant, overwhelmingly rural, white Angle-Saxon Protestant establishment, aware that its privileges and natural right to rule were being increasingly threatened by the massive arrival of largely despised (and feared) beer-swilling, wine-drinking new American immigrants." Behr, *Prohibition*, 3.
7. Alan P. Grimes, *The Puritan Ethic and Woman Suffrage* (New York: Oxford University Press, 1967), 132.
8. Hofstadter, *Age of Reform*, 288–89.
9. McGirr, *The War on Alcohol*, 12.
10. Pegram, *Battling Demon Rum*, 103–4.

11. McGirr, *The War on Alcohol*, 15.
12. Chandler and Kennedy, *Murder and Scandal in Prohibition Portland*, 71.
13. Floyd R. Marsh, *20 Years a Soldier of Fortune* (Portland: Binford & Mort, 1976), xv, 180–81, 192 (quote from 181).
14. Marsh, *20 Years a Soldier of Fortune*, 181–86. See also E. Kimbark MacColl, *The Growth of a City: Power and Politics in Portland, Oregon, 1915 to 1950* (Portland: Georgian Press, 1979), 276.
15. McGirr reminds us, "Enforcement hit working-class, urban immigrants, and poor communities hardest. [Prohibition] was, after all, enacted to discipline their leisure in the first place." McGirr, *The War on Alcohol*, xviii.
16. McGirr, *The War on Alcohol*, 89.
17. Chandler and Kennedy, *Murder and Scandal in Prohibition Portland*, 52.
18. Chandler and Kennedy, *Murder and Scandal in Prohibition Portland*, 114.
19. Quoted in Chandler and Kennedy, *Murder and Scandal in Prohibition Portland*, 103.
20. Marsh, *20 Years a Soldier of Fortune*, 182, 187–89.
21. Chandler and Kennedy, *Murder and Scandal in Prohibition Portland*, 89, 91.
22. J. D. Chandler, *Portland Rogues Gallery: A Baker's Dozen Arresting Criminals from Portland's History* (n.p.: America Through Time, 2021), 101.
23. Chandler and Kennedy, *Murder and Scandal in Prohibition Portland*, 71, 85. After the story appeared in the paper, Mayor Baker suspended Circle for ten days and reassigned him to the St. Johns neighborhood. MacColl, *The Growth of a City*, 278.
24. On the status of the job, see Larry Tye, *Rising from the Rails: Pullman Porters and the Making of the Black Middle Class* (New York: Picador, 2004), 73, 76–77. On the significance of porters in the emerging civil rights movement, see 199–227.
25. Chandler and Kennedy, *Murder and Scandal in Prohibition Portland*, 26, 73; and J. D. Chandler and J. B. Fisher, *Portland on the Take: Mid-Century Crime Bosses, Civic Corruption and Forgotten Murders* (Charleston, SC: The History Press, 2014), 44.
26. Chandler and Kennedy, *Murder and Scandal in Prohibition Portland*, 73.
27. Chandler and Kennedy, *Murder and Scandal in Prohibition Portland*, 26.
28. Chandler and Kennedy, *Murder and Scandal in Prohibition Portland*, 68–69.
29. Quoted in Chandler and Kennedy, *Murder and Scandal in Prohibition Portland*, 78.
30. Joseph S. Uris, "Trouble in River City: An Analysis of an Urban Vice Probe" (PhD diss., Portland State University, 1981), 217. See also Uris, "Trouble in River City," 57–58, 71; and Robert Dietsche, *Jumptown: The Golden Years of Portland Jazz, 1942–1957* (Corvallis: Oregon State University Press, 2005), 103–4.
31. Twice jurors drank confiscated liquor and then acquitted for lack of evidence. Chandler and Kennedy, *Murder and Scandal in Prohibition Portland*, 49.
32. Even apart from the gangland killings, the enforcement of prohibition often proved deadly. One agent estimated that between 1924 and 1934 the Border Patrol killed five hundred "contrabandistas" smuggling alcohol from Mexico. McGirr, *The War on Alcohol*, 209. Prohibition agents killed 135 people over the same period, and 55 agents had been killed. Mabel Walker Willebrandt, "The Danger of Unlawful Prohibition Agents," in *Prohibition*, edited by Dennis Nishi (San Diego: Greenhaven Press, 2003), 109–10.
33. Behr, *Prohibition*, 83; McGirr, *The War on Alcohol*, 208; Woog, *Prohibition*, 60; and Asbury, *The Great Illusion*, 174–75. In 1927, when a civil service exam was finally applied to the Prohibition Bureau, only 41 percent of its agents received passing scores. McGirr, *The War on Alcohol*, 208.
34. Willebrandt, "The Danger of Unlawful Prohibition Agents," 115.

35. Quoted in Judy Blankenship, *Intersections: TriMet Interstate MAX Lightrail Community History Project* (Portland: Tri-County Metropolitan Transportation District of Oregon, 2003), 61.
36. McGirr, *The War on Alcohol*, xxi, 89, 208; and David A. Gerber, *American Immigration: A Very Short Introduction* (Oxford: Oxford University Press, 2011), 57.
37. Pegram, *Battling Demon Rum*, 167–68.
38. Robert C. Donnelly, *Dark Rose: Organized Crime and Corruption in Portland* (Seattle: University of Washington Press, 2011), 44; and Chandler and Kennedy, *Murder and Scandal in Prohibition Portland*, 125.
39. Chandler and Kennedy, *Murder and Scandal in Prohibition Portland*, 116–17.
40. Hofstadter, *Age of Reform*, 290–91.
41. Kristofer Allerfeldt, *Race, Radicalism, Religion, and Restriction: Immigration in the Pacific Northwest, 1890–1924* (Westport, CT: Praeger, 2003), 44–45, 102, 115, 120, 140–41; Leeson, *Rose City Justice*, 101–3; Kenneth T. Jackson, *The Ku Klux Klan in the City, 1915–1930* (New York: Oxford University Press, 1967), 200–201; Kelly J. Baker, *Gospel According to the Klan: The KKK's Appeal to Protestant America, 1915–1930* (Lawrence: University Press of Kansas, 2011), 6; and MacColl, *The Growth of a City*, 154.
42. Quoted in Jackson, *The Ku Klux Klan in the City*, 200.
43. Quoted in MacColl, *The Growth of a City*, 162.
44. Jackson, *Ku Klux Klan in the City*, 198–200, 208.
45. Quoted in Lawrence J. Saalfeld, *Forces of Prejudice in Oregon, 1920–1925* (Portland: Archdiocesan Historical Commission, 1984), 102. In contrast, when the Klan threatened C. M. Raynerson, the managing editor of the *Oregon Labor Press*, the sheriff deputized him and issued him a badge and a gun. Malcolm Clark Jr., "The Bigot Disclosed: 90 Years of Nativism," *Oregon Historical Quarterly* 75, no. 2 (June 1974): 155.
46. Elizabeth McLagan, *A Peculiar Paradise: A History of Blacks in Oregon, 1788–1940* (Portland: Georgian Press, 1980), 138–40; Clark, "The Bigot Disclosed," 163; Dick Pintarich, "The Struggle of Blacks in Oregon," in *Great and Minor Moments in Oregon History: An Illustrated Anthology of Illuminating Glimpses into Oregon's Past from Prehistory to Present* (Portland: New Oregon Publishers, 2008), 291; David A. Horowitz, "Social Morality and Personal Revitalization: Oregon's Ku Klux Klan in the 1920s," *Oregon Historical Quarterly* 90, no. 4 (Winter 1989): 372–73; and Chandler and Kennedy, *Murder and Scandal in Prohibition Portland*, 112.
47. Quoted in Steve Law, "When the Labor Press Battled the Klan," *Northwest Labor Press*, January 6, 2023.
48. Chandler, and Kennedy, *Murder and Scandal in Prohibition Portland*, 112.
49. Quoted in Jackson, *Ku Klux Klan in the City*, 285n29.
50. Jackson, *Ku Klux Klan in the City*, 209; and Saalfeld, *Forces of Prejudice in Oregon*, 47. The *Spectator* accused Governor Walter M. Pierce of granting state police authority to the Black Patrol, but it was never proven. Saalfeld, *Forces of Prejudice in Oregon*, 47.
51. Chandler and Kennedy, *Murder and Scandal in Prohibition Portland*, 111.
52. Quoted in Jackson, *The Ku Klux Klan in the City*, 208.
53. MacColl, *The Growth of a City*, 165; and Clark, "The Bigot Disclosed," 156. Clark believes this figure to be exaggerated.
54. Charles Easton Rothwell, "The Ku Klux Klan in the State of Oregon" (undergraduate thesis, Reed College, 1924), 121. Despite the organization's law-and-order politics, the *Spectator* reported in January 1925, "More than anything else, the Klan influence has been responsible for the lack of discipline in the police department, and the fact that the criminal element

has enjoyed freedom of the city. When the dragons and the griffins can go to headquarters and order their poor satellites to 'lay off' this disorderly house or that bootleg joint, we can hardly expect a spotless town." Quoted in Saalfeld, *Forces of Prejudice in Oregon*, 29.

55. Jackson, *The Ku Klux Klan in the City*, 208, 285n25. Chandler and Kennedy (*Murder and Scandal in Prohibition Portland*, 106) and MacColl (*The Growth of a City*, 163–64) consider the famous Klan photo a setup. Looking at the photo, however, it evinces none of the surprise, confusion, or awkwardness that one might expect from men who find themselves unexpectedly among hooded Klanners.

56. Saalfeld, *Forces of Prejudice in Oregon*, 29; Jackson, *Ku Klux Klan in the City*, 203, 207–8, 283n6; Jewel Lansing, *Portland: People, Politics, and Power, 1851–2001* (Corvallis: Oregon State University Press, 2003), 310; Gordon DeMarco, *A Short History of Portland* (San Francisco: Lexikos, 1990), 115; and Rothwell, "The Ku Klux Klan in the State of Oregon," 133. Gifford, the Exalted Cyclops, and Lem Dever, the editor of the Klan's *Western American*, said that Baker was a member. Baker, as mentioned above, denied it. None of these men, however, are what you might call unimpeachable sources. DeMarco, *A Short History of Portland*, 115; and Saalfeld, *Forces of Prejudice in Oregon*, 29. MacColl thinks it more likely than not that Baker did join the Klan. MacColl, *The Growth of a City*, 167.

57. Jackson, *The Ku Klux Klan in the City*, 203; Carl Abbott, *Portland in Three Centuries: The Place and the People* (Corvallis: Oregon State University Press, 2011), 101; and MacColl, *The Growth of a City*, 168.

58. Jackson, *The Ku Klux Klan in the City*, 207–8; and DeMarco, *A Short History of Portland*, 114, 123. As with Black and Chinese exclusion, economic conflicts lay just beneath the surface of racial hatred. Many of the Japanese who immigrated to Oregon were farmers, and land ownership had been an issue since the 1870s. DeMarco, *A Short History of Portland*, 123. "In Oregon, the old conflict of Portland's commercial interests struggling with the Salem 'populists', which underlay much of Oregon's early history, smoldered beneath the issue of anti-Japanese discrimination. . . . Portland's conservative business community saw no advantage in persecuting the Japanese and set themselves against the intensely nativist sentiments of the population at large." Allerfeldt, *Race, Radicalism, Religion, and Restriction*, 198. Perhaps more than anything else, the business community worried about possible ramifications such discrimination would have on trade with Japan. The *Oregon Voter* summed it up neatly as "the Portland Chamber of Commerce" against "the American Legion boys." Allerfeldt, *Race, Radicalism, Religion, and Restriction*, 197–98.

59. Quoted in MacColl, *The Growth of a City*, 156.

60. Jewel Lansing and Fred Leeson, *Multnomah: The Tumultuous Story of Oregon's Most Populous County* (Corvallis: Oregon State University Press, 2012), 73–76; and Jackson, *Ku Klux Klan in the City*, 212.

61. DeMarco, *A Short History of Portland*, 116.

62. Rothwell, "The Ku Klux Klan in the State of Oregon," 138.

63. Jackson, *Ku Klux Klan in the City*, 210–12; and Clark, "The Bigot Disclosed," 179.

64. Lawrence M. Lipin, *Eleanor Baldwin and the Woman's Point of View: New Thought Radicalism in Portland's Progressive Era* (Corvallis: Oregon State University Press, 2017), viii, ix, 165, 187–88; and Robert D. Johnston, *The Radical Middle Class: Populist Democracy and the Question of Capitalism in Progressive Era Portland, Oregon* (Princeton: Princeton University Press, 2003), 241.

65. On the Klan's defense of corporate monopolies, see Johnston, *The Radical Middle Class*, 244–45.

66. Johnston, *The Radical Middle Class*, 238.

67. Johnston, *The Radical Middle Class*, 222, 230; Paula Abrams, *Cross Purposes:* Pierce v. Society of Sisters *and the Struggle over Compulsory Public Education* (Ann Arbor: University of Michigan Press, 2009), 40; and David A. Horowitz, "The Klansman as Outsider: Ethnocultural Solidarity and Antielitism in the Oregon Ku Klux Klan of the 1920s," *Pacific Northwest Quarterly* 80, no. 1 (January 1989): 12–20. The confluence was crucial to the school bill's success: "Populist and progressive politics, anti-Catholic and nativist sentiments, and fears of radicalism all met the same fertile ground for adoption of compelled public education, as did the Oregon initiative process, one of the country's most vigorous experiments in direct democracy." Abrams, *Cross Purposes*, 3.
68. Johnston, *The Radical Middle Class*, 222, 228.
69. Johnston, *The Radical Middle Class*, 224.
70. "At least some of the opposition to privileged Portlanders had its foundation, as befit a republican tradition that was so often exclusionary, in racism and xenophobia. Much of the racist revolt, in turn, drew on middling-class language, revealing the social base of petit bourgeois ideas as well as their potentially reactionary nature." Johnston, *The Radical Middle Class*, 95.
71. Johnston, *The Radical Middle Class*, 252–53. The Klan's leaders were former union officials, promoted to management and turned loyal company men. Johnston, *The Radical Middle Class*, 239–41; and Clark, "The Bigot Disclosed," 159–60.
72. "For some [Progressives]," historian Lawrence Lipin writes, "the Klan represented a change in emphasis, but not necessarily a new outlook." Lipin, *Eleanor Baldwin*, 165.

Chapter 8: Depression and Repression

1. Lori Shea Kuechler, *The Portland Police Sunshine Division: An Early History* (Portland: Sunshine Division, 2003), 18–23; Malcolm Clark Jr., "The Bigot Disclosed: 90 Years of Nativism," *Oregon Historical Quarterly* 75, no. 2 (June 1974): 157. Quote from Kuechler, *The Portland Police Sunshine Division*, 19.
2. Kuechler, *The Portland Police Sunshine Division*, 19, 55–57; Melvin E. DeGraw, *The Portland Vigilance Police* (n.p., 1991), unpaged (Oregon Historical Society research library, Portland); Kenneth T. Jackson, *The Ku Klux Klan in the City, 1915–1930* (New York: Oxford University Press, 1967), 208–9; Lawrence J. Saalfeld, *Forces of Prejudice in Oregon, 1920–1925* (Portland: Archdiocesan Historical Commission, 1984), 29, 47; Clark, "The Bigot Disclosed," 157.
3. J. D. Chandler, *Portland Rogues Gallery: A Baker's Dozen Arresting Criminals from Portland's History* (n.p.: America Through Time, 2021), 101; and Kuechler, *The Portland Police Sunshine Division*, 9–11 (quote on 11).
4. Kuechler, *The Portland Police Sunshine Division*, 61–62; and Hamish Scott MacKay, "From *My Experiences in the United States*," in *A Richer Harvest: An Anthology of Work in the Pacific Northwest*, edited by Craig Wollner and W. Tracy Dillon (Corvallis: Oregon State University Press, 1999), 173–74.
5. Kuechler, *The Portland Police Sunshine Division*, 75, 77, 83.
6. Kuechler, *The Portland Police Sunshine Division*, 96, 102.
7. William H. Mullins, *The Depression and the Urban West Coast, 1929–1933: Los Angeles, San Francisco, Seattle and Portland* (Bloomington: Indiana University Press, 1991), 82.
8. Quoted in Kuechler, *The Portland Police Sunshine Division*, 109.
9. Mullins, *The Depression and the Urban West Coast*, 92, 112.
10. Mackay, "From *My Experiences in the United States*," 166, 172–75.

11. Mullins, *The Depression and the Urban West Coast*, 27.
12. Mackay, "From *My Experiences in the United States*," 177–78.
13. Mackay, "From *My Experiences in the United States*," 161; and Michael Munk, *The Portland Red Guide: Sites and Stories of Our Radical Past* (Portland: Ooligan Press, 2007), 163.
14. *Rose City Rising: Portland Memories III: The 1950s*, compiled by OregonLive and the *Oregonian* (n.p.: Pediment Publishing, 2018), 108.
15. E. Kimbark MacColl, *The Growth of a City: Power and Politics in Portland, Oregon, 1915 to 1950* (Portland: Georgian Press, 1979), 468–69; and Robin Cody, "Division on the Docks," in *Great and Minor Moments in Oregon History: An Illustrated Anthology of Illuminating Glimpses into Oregon's Past from Prehistory to Present*, edited by Dick Pintarich (Portland: New Oregon Publishers, 2008), 277–78.
16. J. D. Chandler and J. B. Fisher, *Portland on the Take: Mid-Century Crime Bosses, Civic Corruption and Forgotten Murders* (Charleston, SC: The History Press, 2014), 15.
17. Quoted in Gordon DeMarco, *A Short History of Portland* (San Francisco: Lexikos, 1990), 122.
18. Quoted in MacColl, *The Growth of a City*, 471. See also Cody, "Division on the Docks," 278–79.
19. Quoted in Harvey Schwartz, *Solidarity Stories: An Oral History of the ILWU* (Seattle: University of Seattle Press, 2009), 106. Michael Munk suspects the union's source within the Portland Police Bureau was Lieutenant William Epps, a former organizer for the mineworkers union who, two years before, convinced his superiors not to break up a demonstration of the unemployed movement. Munk, *Portland Red Guide*, 102.
20. MacColl, *The Growth of a City*, 472.
21. Quoted in Schwartz, *Solidarity Stories*, 106.
22. MacColl, *The Growth of a City*, 471–72; William W. Pilcher, *The Portland Longshoremen: A Dispersed Urban Community* (New York: Holt, Rinehart and Winston, 1972), 44–46; and Cody, "Division on the Docks," 277. Quote from Pilcher, *The Portland Longshoremen*, 46. At least one scholar of the strike describes the union's actions as a form of policing: "The strikers were organized into two action groups, picket squads and 'riot' or 'flying' squads. The picket squads were the men who did the actual picketing, and the 'riot' squads performed military and police functions. Indeed, these 'riot' squads actually policed the waterfront and kept order during most of the strike. . . . their chief task was to harass actual or potential strikebreakers and to protect the picket squads from violence on the part of the employers' men. They were very successful at this." Pilcher, *The Portland Longshoremen*, 44.
23. Jewel Lansing, *Portland: People, Politics, and Power* (Corvallis: Oregon State University Press, 2003), 330.
24. MacColl, *The Growth of a City*, 475–78; Cody, "Division on the Docks," 280; and Chandler and Fisher, *Portland on the Take*, 24. Quotes from MacColl, *The Growth of a City*, 476–78.
25. Portland Police Survey Commission, *Survey of the Portland Police Bureau* (1934), 37–38.
26. Munk, *Portland Red Guide*, 99–100; Susan G. Hauser, *Pickets, Pistols and Politics: A History of the Portland Police Association* (Portland: Portland Police Association, 1996), 3; and Cody, "Division on the Docks," 279–80. Seven were killed during the strike, four in San Francisco. David H. Selvin, *A Terrible Anger: The 1934 Waterfront and General Strikes in San Francisco* (Detroit: Wayne State University Press, 1996), 233.
27. MacColl, *The Growth of a City*, 475. One striker disputes this account. "Aw, they could have pushed that train through, all right," Toby Christiansen later told an interviewer, "but the engineer was on our side." Quoted in Cody, "Division on the Docks," 280.

28. Fred Leeson, *Rose City Justice: A Legal History of Portland, Oregon* (Portland: Oregon Historical Society Press and the Oregon State Bar, 1998), 129; and Mackay, "From *My Experiences in the United States*," 168.
29. Gary Murrell, "Hunting Reds in Oregon, 1935–1939," *Oregon Historical Quarterly* 100, no. 4 (Winter 1999): 390–91; MacColl, *The Growth of a City*, 483–84; and Munk, *Portland Red Guide*, 102–3. Quote from Murrell, "Hunting Reds," 390.
30. MacColl, *The Growth of a City*, 474, 478–80; Carl Abbott, *Portland in Three Centuries: The Place and the People* (Corvallis: Oregon State University Press, 2011), 114; DeMarco, *A Short History of Portland*, 122–24; and Chandler and Fisher, *Portland on the Take*, 23. Toby Christiansen, a longshore worker riding in the car with Wagner, later said that there was no way to know which side was doing the shooting. Cody, "Division on the Docks," 282.
31. MacColl, *The Growth of a City*, 480.
32. Cody, "Division on the Docks," 282.
33. Munk, *Portland Red Guide*, 100–101.
34. Schwartz, *Solidarity Stories*, 107.
35. Lansing, *Portland*, 330, 336; and Leeson, *Rose City Justice*, 128.
36. MacColl, *The Growth of a City*, 483–84; and Munk, *Portland Red Guide*, 102–3.
37. Eric Rauchway, *The Great Depression and the New Deal: A Very Short Introduction* (Oxford: Oxford University Press, 2008), 95, 141.
38. Pilcher, *The Portland Longshoremen*, 115.
39. Chandler and Fisher, *Portland on the Take*, 25.
40. Quoted in MacColl, *The Growth of a City*, 481–82.
41. National Lawyers Guild, Oregon Chapter, "Report of the Civil Liberties Committee," May 24, 1938, 10. Among the authors of the NLG report was Gus Solomon. National Lawyers Guild, "Report of the Civil Liberties Committee," 53. In 1948, when President Truman nominated Solomon to the US District Court, Odale suggested to Senate investigators that Solomon was a Communist. Solomon denied it in absolute terms and was confirmed without a single dissenting vote. He served until 1987. A federal courthouse now bears his name. Leeson, *Rose City Justice*, 141–42.
42. National Lawyers Guild, "Report of the Civil Liberties Committee," 6–9, 48.
43. National Lawyers Guild, "Report of the Civil Liberties Committee," 27–29, 35.
44. Quoted in National Lawyers Guild, "Report of the Civil Liberties Committee," 17 ("many small groups"), 20 ("build communism").
45. Both quoted in National Lawyers Guild, "Report of the Civil Liberties Committee," 12.
46. National Lawyers Guild, "Report of the Civil Liberties Committee," 15.
47. MacColl, *The Growth of a City*, 465.
48. Murrell, "Hunting Reds in Oregon," 376–79; and Ken Bilderback and Kris Bilderback, *Law and Order at the End of the Oregon Trail* (K. Bilderback, 2015), 125. Quoted from Murrell, "Hunting Reds in Oregon," 376 ("iron pants"), 386 ("Jew Communists").
49. Quoted in Bilderback, *Law and Order at the End of the Oregon Trail*, 126.
50. National Lawyers Guild, "Report of the Civil Liberties Committee," 10–11, 37.
51. Quoted in National Lawyers Guild, "Report of the Civil Liberties Committee," 12.
52. National Lawyers Guild, "Report of the Civil Liberties Committee," 6–7.
53. Quoted in National Lawyers Guild, "Report of the Civil Liberties Committee," 18–19.
54. Shane Burley and Alexander Reid Ross, "From Nativism to White Power: Mid-Twentieth Century White Supremacist Movements in Oregon," *Oregon Historical Quarterly* 120, no. 4 (Winter 2019): 570. The Silver Shirts (formally the Silver Legion), in the estimation of the

Manchester Guardian, was at the time "the largest American fascist organization." Quoted in Bradley W. Hart, *Hitler's American Friends: The Third Reich's Supporters in the United States* (New York: Thomas Dunne Books, 2018), 66. For a short history of the organization, see Hart, *Hitler's American Friends*, 49–67.

55. National Lawyers Guild, "Report of the Civil Liberties Committee," 7, 48–50.
56. Burley and Ross, "From Nativism to White Power," 571. Americans, Inc., was founded in the fall of 1937. Nelson W. Hibbs, the naval aide to Governor Charles Martin, served as president; Captain R. F. Caples, vice president; George Stroup, secretary; and the American Legion's Harvey Swan, treasurer. The board of directors consisted of George Neher (president of Columbia Press), Charles Peabody (ILA secretary), E. O. Arnold (American Legion), and William Blackwell (Teamsters). A February 24, 1939, rally of Americans, Inc., was led by then-former Governor Charles Martin and Mayor Joseph Carson. Burley and Ross, "From Nativism to White Power," 572.
57. National Lawyers Guild, "Report of the Civil Liberties Committee," 50–51 (*Radical Activities Bulletin* quoted on 52).
58. Charles P. Larrowe, *Harry Bridges: The Rise and Fall of Radical Labor in the United States* (Westport, CT: Lawrence Hill, 1972), 139–42.
59. Larrowe, *Harry Bridges*.
60. Larrowe, *Harry Bridges*, 147, 149.
61. Quoted in Larrowe, *Harry Bridges*, 151.
62. Larrowe, *Harry Bridges*, 151–53; Murrell, "Hunting Reds in Oregon," 390–91; and Munk, *Portland Red Guide*, 103. Quotes from Larrowe, *Harry Bridges*, 153 ("my duty") and 154 ("self-confessed liar"). Merriel Bacon also once testified that, from 1930 to 1937, he had acted as a provocateur within the Communist Party. Chandler and Fisher, *Portland on the Take*, 34, 61.
63. Larrowe, *Harry Bridges*, 155, 167–68, 203–8.
64. Larrowe, *Harry Bridges*, 191–92.
65. Larrowe, *Harry Bridges*, 153, 195–97, 207; and Murrell, "Hunting Reds in Oregon," 388, 392. The bug had apparently caught Bridges in an illicit liaison. But James Houghteling, head of the immigration service, absolutely refused to make use of it. "No," he said definitively, "not by such methods." Quoted in Larrowe, *Harry Bridges*, 140.
66. Quoted in Larrowe, *Harry Bridges*, 215–16.
67. Quoted in Larrowe, *Harry Bridges*, 177.
68. Griffin Fariello, *Red Scare: Memories of the American Inquisition* (New York: W.W. Norton, 1995), 18.
69. Quoted in Larrowe, *Harry Bridges*, 222.
70. Quoted in Larrowe, *Harry Bridges*, 237–38.
71. Larrowe, *Harry Bridges*, 244–48.

Chapter 9: Professionalism and Unionization

1. Portland Police Survey Commission, *Survey of the Portland Police Bureau* (1934), ii.
2. Portland Police Survey Commission, *Survey of the Portland Police Bureau*, 7.
3. J. D. Chandler and Theresa Griffin Kennedy, *Murder and Scandal in Prohibition Portland: Sex, Vice and Misdeeds in Mayor Baker's Reign* (Charleston, SC: The History Press, 2016), 123–24; and J. D. Chandler, *Portland Rogues Gallery: A Baker's Dozen Arresting Criminals from Portland's History* (n.p.: America Through Time, 2021), 72.

4. Portland Police Survey Commission, *Survey of the Portland Police Bureau*, 56.
5. Portland Police Survey Commission, *Survey of the Portland Police Bureau*, 3–4.
6. Susan G. Hauser, *Pickets, Pistols and Politics: A History of the Portland Police Association* (Portland: Portland Police Association, 1996), 6.
7. Hauser, *Pickets, Pistols and Politics*, 6–7; and J. D. Chandler and J. B. Fisher, *Portland on the Take: Mid-Century Crime Bosses, Civic Corruption and Forgotten Murders* (Charleston, SC: The History Press, 2014), 61, 65.
8. Dana E. Jewell, "What the Public Expects of the Police and Their Duties," in *Training Oregon's Police: Report, Summary, and Proceedings of the Oregon Police Training Schools Conducted During March, April, and May 1937* (Eugene: League of Oregon Cities, 1937), I-1.
9. Portland Police Survey Commission, *Survey of the Portland Police Bureau*, 56.
10. W. C. Epps, "General Police Problems," in *Training Oregon's Police: Report, Summary, and Proceedings of the Oregon Police Training Schools Conducted During March, April, and May 1937* (Eugene: League of Oregon Cities, 1937), IX-1–IX-2.
11. Jewell, "What the Public Expects," I-1.
12. Portland Police Survey Commission, *Survey of the Portland Police Bureau*, 56–58.
13. Hauser, *Pickets, Pistols and Politics*, 6–7.
14. V. E. Kuhn, et al., foreword to *Training Oregon's Police: Report, Summary, and Proceedings of the Oregon Police Training Schools Conducted During March, April, and May 1937* (Eugene: League of Oregon Cities, 1937), i.
15. "Instructors and Subjects," in *Training Oregon's Police: Report, Summary, and Proceedings of the Oregon Police Training Schools Conducted During March, April, and May 1937* (Eugene: League of Oregon Cities, 1937), ii.
16. "List of Certificates Awarded," in *Training Oregon's Police: Report, Summary, and Proceedings of the Oregon Police Training Schools Conducted During March, April, and May 1937* (Eugene: League of Oregon Cities, 1937), v–viii.
17. "Instructors and Subjects," in *Training Oregon's Police*, ii.
18. Jewell, "What the Public Expects," I-1.
19. Jewell, "What the Public Expects," I-1; C. C. Spears, "Federal Bureau of Investigation and Services to Local Police," in *Training Oregon's Police*, VIII-1; and Epps, "General Police Problems," IX-1.
20. Jewell, "What the Public Expects," I-2.
21. Orville R. Williams, "The Law of Arrests, Searches and Seizures," in *Training Oregon's Police: Report, Summary, and Proceedings of the Oregon Police Training Schools Conducted During March, April, and May 1937* (Eugene: League of Oregon Cities, 1937), V-1.
22. Epps, "General Police Problems," IX-3.
23. Chandler and Fisher, *Portland on the Take*, 65.
24. Hauser, *Pickets, Pistols and Politics*, 8–9.
25. Hauser, *Pickets, Pistols and Politics*, 14.
26. Hauser, *Pickets, Pistols and Politics*, 18. For details of the campaign, see Chandler and Fisher, *Portland on the Take*, 67. Concerning the Boston police strike, see Richard L. Lyons, "The Boston Police Strike of 1919," *New England Quarterly*, June 1947, 147–168; and Francis Russell, *A City in Terror: 1919, the Boston Police Strike* (New York: Viking Press, 1975).
27. Hauser, *Pickets, Pistols and Politics*, 4.
28. Hauser, *Pickets, Pistols and Politics*, 20–21.
29. Quoted in Hauser, *Pickets, Pistols and Politics*, 24.
30. Hauser, *Pickets, Pistols and Politics*, 18–19, 25–27. The uniform allowance was instituted in

1946, and in 1953 the department began providing uniforms for free. Hauser, *Pickets, Pistols and Politics*, 25.

31. Hauser, *Pickets, Pistols and Politics*, 22–23.
32. Quoted in Beverly Gage, *G-Man: J. Edgar Hoover and the Making of the American Century* (New York: Viking, 2022), 207.
33. Bradley W. Hart, *Hitler's American Friends: The Third Reich's Supporters in the United States* (New York: Thomas Dunne Books, 2018), 31–32, 37; and Gage, *G-Man*, 208. For a short history of the German American Bund, see Hart, *Hitler's American Friends*, 23–48.
34. Quoted in Walter Goodman, *The Committee: The Extraordinary Career of the House Committee on Un-American Activities* (New York: Farrar, Straus and Giroux, 1968), 115. See also Hart, *Hitler's American Friends*, 28.
35. Hauser, *Pickets, Pistols and Politics*, 29–34. Hauser was the wife of the red squad commander, Winfield Falk (150).
36. Hauser, *Pickets, Pistols and Politics*, 24, 27.
37. Julian Go, "The Imperial Origins of American Policing: Militarization and Imperial Feedback in the Early 20th Century," *American Journal of Sociology* 125, no. 5 (March 2020): 1206–7, 1212; Gene E. Carte and Elaine H. Carte, *Police Reform in the United States: The Era of August Vollmer, 1905–1932* (Berkeley: University of California Press, 1975), 62–63; Stuart Schrader, *Badges Without Borders: How Global Counterinsurgency Transformed American Policing* (Oakland: University of California Press, 2019), 67–68; and Lee P. Brown, *Policing in the 21st Century: Community Policing* (Bloomington, Indiana: AuthorHouse, 2012), 314. Quote from Go, "Imperial Origins of American Policing," 1199. For a chronology of Vollmer's career, beginning with the North Berkeley Volunteer Fire Department in 1896, see Carte and Carte, *Police Reform in the United States*, 125–28.
38. Carte and Carte, *Police Reform in the United States*, 2.
39. Go, "The Imperial Origins of American Policing," 1203–9; and Carte and Carte, *Police Reform in the United States*, 46–49. One Berkeley officer later recalled, "On force, the rule was very simple. . . . It was that no Berkeley policeman should ever strike any person, particularly a prisoner, except in extreme self-defense; and then [Chief Vollmer] said, if you ever do, you have just resigned. You needn't bother to come in and discuss it." Quoted in Carte and Carte, *Police Reform in the United States*, 46.
40. Go, "The Imperial Origins of American Policing," 1207, 1214, 1217, 1238; and Schrader, *Badges Without Borders*, 67.
41. August Vollmer and Addison H. Fording, *Police Bureau Survey: City of Portland, Oregon* (Portland: Bureau of Municipal Research and Service, Portland Branch, University of Oregon, 1947), vii–viii.
42. Vollmer and Fording, *Police Bureau Survey*, ix.
43. Robert C. Donnelly, *Dark Rose: Organized Crime and Corruption in Portland* (Seattle: University of Washington Press, 2011), 50.
44. Vollmer and Fording, *Police Bureau Survey*, 35.
45. Portland Police Survey Commission, *Survey of the Portland Police Bureau*, 77, 80.
46. Vollmer and Fording, *Police Bureau Survey*, 37–38.
47. Vollmer and Fording, *Police Bureau Survey*, 39–48.
48. Vollmer and Fording, *Police Bureau Survey*, xix.
49. I make this argument in detail in Kristian Williams, *Our Enemies in Blue: Police and Power in America*, 3rd ed. (Oakland: AK Press, 2015), 221–22.
50. Hauser, *Pickets, Pistols and Politics*, 6.

Chapter 10: The Color Line on the Home Front

1. J. D. Chandler, *Hidden History of Portland Oregon* (Charleston, SC: The History Press, 2013), 127–28.
2. Lee P. Brown, "Neighborhood Team Policing and Police Reserves," in *Neighborhood Team Policing: The Multnomah County Experience*, ([Portland]: Multnomah County Sheriff's Office, 1976), 86.
3. Richard Reeves, *Infamy: The Shocking Story of the Japanese American Internment in World War II* (New York: Henry Holt, 2015), 12, 25; Greg Robinson, *Tragedy of Democracy: Japanese Confinement in North America* (New York: Columbia University Press, 2009), 60–62; Roger Daniels, "Words Do Matter: A Note on Inappropriate Terminology and the Incarceration of the Japanese Americans," in *Nikkei in the Pacific Northwest: Japanese Americans and Japanese Canadians in the Twentieth Century*, edited by Louis Fiset and Gail M. Nomura (Seattle: Center for the Study of the Pacific Northwest and University of Washington Press, 2005), 194; and Chandler, *Hidden History*, 127.
4. Fred Leeson, *Rose City Justice: A Legal History of Portland, Oregon* (Portland: Oregon Historical Society Press and the Oregon State Bar, 1998), 137.
5. Robinson, *Tragedy of Democracy*, 47.
6. Daniels, "Words Do Matter," 194.
7. Quoted in Leeson, *Rose City Justice*, 135–37.
8. Chandler, *Hidden History*, 127; and Robinson, *Tragedy of Democracy*, 61–62.
9. In 1984, the federal government finally vacated Yasui's conviction. Deena K. Nakata, *The Gift: The Oregon Nikkei Story Retold* (n.p., 1995), 97–98; Leeson, *Rose City Justice*, 135–37; and Jewel Lansing and Fred Leeson, *Multnomah: The Tumultuous Story of Oregon's Most Populous County* (Corvallis: Oregon State University Press, 2012), 91.
10. Michael Munk, *The Portland Red Guide: Sites and Stories of Our Radical Past* (Portland: Ooligan Press, 2007), 139–40.
11. Quoted in Reeves, *Infamy*, xx; and Nakata, *The Gift*, 130.
12. Daniels, "Words Do Matter," 190–95.
13. Daniels, "Words Do Matter," 193–95.
14. Robinson, *Tragedy of Democracy*, 1; Leeson, *Rose City Justice*, 137; Reeves, *Infamy*, xx; and Nakata, *The Gift*, 129.
15. Nakata, *The Gift*, 99; and Reeves, *Infamy*, 12–16.
16. Robinson, *Tragedy of Democracy*, 55.
17. In the entire United States, only nineteen people were arrested as Japanese agents during World War II. Eleven were convicted. All were white. Robinson, *Tragedy of Democracy*, 46.
18. Allan Wesley Austin, "Loyalty and Concentration Camps in America: The Japanese American Precedent and the Internal Security Act of 1950," in *Last Witness: Reflections on the Wartime Internment of Japanese Americans*, edited by Erica Harth (New York: Palgrave, 2001), 255.
19. Quoted in Reeves, *Infamy*, 41.
20. "Damned nonsense" quoted in John Tateishi, "Afterword," in *Placing Memory: A Photographic Exploration of Japanese American Internment*, by Todd Stewart et al. (Norman: University of Oklahoma Press, 2008), 105; "hysteria" quoted in Nakata, *The Gift*, 99.
21. Robinson, *Tragedy of Democracy*, 104–5, 125–27; and Reeves, *Infamy*, 64, 99. Quote from Robinson, *Tragedy of Democracy*, 93.
22. Quoted in Charles E. Mershon, *Along the Sandy: Our Nikkei Neighbors* (Portland: Guardian Peaks Enterprises, 2006), 128.

23. Nakata, *The Gift*, 105; Wendy Ng, *Japanese American Internment During World War II: A History and Reference Guide* (Westport, CT: Greenwood Press, 2002), 34; Robinson, *Tragedy of Democracy*, 122–24; and Mershon, *Along the Sandy*, 128–29.
24. Quoted in Robinson, *Tragedy of Democracy*, 107.
25. Robinson, *Tragedy of Democracy*, 124, 257.
26. Mershon, *Along the Sandy*, 130–33; Robinson, *Tragedy of Democracy*, 129; Ng, *Japanese American Internment*, 35; Nakata, *The Gift*, 105; and Gordon DeMarco, *A Short History of Portland* (San Francisco: Lexikos, 1990), 132. "It was filthy" quoted in Ng, *Japanese American Internment*, 34; "It stank" quoted in Nakata, *The Gift*, 106.
27. Robinson, *Tragedy of Democracy*, 130–31; Nakata, *The Gift*, 106–7; and Lansing and Leeson, *Multnomah*, 90.
28. Nakata, *The Gift*, 116, 118; Robinson, *Tragedy of Democracy*, 156–57; Mershon, *Along the Sandy*, 134; DeMarco, *A Short History of Portland*, 132; and Reeves, *Infamy*, 104.
29. City of Portland Bureau of Planning, *History of Portland's African American Community (1805 to the Present)* (City of Portland, 1993), 59.
30. Jewel Lansing, *Portland: People, Politics, and Power* (Corvallis: Oregon State University Press, 2003), 343.
31. Quoted in Elizabeth McLagan, *A Peculiar Paradise: A History of Blacks in Oregon, 1788–1940* (Portland: Georgian Press, 1980), 173.
32. Carl Abbott, *Portland in Three Centuries: The Place and the People* (Corvallis: Oregon State University Press, 2011), 43; and Franz M. Schneider, "The 'Black Laws' of Oregon" (master's thesis, University of Santa Clara, 1970), 45.
33. Kimberly Mangun, *A Force for Change: Beatrice Morrow Cannady and the Struggle for Civil Rights in Oregon, 1912–1936* (Corvallis: Oregon State University Press, 2010), 20.
34. McLagan, *A Peculiar Paradise*, 131–32 (quotes from 132).
35. Mangun, *A Force for Change*, 20.
36. DeMarco, *A Short History of Portland*, 135.
37. *Portland Memories, Volume II: The 1940s*, compiled by OregonLive and the *Oregonian* (n.p.: Pediment Publishing, 2017), 143.
38. Quoted in Lucas N. N. Burke and Judson L. Jeffries, *The Portland Black Panthers: Empowering Albina and Remaking a City* (Seattle: University of Washington Press, 2016), 31.
39. Quoted in J. D. Chandler and J. B. Fisher, *Portland on the Take: Mid-Century Crime Bosses, Civic Corruption and Forgotten Murders* (Charleston, SC: The History Press, 2014), 71.
40. Portland Bureau of Planning, *History of Portland's African American Community*, 64–65.
41. *Oregon Experience: Vanport*, directed by Nadine Je Ising et al. (Portland: Oregon Public Broadcasting and the Oregon Historical Society, 2016); Zita Podany, *Vanport* (Charleston, SC: Arcadia, 2016) 55, 69, 71; and Lansing and Leeson, *Multnomah*, 89.
42. Justin LeGrand Vipperman, "'On This, We Shall Build': The Struggle for Civil Rights in Portland, Oregon, 1945–1953" (master's thesis, Portland State University, 2016), 37–38.
43. *Oregon Experience: Vanport.*
44. Lansing and Leeson, *Multnomah*, 94–95.
45. The following year's city budget included funds for overtime paid at time-and-a-half. Susan G. Hauser, *Pickets, Pistols and Politics: A History of the Portland Police Association* (Portland: Portland Police Association, 1996), 32–33.
46. Lansing and Leeson, *Multnomah*, 94–96; and *Oregon Experience: Vanport.*
47. Introduction to *The FBI's RACON: Racial Conditions in the United States During World War II*, edited by Robert A. Hill (Boston: Northeastern University Press, 1995), 4–5.

48. "Section I. Survey of the Racial Conditions in the United States," in *The FBI's RACON: Racial Conditions in the United States During World War II*, edited by Robert A. Hill (Boston: Northeastern University Press, 1995), 382–84.
49. Committee on Race Relations, "The Negro in Portland," *Portland City Club Bulletin*, July 20, 1945, 52, 69.
50. Committee on Race Relations, "The Negro in Portland," 57–64.
51. Quoted in Vipperman, "'On This, We Shall Build'," 63.
52. Committee on Race Relations, "The Negro in Portland," 67–69. The Portland City Club would grow to become, in the view of journalist Floyd McKay, "the most influential civic organization in the state." Floyd J. McKay, *Reporting the Oregon Story: How Activists and Visionaries Transformed a State* (Corvallis: Oregon State University Press, 2016), 216.
53. Vipperman, "On This, We Shall Build," 14–18, 21–22.
54. Vipperman, "On This, We Shall Build," 43–47; quote from J. D. Chandler, *Murder and Mayhem in Portland Oregon* (Charleston, SC: The History Press, 2013), 118–20. A coerced confession would hardly be anomalous. The sheriff's offices at the courthouse had since 1941 included a soundproofed interrogation room. "Criminal defendants were not advised they had a right to remain silent, and some deputy sheriffs used extraordinary measures to obtain statements." Lansing and Leeson, *Multnomah*, 68.

Chapter 11: The No-Sin Mayor and the Vice Czar

1. Robert C. Donnelly, *Dark Rose: Organized Crime and Corruption in Portland* (Seattle: University of Washington Press, 2011), 48.
2. Quoted in Phil Stanford, *Portland Confidential: Sex, Crime, and Corruption in the Rose City* (Portland: Ptown Books, 2010), 24.
3. Quoted in Donnelly, *Dark Rose*, 57–58.
4. Stanford, *Portland Confidential*, 26.
5. J. D. Chandler, *Murder and Mayhem in Portland Oregon* (Charleston, SC: The History Press, 2013), 115.
6. Quoted in Donnelly, *Dark Rose*, 59.
7. Paul C. Pitzer, "Dorothy McCullough Lee: The Successes and Failures of 'Dottie-Do-Good,'" *Oregon Historical Quarterly*, 91, no. 1 (Spring 1990): 10.
8. Quoted in Pitzer, "Dorothy McCullough Lee," 5.
9. Quoted in Pitzer, "Dorothy McCullough Lee," 14.
10. Pitzer, "Dorothy McCullough Lee," 10, 27. Mayor Lee opened an inquiry into racial discrimination her first month in office and six months later appointed the Committee on Inter-Group Relations. Justin LeGrand Vipperman, "'On This, We Shall Build': The Struggle for Civil Rights in Portland, Oregon, 1945–1953" (master's thesis, Portland State University, 2016), 66.
11. Pitzer, "Dorothy McCullough Lee," 15.
12. Pitzer, "Dorothy McCullough Lee," 5, 24, 27; and Joe Streckert, *Storied and Scandalous Portland, Oregon: A History of Gambling, Vice, Wits, and Wagers* (Guilford, CT: Globe Pequot, 2020), 111.
13. Gary Murrell, "Hunting Reds in Oregon, 1935–1939," *Oregon Historical Quarterly* 100, no. 4 (Winter 1999): 383–84.
14. Pitzer, "Dorothy McCullough Lee," 16; Jewel Lansing, *Portland: People, Politics, and Power*

(Corvallis: Oregon State University Press, 2003), 355–56; and E. Kimbark MacColl, *The Growth of a City: Power and Politics in Portland, Oregon, 1915 to 1950* (Portland: The Georgian Press, 1979), 651.

15. J. D. Chandler and J. B. Fisher, *Portland on the Take: Mid-Century Crime Bosses, Civic Corruption and Forgotten Murders* (Charleston, SC: The History Press, 2014), 98.
16. Pitzer, "Dorothy McCullough Lee," 16; and Lansing, *Portland*, 360.
17. Quoted in Rickie Solinger, *The Abortionist: A Woman Against the Law* (Berkeley: University of California Press), 158. The Portland City Club observed: "Public interest and apathy follow a regular pattern, like the peaks and valleys on a seismograph. Every manifestation of an aroused public opinion produces a violent reaction in the police department and a rash of publicity about raids and arrests. The excitement soon subsides and the underworld settles back into its accustomed methods of operation until public opinion again awakens." Quoted in MacColl, *The Growth of a City*, 610–11.
18. Pitzer, "Dorothy McCullough Lee," 16; and Fred Leeson, *Rose City Justice: A Legal History of Portland, Oregon* (Portland: Oregon Historical Society Press and the Oregon State Bar, 1998), 145.
19. Quoted in Donnelly, *Dark Rose*, 67.
20. Streckert, *Storied and Scandalous Portland, Oregon*, 109; and Phil Stanford, "The Rise and Fall of Big Jim Elkins," in *Great and Minor Moments in Oregon History: An Illustrated Anthology of Illuminating Glimpses into Oregon's Past from Prehistory to the Present*, edited by Dick Pintarich (Portland: New Oregon Publishers, 2003), 329.
21. Donnelly, *Dark Rose*, 67–68; and Leeson, *Rose City Justice*, 145.
22. Stanford, "The Rise and Fall of Big Jim Elkins," 329; and Pitzer, "Dorothy McCullough Lee," 29.
23. Quoted in George Painter, *The Vice Clique: Portland's Great Sex Scandal* (Portland: Espresso Book Machine, 2013), 194. See also Faolán M. Thompson, "Polishing the Tarnished Rose: Police Sergeant Earl R. Biggs, Moral Panic, and Sexuality in Cold War Portland, Oregon" (undergraduate thesis, Lewis and Clark College, 2013), 55.
24. Streckert, *Storied and Scandalous Portland, Oregon*, 108. Lee quoted in Chandler and Fisher, *Portland on the Take*, 97.
25. Painter, *Vice Clique*, 195–96; and Thompson, *Polishing the Tarnished Rose*, 6.
26. Chandler and Fisher, *Portland on the Take*, 135–37; and Solinger, *The Abortionist*, 171.
27. Solinger, *The Abortionist*, 155–57.
28. Solinger, *The Abortionist*, 5, 9–10, 14–15, 36, 150–51 (quote on 14).
29. Solinger, *The Abortionist*, 164.
30. Solinger, *The Abortionist*, 218.
31. Solinger, *The Abortionist*, 219–23, 227–30.
32. Chandler and Fisher, *Portland on the Take*, 138.
33. Solinger, *The Abortionist*, 4–5, 29.
34. Solinger, *The Abortionist*, 192.
35. Donnelly, *Dark Rose*, 66; and Stanford, "The Rise and Fall of Big Jim Elkins," 329. For details of Winter's career, see Chandler and Fisher, *Portland on the Take*, 48–49.
36. John Gordon King, "The History of the Office of Multnomah County Sheriff; Multnomah County, Oregon" (undergraduate thesis, Lewis and Clark College, 1965), 77.
37. Pitzer, "Dorothy McCullough Lee," 23; Stanford, *Portland Confidential*, 92; Donnelly, *Dark Rose*, 66–67; and Jewel Lansing and Fred Leeson, *Multnomah: The Tumultuous Story of Oregon's Most Populous County* (Corvallis: Oregon State University Press, 2012), 97. Quote from Chandler and Fisher, *Portland on the Take*, 97.

38. Stanford, *Portland Confidential*, 92–94; Pitzer, "Dorothy McCullough Lee," 23; Donnelly, *Dark Rose*, 66–67; Chandler and Fisher, *Portland on the Take*, 97; Lansing, *Portland*, 356; and Lansing and Leeson, *Multnomah*, 97–98. Elliott, who advertised himself as a college graduate and a marine combat vet, had never finished the tenth grade and received a bad conduct discharge for absenteeism and drunkenness. MacColl, *The Growth of a City*, 653.
39. MacColl, *The Growth of a City*, 653.
40. Lansing and Leeson, *Multnomah*, 99.
41. Schrunk quoted in Lucas N. N. Burke and Judson L. Jeffries, *The Portland Black Panthers: Empowering Albina and Remaking a City* (Seattle: University of Washington Press, 2016), 49. Urban League quoted in "Sheriff's Action Lauded in Grag Case," *Interracial Progress*, June 1953, 3.
42. Quoted in Lansing and Leeson, *Multnomah*, 98–99.
43. Stanford, *Portland Confidential*, 94–95; and Donnelly, *Dark Rose*, 138.
44. Donnelly, *Dark Rose*, 4. During the "Beer Wars" of 1935, a jurisdictional dispute with the Brewery Union led to strikes and violence, including beatings with blackjacks, billy clubs, and tire irons, bricks thrown through windows, and at least four bombings. Chandler and Fisher, *Portland on the Take*, 30–33.
45. Donnelly, *Dark Rose*, 85–87, 132–33; Joseph S. Uris, "Trouble in River City: An Analysis of an Urban Vice Probe" (PhD diss., Portland State University, 1981), 97, 100, 166; and C. David Heymann, *RFK: A Candid Biography of Robert F. Kennedy* (New York: Dutton, 1998), 122.
46. Donnelly, *Dark Rose*, 92–93.
47. Quotes from Pitzer, "Dorothy McCullough Lee," 16–17; and Chandler and Fisher, *Portland on the Take*, 79.
48. Pitzer, "Dorothy McCullough Lee," 25; and Uris, "Trouble in River City," 62.
49. Pitzer, "Dorothy McCullough Lee," 30–32 (quotes from 31).
50. The Internal Security Act of 1950 (McCarran Act) gave the president and attorney general the authority to confine anyone considered a threat to national security. That provision (Title II) was modeled on Executive Order 9066, which had authorized the detention of Japanese Americans during the war. (Tule Lake, one of the wartime concentration camps, was again selected as a potential site.) The law was never used to detain suspected subversives, and no individual or organization ever actually registered. In 1965, the courts overturned its registration requirements on Fifth Amendment grounds. Griffin Fariello, *Red Scare: Memories of the American Inquisition: An Oral History* (New York: W. W. Norton, 1995), 17–18; Samuel Walker, *In Defense of American Liberties: A History of the ACLU*, 2nd ed. (Carbondale: Southern Illinois University Press, 1999), 198, 246; Walter Goodman, *The Committee: The Extraordinary Career of the House Committee on Un-American Activities* (New York: Farrar, Straus and Giroux, 1968), 294; Robert Justin Goldstein, *American Blacklist: The Attorney General's List of Subversive Organizations* (Lawrence: University of Kansas Press, 2008), 267; Greg Robinson, *Tragedy of Democracy: Japanese Confinement in North America* (New York: Columbia University Press, 2009), 290; and Allan Wesley Austin, "Loyalty and Concentration Camps in America: The Japanese American Precedent and the Internal Security Act of 1950," in *Last Witness: Reflections on the Wartime Internment of Japanese Americans*, edited by Erica Harth (New York: Palgrave, 2001), 259, 262–63.
51. Pitzer, "Dorothy McCullough Lee," 32–33; and Leeson, *Rose City Justice*, 146.
52. Stanford, *Portland Confidential*, 45, 49, 64, 66; Donnelly, *Dark Rose*, 107–8; J. D. Chandler and Theresa Griffin Kennedy, *Murder and Scandal in Prohibition Portland: Sex, Vice and Misdeeds in Mayor Baker's Reign* (Charleston, SC: The History Press, 2016) 139, 142; and

Douglas Perry, "Portland Police Waged 'Crime War' in 1947 with Roving Shotgun Squads, Bridge Blockades, But Violence Raged On," *Oregonian*, March 19, 2021.

53. Donnelly, *Dark Rose*, 2, 60; and Chandler and Fisher, *Portland on the Take*, 13–14. Zusman's club, the Desert Room, was known to bring together gangsters, politicians, and cops. Stanford, "The Rise and Fall of Big Jim Elkins," 337–38.
54. Quoted in Donnelly, *Dark Rose*, 62–63.
55. Donnelly, *Dark Rose*, 88–89; and Uris, "Trouble in River City," 122–23.
56. Stanford, *Portland Confidential*, 31, 41; Chandler and Fisher, *Portland on the Take*, 72; Donnelly, *Dark Rose*, 62; and Chandler and Kennedy, *Murder and Scandal in Prohibition Portland*, 138–9.
57. Streckert, *Storied and Scandalous Portland, Oregon*, 119–20.
58. Donnelly, *Dark Rose*, 81, 84, 114–17; and Stanford, *Portland Confidential*, 104.
59. Uris, "Trouble in River City," 71–74.
60. Donnelly, *Dark Rose*, 14, 79–80, 89–91, 97, 103, 133–34; and Uris, "Trouble in River City," 97, 113, 131, 159–64, 180.
61. Streckert, *Storied and Scandalous Portland, Oregon*, 121–23.
62. Donnelly, *Dark Rose*, 74, 100. *The Oregonian* favored Peterson, and its reporting focused on the Teamsters. The *Oregon Journal* backed Schrunk and focused its scrutiny on Elkins. Uris, "Trouble in River City," 54, 90, 173; and Stanford, "The Rise and Fall of Big Jim Elkins," 341.
63. Donnelly, *Dark Rose*, 130; and Heymann, *RFK*, 121.
64. James B. Jacobs, *Mobsters, Unions, and Feds: The Mafia and the American Labor Movement* (New York: New York University Press, 2006), 14; and Streckert, *Storied and Scandalous Portland, Oregon*, 126–27.
65. Donnelly, *Dark Rose*, 14, 132–38, 147; Uris, "Trouble in River City," 134–35; Stanford, *Portland Confidential*, 160; Lansing and Leeson, *Multnomah*, 100; and Heymann, *RFK*, 122. I am chiefly following Donnelly's assessment of Schrunk's involvement, as his book on the subject, *Dark Rose*, is the most thorough of the several I reviewed. Other authors were not so sure. Phil Stanford thought it was "probably right" that Schrunk was acquitted, though later he shrugged that "of course" Schrunk accepted bribes. Stanford, *Portland Confidential*, 176; and Phil Stanford, *Rose City Vice: Portland in the '70s—Dirty Cops and Dirty Robbers* (Port Townsend, Wash.: Feral House, 2017), 3. Joe Uris says simply, "Mayor Terry Schrunk's role in the Portland vice situation remains unclear." Uris, "Trouble in River City," 201. Police were divided as well, seemingly along departmental lines. "*Nobody* in the sheriff's office believed the charges," according to then-Deputy and later-Sheriff Don Clark, "whether or not they supported Schrunk politically. . . . Everyone at the sheriff's office was convinced it was a frame-up." Quoted in Lansing, *Portland*, 373. Clark further said that, after Schrunk put him in charge of pinball enforcement, "He didn't tell me where to go. . . . I was impressed that were weren't any off-limits places, everybody was subject to arrest." Quoted in "Oral History Interview with Don E. Clark" [transcription], interviews conducted by George M. Joseph, August 30, 1994–March 27, 1998, Archives West, SR1166, 99. In contrast, Portland Police Officer Dick Sutter, who testified to seeing Schrunk accept a payoff, described him as a "crooked son-of-a-bitch." Quoted in Donnelly, *Dark Rose*, 136.
66. Quoted in Donnelly, *Dark Rose*, 4.
67. Quoted in Donnelly, *Dark Rose*, 144.
68. Jacobs, *Mobsters, Unions, and Feds*, 119–20, 258; Chris Hedges, *Death of the Liberal Class* (New York: Nation Books, 2010), 107–8; Edwin O. Guthran and C. Richard Allen, eds., *RFK: His Words for Our Times* (New York: William Morrow, 2018), 48; Larry Tye, *Bobby*

Kennedy: The Making of a Liberal Icon (New York: Random House, 2016), 84; and Donnelly, *Dark Rose*, 142.

69. Heymann, *RFK*, 135.
70. Robert F. Kennedy, *The Pursuit of Justice*, edited by Theodore J. Lowi (New York: Harper & Row, 1964), 53.
71. Quoted in Tye, *Bobby Kennedy*, 83. Stone was both a critic and a target of the Red Scare. In the 1950s, J. Edgar Hoover placed him on the Security Index, to be immediately detained in event of a national emergency. FBI agents bugged his phone, searched his trash, opened his mail, and interviewed his friends, family, and colleagues. Over the course of his career, his file grew to more than five thousand pages. Ivan Greenberg, *Surveillance in America: Critical Analysis of the FBI, 1920 to the Present* (Lanham, MD: Lexington Books, 2014), 103; and Hedges, *Death of the Liberal Class*, 166.
72. Quoted in Frank Donner, *Protectors of Privilege: Red Squads and Police Repression in Urban America* (Berkeley: University of California Press, 1990), 72.
73. Guthran and Allen, eds., *RFK: His Words for Our Times*, 37–38; Tye, *Bobby Kennedy*, 34–53; and Heymann, *RFK*, 74.
74. Kennedy, *The Pursuit of Justice*, 141–46.
75. Donnelly, *Dark Rose*, 100, 150; Stanford, *Portland Confidential*, 160, 175; and Streckert, *Storied and Scandalous Portland, Oregon*, 127.
76. Donnelly, *Dark Rose*, 113, 116, 138; and Chandler and Fisher, *Portland on the Take*, 97. Quote from Donnelly, *Dark Rose*, 138.
77. Quoted in Donnelly, *Dark Rose*, 118.
78. Donnelly, *Dark Rose*, 139.
79. Stanford, *Portland Confidential*, 117, 120, 148, 159, 186–87; Donnelly, *Dark Rose*, 70–71, 115; and Uris, "Trouble in River City," 174–76. Quote from Donnelly, *Dark Rose*, 71.
80. Donnelly, *Dark Rose*, 146, 152, 156, 158; Stanford, *Portland Confidential*, 176–78; Lansing, *Portland*, 373; and Uris, "Trouble in River City," 226.
81. Uris, "Trouble in River City," 94–95.
82. Quoted in Donnelly, *Dark Rose*, 150–51.
83. Donnelly, *Dark Rose*, 156, 158; and Lansing, *Portland*, 373. Elkins never rebuilt his criminal empire, but the Teamsters continued to harass him and threaten his family. Officially, his death—which occurred in Arizona in 1968—would be deemed an auto accident, but one Portland police detective claims to have seen evidence that he was shot, and another denies that the body was even his. Donnelly, *Dark Rose*, 150, 159–61; Stanford, *Portland Confidential*, 187; and, Uris "Trouble in River City," 193.
84. Uris, "Trouble in River City," 183.
85. Donnelly, *Dark Rose*, 5.
86. Jacobs, *Mobsters, Unions, and Feds*, 257–58. Preoccupied with Communist conspiracies, the FBI largely neglected organized crime. When the bureau did eventually take up the issue of labor racketeering after the 1975 disappearance of Teamsters president Jimmy Hoffa, it focused entirely on union corruption and ignored management's role. Jacobs, *Mobsters, Unions, and Feds*, 10–12, 257.

Chapter 12: Unamerican, Antiwar, Counterculture

1. Matt Nelson and Bill Nygren, *Radicals in the Rose City: Portland's Revolutionaries 1960–1975* (Portland: Northwest History Press, 2013), 21, 280; and Michael Munk, *The Portland*

Red Guide: Sites and Stories of Our Radical Past (Portland: Ooligan Press, 2007), 138, 156–57. For context concerning the committee's investigations into higher education, see Walter Goodman, *The Committee: The Extraordinary Career of the House Committee on Un-American Activities* (New York: Farrar, Straus and Giroux, 1968), 325–32.

2. Ellen W. Schrecker, *No Ivory Tower; McCarthyism and the Universities* (New York: Oxford University Press, 1986), 236–37 (quote on 237.)
3. Quoted in Schrecker, *No Ivory Tower*, 239–40. Moore went on to teach at Barnard College, and in 1978 Reed passed a resolution expressing regret at his dismissal. Schrecker, *No Ivory Tower*, 288, 388.
4. Schrecker, *No Ivory Tower*, 240.
5. Schrecker, *No Ivory Tower*, 238, 269.
6. Nelson and Nygren, *Radicals in the Rose City*, 21.
7. Quoted in Douglas Perry, "Views on Street Scenes," in *Rose City Rising: Portland Memories III, the 1950s*, compiled by OregonLive and the *Oregonian* (n.p.: Pediment Publishing, 2018), 7.
8. Nelson and Nygren, *Radicals in the Rose City*, 14, 22–23, 26–27 (quotes from 23).
9. Chris Hedges, *Death of the Liberal Class* (New York: Nation Books, 2010), 106–7.
10. Leanne C. Serbulo and Karen J. Gibson, "Black and Blue: Police-Community Relations in Portland's Albina District, 1964–1985," *Oregon Historical Quarterly* 114, no. 1 (Spring 2013): 12.
11. Quoted in Polina Olsen, *Portland in the 1960s: Stories from the Counterculture* (Charleston, SC: The History Press, 2012), 102.
12. Olsen, *Portland in the 1960s*, 100–101.
13. Quoted in Olsen, *Portland in the 1960s*, 116.
14. Nelson and Nygren, *Radicals in the Rose City*, 278.
15. Serbulo and Gibson, "Black and Blue," 12.
16. Both quoted in Nelson and Nygren, *Radicals in the Rose City*, 52–53.
17. Quoted in Olsen, *Portland in the 1960s*, 102.
18. Quoted in Nelson and Nygren, *Radicals in the Rose City*, 42.
19. Nelson and Nygren, *Radicals in the Rose City*, 46–47.
20. Nelson and Nygren, *Radicals in the Rose City*, 53–4.
21. Quoted in Olsen, *Portland in the 1960s*, 102.
22. Nelson and Nygren, *Radicals in the Rose City*, 53–54.
23. Quoted in Nelson and Nygren, *Radicals in the Rose City*, 47.
24. Stephan Leflar, *A History of South Portland* (N.p: 2010) 177–78; Olsen, *Portland in the 1960s*, 16; and Carl Abbott, *Portland in Three Centuries: The Place and the People* (Corvallis: Oregon State University Press, 2011), 139. "Haight-Ashbury" quote from Ryan Tobias, "Cabarets, Social Clubs, Coffee Houses and Discos: How Liquor Laws Influence Local Music," in *Northwest Passage: 50 Years of Independent Music from the Rose City*, edited by Marc Moscato (Portland: Dill Pickle Club, [2010]), 15.
25. Abbott, *Portland in Three Centuries*, 139; Leflar, *A History of South Portland*, 177; Tobias, "Cabarets, Social Clubs, Coffee Houses and Discos,"15; and Jewel Lansing, *Portland: People, Politics, and Power* (Corvallis: Oregon State University Press, 2003), 387. Quote from Olsen, *Portland in the 1960s*, 17.
26. "A Paraphrase of a Lecture by Valerie Brown," in *Northwest Passage: 50 Years of Independent Music from the Rose City*, edited by Marc Moscato (Portland: Dill Pickle Club, [2010]), 39.
27. Lansing, *Portland*, 416.

28. Floyd J. McKay, *Reporting the Oregon Story: How Activists and Visionaries Transformed a State* (Corvallis: Oregon State University Press, 2016), 225–26.
29. Quoted in Olsen, *Portland in the 1960s*, 77.
30. Quoted in Olsen, *Portland in the 1960s*, 79.
31. Olsen, *Portland in the 1960s*, 25–26.
32. Penny Harrington, *Triumph of Spirit: An Autobiography* (Chicago: Brittany Publications, 1999), 37.
33. Howard Zinn, *A People's History of the United States, 1492–Present*, rev. ed. (New York: HarperCollins, 1995), 481.
34. Lansing, *Portland*, 387; and Brent Walth, *Fire at Eden's Gate: Tom McCall and the Oregon Story* (Portland: Oregon Historical Society Press, 1994), 284–85.
35. Quoted in Nelson and Nygren, *Radicals in the Rose City*, 126–27.
36. Nelson and Nygren, *Radicals in the Rose City*, 126; and Olsen, *Portland in the 1960s*, 109–10.
37. Quoted in Nelson and Nygren, *Radicals in the Rose City*, 135–36.
38. Quoted in Olsen, *Portland in the 1960s*, 109.
39. Nelson and Nygren, *Radicals in the Rose City*, 127; and Walth, *Fire at Eden's Gate*, 286.
40. Quoted in Nelson and Nygren, *Radicals in the Rose City*, 135–36.
41. Nelson and Nygren, *Radicals in the Rose City*, 127–28; and "Oregon in the 70s—Part I," in *Great and Minor Moments in Oregon History: An Illustrated Anthology of Illuminating Glimpses into Oregon's Past from Prehistory to Present*, edited by Dick Pintarich (Portland: New Oregon Publishers, 2008), 372; *Oregon Experience: Vortex I*, directed by Eric Cain et al. (Portland: Oregon Public Broadcasting and the Oregon Historical Society, 2010); and Joe Streckert, *Storied and Scandalous Portland, Oregon: A History of Gambling, Vice, Wits, and Wagers* (Guilford, CT: Globe Pequot, 2020), 134–35.
42. Nelson and Nygren, *Radicals in the Rose City*, 128.
43. Olsen, *Portland in the 1960s*, 111.
44. Nelson and Nygren, *Radicals in the Rose City*, 131, 144.
45. Walth, *Fire at Eden's Gate*, 286; and Streckert, *Storied and Scandalous Portland, Oregon*, 135.
46. Olsen, *Portland in the 1960s*, 112.
47. Quoted in Nelson and Nygren, *Radicals in the Rose City*, 63.
48. Olsen, *Portland in the 1960s*, 113.
49. Lansing, *Portland*, 388; *Oregon Experience: Vortex I*; and Walth, *Fire at Eden's Gate*, 286–87. Quote from Tom McCall and Steve Neal, *Tom McCall: Maverick* (Portland: Binford & Mort, 1977), 143.
50. Olsen, *Portland in the 1960s*, 113. To be fair, McCall insists that he only asked the activists "to reschedule" for a time when the Legion would not also be present. He did also ask Nixon to cancel, and the president's refusal led him to suspect that he *wanted* a confrontation to feed his "law and order" campaign narrative. McCall, *Tom McCall*, 133; and Walth, *Fire at Eden's Gate*, 290.
51. Abbott, *Portland in Three Centuries*, 142; and Walth, *Fire at Eden's Gate*, 290.
52. Quoted in *Oregon Experience: Vortex I*.
53. Quoted in Olsen, *Portland in the 1960s*, 117.
54. Quoted in *Oregon Experience: Vortex I*.
55. *Tom McCall*, directed by Eric Cain (Portland: Oregon Public Broadcasting and the Oregon Historical Society, 2013); Lansing, *Portland*, 388; Abbott, *Portland in Three Centuries*, 142; Walth, *Fire at Eden's Gate*, 291; and Streckert, *Storied and Scandalous Portland, Oregon*, 136. Westerdahl quoted in *Oregon Experience: Vortex I*; Ivancie quoted in Lansing, *Portland*, 388.
56. *Oregon Experience: Vortex I*; and Olsen, *Portland in the 1960s*, 118.

57. Quoted in Streckert, *Storied and Scandalous Portland, Oregon*, 139. Things were not so peaceful elsewhere in the country. In his memoirs, McCall offers a brief "survey of national violence during the week of Vortex": "In Madison, Wisconsin, a plastic bomb rocked the University of Wisconsin's Mathematics Research Center. The blast killed a graduate student and injured four others. In Minneapolis, a bomb damaged the Old Federal Office Building. At Harvard University a bomb was discovered in the John F. Kennedy School of Government. In Radford, Virginia, an army arsenal was rocked by an explosion that killed two people and injured four others. An American Legion headquarters was bombed in Seattle. A school was bombed in Rocky Mount, North Carolina. A journalist was killed in an East Los Angeles riot. Policemen were slain in Berkeley, Omaha, Chicago, and Philadelphia. And in Portland: one broken window." McCall, *Tom McCall*, 143.
58. Quoted in Olsen, *Portland in the 1960s*, 120.
59. Olsen, *Portland in the 1960s*, 117; and Walth, *Fire at Eden's Gate*, 300.
60. Quoted in Nelson and Nygren, *Radicals in the Rose City*, 72.
61. Quoted in *Oregon Experience: Vortex I.*
62. Quoted in Olsen, *Portland in the 1960s*, 120–21.
63. Walth, *Fire at Eden's Gate*, 302.
64. Walth, *Fire at Eden's Gate*, 287.
65. Nelson and Nygren, *Radicals in the Rose City*, 72–73. Peter Fornara, one PAJ organizer, explained, "We had heard that the Legion expected to bring twenty-five thousand people to Portland. . . . So we just doubled the number, made it up out of thin air. The number meant nothing. It wasn't real." Quoted in Walth, *Fire at Eden's Gate*, 288.
66. Abbott, *Portland in Three Centuries*, 142.
67. Quoted in Olsen, *Portland in the 1960s*, 120.

Chapter 13: An Occupying Army and Self-Defense

1. Joshua Joe Bryan, "Portland, Oregon's Long Hot Summers: Racial Unrest and Public Response, 1967–1969" (graduate thesis, Portland State University, 2013), 20–26; City of Portland Bureau of Planning, *History of Portland's African American Community* (Portland: Portland Bureau of Planning, 1993), 124–25; Leanne C. Serbulo and Karen J. Gibson, "Black and Blue: Police-Community Relations in Portland's Albina District, 1964–1985," *Oregon Historical Quarterly* 114, no. 1 (Spring 2013), 13; and Lucas N. N. Burke and Judson L. Jeffries, *The Portland Black Panthers: Empowering Albina and Remaking a City* (Seattle: University of Washington Press, 2016), 18.
2. Bryan, "Portland, Oregon's Long Hot Summers," 26–42; Burke and Jeffries, *The Portland Black Panthers*, 52–53; Julie Lorana Buhler, "The Civil Rights Movement in Portland, Oregon, 1955–1968" (honors thesis, University of Oregon, 1983), 33–35; and Don DuPay, *Behind the Badge in River City: A Portland Police Memoir*, 2nd ed. (Portland: Oregon Greystone Press, 2016), 167. "Whitey" quote from Burke and Jeffries, *The Portland Black Panthers*, 53; Schrunk quoted in Bryan, "Portland, Oregon's Long Hot Summers," 42.
3. *Portland Civil Rights: Lift Ev'ry Voice* (Portland: Oregon Public Broadcasting, 2015), DVD.
4. City Club of Portland, "The Negro in Portland: A Progress Report 1945–1957," (1957), 357–59.
5. Kenneth R. Coleman, *Dangerous Subjects: James D. Saules and the Rise of Black Exclusion in Oregon* (Corvallis: Oregon State University Press, 2017), 161. Statistics from Burke and Jeffries, *The Portland Black Panthers*, 28, 37.

6. Serbulo and Gibson, "Black and Blue," 17.
7. Quoted in Burke and Jeffries, *The Portland Black Panthers*, 13.
8. Quoted in Serbulo and Gibson, "Black and Blue," 13.
9. Bryan, "Portland, Oregon's Long Hot Summers," 18–19.
10. Serbulo and Gibson, "Black and Blue," 13.
11. Bureau of Planning, *History of Portland's African American Community*, 127; Bryan, "Portland, Oregon's Long Hot Summers," 47–49; Burke and Jeffries, *The Portland Black Panthers*, 189; and Buhler, "The Civil Rights Movement in Portland," 35–36.
12. Quoted in Serbulo and Gibson, "Black and Blue," 8.
13. Coleman, *Dangerous Subjects*, 161.
14. Bryan, "Portland, Oregon's Long Hot Summers," 54–55; Serbulo and Gibson, "Black and Blue," 15; and Charles Moose, "The Theory and Practice of Community Policing: An Evaluation of the Iris Court Demonstration Project" (PhD diss., Portland State University, 1993), 60–61.
15. Quoted in Moose, "The Theory and Practice of Community Policing," 60–61.
16. Quoted in Moose, "The Theory and Practice of Community Policing," 62.
17. Serbulo and Gibson, "Black and Blue," 17.
18. Burke and Jeffries, *The Portland Black Panthers*, 131; and Joe Biel, *The Enduring Legacy of Portland's Black Panthers: The Roots of Free Healthcare, Free Breakfast, and Neighborhood Control in Oregon* (Portland: Microcosm, 2023), 65.
19. Serbulo and Gibson, "Black and Blue," 12, 15–16.
20. Quoted in Serbulo and Gibson, "Black and Blue," 17.
21. Burke and Jeffries, *The Portland Black Panthers*, 195.
22. Bryan, "Portland, Oregon's Long Hot Summers," 92–95, 99–103. Burke and Jeffries, *The Portland Black Panthers*, 62–63; *Portland Civil Rights: Lift Ev'ry Voice*; and Biel, *Enduring Legacy*, 59. Quotes from Bryan, "Portland, Oregon's Long Hot Summers," 95 (Walker), 99 (Davis).
23. Bryan, "Portland, Oregon's Long Hot Summers," 105–7, 110.
24. Burke and Jeffries, *The Portland Black Panthers*, 75–76.
25. Quoted in Jules Boykoff and Martha Gies, "'We're Going to Defend Ourselves': The Portland Chapter of the Black Panther Party and the Local Media Response," *Oregon Historical Quarterly* 111, no. 3 (2010), 286.
26. Boykoff and Gies, "'We're Going to Defend Ourselves,'" 288–90; Burke and Jeffries, *The Portland Black Panthers*, 99–100; and Biel, *Enduring Legacy*, 70–78. Quote from Boykoff and Gies, "We're Going to Defend Ourselves," 289.
27. Quoted in Burke and Jeffries, *The Portland Black Panthers*, 85–86.
28. Quoted in Burke and Jeffries, *The Portland Black Panthers*, 134. "Pocket Lawyer" is reprinted in Matt Nelson and Bill Nygren, *Radicals in the Rose City: Portland's Revolutionaries 1960–1975* (Portland: Northwest History Press, 2013), 183.
29. Kent Ford later recalled, "When they stopped somebody, we pulled over. We asked . . . what they were stopped for, what they were charged with. And if they take them to jail, we'd say, 'Don't worry, we'll be right down to get you out.' That's the kind of stuff we did." *Arresting Power: Resisting Police Violence in Portland, Oregon*, directed by Jodi Darby et al. (Portland: Collective Eye, 2015), DVD.
30. Sarah Mirk and Khris Soden, *Portland's Black Panthers* ([Portland]: Dill Pickle Club, [2011]) unpaged; Biel, *Enduring Legacy*, 82; and Lee P. Brown, *Policing in the 21st Century: Community Policing* (Bloomington, Ind.: AuthorHouse, 2012), 343.
31. Burke and Jeffries, *The Portland Black Panthers*, 149, 170.

32. Biel, *Enduring Legacy*, 108; and Burke and Jeffries, *The Portland Black Panthers*, 172 (quote).
33. Quoted in Burke and Jeffries, *The Portland Black Panthers*, 170.
34. Burke and Jeffries, *The Portland Black Panthers*, 74, 219. Even before the group's founding, Kent Ford had come under suspicion. After he reported a burglary at his home in 1967, the responding cops filed a report on a "Possible Subversive Subject," noting "two large poster size pictures of Ho Chi Minh, Presidency [*sic*] of North Viet Nam, and the other of Mao, the Premier of Community [*sic*] China," as well as "numerous pamphlets and literature which appeared to be concerning Black Power and this sort of thing." Quoted in Burke and Jeffries, *The Portland Black Panthers*, 66.
35. Quoted in Burke and Jeffries, *The Portland Black Panthers*, 149.
36. Avel Louise Gordly and Patricia A. Schechter, *Remembering the Power of Words: The Life of an Oregon Activist, Legislator, and Community Leader* (Corvallis: Oregon State University Press, 2011), 69.
37. Quoted in Ben Jacklet, "A Legacy of Suspicion," *Portland Tribune*, September 20, 2002.
38. Ben Jacklet, "The Secret Watchers," *Portland Tribune*, September 13, 2002; Ben Jacklet, "'It Should Be Noted,'" *Portland Tribune*, September 17, 2002; and Ben Jacklet, "In Case You Were Wondering," *Portland Tribune*, September 27, 2002. See also Nelson and Nygren, *Radicals in the Rose City*, 278–80. Quote is from Jacklet, "The Secret Watchers." The *Tribune's* five-part exposé is available at http://www.portlandtribune.com/.
39. Jacklet, "The Secret Watchers"; Jacklet, "'It Should Be Noted'"; and Jacklet, "A Legacy of Suspicion."
40. Quoted in American Friends Service Committee Program on Government Surveillance and Citizens' Rights, *The Police Threat to Political Liberty: Discoveries and Actions of the American Friends Service Committee Program on Government Surveillance and Citizens' Rights* (Philadelphia: American Friends Service Committee, 1979), 27.
41. Frank Donner, *Protectors of Privilege: Red Squads and Police Repression in Urban America* (Berkeley: University of California Press, 1990), 357.
42. Donner, *Protectors of Privilege*, 286–67.
43. Jacklet, "'It Should Be Noted.'"
44. Aaron J. Leonard with Conor A. Gallagher, *Heavy Radicals: The FBI's Secret War on America's Maoists: The Revolutionary Union/Revolutionary Communist Party, 1968–1980*, rev. ed. (Winchester, UK: Zero Books, 2022), 240.
45. Jacklet, "In Case You Were Wondering." On Posse Comitatus, see Spencer Sunshine, et al., *Up in Arms: A Guide to Oregon's Patriot Movement* (Scappoose, OR: Rural Organizing Project, and Somerville, MA: Political Research Associates, 2016), 15.
46. Quoted in Jacklet, "The Secret Watchers."
47. Quoted in Jacklet, "'It Should Be Noted.'"
48. Quoted in Burke and Jeffries, *The Portland Black Panthers*, 169. Nationwide, twenty-eight Panthers were killed by law enforcement. Ivan Greenberg, *The Dangers of Dissent: The FBI and Civil Liberties Since 1965* (Lanham, MD: Lexington Books, 2013), 40. For an overview of COINTELPRO, see Ward Churchill and Jim Vander Wall, *The COINTELPRO Papers: Documents from the FBI's Secret Wars Against Domestic Dissent* (Boston: South End Press, 1990).
49. Burke and Jeffries, *The Portland Black Panthers*, 165–66; and Boykoff and Gies, "We're Going to Defend Ourselves," 290.
50. Ward Churchill, "'To Disrupt, Discredit, and Destroy': The FBI's Secret War Against the Black Panther Party," in *Liberation, Imagination, and the Black Panther Party: A New Look at the Panthers and Their Legacy*, edited by Kathleen Cleaver and George Katsiaficas (New York: Routledge, 2001), 87–89; Burke and Jeffries, *The Portland Black Panthers*, 124–25,

171–72; Biel, *Enduring Legacy*, 94–95; *Portland Civil Rights: Lift Ev'ry Voice*; and Mirk and Soden, *Portland's Black Panthers*, unpaged.

51. Biel, *Enduring Legacy*, 126.
52. Quoted in Burke and Jeffries, *The Portland Black Panthers*, 126.
53. Quoted in Burke and Jeffries, *The Portland Black Panthers*, 216.
54. Quoted in Joshua Bloom and Waldo E. Martin Jr., *Black Against Empire: The History and Politics of the Black Panther Party* (Berkeley: University of California Press, 2013), 177.
55. Quoted in Serbulo and Gibson, "Black and Blue," 17. See also Biel, *Enduring Legacy*, 66–67.
56. Serbulo and Gibson, "Black and Blue," 17.
57. Biel, *Enduring Legacy*, 67.
58. Serbulo and Gibson, "Black and Blue," 18.
59. Reproduced in Fedor Zarkhin, "The Forgotten Four, Part Three: The House on Genenbein," oregonlive.com, October 19, 2023.
60. Fedor Zarkhin, "The Forgotten Four, Part Two: 44 Days," oregonlive.com, October 18, 2023.
61. All quotes from Zarkhin, "The Forgotten Four, Part Two: 44 Days."
62. Zarkhin, "The Forgotten Four, Part Two: 44 Days."
63. Fedor Zarkhin, "The Forgotten Four, Part One: The Teenager and the Cop," oregonlive.com, October 16, 2023; Zarkhin, "The Forgotten Four, Part Three: The House on Genenbein"; and Fedor Zarkhin, "The Forgotten Four, Part Four: 'They Always Find Them Not Guilty,'" oregonlive.com, October 20, 2023.

    The shooting took a toll on Sanford. He developed a stutter, had trouble sleeping, drank heavily, and by 1976 his wife had left him. He was given a desk assignment running background checks. A year later he briefly returned to patrol, but in August 1977 he was suspended for an off-duty incident. "At great discredit to the bureau," Commissioner Charles Jordan wrote in his reprimand, "you allowed yourself to become intoxicated to the extent that . . . you had to be physically subdued by fellow on-duty officers." After receiving a diagnosis of trauma-induced depression, Sanford resigned. What followed were a string of drunk-driving convictions and, according to a 2005 psychological evaluation, "flashbacks, intrusive memories, crying spells, some nightmares, chronic problems with depression, and panic attacks." Zarkhin, "The Forgotten Four, Part Four: 'They Always Find Them Not Guilty.'"
64. Zarkhin, "The Forgotten Four, Part Three: The House on Genenbein."
65. Serbulo and Gibson, "Black and Blue," 20.
66. Quoted in Zarkhin, "The Forgotten Four, Part Four: 'They Always Find Them Not Guilty.'"
67. Zarkhin, "The Forgotten Four, Part Three: The House on Genenbein."
68. Zarkhin, "The Forgotten Four, Part Four: 'They Always Find Them Not Guilty'"; Serbulo and Gibson, "Black and Blue," 18; *Portland Civil Rights: Lift Ev'ry Voice*; and Burke and Jeffries, *The Portland Black Panthers*, 200–202. Quote from Zarkhin, "The Forgotten Four, Part Four: 'They Always Find Them Not Guilty.'"
69. Quoted in Zarkhin, "The Forgotten Four, Part Three: The House on Genenbein."

Chapter 14: Full-Service Problem-Solvers

1. John Gordon King, "The History of the Office of Multnomah County Sheriff; Multnomah County, Oregon" (undergraduate thesis, Lewis and Clark College, 1965), 82; and "Oral History Interview with Don E. Clark [transcription]," interviews conducted by George M. Joseph, August 30, 1994–March 27, 1998, Archives West, SR1166, 125.

2. King, *The History of the Office of Multnomah County Sheriff*, 84–87; "Oral History Interview with Don E. Clark," 129; and J. B. Fisher, *Echo of Distant Water: The 1958 Disappearance of Portland's Martin Family* (Walterville, OR: TrineDay, 2019), 137.
3. "Oral History Interview with Don E. Clark," 96, 126–28, 185.
4. "Oral History Interview with Don E. Clark," 126.
5. "Oral History Interview with Don E. Clark," 61.
6. "Oral History Interview with Don E. Clark," 119–21.
7. "Oral History Interview with Don E. Clark," 130.
8. Jewel Lansing and Fred Leeson, *Multnomah: The Tumultuous Story of Oregon's Most Populous County* (Corvallis: Oregon State University Press, 2012) 124–25; and "Oral History Interview with Don E. Clark," 135, 143, 148.
9. Quoted in Lansing and Leeson, *Multnomah*, 124–25.
10. "Oral History Interview with Don E. Clark," 365, 381.
11. "Oral History Interview with Don E. Clark," 277.
12. "Oral History Interview with Don E. Clark," 359–60.
13. "Oral History Interview with Don E. Clark," 250–51. On the events in Selma, see Howard Zinn, "Selma, Alabama," in *You Can't Be Neutral on a Moving Train: A Personal History of Our Time* (Boston: Beacon Press, 2018), 56–68.
14. Quoted in Dean S. Smith et al., *Columbia Villa Community Services Project: A Model for a Troubled Time* (Portland: Housing Authority of Portland, 1992), 41.
15. "Oral History Interview with Don E. Clark," 121, 187–89, 197, 210, 228, 231–32.
16. Quoted in King, *The History of the Office of Multnomah County Sheriff*, 68–69.
17. King, *The History of the Office of Multnomah County Sheriff*, 35; and "Oral History Interview with Don E. Clark," 197.
18. "Oral History Interview with Don E. Clark," 313.
19. "Oral History Interview with Don E. Clark," 190–92, 279, 314.
20. "Oral History Interview with Don E. Clark," 107–8.
21. "Oral History Interview with Don E. Clark," 315–16.
22. "Oral History Interview with Don E. Clark," 238–39.
23. "Oral History Interview with Don E. Clark," 110; and Lee P. Brown, "The Changing Role of the County Sheriff," in *Neighborhood Team Policing: The Multnomah County Experience*, edited by Lee P. Brown ([Portland]:[Multnomah County Sheriff's Office], 1976), 4.
24. "Oral History Interview with Don E. Clark," 301.
25. "Oral History Interview with Don E. Clark," 299–307, 312.
26. "Oral History Interview with Don E. Clark," 317.
27. "Oral History Interview with Don E. Clark," 199–200.
28. Lansing and Leeson, *Multnomah*, 125.
29. "Oral History Interview with Don E. Clark," 200.
30. "Oral History Interview with Don E. Clark," 230.
31. "Oral History Interview with Don E. Clark," 345, 354.
32. Don DuPay, *Behind the Badge in River City: A Portland Police Memoir*, 2nd ed. (Portland: Oregon Greystone Press, 2016), 11.
33. DuPay, *Behind the Badge*, 5.
34. DuPay, *Behind the Badge*, 234–35.
35. Don DuPay, "Integrity in Policing Yesterday and Today," salem-news.com, May 5, 2013.
36. Quoted in DuPay, *Behind the Badge*, 95–96.
37. DuPay, *Behind the Badge*, 114, 148, 191–94; and DuPay, "Integrity in Policing."
38. DuPay, *Behind the Badge*, 308.

Chapter 15: New Leadership, Civic Engagement

1. "Oral History Interview with Don E. Clark" [transcription], interviews conducted by George M. Joseph, August 30, 1994–March 27, 1998, Archives West, SR1166, 341–344; and Lee P. Brown and Joseph Green Bishop, *Outhouse to the White House* (Bloomington, Ind.: AuthorHouse, 2022), 60. Quote from "Oral History Interview with Don E. Clark," 345.
2. Quoted in Avel Louise Gordly and Patricia A. Schechter, *Remembering the Power of Words: The Life of an Oregon Activist, Legislator, and Community Leader* (Corvallis: Oregon State University Press, 2011), 71.
3. Brown, *Outhouse to the White House,* 38–39, 42, 54, 57–58.
4. Quoted in Brown, *Outhouse to the White House,* 61.
5. Lee P. Brown, *Policing in the 21st Century: Community Policing* (Bloomington, Ind.: AuthorHouse, 2012), xvii, 321–22; and Brown, *Outhouse to the White House,* 48, 62, 65–67.
6. Jewel Lansing and Fred Leeson, *Multnomah: The Tumultuous Story of Oregon's Most Populous County* (Corvallis: Oregon State University Press, 2012), 149–50; Brown, *Policing in the 21st Century,* xvii, 321–22; and Brown, *Outhouse to the White House,* 86.
7. Brown, *Outhouse to the White House,* 90.
8. "Oral History Interview with Don E. Clark," 212.
9. Four years later, the court complicated the standard, to include "the severity of the crimes at issue, whether the suspect poses an immediate threat to the safety of the officers or others, and whether he is actively resisting arrest . . . or attempting to evade arrest by flight." Both quoted in Joanna Schwartz, *Shielded: How the Police Became Untouchable* ([New York]: Viking, 2023), 63.
10. Lee P. Brown, "The Changing Role of the County Sheriff," in *Neighborhood Team Policing: The Multnomah County Experience* ([Portland: Multnomah County Sheriff's Office], 1976), 5–6; Lee P. Brown and Edgar E. Martin, "Neighborhood Team Policing: A Viable Concept," in *Neighborhood Team Policing: The Multnomah County Experience* ([Portland: Multnomah County Sheriff's Office], 1976), 15; Lee P. Brown, "Team Policing: Community Involvement under Neighborhood Team Policing," in *Neighborhood Team Policing: The Multnomah County Experience* ([Portland: Multnomah County Sheriff's Office], 1976), 95–96; Robert Kauffman, "The Generalist Investigator: A New Role for the Patrol Officer under Neighborhood Team Policing," in *Neighborhood Team Policing: The Multnomah County Experience* ([Portland: Multnomah County Sheriff's Office], 1976), 44; Dennis Brand and John M. Koroloff, "Management of Criminal Investigation," in *Neighborhood Team Policing: The Multnomah County Experience* ([Portland: Multnomah County Sheriff 's Office], 1976), 50; Harold Amidon and Gary Strudler, "Neighborhood Team Policing: The Role of the Detective Team," in *Neighborhood Team Policing: The Multnomah County Experience* ([Portland: Multnomah County Sheriff's Office], 1976), 56; and Brown, *Policing in the 21st Century,* 132. Team policing was the innovation of James McConnach, chief constable in Aberdeen, Scotland, in 1948. He arrived at the idea by drawing on his experience in the military, where units often have to act without centralized direction. Brown, *Policing in the 21st Century,* 131.
11. Lee P. Brown, "Neighborhood Team Policing and Management by Objectives," in *Neighborhood Team Policing: The Multnomah County Experience* ([Portland: Multnomah County Sheriff's Office], 1976), 66.
12. Brown and Martin, "Neighborhood Team Policing: A Viable Concept," 15.
13. Brown, "The Changing Role of the County Sheriff," 6.
14. Brown, "The Changing Role of the County Sheriff," 5.

15. "Oral History Interview with Don E. Clark," 456–70.
16. Robert D. Putnam et al., *Better Together: Restoring the American Community* (New York: Simon & Schuster, 2003), 241, 247; and, Mathew Witt, "Dialectics of Control: The Origins and Evolution of Conflict in Portland's Neighborhood Association Program," in *The Portland Edge: Challenges and Successes in Growing Communities*, edited by Connie P. Ozawa (Washington, D.C.: Island Press, 2004), 85. Quote from Putnam, *Better Together*, 247.
17. Carl Abbott, *Portland in Three Centuries: The Place and the People* (Corvallis: Oregon State University Press, 2011), 148–49.
18. Putnam, *Better Together*, 241.
19. Putnam, *Better Together*, 241–44.
20. Abbott, *Portland in Three Centuries*, 146; and Putnam, *Better Together*, 247.
21. Lucas N. N. Burke and Judson L. Jeffries, *The Portland Black Panthers: Empowering Albina and Remaking a City* (Seattle: University of Washington Press, 2016), 186.
22. Floyd J. McKay, *Reporting the Oregon Story: How Activists and Visionaries Transformed a State* (Corvallis: Oregon State University Press, 2016), 217.
23. Phil Stanford, *Rose City Vice: Portland in the '70s—Dirty Cops and Dirty Robbers* (Port Townsend, Wash.: Feral House, 2017), 12–13.
24. Phil Stanford, *The Peyton-Allan Files* (Portland: Ptown Books, 2010), 98–111; and Stanford, *Rose City Vice*, 13, 67. The men convicted of the murders were sentenced to twenty-five years to life, but both had been released on parole by 1977. Even in prison, it was widely understood—by inmates and staff alike—that they had been set up, and they were granted special privileges accordingly. Stanford, *The Peyton-Allan Files*, 171.
25. Stanford, *Rose City Vice*, 13.
26. Stanford, *Rose City Vice*, 13.
27. Stanford, *The Peyton-Allan Files*, 170.
28. Stanford, *Rose City Vice*, 17. Michael Schrunk always insisted that the charges against his father had been "trumped up." But then, the younger Schrunk had made his career (in the words of Phil Stanford) by "sweeping accusations against police and other public officials . . . under the rug." Stanford, *Rose City Vice*, 84.
29. Stanford, *Rose City Vice*, 17–18.
30. Don DuPay, *Behind the Badge in River City: A Portland Police Memoir*, 2nd ed. (Portland: Oregon Greystone Press, 2016), 8–11, 94, 99–101.
31. DuPay, *Behind the Badge*, 95–97. Punctuation in quotation altered for clarity. By the time he left the vice squad, Don DuPay worried that drinking was affecting his judgment, sometimes leading to unnecessary violence. He disliked lying and hated the feeling of hypocrisy inherent to the work. He increasingly felt "trapping gay people and trapping prostitutes [was] wrong," saying that "any law that interferes with the sexual activities of consenting adults, whatever their sexual persuasion, is bullshit and unconscionable." In the case of sex workers, he felt it was likely counterproductive as well. "Prostitutes need social services, not arrest." DuPay, *Behind the Badge*, 101–2, 109, 113, 346.

    DuPay later managed a homeless shelter for Transition Projects and became an advocate for medical marijuana. After Oregon legalized the drug for medical purposes, his home was raided by the DEA. No charges were filed. Douglas Perry, "The Detective Who Knew Too Much: Don DuPay's Portland Police Career Haunts Him. He's Still Trying to Get Justice," oregonlive.com, September 5, 2021; and Stanford, *Rose City Vice*, 91n27.
32. Stanford, *Rose City Vice*, 26–28; and Douglas Perry, "Sex, Drugs and Police Corruption in Portland: How the Wild 1970s Paved the Way to the City's Future," oregonlive.com, July 1, 2019. Quotes from Stanford, *Rose City Vice*, 26.

33. Stanford, *Rose City Vice*, 17–18.
34. Stanford, *Rose City Vice*, 18–19; Burke and Jeffries, *The Portland Black Panthers*, 187–88; and Putnam, *Better Together*, 247.
35. K. C. Cowan et al., *Portland: The Riches of a City* (Portland: Portland Metropolitan Chamber of Commerce, 1998), 33.
36. R. Bruce Stephenson, *Portland's Good Life: Sustainability and Hope in an American City* (Lanham, MD: Lexington Books, 2021), 37. For more on the downtown plan, see Carl Abbott, "Centers and Edge: Reshaping Downtown Portland," in *The Portland Edge: Challenges and Successes in Growing Communities*, edited by Connie P. Ozawa (Washington, D.C.: Island Press, 2004).
37. Cowan, *Portland*, 36.
38. Quoted in Burke and Jeffries, *The Portland Black Panthers*, 194.
39. Loren W. Christensen, introduction to *Skid Row Beat: A Street Cop's Walk on the Wild Side* (Boulder, Colo.: Paladin Press, 1999), 3.
40. Loren W. Christensen, "Halloween," in *Skid Row Beat: A Street Cop's Walk on the Wild Side* (Boulder, Colo.: Paladin Press, 1999), 168.
41. "Oral History Interview with Don E. Clark," 716.
42. "Oral History Interview with Don E. Clark," 294.
43. "Oral History Interview with Don E. Clark," 285 (quotes), 294.
44. "Oral History Interview with Don E. Clark," 474–75.
45. DuPay, *Behind the Badge*, 325.
46. "Oral History Interview with Don E. Clark," 823–24; 828–29.
47. Lansing and Leeson, *Multnomah*, 139; and Lindsay Nadrich, "Central City Concern Closes Portland Sobering Station," kgw.com, January 8, 2020.
48. Quoted in Loren W. Christensen, "Fun with Prisoners," in *Skid Row Beat: A Street Cop's Walk on the Wild Side* (Boulder, Colo.: Paladin Press, 1999), 37. The Hooper sobering station was closed in January 2020, purportedly owing to safety concerns. Nadrich, "Central City Concern Closes Portland Sobering Station."
49. Loren W. Christensen, "Just Sittin' in the Sun," in *Skid Row Beat: A Street Cop's Walk on the Wild Side* (Boulder, Colo.: Paladin Press, 1999), 56–57.
50. Charles Moose, "The Theory and Practice of Community Policing: An Evaluation of the Iris Court Demonstration Project" (PhD diss., Portland State University, 1993), 63–64; Stanford, *Rose City Vice*, 18–19; and Burke and Jeffries, *The Portland Black Panthers*, 195–96.
51. Charles A. Moose and Charles Fleming, *Three Weeks in October: The Manhunt for the Serial Sniper* (New York: Dutton, 2003), 94.
52. Stanford, *Rose City Vice*, 43–45; and Perry, "Sex, Drugs and Police Corruption." On Director's role in the gay community, see "Sanford Director, Portland's Gay Mayor," Gay and Lesbian Archives of the Pacific Northwest, https://www.glapn.org/6475SanfordDirector.html, 2014.
53. Stanford, *Rose City Vice*, 10, 48–50.
54. Stanford, *Rose City Vice*, 51–52, 68–69.
55. Stanford, *Rose City Vice*, 52–53; McKay, *Reporting the Oregon Story*, 245; and "Victims," *Murder in Oregon*, podcast, December 25, 2019, iheart.com. "He'd pick me up . . . in a black car," she later recalled. "He always had a driver." Quoted in Margie Boulé, "Neil Goldschmidt's Sex-Abuse Victim Tells of the Relationship that Damaged Her Life," oregonlive.com, February 1, 2011.
56. Stanford, *Rose City Vice*, 52–53; Boulé, "Neil Goldschmidt's Sex-Abuse Victim"; "Victims," *Murder in Oregon*; and McKay, *Reporting the Oregon Story*, 245. Quote from "Victims."

Other sources, such as *Willamette Week*, say that she was fourteen. Goldschmidt himself contends that she was fifteen. In any case, the age of consent was sixteen. Nigel Jaquiss, "The 30-Year Secret: A Crime, a Cover-Up and the Way It Shaped Oregon," *Willamette Week*, May 11, 2004; and Boulé, "Neil Goldschmidt's Sex-Abuse Victim."

57. Boulé, "Neil Goldschmidt's Sex-Abuse Victim"; Jaquiss, "The 30-Year Secret"; "Victims," *Murder in Oregon*; Nigel Jaquiss, "Who Knew," *Willamette Week*, December 14, 2004; and Stanford, *Rose City Vice*, 85. Quote from Jaquiss, "The 30-Year Secret."
58. Quoted in "Victims," *Murder in Oregon*.
59. "Victims," *Murder in Oregon*.

Chapter 16: Collective Bargaining and Affirmative Action

1. Penny Harrington, *Triumph of Spirit: An Autobiography* (Chicago: Brittany Publications, 1999), 44.
2. Susan G. Hauser, *Pickets, Pistols and Politics: A History of the Portland Police Association* (Portland: Portland Police Association, 1996), 50–51; and Harrington, *Triumph of Spirit*, 44.
3. Hauser, *Pickets, Pistols and Politics*, 74–75.
4. Harrington, *Triumph of Spirit*, 48–49, 66.
5. Hauser, *Pickets, Pistols and Politics*, 67.
6. Hauser, *Pickets, Pistols and Politics*, 3–4.
7. Hauser, *Pickets, Pistols and Politics*, 71–72.
8. Hauser, *Pickets, Pistols and Politics*, 72. The Multnomah County sheriff's deputies left AFSCME in 1959 and affiliated with the AFL-CIO's Policeman's Union Local 117. John Gordon King, "The History of the Office of Multnomah County Sheriff; Multnomah County, Oregon" (undergraduate thesis, Lewis and Clark College, 1965), 36.
9. Hauser, *Pickets, Pistols and Politics*, 73. On Cassese and the review board, see William J. Bopp, "The New York City Referendum on Civilian Review," in *The Police Rebellion* (Springfield, Ill.: Charles C. Thomas, 1971), 119–33; Jerome H. Skolnick, *Politics of Protest: Violent Aspects of Protest and Confrontation* (Washington, D.C.: Government Printing Office, 1969), 209; and Algernon D. Black, *The People and the Police* (New York: McGraw-Hill, 1968), 210–11.
10. Hauser, *Pickets, Pistols and Politics*, 73.
11. Hauser, *Pickets, Pistols and Politics*, 135–6.
12. Hauser, *Pickets, Pistols and Politics*, 141.
13. Hauser, *Pickets, Pistols and Politics*, 82.
14. Harrington, *Triumph of Spirit*, 195.
15. Quoted in Hauser, *Pickets, Pistols and Politics*, 93.
16. Leanne C. Serbulo and Karen J. Gibson, "Black and Blue: Police-Community Relations in Portland's Albina District, 1964–1985," *Oregon Historical Quarterly* 114, no. 1 (Spring 2013): 21.
17. "Portland Policeman Files $2.5 Million Libel Suit," *Oregon Journal*, July 5, 1981; "Newspaper Sued," *Oregonian*, July 15, 1981; and Serbulo and Gibson, "Black and Blue," 21.
18. Hauser, *Pickets, Pistols and Politics*, 90, 94.
19. Quoted in Hauser, *Pickets, Pistols and Politics*, 86. This was one of his favorite tactics. Mayor Bud Clark later recalled their first meeting: "The first thing Stan Peters did was reach around behind him, pull out his gun from underneath his shirt, and put in on the table between us. . . . And I think he did it any time I ever met with him." Quoted in Nigel Jaquiss and Tess Riski, "For Nearly 80 Years, the Portland Police Association Has

Wielded Power in a Town That Doesn't Like Cops. That Power Is Now Under Siege," *Willamette Week*, June 24, 2020.

20. Hauser, *Pickets, Pistols and Politics*, 53–54.
21. Phil Stanford, *Rose City Vice: Portland in the '70s—Dirty Cops and Dirty Robbers* (Port Townsend, Wash.: Feral House, 2017), 55. In the late seventies, a regular snitch—a biker called Animal, a member of the Gypsy Jokers—told his handler that he was regularly delivering cocaine to the mayor's residence. Neil Van Horn, the federal agent who took this report, was initially skeptical, but Animal offered a detailed description of the building's interior. Stanford, *Rose City Vice*, 55.
22. Stanford, *Rose City Vice*, 52–53; Ben Jacklet, "A Legacy of Suspicion," *Portland Tribune*, September 20, 2002; and Margie Boulé, "Neil Goldschmidt's Sex-Abuse Victim Tells of the Relationship That Damaged Her Life," oregonlive.com, February 1, 2011.
23. Cara Rabe-Hemp, *Thriving in an All-Boys Club: Female Police and Their Fight for Equality* (Lanham, MD: Rowman & Littlefield, 2018), 14–15; Harrington, *Triumph of Spirit*, 27; and Ivonne Roman, "A Police Pioneer on Her Unfinished Business," themarshallproject.org, September 5, 2018.
24. Harrington, *Triumph of Spirit*, 26.
25. Quoted in Don DuPay, *Behind the Badge in River City: A Portland Police Memoir*, 2nd ed. (Portland: Oregon Greystone Press, 2016), 217. Similar controversies were alive in police agencies across the country. However, of nine major studies conducted throughout the 1970s, eight concluded that "the sexes were equally capable" of police work. The outlier was a study commissioned by the Philadelphia Police Department as part of its defense against a discrimination case. (The judge rejected its findings.) Broadly equal competence, however, does not imply that the studies found no differences. "Women weren't as good with firearms and had more accidents. Women had higher attrition rates and more costly injuries. Women made fewer arrests and traffic stops and issued fewer citations. Women's partners made more decisions and gave more instructions out in the field and did more necessary strenuous activity. On the other hand, women had a less aggressive style of policing and were viewed more favorably by the public. Women were less frequently charged with serious misconduct, they received fewer citizen complaints, and they met with less resistance." Patricia W. Lunneborg, *Women Police Officers: Current Career Profile* (Springfield, Ill.: Charles C. Thomas, 1989), 21–24.
26. Harrington, *Triumph of Spirit*, 62.
27. Rabe-Hemp, *Thriving in an All-Boys Club*, 15.
28. Harrington, *Triumph of Spirit*, 52–53, 68, 119–20, 138.
29. Quoted in Roman, "A Police Pioneer on Her Unfinished Business."
30. Quoted in DuPay, *Behind the Badge*, 216.
31. Quoted in Roman, "A Police Pioneer on Her Unfinished Business."
32. Roman, "A Police Pioneer on Her Unfinished Business."
33. Quoted in DuPay, *Behind the Badge*, 218.
34. All quoted in Harrington, *Triumph of Spirit*, 83–84.
35. Quoted in Harrington, *Triumph of Spirit*, 144. There is some empirical evidence that female officers "used less force . . . than male officers." Additionally, the Bureau of Justice Statistics calculates that 98 percent of officers who shoot civilians are men. Rabe-Hemp, *Thriving in an All-Boys Club*, 124–25, 129, 158.
36. Harrington, *Triumph of Spirit*, 84.
37. Hauser, *Pickets, Pistols and Politics*, 95–96. Quote from Harrington, *Triumph of Spirit*, 113. Orazetti and Ledyar's reply appears at Harrington, *Triumph of Spirit*, 114.

38. Harrington, *Triumph of Spirit*, 77–78.
39. Lee P. Brown and Joseph Green Bishop, *Outhouse to the White House* (Bloomington, Ind.: AuthorHouse, 2022), 88–89; and Floyd J. McKay, *Reporting the Oregon Story: How Activists and Visionaries Transformed a State* (Corvallis: Oregon State University Press, 2016), 224.
40. Harrington, *Triumph of Spirit*, 146–47.
41. Serbulo and Gibson, "Black and Blue," 22.
42. Quoted in Serbulo and Gibson, "Black and Blue," 20.
43. Quoted in Hauser, *Pickets, Pistols and Politics*, 93.
44. Serbulo and Gibson, "Black and Blue," 19. Quote from Fedor Zarkhin, "The Forgotten Four, Part Three: The House on Genenbein," oregonlive.com, October 19, 2023.
45. Both quoted in Serbulo and Gibson, "Black and Blue," 19.
46. Quoted in *Portland Civil Rights: Lift Ev'ry Voice* (Portland: Oregon Public Broadcasting, 2015), DVD.
47. Quoted in Serbulo and Gibson, "Black and Blue," 20.
48. Charles A. Moose and Charles Fleming, *Three Weeks in October: The Manhunt for the Serial Sniper* (New York: Dutton, 2003), 150.
49. Hauser, *Pickets, Pistols and Politics*, 96.

Chapter 17: Drugs and Motorcycles

1. Charles A. Moose and Charles Fleming, *Three Weeks in October: The Manhunt for the Serial Sniper* (New York: Dutton, 2003), 140; and Phil Stanford, *Rose City Vice: Portland in the '70s—Dirty Cops and Dirty Robbers* (Port Townsend, Was.: Feral House, 2017), 44. Don DuPay, a former vice cop, agreed: "All this drug money went straight to the top." Quoted in Douglas Perry, "Sex, Drugs and Police Corruption in Portland: How the Wild 1970s Paved the Way to the City's Future," oregonlive.com, July 1, 2019.
2. Moose and Fleming, *Three Weeks in October*, 95–96, 137–40.
3. David Whitney, "Police Misconduct: Complaints Triggered Probe," *Sunday Oregonian*, May 31, 1981; and Stanford, *Rose City Vice*, 56–57.
4. Stanford, *Rose City Vice*, 40. When a member of the Free Souls threatened a state trooper, the cop went to meet with the club president. "He told me that the Free Souls had worked the guy over after he got out of jail—they did not want trouble from the cops." Mike Davis, *Hunting Men: The Career of an Oregon State Police Detective* (Bloomington, Ind.: Abbott Press, 2014), 19.
5. J. D. Chandler, *Portland Rogues Gallery: A Baker's Dozen Arresting Criminals from Portland's History* (n.p.: America Through Time, 2021), 130.
6. Stanford, *Rose City Vice*, 38–39.
7. Don DuPay, *Behind the Badge in River City: A Portland Police Memoir*, 2nd ed. (Portland: Oregon Greystone Press, 2016), 346. Mike Davis, a retired detective with the Oregon State Police, disagrees, claiming that while he was undercover, he never used drugs himself. Davis, *Hunting Men*, 58, 104.
8. Moose and Fleming, *Three Weeks in October*, 96.
9. Penny Harrington, *Triumph of Spirit: An Autobiography* (Chicago: Brittany Publications, 1999), 158.
10. Stanford, *Rose City Vice*, 36, 39.
11. Stanford, *Rose City Vice*, 63–64; Moose and Fleming, *Three Weeks in October*, 138–39; Harrington, *Triumph of Spirit*, 154; and Perry, "Sex, Drugs and Police Corruption."

12. Moose and Fleming, *Three Weeks in October*, 138.
13. Leonard G. Collins, "Biker Wars," in *Portland Police Stories* (self-published, 2013), 448–53.
14. Stanford, *Rose City Vice*, 15, 36, 63–64; and Chandler, *Portland Rogues Gallery*, 131. Penland's handler was Portland Police drug Detective John Giani ("Uncle Johnny"). Giani, for his part, was known to extort money from sex workers, steal merchandise from drug dealers, and arrest rivals in the narcotics trade. He soon cornered the heroin market. Chandler, *Portland Rogues Gallery*, 121–31; and Stanford, *Rose City Vice*, 37.

    In June 1983, Harold Penland and his wife Laura were found dead in their home. The case was never solved, but Stanford names two suspects—both snitches for the narcotics unit. Stanford, *Rose City Vice*, 76–77, 92n36.
15. Moose and Fleming, *Three Weeks in October*, 139; and Stanford, *Rose City Vice*, 65. After this fiasco, the cops started wearing jackets emblazed with the word "Police" during these sorts of raids. Moose and Fleming, *Three Weeks in October*, 141.
16. Stanford, *Rose City Vice*, 64.
17. Richard Brown and Brian Benson, *This Is Not For You: An Activist's Journey of Resistance and Resilience* (Corvallis: Oregon State University Press, 2021), 46.
18. Whitney, "Police Misconduct"; "Pardons Sought for 59 Drug Cases Listed by District Attorney," *Sunday Oregonian*, May 31, 1981; Stanford, *Rose City Vice*, 70; and Harrington, *Triumph of Spirit*, 154–57. Years later, David Bishop, a former detective with Connall's task force and later chief of police in Beaverton, ran into Gearheart. He said Gearheart began reminiscing about all the things they had gotten away with, himself and the other narcs—including a certain chief of police, whom Bishop declined to name. Stanford, *Rose City Vice*, 81–82.
19. Whitney, "Police Misconduct"; "Pardons Sought for 59 Drug Cases"; Susan G. Hauser, *Pickets, Pistols and Politics: A History of the Portland Police Association* (Portland: Portland Police Association, 1996), 79; Stanford, *Rose City Vice*, 70; and Harrington, *Triumph of Spirit*, 157–58.
20. Stanford, *Rose City Vice*, 70.
21. Phil Stanford, *The Peyton-Allan Files* (Portland: Ptown Books, 2010), 32; and Stanford, *Rose City Vice*, 66. Son had once been suspended for trying to bribe a judge. Stanford, *The Peyton-Allan Files*, 33.
22. We cannot know for certain what two murders Son was referring two, but his notes indicate that he was looking into the 1979 stabbing death of a sex worker named Toni Parker and the 1980 death of a cocaine dealer named Harry Foss. Gearheart, Son wrote, was "bedding" Parker; Foss's connection remains obscure. Stanford, *Rose City Vice*, 71–72.
23. Stanford, *Rose City Vice*, 73. In October 2013, Connall resigned from the bar during an ethics investigation. He died two months later. Stanford, *Rose City Vice*, 74.
24. Harrington, *Triumph of Spirit*, 153.
25. Moose and Fleming, *Three Weeks in October*, 140.
26. Moose and Fleming, *Three Weeks in October*, 138–39.
27. Stanford, *Rose City Vice*, 54–55.
28. Moose and Fleming, *Three Weeks in October*, 92, 140. Retired Police Bureau Officer Leonard Collins reasons, "Either the other officers on the shift turned their heads at the illegal conduct, or it never happened." Leonard G. Collins, "Accidents and Such," in *Portland Police Stories* (L. Collins, 2013), 209.
29. Moose and Fleming, *Three Weeks in October*, 93–94, 99.

Chapter 18: Internal Conflict and External Review

1. Penny Harrington, *Triumph of Spirit: An Autobiography* (Chicago: Brittany Publications, 1999), 149; Leanne C. Serbulo and Karen J. Gibson, "Black and Blue: Police-Community Relations in Portland's Albina District, 1964–1985," *Oregon Historical Quarterly* 114, no. 1 (Spring 2013): 22–23; Charles A. Moose and Charles Fleming, *Three Weeks in October: The Manhunt for the Serial Sniper* (New York: Button, 2003), 149; *Arresting Power: Resisting Police Violence in Portland, Oregon*, directed by Jodi Darby et al. (Collective Eye, 2015), DVD; Susan G. Hauser, *Pickets, Pistols and Politics: A History of the Portland Police Association* (Portland: Portland Police Association, 1996), 77–78; and Richard Brown and Brian Benson, *This Is Not For You: An Activist's Journey of Resistance and Resilience* (Corvallis: Oregon State University Press, 2021), 160–61.
2. Hauser, *Pickets, Pistols and Politics*, 80–81; *Portland Civil Rights: Lift Ev'ry Voice* (Portland: Oregon Public Broadcasting, 2015), DVD; and Harrington, *Triumph of Spirit*, 151. Quote from Hauser, *Pickets, Pistols and Politics*, 81.
3. Hauser, *Pickets, Pistols and Politics*, 97; and Serbulo and Gibson, "Black and Blue," 22–23. See also Moose and Fleming, *Three Weeks in October*, 149.
4. *Portland Civil Rights: Lift Ev'ry Voice*; and Hauser, *Pickets, Pistols and Politics*, 98. Footage of the protests is featured in *Arresting Power*.
5. Jewel Lansing, *Portland: People, Politics, and Power* (Corvallis: Oregon State University Press, 2003), 417–18; Hauser, *Pickets, Pistols and Politics*, 98–100; and Harrington, *Triumph of Spirit*, 152. Aitchison paraphrase from Hauser, *Pickets, Pistols and Politics*, 100.
6. Quoted in Serbulo and Gibson, "Black and Blue," 24. See also Harrington, *Triumph of Spirit*, 157.
7. Harrington, *Triumph of Spirit*, 157.
8. Serbulo and Gibson, "Black and Blue," 24–25.
9. Harrington, *Triumph of Spirit*, 163–65.
10. Quoted in Hauser, *Pickets, Pistols and Politics*, 101. See also Samuel Walker, *Police Accountability: The Role of Citizen Oversight* (Belmont, Ca: Wadsworth, 2001), 36; and Serbulo and Gibson, "Black and Blue," 22. The committee's activities were closely monitored by the police bureau's intelligence unit and filed under "Police–Anti." Ben Jacklet, "A Legacy of Suspicion," *Portland Tribune*, September 20, 2002.
11. Charles Moose, "The Theory and Practice of Community Policing: An Evaluation of the Iris Court Demonstration Project" (PhD diss., Portland State University, 1993), 66–67; Hauser, *Pickets, Pistols and Politics*, 101; and Serbulo and Gibson, "Black and Blue," 25. Quote from Colette Gordon, "Mobilizing Beyond Crisis: Police Accountability Organizing in Portland, Oregon" (undergraduate thesis, Reed College, 2005), 26. For a concise history of PIIAC, see Gordon, "Mobilizing Beyond Crisis," 25–33.
12. Walker, *Police Accountability*, 36.
13. Hauser, *Pickets, Pistols and Politics*, 102.
14. Walker, *Police Accountability*, 36; Hauser, *Pickets, Pistols and Politics*, 102; and Serbulo and Gibson, "Black and Blue," 25.
15. Walker, *Police Accountability*, 36.
16. Gordon, "Mobilizing Beyond Crisis," 27. Parenthetical citations omitted.
17. Serbulo and Gibson, "Black and Blue," 25.
18. Hauser, *Pickets, Pistols and Politics*, 102–3.
19. Walker, *Police Accountability*, 37.
20. Quoted in Gordon, "Mobilizing Beyond Crisis," 28.

21. Walker, *Police Accountability*, 38.
22. Harrington, *Triumph of Spirit*, 176.
23. Quoted in Ivonne Roman, "A Police Pioneer on Her Unfinished Business," themarshall project.org, September 5, 2018.
24. Carl Abbott, *Portland in Three Centuries: The Place and the People* (Corvallis: Oregon State University Press, 2011), 163; and Harrington, *Triumph of Spirit*, 176.
25. Harrington, *Triumph of Spirit*, 12, 184–86; Lansing, *Portland*, 432; Cara Rabe-Hemp, *Thriving in an All-Boys Club: Female Police and Their Fight for Equality* (Lanham, Md: Rowman & Littlefield, 2018), 101; and Allan T. Duffin, *History in Blue: 160 Years of Women Police, Sheriffs, Detectives, and State Troopers* (New York: Kaplan, 2010), 232.
26. Harrington, *Triumph of Spirit*, 167.
27. Harrington, *Triumph of Spirit*, 169–71, 175, 193, 230–31; and Duffin, *History in Blue*, 231.
28. Harrington, *Triumph of Spirit*, 117.
29. Harrington, *Triumph of Spirit*, 167.
30. For an analysis of similar dynamics in Los Angeles, see Luis Daniel Gascón and Aaron Rousell, *The Limits of Community Policing: Civilian Power and Police Accountability in Black and Brown Los Angeles* (New York: New York University Press, 219), 5–6.
31. Harrington, *Triumph of Spirit*, 189–92, 196–98; Hauser, *Pickets, Pistols and Politics*, 107–9; and Duffin, *History in Blue*, 230–31.
32. Harrington, *Triumph of Spirit*, 224–26; and Duffin, *History in Blue*, 231.
33. Harrington, *Triumph of Spirit*, 193–94, 199.
34. Harrington, *Triumph of Spirit*, 188.
35. Douglas Perry, "Sex, Drugs, and Police Corruption in Portland: How the Wild 1970s Paved the Way to the City's Future," oregonlive.com, July 1, 2019.
36. Quoted in Harrington, *Triumph of Spirit*, 233.
37. Harrington, *Triumph of Spirit*, 213.
38. Hauser, *Pickets, Pistols and Politics*, 104–5; Serbulo and Gibson, "Black and Blue," 27; Harrington, *Triumph of Spirit*, 210–11; *Portland Civil Rights: Lift Ev'ry Voice*. Accounts of the incident vary considerably. For contrasting versions, see Serbulo and Gibson, "Black and Blue," 25; and Harrington, *Triumph of Spirit*, 202–3.
39. Harrington, *Triumph of Spirit*, 207–8. See also Hauser, *Pickets, Pistols and Politics*, 104–5, 203–5.
40. Quoted in Hauser, *Pickets, Pistols and Politics*, 105.
41. Serbulo and Gibson, "Black and Blue," 26; Harrington, *Triumph of Spirit*, 208; Hauser, *Pickets, Pistols and Politics*, 106; Lansing, *Portland*, 432–33; Elinor Langer, *A Hundred Little Hitlers: The Death of a Black Man, the Trial of a White Racist, and the Rise of the Neo-Nazi Movement in America* (New York: Picador, 2003), 218; and Brown, *This Is Not For You*, 183–84.
42. *Portland Civil Rights: Lift Ev'ry Voice*.
43. Quoted in Harrington, *Triumph of Spirit*, 208.
44. Hauser, *Pickets, Pistols and Politics*, 106; Harrington, *Triumph of Spirit*, 213; Lansing, *Portland*, 432–3;3 and *Portland Civil Rights: Lift Ev'ry Voice*. Quote from Harrington, *Triumph of Spirit*, 213; parentheses in original.
45. Harrington, *Triumph of Spirit*, 216–21.
46. Harrington, *Triumph of Spirit*, 221.
47. Harrington, *Triumph of Spirit*, 183–84.
48. Harrington, *Triumph of Spirit*, 214–15, 235–36; and Duffin, *History in Blue*, 231.
49. Harrington, *Triumph of Spirit*, 238–39, 242–45; and Roman, "A Police Pioneer on Her

Unfinished Business" (quote). An *Oregonian* poll had earlier found that 25 percent of Portland Police officers thought morale would improve if Harrington were replaced. Harrington, *Triumph of Spirit*, 222.

50. Lansing, *Portland*, 436; Harrington, *Triumph of Spirit*, 239. Tim Gallagher, who served on both Ivancie and Clark's mayoral staff, had been caught in a cocaine bust in Gresham. "Oral History Interview with Don E. Clark" [transcription], interviews conducted by George M. Joseph, August 30, 1994–March 27, 1998, Archives West, SR1166, 847.
51. Harrington, *Triumph of Spirit*, 239.
52. Lansing, *Portland*, 437.
53. Quoted in Harrington, *Triumph of Spirit*, 12.
54. Harrington, *Triumph of Spirit*, 257, 264–65; Roman, "A Police Pioneer on Her Unfinished Business"; and Duffin, *History in Blue*, 232.
55. Harrington, *Triumph of Spirit*, 250, 257.
56. Lansing, *Portland*, 437.
57. Quoted in Harrington, *Triumph of Spirit*, 248.

Chapter 19: Community Policing and Public Housing

1. Dean S. Smith et al., *Columbia Villa Community Services Project: A Model for a Troubled Time* (Portland: Housing Authority of Portland, December 1992) vi, 8; and "Oral History Interview with Don E. Clark" [transcription], interviews conducted by George M. Joseph, August 30, 1994–March 27, 1998, Archives West, SR1166, 901–2 (quote).
2. "Oral History Interview with Don E. Clark," 874, 893–95; and Smith, *Columbia Villa Community Services Project*, 7. In 1987, the Portland Police Bureau's Gang Intelligence Unit identified seventy "original gangsters" who had moved to Portland from Los Angeles. Two years later, the cops estimated that fourteen hundred local Black youth were involved in gangs, though others considered that a gross exaggeration. Smith, *Columbia Villa Community Services Project*, 4.

   Within a few years, the Gang Enforcement Team had twenty-eight hundred names on its gang list. Appearing there could lead to stricter probation, and cops would sometimes call employers. In 1993, Ernesto Ysaga sued after the cops had him fired. A judge ordered the police to apply standard criteria in deciding whom to list, required them to notify those listed, and created an appeals process. That system, established in 1996, continued until 2020. Carli Brousseau, "'I Was Pulled Over Again': Letters from Portland's Gang List," oregonlive.com, November 10, 2016; Carli Brousseau, "'Labelled as Someone I am Not': Letters from Portland's Gang List," oregonlive.com, November 5, 2016; Carli Brousseau, "'It Offers No Hope': Letters from Portland's Gang List," oregonlive.com, November 8, 2016; and Carli Brousseau, "'A Policy of Wide-Scale Racial Profiling'? Letters from Portland's Gang List," oregonlive.com, November 7, 2016.
3. Smith, *Columbia Villa Community Services Project*, v–vi, 1, 4–5, 27.
4. Smith, *Columbia Villa Community Services Project*, 6, 16. Quotes in "Oral History Interview with Don E. Clark," 910–12.
5. Smith, *Columbia Villa Community Services Project*, 25.
6. "Oral History Interview with Don E. Clark," 927–28.
7. "Oral History Interview with Don E. Clark," 905–9.
8. "Oral History Interview with Don E. Clark," 931.
9. Smith, *Columbia Villa Community Services Project*, 22–23, 29.

10. Smith, *Columbia Villa Community Services Project*, 42–64.
11. "Oral History Interview with Don E. Clark," 917.
12. Smith, *Columbia Villa Community Services Project*, 33–34. Quote from 34.
13. Smith, *Columbia Villa Community Services Project*, 34, 36; and "Oral History Interview with Don E. Clark," 929–30.
14. Smith, *Columbia Villa Community Services Project*, 60.
15. Smith, *Columbia Villa Community Services Project*, 36–37.
16. Smith, *Columbia Villa Community Services Project*, 37–38.
17. Smith, *Columbia Villa Community Services Project*, 37.
18. Quoted in Smith, *Columbia Villa Community Services Project*, 77.
19. Smith, *Columbia Villa Community Services Project*, 36–38. There was undoubtedly an element of territorialism alongside the culture clash and usual interagency rivalry. It had only been a few years since 1983's Resolution A had finally established an agreed-upon division of labor between the county and the city governments. Henceforth, Portland would be responsible for policing, firefighting, transportation, parks, water, and sewers. The county would fulfill state-mandated duties and provide "human and justice services," including social services, libraries, tax collection, elections, and jails. The county sheriff retained responsibility for river patrols, special investigations, and policing unincorporated areas. The Multnomah County Sheriff's Office shrank from 220 officers to 87, as many deputies were transferred to the Portland or Gresham police departments. Jewel Lansing and Fred Leeson, *Multnomah: The Tumultuous Story of Oregon's Most Populous County* (Corvallis: Oregon State University Press, 2012), 178–180.
20. Smith, *Columbia Villa Community Services Project*, 21, 36; and "Oral History Interview with Don E. Clark," 928.
21. Smith, *Columbia Villa Community Services Project*, 57.
22. Smith, *Columbia Villa Community Services Project*, 38.
23. Smith, *Columbia Villa Community Services Project*, 62–63.
24. Quoted in Smith, *Columbia Villa Community Services Project*, 79–80.
25. Smith, *Columbia Villa Community Services Project*, 58.
26. "Oral History Interview with Don E. Clark," 932, 934.
27. Smith, *Columbia Villa Community Services Project*, 49.
28. Smith, *Columbia Villa Community Services Project*, 59.
29. Quoted in Smith, *Columbia Villa Community Services Project*, 65.
30. Charles Moose, "The Theory and Practice of Community Policing: An Evaluation of the Iris Court Demonstration Project" (PhD diss., Portland State University, 1993), 70, 72.
31. Quoted in Moose, "The Theory and Practice of Community Policing," 5–6. Over six months at the end of 1989 and the very beginning of 1990, the Portland City Council passed a series of resolutions setting community policing goals for the following five years and adopting Potter's transition plan. Moose, "The Theory and Practice of Community Policing," 74.
32. Moose, "The Theory and Practice of Community Policing," 74, 78–79.
33. Charles A. Moose and Charles Fleming, *Three Weeks in October: The Manhunt for the Serial Sniper* (New York: Button, 2003), 187.
34. Quoted in Moose, "The Theory and Practice of Community Policing," 89. "Quality of life was to be gauged by the following indicators[:] income, employment, health and education." Moose, "The Theory and Practice of Community Policing," 89.
35. Moose, "The Theory and Practice of Community Policing," 90–93.
36. Moose, "The Theory and Practice of Community Policing," 94–99.

37. Moose and Fleming, *Three Weeks in October*, 187–88. Concerning the substation and the television, see also Moose, "The Theory and Practice of Community Policing," 114, 122. On the laundry room, see Moose, "The Theory and Practice of Community Policing," 122–23.
38. Moose, "The Theory and Practice of Community Policing," 122–27; Moose and Fleming, *Three Weeks in October*, 187–88; and Doug Kenck-Crispin, "Charles Moose Had a Radical Idea for What Portland Police Officers Should Do: Live Here," *Willamette Week*, December 1, 2021.
39. Moose and Fleming, *Three Weeks in October*, 187–88.
40. Moose, "The Theory and Practice of Community Policing," 115–16.
41. Moose, "The Theory and Practice of Community Policing," 116–17.
42. Moose, "The Theory and Practice of Community Policing," 119–20.
43. Moose, "The Theory and Practice of Community Policing," 121, 145, 155.
44. Moose and Fleming, *Three Weeks in October*, 189.
45. See Moose, "The Theory and Practice of Community Policing."
46. Moose and Fleming, *Three Weeks in October*, 189, 194.
47. This lineage was not always perfectly linear. The lines of influence sometimes looped back around. Lee Brown considered Don Clark a mentor. But in the late eighties, Brown—by that point, the chief of police in Houston—was sending both Clark and Portland Police captain Tom Potter materials he collected while researching community policing. This research, as well as the practical example of Columbia Villa, would help inform Potter's approach. "Oral History Interview with Don E. Clark," 844, 914; and Lansing and Leeson, *Multnomah*, 149–50.
48. Smith, *Columbia Villa Community Services Project*, 51. Portland and Gresham police applied the model in five locations: Rockwood, Brentwood-Darlington, Hillsdale Terrace, David Douglas School District, and Iris Court. Smith, *Columbia Villa Community Services Project*, 64–65.
49. Smith, *Columbia Villa Community Services Project*, 64–55.
50. "When now-Capt. Charles Moose went to Iris Court in July 1990, he used basically the same mission statement and procedural protocols as were used at Columbia Villa." Smith, *Columbia Villa Community Services Project*, 65.
51. Moose and Fleming, *Three Weeks in October*, 205.

Chapter 20: Enforcing Quality of Life

1. Quoted in Holly Danks, "Repercussions of Laurelhurst Raid Still Reverberate," *Oregonian*, November 28, 1993. See also Colette Gordon, "Mobilizing Beyond Crisis: Police Accountability Organizing in Portland, Oregon" (undergraduate thesis, Reed College, 2005), 26.
2. Quoted in Danks, "Repercussions of Laurelhurst Raid Still Reverberate."
3. Steve Duin, "Nathan Thomas's Parents Reflect on His Death, Whether Portland Police Learned Anything From It," oregonlive.com, September 19, 2020; and Danks, "Repercussions of Laurelhurst Raid Still Reverberate."
4. People Overseeing Police Study Group [Portland Copwatch], "Shooter Cop Reinstated: What's Wrong with This Picture?" *People's Police Report*, no. 6 (Second Trimester 1995), 1–2.
5. "Setback for Police, Public," *Oregonian*, May 5, 1995.
6. Danks, "Repercussions of Laurelhurst Raid Still Reverberate."

7. Gordon, "Mobilizing Beyond Crisis," 26–27.
8. Gordon, "Mobilizing Beyond Crisis," 34–35.
9. Richard Brown and Brian Benson, *This Is Not For You: An Activist's Journey of Resistance and Resilience* (Corvallis: Oregon State University Press, 2021), 216. Parentheses in original.
10. Portland Copwatch, "New Mayor Is Former Top Cop," *People's Police Report*, no. 34 (January 2005), 5.
11. Avel Louise Gordly and Patricia A. Schechter, *Remembering the Power of Words: The Life of an Oregon Activist, Legislator, and Community Leader* (Corvallis: Oregon State University Press, 2011), 88, 97, 107–8; and Brown, *This Is Not For You*, 163–64, 181–83, 189–90.
12. Brown, *This Is Not For You*, 16–17.
13. Brown, *This Is Not For You*, 232–33.
14. Brown, *This Is Not For You*, 220.
15. Brown, *This Is Not For You*, 45–46, 227.
16. Portland Copwatch, "Late Breaking News: 100% African American Citations; Civilian Investigator Flap and Audit of IPR," *People's Police Report*, no. 41 (May 2007), 11.
17. Brown, *This Is Not For You*, 45, 219, 240.
18. Samuel Walker, *Police Accountability: The Role of Citizen Oversight* (Belmont, Ca: Wadsworth, 2001), 107, 147, 169–70.
19. Portland Copwatch, "In Historic Hearing, Council Votes to Hold Officer Accountable for Misconduct," *People's Police Report*, no. 78 (September 2019), 3; and Gordon, "Mobilizing Beyond Crisis," 26–28.
20. Walker, *Police Accountability*, 78; and Portland Copwatch/POPSG, "Rapping Back: Police Complain About . . . You Guessed It . . . Internal Affairs," *People's Police Report*, no. 11 (April 1997), 6.
21. Quoted in Gordon, "Mobilizing Beyond Crisis," 26.
22. Former chief Charles Moose later wrote: "The alternative I favored was to go to the same area with uniformed officers and with members of the gay and lesbian community and say, 'This park may have been the place where this kind of activity was the status quo, but things have changed. There are other people using this park now, and that kind of behavior, in public, is no longer acceptable.'" Charles A. Moose and Charles Fleming, *Three Weeks in October: The Manhunt for the Serial Sniper* (New York: Dutton, 2003), 263.
23. Leonard G. Collins, "Hamburger Mary's," in *Portland Police Stories* (L. Collins, 2013), 476.
24. Phil Stanford, "Just a Little Cruise Down Broadway," in *Do You Know How Much a Light Year Is?* (Beaverton, Or: Touchstone Press, 1991), 47.
25. Portland Copwatch, "Portland Police Target 'Zoobombers,'" *People's Police Report*, no. 31 (January 2004), 5; and Portland Copwatch, "Cops Target Zoobombers Again," *People's Police Report*, no. 39 (September 2006), 5. For more on the Zoobombers, see Shawn Granton, *The Zinester's Guide to Portland* (Portland: Microcosm, [2016]), 47–48.
26. Portland Copwatch, "Three Portland Beatings Raise Serious Questions About Community Policing," *People's Police Report*, no. 24 (August 2001), 12. I remember seeing an unenthusiastic group in safety orange vests walking along Southeast Belmont Street, tearing off the accumulated fliers. Strangely, no one had seen fit to send them with trash bags, so they just left the resulting litter piled in the street, on sidewalks, and in my front yard.
27. "Sometimes," they wrote, "what [a policeman] did could be described as 'enforcing the law,' but just as often it involved taking informal or extralegal steps to help protect what the neighborhood had decided was the appropriate level of public order. Some of the things he did probably would not withstand a legal challenge." George L. Kelling and James Q. Wilson, "Broken Windows," theatlantic.com, March 1982.

28. Bernard E. Harcourt, *Illusion of Order: The False Promise of Broken Windows Policing* (Cambridge, Ma: Harvard University Press, 2001), 7, 88–89.
29. Moose and Fleming, *Three Weeks in October*, 205.
30. "Oral History Interview with Don E. Clark" [transcription], interviews conducted by George M. Joseph, August 30, 1994–March 27, 1998, Archives West, SR1166, 929; and Dean S. Smith et al., *Columbia Villa Community Services Project: A Model for a Troubled Time* (Portland: Housing Authority of Portland, 1992), 39.
31. Harcourt, *Illusion of Order*, 18–19, 242.
32. Mark Neocleous notes that, as vagrancy and the enclosures arose together, the vagrant holds a special role in the conceptual world of policing. Mark Neocleous, *A Critical Theory of Police Power: The Fabrication of Social Order* (London: Verso, 2021), 12.
33. Portland Copwatch, "Sidewalk Management Plan: Sit/Lie 4.0," *People's Police Report*, no. 49 (January 2010), 1, 8. On earlier efforts, see "Updated: Eight Years of Sit-Lie History," *Street Roots*, May 5, 2010, streetroots.wordpress.com.
34. All quoted in Portland Copwatch, "Sit/Lie Report: Sign Boards Okay, Homeless Not," *People's Police Report*, no. 46 (January 2009), 7.
35. Portland Copwatch, "Sit/Lie Put on Hold After Public Objection," *People's Police Report*, no. 27 (August 2002), 2.
36. Portland Copwatch, "Sit/Lie Report," 7. In the summer of 2005, Portland Copwatch conducted a survey of downtown sidewalks and found numerous businesses in violation of the sit/lie law's requirement for six feet of free passage: Big Town Hero, the Daily Grill, the Virginia Cafe, the Starbucks at Southwest Ninth and Taylor, South Park, and the Greek Cusina all set up outdoor seating that crowded the sidewalk illegally. Portland Copwatch, "Sit-Lie Warnings Handed Out; Portland Copwatch Notes Obstructive Eateries," *People's Police Report*, no. 36 (September 2005), 5.
37. Portland Copwatch, "More Targeting 'Youth Crimes,'" *People's Police Report*, no. 15 (August 1998), 7.
38. Portland Copwatch, "Perceptions and Reality in Downtown Portland: Crackdown Means Favors for Business, Shoppers, While Poor Suffer," *People's Police Report*, no. 37 (January 2006), 9.
39. People Overseeing Police Study Group [Portland Copwatch], "Policing the Homeless Community: Camp Sweeps and Trespass Tickets," *People's Police Report*, no. 8 (First Trimester, 1996), 7.
40. Portland Copwatch/POPSG, "Police Harass Homeless at Community Dining Hall," *People's Police Report*, no. 15 (August 1998), 8.
41. Tracy J. Prince, "Portland's Response to Homeless Issues and the 'Broken Windows' Theory," in *The Portland Edge: Challenges and Successes in Growing Communities*, edited by Connie P. Ozawa (Washington, D.C.: Island Press, 2004), 293.
42. Wade Nkrumah, "Residents Push to Stop Meals for Homeless," *Oregonian*, January 13, 2000; and Steve Duin, "Sunnyside Case the Tip of a Very Cold Shoulder," *Oregonian*, February 8, 2000.
43. Wade Nkrumah, "Issues Simmering in Sunnyside," *Oregonian*, February 21, 2000.
44. Steven Reed Johnson, "The Myth and Reality of Portland's Engaged Citizenry and Process-Oriented Governance," in *The Portland Edge: Challenges and Successes in Growing Communities*, edited by Connie P. Ozawa (Washington, D.C.: Island Press, 2004), 103, 112–13.
45. Quoted in Duin, "Sunnyside Case the Tip." The reference is to the Parable of the Good Samaritan, Luke 10:25–37.

46. Duin, "Sunnyside Case the Tip" (quote); Nkrumah, "Residents Push to Stop Meals for Homeless"; Nkrumah, "Issues Simmering in Sunnyside"; and "Loving Your Neighbor (hood)," editorial, *Oregonian*, February 15, 2000.
47. Quoted in Wade Nkrumah, "Hearings Officer Rules Against Church Meals," *Oregonian*, January 17, 2000.
48. Portland Copwatch/POPSG, "Police Commendations: What's Really Important???," *People's Police Report*, no. 14 (April 1998), 10.
49. Portland Copwatch, "Sgt. Pool: In One End and Out the Other," *People's Police Report*, no. 26 (April 2002), 2.
50. Portland Copwatch, "Rogue 'Solutions Guy' Officer Targets Homeless," *People's Police Report*, no. 31 (January 2004), 11; Portland Copwatch, "Secret List Allowed to Continue, with Reservations, in Judge's Ruling," *People's Police Report*, no. 47 (May 2009), 1, 4; and, Phil Busse, "Who Is Portland's Most Rotten Cop?" portlandmercury.com, February 19, 2004. Quotes from Portland Copwatch, "Secret List," 1.
51. Portland Copwatch, "Rogue 'Solutions Guy' Officer Targets Homeless," 11.
52. Portland Copwatch, "Cops Create Rules or Secret List of 'Dirty 30' Suspects, Five Years Later," *People's Police Report*, no. 46 (January 2009), 2; and Portland Copwatch, "Secret List Allowed to Continue," 1, 4.
53. Oregonian Editorial Board, "Clipping Wings of Frequent Fliers," oregonlive.com, January 8, 2009.
54. Quoted in Portland Copwatch, "Public Defender Takes Commissioner Leonard to Task on Drug-Free Zone Alternative Plan," *People's Police Report*, no. 44 (May 2008), 7.
55. Portland Copwatch, "Not So Secret List," *People's Police Report*, no. 49 (January 2010), 6.
56. Harcourt, *Illusion of Order*, 17. Police Chief Charles Moose was frank about the political and specifically class considerations inherent to the construction of the related category of "crime": "To many people, serious crime means violence, open drug dealing, burglary to our homes, and kindred offenses, while to others, serious crime may mean 'red lining' in the real estate industry, industrial pollution that will destroy the ozone layers, or tax evasion. The question is, how do the police resolve conflicting definitions of 'the crime problem,' and what if no identifiable 'community' exists?" Charles Moose, "The Theory and Practice of Community Policing: An Evaluation of the Iris Court Demonstration Project" (PhD diss., Portland State University, 1993), 41.
57. Quoted in "Michael D. Schrunk, District Attorney, Portland, Oregon," Center for Justice Innovation, February 2007, innovatingjustice.org.
58. Matthew Robinson, "Lawyers We Like," *City Journal*, August 1997; "Michael D. Schrunk, District Attorney," Center for Justice Innovation; Lee P. Brown, *Policing in the 21st Century: Community Policing* (Bloomington, Ind.,: AuthorHouse, 2012), 517–20; and Alex Zielinski, "Portland DA Seeks to Revive a Conservative Policing Tactic with 'Neighborhood Prosecutors,'" *Portland Mercury*, May 25, 2022.
59. Emily Green, "Broken Windows Prosecuting," streetroots.org, April 15, 2016; Zielinski, "Portland DA Seeks to Revive a Conservative Policing Tactic"; and Brown, *Policing in the 21st Century*, 520. The idea of neighborhood prosecutors was resuscitated in 2022, under progressive DA Mike Schmidt, who promised to "problem-solve individual, neighborhood or community issues that may or may not be criminal in nature but impact the quality of life." Quoted in Zielinski, "Portland DA Seeks to Revive a Conservative Policing Tactic." The ACLU was skeptical, worrying that "while well-intentioned, [the Program] will have harmful impacts on the same communities that prosecutors have harmed for

generations." Quoted in Julie Sabatier, "Multnomah County District Attorney Seeks Funding for New Neighborhood Prosecutor program," opb.org, June 2, 2022.

60. Sarah Mirk, "Portland Business Alliance Is City's #1 Lobbyist," *Portland Mercury*, October 19, 2009; Matt Davis, "The Portland Business Alliance: Still Lobbying Harder than Anyone Else," *Portland Mercury*, February 11, 2010; Phil Busse, "The Alliance," *Portland Mercury*, February 6, 2003; Alex Zielinski, "Q&A: Small Business Advocate Ashley Henry on How City Money Goes into the Pockets of the PBA," *Portland Mercury*, December 2, 2022; and Portland Copwatch, "Sit/Lie Law Put on Hold," 2. Quotes from Busse, "The Alliance."
61. K. C. Cowan et al., *Portland: The Riches of a City* (Portland: Portland Metropolitan Chamber of Commerce, 1998), 36.
62. Portland Copwatch, "Will the Real Cop Please Stand Up?," *People's Police Report*, no. 42 (September 2007), 11. See also Michelle Martin, "A Message from the Chair," *BID News*, April–May 2010, http://www.portlandalliance.com/news_cals/BIDnewsletter_may2010.html.
63. Quoted in Matt Davis, "Wake Up! Rent-a-Cops Paid to Harass the Homeless," *Portland Mercury*, May 31, 2007.
64. Portland Copwatch/POPSG, "Special Duty," *People's Police Report*, no. 12 (August 1997), 6.
65. Quoted in Alex Zielinski, "City Hears Opposition to Continuation of Downtown Clean & Safe's Contract," *Portland Mercury*, July 28, 2021.
66. Quoted in Portland Copwatch/POPSG, "Chief Moose Cuts Loose—Leaving Legacy of Mixed Messages," *People's Police Report*, no. 18 (August 1999), 8. Moose was later chief of police in Montgomery County, Maryland, during the "DC Sniper" investigation. He left that position when it was determined that it would be unethical for him to write a book on the experience. Moose and Fleming, *Three Weeks in October*, 308.

Chapter 21: Militarizing Prohibition, Sexual Misconduct, and Exclusion Zones

1. Charles A. Moose and Charles Fleming, *Three Weeks in October: The Manhunt for the Serial Sniper* (New York: Dutton, 2003), 190–92. Vera Katz was born in Germany and fled the Nazis as a child. She was later active in Robert Kennedy's presidential campaign and then the United Farm Workers grape boycott. For a profile of Mayor Katz, see Floyd J. McKay, *Reporting the Oregon Story: How Activists and Visionaries Transformed a State* (Corvallis: Oregon State University Press, 2016), 164–66.
2. Quoted in Moose and Fleming, *Three Weeks in October*, 197. Moose's dream was to have a cop living on every block. He partnered with banks to create a "Police at Home" program, making no-money-down mortgages available for cops buying homes in eight targeted neighborhoods. Only twenty-two officers ever took advantage of the program. Doug Kenck-Crispin, "Charles Moose Had a Radical Idea for What Portland Police Officers Should Do: Live Here," *Willamette Week*, December 1, 2021.
3. Sophie Bernard, et al., *The State of Our Children: African American Children in Multnomah and Washington Counties* (Portland: Center of Community Research [and the Urban League of Portland], [1997?]), 75.
4. Moose and Fleming, *Three Weeks in October*, 194–95.
5. Susan G. Hauser, *Pickets, Pistols and Politics: A History of the Portland Police Association* (Portland: Portland Police Association, 1996), 125.

6. Moose and Fleming, *Three Weeks in October*, 298; and Kenck-Crispin, "Charles Moose Had a Radical Idea." The simultaneous move toward militarization and community policing fits a pattern seen across the country. See Kristian Williams, *Our Enemies in Blue: Police and Power in America*, 3rd ed. (Oakland: AK Press, 2015), 321–61.
7. Portland police officers killed nine people in the nineteen thirties; fifteen in the forties; two in the fifties; three in the sixties; ten in the seventies; and twelve in the eighties—then twenty-four in the nineties; twenty-two in the first decade of the twenty-first century; twenty-five in the teens; and ten in the first three years in the twenties. Fedor Zarkhin, "The Forgotten Four, Part Four: 'They Always Find Them Not Guilty,'" oregonlive.com, October 20, 2023.
8. Lee P. Brown, *Policing in the 21st Century: Community Policing* (Bloomington, Ind.: AuthorHouse, 2012), xvii, 322–23; Lee P. Brown and Joseph Green Bishop, *Outhouse to the White House* (Bloomington, Ind.: AuthorHouse, 2022) 160–63, 272; and Jewel Lansing and Fred Leeson, *Multnomah: The Tumultuous Story of Oregon's Most Populous County* (Corvallis: Oregon State University Press, 2012), 149–50. "Father of community policing": Avel Louise Gordly and Patricia A. Schechter, *Remembering the Power of Words: The Life of an Oregon Activist, Legislator, and Community Leader* (Corvallis: Oregon State University Press, 2011), 71.

   "The Weed and Seed strategy is based on a two-pronged approach: 1. Law enforcement agencies and criminal justice officials cooperate with local residents to 'weed out' criminal activity in the designated area. 2. Social service providers and economic revitalization efforts are introduced to 'seed' the area, ensuring long-term positive change and a higher quality of life for residents." Community Capacity Development Office, *Weed and Seed Implementation Manual* (Washington, D.C.: U.S. Department of Justice, August 2005), 1. I have written about Weed and Seed as an application of counterinsurgency in Williams, *Our Enemies in Blue*, 356–57; and Kristian Williams, "The Other Side of the Coin: Counterinsurgency and Community Policing," in *Gang Politics: Revolution, Repression, and Crime* (Chico, Ca: AK Press, 2022), 31–32. On New York's experience with zero-tolerance policing, see Christian Parenti, *Lockdown America: Police and Prisons in the Age of Crisis* (London; Verso, 1999), 75–82.
9. Brown, *Outhouse to the White House*, 359.
10. Brown, *Outhouse to the White House*, 393–94; and Parenti, *Lockdown America*, 65–66.
11. Elizabeth Hinton, *America on Fire: The Untold History of Police Violence and Black Rebellion Since the 1960s* (New York: Liveright, 2021), 271.
12. Parenti, *Lockdown America*, 65–66.
13. Michelle Alexander, *The New Jim Crow: Mass Incarceration in the Age of Colorblindness* (New York: New Press, 2010), 253.
14. Hinton, *America on Fire*, 271.
15. Quoted in Alexander, *The New Jim Crow*, 56.
16. State of Oregon Criminal Justice Commission, "Longitudinal Study of Measure 11 and Mandatory Minimums in Oregon," March 2011, viii, 2, 41; Kelly Officer et al., "Updated Measure 11 Indictments, Convictions, and Sentencing Trends, 2013–2018," Oregon Criminal Justice Commission, March 2021, 9; Clayton James Szczech, "Beyond Autonomy and Dominance: The Political Sociology of Prison Expansion" (undergraduate thesis, Reed College, 2000), 45–46; Bernard, *The State of Our Children*, 77; Edward Jones, "Opinion: DA's Defense of Measure 11 Serves Prosecutors, Not Justice," *Oregonian*, March 2, 2021; and Lea Zaitz, "Measure 11: Is It Really Working?," *Oregonian*, March 14, 2011.
17. Criminal Justice Commission, "Longitudinal Study of Measure 11," 30.

18. Bernard, *The State of Our Children*, 76; and Szczech, "Beyond Autonomy and Dominance," 45.
19. "Historical Prison and Community Corrections Populations," oregon.gov, accessed March 2024; and, Criminal Justice Commission, "Longitudinal Study of Measure 11," xi.
20. Officer, "Updated Measure 11 Indictments," 1, 4–5, 8; and Criminal Justice Commission, "Longitudinal Study of Measure 11," x.
21. "Quick Facts: Multnomah County, Oregon," US Census Bureau, https://www.census.gov/quickfacts/fact/table/multnomahcountyoregon/PST045222.
22. Quoted in Midge Purcell et al., eds., *The State of Black Oregon* (Portland: Urban League, [2009]), 46.
23. Kelly Officer and Michael Weinerman, "Research Review: Impacts of Measure 11 and Other Factors on Crime," Oregon Criminal Justice Commission, March 2021, 3.
24. See, for instance, Peter B. Kraska, "Crime Control as Warfare: Language Matters," in *Militarizing the American Criminal Justice System: The Changing Roles of the Armed Forces and Police*, edited by Peter B. Kraska (Boston: Northeastern University Press, 2001).
25. Portland Copwatch/POPSG, "'Grow Light' Store Busted After Filing Suit," *People's Police Report*, no. 18 (August 1999), 4.
26. Portland Copwatch/POPSG, "Politically Motivated Persecution of Hemp Activists," *People's Police Report*, no. 13 (January 1998), 3.
27. Portland Copwatch/POPSG, "Police Shot in Botched Warrantless Search; Suspect Supposedly Strangles Self," *People's Police Report*, no. 14 (April 1998), 1, 6.
28. Portland Copwatch/POPSG, "Police Shot in Botched Warrantless Search," 6.
29. Mike Davis, *Hunting Men; The Career of an Oregon State Police Detective* (Bloomington, Ind.: Abbott Press, 2014), 124–26, 131.
30. Portland Copwatch, "SERT Hazing Investigation 'Drags' On," *People's Police Report*, no. 25 (December 2001), 9; Portland Copwatch, "Swat My Backside, the SERT Team's Been Disbanded," *People's Police Report*, no. 24 (August 2001), 11; and Portland Copwatch, "Where's the Justice for Whistleblowers? First Female SERT Officer Loses Lawsuit, Officers File for Whistleblower Protection," *People's Police Report*, no. 36 (September 2005), 5. *Oregonian* quoted in Portland Copwatch, "Where's the Justice for Whistleblowers?" 5.

    The Multnomah County Sheriff's Office's Corrections Emergency Response Team (CERT) had its own hazing scandal in 2002, after several deputies were sent to the hospital with injuries—including cracked ribs, a dislocated elbow, kidney failure, a fractured spine, and a probable concussion—incurred in the course of a training exercise called "bull in a ring": deputies would surround an officer and try to knock him down. Multnomah County Deputy Vera Pool and Washington County Commander Rob Gordon both described the training as a hazing ritual, and I will add that it does sound a bit like being "jumped in" to a gang. Washington County had already ended the practice after numerous injuries. Portland Copwatch, "Wacky Sheriffs and Their Shenanigans," *People's Police Report*, no. 27 (August 2002), 11.
31. Portland Copwatch, "Drug Free Zones to Expand?," *People's Police Report*, no. 27 (August 2002), 9; Portland Copwatch, "Drug-Free Zones Prove Racially Biased, Get Smacked Down by Mayor," *People's Police Report*, no. 43 (January 2008), 1; and Bernard, *The State of Our Children*, 89–90.
32. All quoted in Portland Copwatch/POPSG, "Fuddy Duddy, the 'Ho Daddy,'" *People's Police Report*, no. 14 (April 1998), 12.
33. Chuck Palahniuk, *Fugitives and Refugees: A Walk in Portland, Oregon* (New York: Crown, 2003), 104–06.

34. Quoted in Anne Gray Fischer, *The Streets Belong to Us: Sex, Race, and Police Power from Segregation to Gentrification* (Chapel Hill: University of North Carolina Press, 2022), 195–96.
35. Rose City Copwatch, *Alternatives to Police* (Portland: Rose City Copwatch, 2008), 20; and Palahniuk, *Fugitives and Refugees*, 103.
36. All quoted in Portland Copwatch/POPSG, untitled short, *People's Police Report*, no. 14 (April 1998), 7.
37. Portland Copwatch, "Police Predator Gets Discipline and Award," *People's Police Report*, no. 22 (December 2000), 10.
38. Portland Copwatch, "Sixth Cop in Three Years Leaves Force for Sexual Misconduct; Previous Pervocop Costs City $27,500," *People's Police Report*, no. 49 (January 2010), 6.
39. Portland Copwatch, "Sixth Cop in Three Years"; Portland Copwatch, "More PervoCops in Oregon," *People's Police Report*, no. 56 (May 2012), 2; Portland Copwatch, "One Pervert Cop Forced to Pay $5000, Another Draws Suit for Underwear Stunt," *People's Police Report*, no. 45 (September 2008), 9; Portland Copwatch, "Cop Arrested for Sex Assault," *People's Police Report*, no. 31 (January 2004), 5; Portland Copwatch, "Officer Gone Wild: Cop Arrested for Sexual Calls," *People's Police Report*, no. 48 (September 2009), 2; and Portland Copwatch, "'Girls Gone Wild' Cop Case Unresolved," *People's Police Report*, no. 41 (May 2007), 4.
40. Portland Copwatch, "More PervoCops in Oregon," 2.
41. Portland Copwatch, "Sexual Perversion in Portland: Two Cops Plead Guilty, One on Leave for Misconduct," *People's Police Report*, no. 40 (January 2007), 2.
42. Andrea J. Ritchie, *Invisible No More: Police Violence Against Black Women and Women of Color* (Boston: Beacon Press, 2017), 107, 109.
43. Portland Copwatch, "Pervocops and the Perv Who Certified Them," *People's Police Report*, no. 51 (September 2010), 9.
44. Palahniuk, *Fugitives and Refugees*, 102, 105.
45. Portland Copwatch, "Drug Free Zones to Expand?," 9.
46. Portland Copwatch, "Drug-Free Zones Prove Racially Biased," 1, 8. Quote on 8.
47. Portland Copwatch, "Neighbors Call for Prostitution Free Zones' Return, Cops Try Other Tactics," *People's Police Report*, no. 46 (January 2009) 7; and Emi Koyama, *Surviving the Witchhunt: Battle Notes from Portland's 82nd Avenue, 2007–2010* (n.p.: Confluence Publications, 2010), 1–2; and Emi Koyama, "Stop the Scapegoating of Women Working on the 82nd (September 15, 2008)," in *Surviving the Witchhunt*, 4.
48. Portland Copwatch, "Help or Coercion for Prostitution Suspects?," *People's Police Report*, no. 47 (May 2009), 4. For a further critique of the treatment model, see Mariame Kaba and Andrea J. Ritchie, *No More Police: A Case for Abolition* (New York: New Press 2022), 158–60.
49. Portland Copwatch, "Of Cossacks, Bad Weather and Pretext Arrests: Selective Enforcement of Sit/Lie 4.0 Continues," *People's Police Report*, no. 53 (May 2011), 8; and Portland Copwatch, "Cops Create Rules for Secret List of 'Dirty 30' Suspects, Five Years Later," *People's Police Report*, no. 46 (January 2009), 2.
50. Portland Copwatch, "Gun Free Zone Committee Reports to Council," *People's Police Report*, no. 54 (September 2011), 7.
51. Loren Christensen, *Skinhead Street Gangs* (Boulder, Colo.: Paladin Press, 1994), 161.
52. Quoted in People Overseeing Police Study Group [Portland Copwatch], "Police Report Shows True Blue Colors," *People's Police Report* no. 4 (Fourth Quarter 1994), 2.
53. Jennifer Anderson, "Cops Jab at Drugs, One Bust at a Time," *Portland Tribune*, December 17, 2002.

Chapter 22: Skin City and Little Beirut

1. Leanne C. Serbulo and Karen J. Gibson, "Black and Blue: Police-Community Relations in Portland's Albina District, 1964–1985," *Oregon Historical Quarterly* 114, no. 1 (Spring 2013): 24–25. Quote on 25.
2. Moe Bowstern et al., *It Did Happen Here: An Antifascist People's History* (Oakland: PM Press, 2023), 29–30.
3. Bowstern, *It Did Happen Here*, 11; and M. Treloar, "Portland History in Review: *A Hundred Little Hitlers*," (n.p.: Anarchist Library, 2009), 3.
4. Loren Christensen, *Skinhead Street Gangs* (Boulder, Colo.: Paladin Press, 1994), 56.
5. Bowstern, *It Did Happen Here*, 198; and Alice Speri, "Life and Death of an Anti-Fascist," *The Intercept*, March 2, 2021, theintercept.com.
6. Quoted in Bowstern, *It Did Happen Here*, 201.
7. Bowstern, *It Did Happen Here*, 258–60; and Elinor Langer, *A Hundred Little Hitlers: The Death of a Black Man, the Trial of a White Racist, and the Rise of the Neo-Nazi Movement in America* (New York: Picador, 2003), 226. Quote from Bowstern, *It Did Happen Here*, 260.
8. Langer, *A Hundred Little Hitlers*, 360–61.
9. See, for instance, Craig Rosebraugh, *Burning Rage of a Dying Planet: Speaking for the Earth Liberation Front* (New York: Lantern Books, 2004), xii–xiii.
10. Loren W. Christensen, *Riot: A Behind-the-Barricades Tour of Mobs, Riot Cops, and the Chaos of Crowd Violence* (Boulder, Colo.: Paladin Press, 2008), 22, 30, 32.
11. Michael Munk, *The Portland Red Guide: Sites and Stories of Our Radical Past* (Portland: Ooligan Press, 2007), 223; John Locanthi, "Big Trouble in Little Beirut," *Willamette Week*, May 4, 2016; and Holley Gilbert, "Demonstrators Take On Slew of Bush Policies," *Oregonian*, September 20, 1991. Quote from Locanthi, "Big Trouble."
12. Quoted in Andy Campbell, *We Are Proud Boys: How a Right-Wing Street Gang Ushered in a New Era of American Extremism* (New York: Hachette, 2022), 78.
13. People Overseeing Police Study Group [Portland Copwatch], "The Resurfacing of Political Surveillance," *People's Police Report*, no. 8 (First Trimester, 1996), 3.
14. Quoted in Mitzi Waltz, "Policing Activists: Think Global, Spy Local," *CovertAction Quarterly*, Summer 1997, 27.
15. Waltz, "Policing Activists," 27; and *X-Ray Visions*, DVD, directed by Benjamin Arthur Ellis (Bloomington, Ind.: Microcosm, 1999).
16. Waltz, "Policing Activists," 27; POPSG [Portland Copwatch], "The Resurfacing of Political Surveillance," 1, 3; and Jim Redden, "Spying on Trial," *Portland Tribune*, September 27, 2002.
17. Portland Copwatch/POPSG, "Portland Police Increase Political Repression," *People's Police Report*, no. 17 (April 1999), 2.
18. Michael Larson, Criminal Intelligence Report, City of Portland, Oregon, Bureau of Police, February 16, 1999, 6.
19. Colette Gordon, "Mobilizing Beyond Crisis: Police Accountability Organizing in Portland, Oregon" (undergraduate thesis, Reed College, 2005), 42–43, 58.
20. Quoted in People Overseeing Police Study Group [Portland Copwatch], "Critical Mass Update," *People's Police Report*, no. 6 (Second Trimester, 1995), 1, 3.
21. *Aftermass: Bicycling in a Post–Critical Mass Portland*, directed by Joe Biel (Bloomington, Ind.: Microcosm, 2013); People Overseeing Police Study Group [Portland Copwatch], "Critical Mass," *People's Police Report*, no. 5 (First Trimester, 1995), 1; and POPSG, "Critical Mass Update," 1, 3. Both quotes from *Aftermass*.

22. Portland Copwatch/POPSG, "Mass Arrest During Critical Mass Ride," *People's Police Report*, no. 17 (April 1999) 8; POPSG, "Critical Mass Update," 1, 3; and, *Aftermass*. Quote from Portland Copwatch/POPSG, "Mass Arrest," 8.
23. Portland Copwatch, "PDX Mayor Hits Critical Mass—BMX Style," *People's Police Report*, no. 35 (May 2005), 5; and *Aftermass* (quotes).
24. Scott Cohen, "Critical Mass in Portland," *Oregon Encyclopedia*, https://www.oregonencyclopedia.org/articles/critical_mass_in_portland.
25. Quoted in *Aftermass*.
26. "A compilation of forty-five street protests in Portland during the 1990s shows that the leading subjects were labor (including globalization) for seventeen, foreign policy for twelve, identity/civil rights for eight, and environment (mainly forest) for seven." Munk, *Portland Red Guide*, 213–14. For an overview of the antiglobalization movement, see Notes from Nowhere, eds., *We Are Everywhere: The Irresistible Rise of Global Anticapitalism* (London: Verso, 2003).
27. I am writing here mainly from my own recollections.
28. Portland Copwatch, "Sgt. Pool: In One End and Out the Other," *People's Police Report*, no. 26 (April 2002), 2.
29. Again, I am writing from direct observation.
30. Richard Brown and Brian Benson, *This Is Not For You: An Activist's Journey of Resistance and Resilience* (Corvallis: Oregon State University Press, 2021), 244; and Portland Copwatch, "New Chief Kroeker: A Politician, a Cop, a White Guy," *People's Police Report*, April 2000, 1, 5.
31. Jewel Lansing and Fred Leeson, *Multnomah: The Tumultuous Story of Oregon's Most Populous County* (Corvallis: Oregon State University Press, 2012), 180.
32. Quotes from Portland Copwatch/POPSG, "Police Rank-and-File Sound Off on Kroeker's New Policies," *People's Police Report*, no. 21 (August 2000), 5.
33. Quoted in Portland Copwatch, "Top Cop a Big Bigot, or, Kroeker's Callous Comments Create Conundrum for Katz," *People's Police Report*, no. 22 (December 2000), 1.
34. Portland Copwatch, "Top Cop a Big Bigot," 1 (quote), 9.
35. Portland Copwatch, "Police Attack May Day Celebration," *People's Police Report*, no. 21 (August 2000), 1, 6.
36. Portland Copwatch, "Police Attack May Day Celebration," 6.
37. Portland Copwatch, "Police Attack May Day Celebration," 6.
38. Portland Copwatch, "Bush Protest, Critical Mass, Union Solidarity Ride Face Violent Police Tactics," *People's Police Report*, no. 28 (January 2003), 7. The quality of the training was questionable. In 2002, the Rapid Response Team, the Mounted Patrol, the Oregon State Police, and the Vancouver (Washington) Police Department held a joint crowd control training, in which University of Portland criminal justice students acted as their opponents in a series of scenarios, playing a drunken Saint Patrick's Day crowd, an animal rights demonstration, and civil disobedience protesters. The students were given tennis balls to throw at the cops, though after the first round the riot squad asked them to toss the missiles more softly. "Just *lob* them," the instructor explained. Portland Copwatch, "Copwatch Observes as Police Stage 'Riot,'" *People's Police Report*, no. 27 (August 2002), 1.
39. Nicholas E. Mitchell, "The Handling of the 2020 Protests and Riots in Portland, Oregon: An Independent Review," Independent Monitoring, LLC, August 9, 2023, 8–9, 24–25.
40. Patrick F. Gillham, "Securitizing America: Strategic Incapacitation and the Policing of Protest Since the 11 September 2001 Terrorist Attacks," *Sociology Compass* 5, no. 7 (2011): 640. I outline the history of crowd control and the emergence and application of strategic

incapacitation in more detail in Kristian Williams, *Our Enemies in Blue: Police and Power in America*, 3rd ed. (Oakland: AK Press, 2015), 287–319.

41. Gillham, "Securitizing America," 643–44.
42. Portland Copwatch, "Police Attack September 26 Street Gathering: Fight for Your Right to Party," *People's Police Report*, no. 22 (December 2000), 4.
43. Quoted in Portland Copwatch, "Police and Crowds: Remembering May Day, September 26, October 22, and New Year's Eve," *Portland Police Report*, no. 23 (April 2001), 6.
44. Portland Copwatch, "Police and Crowds," 6; and Portland Copwatch, "Portland Marches Against Police Violence Once Again," *People's Police Report*, no. 22 (December 2000), 7.
45. Portland Copwatch, "Police and Crowds," 6–7.
46. Portland Copwatch, "Police and Crowds," 6.
47. David Fort, "Interview with David Howe," Portland Police Bureau Tactical Operations Division, taped interview transcription, April 4, 2001; David Fort, "Report to Portland Police Bureau," March 30, 2001; Walidah Imarisha, "Two People Facing Charges Because of Portland Police Assault," www.nyc.indymedia.org, accessed April 24, 2001; Chaz Johnson, "Thinly Disguised Political Crackdown Hits Subculture," *Portland Alliance*, September 2001; Jason Roberts, "Interview with Howe and Stradley," Portland Police Tactical Operations Division, taped interview transcription, April 4, 2001; Norman Sharp, "Use of Mace—Use of Baton—Riot," report to Portland Police Bureau, March 30, 2001; Portland Copwatch, "Cops Step Up Campaign Against Counter-Culture," *People's Police Report*, no. 24 (August 2001), 12, 14; and "The Troubles," *Life During Wartime*, July 1, 2003, kboo.fm. I discuss this period in more detail in Kristian Williams, "The Criminalization of Anarchism, Part Two; Guilt by Association, Questionable Confessions, and Mandatory Minimums," in *Confrontations; Selected Journalism* (Portland: Tarantula, 2007), 37–49.
48. Portland Copwatch, "Northeast House Party Raid Saga Ends with Plea Bargain," *People's Police Report*, no. 25 (December 2001), 7.
49. Ian Thomas, "End of Story: District Attorney Drops Kidnapping Charges," *Portland Mercury*, September 20, 2001.
50. Portland Copwatch, "May Day 2001: Police Back Off, City Council Gives In," *People's Police Report*, no. 24 (August 2001), 2, 15. On May Day's origins, see Howard Zinn, *A People's History of the United States, 1492–Present*, rev. ed. (New York: HarperCollins, 1995), 263–66.
51. Portland Copwatch, "May Day 2001," 2 (quote), 15.
52. Portland Copwatch, "Protests, Crowd Control, and the Siege of a Neighborhood," *People's Police Report*, no. 26 (April 2002), 2.
53. Portland Copwatch, "Bush Protest, Critical Mass, Union Solidarity Ride," 7.
54. Quoting from memory.
55. Portland Copwatch, "Sheriff Uses Fear to Get More Funds," *People's Police Report*, no. 29 (May 2003), 7.
56. Portland Copwatch, "Anti-War Protests Marred by Police Violence," *People's Police Report*, no. 29 (May 2003), 4.
57. Quoted in Portland Copwatch, "Undercover Tales: Retired Cop Enjoyed Violating Your Civil Rights," *People's Police Report*, no. 40 (January 2007), 11.
58. Maxine Bernstein, "Portland Police Panel Finds Capt. Mark Kruger Brought Discredit and Disgrace upon the City by Erecting a Memorial to Nazi Soldiers," oregonlive.com, October 8, 2010; Nick Budnick, "The Cop Who Liked Nazis," *Willamette Week*, February 11, 2004; and Portland Copwatch, "Officer Kruger's Interest in Nazis Confirmed by Another Acquaintance," *People's Police Report*, no. 32 (May 2004), 11. Robert Seaver (formerly Seaburg), one

of the friends in question, had been working as a clerk in the district attorney's office but was dismissed after the story came to light. Portland Copwatch, "Strange Twists in 2002 Bush Protest Lawsuit," *People's Police Report*, no. 31 (January 2004), 9.

59. Portland Copwatch, "Retaliatory Nazi-Enthusiast Captain's Discipline Purged: Harassing Road-Ragey Captain Re-Promoted," *People's Police Report*, no. 63 (September 2014), 7; Bernstein, "Portland Police Panel"; and Portland Copwatch, "City Pays Demonstrators $300,000 for Pepper Spray, Abuses at Protests," *People's Police Report*, no. 34 (January 2005), 1, 6.

Chapter 23: The Local War on Terror

1. Portland Copwatch/POPSG, "Raids on Organizers' Office and Activist's Home: The FBI Still Hates Protestors," *People's Police Report*, no. 20 (April 2000), 1, 7; and Craig Rosebraugh, *Burning Rage of a Dying Planet: Speaking for the Earth Liberation Front* (New York: Lantern Books, 2004), 137.
2. Rosebraugh, *Burning Rage of a Dying Planet*, 37–40; 48–60, 114–16.
3. Rosebraugh, *Burning Rage of a Dying Planet*, 30–32.
4. Portland Copwatch/POPSG, "Mounted Patrol and Riot Police Attack Peaceful Protest," *People's Police Report*, no. 19 (December 1999), 6. After a meticulous review of the trial transcript and documentary evidence, Amnesty International concluded that "numerous aspects" of Mumia Abu-Jamal's conviction and sentencing "clearly failed to meet minimum international standards" of fairness. Amnesty International, *A Life in the Balance: The Case of Mumia Abu-Jamal* ([Amnesty International], 2000); https://www.amnesty.org/fr/wp-content/uploads/2021/06/amr510012000en.pdf.
5. Rosebraugh, *Burning Rage of a Dying Planet*; Portland Copwatch, "The Trials and Tribulations of Craig Rosebraugh," *People's Police Report*, no. 21 (August 2000), 9; Jules Boykoff, *Beyond Bullets: The Suppression of Dissent in the United States* (Oakland: AK Press, 2007), 141; and Portland Copwatch, "FBI, Police Raid Activist's Home, Bakery," *People's Police Report*, no. 24 (August 2001), 6.
6. Reproduced in Leslie James Pickering, *The Earth Liberation Front, 1997–2002* (Portland: Arissa, 2007), unpaged frontmatter.
7. Quoted in Will Potter, *Green Is the New Red: An Insider's Account of a Social Movement Under Siege* (San Francisco: City Lights Books, 2011), 44–45.
8. "FBI Releases Its 2005 Statistics on Hate Crimes," press release, FBI, October 16, 2006.
9. Mike German, *Disrupt, Discredit, and Divide: How the New FBI Damages Democracy* (New York: New Press, 2019), 237.
10. Jeffrey St. Clair, "The Cancer Agents of the FBI: The Great Green Scare," in *Born Under a Bad Sky: Notes from the Dark Side of the Earth* (Petrolia, CA: Counterpunch; and Oakland: AK Press, 2008), 56.
11. Mike Romano, "Who Killed the Timber Task Force?," *Seattle Weekly*, October 9, 2006; and Jeffrey St. Clair, "Steal a Tree, Go to Jail; Steal a Forest, Meet the President: The Politics of Timber Theft," in *Born Under a Bad Sky: Notes from the Dark Side of the Earth* (Petrolia, Ca: Counterpunch, 2008), 165–66.
12. Quoted in Rosebraugh, *Burning Rage of a Dying Planet*, 114.
13. Rosebraugh, *Burning Rage of a Dying Planet, en passim*; Portland Copwatch, "The Trials and Tribulations of Craig Rosebraugh," 9; and Boykoff, *Beyond Bullets*, 141.
14. For details of the grand jury process, see Boykoff, *Beyond Bullets*, 141; and Rosebraugh, *Burning Rage of a Dying Planet*, 42–43.

15. Quoted in Pickering, *The Earth Liberation Front,* 80, 83, and 152–55. For lists of the grand juries' questions, see Pickering, *The Earth Liberation Front,* 80–83. For the questions posed by Congress, see Pickering, *The Earth Liberation Front,* 152–57.
16. Rosebraugh, *Burning Rage of a Dying Planet,* 234.
17. Matthew Wolfe, "The Rise and Fall of America's Environmentalist Underground," *New York Times Magazine,* May 26, 2022; and Leah Sottile, *Burn Wild* podcast, bbc.co.uk, August–November 2022.
18. Josef Schneider, "Portland Withdraws from Terrorism Task Force," *Z Magazine,* July–August 2005, 75; and Portland Copwatch, "FBI 'Domestic Terrorism' Squad Deputizes Portland Police Officers," *People's Police Report,* no. 23 (April 2001), 1.
19. Schneider, "Portland Withdraws from Terrorism Task Force," 75; Portland Copwatch, "Joint Terrorism Task Force Its own Worst Enemy," *People's Police Report,* no. 24 (August 2001), 6; and Adam J. Hodges, *World War I and Urban Order: The Local Class Politics of National Mobilization* (Houndmills, UK: Palgrave Macmillan, 2016), 149.
20. Portland Copwatch, "Local News in the 'War on Civil Liberties'—er—'Terrorism,'" *People's Police Report,* no. 27 (August 2002), 8.
21. Richard W. Stevenson, "Signing Homeland Security Bill, Bush Appoints Ridge as Secretary," *New York Times,* November 26, 2002; "U.S. Homeland Security Bill: Civil Rights Vulnerable and Immigrant Children Not Protected," Human Rights Watch, November 21, 2002, https://www.hrw.org; and Amanda Chicago Lewis, "The 20-Year Boondoggle," theverge.com, November 16, 2022.
22. Nancy Chang, "The USA Patriot Act: What's So Patriotic About Trampling on the Bill of Rights?," *CovertAction Quarterly,* Winter 2001, 14–18; and American Civil Liberties Union, "USA Patriot Act Boosts Government Powers While Cutting Back on Traditional Checks and Balances: An ACLU Legislative Analysis," archive.aclu.org, accessed December 22, 2002.
23. Glenn Greenwald, *No Place to Hide: Edward Snowden, the NSA, and the U.S. Surveillance State* (New York: Metropolitan Books, 2014), 99, 116.
24. John Ashcroft, quoted in Eric Lichtblau et al., "Response to Terror: Justice Dept. to Tighten Focus on Terrorism Law," *Los Angeles Times,* November 9, 2001.
25. "Reaction Universal, Personal," *Oregonian,* September 12, 2001.
26. David Harris, *Good Cops: The Case for Preventive Policing* (New York: New Press, 2005), 10. A transcript of one such interview, conducted by the FBI, appears in Harris, *Good Cops,* 174–80.
27. German, *Disrupt, Discredit, and Divide,* 33, 151–52.
28. Schneider, "Portland Withdraws from Terrorism Task Force," 76; Portland Copwatch, "Updates on Portland, the 'War on Terrorism,' and Police Spying," *People's Police Report,* no. 29 (May 2003), 6.
29. One of the seven was Patrice Lumumba Ford, the son of Kent Ford, former leader of the Portland chapter of the Black Panther Party. Boykoff, *Beyond Bullets,* 267–69; and Lucas N. N. Burke and Judson L. Jeffries, *The Portland Black Panthers: Empowering Albina and Remaking a City* (Seattle: University of Washington Press, 2016), 225–27.
30. Ivan Greenberg, *The Dangers of Dissent: The FBI and Civil Liberties Since 1965* (Lanham, Md: Lexington Books, 2013), 281; and Portland Copwatch, "Joint Terrorism Task Force Screws Up: False Fingerprint Puts Lawyer in Jail," *People's Police Report,* no. 33 (September 2004) 5. Quote from Portland Copwatch, "Joint Terrorism Task Force Screws Up," 5.
31. Schneider, "Portland Withdraws from Terrorism Task Force," 76; Greenberg, *The Dangers of Dissent,* 281; Portland Copwatch, "Lawyer Falsely Accused of Terrorism Sues FBI,"

People's Police Report, no. 34 (January 2005), 3; Portland Copwatch, "Portland Officers Withdrawn from Joint Terrorism Task Force," *People's Police Report*, no. 36 (September 2005), 6; and Portland Copwatch, "Judge in Mayfield Case Finds Portion of PATRIOT Act Unconstitutional," *People's Police Report*, no. 43 (January 2008), 9.

32. Portland Copwatch, "Lawyer Falsely Accused of Terrorism Sues FBI," 3.
33. Quoted in Portland Copwatch, "Portland Officers Withdrawn," 6.
34. Portland Copwatch, "Portland Officers Withdrawn," 1; and Schneider, "Portland Withdraws from Terrorism Task Force."
35. Quoted in Portland Copwatch, "City Renews FBI-Police 'Joint Terrorism Task Force' After Considerable Community Opposition," *People's Police Report*, no. 25 (December 2001), 1.
36. Quoted in Portland Copwatch, "Local and National Spying Challenged," *People's Police Report*, no. 39 (September 2006) 9. Potter was hardly being paranoid. The FBI had tapped Mayor Goldschmidt's phone in 1976. It is not known whether they collected evidence concerning his sexual relationship with an underage girl. Portland Copwatch, "Local and National Spying Challenged," 9.
37. Quoted in Schneider, "Portland Withdraws from Terrorism Task Force," 78.
38. Quoted in Portland Copwatch, "Local and National Spying Challenged," 9.
39. Trevor Aaronson, *The Terror Factory: Inside the FBI's Manufactured War on Terrorism* (Brooklyn: Ig Publishing, 2013), 184–88; and German, *Disrupt, Discredit, and Divide*, 266.
40. Quoted in Nigel Duara, "Oregon Man Gets 30 Years in Christmas Bomb Plot," AP, apnews.com, October 1, 2014.
41. Aaronson, *The Terror Factory*, 204–5.
42. Quoted in Aaronson, *The Terror Factory*, 195.
43. German, *Disrupt, Discredit, and Divide*, 161, 266–67.
44. Aaronson, *The Terror Factory*, 205; Portland Copwatch, "City Releases Disappointingly Vague Reports on Joint Terrorism Task Force," *People's Police Report*, no. 56 (May 2012), 1; Portland Copwatch, "Portland Re-joins Terrorism Task Force Despite Itself," *People's Police Report*, no. 54 (September 2011), 7. Concerning more recent iterations of this pattern, see Portland Copwatch, "In Narrow Vote, Portland Re-Joins Joint Terrorism Task Force," 1, 6; and Portland Copwatch, "City Council Votes to Get Portland Out of The Terrorism Task Force," *People's Police Report*, no. 77 (May 2019), 1, 5.

Chapter 24: North Star, Whistle-Blowers, and Cover-Ups

1. Roxanne Lynn Doty, "Divided Lines: The Politics of Immigration Control in the United States," in *Immigration and the Law: Race, Citizenship, and Social Control*, edited by Sofía Espinoza Álvarez and Martin Guevara Urbina (Tucson: University of Arizona Press, 2018), 63; and Ruth Gomberg-Muñoz, "Building America; Immigrant Labor and the U.S. Economy," in *Immigration and the Law: Race, Citizenship, and Social Control*, edited by Sofía Espinoza Álvarez and Martin Guevara Urbina (Tucson: University of Arizona Press, 2018), 108. See also Geo Maher, *A World Without Police: How Strong Communities Make Cops Obsolete* (London: Verso, 2021), 187.
2. Jennifer Bjorhus, "Joint Efforts by Police, INS Concern Immigrant-Rights Groups," *Oregonian* November 2, 1997; Maya Blackmun, "Activists Charge INS Tactics Violate Rules," *Oregonian*, May 31, 1997; Richard Read, "Overwhelmed, I.N.S. Develops Culture of Abuse,

Racism," *Oregonian*, December 14, 2000; and Alex Pulaski, "Immigration Raids Hit Workplace," *Oregonian*, November 9, 1997.

3. Dan Hortsch, "Angry Workers Group Condemns INS Raid Tactics," *Oregonian*, March 25, 1998; John Snell and David R. Anderson, "INS Raids 'Job Corner' on Northeast Burnside," *Oregonian*, July 10, 1997; Portland Copwatch/POPSG, "¡Raza Sí! ¡Migra No! Day Laborers Resist INS Raids," *People's Police Report*, no. 12 (August 1997), 3; Portland Copwatch/POPSG, "INS Declares Open Season on Latinos," *People's Police Report*, no. 14 (April 1998), 11; and Christian Parenti, *Lockdown America: Police and Prisons in the Age of Crisis* (London; Verso, 1999), 150. Ramirez quoted in Blackmun, "Activists Charge INS Tactics Violate Rules."
4. Hortsch, "Angry Workers Group Condemns INS Raid Tactics"; Portland Copwatch/POPSG, "¡Raza Sí! ¡Migra No!," 3; Portland Copwatch/POPSG, "INS Declares Open Season on Latinos," 11; and Portland Copwatch/POPSG, "The INS Versus Workers' Rights: La Lucha Sigue," *People's Police Report*, no. 15 (August 1998), 7–8. Beebe quoted in Blackmun, "Activists Charge INS Tactics Violate Rules."
5. Maher, *A World Without Police*, 195. See also Parenti, *Lockdown America*, 152–54.
6. Quoted in Kale Williams, "Portland Police Won't Cooperate with Feds on Potential ICE Raids, Chief Says," oregonlive.com, July 14, 2019.
7. Bjorhus, "Joint Efforts by Police, INS"; and Ashbel S. Green, "Immigrants Swept Up in Drug Raid," *Oregonian*, September 30, 1997.
8. Green, "Immigrants Swept Up in Drug Raid."
9. Portland Copwatch/POPSG, "¡Raza Sí! ¡Migra No!," 3.
10. Quoted in Portland Copwatch/POPSG, "Rapping Back: Watch Out for Open Face Sores," in *People's Police Report*, no. 11 (April 1997), 6.
11. Green, "Immigrants Swept Up in Drug Raid."
12. Quoted in Portland Copwatch/POPSG, "¡Raza Sí! ¡Migra No!," 3.
13. Maxine Bernstein, "30 Officers Falsified Overtime, Review Finds," *Oregonian*, August 7, 1999; Maxine Bernstein, "Inquiry Details City's Police Overtime Ruses," *Oregonian*, August 2, 2000 (quote); and, Maxine Bernstein, "Officers Won't Face Charges in Pay Abuse," *Oregonian*, February 17, 2001.
14. Bernstein, "Inquiry Details City's Police Overtime Ruses."
15. Quoted in Bernstein, "30 Officers Falsified Overtime."
16. Quoted in Bernstein, "Officers Won't Face Charges in Pay Abuse."
17. Bernstein, "30 Officers Falsified Overtime"; Bernstein, "Inquiry Details City's Police Overtime Ruses"; Bernstein, "Officers Won't Face Charges in Pay Abuse"; Portland Copwatch/POPSG, "Police Cheat on Overtime," *People's Police Report*, #18 (August 1999), 11; Portland Copwatch/POPSG, "Overtime Scandal Investigations Turns to Possible Criminal Activity," *People's Police Report*, no. 19 (December 1999), 8; and Portland Copwatch, "Three Portland Police Officers Fired for Unsatisfactory Performance," *People's Police Report*, no. 21 (August 2000), 8.
18. Quoted in Maxine Bernstein, "Policeman Sues City, Supervisors." *Oregonian*, July 1, 2000.
19. Bernstein, "Inquiry Details City's Police Overtime Ruses."
20. Maxine Bernstein, "Audit Says Police Can Curb Costs of Overtime," *Oregonian*, November 13, 2000; and Portland Copwatch/POPSG, "Second Overtime Scandal Exposed; Stress Disability Awarded to Two," *People's Police Report*, no. 20 (April 2000), 4.
21. Nick Budnick, "Crossing the Line," *Willamette Week*, February 5, 2002; and Bernstein, "Inquiry Details City's Police Overtime Ruses."
22. Budnick, "Crossing the Line."
23. Quotes from Budnick, "Crossing the Line."

24. Budnick, "Crossing the Line"; and Portland Copwatch, "SERT and Woodcock Scandals 'Resolved': PPB Discrimination and Retaliation Against Two Sexual Minority Whistleblowers," *People's Police Report*, no. 26 (April 2002), 5.
25. Loren W. Christensen, "Officer Cocky Hat," in *Skid Row Beat: A Street Cop's Walk on the Wild Side* (Boulder, Colo.,: Paladin Press, 1999), 158–59.
26. People Overseeing Police Study Group [Portland Copwatch], "Portland Pays Through the Nose Again in '93 for Improper Police Actions," *People's Police Report*, no. 1 (First Quarter, 1994) 2; and Budnick, "Crossing the Line."
27. Nick Budnick, "Gross Violation," *Willamette Week*, December 24, 2002; Chris Lydgate and Nick Budnick, "Rubbish!," *Willamette Week*, December 24, 2002; Portland Copwatch, "'Bad Pig' . . . or Sacrificial Lamb?," *People's Police Report*, no. 27 (August 2002), 11; and Portland Copwatch, "Where's the Justice for Whistleblowers? First Female SERT Officer Loses Lawsuit, Officers File for Whistleblower Protection," *People's Police Report*, no. 36 (September 2005), 5.
28. Quoted in Portland Copwatch, "Whistleblower Cop Trainee Loses Harassment Suit Against City," *People's Police Report*, no. 54 (September 2011), 2.
29. Quoted in Portland Copwatch, "Citizen Review Committee Analyzes Whistleblower Case (but No Appeals); Holds Retreat, Forum," *People's Police Report*, no. 54 (September 2011), 3.
30. Portland Copwatch, "Cops End Free Ride on Sodas at Convenience Store," *People's Police Report*, no. 45 (September 2008), 9.
31. Portland Copwatch, "Off-Duty Beating Cover-Up Cops Punished, City Pays Victim $75,000," *People's Police Report*, no. 31 (January 2004), 7.
32. Portland Copwatch, "Savage Beating, Cover-Up Highlight Problems with Police Bureau," *People's Police Report*, no. 27 (August 2002), 1–2.
33. Portland Copwatch, "Investigation Closed on Police Cover-Up of Assault by Off-Duty Officers," *People's Police Report*, no. 28 (January 2003), 6; and Portland Copwatch, "Off-Duty Beating Whistleblower Punished," *People's Police Report*, no. 29 (May 2003), 5. Both quotes from Portland Copwatch, "Savage Beating, Cover-Up," 1–2.
34. Portland Copwatch, "Investigation Closed on Police Cover-Up," 6; Portland Copwatch, "Off-Duty Beating Cover-Up Cops Punished," 7; Portland Copwatch, "Savage Beating, Cover-Up," 2; and Portland Copwatch, "Off-Duty Beating Whistleblower Punished," 5.
35. Quoted in Budnick, "Gross Violation."
36. Read, "Overwhelmed, I.N.S. Develops Culture of Abuse."
37. Read, "Overwhelmed, I.N.S. Develops Culture of Abuse."
38. Read, "Overwhelmed, I.N.S. Develops Culture of Abuse."
39. Portland Copwatch, "Bye-Bye Beebe: INS Chief Scandalized, Whole Agency in Disarray," *People's Police Report*, no. 22 (December 2000), 8.
40. Associated Press, "More than 165 Workers Detained After Agents Raid Portland Food Plant," *Seattle Times*, June 13, 2007.
41. Brent Hunsberger, "Del Monte Settlement Considered Victory for Low-Wage Workers," oregonlive.com, August 10, 2006.
42. Quoted in Brent Hunsberger, "Will Del Monte Raid Keep Workers from Reporting Abuses?" blog.oregonlive.com, June 14, 2007.
43. Quoted in Don McIntosh, "Del Monte Raid Puts Portland at Center of Immigration Debate," nwlaborpress.org, July 6, 2007.
44. Associated Press, "Oregon Supreme Court Declines to Review Del Monte Fresh Produce Verdict," oregonlive.com, May 10, 2014.

Chapter 25: Accountability and Reform

1. Portland Copwatch, "Police Shoot Man Inside Psychiatric Hospital," *People's Police Report*, no. 24 (August 2001), 1, 8 (quote).
2. Portland Copwatch, "Police Shoot Man Inside Psychiatric Hospital," 8–9; and Colette Gordon, "Mobilizing Beyond Crisis: Police Accountability Organizing in Portland, Oregon" (undergraduate thesis, Reed College, 2005), 59.
3. Merlin Douglass, "Mental Health in Crisis," *Portland Business Journal*, September 16, 2001; Portland Copwatch, "Police Shoot Man Inside Psychiatric Hospital," 9; and, Portland Copwatch, "Awards to Police Who Killed José Mejía Spark Outrage," *People's Police Report*, no. 28 (January 2003), 1.
4. Portland Copwatch, "Tasers Hit the Streets Before Police Are Ready; Electroshock Weapons Possibly Linked to Deaths Elsewhere," *People's Police Report*, no. 27 (August 2002), 1. On the history of the taser and its use as an instrument of torture, see Darius Rejali, *Torture and Democracy* (Princeton, NJ: Princeton University Press), 225–47.
5. Portland Copwatch, "Tasers Continue Causing Static: Local, National Attention to Electroshock Devices Extends Debate," *People's Police Report*, no. 32 (May 2004), 1, 8.
6. Portland Copwatch, "Tasers Zapped by Bad Publicity," *People's Police Report*, no. 33 (September 2004), 9.
7. Quoted in Portland Copwatch, "Taser Danger Probe: More Portland Cases Make Headlines as the Manufacturer Expands Its Arsenal," *People's Police Report*, no. 46 (January 2009), 9.
8. Portland Copwatch, "Use of Force Report Shows Tasers as Prevalent While Other Force Down," *People's Police Report*, no. 48 (September 2009), 5.
9. Portland Copwatch, "Portland Police Experience First Taser-Related Death," *People's Police Report*, no. 38 (May 2006), 1, 7. Amnesty International documented more than five hundred taser-related deaths in North America during the period 2001–15. David Correia and Tyler Wall, *Police: A Field Guide* (London: Verso, 2018), 18.
10. Portland Copwatch, "Taser Updates: Supreme Court Refuses Appeal by Seattle Cops; Portland Lawsuit Taser Totals Examined," *People's Police Report*, no. 57 (September 2012), 8.
11. Portland Copwatch, "Lawsuits Continue to Rack Up Against Portland," *People's Police Report*, no. 53 (May 2011), 1.
12. Portland Copwatch, "Another Taser Incident Costs Portland $200,000," *People's Police Report*, no. 56 (May 2012), 1, 9.
13. Quote in Portland Copwatch, "Tasers Zapped by Bad Publicity," 1, 9.
14. Quoted in Gordon, "Mobilizing Beyond Crisis," 27–29.
15. Gordon, "Mobilizing Beyond Crisis," 30.
16. Twice (in 2000 and 2002) the Police Accountability Campaign, headed by Jo Ann Bowman (later, Hardesty) and the *Portland Alliance*'s Dave Mazza, collected signatures for a ballot measure. Each time, the proposals failed to qualify by a painfully narrow margin. Gordon, "Mobilizing Beyond Crisis," 46.
17. Gordon, "Mobilizing Beyond Crisis," 31; and Portland Copwatch, "In Historic Hearing, Council Votes to Hold Officer Accountable for Misconduct . . . as the Entire Oversight Body Management Quits, and Review Committee Continues Work," *People's Police Report*, no. 78 (September 2019), 1–3.
18. Portland Copwatch, "Police Review Division Director Covers Up Missing Files, Stalls Citizen Committee," *People's Police Report*, no. 30 (September 2003), 1, 9.

19. Portland Copwatch, "Police Review Board Challenges System; Citizen Review Board Takes Firm Stands on Mejía and Bonneau Cases," *People's Police Report*, no. 29 (May 2003), 1, 3.
20. Quoted in Portland Copwatch, "Five Citizen Review Committee Members Resign in Protest," *People's Police Report*, no. 30 (September 2003), 3.
21. Portland Copwatch, "Former Review Board Members Hold Hearing on Mejía Beating," *People's Police Report*, no. 32 (May 2004), 4.
22. A report commissioned by the city after the 2020 George Floyd protests is similarly frank: "Portland has a dizzying variety of committees with sometimes overlapping mandates," resulting in an "alphabet soup of community engagement." Nicholas E. Mitchell, "The Handling of the 2020 Protests and Riots in Portland, Oregon: An Independent Review," Independent Monitoring, LLC, August 9, 2023, 25.
23. Thomas E. Perez and Amanda Marshall, "Re: Investigation of the Portland Police Bureau [letter of findings]," US Department of Justice, Civil Rights Division, September 12, 2012, 26.
24. Perez and Marshall, "Re: Investigation of the Portland Police Bureau," 28–30.
25. Perez and Marshall, "Re: Investigation of the Portland Police Bureau," 33–34.
26. Perez and Marshall, "Re: Investigation of the Portland Police Bureau," 34–35. Parallel to this system of non-accountability, the Police Review Board "reviews certain PPB incidents with the stated goal of making recommendations to the Chief regarding findings on those incidents and proposed discipline. . . . It has no ultimate decision making authority." Perez and Marshall, "Re: Investigation of the Portland Police Bureau," 32.
27. Perez and Marshall, "Re: Investigation of the Portland Police Bureau," 26–27, 35.
28. Gordon, "Mobilizing Beyond Crisis," 78–80.

Chapter 26: Deadly Profiles

1. Colette Gordon, "Mobilizing Beyond Crisis: Police Accountability Organizing in Portland, Oregon" (undergraduate thesis, Reed College, 2005), 42–43, 58.
2. McCollister quoted in "The Officer Who Shot Kendra James Describes What Happened the Night She Died," *Oregonian*, May 20, 2003. See also Portland Copwatch, "Kendra James Case Continues to Reverberate," *People's Police Report*, no. 31 (January 2004), 8; and *Arresting Power: Resisting Police Violence in Portland, Oregon*, directed by Jodi Darby et al. (Collective Eye, 2015), DVD.
3. Portland Copwatch, "Police Shooting of Young Woman Draws Intense Community Criticism," *People's Police Report*, no. 30 (September 2003), 1, 8; and Gordon, "Mobilizing Beyond Crisis," 59.
4. "Critiquing Portland Police," *Oregonian*, August 26, 2003.
5. Quoted in Maxine Bernstein, "Report Finds Glaring Deficiencies in Inquiries into Police Shootings," *Oregonian*, August 21, 2003.
6. Portland Copwatch, "Kendra James Case Continues to Reverberate," 1, 8.
7. Maxine Bernstein, "Kroeker Forced Out," *Oregonian*, August 30, 2003; and Portland Copwatch, "Chief Kroeker Resigns Under Pressure," *People's Police Report*, no. 31 (January 2004), 6.
8. Quoted in Portland Copwatch, "Chief Kroeker Resigns Under Pressure," 6.
9. Portland Copwatch, "Two Die in 32 Hours After Police Gunfire; One Officer Also Shot Kendra James," *People's Police Report*, no. 45 (September 2008), 1.

10. Portland Copwatch, "Chief Kroeker Resigns Under Pressure," 6; and Nick Budnick, "Black and Blue," *Willamette Week*, October 8, 2003; and Portland Copwatch, "Police Shoot 'Non-Lethal' Rounds into Crowd of Protesters," *People's Police Report*, no. 16 (December 1998), 1, 5.
11. Portland Copwatch, "Chief Kroeker Resigns Under Pressure," 6.
12. Budnick, "Black and Blue."
13. Portland Copwatch, "Foxworth's Foxhole: Old Political and Personal Problems Plague Portland Police Chief," *People's Police Report*, no. 34 (January 2005), 5. That inquiry was itself a spin-off from a different investigation, one looking into the behavior of Commander Mike Garvey, who was suspected of cavorting with male "escorts." The investigation largely flopped: the only misconduct it found was Garvey's use of his bureau-issued cell phone to conduct a separate business. Regardless, he was demoted to captain and removed from the police honor guard. He later sued, alleging discrimination based on his sexual orientation. Portland Copwatch/POPSG, "Capt. Garvey Sues for Discrimination," *People's Police Report*, no. 15 (August 1998), 7; and Portland Copwatch, "Foxworth's Foxhole: Old Political and Personal Problems," 5.
14. Portland Copwatch, "Foxworth's Foxhole: Portland's Chief Takes Control in More Ways than One," *People's Police Report*, no. 33 (September 2004), 6.
15. Portland Copwatch, "Police Shoot and Kill Third Unarmed Young Black Person in 3 Years," *People's Police Report*, no. 32 (May 2004), 1.
16. Portland Copwatch, "Perez Shooting Prompts Change," *People's Police Report*, no. 33 (September 2004), 1, 7; and Nick Budnick, "One Trigger Finger, One Hired Gun," *Willamette Week*, May 15, 2004. Martin Dennis, who witnessed the attack and managed to capture part of it on an audio recording, insists that Perez's hands were visible and that Sery "had the gun out as soon as he got out of the car." As he tells it, "There was no struggle. This guy walked up to the car and tried to pull him out. Then he stepped back, and Sery shot him." Quoted in Jim Redden, "Eyewitness to Chaos," *Portland Tribune*, April 6, 2004.
17. Budnick, "One Trigger Finger" (quote); and Portland Copwatch, "Perez Shooting Prompts Change," 7.
18. Portland Copwatch, "New Racial Profiling Statistics Show Little Change Since 2001," *People's Police Report*, no. 39 (September 2006), 1. The numbers were stubbornly consistent over time. Statistics from 2001 showed African Americans to be 2.6 times as likely as whites to be stopped by the police; on the west side, they were stopped at an astonishing *five times* the white rate. Portland Copwatch, "Racial Profiling Proven: African Americans 260% More Likely to Be Pulled Over in Portland," *People's Police Report*, no. 24 (August 2001), 1; and Portland Copwatch, "Racial Profiling: Chief Kroeker Continues to Discount Statistics, and Other Stories," *People's Police Report*, no. 25 (December 2001), 4.
19. Portland Police Bureau, "Kendra James Community Forum," information packet, July 1, 2003, 13.
20. Portland Copwatch, "New Use of Force Report Shows Disparities in Who Gets Hit," *People's Police Report*, no. 48 (September 2009), 1.
21. Portland Copwatch, "Foxworth's Foxhole: Portland's (Ex?) Chief Has Police, Public Perception Issues," *People's Police Report*, no. 38 (May 2006), 9.
22. Lisa K. Bates, Ann Curry-Stevens, and Coalition of Communities of Color, *The African American Community in Multnomah County* (Portland: Portland State University, 2010), 78.
23. Portland Copwatch, "Chief Sizer Finally Releases (Good Beginning of) Racial Profiling Plan . . . on the Same Day the Police Review Board Publishes Its 'Bias Based Policing' Report," untitled sidebar, *People's Police Report*, no. 47 (May 2009), 6.

24. Quoted in Portland Copwatch, "Rapping Back: 'No Such Thing as Racial Profiling,'" *People's Police Report*, no. 27 (August 2002), 12.
25. Bates, Curry-Stevens, and Coalition of Communities of Color, *The African American Community in Multnomah County*, 79.
26. Portland Copwatch, "New Racial Profiling Statistics Show Little Change," 8.
27. Midge Purcell et al., eds., *The State of Black Oregon* (Portland: Urban League, [2009]), 2.
28. Portland Copwatch, "Perez Shooting Prompts Change," 1, 7 (quote); and Gordon, "Mobilizing Beyond Crisis," 59–60.
29. Quoted in *Arresting Power*.
30. Gordon, "Mobilizing Beyond Crisis," 46–47, 57, 61. I was a member of Rose City Copwatch from its founding in 2003 until its dissolution in 2012. Concerning my time with the group, see Kristian Williams, "*Our Enemies in Blue*: A Short Retrospective," in *Fire the Cops! Essays, Lectures, and Journalism* (Montreal: Kersplebedeb, 2014), 11–12; and Kristian Williams, acknowledgements in *Fire the Cops!*, 192–93. For more on RCCW and its politics, see "What We Want," Rose City Copwatch, rosecitycopwatch.wordpress.com/about.
31. Gordon, "Mobilizing Beyond Crisis," 60–61.
32. Portland Copwatch, "Shootings, Death in Custody Updates," untitled sidebar, *People's Police Report*, no. 32 (May 2004), 6.
33. See "Rogues of the Week," *Willamette Week*, April 14, 2004; and "A Dangerous Antipolice Stunt," *Oregonian*, February 21, 2004.
34. *Arresting Power*. The posters can be seen at "Past Events and Projects," Rose City Copwatch, rosecitycopwatch.wordpress.com/projects.
35. I wrote about this moment of stressed uncertainty in Kristian Williams, "Will Portland Burn?," in *Fire the Cops! Essays, Lectures, and Journalism* (Montreal: Kersplebedeb, 2014), 21–31.
36. Quoted in Redden, "Eyewitness to Chaos."
37. Quoted in Williams, "Will Portland Burn?," 22.
38. Quoted in Williams, "Will Portland Burn?," 29–30.
39. All quoted in Williams, "Will Portland Burn?," 28.
40. David R. Anderson, "Officer Who Killed Motorist Gets New Police Job," *Oregonian*, January 16, 2008. More than a year after Sery's departure, Chief Foxworth released a report stating that "the use of deadly force and the use of the Taser [in the Perez case] were within current policies and procedures." Portland Police Bureau, *A Report to the Community: James Jahar Perez* (Portland: Portland Police Bureau, 2005), 17.
41. All quotes from Lucas Manfield, "Derrick Foxworth Prefers to Leave His Erotic Prose in the Past," *Willamette Week*, October 4, 2023.
42. Portland Copwatch, "Chief Sizer Permanently Appointed; Foxworth Demoted for Rumor," *People's Police Report*, no. 39 (September 206), 1.
43. Richard Brown and Brian Benson, *This Is Not For You: An Activist's Journey of Resistance and Resilience* (Corvallis: Oregon State University Press, 2021), 251–52.
44. Portland Copwatch, "Deaths and Beatings in County Jail: Dangerous Tattooed Gang Roves Hallways," *People's Police Report*, no. 22 (December 2000), 1, 8; and Portland Copwatch, "Multnomah Sheriff Fires Four Deputies in Beating; Grand Juries Clear Cops in Jail Deaths," *People's Police Report*, no. 23 (April 2001), 11.
45. Portland Copwatch, "Deaths and Beatings in County Jail," 8; and Portland Copwatch, "Multnomah Sheriff Fires Four Deputies," 11.
46. Portland Copwatch, "Bernie Giusto: 'The Teflon Sheriff' aka 'Porno Pants,'" *People's Police Report*, no. 41 (May 2007), 3; Portland Copwatch, "Multiple Lawsuits, High Visibility

Incidents Rock Sheriff's Office," *People's Police Report*, no. 43 (January 2008), 4 (quote); and Portland Copwatch, "Bedtime for Bernie: Sheriff Giusto to Resign as Investigation Winds Down," *People's Police Report*, no. 44 (May 2008), 8.

47. Jewel Lansing and Fred Leeson, *Multnomah: The Tumultuous Story of Oregon's Most Populous County* (Corvallis: Oregon State University Press, 2012), 231.
48. Portland Copwatch, "Need Headlines? Go for the Giusto!" *People's Police Report*, no. 36 (September 2005), 7; and Portland Copwatch, "Weekend at Bernie's: Can Multnomah County's Sheriff Keep His Career from Dying?," *People's Police Report*, no. 38 (May 2006), 2.
49. Portland Copwatch, "Bernie Giusto: 'The Teflon Sheriff,'" 3.
50. Lansing and Leeson, *Multnomah*, 231–32; Portland Copwatch, "Bernie Under Fire: Sheriff Giusto's Jails Slammed in DA's Report," *People's Police Report*, no. 40 (January 2007), 9; and Portland Copwatch, "Bedtime for Bernie," 1, 8. "Violent and costly" quoted in Lansing and Leeson, *Multnomah*, 231; "jailin' system" quoted in Portland Copwatch, "Bernie Under Fire," 9.
51. Portland Copwatch, "Need Headlines? Go for the Giusto!," 7; and Portland Copwatch, "Weekend at Bernie's," 2. Both quotes from Portland Copwatch, "Bernie Giusto: 'The Teflon Sheriff,'" 3.
52. Portland Copwatch, "Sheriff Checks Out Accuser in Criminal Database," *People's Police Report*, no. 42 (September 2007), 9 (quote); Nigel Jaquiss, "Who Knew," *Willamette Week*, December 14, 2004; Lansing and Leeson, *Multnomah*, 231–32; and Portland Copwatch, "There's a New Sheriff in Town: It's Bye, Bye Bernie! As Skipper Takes the Wheel," *People's Police Report*, no. 45 (September 2008), 9. The misuse of police files for personal or political purposes is undoubtedly common. Even the quintessential reformer, Don Clark, when facing a recall petition, asked a sheriff's department sergeant to look into it. The sergeant accessed the Columbia Region Information System to access the records of those circulating the petition. Clark faced a minor scandal. After an investigation headed by Lee Brown, the sergeant was reprimanded and reassigned. "Oral History Interview with Don E. Clark" [transcription], interviews conducted by George M. Joseph, August 30, 1994–March 27, 1998, Archives West, SR1166, 649; and Lee P. Brown and Joseph Green Bishop, *Outhouse to the White House* (Bloomington, Ind.: AuthorHouse, 2022), 95–96.
53. Quoted in Lansing and Leeson, *Multnomah*, 232.
54. Portland Copwatch, "New Sheriff Dealing with Scandals," *People's Police Report*, no. 49 (January 2010), 4.
55. Portland Copwatch, "New Sheriff Dealing with Scandals," 4.
56. Portland Copwatch, "Another Sheriff Hits the Dusty Trail," *People's Police Report*, no. 69 (September 2016), 5.
57. Portland Copwatch, "Third Sheriff in a Row Rocked by Scandals, May Resign," *People's Police Report*, no. 68 (May 2016), 1, 5.
58. Quoted in Nigel Jaquiss, "Oregon State Fraternal Order of Police Issues Statement on Sheriff Dan Staton," wweek.com, February 29, 2016.

Chapter 27: Public Order and Mental Disorder

1. Quoted in *Alien Boy: The Life and Death of James Chasse*, directed by Brian Lindstrom (Philadelphia: Breaking Glass Pictures, 2014), DVD.
2. Portland Copwatch, "Man Dies from Internal Injuries After Portland Police Tackle, Beat Him for 'Acting Bizarre,'" *People's Police Report*, no. 40 (January 2007), 1, 7; Mark Sten, *All*

Ages: The History of Portland Punk, 1977–1981 (Portland: Reptilicus Press, 2015), 90–104; and *Arresting Power: Resisting Police Violence in Portland, Oregon,* directed by Jodi Darby et al. (Portland: Collective Eye, 2015), DVD.

3. Quoted in *Alien Boy.*
4. *Arresting Power*; Nick Budnick, "Why Did James Chasse Die?," *Portland Tribune,* September 11, 2008; and Portland Copwatch, "Man Dies From Internal Injuries," 1.
5. Quoted in *Alien Boy.* For detailed composite accounts from the police perspective, see Maxine Bernstein, "Police Missed Clues to Chasse's Mental Illness," *Oregonian,* October 20, 2006; and Maxine Bernstein, "No Indictment in Chasse Death," *Oregonian,* October 18, 2006.
6. Quoted in Portland Copwatch, "Chasse, Kaady Families Get Partial Settlements of Roughly $1 Million Each," *People's Police Report,* no. 48 (September 2009), 6.
7. Portland Copwatch, "Man Dies From Internal Injuries," 1, 7; Budnick, "Why Did James Chasse Die?"; and *Arresting Power.*
8. Quoted in *Alien Boy.*
9. Ian Demsky, "Why Did James Chasse Jr. Die?," *Willamette Week,* November 1, 2006; *Alien Boy*; Portland Copwatch, "Man Dies From Internal Injuries," 1, 7; Portland Copwatch, "More details on How James Chasse Died: Lawyers Say Police Cover-Up Killed Him," *People's Police Report,* no. 52 (January 2011), 1, 7; and *Arresting Power.*
10. Quoted in Portland Copwatch, "Chasse, Kaady Families Get Partial Settlements," 6.
11. The *Oregonian* paraphrased Henderson saying "Humphreys' actions were not unreasonable considering the Transit Division's proactive attempts to eradicate drug dealing and other nuisance behavior." Maxine Bernstein, "Portland Officer Chris Humphreys' Decision to Chase James Chasse and Knock Him Down Was 'Inconsistent' with His Training, Review Says," *Oregonian,* August 8, 2010.
12. Quoted in *Arresting Power.*
13. Bruce Johnson, *The Pearl District: Placemaking from the Ground Up* (Portland: Pearl Light, 2022), 321–22, 330–31.
14. *Alien Boy*; Maxine Bernstein, "Police Punishment Reversed," *Oregonian,* July 13, 2012; and Portland Copwatch, "Three Years Later, Chasse Case Stirs More Controversy," *People's Police Report,* no. 49 (January 2010), 1. Saltzman later complained, "Anything we did, it always seemed like there was a high likelihood to be overturned by an arbitrator. . . . We were always going to lose." Quoted in Nigel Jaquiss and Tess Riski, "For Nearly 80 Years, the Portland Police Association Has Wielded Power in a Town That Doesn't Like Cops. That Power Is Now Under Siege," *Willamette Week,* June 24, 2020.
15. Quoted in Portland Copwatch, "Three Years later, Chasse Case Stirs More Controversy," 7 Westerman would later be fired after a pair of road rage incidents involving the same driver, and for lying to investigators. Portland Copwatch, "Road Rage Cops: Sgt. Scott Westerman Fired, Traffic Captain Todd Wyatt Indicted," *People's Police Report,* no. 55 (January 2012), 10.
16. *Alien Boy*; and Portland Copwatch, "Three Years Later, Chasse Case Stirs More Controversy," 7.
17. Portland Copwatch, "Three Years Later, Chasse Case Stirs More Controversy," 7; Dan Handelman, "Rapping Back: Chasse/Beanbag Cop's Punishment Pushes Police Protest," *People's Police Report,* no. 50 (May 2010), 12; Maxine Bernstein, "Long Blue Line Walks in Protest," *Oregonian,* November 25, 2009; "A 'Win' for the Police, a Loss for the Community," *Oregonian,* December 2, 2009; Maxine Bernstein, "Beanbag Use on Girl 'Consistent' with Policy," *Oregonian,* September 16, 2010; Maxine Bernstein, "Portland Police Promise Improved Approach to Mental Illness After Scathing Justice Department Report,"

oregonlive.com, September 13, 2012; Stuart Tomlinson, "Ex-Portland Cop Elected Wheeler Sheriff," *Oregonian*, November 8, 2012; and James Pitkin, "Sizer Matters," *Willamette Week*, December 9, 2009.

18. Tomlinson, "Ex-Portland Cop Elected Wheeler Sheriff."

19. James Pitkin, "'We're Better Than All This': And Nine Other Things We've Learned in the Past Week About the Fatal Police Shooting of Aaron Campbell," *Willamette Week*, February 23, 2010; *Arresting Power*; and Portland Copwatch, "'Basically We Shot an Unarmed Black Guy Running Away from Us': Aaron Campbell Killed in Third Avoidable Sniper Shooting in Five Years," *People's Police Report*, no. 50 (May 2010), 1, 6. Quote from Portland Copwatch, "Basically We Shot an Unarmed Black Guy," 1.

    Campbell's mother suspects that the murder was premeditated. She claims that a gang intervention worker told her that the cops went to the Sandy Terrace that night intending to kill her son. Aaron Campbell had a history with the Portland Police. He had once been arrested in connection with a shooting, and his mother says that she saw the cops plant evidence while searching his room. He was acquitted at trial when the victim testified in his defense. Marva Davis, *Two Sons Set in a Day* (n.p., 2020), 39–41.

20. Grand Jury 1, Session 1, 2010, "Aaron Campbell Grand Jury Letter" (February 10, 2010), scribd.com/document/27133490/Aaron-Campbell-Grand-Jury-Letter, accessed December 8, 2023.

21. Grand Jury 1, Session 1, 2010, "Aaron Campbell Grand Jury Letter"; James Pitkin, "'We're Better Than All This'"; and Maxine Bernstein, "Portland Police Deputy Chief Robert Day to Retire in Early May," oregonlive.com, March 27, 2019.

22. George Ciccariello-Maher, "Oakland's Not for Burning? Popular Fury at Yet Another Police Murder," in *Raider Nation*, vol. 1, *From the January Rebellions to Lovelle Mixon and Beyond* (Oakland: Raider Nation Collective, 2010).

23. Just two months after Grant's death, Lovelle Mixon killed two Oakland cops at a traffic stop, then two more during the SWAT raid that also killed him. That October, several unoccupied police cars were firebombed in Seattle; a few days later, two cops were shot in a drive-by attack, and one died. The following month Maurice Clemmons ambushed four cops in a Lakewood, Washington, coffee shop, killing them all. I discuss this whole sequence of events in more detail in Kristian Williams, "Cop Killers and Killer Cops: Political Considerations," in *Fire the Cops! Essays, Lectures, and Journalism* (Montreal: Kersplebedeb, 2014), 32–51.

24. Both quotes from Helen Jung, "Permitting Portland Officer's Return to Work a Political, 'Not a Wise' Decision, Jesse Jackson Says," *Oregonian*, February 17, 2010.

25. "Jack Collins: Officer Involved Shooting Summary," PPB Open Data, Portland Police Bureau, https://www.portland.gov/police/open-data/jack-collins, accessed December 1, 2023; and Portland Copwatch, "Second Shooting of 2010 Leaves Homeless Man Dead," *People's Police Report*, no. 50 (May 2010), 1, 7.

26. "Anti-Police Activity in the Northwest + Beyond," *Fire to the Prisons* (Summer 2010), 29–34.

27. "Anti-Police Activity in the Northwest + Beyond," 29–34.

28. Brian Michael Bendis and Alex Maleev, *Scarlet* (Milwaukie, OR: Dark Horse Comics, 2022).

    Bendis said in an interview that he was moved to write the series after seeing a young woman arrested in Pioneer Square ("it got hostile and rough"). Quoted in Forrest Helvie, "Bendis and Maleev Stage an Apolitical Revolution for the People in *Scarlet*," in Bendis and Maleev, *Scarlet*, unpaged.

29. Bernie Foster, "Having an Emergency? Don't Call the Police," *Skanner*, February 15, 2010.
30. Interview with Genevieve Goffman, October 1, 2014; Tabatha Millican, in conversation, November 1, 2014; and [Tabatha Millican], "Survivor Support Group," interview with Kat of Hysteria, *Altjustice*, July 12, 2010, altjustice.wordpress.com.
31. Portland Copwatch, "Police Review Board to Get Some Teeth—Nine Years Later," *People's Police Report*, no. 50 (May 2010), 1–2.
32. *Alien Boy*.
33. Adams proposed a $4.9 million reduction in the police budget (approximately 3.8 percent) to offset $5 million in excess overtime costs. Sizer estimated that the cuts would result in the elimination of twenty-five officers and twelve other staff, the Cold Case Homicide Squad, the Mounted Patrol, and the drug task force. Maxine Bernstein, "Portland Police Chief Rosie Sizer Upset at Proposed Cuts in Police Bureau," *Oregonian*, May 11, 2010.
34. Steve Duin, "Rose Sizer Defended 'Demonized' Portland Police Bureau to the Bitter End," *Oregonian*, May 12, 2020.
35. Sam Adams, "From Sam Adams: A New Police Chief for a New Direction," *Oregon Mental Health Archive*, oregonarchive.org, May 12, 2020.
36. Maxine Bernstein, "Police Stop Went Bad Almost Instantly," *Oregonian*, June 2, 2010; and Portland Copwatch, "Portland Police Shoot, Kill Third Person in Mental Health Crisis in 2010," *People's Police Report*, no. 51 (September 2010), 1, 6. Quotes (from Detective Arjay Dran, May 12, 2010, and Detective Meredith Hopper, May 13, 2010): "Confidential Taped Statement Transcription: Case No. 10-38353," in Portland Police Bureau, *Detective Investigation: Keaton Otis* (2010), portland.gov/police/open-documents/keaton-otis-investigative-book-1/download.
37. Portland Copwatch, "Police Kill Suicidal Man, Wound Robbery Suspect; SWAT Team Shoots Man on His Porch," *People's Police Report*, no. 56 (May 2012), 1. Cody Berne, one of the cops who shot Keaton Otis, went on to become a prosecuting attorney with the Multnomah County DA's office. Portland Copwatch, "PPB Shoots, Kills Man [for] First Time in a Year; Former Chief Indicted in Off-Duty Shooting," *People's Police Report*, no. 70 (January 2016), 6; and Portland Copwatch, "Otis Shooter Cop Turned Lawyer Interviewed," *People's Police Report*, no. 71 (May 2017), 6.
38. *Arresting Power*. One witness to the shooting told Detective Erica Hurley, "I never seen a gun. I never seen the boy with a gun. What made them start shooting, I don't know." Quoted in "Confidential Taped Statement Transcript; Case no. 10-38353," (May 13, 2010), in Portland Police Bureau, *Detective Investigation: Keaton Otis* (May 2010), portland.gov/police/open-documents/keaton-otis-investigative-book-1/download.
39. Portland Copwatch, "Portland Police Shoot, Kill Third Person," 6.
40. Quoted in "Albina Ministerial Alliance: 'Keaton Otis Did Not Have to Die'," *Willamette Week*, June 8, 2010.
41. Ryan Foote (May 13, 2010) and James Defrain (May 15, 2010), in "Confidential Taped Statement Transcript: Case No. 10-38353," Portland Police Bureau, *Detective Investigation: Keaton Otis* (May 2010), portland.gov/police/open-documents/keaton-otis-investigative-book-1/download; and Portland Copwatch, "Portland Police Shoot, Kill Third Person," 1.
42. Quoted in Defrain, "Confidential Taped Statement Transcription."
43. Portland Copwatch, "Portland Police Shoot, Kill Third Person," 6.
44. Quoted in Bernstein, "Police Stop Went Bad Almost Instantly."
45. Quoted in James Pitkin, "Black and Blue," *Willamette Week*, January 28, 2009.
46. Portland Copwatch, "Chief Sizer Finally Releases (Good Beginning of) Racial Profiling

Plan . . . on the Same Day the Police Review Board Publishes Its 'Bias Based Policing' Report," untitled sidebar, *People's Police Report*, no. 47 (May 2009), 6.

47. Lisa K. Bates, Ann Curry-Stevens, and Coalition of Communities of Color, *The African American Community in Multnomah County* (Portland: Portland State University, 2010), 78–79.

Two years later, in 2011, African Americans were the subject of 11.8 percent of all traffic stops and 19.5 percent of all pedestrian stops, though they constituted only 6.3 percent of the local population. They were searched in 12.6 percent of the these stops, which is 3.7 times the rate at which white people were searched. Latinos were stopped at a rate below their portion of the population (6.2 percent of traffic and 6 percent of pedestrian stops, as opposed to 9.2 percent of the census total), but they were searched 8 percent of the time (2.7 times the white rate). Police were more likely to find contraband on whites (42.7 percent of searches) than Blacks (30.5 percent) or Latinos (29.8 percent). Greg Stewart and Emily Covelli, *Stops Data Collection: The Portland Police Bureau's Response to the Criminal Justice Policy and Research Institute's Recommendations* (Portland: Portland Police Bureau, 2014), 11, 13, 15–17.

48. As University of Pittsburgh law professor David Harris explains, "In the case of consensual crimes such as drug activity and weapons offenses, arrest and incarceration rates are particularly poor measures of criminal activity. They are much better measures of *law enforcement activity*. . . . Arrest statistics tell us that police arrest disproportionate numbers of African American males for drug crimes. This reflects decisions made by someone in the police department . . . to concentrate enforcement activity on these individuals." David A. Harris, *Profiles in Injustice: Why Racial Profiling Cannot Work* (New York: New Press, 2002), 78. Emphasis in original.

49. Midge Purcell et al., eds., *The State of Black Oregon* (Portland: Urban League, [2009]), unpaged.

50. Quoted in Thor Benson, "Portland Has a Hip-Hop Problem," vice.com, September 18, 2013.

51. Quoted in "Why Portland?," *Uprising: A Guide from Portland*, podcast, November 22, 2020, iheart.com.

52. Anika Bent-Albert et al., "Policy Review: Portland Police Bureau Policies and Practices Related to Hip-Hop Events," Office of the City Auditor, Independent Police Review, undated, 7.

53. Quoted in Matthew Singer, "Illmaculate Declares 'I Will Not Perform'," *Willamette Week*, March 2, 2014.

54. Bent-Albert, "Policy Review," 17–20; Singer, "Illmaculate Declares 'I Will Not Perform'"; and David Greenwald, "The Blue Monk Closing April 29," oregonlive.com, April 22, 2014.

55. Leah Sottile, "Racist Policing Plagues Portland's Nightclubs," *High Country News*, hcn.org, February 2, 2019; Alex Zielinski, "Discriminatory Club Policies Are Pushing African Americans Out of Portland's Nightlife," *Portland Mercury*, July 4, 2019 (quote); and Sarah Mirk, "How to Dress Like a Gang Member," *Portland Mercury*, May 12, 2011.

56. Maxine Bernstein, "Owner of Portland's Seeznin's Bar and Lounge Said OLCC Restrictions Will Force Him to Close Down," oregonlive.com, July 5, 2011; Sottile, "Racist Policing Plagues Portland's Nightclubs" (quotes); and, Zielinski, "Discriminatory Club Policies."

57. Quoted in Cary Clarke and Terrence Scott, "An Interview with Cool Nutz," in *Northwest Passage: 50 Years of Independent Music from the Rose City*, edited by Marc Moscato (Portland: Dill Pickle Club, [2010]), 78.

58. Zielinski, "Discriminatory Club Policies."

59. Grand Jury 1, Session 1, 2010, "Aaron Campbell Grand Jury Letter"; Pitkin, "'We're Better Than All This'"; and Bernstein, "Portland Police Deputy Chief Robert Day to Retire." Some cops further questioned Reyna's decision not to summon the Special Emergency Reaction Team, attributing it to a grudge derived from her experience of hazing when she was part of the unit. Pitkin, "'We're Better Than All This.'"
60. Portland Copwatch, "Police Kill Suicidal Man," 1; and Portland Copwatch, "Officer Who Shot Aaron Campbell in the Back Reinstated: City's Inability to Fire Ron Frashour Prompts Protests, Appeal," *People's Police Report*, no. 58 (January 2013), 10.
61. Quoted in Jaquiss and Riski, "For Nearly 80 Years."
62. Lisa Loving, "US Department of Justice Confirms 'Pattern and Practices' Probe of Portland Police," *Skanner*, July 23, 2010.
63. Portland Copwatch, "Department of Justice Investigates Portland Police Use of Force," *People's Police Report*, no. 54 (September 2011), 1, 11.
64. Thomas E. Perez and Amanda Marshall, "Re: Investigation of the Portland Police Bureau [letter of findings]," US Department of Justice, Civil Rights Division, September 12, 2012), 2–3, 19, 25.
65. Office of Public Affairs, US Department of Justice, "Justice Department and the City of Portland, OR, Reach Preliminary Agreement on Reforms Regarding Portland Police Bureau's Use of Force Against Persons with Mental Illness," press release, justice.gov, September 13, 2012.
66. Quoted in *Alien Boy*.
67. Lucas Manfield, "State Records Suggest Multnomah County Deputies Let Hoover Gang Members Beat Up Jailhouse Rivals," *Willamette Week*, February 20, 2024 (quotes); Multnomah County Sheriff's Office, "Statement on Alleged Misconduct by Three Corrections Deputies," news release, flashalert.net/id/MCSO/170164, February 20, 2024; Lucas Manfield, "Jail Deputies Were Also Accused of Doing Favors for Gypsy Jokers Motorcycle Gang," *Willamette Week*, March 16, 2024; and Lucas Manfield, "Multnomah County Sheriff's Office Received State Report on Deputy Abuses Three Months Before the Sheriff Read It," *Willamette Week*, February 23, 2024.
68. Manfield, "State Records Suggest Multnomah County"; and Manfield, "Multnomah County Sheriff's Office Received State Report."

Chapter 28: Redevelopment, Homelessness, and the Occupy Movement

1. Margaret Haberman, "Occupy Portland Hits Town with a Cast of Thousands for Massive, Peaceful Demonstration," *Oregonian*, October 7, 2011; and "Occupy Portland: Police Raze Camps, Drive Protestors from 2 Squares," oregonlive.com, November 13, 2011.
2. For a timeline of the Occupy movement, see Writers for the 99%, *Occupying Wall Street: The Inside Story of an Action That Changed America* (Chicago: Haymarket Books, 2011), 206–12.
3. David Harvey, *Rebel Cities: From the Right to the City to the Urban Revolution* (London: Verso, 2012), 161.
4. For a brief overview, see Mike King, *When Riot Cops Are Not Enough: The Policing and Repression of Occupy Oakland* (New Brunswick, NJ: Rutgers University Press, 2017), 3–6. For a sampling of the multiplicity of the movement, see Kate Khatib et al., eds., *We Are Many: Reflections on Movement Strategy from Occupation to Liberation* (Oakland: AK Press, 2012).

5. "Occupy Portland: Police Raze Camps"; Portland Copwatch, "Police Brutality at Occupy Portland," *People's Police Report*, no. 55 (January 2012), 8; and "Police Close Down Occupy Portland Protest Camp," bbc.com, November 14, 2011.
6. Portland Copwatch, "Over-Policing of Occupy and Related Protests Continues Post-Eviction," *People's Police Report*, no. 56 (May 2012), 7.
7. Portland Copwatch, "Police Brutality at Occupy Portland," 8.
8. King, *When Riot Cops Are Not Enough*, 65–67.
9. Hannah Hoffman and Aaron Mesh, "Pearl District Occupation Ends with 27 Arrests," *Willamette Week*, October 30, 2011.
10. King, *When Riot Cops Are Not Enough*, 76–80. Quotes on 78 (Wexler) and 80 (Adams).
11. King, *When Riot Cops Are Not Enough*, 80–83. Adams quoted in "Police Close Down Occupy Portland Protest Camp," bbc.com. On the identification of dirt with disorder, see Mark Neocleous, *A Critical Theory of Police Power: The Fabrication of Social Order* (London: Verso, 2021), 176–77.
12. Portland Copwatch, "Reese's Pieces: Reese's Mayoral Hopes Dashed After He Blames Occupy Protests for Lack of Patrol Cops," *People's Police Report*, no. 55 (January 2012), 9.
13. Andrew Dickson recalls living in Portland in the mid-nineties: "I was playing in three bands, making my own movies and living with friends in a 5000 square foot warehouse for a few hundred dollars a month." Alexander Barrett and Andrew Dickson, *This Is Portland: The City You've Heard You Should Like*, 2nd ed. (Portland: Microcosm Publishing, 2018), 4.
14. R. Bruce Stephenson, *Portland's Good Life: Sustainability and Hope in an American City* (Lanham, Md: Lexington Books, 2021), 134–36, 139.
15. Stephenson, *Portland's Good Life*, 134–35, 138.
16. Portland Copwatch, "Sit/Lie 4.0: Pitting People with Disabilities Against Those Without Homes," *People's Police Report*, no. 51 (September 2010), 1, 8.
17. Michelle Martin, "A Message from the Chair," *BID News*, April–May 2010, http://www.portlandalliance.com/news_cals/BIDnewsletter_may2010.html.
18. Portland Copwatch, "Sit/Lie Targets Homeless People—and African Americans," *People's Police Report*, no. 55 (January 2012), 5; Portland Copwatch, "More Misery for Poor and Homeless Portlanders: PCW Holds 'Public Meeting' with the Mayor to Change Bad Policies," *People's Police Report*, no. 64 (January 2015), 9; and Portland Copwatch, "The Portland Police Bureau and 'Union' vs. Houseless People," *People's Police Report*, no. 75 (September 2018), 4.
19. Portland Copwatch, "Sit/Lie Targets Homeless People," 5; and Portland Copwatch, "Homeless Continue to Be Targets of the Powers That Be," *People's Police Report*, no. 56 (May 2012), 9.
20. Stephenson, *Portland's Good Life*, 128.
21. Stephenson, *Portland's Good Life*, 127. Northparkblocks.org is still active, with information about neighborhood clean-ups, a volunteer "Pearl Foot Patrol," and instructions for "report[ing] and [*sic*] encampment or tent on the sidewalk." northparkblocks.org, accessed December 19, 2023.
22. Stephenson, *Portland's Good Life*, 128.
23. Bruce Johnson, *The Pearl District: Placemaking from the Ground Up* (Portland: Pearl Light, 2022), 99.
24. Tracy J. Prince, "Portland's Response to Homeless Issues and the 'Broken Windows' Theory," in *The Portland Edge: Challenges and Successes in Growing Communities*, edited by Connie P. Ozawa (Washington, D.C.: Island Press, 2004), 286–87.
25. Johnson, *The Pearl District*, 296, 303–4.

26. Portland Copwatch, "Sweeps Continue Even as City Unveils More Relaxed Rules for Houseless Campers," *People's Police Report*, no. 68 (May 2016), 5.
27. Quoted in Stephenson, *Portland's Good Life*, 137–38.
28. Portland Copwatch, "Mayor Caves to Business Demands on Pushing Houseless Out of Downtown," *People's Police Report*, no. 73 (January 2018), 7.
29. Rebecca Woolington and Melissa Lewis, "Portland Homeless Accounted for Majority of Police Arrests in 2017, Analysis Finds," oregonlive.com, June 27, 2018; and Rebecca Woolington, "Half the Arrests in Portland Last Year Were of Homeless People. Mayor Ted Wheeler Says That's a Problem," oregonlive.com, July 13, 2018. Quote from Woolington, "Half the Arrests."
30. Quoted in Rebecca Woolington, "Portland Police Union Leader Calls City 'Cesspool,' Slams Mayor's Response to Homelessness," oregonlive.com, July 16, 2018.
31. Portland Copwatch, "Interfering with Homeless People's Lives: Portland's Ongoing War on the Poor," *People's Police Report*, no. 63 (September 2014), 9; Portland Copwatch, "More Misery for Poor and Homeless Portlanders," 9; and Portland Copwatch, "Houseless Woes: Sweeps Continue, Boulders Planted," *People's Police Report*, no. 78 (September 2019), 2.
32. Portland Copwatch, "PPB Sweeps Homeless People from Springwater Corridor," *People's Police Report*, no. 70 (January 2015), 5; Portland Copwatch, "Continued Plight of the Houseless: RV Crackdown, R2DToo Moves," *People's Police Report*, no. 72 (September 2017), 7; and Portland Copwatch, "Vigilante 'Community' Groups Join War on Portland's Unhoused," *People's Police Report*, no. 76 (January 2019), 7.
33. Portland Copwatch, "Houseless Woes," 2.
34. Amelia Templeton, "Portland Wants Your Rundown RV," opb.org, October 27, 2017.
35. Dirk Vanderhart, "RV Camping Has Exploded on Portland Streets," *Portland Mercury*, July 12, 2017.
36. Quoted in Portland Copwatch, "Continued Plight of the Houseless."
37. Quoted in Heather Mack et al., *Decriminalizing Homelessness: Why Right to Rest Legislation Is the High Road for Oregon* (Portland: ACLU of Oregon, 2017), 6.

Chapter 29: Between Occupy and Uprising

1. Portland Copwatch, "Over-Policing of Occupy and Related Protests Continues Post-Eviction," *People's Police Report*, no. 56 (May 2012), 7.
2. Portland Copwatch, "May Day Melee Elevates Tensions," *People's Police Report*, no. 57 (September 2012), 1, 5.
3. Mike German, *Disrupt, Discredit, and Divide: How the New FBI Damages Democracy* (New York: New Press, 2019), 205; "Attachment B: Items to Be Seized," in Kris Hermes, "Chasing Anarchists: May Day and the Federal Government's Use of Grand Juries as Political Counterintelligence," huffingtonpost.com, April 30, 2013; and Brendan Kiley, "Christmas in Prison," *Stranger*, December 19, 2012. Jones quoted in Hermes, "Chasing Anarchists."
4. German, *Disrupt, Discredit, and Divide*, 204–5.
5. German, *Disrupt, Discredit, and Divide*, 205; Levi Pulkkinen, "Agent: FBI Tailed Anarchists Headed to May Day Riot," *Seattle Post-Intelligencer*, October 18, 2012; Mike, "Tell It Like It Isn't: Portland Police and Press Smear Anarchist Squatters," *The Portland Radical*, August 2012, portlandradical.wordpress.com; Everton Bailey Jr., "Police Arrest Man, 25, Stemming from Investigation of Multiple Portland ATM, Bank Vandalisms," oregonlive.com, May 3,

2012; Sarah Mirk, "Portland Activist Charged with 72 Felonies Gets Plea Deal," *Portland Mercury*, October 5, 2012; and Portland Police Bureau, "Portland Police Arrest Protesters," portlandoregon.gov, July 9, 2010.

6. "The Shooting of a Missouri Teenager," *New York Times*, August 14, 2014; Annie Karni et al., "Two Cops Pulled Off Streets, Staten Island DA Looking into Death of Dad of Six After NYPD Cop Put Him in a Chokehold During Sidewalk Takedown," *Los Angeles Daily News*, July 18, 2014; and Steve Almasy and Holly Yan, "Protestors Fill Streets Across Country as Ferguson Protests Spread Coast to Coast," cnn.com, November 26, 2014.

7. Darlena Cunha, "Ferguson: In Defense of Rioting," *Time*, November 25, 2014, time.com.

8. Instead of police, they offered six alternatives: "1. Unarmed mediation and intervention teams.... 2. Decriminalization of almost every crime.... 3. Restorative Justice.... 4. Direct democracy at the community level.... 5. Community patrols.... 6. Mental health care." José Martín, "Policing Is a Dirty Job, but Nobody's Gotta Do It: 6 Ideas for a Cop-Free World," *Rolling Stone*, December 16, 2014, rollingstone.com.

9. Portland Copwatch, "PPB Attacks Portland Michael Brown/Eric Garner Protests," *People's Police Report*, no. 64 (January 2015), 8; Portland Copwatch, "Bureau Boycotts Citizen Review Committee, Which in Turn Compels Officers to Attend," *People's Police Report*, no. 68 (May 2016), 3; and Portland Copwatch, "Police Oversight Panel Makes Mixed Recommendations, Gets New Members," *People's Police Report*, no. 70 (January 2017), 3 (Marshman quote). For a description of a demonstration blocking traffic without police interference, see Deke N. Blue, *Just Drive: Life in the Bus Lane* (Oregon City: Just Zakanna Productions, 2017), 160–61.

10. See, for example, ABC News, "How Donald Trump Perpetuated the 'Birther' Movement for Years," abcnews.go.com, September 16, 2016; Michael Lesher, "Donald Trump's Conspiracy Theories," *New York Times*, February 29, 2016; and Sally Kohn, "Nothing Donald Trump Says on Immigration Holds Up," *Time*, June 29, 2016, time.com.

11. Terrence Petty and Robert Jablon, "Oregon Is Epicenter as Trump Protests Surge Across Nation," AP, November 11, 2016, apnews.com; Eder Campuzano, "Portland Protests: 18 Key Demonstrations Since Donald Trump Was Elected President," oregonlive.com, November 8, 2017; and Portland Copwatch, "PPB Violence at Post-Election Protests Makes International News," *People's Police Report*, no. 70 (January 2017), 9.

12. Petty and Jablon, "Oregon Is Epicenter"; Mat dos Santos, "Sunday's Protests in Portland Were a Trial for the First Amendment and Policing," ACLU Oregon, June 6, 2017, aclu-or.org; and Portland Copwatch, "PPB Violence at Post-Election Protests," 9.

13. Campuzano, "Portland Protests."

14. Portland Police training documents identify the governing strategy as the "Negotiated Management Model," characterized by a "non-confrontational approach" and "emphasiz[ing] prevention and accommodation" with "closer communication and cooperation between police and organizers," resulting in a "minimum use of force" and a "reduced tendency to make arrests." However, the materials also describe this as an "Iron Fist in the Velvet Glove." Portland Police Bureau, *Protests and Riots*, undated, documentcloud.org/documents/21180085-protests_riots_powerpoint_reduced_size_final, 16–18, accessed February 23, 2024. For details of the negotiated management model, see Clark McPhail et al., "Policing Protest in the United States: 1960–1995," in *Policing Protest: The Control of Mass Demonstrations in Western Democracies*, edited by Donnatella della Porta and Herbert Reiter (Minneapolis: University of Minnesota Press, 1998), 49–69.

15. Quoted in Portland Copwatch, "Portland Protests Met with Violence or Hugs, Depending on Permit," *People's Police Report*, no. 71 (May 2017), 4. Emphasis in original.

16. Southern Poverty Law Center, "SPLC Statement on Proud Boys Rally in Portland, OR," September 25, 2020, splcenter.org.
17. David Neiwert, *The Age of Insurrection: The Radical Right's Assault on American Democracy* (Brooklyn: Melville House, 2023), 179–80; Laura Jedeed, "Making Monsters: Right-Wing Creation of the Liberal Enemy" (undergraduate thesis, Reed College, 2019), 92, 99–104, 122; Daniel Martinez HoSang and Joseph E. Lowndes, *Producers, Parasites, Patriots: Race and the New Right-Wing Politics of Precarity* (Minneapolis: University of Minnesota Press), 2, 154–5; and Jane Coaston, "The Pro-Trump, Anti-Left Patriot Prayer Group, Explained," *Vox*, September 8, 2020, vox.com.
18. Portland City Auditor and Independent Police Review, *Policy Review: Portland Police Can Improve Its Approach to Crowd Control During Street Protests* (2018), https://www.portland.gov, 2; Doug Brown, "Photos and Video: Saturday's Right-Wing March, Left Protest in Montavilla," *Portland Mercury*, April 29, 2017; and Eder Campuzano, "Opposing Protests March Down 82nd Avenue in Fits, Starts and Shouts," oregonlive.com, April 29, 2017.
19. "Police Declare Riot as Protestors Set Fires in Downtown Portland," oregonlive.com, May 1, 2017; and Campuzano, "Portland Protests."
20. Neiwert, *Age of Insurrection*, 179, 399–401; "The Birth of an Uprising," *Uprising: A Guide from Portland*, podcast, December 6, 2020, iheart.com; Kale Williams, "Video: Portland Max Stabbing Suspect Made Threats Hours Before Slayings," orgonlive.com, May 28, 2017; and Jason Wilson, "Suspect in Portland Double Murder Pushed White Supremacist Material Online," *Guardian*, May 28, 2017. Christian was sentenced to life in prison without the possibility of parole. Neiwert, *Age of Insurrection*, 407.
21. Portland City Auditor and Independent Police Review, *Policy Review*, 2–5; National Police Foundation, "Preparing for and Responding to Mass Demonstrations and Counter-Demonstrations in Portland, Oregon: A Review of the Portland Police Bureau's Response to Demonstrations on June 4, 2017, August 4, 2018, and August 17, 2019," December 2020, 20–22; Andrea Damewood and Eric Berry, Confidential Investigative Report (Portland: Independent Police Review, 2019), 24; Neiwert, *Age of Insurrection*, 179–80; Andy Campbell, *We Are Proud Boys: How a Right-Wing Street Gang Ushered in a New Era of American Extremism* (New York: Hachette, 2022), 86; and Jedeed, "Making Monsters," 95.
22. Dos Santos, "Sunday's Protests in Portland"; Portland City Auditor and Independent Police Review, *Policy Review*, 5–7; Campbell, *We Are Proud Boys*, 148–49; German, *Disrupt, Discredit, and Divide*, 240; and National Police Foundation, "Preparing for and Responding to Mass Demonstrations," 21.
23. Quoted in Damewood and Berry, *Confidential Investigative Report*, 19, 23.
24. Neiwert, *Age of Insurrection*, 192–95, 402–3.
25. Campbell, *We Are Proud Boys*, 88.
26. Quoted in Dan Handelman, "Rapping Back," *People's Police Report*, no. 77 (May 2019), 12.
27. Katie Shepherd, "Portland Police Launched a Criminal Investigation After Joey Gibson Complained About an Antifascist Demonstrator," *Willamette Week*, July 31, 2019.
28. Katie Shepherd, "Portland Police Declare a Riot After Right-Wing Marchers Begin Beating Antifascists with Flag Poles," *Willamette Week*, June 30, 2018.
29. Campbell, *We Are Proud Boys*, 91.
30. Neiwert, *Age of Insurrection*, 406.
31. Jared Cowley and Nate Hanson, "Timeline: 13 Arrested During Dueling Demonstrations in Portland on August 17," kgw.com, August 19, 2019. A recording of police radio chatter, captured by their own spy plane, revealed the cops deciding to make arrests without

probable cause. Lucas Manfield, "Recordings from a Police Plane Show Officers Looking for Reasons to Arrest the Leftist Protestors Below," *Willamette Week*, March 12, 2024.

32. Quoted in Meerah Powell et al., "Portland Police Arrest at Least 13 in Downtown Portland Rally," opb.org, August 16, 2019.
33. Alex Zielinski, "The Proud Boys Came to Portland and Are Threatening to Return. Now What?" *Portland Mercury*, August 19, 2019.
34. Trump quoted in Cowley and Hanson, "Timeline: 13 Arrested." On the legal arguments, see Nur Ibrahim, "Can Trump Designate Antifa as a 'Terrorist Organization'?," snopes.com, June 3, 2020.
35. Alex Zielinski, "Portland Police Offer No Proof That Protesters Had Milkshakes with 'Quick-Dry Cement,'" *Portland Mercury*, June 20, 2019; and Portland Copwatch, "Officer Violence, Tainted Milkshake Tweet Impact Anti-Fascist Protest," *People's Police Report*, no. 78 (September 2019), 4.
36. German, *Disrupt, Discredit, and Divide*, 240.
37. Damewood and Berry, *Confidential Investigative Report*, 11 (quote), 23.
38. Jonathan Levinson, "Dozens of Oregon Law Enforcement Officers Have Been Members of the Far-Right Oath Keepers Militia," opb.org, October 15, 2021. On the Oathkeepers, see Neiwert, *Age of Insurrection*, 148–53.
39. Quoted in Katie Shepherd, "Portland Police Chief Says Protestors Went Off to 'Whine and Complain' Last Week Because Officers 'Kicked Your Butt,'" *Willamette Week*, August 18, 2018. Outlaw came to Portland after twenty years with the Oakland Police Department, where she had avoided scandal and earned the respect of civil rights lawyers and members of the review board. But as the captain overseeing Internal Affairs during the Occupy protests, she concluded that more should be done to protect private property. She later said that she applied for the Portland Police Bureau job because of the city's reputation as a center of protest. Katie Shepherd, "She Learned the Ropes at One of the Most Corrupt Police Departments in the Country. Now Danielle Outlaw Runs the Portland Police—and She Wants More Power," *Willamette Week*, November 7, 2018.

    After Outlaw left Portland, she became chief of the Philadelphia Police Department, whose handling of the 2020 George Floyd protests resulted in $9.2 million in settlements. Associated Press, "Danielle Outlaw, Former Portland Police Chief, Quits Top Cop Job in Philadelphia After Three Turbulent Years," oregonlive.com, September 5, 2023.
40. German, *Disrupt, Discredit, and Divide*, 240–41.
41. Maxine Bernstein, "Portland Police Training on Protests Ends with Slide Showing Mock Prayer for 'Dirty Hippy,' Prompts Investigation," oregonlive.com, January15, 2022. The image appears at: Portland Police Bureau, *Protests and Riots*, undated, documentcloud .org/documents/21180085-protests_riots_powerpoint_reduced_size_final, 110, accessed February 23, 2024.
42. Lucas Manfield, "A Police Sergeant Suspended for Glorifying Violence Against Protestors Was Repeatedly Sued for His Use of Force," *Willamette Week*, March 1, 2023; and Lucas Manfield, "Portland Police Bureau Suspends Officer It Believes Responsible for Adding 'Dirty Hippy' Meme to Training Materials," *Willamette Week*, February 22, 2023.
43. Jo Ann Hardesty, "Statement from Commissioner Jo Ann Hardesty Regarding PPB Texts with Patriot Prayer Leader," news release, portlandoregon.gov, February 14, 2019.
44. Alex Zielinski, "Texts Show Protective Relationship Between Portland Cops and Patriot Prayer," *Portland Mercury*, February 14, 2019; and Kelly Weill, "Antifa: Portland Police 'Protect White Supremacy' by Passing Intel to Patriot Prayer," thedailybeast.com, February 15, 2019.

45. Quoted in Damewood and Berry, *Confidential Investigative Report*, 12. Toese would eventually be sentenced to eight years for riot, assault, criminal mischief, and weapons charges. April Ehrlich, "Proud Boy Tusitala 'Tiny' Toese Sentenced to 8 Years for Violence at Portland Rallies," opb.org, July 21, 2023. On his role in the movement, see HoSang and Lowndes, *Producers, Parasites, Patriots*, 118–21.
46. Quoted in Damewood and Berry, *Confidential Investigative Report*, 4.
47. Damewood and Berry, *Confidential Investigative Report*, 24; and Maxine Bernstein, "Cop Cleared in Controversy over His Friendly Texts with Patriot Prayer's Joey Gibson Before, During, Protests," oregonlive.com, July 13, 2019. Quote from Zielinski, "Texts Show Protective Relationship."

    Niiya has since left the Portland Police Bureau and works as a police officer in Boise, Id. Neiwert, *Age of Insurrection*, 405.
48. Quoted in Damewood and Berry, *Confidential Investigative Report*, 24 ("assign peacekeepers") and 27 ("bluntly").
49. Quoted in Damewood and Berry, *Confidential Investigative Report*, 8–9. Emphasis added.
50. Clifford Stott, "Crowd Dynamics and Public Order Policing," in *Preventing Crowd Violence*, edited by Tamara D. Madensen and Johannes Knutsson (Boulder, Colo.: Lynne Rienner, 2011), 41–42.
51. Stefan Holgersson and Johannes Knutsson, "Dialogue Policing: A Means for Less Crowd Violence?," in *Preventing Crowd Violence*, edited by Tamara D. Madensen and Johannes Knutsson (Boulder, Colo.: Lynne Rienner, 2011), 191–216; Stott, "Crowd Dynamics and Public Order Policing," 41–42; and, Ingrid Hylander and Kjell Granström, "Police Use of Active and Passive Mitigation Strategies at Crowd Events," in *Preventing Crowd Violence*, edited by Tamara D. Madensen and Johannes Knutsson (Boulder, Colo.: Lynne Rienner, 2011), 70.
52. Bernstein, "Cop Cleared in Controversy."
53. Quoted in Damewood and Berry, *Confidential Investigative Report*, 24.
54. Quoted in Portland Copwatch, "Police Release Info on Political Affiliations During Scandal over Protest-Related Texts," *People's Police Report*, no. 77 (May 2019), 1.
55. Quoted in Damewood and Berry, *Confidential Investigative Report*, 19–20.
56. Quoted in Damewood and Berry, *Confidential Investigative Report*, 21.
57. Damewood and Berry, *Confidential Investigative Report*, 2, 16, 22–23. Niiya quoted on 7 and 23.
58. Corey Pein, "A Multnomah County Sheriff's Deputy Allegedly Aided Federal Agents in Courthouse Immigration Sting," *Willamette Week*, January 31, 2017; and Campuzano, "Portland Protests."
59. Jessica Floum, "City Council to Declare Portland a 'Sanctuary City,'" oregonlive.com, March 21, 2017. Reese quoted in Pein, "A Multnomah County Sheriff's Deputy Allegedly Aided Federal Agents"; ICE quoted in Katie Shepherd, "Despite Oregon's Sanctuary Laws, Emails Show Portland Prosecutors Volunteered Information to ICE Agents," *Willamette Week*, June 6, 2018.
60. Shepherd, "Despite Oregon's Sanctuary Laws."
61. Geo Maher, *A World Without Police: How Strong Communities Make Cops Obsolete* (London: Verso, 2021), 190.
62. Rachel Monahan, "Portland Mayor Announces Plans to Sweep Out the Occupy ICE Camp," *Willamette Week*, July 23, 2018; and "The ICE Age Is Over: Reflections from the ICE Blockades," crimethinc.com, July 1, 2018.
63. Quoted in Gordon R. Friedman, "Portland Mayor, Decrying Immigration Agency, Sides with Demonstrators," oregonlive.com, June 20, 2018.

64. Lydia Gerike, "Occupy ICE PDX: A Timeline of the Portland Encampment," oregonlive .com, July 25, 2018; and Katie Shepherd, "After Dawn Raid, Federal Agents in Riot Gear Stand Watch Over 'Very, Very Peaceful' Protest at Portland ICE Building," *Willamette Week*, July 28, 2018.
65. National ICE Council quoted in Katie Shepherd, "Portland Police Refused to Respond When ICE Agents Called 911 During Protest, Letter Says," *Willamette Week*, July 30, 2018; Wheeler quoted in Katie Shepherd, "Portland Mayor Calls ICE Allegations that Police Ignored 911 Calls 'Inaccurate and Inflammatory,'" *Willamette Week*, July 31, 2018.
66. "The ICE Age is Over," crimethinc.org; Shepherd, "After Dawn Raid"; Gerike, "Occupy ICE PDX"; and "Occupy ICE Portland: Policing Revolution—Some Critical Reflections," crimethinc.com, July 9, 2018. Quote from Shepherd, "After Dawn Raid."
67. Monahan, "Portland Mayor Announces Plans"; Katie Shepherd, "Mayor Ted Wheeler Sends Portland Police to Occupy ICE Camp After Patriot Prayer Leader Said He Would Show Up to 'Talk with Protestors,'" *Willamette Week*, July 20, 2018; and Gerike, "Occupy ICE PDX." Wheeler quoted in Shepherd, "Mayor Ted Wheeler Sends Portland Police."
68. Quoted in Shepherd, "Portland Police Chief Says Protestors Went Off to 'Whine and Complain.'"

Chapter 30: Can't Breathe

1. Lawrence Wright, "The Plague Year: The Mistakes and Struggles Behind America's Coronavirus Tragedy," *New Yorker*, December 28, 2020, newyorker.com; and Gabriel Granillo and Margaret Seller, "Six Months Later: A Quick Look at Coronavirus in Oregon," pdxmonthly.com, August 7, 2020.
2. Maggie Vespa, "'This Really Isn't Social Distancing': What to Do If You Come Across Social Distancing Violations," kgw.com, April 14, 2020. Quote from David Crow and Patti Waldmeir, "US Anti-Lockdown Protests: 'If You Are Paranoid About Getting Sick, Just Don't Go Out,'" *Financial Times*, April 22, 2020, ft.com.
3. Maggie Vespa, "Portland, Multnomah County Drop Vaccine Mandate for Law Enforcement After State Says Officers Are 'Probably Not' Eligible," kgw.com, September 9, 2021; Rebecca Ellis, "Portland Will Not Enforce Citywide Vaccine Mandate on Police Officers," opb.org, September 8, 2021; and Tess Riski, "Portland Police Union to City: Vaccine Mandate Will 'Exacerbate an Already Dangerous Staffing Crisis,'" *Willamette Week*, September 1, 2021.
4. KATU Staff, "Governor Meets with Oregon State Police Troopers Who Defied Mask Order," katu.com, July 3, 2020.
5. Bob Heye, "Coronavirus and Crime: Jail Releases, a Rash of Break-Ins, and One Encouraging Trend," katu.com, March 23, 2020; and Emily Widra, "As COVID-19 Continues to Spread Rapidly, State Prisons and Local Jails Have Failed to Mitigate the Risk of Infection Behind Bars," prisonpolicy.org, December 12, 2020.
6. Tess Riski, "Portland Police Will Not Take Misdemeanor Arrests to Jail During the Covid-19 Outbreak, to Avoid Overcrowding," *Willamette Week*, March 20, 2020; Aimee Green, "Portland Police Will Stop Responding to Calls That Aren't Life-Threatening, Citing Coronavirus Concerns," kgw.com, March 13, 2020; and Keaton Thomas, "Portland Not Asking Homeless to Move During Coronavirus Pandemic," katu.com, May 5, 2020.
7. Conrad Wilson, "Oregon Prisons to Release More Inmates as COVID-19 Outbreaks Continued," opb.org, December 15, 2020; Tess Riski, "Jay Inslee Released Many Nonviolent Offenders to Stem the Spread of COVID-19. Kate Brown Hasn't Yet," *Willamette*

Week, September 2, 2020; Maxine Bernstein, "Oregon Inmate with Coronavirus: 'They Told Us We'd Be Treated Humanely. That's Not the Case,'" oregonlive.com, May 30, 2020; and Beth Schwartzapfel et al., "1 in 5 Prisoners in the U.S. Has Had COVID-19," themarshallproject.org, December 18, 2020. On the relationship between incarceration and Covid outcomes, see Arvind Krishnamuthy, "COVID-19, Race, and Mass Incarceration," in *The Pandemic Divide: How Covid Increased Inequality in America*, edited by Gwendolyn L. Wright et al. (Durham: Duke University Press, 2022), 87–108.

8. Juana Summers, "Timeline: How Trump Has Downplayed the Coronavirus Pandemic," npr.org, October 2, 2020; Cameron Peters, "A Detailed Timeline of All the Ways Trump Failed to Respond to the Coronavirus," *Vox*, June 8, 2020, vox.com; Christian Paz, "All the President's Lies About the Coronavirus," *Atlantic*, November 2, 2020, theatlantic.com; Oliver Holmes, "What Donald Trump Has Said About Covid-19: A Recap," *Guardian*, October 2, 2020; and Joel Rose, "Immigration Grinds to a Halt as President Trump Shuts Border," npr.org, March 18, 2020.
9. "The profit motive is at odds with the requirements of public health." Jennifer Cohen, "COVID-19 Capitalism: The Profit Motive Versus Public Health," *Public Health Ethics*, September 20, 2020. On inequality, see Mary T. Bassett, foreword to *The Pandemic Divide: How Covid Increased Inequality in America*, edited by Gwendolyn L. Wright et al. (Durham: Duke University Press, 2022); Keisha L. Bentley-Edwards et al., "How Systemic Racism and Preexisting Conditions Contributed to COVID-19 Disparities for Black Americans" in *The Pandemic Divide: How Covid Increased Inequality in America*, edited by Gwendolyn L. Wright et al. (Durham: Duke University Press, 2022), 29–45; Ellie Hu, "How Covid-19 Has Magnified Pre-Existing Inequalities in the US," bu.edu, March 10, 2022; David Blumenthal et al., "COVID-19—Implications for the Healthcare System," nejm.org, October 8, 2020; and Joe Nocera and Bethany McLean, *The Big Fail: What the Pandemic Revealed About Who America Protects and Who It Leaves Behind* (n.p.: Portfolio/Penguin, 2023), 414–17.
10. John Hull, "Mutual Aid Groups Form in the Portland Metro Area Amidst the Pandemic to Help Reach People in Need," opb.org, December 23, 2021; Lucy Diavolo, "People Are Fighting Coronavirus with Mutual Aid Efforts to Help Each Other," teenvogue.com, March 16, 2020; and Rosehip Medic Collective, rosehipmedics.org, accessed March 1, 2024.
11. Granillo and Seller, "Six Months Later"; and Erin K. Stokes et al., "Coronavirus Disease 2019 Case Surveillance—United States, January 22–May 30, 2020," *Morbidity and Mortality Weekly Report*, June 19, 2020.
12. William Wan, "The Coronavirus Pandemic Is Pushing America into a Mental Health Crisis," *Washington Post*, May 14, 2020; Grace Hauck, "Americans Are Using Alcohol to Cope with Pandemic Stress: Nearly 1 in 5 Report 'Heavy Drinking,'" *USA Today*, November 22, 2021; and Noelle Crombie, "Calls to Oregon's Domestic Violence Crisis Line Spike amid Coronavirus Crisis," oregonlive.com, May 14, 2020. Curiously, the rise in domestic violence began *before* the lockdown order.
13. In April, 20.5 million Americans lost their jobs. The unemployment rate reached 14.7 percent. Nocera and McLean, *The Big Fail*, 166. By August, Oregonians had filed 658,000 unemployment claims. Granillo and Seller, "Six Months Later."
14. Jesse Kavadlo, "For Don DeLillo, 'The Silence' Is Deafening," popmatters.com, September 30, 2020.
15. Keith Ellison, *Break the Wheel: Ending the Cycle of Police Violence* (New York: Twelve, 2023), 14, 25; and Angela Harrelson and Michael Levin, *Lift Your Voice: How My Nephew George Floyd's Murder Changed the World* (New York: Post Hill Press, 2022), 1. The full sequence of events is described in detail in Ellison, *Break the Wheel*, 25–43. A transcript of

the video is included on pages 34–42. "I can't breathe" appears fourteen times on pages 34–37. "They're gonna kill me" appears twice on page 36.

16. Derek Chauvin was convicted of "unintentional second-degree murder while committing a felony," "third-degree murder perpetrating an imminently dangerous act," and "second degree manslaughter, culpable negligence, creating an unreasonable risk." He later pled guilty to federal civil rights charges as well. He is serving a sentence of twenty-one years. The other officers were tried and convicted on federal civil rights charges and pled guilty to manslaughter at the state level. They were each sentenced to two or three years. Ellison, *Break the Wheel*, 265–68.

17. Police Executive Research Forum, *Rethinking the Police Response to Mass Demonstrations: 9 Recommendations* ([Portland]: Police Executive Research Forum, 2022), 17; Elizabeth Hinton, *America on Fire: The Untold History of Police Violence and Black Rebellion Since the 1960s* (New York: Liveright, 2021), 288; Ellison, *Break the Wheel*, 57; and Cedric Johnson, *After Black Lives Matter: Policing and Anti-Capitalist Struggle* (London: Verso, 2023), 24.

18. Portland Police Bureau, *Community Engagement and Inclusion* (Portland: Portland Police Bureau, [2019]), 23; and Alex Zielinski, "Report Shows Concerning Divide Between Portland Cops and the Public," *Portland Mercury*, March 20, 2019. Another survey with more favorable numbers still offered plenty of reason to worry. True, 87 percent said they would call the police to report a crime, and 86 percent said they would work with police to reduce crime—but those large majorities may reflect a perceived lack of alternatives rather than eager support for the Portland Police. Equally notable is that more than one person in ten would *not* seek their assistance or assist them if asked. Likewise, while 73 percent said that they expected to be "treated fairly" by police, more than a quarter of the people in the city did not expect the same. And while a majority (56 percent) believed the city's police were trustworthy, a remainder of 44 percent does not bespeak overwhelming public confidence. Michael Geanaco et al., *An Independent Review of the Portland Police Bureau: Agency Culture, Community Perception, and Public Safety in a Time of Change* (Playa del Rey, Ca: OIR Group, 2022), 70–71.

19. Portland Police Bureau, *Community Engagement and Inclusion*, 19; Maxine Bernstein, "Community Distrusts Portland Police; Police Say Community Doesn't Understand Their Jobs," *Oregonian*, March 20, 2019; and Zielinski, "Report Shows Concerning Divide."

20. Portland Copwatch, "Bureau Continues Hiding Racial Imbalance of Force Use, Training Advisory Council Pushes Back," *People's Police Report*, no. 77 (May 2019), 4; and Portland Copwatch, "Portland Police Implicated in West Linn Racial Bias Case; Latest Stop Data Show No Changes in Over-Policing; City Considers Facial Recognition Ban," *People's Police Report*, no. 80 (May 2020), 2.

Data on police stops reveal similar patterns. In 2019, Portland Police stopped 36,517 people. Two-thirds were white, but disproportionately many were Black (17.1 percent) or Latino (10.2 percent). The Multnomah County Sheriff's Office, with far fewer stops (9,791), showed less bias against Blacks (8.7 percent of stops) and more against Latinos (12.3 percent). Only 6 percent of the county's population was Black, and 10 percent was Latino. Kelly Officer et al., "Statistical Transparency of Policing Report," Oregon Criminal Justice Commission, December 8, 2020, 7; and Alex Zielinski, "Black Adults Are Increasingly Overrepresented in Multnomah County Jails, Report Finds," *Portland Mercury*, November 25, 2019.

Such disparities pervade the local legal system. A report from the W. Haywood Burns Institute for Justice Fairness and Equity found that disparities in Multnomah County jails had worsened over five years. Blacks were 8.3 times as likely as whites to be held before trial in 2019, as compared to 7.0 times as likely in 2014. Latinos were 1.8 times as likely in 2019, up from 1.5 times in 2014. People of color were also held for longer. The average stay for whites was 11.9 days; for Blacks, 16.8 days; and for Latinos, 17 days. Whites were more likely to be offered a diversion program in lieu of prosecution (1.3 times as likely as Blacks). People of color, and especially African Americans, were more likely to be convicted and incarcerated. The report's authors suggest that these difference point to the institutions' historical functions: "The racial and ethnic disparities that exist in the justice system today are symptoms of a system that, from its inception, was a tool of social control for people of color and that continues to harm people of color." W. Haywood Burns Institute for Justice Fairness and Equity, *Racial and Ethnic Disparities in Multnomah County* (W. Haywood Burns Institute for Justice Fairness and Equity, 2019), 5, 9–10, 14, 27, 29, 31, 39.

21. Geanaco et al., *An Independent Review of the Portland Police Bureau*, 13.

22. Portland Copwatch, "Tenth Deadly Force Incident in Ten Months; Portland Police Level of Violence Unheard of Since 2001," *People's Police Report*, no. 78 (September 2019), 1.

23. "Why Portland?," *Uprising: A Guide from Portland*, podcast, November 22, 2020, iheart.com; Nicholas E. Mitchell, "The Handling of the 2020 Protests and Riots in Portland, Oregon: An Independent Review," Independent Monitoring, 2023, 11–12; Rian Dundon, *Protest City: Portland's Summer of Rage* (Corvallis: Oregon State University Press, 2023), xxiii; Eder Campuzano et al., "100 Days of Protests in Portland," oregonlive.com, September 5, 2020; and Tommy Clark, *The 2020 Portland Riots: A Fight Against Domestic Terrorism; An Officer's Memoir* (n.p.: McHenry Press, 2020), 26.

24. "We Do This Every Night," *Uprising: A Guide from Portland*, podcast, November 29, 2020, iheart.com; "Why Portland?"; and Campuzano, "100 Days of Protests in Portland."

25. "Tactics and Teargas," *Uprising: A Guide from Portland*, podcast, February 6, 2021, iheart.com; "We Do This Every Night"; and "Why Portland?" Researchers with Forensic Architecture sampled fifteen locations and found than many exceeded 100 mg/m^3 of CS gas, with the highest reaching 4500 mg/m.^{3} (Federal regulators consider anything above 2 mg/m^3 "immediately dangerous to life or health.") Sam Levin and Forensic Architecture, "What Happened When US Police Teargassed Protesters: A Visual Investigation," *Guardian*, April 17, 2023.

26. Mitchell, "The Handling of the 2020 Protests," 1, 12; "We Do This Every Night"; "The Birth of an Uprising," *Uprising: A Guide from Portland*, December 6, 2020, iheart.com; Campuzano, "100 Days of Protests in Portland"; "Tactics and Teargas"; "Why Portland?"; and Joseph V. Cuffari, "DHS Had Authority to Deploy Federal Law Enforcement Officers to Protect Federal Facilities in Portland, Oregon, But Should Engage Better Planning and Execution in Future Cross-Component Activities," US Department of Homeland Security, Officer of the Inspector General, March 16, 2021, 3.

27. Mitchell, "The Handling of the 2020 Protests," 19, 53; Monique Queen, "Showing Up and Showing Out: Predictors of Black Lives Matter Protest Endorsement and Protest Behavior in Portland, OR" (undergraduate thesis, Reed College, 2022), 9; Alex Zielinski, "Portland Police Have Used Force Against Protestors More than 6,000 Times in 2020," *Portland Mercury*, November 16, 2020; Karina Brown, "Judge Holds Portland in Contempt Over Violent Policing of Protests," courthousenews.com, December 1, 2020; "Tactics and Teargas"; "We Do This Every Night"; and Campuzano, "100 Days of Protests in Portland."

28. Carrie Belding, public information officer, City of Portland, Officer of Management and Finance, communication with author, March 7, 2024. For the stories of some of those injured, see Shane Dixon Kavanaugh et al., "Burns, Bloody Wounds, Broken Bones: Injuries Mount at Portland Protests," oregonlive.com, January 21, 2021.

29. Catalina Gaitán, "Portland Expected to Pay $300K to Settle 2020 Police Brutality

Lawsuit by Protester," oregonlive.com, October 31, 2023; Claire Rush, "Portland Settles Lawsuit over Police Use of Tear Gas," *Skanner*, November 30, 2022; John Ross Ferrara, "City of Portland Settles $95K Lawsuit with Protestor Injured by Cop in 2020," koin.com, July 26, 2023; Maxine Bernstein, "Man Shot with Munitions During Portland Riot in 2020 Will Get $80,000 from Portland, Multnomah County," oregonlive.com, February 22, 2023; Alex Zielinski, "City Council Set to Approve $47,000 to Settle Police Abuse Case," *Portland Mercury*, October 25, 2022; Maxine Bernstein, "Portland Protester Arrested for Twerking in Bike Lane Gets $75,000; Woman Hit with Plastic Buck Shot to Receive $30,000," oregonlive.com, June 22, 2022; Savannah Eadens, "Portland Pays $55K to Settle Lawsuit Brought by 2 Independent Reporters over Injuries from 2020 Protests," oregonlive.com, July 20, 2022; Galen Ettlin, "Portland Approves $100K Settlement to Protester Pepper Sprayed and Arrested by Police in 2020," kgw.com, December 22, 2021; Maxine Bernstein, "City of Portland Set to Pay $100,000 to Settle Suit Filed by Man Arrested After Refusing to Relinquish Sign During Protest," oregonlive.com, December 20, 2021; and Maxine Bernstein, "Portland to Pay $5000 to Settle Suit by Montana Man Chased by Police While Holding 'Accountability' Sign After Protest," oregonlive.com, September 22, 2021.

30. Mitchell, "The Handling of the 2020 Protests," *en passim*.
31. Mitchell, "The Handling of the 2020 Protests," 39–40.
32. "Tactics and Teargas"; "We Do This Every Night"; "The Birth of an Uprising"; and Sarah Jeong and Sergio Olmos, "The Portland Van Abductions," theverge.com, October 19, 2022.
33. "Resistance Through Mutual Aid," *Uprising: A Guide from Portland*, podcast, January 19, 2021, iheart.com.
34. Clark, *The 2020 Portland Riots*, 25, 43–45; Physicians for Human Rights, "'Now They Seem to Just Want to Hurt Us,'" phr.org, October 8, 2020; "We Do This Every Night"; "Tactics and Teargas"; "Resistance Through Mutual Aid"; and Campuzano, "100 Days of Protests in Portland."
35. "We Do This Every Night"; and Dundon, *Protest City*, xxiv.
36. Mitchell, "The Handling of the 2020 Protests," 1.
37. Clark, *The 2020 Portland Riots*, 18, 58.
38. Quoted in "Chief Chuck Lovell, Portland Police Bureau," Police Executive Research Forum, policeforum.org/criticalissuessep3, accessed February 10, 2024.
39. Campuzano, "100 Days of Protests in Portland"; Mitchell, "The Handling of the 2020 Protests," 13; "The Birth of an Uprising"; and "Why Portland?"
40. Quoted in "The Birth of an Uprising."
41. Cuffari, "DHS Had Authority," 4, 7.
42. Mitchell, "The Handling of the 2020 Protests," 14; and Jo Ann Hardesty, "What's Wrong with Policing in Portland?," panel discussion, March 9, 2024, Policing in Portland: A Community Conversation, Portland Institute for Contemporary Art.
43. Lawrence Hurley, "Portland Protesters Were Beaten, Shot at and Snatched. Years Later, They Are Frustrated by Legal Blockades to Accountability," nbcnews.com, December 12, 2023; "The Fed War, Part One," *Uprising: A Guide from Portland*, podcast, December 20, 2020, iheart.com; Campuzano, "100 Days of Protests in Portland"; Mitchell, "The Handling of the 2020 Protests," 14; and Dundon, *Protest City*, xxv. LaBella's mother describes him as "irreparably damaged," with changes to his personality and an inability to work, leading to homelessness. Conrad Wilson, "Man Shot in Head by Federal Officers During 2020 Protest Files Lawsuit," opb.org, November 18, 2021.
44. "Why Portland?"

45. Quoted in Physicians for Human Rights, "Now They Seem to Just Want to Hurt Us." Numerous injuries are documented in that report.
46. Reece Jones, *Nobody Is Protected: How the Border Patrol Became the Most Dangerous Police Force in the United States* (Berkeley: Counterpoint, 2022), 7–9, 232–35; Jeong and Olmos, "The Portland Van Abductions"; Jonathan Levison and Conrad Wilson, "Federal Law Enforcement Use Unmarked Vehicles to Grab Protestors Off Portland Streets," opb.org, July 16, 2020; and "The Fed War, Part One."
47. "The Fed War, Part One"; Jeong and Olmos, "The Portland Van Abductions"; "Why Portland?"; and Campuzano, "100 Days of Protests in Portland" (quote).
48. Kavanaugh, "Burns, Bloody Wounds, Broken Bones"; Cuffari, "DHS Had Authority," 12; and Mitchell, "The Handling of the 2020 Protests," 1.
49. US Department of Homeland Security, Office of Intelligence and Analysis, "Office of Intelligence and Analysis Operations in Portland," April 20, 2021, 6–8. See also Mike Baker et al., "The FBI Deployed Surveillance Teams Inside Portland Protests" *New York Times*, December 22, 2021; Mattathias Schwartz, "The FBI Team Sent to 'Exploit' Protesters' Phones in Portland," *New York Review of Books*, October 8, 2020; and Campuzano, "100 Days of Protests in Portland."
50. Department of Homeland Security, "Report on DHS Administrative Review into I&A Open Source Collection and Dissemination Activities During Civil Unrest, Portland, Oregon, June through July 2020," January 6, 2021, 5, 48, 54–59.
51. Department of Homeland Security, "Report on DHS Administrative Review," 64. The phrase "Violent Antifa Anarchists Inspired" appears on pages 51, 63, and 64. For an account of the dispute see 54–77. The FBI too concluded that there was no organized Antifa contingent. David Neiwert, *The Age of Insurrection: The Radical Right's Assault on American Democracy* (Brooklyn: Melville House, 2023), 342.
52. Quoted in Neiwert, *The Age of Insurrection*, 344.
53. Department of Homeland Security, "Report on DHS Administrative Review," 5. For details, see pages 61–64.
54. Elizabeth Pape and Bob MacKay, "Police Intelligence-Gathering and Surveillance: Better Management Needed to Protect Civil Rights," Portland City Auditor, Audit Services, April 2022, 1, 4, 6; and Alex Zielinski, "Portland Police Violated State Law by Livestreaming Protests, Court Finds," *Portland Mercury*, September 21, 2021.
55. Henry Brannan, "Portland Police Are No Better than the Feds, Activists Say," streetroots.org, August 1, 2020; "The Fed War, Part Two"; and Campuzano, "100 Days of Protests in Portland."
56. Alex Zielinski, "For Portland Police, Indiscriminate Use of Tear Gas During Protests Is Unavoidable," *Portland Mercury*, July 9, 2020; "The Birth of an Uprising"; Mitchell, "The Handling of the 2020 Protests," 19–20 (quotes); J. Ashlee Albies, "Police Reform and Accountability: Where Are We?," panel discussion, March 9, 2024, Policing in Portland: A Community Conversation, Portland Institute for Contemporary Art; and Brown, "Judge Holds Portland in Contempt."
57. "The Fed War, Part Two"; Campuzano, "100 Days of Protests in Portland"; and Mitchell, "The Handling of the 2020 Protests," 15. OSP quoted in Tess Riski, "Gov. Kate Brown Says Feds Have Agreed to 'Phased Withdraw' from Portland Starting Tuesday," *Willamette Week*, July 29, 2020.
58. "Why Portland?"; "We Do This Every Night"; and "Tactics and Teargas."
59. Quoted in Mitchell, "The Handling of the 2020 Protests," 21. See also Maxine Bernstein, "Hundreds of Portland Protesters Will See Their Criminal Cases Dropped as DA Announces Plan to 'Recognize the Right to Speak'," oregonlive.com, August 11,

2020; "Resistance Through Mutual Aid"; and Campuzano, "100 Days of Protests in Portland."

60. "The Fed War, Part One"; Mitchell, "The Handling of the 2020 Protests," 16; "Why Portland?"; Campuzano, "100 Days of Protests in Portland"; Dundon, *Protest City*, xx; and "The Birth of an Uprising."

61. "The Return of the Right," *Uprising: A Guide from Portland*, podcast, January 25, 2021, iheart.com; Campuzano, "100 Days of Protests in Portland"; Dundon, *Protest City*, xxv–xxvi; Jaimie Ding, "Man Who Fired Gun at Downtown Portland Protest Gets Probation," oregonlive.com, September 8, 2021; "Why Portland?"; Andy Campbell, *We Are Proud Boys: How a Right-Wing Street Gang Ushered in a New Era of American Extremism* (New York: Hachette, 2022), 156; and Jeong and Olmos, "The Portland Van Abductions."

62. Neiwert, *Age of Insurrection*, 80–81, 361–62, 373–74; "The Return of the Right"; Dundon, *Protest City*, xxvi; and Campuzano, "100 Days of Protests in Portland."

63. "The Return of the Right"; Bryan Denson and Conrad Wilson, "New Eyewitness Accounts: Feds Didn't Identify Themselves Before Opening Fire on Portland Antifa Suspect," propublica.org, October 10, 2020; Evan Hall et al., "'Straight to Gunshots': How a U.S. Task Force Killed an Antifa Activist," *New York Times*, October 13, 2020; Maxine Bernstein, "Michael Reinoehl, Sought in Fatal Portland Shooting After Trump Rally, Killed by Officers in Washington," oregonlive.com, September 3, 2020; and Tim Marchman, "Docs Reveal Chaotic Planning, Execution of Raid That Killed Portland Antifa Shooter," vice.com, May 27, 2022.

64. Quotes from "The Return of the Right"; and Neiwert, *Age of Insurrection*, 376. Trump was not good with details: it seems that the US Marshals did not fire their weapons, though two Pierce County sheriff's deputies, a Lakewood police officer, and an officer with the Washington Department of Corrections did. Denson and Wilson, "New Eyewitness Accounts."

65. Mitchell, "The Handling of the 2020 Protests," 16; "Resistance Through Mutual Aid"; and Jeong and Olmos, "The Portland Van Abductions."

66. K. Rambo, "Rumors About 'Antifa' Wildfires in Oregon are False, Law Enforcement Says," oregonlive.com, August 2, 2024; Melissa Gira Grant, "The Era of Disaster Militarism in America," *New Republic*, September 15, 2020; and Neiwert, *Age of Insurrection*, 354–55.

    Clackamas County Sheriff Craig Roberts said the rumors were absolutely false. However, his department's Captain Jeff Smith told a public meeting that there were "reliable sightings and reports" of Antifa agents cutting down power lines and hiding gas cans for later use. Quoted in Everton Bailey Jr., "Before a Clackamas County Sheriff's Deputy Spread Unfounded Antifa Wildfire Rumors, a Supervisor Did—In a Public Meeting," oreonlive.com, September 14, 2020. Likewise, the FBI stated clearly, "There is no indication that the fires are the result of coordinated criminal activity." But, as the *Guardian*'s Jason Wilson noted, these rumors seemed to build on equally unfounded conspiracy theories appearing in intelligence reports distributed by the Department of Homeland Security, the National Counterterrorism Center, and the FBI itself. Jason Wilson, "Officials Baselessly Linked 'Antifa' to Arson Before Wildfires, Documents Show," *Guardian*, theguardian.com, September 19, 2020. FBI quote from Rambo, "Rumors About 'Antifa' Wildfires."

67. Jeong and Olmos, "The Portland Van Abductions"; "Why Portland?"; and "Resistance Through Mutual Aid."

68. "Why Portland?"; and Dundon, *Protest City*, xxvii.

69. Mitchell, "The Handling of the 2020 Protests," 16.

70. Quoted in Campuzano, "100 Days of Protests in Portland."

Chapter 31: Aftermath

1. Everton Bailey Jr., "Portland Approved Budget with Millions in Cuts to Police, but Short of Public Demand for $50 Million Reduction," oregonlive.com, June 17, 2020; and Eder Campuzano et al., "100 Days of Protests in Portland," oregonlive.com, September 5, 2020.
2. Mike Rogoway, "From Hate Crimes to Cold Medicine, Many New Oregon Laws Take Effect Jan. 1," kgw.com, December 29, 2021; Alex Zielinski and Isabella Garcia, "What Was Accomplished (and What Wasn't) in Oregon's 2022 Legislative Session," *Portland Mercury*, March 9, 2022; and Portland Copwatch, "State Legislature Passes Package of Mild Accountability Bills," *People's Police Report*, no. 81 (September 2020), 4.
3. Eder Campuzano, "Portland Superintendent Says He's 'Discontinuing' Presence of Armed Police Officers in Schools," oregonlive.com, June 4, 2020; Rachel Saslow, "Portland Public Schools Replaced Cops with a Vast, Unarmed Security Team. Is It Enough?," *Willamette Week*, September 20, 2023; "We Do This Every Night," *Uprising: A Guide from Portland*, podcast, November 29, 2020, iheart.com; Blair Stenvick, "Portland Police Are Leaving the Transit Division. What Does That Mean for TriMet Security?" *Portland Mercury*, June 9, 2020; and Isabella Garcia, "Transit Rider Advocates Question Training Process for New Transit Security Team," *Portland Mercury*, December 12, 2021.
4. Campuzano, "100 Days of Protests in Portland."
5. Quoted in Maxine Bernstein, "Jami Resch Resigned as Portland Police Chief a Day After Letter from Black Leaders Condemned Her All-White Command Staff," oregonlive.com, June 10, 2020.
6. Campuzano, "100 Days of Protests in Portland'; Nicholas E. Mitchell, "The Handling of the 2020 Protests and Riots in Portland, Oregon: An Independent Review," Independent Monitoring, LLC, August 9, 2023, 13; and Bernstein, "Jami Resh Resigned."
7. Noelle Crombie, "Multnomah County DA Mike Schmidt Hires Criminal Defense Lawyer to Review Past Convictions, Sentences," oregonlive.com, September 1, 2021; and Tess Riski, "A Precinct Commander for the Portland Police Bureau Suggested Residents Should Vote Out the District Attorney for Being Soft on Crime," *Willamette Week*, March 17, 2021.

   As DA, Schmidt would lobby for a new law allowing prosecutors to review old convictions for reduced sentencing and created a unit in his office to reclassify old felonies as misdemeanors. He introduced a restorative justice program for low-level violent offences, and diversion programs where people could seek treatment rather than go to prison. He also started a campaign to pursue wage theft. Crombie, "Multnomah County DA Mike Schmidt Hires Criminal Defense Lawyer"; Lucas Manfield, "Portland Crime Victims Have a New Alternative to Prosecution: Restorative Justice," *Willamette Week*, January 27, 2023; Lucas Manfield, "Multnomah County's Top Prosecutor Is Betting His Future on an Aggressive Program Designed to Keep Violent Offenders Out of Prison," *Willamette Week*, January 25, 2023; and Colin Staub, "Wage Theft Will Soon Face Criminal Prosecution in Multnomah County," *Willamette Week*, August 17, 2022.
8. Mitchell, "The Handling of the 2020 Protests," 22; Pat Dooris and Jamie Parfitt, "Ad Campaign Targets Multnomah County Officials, Pressuring Them to Act on Crime," kgw.com, March 8, 2023; Joseph V. Cuffari, "DHS Had Authority to Deploy Federal Law Enforcement Officers to Protect Federal Facilities in Portland, Oregon, but Should Engage Better Planning and Execution in Future Cross-Component Activities," US Department of Homeland Security, Officer of the Inspector General, March 16, 2021, 6; Alice Speri, "A Progressive Prosecutor Faces Off with Portland's Aggressive Police," theintercept.com, September 16, 2020.

Months later, the federal government would make the same decision, though with none of the controversy, dismissing sixty-two of the ninety-six federal prosecutions. Maxine Bernstein, "Texas Man Pleads Guilty to Assaulting Federal Officer with Hammer During Protest Outside Courthouse in Portland," oregonlive.com, September 8, 2021; and Kyle Iboshi, "Feds Quietly Dismiss Dozens of Portland Protest Cases," kgw.com, March 2, 2021.

9. Dooris and Parfitt, "Ad Campaign Targets Multnomah County Officials"; "Six Public Safety Unions Endorse Nathan Vasquez," *Willamette Week*, February 12, 2024; Lucas Manfield, "Lead Advocate in the Multnomah County Victims Assistance Unit Blasts DA Mike Schmidt in Resignation Letter," *Willamette Week*, July 7, 2022; Dan Tilkin and Kaitlin Flanigan, "'Bullies Abound': Survey Results Reveal Low Morale in Mult Co. District Attorney's Office," koin.com, March 19, 2023; Lucas Manfield, "Multnomah County Prosecutors' Union Endorses Nathan Vasquez's Candidacy to Unseat Their Boss," *Willamette Week*, January 29, 2024; Lucas Manfield, "In an Unusual Email, Police Chief Chuck Lovell Told His Troops to Stop Badmouthing DA Mike Schmidt and the City of Portland," *Willamette Week*, August 8, 2023; and John Ross Ferrara, "DA Schmidt Responds to Downtown's Enormous 'Schmidt Show' Billboard," koin.com, April 5, 2023.

10. Michael Geanaco et al., *An Independent Review of the Portland Police Bureau: Agency Culture, Community Perception, and Public Safety in a Time of Change* (Playa del Rey, Ca: OIR Group, 2022), 15; Conrad Wilson and Jonathan Levinson, "DA Mike Schmidt Declines Charges in 12 Cases Against Portland Police Officers," opb.org, September 3, 2021; and Speri, "A Progressive Prosecutor Faces Off with Portland's Aggressive Police."

11. Wilson and Levinson, "DA Mike Schmidt Declines Charges"; Tess Riski, "District Attorney Declines to Prosecute Portland Police Officers After Criminal Probe of Excessive Use of Force at Protests," *Willamette Week*, September 3, 2021; and Jonathan Levinson, "Retired Portland Police Officer Pleads Guilty to 2020 Assault Charge," opb.org, July 25, 2022 (quote).

12. "Disquieting" from Geanaco, *An Independent Review of the Portland Police Bureau*, 16. See also Mitchell, "The Handling of the 2020 Protests," 18; Tess Riski and Sophie Peel, "Portland Police Officers Vote to Disband Rapid Response Team, Multiple Sources Say," *Willamette Week*, June 17, 2021; and Courtney Vaughn, "Portland Police Officer Apologizes to Photographer Struck in Head with Baton During 2020 Protests," *Portland Mercury*, July 12, 2023.

In 2024 the specialized riot squad would be reconstituted as the "Public Order Team," and cops who volunteered for the duty would receive a 6 percent raise in pay. Alex Zielinski, "Portland Will Reinstate Protest Response Team Ahead of 2024 Elections," opb.org, March 20, 2024; and Joelle Jones, "Some Community Members 'Don't Have Trust' in Portland's Newly Minted Crowd Control Cop Team," koin.com, March 20, 2024.

13. Alex Zielinski, "Most Officers Who Used Force During 2020 Protests Have Been Cleared by the City of Misconduct. Here's Why," *Portland Mercury*, January 19, 2022.

14. Wilson and Levinson, "DA Mike Schmidt Declines Charges."

15. Mitchell, "The Handling of the 2020 Protests," 7; Alex Zielinski, "Portland Police Are Out of Compliance with DOJ Agreement After Heavy-Handed Response to 2020 Protests," *Portland Mercury*, February 11, 2021; Alex Zielinski, "Portland Remains Out of Compliance with DOJ Settlement," *Portland Mercury*, June 30, 2022; and Alex Zielinski, "City Blames Protesters, Not Police, for Officers' Inability to Meet DOJ Settlement Standards," *Portland Mercury*, March 24, 2021.

16. Alex Zielinski, "Portland Moves Toward Adopting New Police Oversight System While City Council Is Lukewarm," opb.org, August 17, 2023.

17. Tony Schick and Conrad Wilson, "Oregon's Drug Decriminalization Aimed to Make Police a Gateway to Rehab, Not Jail. State Leaders Failed to Make It Work," opb.org, February 14, 2024; and Hope M. Smiley-McDonald et al., "'All Carrots and No Stick': Perceived Impact, Changes in Practices, and Attitudes Among Law Enforcement Following Drug Decriminalization in Oregon State, USA," *International Journal of Drug Policy* 118 (2023): 2, 8; Amelia Templeton, "Oregon's First Round of Measure 110 Funding Is Finally Out the Door," opb.org, September 20, 2022; and Dirk VanderHart, "Oregon's Pioneering Drug Law Raises More Questions than It Answers in Early Months," opb.org, October 27, 2021. Quote from text of Ballot Measure 110, "Drug Addiction Treatment and Recovery Act," oregon.gov, accessed February 16, 2025.
18. Schick and Wilson, "Oregon's Drug Decriminalization" (Marshall quote); and Smiley-McDonald, "'All Carrots and No Stick,'" 5.
19. Emily Green, "Money for Measure 110 Addiction Services Finally Arrives; Oregon Auditors Spot Problems," opb.org, June 2, 2022; and Nigel Jaquiss, "As Meth and Fentanyl Tighten Their Grips on Oregon, the State Scrambles to Implement Treatment Services," *Willamette Week*, January 26, 2022.
20. Smiley-McDonald, "'All Carrots and No Stick,'" 6.
21. Kelsey S. Henderson et al., "Key Points in Preparation for Oregon Legislative Session (2024): Examining the Multifaceted Impacts of Drug Decriminalization on Public Safety, Law Enforcement, and Prosecutorial Discretion," *Criminology and Criminal Justice Faculty Publications and Presentations*, no. 118 (2023): 2; and Nigel Jaquiss, "Initial Research on Measure 110 Finds No Correlation Between Drug Decriminalization and Calls for Police Service," *Willamette Week*, October 12, 2022.
22. Smiley-McDonald, "'All Carrots and No Stick,'" 6–7. See also Nigel Jaquiss, "Researchers Release Second Round of Findings on Measure 110; Police Don't Like It," *Willamette Week*, June 23, 2023.
23. Quoted in Smiley-McDonald, "'All Carrots and No Stick,'" 4. For critiques of mandatory treatment, see Maya Schenwar and Victoria Law, *Prison by Any Other Name: The Harmful Consequences of Popular Reforms* (New York: New Press, 2020), 18, 54, 59–60; and Boston University Medical Center, "Mandatory Treatment Not Effective at Reducing Drug Use, Violates Human Rights, Researchers Say," press release, bumc.bu.edu, June 21, 2016.
24. Conrad Wilson, "Oregon Governor Will Sign Bill to Recriminalize Drugs, Expand Treatment," opb.org, March 8, 2024.
25. Spruha Joshi et al., "One Year Association of Drug Possession Law Change with Fatal Drug Overdoses in Oregon and Washington," *JAMA Psychiatry* 80, no. 12 (September 27, 2023), 1277–1283. Initial data comparing overdose deaths in other states was mixed. A CDC study looking at data from February 2021 to March 2022 found that overdose deaths in Oregon and Washington, two states that had recently reformed their drug laws, were no more prevalent than elsewhere. Data from the following year, on the other hand, found unusually high rates of overdose deaths in Oregon, Washington, and Nevada. (Nevada had not reformed its drug laws.) The CDC tentatively concluded that there was not sufficient evidence to find "an association between legal changes that reversed or substantially reduced criminal penalties for drug possession in Oregon and Washington and fatal drug overdose rates." Quoted in Courtney Vaughn, "New Research Finds No Link Between Measure 110 and Overdose Deaths," *Portland Mercury*, September 27, 2023.
26. Jaquiss, "As Meth and Fentanyl Tighten Their Grips." PSU researchers note: "Drug overdose deaths have increased since M110, however, [that rate] appears to be following a

significant upward trend that began with [the] COVID-19 lockdown." Henderson, "Key Points in Preparation," 2. Italics omitted.

27. Conrad Wilson and Dirk VanderHart, "Oregon's New Drug Penalties Would Mean Surge in Convictions, Jail Stints, State Estimates Suggest," opb.org, March 4, 2024.
28. Piper McDaniel, "Portland Police Bureau's Budget Reduction Was Slight and Short-Lived," streetroots.org, August 3, 2022; and Saundra Sorensen, "City's Budget Windfall Means More for Police, Despite NAACP Demands," *Skanner*, November 24, 2021.
29. Zielinski, "Portland Moves Toward Adopting New Police Oversight System"; Saundra Sorensen, "As City Approves Major Changes to Proposed Police Oversight System, BIPOC Leaders and Voters' Rights Advocates Call Foul," *Skanner*, November 22, 2023 (quotes); Amy-Xiaoghi DePaola, "Portland City Council Unanimously Approves Updated Language for Police Oversight Committee," kgw.com, November 15, 2023; Katherine McDowell, "Police Reform and Accountability: Where Are We?," panel discussion, March 9, 2024, Policing in Portland: A Community Conversation, Portland Institute for Contemporary Art; and Alex Zielinski, "Portland City Council Approves New Police Oversight System, Despite Public Concerns," opb.org, November 16, 2023.
30. "Portland Street Response: A Plan For the Future of Crisis and Disorder Intervention in Public Spaces," streetroots.org, accessed February 8, 2024.
31. Kaia Sand, "Portland Needs Big Action on Street Response—Now," streetroots.org, March 15, 2019. CAHOOTS originated in the early eighties, when the city was facing simultaneous rises in drug use, mental health crises, and homelessness. City manager Mike Gleason started looking for alternatives to arrest and turned to the White Bird Clinic for help. Inspired by the Haight-Ashbury community clinic, White Bird had been founded in 1968 by graduate students in the University of Oregon's psychology program. It offered free medical care and referrals for social services. It soon created an informal "Bummer Squad" to respond to people having bad drug experiences. Rowan Moore Gerety, "An Alternative to Police the Police Can Get Behind," *Atlantic*, December 28, 2020, theatlantic.com.
32. "CAHOOTS: Crisis Assistance Helping Out On The Streets," whitebirdclinic.org/cahoots, accessed February 8, 2024.
33. Emily Green, "The Need for a Better First Response on Portland's Streets," streetroots.org, March 15, 2019; Geo Maher, *A World Without Police: How Strong Communities Make Cops Obsolete* (London: Verso, 2021), 142; and Sand, "Portland Needs Big Action."

    In early April 2025, Eugene and its CAHOOTS partner White Bird Clinic ended the program, citing financial problems. "CAHOOTS Service Update," City of Eugene, April 7, 2025, https://www.eugene-or.gov/5129/CAHOOTS.
34. Greg Townley and Emily Leickly, "Portland Street Response: Year Two Program Evaluation," Portland State University Homelessness Research & Action Collaborative, June 2023, 13.
35. Portland City Auditor, "Portland Fire and Rescue: Community Health Division Programs Need Guidance and Leadership to Provide Portlanders with the Services They Need and Reduce Demands on Firefighters," portland.gov, January 10, 2024, 8.
36. Townley and Leickly, "Portland Street Response," 7–8.
37. "Survey of Portland Voters Shows Stunning Support for Non-Police First Responders to Street Crises," portlandstreetresponse.org, March 16, 2021; and Alex Zielinski, "Former Portland Street Response Manager Blames Exit on City Leadership Shortfalls," opb.org, July 27, 2023.
38. Townley and Leickly, "Portland Street Response," 90–92.

39. Portland City Auditor, "Portland Fire and Rescue," 8; Zielinski, "Former Portland Street Response Manager"; Courtney Vaughn, "Commissioner Gonzales Shows Little Interest in Heeding Auditor's Recommendations for Portland Street Response," *Portland Mercury*, January 11, 2024; Courtney Vaughn, "Despite Being Safe from Deep Budget Cuts, Fire Bureau Puts Health Services on Chopping Block," *Portland Mercury*, February 13, 2024; and Townley and Leickly, "Portland Street Response," 78–79.

    To justify his tent embargo, Gonzalez cited an increase in tent fires: 1,277 reported between 2019 and 2022, injuring thirty and killing two. However, during that same period eleven people in Multnomah County died of hypothermia. Isaac McLennan, president of the Portland Fire Fighters Association, argued that the fire-or-ice debate assumed a false dilemma and that the real solution was to provide people with housing. Catalina Gaitán, "A Portland City Commissioner Banned Tent, Tarp Distribution. Then It Snowed 11 Inches," oregonlive.com, February 25, 2023; Isabella Garcia, "Majority of Portland Street Response Workers Condemn Commissioner Gonzales' Tent Ban," *Portland Mercury*, March 30, 2023; and Sophie Peel, "Rene Gonzalez Explains Reasoning Behind Tent Ban," *Willamette Week*, February 20, 2023.

40. Alex Zielinski, "Portland Street Response, Despite Successes, Faces an Uncertain Future," opb.org, June 27, 2023; and Alex S. Vitale, "Community Centered Public Safety: The Movement for a Police Free Future," lecture, Policing in Portland: A Community Conversation, Portland State University, March 8, 2024.
41. Street Roots Editorial Board, "Police Trust, Efficiency All More Reason for Better Street Response," streetroots.org, March 22, 2019.
42. Geanaco, *An Independent Review of the Portland Police Bureau*, 4, 47–49.
43. Geanaco, *An Independent Review of the Portland Police Bureau*, 47–49. Not even a quarter of officers (21.19 percent) agree they "feel supported by the senior leadership of the Bureau," and a solid majority (59.11 percent) say they do not. Geanaco, *An Independent Review of the Portland Police Bureau*, 45.
44. Maxine Bernstein, "Police Union Has Moved Out of North Portland Office, Plans To Sell It After Repairing Protest Damage," oregonlive.com, June 9, 2021.
45. Zielinski, "Portland Remains Out of Compliance."
46. Charles Fain Lehman, "Portland's Police Staffing Crisis: What It Is, Why It Is, and How to Fix It," manhattan.institute, September 14, 2023; Alex Zielinski, "Portland's Crime Rate Isn't Impacted by Size of Police Force, Data Finds," November 9, 2021, portlandmerrcury.com; and Saundra Sorenson, "City Council Accepts 2020 Police Report Citing Staffing Shortages, Resource-Drain from Protests," *Skanner*, August 25, 2021.
47. Amanda Arden, "PPB Officer Numbers Continue to Drop. Here's Why Some Say They're Leaving," koin.com, October 15, 2021; Amanda Arden, "Former PPB Staff Say Work Experience Was Good, but They Have Several Complaints," koin.com, October 25, 2022; and Maxine Bernstein, "'Overworked, Overwhelmed and Burned Out': Why Portland Cops Say They're Leaving in Droves," oregonlive.com, April 5, 2021.
48. Alex Zielinski, "Portland Will Reinstate Protest Response Team Ahead of 2024 Elections." Writing for the conservative Manhattan Institute, Charles Fain Lehman blames "the city's particularly harmful riots" and "its leadership's embrace of the 'defund the police' movement" for "deal[ing] a massive blow to police morale, driving mass resignations and retirements, which have continued to hamstring operations." Lehman, "Portland's Police Staffing Crisis."
49. For example, police failed to respond to calls about an armed man driving down a closed road and about drag racing on Sandy Boulevard. In both instances, the bureau blamed

short staffing. Lucas Manfield, "Mayor Rebukes Portland Police Citing Understaffing as Reason for Slow Response: 'Bullshit'," *Willamette Week*, August 31, 2022. City Commissioner Jo Ann Hardesty, on her way out of office stated, however: "I believe [the] Portland Police Bureau is still on strike and has been on strike since the summer of 2020. . . . I continue to get calls from small businesses and from community members, when they call the police and they still get the line, 'We've been defunded. We don't have enough officers.'" Quoted in Shane Dixon Kavanaugh, "Portland Commissioner Jo Ann Hardesty In Her Own Words," *Oregonian*, December 28, 2022. At least one officer has admitted to overstating the reduction of services for political purposes: "We needed to create a stir to get some change, to get them to fund us back up." Quoted in Jonathan Maus, "Portland Police Bureau Officer Admits Traffic Enforcement Messaging Was Politically Motivated," bikeportland.org, August 8, 2023.

50. League of Women Voters, "Top Ten Reasons We Support Charter Reform," lvwpdx.org, accessed March 28, 2024; and Community Alliance of Tenants, "Portland Charter Reform Passes—a WIN for Representation," oregoncat.org, accessed March 3, 2024.

Conspectus: Policing and Progress

1. The classic text on the Protestant ethic is Max Weber, *The Protestant Ethic and the Spirit of Capitalism*, translated by Talcott Parsons (London: Routledge, 2005).
2. US Department of Homeland Security, "DHS Strategic Framework for Addressing Climate Change," dhs.gov, October 21, 2021; "Findings for Select Government Reports: The National Security Implications of a Changing Climate," obamawhitehouse.archives.gov, May 2015; Office of the Director of National Intelligence, National Intelligence Council, "National Intelligence Estimate: Climate Change and International Responses Increasing Challenges to US Security Through 2040," [2021]; Oregon Climate Change Research Institute, *Sixth Oregon Climate Assessment* (Corvallis: Oregon State University, January 2023); and Josh Howe, "Climate Change in Oregon," oregonencyclopedia.org, December 29, 2023.

Index

"Passim" (literally "scattered") indicates intermittent discussion of a topic over a cluster of pages.

D

E

F

H

K

L

N

Q

R

S

Y

Z

Also by Kristian Williams

The Illuminist: Philosophical Explorations in the Work of Alan Moore (Emergency Hearts, 2024)

Gang Politics: Revolution, Repression, and Crime (AK Press, 2022)

Resist Everything Except Temptation: The Anarchist Philosophy of Oscar Wilde (AK Press, 2020)

Whither Anarchism? (AK Press, 2018)

Between the Bullet and the Lie: Essays on Orwell (AK Press, 2017)

Our Enemies in Blue: Police and Power in America, 3rd ed. (AK Press, 2015)

Fire the Cops: Essays, Lectures, and Journalism (Kersplebedeb, 2014)

Witness to Betrayal/Profiles of Provocateurs (with scott crow) (Emergency Hearts, 2014)

Hurt: Notes on Torture in a Modern Democracy (Microcosm, 2012)

American Methods: Torture and the Logic of Domination (South End Press, 2006)